RACE, GENDER AND CLASS

Race, Gender and Class

Theory and Methods of Analysis

BART LANDRY

University of Maryland

Upper Saddle River, New Jersey 07458

Library of Congress Cataloging-in-Publication Data

Landry, Bart.
Race, gender and class : theory and methods of analysis / Bart Landry.
p. cm.
ISBN 0-13-048761-9
1. United States—Social conditions—1980- 2. United States—Race relations—Study and teaching (Higher) 3. Social classes—Study and teaching (Higher)—United States. 4. Sex role—Study and teaching (Higher)—United States. 5. Homosexuality—Study and teaching (Higher)—United States. 6. Discrimination—Study and teaching (Higher)—United States. I. Title.
HN59.2.L365 2006
306.072'073—dc22

2006013515

Publisher: Nancy Roberts
Editorial Assistant: Lee Peterson
Executive Marketing Manager: Marissa Feliberty
Marketing Assistant: Anthony DeCosta
Production Liaison: Marianne Peters-Riordan
Manufacturing Buyer: Brian Mackey
Art Director: Jayne Conte
Cover Design: Bruce Kenselaar
Cover Illustration/Photo: Lisa Henderling/Stock Illustration Source, Inc.
Manager, Cover Visual Research & Permissions: Karen Sanatar
Composition/Full-Service Project Management: Sarvesh Mehrotra/Techbooks
Printer/Binder: Courier Companies, Inc.

Credits and acknowledgments borrowed from other sources and reproduced, with permission, in this textbook appear on appropriate page within text .

Pearson Education LTD.
Pearson Education Singapore, Pte. Ltd
Pearson Education, Canada, Ltd
Pearson Education-Japan
Pearson Education Australia PTY, Limited
Pearson Education North Asia Ltd
Pearson Educación de Mexico, S.A. de C.V.
Pearson Education Malaysia, Pte. Ltd
Pearson Education, Upper Saddle River, New Jersey

10 9 8 7 6 5 4 3 2 1
ISBN: 0-13-048761-9

For Ayo

CONTENTS

FOREWORD

In the last 30 to 35 years, the study of race, class, gender, and other dimensions of social inequality as simultaneously expressed socially constructed systems of power relationships has grown to a powerful scholarship that has permeated the humanities, the social sciences, and, more recently, the sciences. Forty years ago if we had been asked to predict where this new study of race, class, and gender would emerge, sociology would have been the obvious disciplinary location. After all, by 1970 sociology had a long tradition of social class/stratification and racial/ethnic studies, and social stratification was seen as the core of the discipline—essential education for all sociologists. Yet the study of the intersections of race, class, and gender did not emerge as a logical outgrowth of sociology's scholarship in stratification in part because "race/ethnicity" and "social class/stratification" had evolved as quite distinct fields of study—as subdisciplines. In the 1960s and 1970s, when the political activity surrounding the women's movement sparked a new scholarship that posed gender as a system of oppression and social inequality, the disciplinary structure to accommodate these kinds of questions was already in place, and another subdiscipline, "sex and gender," was born.

The very core of the discipline had already been structured in ways that could both accommodate and marginalize this new scholarly challenge. Questions of gender were easily segregated and marginalized relative to the more central social class/stratification studies—on which the focus was the social significance of white men—and even to the long-standing subdiscipline of race and ethnicity—on which the focus was the cultural practices and traditions of racial and ethnic communities represented in the experiences of men. In that separate space carved out by gender studies, the limitations to knowledge that accompanied the largely white and middle-class thrust of the scholarship and the women who conducted it was not seen as particularly problematic until the groups who had been left out of the whole structure, who lived "at the intersections," got a voice.

By the 1970s and 1980s, women of color (a large percentage of whom were poor or working class) had entered and risen in the academy in much greater numbers than ever in the past, and they were especially vehement in voicing their opposition to theories of and perspectives on social reality that focused on a single dimension of inequality, most especially on gender but also on race or class, and more recently on sexuality. They argued that the multidimensionality and interconnected nature of race, class, and gender hierarchies were especially visible to those who faced oppression along more than one dimension of inequality.

The irony of ignoring groups whose experiences typically reflected the confluence of three major dimensions of inequality was captured in the often-cited title of one of the first anthologies about black women's studies: *All the Women Were White, All the Blacks Were Men, But Some of Us Are Brave: Black Women's Studies* (Hull, Scott, and Smith 1982). By the mid-1980s some notable lesbian authors of color such as Gloria Anzaldúa (1987a, 1987b) and Audre Lorde (1985) had bridged the gap between developing gay and lesbian studies and the writings of women of color that tended to ignore heterosexism.

When black women began to critique the emerging gender scholarship for its exclusionary practices, they focused on conducting analyses that began from the experiences of black women, putting black women at center stage. *The Black Woman* (Cade 1970), *Ain't I a Woman* (hooks 1981), *The Black Woman* (Rodgers-Rose 1980), and "The Dialectics of Black Womanhood" and (1983) "The Prospects for an All-Inclusive Sisterhood" (Dill 1979) were among the first critical perspectives on black women published in books and major feminist journals.

Thus it was in women's studies and in the scholarship of women of color in many different disciplines that race, class, and gender studies first emerged. Because of its critical stance toward knowledge in the traditional disciplines, its interdisciplinary approach, and its orientation toward social change and social betterment, women's studies was more open to self-critique for its exclusion of multiple oppressed groups such as women of color, working-class women, and lesbians (see Baca Zinn et al. 1986).

One of the galvanizing forces behind this critical perspective was the Center for Research on Women, founded at the University of Memphis in 1982, with funding from the Ford Foundation (see Weber, Higginbotham, and Dill 1997). The center, cofounded by Bonnie Thornton Dill, Elizabeth Higginbotham, and me—all sociologists—gave us the resources to facilitate scholarship and curriculum change at the intersections of race, class, and gender. Although there were already 25 centers for research on women all over the country at the time, none focused on women of color, none were in the South, and few were led by social scientists. We became the first in the nation to focus on women of color and on the intersections of race, class, and gender. During the 1980s and early 1990s, the center sponsored many three-day to week-long workshops for graduate students and faculty from across the nation to come together and discuss our developing efforts to understand race, class, and gender largely through the eyes of women of color. Many of today's leading race, class, and gender scholars were deeply involved with the work of the center, serving on the faculty, on the advisory board, as visiting scholars, and as curriculum workshop leaders and participants: Bernice Barnett, Esther Chow, Patricia Hill Collins, Cheryl Gilkes, Evelyn Nakano Glenn, Kenneth Goings, Sharon Harley, Elaine Bell Kaplan, Sandra Morgen, Leith Mullings, Judith Rollins, Mary Romero, Sheryl Ruzek, Denise Segura, Kathy Ward, Ruth Zambrana, Maxine Baca Zinn, and many others.

In 1993, for the pioneering research of the center, Bonnie, Elizabeth, and I received the Jessie Bernard Award from the American Sociological Association, and in the same year we received the ASA's Distinguished Contributions to Teaching Award—a dual honor never bestowed before or since. This honor recognized that the work of the center had facilitated the growth of an entirely new perspective on social inequality by providing forums for marginalized groups to fully explore and to express their social worlds outside the constraints of traditional disciplinary and institutional structures. The interactions among graduate students and faculty from different disciplines and from across the country provided the intellectual space and social support to foster collaborative, interdisciplinary, border-challenging approaches to traditional scholarships.

Today race, class, gender, and sexuality scholarship has permeated virtually every traditional discipline as well as numerous interdisciplinary fields (American studies, ethnic studies, cultural studies, justice studies, environmental studies, and women's studies). Scholars conducting research on race, class, gender, and sexuality have explored these dynamics in every social institution—education, economy and work, family, politics, and religion. They have focused attention on the lives and perspectives of people situated in many different locations in the relations of race, class, gender, and sexuality. They use many different methodologies—from quantitative analyses of large-scale national surveys and census data to textual analysis of a culture's music, and from life history interviews to participatory research. In fact, the body of scholarship and the university course offerings on race, class, gender, and sexuality are extensive enough that we now refer to the field of race, class, and gender studies, and increasingly of race, class, gender, and sexuality studies.

The rapid growth and extensive reach of race, class, gender, and sexuality throughout the disciplines in research and in the curriculum is nothing short of phenomenal. Today, searches of research publication databases will turn up hundreds of citations on the topic across a wide array of disciplines. Curricula also have been reshaped by this work. For example, in 1999 when the women's studies program that I now direct at the University of South Carolina decided to implement a new BA degree to accompany our graduate certificate degree, we surveyed programs across the country to identify the typical core requirements in these relatively new degrees. We found three common courses in almost all degree programs: introduction to women's studies, feminist theory, and race, class, and gender (sometimes labeled as *multicultural feminism*).

Race, class, gender, and sexuality scholarship has been integrated into graduate and undergraduate education in a wide range of disciplines. In the fall of 2004 the USC women's studies program advertised an assistant professor position in race, class, gender, and sexuality that was to be a joint appointment with Women's Studies and any other appropriate department. We received more than 360 applications for the position from young scholars representing 15 different disciplines and interdisciplinary programs. These future leaders in the academy were striking for the breadth of their work and the nature of their educations—many had degrees in interdisciplinary fields—graduate and undergraduate certificates, BAs, MAs, and PhDs in women's studies, feminist studies, cultural studies, ethnic studies, film studies, peace studies, American studies, and area studies. Many had combined these interdisciplinary degrees with degrees in traditional disciplines, whereas others had focused their entire academic lives in interdisciplinary fields—an option that has only recently become available.

This next generation of race, class, gender, and sexuality scholars is ready to move us forward into more complex and nuanced analyses, using new theoretical perspectives and new empirical applications, and developing new activist agendas. These scholars are less likely to rely on a single research method or to view qualitative and quantitative methods as oppositions and are more likely to employ mixed-methods research that draws from multiple disciplinary traditions, examines macro as well as micro levels of analysis, attends to the perspectives of oppressed groups, and integrates sexuality more fully into the race, class, and gender paradigm. This new work provides clear evidence that intersectional scholarship is neither a fad nor a limited perspective but instead is a powerful paradigm for understanding the complexities of life in the twenty first century.

References

Anzaldúa, Gloria. 1987a. *Borderlands/La Frontera: The new mestiza.* San Francisco: Spinsters/AuntLute.

———, ed. 1987b. *Making faces, making soul/Haciendo caras: Creative and critical perspectives by women of color.* San Francisco: Spinsters/AuntLute.

Baca Zinn, Maxine, Lynn Weber Cannon, Elizabeth Higginbotham, and Bonnie Thornton Dill. 1986. The costs of exclusionary practices in women's studies. *Signs: Journal of Women in Culture and Society* 11 (Winter): 290–303.

Cade, Toni, ed. 1970. *The black woman.* New York: Signet.

Dill, Bonnie Thornton. 1979. The dialectics of black womanhood. *Signs: Journal of Women in Culture and Society* 4: 543–55.

———. 1983. Race, class and gender: Prospects for an all-inclusive sisterhood. *Feminist Studies* 9 (Spring): 131–50.

Hull, Gloria, Patricia Bell Scott, and Barbara Smith, eds. 1982. *All the women are white, all the blacks are men, but some of us are brave: Black women's studies.* Old Westbury, NY: Feminist Press.

hooks, bell. 1981. *Ain't I a woman.* Boston: South End Press.

Lorde, Audre. 1985. *I am your sister: Black women organizing across sexualities.* New York: Kitchen Table, Women of Color Press.

Rodgers-Rose, LaFrances, ed. 1980. *The black woman.* Beverly Hills, CA: Sage Publications.

Weber, Lynn, Elizabeth Higginbotham, and Bonnie Thornton Dill. 1997. Sisterhood as collaboration: Building the Center for Research on Women at the University of Memphis. In *Feminist sociology: Life histories of a movement,* ed. Barbara Laslett and Barrie Thorne, 229–56. New Brunswick, NJ: Rutgers University Press.

LYNN WEBER CANNON
Women's Studies Department
University of South Carolina

PREFACE

The purpose of this volume is to provide a comprehensive methodological text for instructors and scholars who wish to teach and/or to adopt the *intersectional approach*[1] in their own research, whether qualitative or quantitative. Recently, Patricia Hill Collins recounted that the most frequent query she hears now is: "How do you do RGC research?"[2] Specifically, my goal is to provide instructors of upper-division undergraduate courses on race, gender, and class with a comprehensive teaching tool—whatever their respective discipline. It is hoped, also, that many who now teach lower-division undergraduate courses on race, gender, and class will see this as an opportunity to expand these courses to the upper-division level. These are students who can be taken a step further and assigned small research projects, at least of a qualitative nature. In undergraduate departments that require statistical courses, it may be possible for students to attempt quantitative studies from an intersectional perspective. An appendix offers some suggestions employing analysis of variance.

On the graduate level, this volume provides instructors with a tool to teach courses on the intersectional approach as well as with a manual for graduate students and faculty who wish to learn and adopt the RGC approach in their own research. At the University of Maryland, I have used these materials in my own graduate seminar and both advised students and participated in MA and PhD committees of graduate students in several departments who were applying the RGC perspective. Finally, this volume can also be used as a supplementary text for those instructors who wish to include the RGC approach as part of courses in women's studies, stratification, race/ethnic studies, and other studies.

From my experience teaching a graduate seminar on race, gender, and class for almost 10 years, I have become convinced that race, gender, and class studies has reached the point where it is now handicapped by the lack of a methodology. The need is for a methodology in the strict meaning of the term (including statistical approaches) as well as for new ways

[1]A variety of terms are currently used for this approach, including *intersectional analysis, intersectional theory,* and *race, gender, and class* (in several versions) *studies.* In this volume I use these terms interchangeably.

[2]Private communication.

of empirical thinking to parallel the theoretical formulations that have been developed with this new paradigm. The foundation of this new approach has been solidly established by a very rich theoretical literature; and although new insights will no doubt continue to emerge from theorists, the RGC approach needs to be put to the test by empirical studies. It is not just *testing* the theory that is needed, however. Ultimately, this new paradigm can bear its richest fruit only through research. Theory and research can be thought of as handmaidens, with each enriching the work of the other. New conceptualizations point the way to fresh approaches for researchers to explore. Researchers, on the other hand, test, clarify, and sometimes expand the new theoretical formulations. This is an extended process, dependent on the cumulative efforts of numerous scholars as each explores the meanings and experiences of individuals and groups at the intersections of race, gender, and class.

After reviewing a large body of qualitative and quantitative articles in the course of teaching my seminar on race, gender, and class, I realized that although these articles often yielded important findings, most fell short of the goals of intersection theory. At times the problem was methodological, at times conceptual, and at other times both methodological and conceptual. Conceptually, most researchers have not been able to move beyond the traditional ways of thinking that we have all learned. As a result, old ways of thinking and conceptualizing are for the most part still the tools being used by those attempting to employ the RGC approach. Here I'm referring especially to the way comparisons between groups have been traditionally made. For instance, in race, gender, *or* class studies comparisons have traditionally been made between what I call *simple social locations:* across race, as in black or white, Latino or African American; across gender, as in female income compared with male income; or across class, as in rates of unionization among working-class versus middle-class employees. Although there is nothing inherently wrong with these comparisons, they are not the type called for when conducting intersectional analysis.

Race, gender, and class studies are concerned with experiences at the *intersections* of race, gender, and class. As I shall discuss in greater detail in later chapters, the intersections of race, gender, and class create *complex social locations.* They push the boundaries beyond dichotomous thinking to an examination of our experiences as complex individuals who are not black, or female, or working class but who may be a working-class white female, or a middle-class Asian male, or a middle-class black female. These three identities (race, gender, and class) combined create complex social locations. The researcher's task is to uncover the varied experiences that occur at these intersections and to compare these experiences across these complex social locations, not simply across dichotomies. Rather than asking if females earn the same incomes as males, the intersectional analyst might compare the incomes of *middle-class* white and black (or Asian or Latino) females with those of *middle-class* white and black (or Asian or Latino) males. Such a comparison might extend to other social locations such as *working-class* Latino females and/or *working-class* Asian females. These comparisons across complex social locations provide more nuanced insights into the distribution of income or some other characteristic or experience, compared with dichotomous comparisons.

Organization

I have organized this volume along theoretical and methodological dimensions rather than by substantive areas of research using the intersectional approach. Although articles using the intersectional approach have appeared in sociological, gender, ethnic, and even legal and medical journals, covering a wide variety of substantive issues, my concern here is *not* with any particular substantive issue or issues. My concern is the degree to which these articles can be said to reflect "sound" intersectional methodology. The articles themselves, therefore, are only of interest methodologically. Thus, I have divided this volume into three parts. The first contains the major articles written by black feminist theorists on intersectionality; the second and third parts present a smorgasbord of qualitative and quantitative articles that use the intersectional approach. The qualitative and quantitative sections are further subdivided by the number of social locations represented in articles. Research using race, gender, and class as dichotomous variables will have eight possible social locations ($2 \times 2 \times 2$). If race or class has more than two groups, or if one of the three identities is excluded, the result will be more or fewer social locations. As will become clear, grouping articles by the number of social locations is a useful device for exploring intersectional analysis.

Each of the three parts opens with an introduction. In the introduction to the first part I attempt to synthesize the theory of intersectional analysis, based on a careful reading of the theoretical articles. The second and third introductions, preceding the qualitative and quantitative sections, offer methodological rules and strategies for the researcher. These two introductions also provide methodological critiques of the articles included in this volume. In doing so, I do not replicate the canons of sound qualitative and quantitative research that should inform any research endeavor. Rather, I attempt to present what I believe to be principles and practices that are unique to intersectional analysis. The articles selected are among the best that my students and I have found in the literatures of a variety of disciplines. From a methodological point of view—the methodology of intersectional analysis—the articles are mixed in their reflection of the intersectional approach. This is the state of the field at this point.

In no way do I consider this text the final word. It is, rather, the beginning of a much-needed addition to the intersectional approach. My own reading and class discussions of articles purporting to apply the intersectional approach left me with the firm conviction that both qualitative and quantitative researchers have been groping in the dark. Without clear methodological (and statistical) guidelines, otherwise fine articles often fall short from an intersectional perspective. It is hoped that this volume will prove useful to instructors and helpful to the many scholars in a large variety of disciplines who see the value of the intersectional approach and wish to incorporate it in their work. I firmly hope that others will add to this beginning.

As with every effort of this kind, many people have contributed to its realization. First of all I wish to acknowledge my students over many semesters, who struggled together during countless hours of discussion to gain a better understanding of intersectionaliy. These discussions sharpened my own thinking as well as provided me with valuable insights. I am especially grateful for the support of my editor, Nancy Roberts, who remained interested in this project in spite of a number of lengthy delays. As always, I take full responsibility for its content.

RACE, GENDER AND CLASS

PART I

The Theory of Intersectional Analysis

INTRODUCTION

Social science research has historically focused on race, gender, *or* class separately. Collectively from this research we have learned a great deal about race and gender in the United States, and somewhat less about class. Nevertheless, some recent scholars have criticized the race, gender, *or* class approach. These theorists, mainly black female academics (Brewer 1993; Collins 1993; King 1988; Zinn and Dill 1996), have championed an approach variously referred to as *intersection theory or intersectional analysis.* They argue that instead of conducting research separately on race, gender, or class we should focus on the *social locations* created by the intersection of these three identities. Research on race, gender, *or* class ignores the multifaceted nature of individual experiences, capturing only part of a more complex whole.

To ignore someone's race and class while studying his or her gender experience, for example, runs the risk of missing variations in gender experience due to that individual's race or class. In addition to being white, an individual is male or female and a member of the upper, middle, or working class. White (R) upper-middle-class (C) females (G), although experiencing some disadvantages based on their gender, lead privileged lives because of their class position compared with white working-class females. Additionally, their race gives them further advantages over Latino and African American females of all classes (Glenn 1992). Gender studies of white middle-class women or of all women together fail to provide an understanding of these different experiences. Similarly, although there is justification for speaking of a historical "black experience" of slavery, discrimination, and racism, blacks, like whites, differ by gender and class. Although a black (R) upper-middle-class (C) male (G) and a black (R) working-class (C) male (G) both may experience discrimination in the housing and labor markets owing to their race, the black upper-middle-class male has greater resources with which to fight this discrimination and enjoys a more affluent living standard. Among blacks, a black woman may be more successful in hailing a cab than a black male, regardless of their class. Although some Asians have achieved notable success as entrepreneurs and professionals, others have been able to find only unskilled working-class jobs (Kwong 1987; Ong, Bonacich, and Cheng 1994; Zhou 1992).

In reality our identities are constructed from many layers. Whether we start from the most micro or the most macro, we are at the same time citizens of a particular nation; residents of a state, city, and neighborhood; members of a family, an ethnic or racial group, as well as of a social class; and a particular gender. Although all these characteristics are important parts of us, some are more significant than others. In the United States an individual's race, gender, and class have historically been particularly salient. Although many call for and others yearn for a "color-blind" society, we have not been so historically and are not so today. As in other societies, we have always classified and still separate individuals by their gender and treat them differently; and class distinctions have become more rather than less important in recent years.[1]

Other characteristics like age, disability, and sexual orientation have also become contentious issues in the United States and very salient aspects of many individuals' lives. Nevertheless, because the purpose of this book is to contribute to the further development of the theory and methodology of intersectionality as originally espoused, I will confine myself to the original characteristics of race, gender, and class. Race, gender, and class, although not exhaustive of our identity, have historically been the three most important characteristics shaping lives and society in the United States. In other countries one may have to substitute ethnicity, caste, or even religion for race, but in the United States race is indisputably one of the most salient characteristics of everyone's identity. Not only is the saliency of race deeply rooted in our collective history, it continues to influence almost every aspect of our lives (Fears 2004; Joyce 2004; Masters 2004; Mayer 2004; Merle 2004).

Interlocking Systems of Oppression and Privilege

Corresponding to our race, gender, and class identities we are confronted on the macro level of society with the systems of racism, patriarchy, and capitalism. Historically these systems have stood out as three of the most powerful forces in our society. Intersectional theorists refer to them as "interlocking" systems of oppression (Collins 1993, 558). Just as we interact with one another as members of a particular race, gender, *and* class, so do the systems of racism, patriarchy, and capitalism function in tandem. And although some writers debate the relative importance of each, it is probably more fruitful to understand how these systems interact with and reinforce each other. Additionally, it is increasingly becoming recognized that racism, patriarchy, and capitalism are both systems of oppression and systems of privilege (Domhoff 1983; Hurtado 1999; Johnson 2006; Leonardo 2004; Rothenberg 2002). To some individuals they provide advantages, to others handicaps.

Race

The concept of *race* has its origin in the notion that different and distinct gene pools exist among humans spread across the globe. European expansion promoted the notion of inherent racial inequality as these nations colonized Africa, India, and the Americas, appropriated land, and exacted forced labor (Harrison 1995). According to Foner and Fredrickson (2004, 3), "The concept of race entered American history in the seventeenth century, when the colonists began to identify themselves as 'white' in distinction from the Indians whose land they were appropriating and the blacks they were enslaving." Thus racism early on became entwined with the anthropological concept of race. The "scientific" concept of race itself became hotly

[1]Witness, for instance, the intense debate between presidential candidates over the recipients of tax cuts.

contested in the twentieth century, culminating in the late 1970s with its rejection as a useful tool for classifying humans (Littlefield, Lieberman, and Reynolds 1982). The term has nevertheless lived on in both popular and scholarly discourse.

Social Darwinists (Claeys 2000; Dennis 1995; Oakes 1985) of the late nineteenth and early twentieth centuries appropriated the concept, using it in a somewhat related yet different way from that used by anthropologists. For them each nationality represented a different "race" of people: Italian immigrants were a race, Polish immigrants were a race, African Americans were a race, and those of Anglo Saxon heritage were still another race. Today we use terms such as *ethnicity* or *ethnic group* rather than race to distinguish individuals with different national and cultural heritages. In the late nineteenth century, however, social Darwinist theorists argued that immigrants from southern and eastern Europe were "races" lower on the evolutionary scale than Anglo Saxons, who had earlier immigrated to the United States. These ideas became the basis for severe discrimination of these immigrants in every aspect of daily life, including schools (Oakes 1985). Here social Darwinist ideas prevailed in motivating the development of a tracking system that provided an inferior education to immigrant children deemed inferior to the native born. Eventually, social Darwinist ideas lost their cogency, and after several generations, immigrants from Europe intermarried and became part of the white population in the United States (Roediger 2005). National origin distinctions persisted in the more benign form of *ethnicity,* preserved in cuisines and festivities that everyone enjoyed. The Saint Patrick's Day Parade in New York City, for instance, is enjoyed by New Yorkers of all backgrounds. Today other heritages are also celebrated in events such as a Puerto Rican Day parade or Caribbean festivals.

Although *ethnicity* replaced *race* as a designation for those of different European origins, it lived on as a distinction between Americans of African versus European descent, resulting largely from the failure to accept freedmen fully into the life of the community following the Civil War (Steinberg 1981). Southern whites and many northerners had developed a stake in preserving the distinction, partly prompted by the need to maintain a cheap labor force to rebuild the cotton industry of the South in the nineteenth century and partly stemming from negative stereotypes and prejudices against blacks that had become part of white culture (Landry 1991).

Unlike in Brazil, which also has a slave history and where race is viewed in "graduated" tones, race in the United States was defined in absolute terms of black or white. Laws passed by Southern states, defining racial identity in terms of percentage of racial ancestry, further institutionalized this racial dichotomy. Eventually referred to as the "one drop rule," these laws designated a person legally black who had even the minutest percentage of black ancestry (Davis 1991). In Louisiana this definition of black led to the practice of "passing" by some mulattoes with such light skin that they were indistinguishable from those individuals who were legally white. Such an individual might have migrated to California and lived as a white person but had to revert to black status when visiting relatives in Louisiana. Southern states further created legal and social barriers against black participation in the civic, social, and economic life of the community. It was a segregated system maintained by Jim Crow laws, custom, and violence (Myrdal [1944] 1972). Thus the concept of *race* lived on in the United States primarily as a term separating blacks and whites.

The social construction of race

Today sociologists think of the concept of race as *socially constructed.* By this they mean that its content or meaning is not absolute, nor is its meaning derived from any facts such as biology. Rather, its meaning springs from its *use* by a particular group of people; it is a social concept rather than a biological one. For instance, the term *race* means different things in the United States, Brazil, and Columbia.[2] In the United States individuals of African descent with brown or black skin are all seen as "black." Brazil has distinct terms for such individuals (Fears 2002). A brown-skinned individual is referred to by the term *moreno,* whereas a very dark-skinned person is called *negro* (black). On a trip to Brazil in 1990 I had the experience of meeting the friend of an American acquaintance who was brown skinned. Sitting across from her over coffee was a strange, almost surreal, experience. As she explained that in Brazil she was not black but *moreno* (brown), I nevertheless saw before me a "black" woman. I could not easily adjust to the idea that the brown-skinned woman sitting before me was not black here in Brazil, because she would certainly have been seen as black in the United States. I was further confused as I listened to her account of her family. Married to a white man, she was accused by some friends, she said, of attempting to *whiten* her offsprings. Such a notion of whitening one's offspring is entirely foreign to the United States context. In Brazil if one is light skinned enough, one is considered white; in the United States the whitest mulatto is still black. Clearly "race" is *constructed* differently in these two countries.

The social construction of gender

Whereas there are thousands of books and articles about race in the United States, social science interest in gender is more recent. Although some attention was given to gender by feminists in the nineteenth and early twentieth centuries, for all practical purposes interest in gender by social scientists can be dated to the publication of *The Second Sex* by Simone de Beauvoir in 1957. Along with Betty Friedan's *The Feminine Mystique,* published in 1963, *The Second Sex* was a radical challenge to current thinking about the position of women in society. Written about the position of women in France, the book was perceived as equally applicable to women in the United States. The feminist movement of the late 1960s and 1970s gave further impetus to the scrutiny of the experiences and position of women in society. One of the gains of the feminist movement was an increase in the number of women entering college and a significant growth in the number of female college and university professors. Many of these academics focused their research on the condition of women, just as black academics had focused earlier on race. Gender studies and women's studies followed the earlier path of black studies and Afro-American studies. A rich tapestry of books and articles poured from the pens of women scholars in the academy.

It may be surprising to learn that one of the conclusions of women scholars is that gender, like race, is *socially constructed.* But unlike race, doesn't gender have a biological foundation? After all, males and females are different biologically. That is true, sociologists contend, but we must distinguish between the concepts of *gender* and *sex.* An individual's sex is biological, but what it *means* to be male or female is socially constructed. It is this area of gender that is contested. When a society assigns roles based on an individual's sex, it has moved from biology to culture. Here we encounter vast differences in a society's beliefs about women's roles across nations (Lindsey 1994). Whether a women should be employed or remain at home is a question of gender rather than sex; whether she should take the initiative in dating, whether she should wear a dress or slacks, whether she should wear a veil are also part of the social construction of gender in a particular society at a particular time. The issue of subordinate or egalitarian relationships between men and women concerns a society's views about gender. In short,

---

[2]See the article by Joel Streicker among the qualitative articles in this volume.

gender refers to a particular society's views of the proper place and roles of women and men.

For example, views about the proper attire for women have varied tremendously in the United States between the nineteenth and early twentieth centuries and today. Everyone has seen pictures of early-twentieth-century beaches with women wading in bathing suits that covered most of their body, or wearing long dresses and carrying umbrellas. Today the burka or veil worn by Muslim women stands in sharp contrast to the sleeveless tank tops and short skirts of Western women. Gender, far from being biological, refers to the *meaning* a society gives to the roles and position of members of each sex. Gender, like race, is socially constructed.

Class

In the 2001 PBS documentary *People Like Us: Social Class in America* the moderator says: "It's basically against the American principal to belong to a class. So naturally Americans have a really hard time talking about the class system, because they really don't want to admit that a class system exists. But the reality is it does." Perhaps the most significant thing about the documentary was that it was made. Twentieth-century Americans (and to a lesser extent those of the twenty-first century) have often thought that ours is a classless society, yet the idea of a classless U.S. society would have struck nineteenth-century Americans as a strange notion (Blumin 1989). Immigrants who came to the United States by the millions in search of economic opportunity had no illusions about the existence of classes. Class differences were obvious in everyday life. The urban tenements of working-class families contrasted sharply with the more affluent homes of the middle and upper classes. In a period before designer labels, class differences were further visible in the clothes worn by the member of different classes. Rather than deny the existence of classes, immigrants aspired to climb the class ladder or at least prepare their children for movement into the middle class. The novels of Horatio Alger ([1872] 1972, 1899, [18??] 1974) promoting the idea of upward mobility were enormously popular in the early twentieth century. "Rags to riches" became the goal of every immigrant or working-class American. In America, at least, class position was not fixed, as in Europe.

Nineteenth-century Americans spoke of the "middling class" or "middling classes" (Blumin 1989). These were individuals with the "good jobs," professionals, managers, workers in sales and even clerical jobs: in short, white-collar workers whose lives stood in sharp contrast to those of factory and domestic workers. *Sister Carrie,* a novel by Theodore Dreiser published in 1900, took for granted class differences of the time. The heroine, Sister Carrie, is a young white girl who leaves a small town in Illinois to seek her fortune in Chicago. Her initial attempts to land a respectable, pleasant job as a department store clerk are frustrated by her lack of experience. In desperation she turns to factory employment but finds the work tedious and the coarse behavior and humor of the working-class girls offensive. Rather than discussing turn-of-the-century class differences, Dreiser simply reveals them in his description of life in Chicago, seen through the eyes of Sister Carrie. The lesson: class differences were part of the fabric of everyday life in America.

Class differences were not eliminated or even diminished in the later twentieth century. In an economy progressively dominated by large corporations, wealth became increasingly concentrated in the hands of a relatively small number of families in the upper class. The middle class continued to grow, fed by the demand for accounts, lawyers, engineers, clerks, sales workers, and countless others needed to run the growing corporations. At the same time, American industry absorbed a steady flow of manual workers to turn out the goods consumed here and abroad. There were, therefore, three clearly distinct classes: an upper class, which owned the corporate wealth of the nation; a middle class of white-collar employees; and a working class of manual or blue-collar workers. These three classes along with small entrepreneurs are the basic classes of an industrial, capitalist society and form one of the important backdrops of everyday life.

The PBS documentary was important for its candid and matter-of-fact portrayal of class in America. At the same time it revealed a level of confusion among Americans about the difference between *class* and *status*. Class, as the preceding discussion indicates, is an objective fact of life. It indicates an individual's place within the economy: as the possessor and controller of great economic wealth and power, as the holder of a position (occupation) in one of the two broad groups of occupations in the labor market, or as a small entrepreneur. Class position determines one's economic resources, which in turn determine one's living standard. In contrast status refers to how other people think of us. It is their evaluation of us as persons based on such things as our family background, our character, our occupation, and residence. Status is therefore subjective rather than objective like class.

The Language of Intersection Theory

Social scientists often use the term *theory* rather loosely. Strictly speaking, a theory is a set of propositions that taken together form an explanation. A *proposition* (or *hypothesis*) is a statement of the expected relationship between two variables, usually expressed as more or less, higher or lower, or in some other wording signifying a direct or indirect relationship. Thus we may say that the higher an individual's education, the higher his or her income. Of course, the perceptive student will immediately recognize that additional factors influence income attainment. To develop a theory of income attainment, therefore, one must include other propositions linking other variables (some of them conditional). How are occupations linked to income? What is the impact of job experience on income? All these relationships and others must be explored to construct a theory of income attainment. Once sufficient research has been conducted to test the many hypotheses involved, a theory may emerge . . . or may not.

We often speak of a theory when in fact we are using a set of assumptions or hypotheses that have yet to be verified through empirical research. Or we may use the term *theory* when we are really referring to a hypothesis. With this distinction in mind we would have to say that intersection theory is not yet a theory but a set of assumptions or hypotheses that are being tested through the efforts of many researchers. However, for simplicity, I shall continue speaking of intersection theory throughout this and the following discussions.

A theory involves new ideas, often new ways of looking at familiar issues and experiences. To express these new ways of looking at society, theorists often invent new terms or use existing ones in different ways. Thus there is a *language* of intersection theory along with a set of *assumptions.* All the concepts of intersection theory are not at the same level, though. There are macro-level concepts such as *racism, patriarchy,* and *capitalism.* Others, like *sexism, racism, privilege, simultaneity,* and *multiplicative* are used at the messo or micro (individual) level.

At the *macro* level intersection theorists see a society in which racism, patriarchy, and capitalism function from the top down, as *systems of oppression* (Baron 1971; Domhoff 1983; Fredrickson 1988; Hartman 1981).[3] Existing at the societal or macro level these systems represent power relationships between whites and blacks, men and women, and capitalists and workers. Essentially, patriarchy, racism, and capitalism are systems of

[3]Heidi Hartmann's (1981, 2) definition of *patriarchy* is often cited: "We can usefully define patriarchy as a set of social relations between men, which have a material base, and which, though hierarchical, establish or create interdependence and solidarity among men that enable them to dominate women."

beliefs and values as well as systems of relationships. Racism and patriarchy are sets of beliefs and values about blacks and whites, and about men and women, respectively. Often, it is the stereotypes of blacks, of women, and of workers as different, as other, and as inferior that support unequal and unjust power relationships between blacks and whites, males and females, and capitalists and workers. (The notion in nineteenth-century America that women had smaller brains than men, and therefore could not bear the stress of higher education, contributed to society's opposition to their admission to colleges.) In their book *For Her Own Good: 150 Years of the Experts' Advice to Women* Ehrenreich and English (1978, 100) provide the following quote from nineteenth-century England:

> Women beware. You are on the brink of destruction. You have hitherto been engaged in crushing your waists, now you are attempting to cultivate your mind. You have been merely dancing all night in the foul air of the ball room; now you are beginning to spend your mornings in study. You have been incessantly stimulating your emotions with concerts and operas; now you are exerting your understanding to learn Greek, and solve propositions in Euclid. Beware!! Science pronounces that the woman who studies is lost.

The "science" referred to was probably from Freud and Darwin, both of whom encouraged this idea of the intellectual inferiority of women, an idea that also became popular in the United States during the Victorian period of the late nineteenth-century.

African Americans, no less than white women, were the objects of negative stereotypes. Slaveholders invented Sambo, the happy-go-lucky but simple-minded male slave. Other images of black slaves as somewhat less than human, or lacking souls or virtue, were all used to justify their subordination. Senator James Henry Hammond, the planter-intellectual and senator for the state of South Carolina, argued on the Senate floor in 1858 (Frederickson 1988, 23):

> We do not think that whites should be slaves either by law or necessity. Our slaves are black, of another, inferior race. The *status* in which we have placed them is an elevation. They are elevated from the condition in which God first created them by being made our slaves.

Racism, patriarchy, and capitalism also represent expected behaviors and relationships. In the cases of racism and patriarchy these belief systems are often acted out in face-to-face interactions as whites and men attempt to coerce blacks and women into conforming to these beliefs (West and Fenstermaker 2002). Likewise, in our capitalist system—a system of relationships among individuals in the marketplace—certain behaviors are sanctioned. Workers are expected to accept the economic dominance of capitalists and to conform to their rules for achieving economic success.

Because these "systems" operate in tandem—white upper-class males may use their command over the economy to control women and minorities, whites may use their superior numbers and positions of authority to discriminate against minorities, and capitalists may use their ownership of economic resources to control workers—intersection theorists view these systems as *interlocking* systems of oppression. In the preceding examples we see that a group of males may use their position as *capitalists* to oppress women (patriarchy). In other instances they may also identify as *white* and use their combined resources to oppress blacks and other minorities (racism). These are shifting alliances that may operate alone or together. Capitalists (both males and females) may join together to oppose legislation benefiting workers, such as proposed legislation for redesigning machinery to limit incidences of carpal tunnel syndrome; or the males among them may invoke their maleness or their whiteness in opposition to gender or racial issues.

The *messo* level refers to the institutions and organizations of society such as education, the health care system, and state and local government agencies, to name but a few. Sociologists customarily use the term *institutions* for those organizations that provide essential services to society such as health care and education. *Organizations* are groups of people united around some common purpose. The purpose may be recreational (Lions or Elks Clubs), religious (Knights of Columbus), social (Jack and Jill), offensive (a paramilitary group), economic (a local chamber of commerce), or dominative (the Ku Klux Klan). Institutions and organizations, although composed of individuals, take on a life of their own that represents the collective. Through rules and customs they "act" on behalf of their members or their mandate. Because they are embodied in rules and customs, voluntary organizations persist as long as there are any members, even though individual members come and go.

Institutions and organizations exist between the macro or societal level and the individual level. They translate or reflect the beliefs and values of the macro systems of society. Their effects are felt by individuals or groups in a particular social location—African American male workers, poor white women, or the broader categories of women, African Americans, Asians, Latinos, or Native Americans. For instance, during the nineteenth and first half of the twentieth centuries blacks were refused entrance into the colleges of the South because of the racist belief that blacks were inferior to whites. Nineteenth-century capitalists sought and received help from the federal government to deny workers the right to organize in unions for self-protection and to improve working conditions and pay (Edwards 1979).

Many nineteenth-century discriminatory practices extended into the twentieth century. Indeed, women did not win the right to vote until 1920, workers did not gain the legal right to unionize until 1935, and blacks were legally segregated until 1964. Having won these legal rights, women, blacks, and workers have had to continue to struggle for their implementation. Part of their struggle has been to alter values, beliefs, and laws at the macro level and have them translated into institutions and organizations at the messo level. To eliminate barriers to education, women and blacks have had to appeal to the federal government to enact policies outlawing these practices. Once such policies were promulgated, women and blacks had to continue struggling at the messo level to gain compliance from schools in their admission policies. Likewise, workers have had to continue their struggle to preserve the right to collective bargaining with capitalists.

Regardless of our gender, race, or class each of us lives our life at the individual or *micro* level (Goffman 1961, 1963). The micro level of face-to-face interactions is operative in the chance encounters of everyday life—on the street, in elevators, in stores, in introductions. When applying for a job we function as individuals at the micro level, within a messo-level organization. Our social lives are lived at the micro level. We go out on dates as individuals, we take classes as individuals, and we graduate as individuals (although we probably had the backing of family, friends, and teachers). It is at this level that we are perceived—and perceive others—as male or female, African American, Asian, Latino or white, upper class, middle class, or working class.

Face-to-face contact also occurs in the more structured encounters of organizational and institutional settings: purchasing an item in stores, talking to a professor after class, applying for a driver's license, or visiting a doctor's office. The distinction between the micro and messo levels may at times be difficult to untangle. I suggest that when an encounter occurs with members of an organization or institution as *representatives* of that organization or institution it is a messo-level encounter. Workers in the organization or institution have the presumptive authority and power of the organization or institution in their favor and perceive themselves as enforcers of/or functioning within the rules of the organization; but this organizational encounter takes place within the larger setting of the society. Thus both macro-level and messo-level norms are brought to bear in the encounter. A white store clerk may follow a black customer because she or he adheres to the societal stereotype that blacks are dishonest and feels free to do so because she or he perceives her- or himself as representing the authority of the store. Conversely, if a black and a white customer meet by chance in the same store, or male and female patients sit in adjacent chairs in a doctor's waiting room, they experience a micro-level, personal encounter. In such encounters the more "powerful" individual may attempt to hold the less powerful accountable to the race, gender, and class norms and stereotypes they hold. At the same time, the less powerful individual may acquiesce, feign acquiescence, or overtly resist these attempts.

The notion of oppression in race, gender, and class relationship is useful and reflects real experiences; however, race, gender, and class analysis can also accommodate more "neutral" experiences of differences or variations in experiences across social locations that are not inherently oppressive. For intersection theory to realize its full potential in social research it must incorporate these other types of relationships. A number of articles in this book fall into the latter category. Rather than detracting from the intersectional approach, the inclusion of nonoppressive experiences encourages the adoption of this perspective over a broader range of societal experiences.

Social locations

Yet, it is not as Latino *or* female *or* working class that we are perceived or that we perceive others. Each of us is met and meets others with a potential recognition of all three characteristics of our identity. The person you meet may be white, female, *and* working class; or the individual seeking a job or an apartment may be seen as Asian, male, *and* middle class. Taken together these three characteristics of our identity define a *social location.* Thus it is immediately evident that each of us "lives in" a unique social location. Into two of these identities—gender and race—we are born and there live out our lives with only rare exception. As Patricia Hill Collins (1998) notes, these social locations usually set the stage for the rest of our lives. The mulatto who moved from Louisiana to California and there lived as a white person was attempting to change from a disadvantaged to an advantaged social location. Even extreme measures like a sex change can be interpreted as an attempt by an individual to modify his or her social location.

We are also born into a class—the class of our parents. Although the majority of children remain in the class of their parents, a significant percentage of working-class children move into the middle class by virtue of obtaining a college education. A smaller percentage of those born middle class experience downward mobility into the working class by failing to attend college to earn a bachelor's degree or by failing to secure a middle-class job. Practically no child from the upper class experiences downward mobility. Once we have completed our education and moved into the labor force as adults we assume our own class position, a position that we are rarely able to change. From that point on, therefore, we are likely to live the remainder of our lives in a *single* social location. We are a Puerto Rican middle-class male, or a black middle-class female, or a white upper-class female. If, for simplicity's sake, we omit the upper class in this discussion, then the three identities yield eight distinct social locations: (1) black[4] middle-class female, (2) white middle-class female, (3) black middle-class male, (4) white middle-class male, (5) black working-class female, (6) white working-class female, (7) black working-class male (8), and white working-class female.[5] From the point of view of importance to the individual, we cannot rank these social locations. Each individual's social location is important to him or to her, it is the "house" in which the person lives out life.

[4]We can, of course, substitute another racial group for black.

[5]Adding upper class would yield four additional social locations.

We may also evaluate these social locations in terms of their experiences in life. Social scientists have moved from the position of focusing only on the disadvantages that some individuals experienced to acknowledging that for every disadvantage suffered there is often some advantage to others (Hurtado 1999; Leonardo 2004; McKinney 2005; Rothenberg 2002). I do not mean to imply that life is a zero-sum game. Zero-sum games exist only when the "good" involved is *fixed*. Although that may be the case in some instances, it is by no means always the case. If there are only 100 taxis on the street but 110 individuals competing for rides, then 10 persons will be losers in this zero-sum game. If 90 are white males and 20 are black males, the game is skewed if 5 of the black males are refused service because of their race, thus increasing the likelihood that proportionally more black than white males will fail to secure a ride home.

Being white *privileges* an individual in situations where race is salient. Being male likewise conveys privileges over females; and those in the upper class have the advantages of power and wealth relative to individuals of all other classes. In general, it should be obvious that white upper-class males are in the most privileged social location, followed by white upper-class females. Conversely, the most disadvantaged are minority working-class males and females. Given that being male trumps being female in our society, minority working-class females are probably in the most disadvantaged of all social locations.

Although we carry our race, gender, and class identities into every situation, all three may not always be salient in a particular encounter (Collins 1993; King 1988). When girls are called on less frequently than boys in class, it is their gender that is salient rather than their race or class. A working-class black couple searching for an apartment may be turned away because of their race and class position. A white upper-middle-class male may receive preferential treatment by his bank because of his connections as a member of the upper middle class and because of his race. Whether all three of these identities affect the outcome of an encounter depends on the particular situation and the individuals involved. The strength of the intersectional approach is its recognition that as individuals we enter life situations with our race, gender, and class identities. To focus on just one is potentially to misinterpret the experience or to fail to understand it fully. In later chapters I will address methods that can be used to apply the insights of intersection theory in research.

The Assumptions of Intersection Theory

As noted previously, new approaches or new theories in the physical and social sciences are accompanied by new concepts or terminologies that become the tools for expressing novel ideas. This is the stage at which race, gender, and class analysis finds itself today. This stage necessarily involves debates, disagreements, criticisms, and revisions. The eventual goal is to arrive at a consensus about the "best" terminology to use, the "most accurate" way to conceptualize relationships, and new ways of thinking about social relations. Debate fosters this process by pushing theorists and researchers to examine their ideas more closely and critically than they would otherwise. It is a process in which no one commands the "truth." It is hoped that over time new insights are achieved, and eventually consensus is reached. Collins (1995, 491) summarizes this challenge:

> The area of race, class, gender studies struggles with the complex question of how to think about intersections of systems of oppression race, class, and gender. We clearly need new models that will assist us in seeing how structures of power organized around intersecting relations of race, class, and gender frame the social positions occupied by individuals; work explaining how interlocking systems of oppression produce social locations for us all.

Simultaneity

Black feminists who introduced the notion of *simultaneity* argue that race, gender, and class cannot be separated. Although sociologists have historically examined the experiences of race, gender, and class separately, this gives the false impression that they function independently of one another. Rather, these black feminists assert that race, gender, and class represent "distinctive yet interlocking structures of oppression" (Collins 1993, 558). Race, gender, and class are salient characteristics of each individual that "accompany" the individual into every interaction or experience.

At the same time it is acknowledged that although all three characteristics of an individual's identity are always present, they are not necessarily all *relevant* in every situation. As King (1988, 48) emphasizes:

> The *importance* of any one factor in explaining black women's circumstances thus *varies* depending on the particular aspect of our lives under consideration and the reference groups to whom we are compared. In some cases, race may be the *more significant* predictor of black women's status; in others gender or class may be more influential (italics added).

Still, Collins (1993, 560–61) cautions against losing sight of at least the potential presence of all three characteristics:

> Race, class and gender may all structure a situation but may not be equally visible and/or important in people's self-definitions. . . . This recognition that one category may have salience over another for a given time and place does not minimize the theoretical importance of *assuming* that race, class and gender as categories of analysis structure all relationships (italics added).

Perhaps the most important word in the preceding quote is *assuming*. Although it may be argued that the researcher should approach each situation with the assumption that race, gender, and class are all relevant, this assumption is open to the test of empirical analysis. In some instances this assumption may prove valid; in others the researcher may discover that only two of the three characteristics are relevant.

A further nuance of the simultaneity assumption is voiced by Zinn and Dill (1996, 326–27):

> People experience race, class, gender, and sexuality differently depending upon their social location in the structures of race, gender, and sexuality. For example, people of the same race will experience race *differently* depending upon their location in the class structure as working class, professional managerial class, or unemployed; in the gender structure as female or male; and in structures of sexuality as heterosexual, homosexual, or bisexual (italics added).

Thus we have some variation in the conceptualization of *simultaneity*. Collins emphasizes the "theoretical importance" of assuming that all three characteristics are present and active. King suggests that one of the three characteristics may be "more significant" in a given situation; and Zinn and Dill propose that one of the three characteristics may be experienced "differently" depending on the individual's social location. It is only by juxtaposing these three different expressions of the idea of simultaneity that these nuances are revealed. Common to all three expressions is the notion that race, gender, and class are all present and that we should approach each situation with the assumption that all three *may* be active; however, this may not be the case. One or two of the three characteristics may be more salient, more significant, or experienced differently. The answer becomes a question that can be resolved only through empirical research. For example, in the case of racial profiling it is probably typically the individual's race and gender (black male) that prompts a police officer to pull him over. If, however, the individual is observed from nearby, the *assumed* working-class position of the black male may also come into play. Perhaps the most important conclusion to draw from this assumption of simultaneity is that the old approach of studying race *or* gender *or* class individually should be replaced with attention to all three in a given project.

Multiplicative versus additive relationships

The term *simultaneity* is dynamic, suggesting *how* social processes operate—not one at a time but together, in tandem. Closely linked to the notion of simultaneity is the idea of multiplicative relationships. This concept suggests the *form* of social processes that involves race, gender, and class, and intersection theorists express this notion in various ways. Brewer (1993), King (1988), and others eschew the idea that the form is additive. Race, gender, and class effects are not added one to another, they maintain. King (1988, 47) argues that "most applications of the concepts of double and triple jeopardy have been overly simplistic in assuming that the relationships among the various discriminations are merely additive." Brewer (1993, 16) writes of the "embeddedness and relationality of race, class and gender and the multiplicative nature of these relationships: race × class × gender" rather than "race + class + gender." Collins (1995, 492) and Zinn and Dill (1996, 327) all use "intersectional" or "intersectionality" to convey the notion of nonadditive relationships. For Collins (1995, 492) "the notion of intersectionality describes micro-level processes—namely, how each individual and group occupies a social position within interlocking structures of oppression described by the metaphor of intersectionality." For Zinn and Dill (1996, 327),

> multiracial feminism emphasizes the intersectional nature of hierarchies at all levels of social life. Class, race, gender, and sexuality are components of both social structure and social interaction. Women and men are differently embedded in locations created by these cross-cutting hierarchies. As a result, women and men throughout the social order experience different forms of privilege and subordination, depending on their race, class, gender, and sexuality. In other words, intersecting forms of domination produce *both* oppression *and* opportunity.

These and other statements by intersectional theorists appear to focus on experiences, experiences in which an individual's race, gender, and class are all implicated.

Zinn and Dill (1996, 327) write:

> Race, class, gender, and sexuality are not reducible to individual attributes to be measured and assessed for their separate contribution in explaining given social *outcomes,* an approach that Elizabeth Spelman calls "popbead metaphysics," where a woman's *identity* consists of the sum of parts neatly divisible from one another. The matrix of domination seeks to account for the multiple ways that women *experience* themselves as gendered, raced, classed, and sexualized (italics added).

Terms like *matrix of domination, intersectional,* or *intersectionality* all seem to be reaching for concepts that express unique forms of experiences and outcomes. At times, however, some writers, while eschewing additive concepts, use language that is additive. Deborah King (1988, 47), after noting, "The modifier 'multiple' refers not only to several, simultaneous oppressions but to the multiplicative relationships among them as well. . . . the equivalent formulation is racism multiplied by sexism multiplied by classism," proceeds to give examples from black women's slave experience. "While black women workers suffered the same demanding physical labor and brutal punishments as black men, as females, we were *also* subject to forms of subjugation only applicable to women (italics added)." She then quotes from Angela Davis's (1983, 47) *Women, Race and Class:* "If the most violent punishments of men consisted in floggings and mutilations, women were flogged *and* mutilated, *as well as* raped (italics added)." It is difficult not to interpret terms such as *and, also,* or *as well as* in a additive sense.

I suggest that the sense of the preceding passages is cumulative rather than multiplicative (in the statistical sense). Female slaves had the cumulative experience of floggings, mutilations, plus rape. It seems to make intuitive sense that somehow these various experiences of female slaves added up or were cumulative to the point that they exceeded even what black male slaves experienced. This cumulative sense of many experiences is one we are all familiar with from everyday life and is conveyed by such expressions as "the straw that broke the camel's back." Adding just one more frustration to our day is sometimes experienced as just "too much" or as "the last straw." Or to think of it in a slightly different way, we may be able to emotionally (or financially, or . . .) bear up to the negative consequences of our race or our gender or our class; but suffering negative consequences in all three areas simultaneously (as sometimes occurs) may be experienced as debilitating or threatening to push us off the edge (poor, black, and female), expressed in laments of "I can't take any more of this." Of course, the opposite is also true. Having positive consequences of our race, gender, and class may be experienced as "too good to be true," or as euphoric (rich, white, and male). If you look at pictures of individuals included in the *Forbes* list of the 400 richest Americans, you find beaming images of very happy, confident, and satisfied individuals (mostly white men).

All these metaphors attempt to convey something cumulative—something more than merely the sum of parts. Whether the experiences and outcomes of race, gender, and class are cumulative in an additive or multiplicative sense, however, is a matter to be determined by research.

The assumption of multiplicative rather than additive experiences and relationships parallels the statistical distinction between *interactive* and *linear*. In the language of statistics, multiplicative means *interactive.* An interactive relationship is one that is conditional. King (1988) offers an example in Table 2 of "Multiple Jeopardy, Multiple Consciousness," where she presents statistics on income for black and white males and females. In this table it becomes clear that the effect of education on income is conditional on the race and gender of the individual. White males with less than a high school education earn more than black males, white females, or black females with the same level of education. In a statistical sense, the relationship of education and income is multiplicative or interactive; that is, the effect of education varies across categories of race and gender. If the relationship between education and income were additive, individuals in all four locations would receive the same income for the same level of education.

From this point of view, the experiences of males and females and blacks and whites, with respect to education and income, can only be understood using interactive (multiplicative) models. Simple additive (linear) models would fail to reveal the conditional nature of the relationship between education and income. This is the sense in which Zinn and Dill (1996, 327) assert that "women and men are differently embedded in locations created by these cross-cutting hierarchies. As a result, women and men throughout the social order experience different forms of privilege and subordination, depending on their race, class, gender, and sexuality." In other words, the returns on education in income depends on an individual's social location. White males receive the greatest return; black males, white females, and black females receive lower returns than white males. In this example only individuals' race and gender are considered. Models with race, gender, and class can also be constructed but are statistically more complicated, as we will see later. It would appear then that the *form* in which individuals experience race, gender, and class may be either additive or multiplicative, depending on the particular experience in question.

Summary

During the past decades a number of black feminists have argued that our historical approach to studying race, gender, or class has been inadequate to an accurate understanding of our experiences. Rather, they argue, that race, gender, and class are identities of each individual that together shape everyday life and experiences. They further argue that these three identities—race, gender, and class—have parallels at the macro level of society as systems of racism, patriarchy, and capitalism and that these systems function in tandem as interlocking systems of oppression. As aspects of our total identity, race, gender, and class emerge as three of the most salient historically and continue to shape our lives in the twenty-first century. These three identities are assumed not only to simultaneously shape our experiences but to do so interactively. That is, these black feminists argue that the effects of race, gender, and class are multiplicative rather than additive. These two assumptions, I have argued, should be taken as hypotheses to be tested in both qualitative and quantitative research. In this way, this promising new approach to social science inquiry will advance and have its greatest impact.

References

Alger, Horatio, Jr. 1899. *Mark Mason's victory; or, The trials and triumphs of a telegraph boy.* New York: A. L. Burt.

———. [19??] 1972. *Strive and succeed; or, The progress of Walter Conrad.* Philadelphia: Porter & Coates.

———. [18??] 1974. *Making his way; or, Frank Courtney's struggle upward.* New York: Arno Press.

Baron, Harold M. 1971. The demand for black labor: Historical notes on the political economy of racism. *Radical America* 5, no. 2 (March–April): 1–46.

Blumin, Stuart M. 1989. The *emergence of the middle class: Social experience in the American city, 1760–1900.* New York: Cambridge University Press.

Brewer, Rose M. 1993. Theorizing race, class and gender: The new scholarship of black feminist intellectuals and black women's labor. In *Theorizing black feminisms: The visionary pragmatism of black women,* ed. Stalie M. James and Abena P. A. Busia, 13–30. London: Routledge.

Claeys, Gregory. 2000. The "survival of the fittest" and the origins of social Darwinism. *Journal of the History of Ideas* 61, no. 2 (April): 223–40.

Collins, Patricia Hill. 1993. Toward a new vision: Race, class, and gender as categories of analysis and connection. *Race, Sex, & Class* 1, no. 1 (Fall): 557–71.

———. 1995. Symposium on West and Fenstermaker's "Doing Difference." *Gender & Society,* 9, no. 4 (August): 491–94.

———. 1998. Some group matters: Intersectionality, situated standpoints, and black feminist thought. In *Fighting words: Black women and the search for justice,* 201–28.

Davis, Angela. 1983. *Women, Race and Class.* New York: Random House.

Davis, James F. 1991. *Who is black? One nation's definition.* University Park: The Pennsylvania State University.

de Beauvoir, Simone. 1957. *The second sex.* New York: Alfred A. Knopf.

Dennis, Rutledge M. 1995. Social Darwinism, scientific racism, and the metaphysics of race. *Journal of Negro Education* 64, no. 3 (Summer): 243–52.

Domhoff, G. William. 1983. *Who rules America now?: A view for the '80s.* Upper Saddle River, NJ: Prentice Hall.

Dreiser, Theodore. [1900] 1981. *Sister Carrie.* Philadelphia: University of Pennsylvania Press.

Edwards, Richard. 1979. *Contested terrain: The transformation of the workplace in the twentieth century.* New York: Basic Books.

Ehrenreich, Barbara, and Deidre English. 1978. *For her own good: 150 years of the experts' advice to women.* Garden City, NJ: Anchor Press.

Fears, Darryl. 2002. People of color who never felt they were black: Racial label surprises many latino immigrants. *Washington Post,* December 26.

———. 2004. Victory slipping away for black farmers. *Washington Post,* July 20.

Foner, Nancy, and Geroge M. Fredrickson, eds. 2004. *Not just black and white: Historical and contemporary perspectives on immigration, race, and ethnicity in the United States.* New York: Russell Sage Foundation.

Frederickson, George M. 1988. *The arrogance of race: Historical perspectives on slavery, racism, and social inequality.* Middletown, CT: Wesleyan University Press.

Friedan, Betty. 1963. *The feminine mystique.* New York: Dell.

Glenn, Evelyn Nakano. 1992. From servitude to service work: Historical continuities in the racial division of paid reproductive labor. *Signs* 18, no. 1 (Autumn): 1–43.

Goffman, Erving. 1961. *Encounters: Two studies in the sociology of interaction.* Indianapolis, IN: Bobbs-Merrill.

———. 1963. *Behavior in public places: Notes on the social organization of gatherings.* New York: Free Press of Glencoe.

Harrison, Faye V. 1995. The persistent power of "race" in the cultural and political economy of racism. *Annual Review of Anthropology* 24:47–74.

Hartmann, Heidi. 1981. The unhappy marriage of Marxism and feminism: Towards a more progressive union. In *Women and revolution,* ed. Lydia Sargent, 2–41. Boston: South End.

Hurtado, A. 1999. *The color of privilege: Three blasphemies on race and feminism.* Ann Arbor: University of Michigan Press.

Johnson, Allen G. 2006. *Privilege, power, and difference,* 2nd ed. New York: McGraw-Hill.

Joyce, Amy. 2004. Lockheed let racism brew, EEOC says. *Washington Post,* July 13.

King, Deborah K. 1988. Multiple jeopardy, multiple consciousness: The context of a black feminist ideology. *Signs: Journal of Women in Culture and Society* 14, no. 1:42–72.

Kwong, Peter. 1987. *The new Chinatown.* New York: Hill and Wang.

Landry, Bart. 1991. The enduring dilemma of race in America. In *America at century's end,* ed. Alan Wolfe, 185–207. Berkeley: University of California Press.

Leonardo, Zeus. 2004. The color of supremacy: Beyond the discourse of "white privilege." *Educational Philosophy and Theory* 36, no. 2:137–52.

Lindsey, Linda L. 1994. *Gender roles: A sociological perspective.* Upper Saddle River, NJ: Prentice Hall.

Littlefield, Alice, Leonard Lieberman, and Larry T. Reynolds. 1982. Redefining race: The potential demise of a concept in physical anthropology. *Current Anthropology* 23, no. 6 (December): 641–55.

Masters, Brooke A. 2004. Wall Street sex-bias case settled. *Washington Post,* July 13.

Mayer, Caroline E. 2004. Study supports race-bias suit against Honda. *Washington Post,* July 28.

McKinney, Karyn D. 2005. *Being white: Stories of race and racism.* New York: Routledge.

Merle, Renae. 2004. Boeing settles sex-bias lawsuit. *Washington Post,* July 17.

Myrdal, Gunnar. [1944] 1972. *An American dilemma: The Negro problem and modern democracy.* Vol. 1. New York: Pantheon Books.

Oakes, Jeannie. 1985. *Keeping track: How schools structure inequality.* New Haven, CT: Yale University Press.

Ong, Paul, Edna Bonacich, and Lucie Cheng. 1994. *The new Asian immigration in Los Angeles and global restructuring.* Philadelphia: Temple University Press.

PBS. 2001. *People like us: Social class in America.* New York: The Center for New American Media.

Roediger, David R. 2005. *Working toward whiteness: How America's immigrants became white.* New York: Basic Books.

Rothenberg, P., ed. 2002. *White privilege: Essential readings on the other side of racism.* New York: Worth Publishers.

Steinberg, Stephen. 1981. The reconstruction of black servitude after the Civil War. Chap. 7 in *The ethnic myth: Race ethnicity and class in America.* Boston: Beacon Press.

Streicker, Joel. 1995. Policing boundaries: Race, class, and gender in Cartagena, Colombia. *American Ethnologist* 22 (1): 54–74.

Taylor, Carol M. 1981. W. E. B. DuBois's challenge to scientific racism. *Journal of Black Studies* 11, no. 4 (June): 449–60.

West, Candace, and Sarah Fenstermaker, eds. 2002. Power, inequality, and the accomplishment of gender: An ethnomethodological view. In *Doing gender, doing difference: Inequality, power, and institutional change,* 41–54. New York: Routledge.

———. 2002. Doing difference. In *Doing gender, doing difference: Inequality, power, and institutional change,* 55–79. New York: Routledge.

Zhou, Min. 1992. *Chinatown: The socioeconomic potential of an urban enclave.* Philadelphia: Temple University Press.

Zinn, Maxine Baca, and Bonnie Thornton Dill. 1996. Theorizing difference from multiracial feminism. *Feminist Studies* 22, no. 2 (Summer): 321–31.

Multiple Jeopardy, Multiple Consciousness
The Context of a Black Feminist Ideology

DEBORAH K. KING

Black women have long recognized the special circumstances of our lives in the United States: the commonalities that we share with all women, as well as the bonds that connect us to the men of our race. We have also realized that the interactive oppressions that circumscribe our lives provide a distinctive context for black womanhood. For us, the notion of double jeopardy is not a new one. Near the end of the nineteenth century, Anna Julia Cooper, who was born a slave and later became an educator and earned a Ph.D., often spoke and wrote of the double enslavement of black women and of our being "confronted by both a woman question and a race problem."[1] In 1904, Mary Church Terrell, the first president of the National Association of Colored Women, wrote, "Not only are colored women ... handicapped on account of their sex, but they are almost everywhere baffled and mocked because of their race. Not only because they are women, but because they are colored women."[2]

The dual and systematic discriminations of racism and sexism remain pervasive, and, for many, class inequality compounds those oppressions. Yet, for as long as black women have known our numerous discriminations, we have also resisted those oppressions. Our day-to-day survival as well as our organized political actions have demonstrated the tenacity of our struggle against subordination. In the mid-nineteenth century, Sojourner Truth, an anti-slavery activist and women's rights' advocate, repeatedly pronounced the strength and perseverance of black women.[3] More than one hundred years later, another black woman elaborated on Truth's theme. In addressing the National Association for the Advancement of Colored People (NAACP) Legal Defense Fund in 1971, Fannie Lou Hamer, the daughter of sharecroppers and a civil rights activist in Mississippi, commented on the special plight and role of black women over 350 years: "You know I work for the liberation of all people because when I liberate myself, I'm liberating other people ... her [the white woman's] freedom is shackled in chains to mine, and she realizes for the first time that she is not free until I am free."[4] The necessity of addressing all oppressions is one of the hallmarks of black feminist thought.

The Theoretical Invisibility of Black Women

Among the first and perhaps most widely used approaches for understanding women's status in the United States has been the race-sex analogy.

I am greatly indebted to Elsa B. Brown, Elaine Upton, Patricia Palmieri, Patricia Hill Collins, Dianne Pinderhughes, Rose Brewer, and *Signs*' referees for their thoughtful and critical comments on this paper.

[1]Gerda Lerner, ed., *Black Women in White America: A Documentary History* (New York: Vintage, 1973), 573.

[2]Mary Church Terrell, "The Progress of Colored Women," *Voice of the Negro* 1, no. 7 (July 1904): 292.

[3]See Lerner, ed., esp. 566–72; and Bert James Loewenberg and Ruth Bogin, eds., *Black Women in Nineteenth-Century American Life* (University Park: Pennsylvania State University Press, 1976), 234–42.

[4]See Lerner, ed., 609, 610, 611.

In essence, the model draws parallels between the systems and experiences of domination for blacks and those for women, and, as a result, it assumes that political mobilizations against racism and sexism are comparable. In 1860, Elizabeth Cady Stanton observed, "Prejudice against color, of which we hear so much, is no stronger than that against sex."[5] Scholars in various disciplines have drawn similar analogies between racism and sexism. Sociologist Helen Hacker and historian William Chafe have both noted that unlike many ethnic groups, women and blacks possess ineradicable physical attributes that function "systematically and clearly to define from birth the possibilities to which members of a group might aspire."[6] In the first formal typology of the race-sex analogy, Helen Hacker identifies four additional dimensions on which the castelike status of blacks and women are similar: (1) ascribed attributes of emotionality, immaturity, and slyness; (2) rationalizations of status as conveyed in the notions of appropriate "place" and the contented subordinate; (3) accommodating and guileful behaviors; and (4) economic, legal, educational, and social discriminations.[7] Feminist theorists, including Simone de Beauvoir, Kate Millett, Mary Daly, and Shulamith Firestone have all drawn extensively on this analogy in their critiques of the patriarchy.[8]

This analogy has served as a powerful means of conveying an image of women's subordinate status, and of mobilizing women and men for political action. The social movements for racial equality in the United States, whether the abolitionist movement in the nineteenth century or the civil rights movement in the mid-twentieth century, were predecessors, catalysts, and prototypes for women's collective action. A significant segment of feminist activists came to recognize and understand their own oppression, as well as to develop important organizing skills through their participation in efforts for racial justice.[9] In sum, the race-sex correspondence has been used successfully because the race model was a well-established and effective pedagogical tool for both the theoretical conceptualization of and the political resistance to sexual inequality.

---

[5]Elizabeth Cady Stanton as quoted by William Chafe, *Women and Equality: Changing Patterns in American Culture* (New York: Oxford University Press, 1977), 44. Some eighty years after Stanton's observation, Swedish social psychologist Gunnar Myrdal, in an appendix to his *An American Dilemma: The Negro Problem and Modern Democracy* (New York: Harper & Row, 1962), also saw the woman problem as parallel to the Negro problem.

[6]Chafe, 77.

[7]Helen Hacker, "Women as a Minority Group," *Social Forces* 30 (1951): 60–69.

[8]For examples of feminist writings using the race-sex analogy or the master-slave model, see Simone de Beauvoir, *The Second Sex,* trans. and ed. H. M. Parshley (New York Random House, 1974); Kate Millett, *Sexual Politics* (New York: Avon, 1969); Shulamith Firestone, *The Dialectics of Sex* (New York: Morrow, 1970); and Mary Daly, *Beyond God the Father: Toward a Philosophy of Women's Liberation* (Boston: Beacon, 1973).

[9]See Sara Evans, *Personal Politics: The Roots of Women's Liberation in the Civil Rights Movement and the New Left* (New York: Vintage, 1980); Catharine Stimpson, "Thy Neighbor's Wife, Thy Neighbor's Servants: Women's Liberation and Black Civil Rights," in *Woman in Sexist Society: Studies in Power and Powerlessness,* ed. Vivian Gornick and Barbara Moran (New York: Basic, 1971), 452–79; and Angela Davis, *Women, Race and Class* (New York: Random House, 1981). Recently, there has been some debate concerning precisely what lessons, if any, women learned from their participation in the abolitionist and civil rights movements. For an argument against the importance of race-oriented movements for feminist politics, see E. C. DuBois, *Feminism and Suffrage* (Ithaca, N.Y.: Cornell University Press, 1978).

We learn very little about black women from this analogy.[10] The experience of black women is apparently assumed, though never explicitly stated, to be synonymous with that of either black males or white females; and since the experiences of both are equivalent, a discussion of black women in particular is superfluous. It is mistakenly granted that either there is no difference in being black and female from being generically black (i.e., male) or generically female (i.e., white). The analogy obfuscates or denies what Chafe refers to as "the profound substantive differences" between blacks and women. The scope, both institutionally and culturally, and the intensity of the physical and psychological impact of racism is qualitatively different from that of sexism. The group experience of slavery and lynching for blacks, genocide for Native Americans, and military conquest for Mexican-Americans and Puerto Ricans is not substantively comparable to the physical abuse, social discrimination, and cultural denigration suffered by women. This is not to argue that those forms of racial oppressions are greater or more unjust but that the substantive differences need to be identified and to inform conceptualizations. Althea Smith and Abigail Stewart point out that "the assumption of parallelism led to research that masked the differences in these processes [i.e., racism, sexism, and their effects on self-image] for different groups."[11] A similar point has been forcefully made by bell hooks: "No other group in America has so had their identity socialized out of existence as have black women. We are rarely recognized as a group separate and distinct from black men, or a present part of the larger group 'women' in this culture. . . When black people are talked about the focus tends to be on black men; and when women are talked about the focus tends to be on white women."[12] It is precisely those differences between blacks and women, between black men and black women, between black women and white women that are crucial to understanding the nature of black womanhood.

The Promise and Limitations of Double Jeopardy

In 1972, Frances Beale, a founding member of the Women's Liberation Committee of the Student Nonviolent Coordinating Committee (SNCC) and, later, a member of the Third World Women's Alliance, introduced the term "double jeopardy" to describe the dual discriminations of racism and sexism that subjugate black women. Concerning black women, she wrote, "As blacks they suffer all the burdens of prejudice and mistreatment that fall on anyone with dark skin. As women they bear the additional burden of having to cope with white and black men."[13] Beale also astutely observed that

---

[10]Other limitations have been noted by Linda LaRue, who contends that the analogy is an abstraction that falsely asserts a common oppression of blacks and women for rhetorical and propagandistic purposes ("The Black Movement and Women's Liberation," in *Female Psychology: The Emerging Self,* ed. Sue Cox [Chicago: Science Research Assoc., 1976]). In *Ain't I a Woman* (Boston: South End Press, 1981), bell hooks questions whether certain women, particularly those self-identified feminists who are white and middle class, are truly oppressed as opposed to being discriminated against. Stimpson bluntly declares that the race-sex analogy is exploitative and racist. See also Margaret A. Simons, "Racism and Feminism: A Schism in the Sisterhood," *Feminist Studies* 5 (1979): 384–401, for a critical review of this conceptual approach in feminist theorizing.

[11]Chafe, 76; Althea Smith and Abigail J. Stewart, "Approaches to Studying Racism and Sexism in Black Women's Lives," *Journal of Social Issues* 39 (1983): 1–15.

[12]hooks, *Ain't I a Woman,* 7.

[13]Frances Beale, "Double Jeopardy: To Be Black and Female," in *The Black Woman: An Anthology,* ed. Toni Cade (New York: New American Library, 1979), 90–100.

the reality of dual discriminations often entailed economic disadvantage; unfortunately she did not incorporate that understanding into the conceptualization. Perhaps she viewed class status as a particular consequence of racism, rather than as an autonomous source of persecution; but such a preponderant majority of black women have endured the very lowest of wages and very poorest conditions of rural and urban poverty that some scholars have argued that economic class oppression must necessarily constitute a third jeopardy.[14] Still others have suggested that heterosexism or homophobia represents another significant oppression and should be included as a third or perhaps fourth jeopardy.[15] The triple jeopardy of racism, sexism, and classism is now widely accepted and used as the conceptualization of black women's status. However, while advancing our understanding beyond the erasure of black women within the confines of the race-sex analogy, it does not yet fully convey the dynamics of multiple forms of discrimination.

Unfortunately, most applications of the concepts of double and triple jeopardy have been overly simplistic in assuming that the relationships among the various discriminations are merely additive. These relationships are interpreted as equivalent to the mathematical equation, racism plus sexism plus classism equals triple jeopardy. In this instance, each discrimination has a single, direct, and independent effect on status, wherein the relative contribution of each is readily apparent. This simple incremental process does not represent the nature of black women's oppression but, rather, I would contend, leads to nonproductive assertions that one factor can and should supplant the other. For example, class oppression is the largest component of black women's subordinate status, therefore the exclusive focus should be on economics. Such assertions ignore the fact that racism, sexism, and classism constitute three, interdependent control systems. An interactive model, which I have termed multiple jeopardy, better captures those processes.[16]

The modifier "multiple" refers not only to several, simultaneous oppressions but to the multiplicative relationships among them as well. In other words, the equivalent formulation is racism multiplied by sexism multiplied by classism. The sexual exploitation of black women in slavery is a historical example. While black women workers suffered the same demanding physical labor and brutal punishments as black men, as females, we were also subject to forms of subjugation only applicable to women. Angela

[14]See, e.g., Beverly Lindsay, "Minority Women in America: Black American, Native American, Chicana, and Asian American Women," in *The Study of Woman: Enlarging Perspectives of Social Reality,* ed. Eloaise C. Synder (New York: Harper & Row, 1979), 318–63. She presents a paradigm wherein whiteness, maleness, and money are advantageous; a poor, black woman is triply disadvantaged. Lindsay argues that triple jeopardy, the interaction of sexism, racism, and economic oppression, is "the most realistic perspective for analyzing the position of black American women; and this perspective will serve as common linkage among the discussions of other minority women" (328).

[15]See Barbara Smith, ed., *Home Girls: A Black Feminist Anthology* (New York: Kitchen Table Press, 1983), esp. sec. 3; and Audre Lorde, "Scratching the Surface: Some Notes on Barriers to Women and Loving," *Black Scholar* 13 (Summer 1982): 20–24, and *Sister Outsider: Essays and Speeches* (Trumansberg, N.Y.: Crossing Press, 1984).

[16]For other attempts at nonadditive models, see Smith and Stewart; Elizabeth M. Almquist, "Untangling the Effects of Race and Sex: The Disadvantaged Status of Black Women," *Social Science Quarterly* 56 (1975): 129–42; Margaret L. Andersen, *Thinking about Women: Sociological and Feminist Perspectives* (New York: Macmillan, 1983). The term "ethnogender" is introduced in Vincent Jeffries and H. Edward Ransford, *Social Stratification: A Multiple Hierarchy Approach* (Boston: Allyn & Bacon, 1980); and Edward Ransford and Jon Miller, "Race, Sex, and Feminist Outlook," *American Sociological Review* 48 (1983): 46–59.

Davis, in *Women, Race and Class,* notes, "If the most violent punishments of men consisted in floggings and mutilations, women were flogged and mutilated, as well as raped."[17] At the same time, our reproductive and child-rearing activities served to enhance the quantity and quality of the "capital" of a slave economy. Our institutionalized exploitation as the concubines, mistresses, and sexual slaves of white males distinguished our experience from that of white females' sexual oppression because it could only have existed in relation to racist and classist forms of domination.

The importance of any one factor in explaining black women's circumstances thus varies depending on the particular aspect of our lives under consideration and the reference groups to whom we are compared. In some cases, race may be the more significant predictor of black women's status; in others, gender or class may be more influential. Table 1 presents the varied and conditional influence of race and gender and, presumably, of racism and sexism on socioeconomic and educational status. White males earn the highest median incomes, followed in decreasing order by black males, white females, and black females. The educational rankings are different. White males are again on top; but whites, males and females, have more years of schooling than black males and females. While gender is more critical in understanding black women's income ranking, race is more important in explaining their level of educational attainment. But in both examples, black females have the lowest status.

Table 2 shows a more complex relationship between race, gender, and class (here represented by educational attainment), and the influence of these variables on income. Overall, education is an important determinant of income, and despite race or gender, those with more education earn more money than those with less. Men earn more than women at the same level of education, and whites earn more than blacks at the same level of education. But among women, the relationship of education to income is confounded by race. Given our subordinate statuses as female and black, we might expect black women to receive the lowest incomes regardless of their educational attainment. However, the returns of postsecondary education, a college degree or higher, are greater for black females than for white females, while among those with less than a college degree, black females earn less than white females. A similar pattern is not found among males. In this three-way analysis, black

TABLE I ■ RACE AND GENDER INTERACTIVE EFFECTS ON SOCIOECONOMIC STATUS

	Economic status ($)	Educational status (yrs.)
White males	16,467	12.7
Black males	9,448	12.2
White females	6,949	12.6
Black females	6,164	12.2

NOTE. Income figures are 1984 median incomes for those fifteen years or older. Educational attainment is for 1984, median years of school completed.

SOURCE. U.S. Department of Commerce. Bureau of the Census, *Statistical Abstract of the United States, 1987* (Washington, D.C.: Government Printing Office, 1987).

[17]Davis, *Women, Race and Class,* 7.

TABLE 2 ■ MULTIPLICATIVE EFFECTS OF RACE, GENDER, AND CLASS ON INCOME

	Income ($)			
	White males	Black males	White females	Black females
Less than a high school diploma	9,525	6,823	3,961	3,618
4 years of high school	13,733	9,260	6,103	5,954
1–3 years of college	14,258	10,532	6,451	6,929
Bachelor's degree	19,783	14,131	9,134	10,692
5 or more years of postbaccalaureate education	23,143	18,970	12,980	14,537

NOTE. Income is 1979 median income. Educational attainment is used as a measure of economic class.

SOURCE. *Detailed Population Characteristics,* U.S. Summary, Sec. A, 1980 (Washington, D.C.: Government Printing Office, 1980).

women are not consistently in the lowest status, evidence that the importance of the multiple discriminations of race, gender, and class is varied and complex.

In the interactive model, the relative significance of race, sex, or class in determining the conditions of black women's lives is neither fixed nor absolute but, rather, is dependent on the socio-historical context and the social phenomenon under consideration. These interactions also produce what to some appears a seemingly confounding set of social roles and political attitudes among black women. Sociologist Bonnie Thornton Dill has discussed the importance of scholars' recognizing, incorporating, and interpreting the complex variety of social roles that black women have performed in reaction to multiple jeopardies. She argues that the constellation of "attitudes, behaviors, and interpersonal relationships . . . were adaptations to a variety of factors, including the harsh realities of their environment, Afro-American cultural images of black womanhood, and the sometimes conflicting values and norms of the wider society."[18]

A black woman's survival depends on her ability to use all the economic, social, and cultural resources available to her from both the larger society and within her community. For example, black women historically have had to assume economically productive roles as well as retain domestic ones, and until recently our labor force participation rate well exceeded that of white women.[19] Labor, whether unpaid and coerced (as under slavery) or paid and necessary employment, has been a distinctive characteristic of black women's social roles. It has earned us a small but significant degree of self-reliance and independence that has promoted egalitarian relations with black men and active

[18]Bonnie Thornton Dill, "The Dialectics of Black Womanhood," *Signs: Journal of Women in Culture and Society* 4 (1979): 43–55, esp. 547. Smith and Stewart, 1, make a similar point.

[19]In slavery, there was 100 percent labor force participation by black women. In 1910, 34 percent were in the official labor force. In 1960, the figure was 40 percent, and by 1980, it was over 50 percent. Comparable figures for white women are 18 percent in 1890, 22 percent in 1910, 37 percent in 1960, and 51 percent in 1980. For a more detailed discussion, see Phyllis A. Wallace, *Black Women in the Labor Force* (Cambridge, Mass.: MIT Press, 1980).

influence within the black family and community.[20] But it also has had costs. For instance, black women have most often had to work in low status and low paying jobs since race and sex discrimination have historically limited our employment options. The legacy of the political economy of slavery under capitalism is the fact that employers, and not black women, still profit the most from black women's labor. And when black women become the primary or sole earners for households, researchers and public analysts interpret this self-sufficiency as pathology, as deviance, as a threat to black family life.[21] Yet, it is black women's well-documented facility to encompass seemingly contradictory role expectations of worker, homemaker, and mother that has contributed to the confusion in understanding black womanhood.[22] These competing demands (each requiring its own set of resistances to multiple forms of oppression) are a primary influence on the black woman's definition of her womanhood, and her relationships to the people around her. To reduce this complex of negotiations to an addition problem (racism + sexism = black women's experience) is to define the issues, and indeed black womanhood itself, within the structural terms developed by Europeans and especially white males to privilege their race and their sex unilaterally. Sojourner's declaration, "ain't I a woman?" directly refutes this sort of conceptualization of womanhood as one dimensional rather than dialectical.

Multiple jeopardy within the politics of liberation

In order to understand the concept of multiple jeopardy, it is necessary to look beyond the social structure and process of the dominant society

[20]Angela Davis, "Reflections of the Black Woman's Role in the Community of Slaves," *Black Scholar* 3 (December 1971): 2–16, offers an enlightening discussion of the irony of independence out of subordination. See also Deborah Gray White, *Ar'n't I a Woman? Female Slaves in the Plantation South* (New York: Norton, 1985), for a more detailed analysis of the contradictions of the black female role in slavery. For a discussion of the role of black women in the family, see Robert Staples, *The Black Woman in America* (Chicago: Nelson Hall, 1973); Robert Hill, *The Strengths of Black Families* (New York: Emerson Hall, 1972); Herbert Guttman, *The Black Family in Slavery and Freedom, 1750 to 1925* (New York: Random House, 1976); Carol Stack, *All Our Kin: Strategies for Survival in a Black Community* (New York: Harper & Row, 1974); and Charles Willie, *A New Look at Black Families* (New York: General Hall, 1976). For a discussion of black women's community roles, see Bettina Aptheker, *Woman's Legacy: Essays on Race, Sex, and Class in American History* (Amherst: University of Massachusetts Press, 1982); Paula Giddings, *When and Where I Enter: The Impact of Black Women on Race and Sex in America* (New York: William Morrow, 1983); Lerner, ed. (n. 1 above); Sharon Harley and Rosalyn Terborg-Penn, eds., *The Afro-American Woman: Struggles and Images* (Port Washington, N.Y.: Kennikat Press, 1978); Linda Perkins, "The Impact of the 'Cult of True Womanhood on the Education of Black Women," *Journal of Social Issues* 39 (1983): 17–28; and the special issue, "The Impact of Black Women in Education," *Journal of Negro Education* 51, no. 3 (Summer 1982).

[21]See Robert Staples, "The Myth of the Black Matriarchy," in his *The Black Family: Essays and Studies* (Belmont, Calif.: Wadsworth, 1971), and *The Black Woman in America.* Also see hooks, *Ain't I a Woman* (n. 10 above); and Cheryl T. Gilkes, "Black Women's Work as Deviance: Social Sources of Racial Antagonism within Contemporary Feminism," Working Paper no. 66 (Wellesley, Mass.: Wellesley College, Center for Research on Women, 1979). However, more recently Robert Staples has argued that black women who are too independent will be unable to find black mates and that black men are justified in their preference for a more traditionally feminine partner ("The Myth of Black Macho: A Response to Angry Black Feminists," *Black Scholar* 10 [March–April 1979]: 24–32).

[22]See White; and Jacqueline Jones, *Labor of Love, Labor of Sorrow: Black Women, Work and the Family, From Slavery to the Present* (New York: Basic, 1985).

that insidiously pervade even the movements for race, gender, and class liberation. Thus, the confrontations among blacks about sexism and classism, among women about racism and classism, and among the various economic classes about racism and sexism compose a second feature of the context of black feminist ideology. A formidable impediment in these battles is the "monist" approach of most liberation ideologies. In *Liberating Theory*, monism is described as a political claim "that one particular domination precipitates all really important oppressions. Whether Marxist, anarchist, nationalist, or feminist, these 'ideal types' argue that important social relations can all be reduced to the economy, state, culture, or gender."[23] For example, during the suffrage debates, it was routinely asserted that only one group might gain voting privileges—either blacks or women, that is black men or white women. For black women, the granting of suffrage to either group would still mean our disenfranchisement because of either our sex or our race. Faced with this dilemma, many black women and most black men believed that the extension of suffrage to black males was imperative in order to protect race interests in the historical period of postbellum America. But because political empowerment for black women would require that both blacks and women gained the right to vote, some of these same black women also lobbied strenuously for women's suffrage.[24]

The contemporary efforts of black women to achieve greater equal opportunity and status present similar dilemmas, whether in the areas of reproductive rights, electoral politics, or poverty. Our history of resistance to multiple jeopardies is replete with the fierce tensions, untenable ultimatums, and bitter compromises between nationalism, feminism, and class politics. In a curious twist of fate, we find ourselves marginal to both the movements for women's liberation and black liberation irrespective of our victimization under the dual discriminations of racism and sexism. A similar exclusion or secondary status typifies our role within class movements. Ironically, black women are often in conflict with the very same subordinate groups with which we share some interests. The groups in which we find logical allies on certain issues are the groups in which we may find opponents on others. To the extent that we have found ourselves confronting the exclusivity of monistic politics, we have had to manage ideologies and activities that did not address the dialectics of our lives. We are asked to decide with whom to ally, which interests to advance. Should black women's primary ideological and activist commitment be to race, sex, or class-based social movements? Can we afford to be monist? Can we afford not to be?

In the following consideration of the dialectics within each of three liberation movements, I hope to describe the tensions and priorities that influence the construction of a black feminist ideology. To the extent that any politic is monistic, the actual victims of racism, sexism, or classism may be absent from, invisible within, or seen as antagonistic to that politic. Thus, prejudicial attitudes and discriminatory actions may be overt, subtle, or covert; and they may have various manifestations through ideological statements, policies and strategies, and interpersonal relations. That is, black and/or poor women may be marginal to monistic feminism, women's concerns may be excluded from nationalistic activism, and indifference to race and gender may pervade class politics. This invisibility may be due to actual exclusion or benign neglect, while marginality

---

[23]Michael Albert et al., *Liberating Theory* (Boston: South End Press, 1986), 6.

[24]For further discussion of suffrage and racism, see Davis, *Women, Race and Class* (n. 9 above); Giddings; Harley and Terborg-Penn; and Barbara H. Andolsen, *"Daughters of Jefferson, Daughters of Bootblacks": Racism and American Feminism* (Macon, Ga.: Mercer University Press, 1986).

is represented in tokenism, minimization, and devalued participation. Antagonism involves two subordinate groups whose actions and beliefs are placed in opposition as mutually detrimental. From this conceptual framework, the following discussion highlights the major aspects of multiple jeopardy within liberation politics.

Intraracial politics

Racial solidarity and race liberation have been and remain a fundamental concern for black Americans. Historically and currently, slavery, segregation, and institutional as well as individual discrimination have been formative experiences in most blacks' socialization and political outlook. The inerasable physical characteristics of race have long determined the status and opportunities of black women in the United States. Since race serves as a significant filter of what blacks perceive and how blacks are perceived, many black women have claimed that their racial identity is more salient than either their gender or class identity.[25] Diane Lewis, an anthropologist, has remarked that when racism is seen as the principal cause of their subordinate status, "their interests as blacks have taken precedence over their interests as women."[26] This political importance of race is evident for other reasons as well. Certainly, the chronological order of the social movements for racial, gender, and class justice in part explains the priority given to racial interests. In both the nineteenth and twentieth centuries, the abolition and civil rights movements predate women's suffrage and the women's movement. Similarly, collective efforts that addressed economic deprivation and exploitation, such as trade unionism beginning in the late 1800s, communist organizing in the 1920s and 1930s, and the anti-imperialist activism of the 1960s were preceded by or simultaneous with race-oriented movements. Considering the order of events, it is reasonable to expect that most black women would have made commitments to and investments in the race movements such that they would not or could not easily abandon those for later movements.

Furthermore, through the necessity of confronting and surviving racial oppression, black women have assumed responsibilities atypical of those assigned to white women under Western patriarchy. Black women often held central and powerful leadership roles within the black community and within its liberation politics. We founded schools, operated social welfare services, sustained churches, organized collective work groups and unions, and even established banks and commercial enterprises. That is, we were the backbone of racial uplift, and we also played critical roles in the struggle for racial justice.[27] Harriet Tubman led slaves to freedom on the underground railroad; Ida Wells Barnett led the crusade against lynching; Fannie Lou Hamer and Ella Baker were guiding political spirits of the southern black efforts that gave birth to SNCC and the Mississippi Freedom Democratic Party; the "simple" act of Rosa Parks catapulted Martin Luther King to national prominence. Black women, therefore, did not experience sexism within the race movement in

---

[25]See Gloria Joseph and Jill Lewis, *Common Differences: Conflicts in Black and White Feminist Perspectives* (New York: Avon, 1981); Diane K. Lewis, "A Response to Inequality: Black Women, Racism, and Sexism," *Signs* 3 (1977): 339–61; and bell hooks, *Feminist Theory: From Margin to Center* (Boston: South End Press, 1984), for extended discussions of the dynamics of structural subordination to and social conflict with varying dominant racial and sexual groups.

[26]Lewis, 343.

[27]Giddings; Harley and Terborg-Penn; and Davis, "Reflections on the Black Woman's Role in the Community of Slaves."

quite the ways that brought many white women to feminist consciousness within either civil rights or New Left politics.[28]

All together this history constitutes a powerful impetus toward a monistic race approach as the means of liberation for black women. Michelle Wallace concludes that black women simply lack a feminist consciousness as a matter of choice, out of ignorance, misguided beliefs, or an inability to recognize sexual domination both within and without the black community.[29] Since the 1800s, however, the writings of such prominent black women as Sojourner Truth, Maria Stewart, Anna Julia Cooper, Josephine St. Pierre Ruffin, Frances Watkins Harper, Pauli Murray, Frances Beale, Audre Lorde, and Angela Davis have described a broader view of black consciousness.[30] Even among those black women who expressed grave reservations about participating in the women's movement, most recognized sexism as a factor of their subordination in the larger society and acknowledged sexual politics among blacks. They could identify the sexual inequities that resulted in the images of black women as emasculating matriarchs; in the rates of sexual abuse and physical violence; and in black men assuming the visible leadership positions in many black social institutions, such as the church, the intelligentsia, and political organizations.[31] During the civil rights and black nationalist movements of the 1960s and 1970s, men quite effectively used the matriarchy issue to manipulate and coerce black women into maintaining exclusive commitments to racial interests and redefining and narrowing black women's roles and images in ways to fit a more traditional Western view of women. Black feminists Pauli Murray and Pauline Terrelonge Stone both agree that the debates over this issue became an ideological ploy to heighten guilt in black women over their supposed collusion with whites in the oppression of black men.[32] Consequently, these intraracial tensions worked against the public articulations of a feminist consciousness by most black women. Nevertheless, a point of concern and contention within

[28]See Evans (n. 9 above); and Clayborne Carson, *In Struggle: SNCC and the Black Awakening of the 1960s.* (Cambridge, Mass.: Harvard University Press, 1981).

[29]Michelle Wallace, *Black Macho and the Myth of the Superwoman* (New York: Dial, 1979). See also Linda C. Powell, "Black Macho and Black Feminism," in Smith, ed. (n. 15 above), 283–92, for a critique of Wallace's thesis.

[30]For statements by Truth, Stewart, Cooper, Ruffin, and Harper, see Loewenberg and Bogin, eds. (n. 3 above); and Lerner, ed. (n. 1 above); for Lorde, see Lorde (n. 15 above); for Davis, see Davis, *Women, Race and Class;* for Beale, see Frances Beale, "Double Jeopardy" (n. 13 above), and "Slave of a Slave No More: Black Women in the Struggle," *Black Scholar* 12, no. 6 (November/December 1981): 16–24; and for Murray, see Pauli Murray, "The Liberation of Black Women," in *Women; A Feminist Perspective,* ed. Jo Freeman (Palo Alto, Calif.: Mayfield, 1975), 351–63.

[31]Regarding the church, see Pauline Terrelonge Stone, "Feminist Consciousness and Black Women," in Freeman, ed., 575–88; Joseph and Lewis; Jacqueline Grant, "Black Women and the Church," in *But Some of Us Are Brave: Black Women's Studies,* ed. Gloria T. Hull et al. (Old Westbury, N.Y.: Feminist Press, 1982), 141–52; and Cheryl Townsend Gilkes, "'Together and in Harness'; Women's Traditions in the Sanctified Church," *Signs* 10, no. 4 (Summer 1985): 678–99. Concerning politics, see LaRue (n. 10 above); Mae C. King, "The Politics of Sexual Stereotypes," *Black Scholar 4* (March/April 1973): 12–22; and Manning Marable, *How Capitalism Underdeveloped Black America* (Boston: South End Press, 1983), esp. chap. 3. For a discussion of sexual victimization, see Barbara Smith, "Notes for Yet Another Paper on Black Feminism, or Will the Real Enemy Please Stand Up," *Conditions* 5 (1979): 123–27, as well as Joseph and Lewis. For a critique of the notion of the matriarch, see Stone; and Staples, "The Myth of the Black Matriarchy" (n. 21 above).

[32]See Murray; and Stone.

the black community was how sexual inequalities might best be addressed, not whether they existed. A few black women responded by choosing monistic feminism, others sought a distinct black feminist activism. While many organized feminist efforts within race-oriented movements, some also adopted a strict nationalist view. Over time, there were also transformations of perspectives. For example, the black women of SNCC created within it a women's liberation group which later became an independent feminists-of-color organization, the Third World Women's Alliance, which is today the only surviving entity of SNCC.

The politics of race liberation have rarely been exclusively race-based. Because so many blacks historically have been economically oppressed, race liberation has out of necessity become more pluralistic through its incorporation of economic interests. Whether civil rights or a nationalist activism, the approach to class injustice generally promotes greater economic opportunities and rewards within the existing capitalist order. At the turn of the century, for instance, the collective action known as racial uplift involved the efforts of educated, middle-class blacks to elevate the moral, physical, social, and economic conditions of lower income blacks. The National Association of Wage Earners was established in the 1920s by women like Nannie Burroughs, Maggie Wallace, and Mary McCleod Bethune to assist black female domestic and factory workers.[33]

The civil rights movement initially seemed to avoid the value-laden implications of this pattern of middle-class beneficence toward those with fewer economic resources. Both Aldon Morris, a sociologist, and Clayborne Carson, a historian, have written of the genuine grass roots orientation of the black southern strategy in the 1950s and early 1960s.[34] The majority of the participants were rural, poorly educated, and economically disadvantaged, but more important, these same individuals set the priorities and the strategies of the movement. The legacy was an affirmation of the strength of seemingly powerless people, and particularly of the black women who were among the principal organizers and supporters.[35]

Despite these auspicious beginnings, Cornell West, a black theologian, described the 1960s as a time when the interests of poor blacks were often betrayed.[36] Middle-class blacks were better able to take advantage of the relatively greater opportunities made possible through the race-oriented, legal liberalism of equal opportunity and affirmative action policies and electoral politics. Only such groups as the Nation of Islam and the League of Revolutionary Black Workers, like Marcus Garvey's United Negro Improvement Association earlier in this century, continued to represent the interests of working class and impoverished blacks. The contemporary controversy over class polarization in the black community is a consequence of the movement not effectively addressing the economic status of all blacks. Given the particularly precarious economic status of black women, this neglect and marginalization of class is especially problematic for them. The National Welfare Rights Organization, founded in 1967, was one of the few successful, though short-lived, efforts to address the class divisions. Only recently have race-focal groups, including the Urban League and the

---

[33]Evelyn Brooks Bennett, "Nannie Burroughs and the Education of Black Woman," in Harley and Terborg-Penn (n. 20 above), 97–108.

[34]Aldon Morris, *The Origins of the Civil Rights Movement: Black Communities Organizing for Change* (New York: Free Press, 1984); and Carson.

[35]See the recent publication by Jo Ann Gibson Robinson, *The Montgomery Bus Boycott and the Women Who Started It* (Knoxville: University of Tennessee Press, 1987).

[36]Cornell West, "The Paradox of the Afro-American Rebellion," in *The Sixties without Apology,* ed. Sohnya Sayres, Anders Stephanson, Stanley Aronowitz, Fredric Jameson (Minneapolis: University of Minnesota Press, 1984).

National Association for the Advancement of Colored People, addressed the plight of impoverished black women.

Racial solidarity has been a fundamental element of black women's resistance to domination. However, the intraracial politics of gender and class have made a strictly nationalistic approach overly restrictive and incalculably detrimental to our prospects for full liberation. Given a social condition that is also compounded by other oppressions, black women have necessarily been concerned with affecting, at the very least, an amelioration of economic and gender discriminations. Consequently, some black women have sought an association with feminism as one alternative to the limitations of monistic race politics.

Politics among women

At one level, black women, other women of color, and white women share many common contemporary concerns about their legal status and rights, encounters with discrimination, and sexual victimization. It is on these shared concerns that feminists have sought to forge a sense of sisterhood and to foster solidarity. This effort is manifest in a variety of ways, but the slogan "sisterhood is powerful" best exemplifies the importance and the hoped for efficacy of such solidarity in the achievement of women's equality and liberation. For example, all-female restrictions for consciousness-raising sessions, intellectual and artistic programs and publications, organizations, businesses, and communities reflect this singular orientation; and lesbian feminist separatism represents the absolute ideological expression of the monistic tendencies in feminism.

Presumably, black women are included in this sisterhood, but, nonetheless, invisibility and marginality characterize much of our relationship to the women's movement. The assertion of commonality, indeed of the universality and primacy of female oppression, denies the other structured inequalities of race, class, religion, and nationality, as well as denying the diverse cultural heritages that affect the lives of many women. While contending that feminist consciousness and theory emerged from the personal, everyday reality of being female, the reality of millions of women was ignored. The phrase "the personal is the political" not only reflects a phenomenological approach to women's liberation—that is, of women defining and constructing their own reality—but it has also come to describe the politics of imposing and privileging a few women's personal lives over all women's lives by assuming that these few could be prototypical. For black women, the personal is bound up in the problems peculiar to multiple jeopardies of race and class, not the singular one of sexual inequality. This has not necessarily meant that black women rejected feminism, but merely that they were not single-mindedly committed to the organizations and some of the agenda that have come to be called the women's movement, that is, the movement of white, often protestant, middle-class women.

Feminism has excluded and devalued black women, our experiences, and our interpretations of our own realities at the conceptual and ideological level. Black feminists and black women scholars have identified and critically examined other serious flaws in feminist theorizing. The assumption that the family is by definition patriarchal, the privileging of an individualistic worldview, and the advocacy of female separatism are often antithetical positions to many of the values and goals of black women and thus are hindrances to our association with feminism.[37] These theoretical blinders

[37]Lorde, *Sister Outsider,* esp. 66–71; hooks, *Feminist Theory* (n. 25 above); Linda Burnharn, "Has Poverty Been Feminized in Black America?" *Black Scholar* 16, no. 2 (March/April 1985): 14–24; Maria C. Lugones and Elizabeth V. Spelman, "Have We Got A Theory for You! Feminist Theory, Cultural Imperialism and the Demand for "The Woman's Voice,' " *Women's Studies International Forum* 6, no. 6 (1983): 573–81.

obscured the ability of certain feminists first to recognize the multifaceted nature of women's oppressions and then to envision theories that encompass those realities. As a consequence, monistic feminism's ability to foresee remedies that would neither abandon women to the other discriminations, including race and class, nor exacerbate those burdens is extremely limited. Without theories and concepts that represent the experiences of black women, the women's movement has and will be ineffectual in making ideological appeals that might mobilize such women. Often, in fact, this conceptual invisibility has led to the actual strategic neglect and physical exclusion or nonparticipation of black women. Most black women who have participated in any organizations or activities of the women's movement are keenly aware of the racial politics that anger, frustrate, and alienate us.

The case of the struggle for suffrage in the nineteenth century again is an instructive example of the complexity of multiple jeopardy and its politics. Initially, there was an alliance of blacks and women for universal suffrage. However, as the campaign ensued, opponents of universal suffrage, and of any extension of voting privileges, were successful in transforming the debate into one of who should receive the vote—women or black males. Many prominent white suffragists, including Elizabeth Cady Stanton, Susan B. Anthony, and Carrie Chapman Catt, abandoned the alliance and demanded a "women only" enfranchisement. The question of black women's suffrage should have been especially problematical for them. In fact, it was never seriously considered. More damning, however, were their politics of expediency. They cooperated with avowed racists in order to gain the southern vote and liberally used racial slurs and epithets arguing that white women's superior character and intellect made them more deserving of the right to vote than blacks, Native Americans, and Eastern European and Asian immigrants.

As Angela Davis observes in her examination of race and class in the early women's rights campaign, even the Seneca Falls Declaration "all but ignored the predicament of white working-class women, as it ignored the condition of black women in the South and North alike."[38] Barbara Andolsen, in one of the most comprehensive studies of racism in the woman suffrage movement observed: "[it] had a bold vision and noble principles . . . but this is a story of a vision betrayed. For the white women who led this movement came to trade upon their privilege as the daughters (sisters, wives, and mothers) of powerful white men in order to gain for themselves some share of the political power those men possessed. They did not adequately identify ways in which that political power would not be accessible to poor women, immigrant women, and black women."[39] Yet despite the blatant racism and class bias of the women's suffrage movement, black women, discouraged and betrayed, continued to work for their right to vote, both as blacks and as women, through their own suffrage organizations.

This history of racism in the early women's movement has been sustained by contemporary white feminists. Within organizations, most twentieth-century black women encounter myriad experiences that deny their reality. In some instances, it is the absence of materials, information, speeches, readings, or persons representing black women. When present at all, women of color are underrepresented and have marginal and subordinate roles. Recently, Paula Giddings has reported that the National Organization of Women (NOW) remains insensitive to such problematic issues as rape, abortion, sterilization, poverty, and unions. Women of color are rarely elected as officers or appointed to major positions, and NOW has actually

---

[38] Davis, *Women, Race and Class* (n. 9 above), 53–54.

[39] Andolsen (n. 24 above), 78.

encouraged minority women's chapters rather than the incorporation of their concerns into the "regular" chapters.[40] Lawyer and educator Mary Frances Berry, in her analysis of the politics of amending the constitution, has argued that one reason for the defeat of the Equal Rights Amendment was the failure of its proponents to campaign, educate, and mobilize the black community, and especially black women.[41]

Many white feminist activists have often assumed that their antisexism stance abolished all racial prejudice or discriminatory behaviors. At best, this presumption is naive and reflects a serious ignorance of the pervasiveness of racism in this society. Many blacks, women and men alike, see such postures as arrogant, racist, and dangerous to their own interests. Diane Lewis concluded that the status of black women and our interests within the women's movement and its organizations essentially replicates our structurally subordinate position to white women in the larger society.[42] Different opportunity structures and life options make interracial alliances and feminist solidarity problematic. Conceptually invisible, interpersonally misunderstood and insulted, and strategically marginal, black women have found that much in the movement has denied important aspects of our history and experience. Yet, despite the critical obstacles and limitations, the imperatives of multiple jeopardy necessitate recognizing and resisting sexism.

Beyond the race politics in feminism, many black women share concerns of impoverished and working-class women about class politics. What has become mainstream feminism rests on traditional, liberal economic aspirations of equal employment opportunities for women. In practice, however, the emphasis is often on the professional careers of those women who are already economically privileged and college educated. It could be argued, for instance, that equal access to all types of vocational training and jobs may not be desirable as a necessary or primary goal. While it is true that men on average earn more than women, all men do not have equally attractive jobs in terms of working conditions, compensation and benefits, prestige, and mobility. Those male jobs may represent, at best, only a minimal improvement over the jobs of many working women. White feminist economic concerns have concentrated on primary sector employment, but these are not the positions that are most critical and accessible to lower- or no-income women. Referring to the equal opportunity approach, Karen Kollias points out that "the majority of nonwhite, lower- and working-class women don't have the power to utilize these benefits because their primary, objective economic conditions haven't changed."[43]

Class stratification becomes an insignificant issue if economic disadvantage is seen as only relevant for feminism to the extent that women are unequal vis-à-vis men. The difference between male and female incomes is dramatically less among blacks than among whites (see Table 1), suggesting that sex alone is not the sole determinant of economic status. From a monist feminist perspective, class exploitation is not understood as an independent system of oppression. Consequently, broad class dynamics are not addressed in liberal and some radical feminisms. Marxist and socialist feminists have

---

[40]Giddings (n. 20 above), 348.

[41]Mary Frances Berry, *Why ERA Failed: Politics, Women's Rights, and the Amending Process of the Constitution* (Bloomington: Indiana University Press, 1986).

[42]Lewis (n. 25 above).

[43]Karen Kollias, "Class Realities: Create a New Power Base," in *Building Feminist Theory: Essays from Quest,* ed. *Quest* staff (New York: Longman, 1981), 125–38, esp. 134.

sought to correct this biased view of class.[44] While the Marxists attempted to incorporate a concern for gender within traditional Marxist analysis, socialist feminists tried to develop a nonmonist perspective of feminism that saw sexism and classism as co-equal oppressions. Ellen Willis concludes that within various feminisms there was limited politics beyond an assertion that class hierarchy was oppressive. A radical feminist, she observes that the consciousness-raising, personal politics approach did not effectively challenge the structural, political economy of class oppression. She concludes that as a consequence, "women were implicated in the class system and had real class interests, that women could oppress men on the basis of class, and that class differences among women could not be resolved within a feminist context alone."[45]

First, the memberships of these class-oriented groups remained mostly middle class. Economically disadvantaged women have not directly contributed to a feminist theoretical understanding of class dynamics or the development of programs and strategies. Black feminist and literary critic bell hooks notes that "had poor women set the agenda for feminist movement, they might have decided that class struggle would be a central feminist issue."[46] She further contends that class oppression has not become central among women liberationists because their "values, behaviors, and lifestyles continue to be shaped by privilege."[47] In a similar fashion, feminist and race politics have not informed or established ties between poor and working-class black and white women. Phyllis M. Palmer reasons that from the perspective of a poor black woman, white women individually may suffer wage discrimination because of their sex, but their relations to white males, the top income earners, as daughters and wives grants them a relatively better quality of material well-being. "Most white women do not *in reality* live on what they earn; they have access to the resources of white male income earners."[48] Rejecting what she views as the hollow efforts of "slumming" or nonhierarchical organizing, she observes that no serious strategies have been developed for convincing bourgeois women that class liberation is critical for women's liberation or for organizing with poor and working-class women.

This lack of attention to economic issues has significant implications for the participation of black women. Many of the differences of priorities between black and white women are related to class. Issues of welfare, hunger, poor housing, limited health care, and transportation are seldom seen as feminist interests and are rarely the subject of feminist social policies. As Brenda Eichelberger maintains, "the black woman's energy output is more often directed toward such basic survival issues, while the

---

[44]See Josephine Donovan, *Feminist Theory: The Intellectual Traditions of American Feminism* (New York: Ungar, 1985); and Lydia Sargent, ed., *Woman and Revolution: A Discussion of the Unhappy Marriage of Marxism and Feminism* (Boston: South End Press, 1981); and Zillah R. Eisenstein, ed., *Capitalist Patriarchy and the Case for Socialist Feminism* (New York: Monthly Review Press, 1979), for fuller discussions.

[45]Ellen Willis, "Radical Feminism and Feminist Radicalism," in Sayres et al., eds. (n. 36 above), 91–118, esp. 110–11.

[46]hooks, *Feminist Theory* (n. 25 above), 60–61.

[47]Ibid., 61.

[48]Phyllis Marynick Palmer, "White Women/Black Women: The Dualism of Female Identity and Experiences in the United States," *Feminist Studies* 91 (Spring 1983): 162.

white woman's is more often aimed at fulfillment."[49] The economic concerns of women from lower-income backgrounds are relatively ignored and distorted in the contemporary women's movement. The feminist interpretation of the "feminization" of poverty is a case in point. While noting that some women, again middle class, have indeed experienced a recent drastic decline in life circumstances as a consequence of divorce, the feminization analysis has misrepresented many of the causes of female poverty. For example, most impoverished women have been poor throughout their lives as a consequence of their class position or of racial oppression. Linda Burnham writes that race and class are more significant causative factors in black women's impoverishment than is gender. In the thesis of the feminization of poverty, she contends, "The vulnerability of white women to impoverishment is overstated; the impoverishment of Black men is ignored or underestimated; and the fundamental basis in working-class exploitation for the continual regeneration of poverty is abandoned for a focus on gender."[50]

In summary, feminism's neglect, misunderstanding, or deemphasis of the politics of race and class have direct implications for the actions of black women in relationship to the movement. Often, our response has been to avoid participation in white female, middle-class dominated organizations and to withhold our support from policies that are not in our race and class interests. Nevertheless, just as the importance of race led many black women to commitments to racially based politics, and gender interests compelled our feminist efforts, economic injustices have brought many to consider class politics as a major avenue of liberation.

Class politics

Economic exploitation is the third societal jeopardy constraining the lives of black women. Historically, the three major movements to address the deprivations of class in the United States have been trade unionism and the anticapitalist politics of the 1930s and 1960s, which are colloquially referred to as the Old and the New Left. Having their origins in responses to the degradations that accompanied urbanization and industrialization, labor unionists and leftists organized to address the problems of wage labor and economic stratification in a capitalistic society, including the excessive working hours in poor, unsafe conditions, low pay and limited job security, fluctuations in the labor demand, the decline in work satisfaction, the loss of worker autonomy, and poverty. Each movement, although monistic, possessed different objectives. Unionism was reformist in orientation, seeking to ameliorate the worst of the above conditions. In contrast, the socialist and communist ideologies of the Left were revolutionary in that they aspired to eradicate capitalism and ostensibly to establish a classless society.

Into the first quarter of this century, organized labor's approach to economic disadvantage held little promise for blacks or women, and thus no promise for black women. Samuel Gompers, the leading force of trade unionism and president of the American Federation of Labor (AFL, founded in 1886), believed that the best means of improving wages for Anglo males was to restrict the labor supply. His strategy was to advocate the return of women to the home and the banning of blacks and Asians from the unions. Although the AFL never formally adopted these restrictions at the national level, many

[49]Brenda Eichelberger, "Voices on Black Feminism," *Quest: A Feminist Quarterly* 4 (1977): 16–28, esp. 16.

[50]Burnham (n. 37 above), 15.

local chapters did so through both formal rules and informal practices.[51] Trade unionists cultivated a cultural image of the worker as a married male who required a family wage to support a wife and children. Labor actively supported protective labor legislation, which effectively excluded women from the jobs that would provide them with sufficient incomes to support themselves and their families. These efforts against women were coupled with the exclusion of blacks, other racial minorities, and initially southern and eastern European immigrant males from the most economically rewarding labor in the unionized crafts and the closed shops. Blacks, in particular, were specifically denied union membership or else relegated to the unskilled, low paying jobs. Consequently, the denial of a family wage to black males exacerbated the circumstances of already economically distressed black families and individuals. In occupations where blacks were well represented, unionization often meant their forceable expulsion. Many of the race riots in the early 1900s were related to the tensions between black laborers and white laborers in competition for employment. So, an effective two-prong strategy for improving white men's income required the demand for a family wage and the restriction of labor competition from women and racial minorities.

In response to union discrimination, white women and black women and men organized. The Working Women's Association, formed in 1868, was one of the earlier attempts at synthesizing feminist and white female workers concerns; the Women's Trade Union League, established in 1903, allied white working- and middle-class women, while the International Ladies' Garment Workers' Union publicized the conditions of white working women, demanded equal pay, demanded female representation in the national labor unions, formed female unions, and organized strikes.[52] Ironically, most of the women's trade union organizations as well as many socialist feminists supported protective legislation but with the mistaken belief that involving the state would ensure safer work environments and reasonable labor requirements for both women and men. However, an unintended consequence of this strategy was that many women's economic situations declined because protective legislation could be used to reinforce occupational segregation and thus limit women's wage earning opportunities.

As the wives and daughters of men who did not earn a family wage, black women's participation in the labor market was crucial to the survival of themselves and their families. Yet, black women benefited little from the unionization efforts among white women. First, they were disproportionately situated in those occupations least likely to be unionized, such as domestic and nonhousehold service and agricultural labor. In

---

[51]For discussion of women, employment, and the labor movement, see Diane Balser, *Sisterhood and Solidarity: Feminism and Labor in Modern Times* (Boston: South End Press, 1987); Carol Groneman and Mary Beth Norton, eds., *"To Toil the Livelong Day": America's Women at Work, 1780–1980* (Ithaca, N.Y.: Cornell University Press, 1987); Philip S. Foner, *Women and the American Labor Movement: From World War I to the Present* (New York: Free Press, 1980); Bettina Berch, *The Endless Day: The Political Economy of Women and Work* (New York: Harcourt Brace Jovanovich, 1982); and Mary Frank Fox and Sharlene Hesse-Biber, *Women at Work* (Palo Alto, Calif.: Mayfield, 1984). For blacks, see Marable (n. 31 above); Richard Polenberg, *One Nation Divisible: Class, Race, and Ethnicity in the United States since 1938* (New York: Penguin, 1980); Philip S. Foner, *Organized Labor and the Black Worker, 1619–1973* (New York: International Publishers, 1976); and Dorothy K. Newman et al., *Protest, Politics, and Prosperity; Black Americans and White Institutions, 1940–75* (New York: Pantheon, 1978).

[52]See Balser for a detailed consideration of the contemporary union activities of women, especially their efforts to organize clerical and other pink collar workers.

large industrial workplaces, they were segregated from white female workers, where the organizing took place, and were often pawns in the labor-management contests.[53] Second, white trade unionists failed actively to recruit black females and they often were denied membership because of their race. The protective legislation further hampered their opportunities by closing off numerous employment opportunities simply on the basis of sex. Black women wanted better paying jobs, but they often had to settle for the jobs that were considered too hazardous, dirty, or immoral for white women, and for which they were not fairly compensated. During the Depression, race-gender discrimination was so pervasive that employment in federal work-relief projects often was closed to them. Thus, significant numbers of black women were unemployed and/or underemployed and, therefore, untouched by union activism.

Despite their exclusion from the major unions, black women and men organized caucuses within predominantly white unions and formed their own unions, such as the Urban League's Negro Workers Councils, African Blood Brotherhood, Negro American Labor Council, National Negro Labor Council, and Dodge Revolutionary Union Movement (DRUM). A. Phillip Randolph, founder of the Brotherhood of Sleeping Car Porters, called for a march on Washington in the 1940s to demand the end of wage and job discrimination, the desegregation of schools and public accommodations, protection of immigrant workers, cessation of lynching, and the unionization of black women. During the Depression, trade unions and unemployed councils held demonstrations demanding immediate cash relief and unemployment compensation, as well as advocating race solidarity. For blacks in the first half of this century, class and race interests were often inseparable. Black women benefited indirectly from black men's labor activism, and they often supported those efforts by participating on picket lines, providing food and clothing for strikers and their families, and, most important, making financial contributions to the households from their own paid labor. Black women also engaged in labor organizing directly, both through existing predominantly white unions and through their own activism. Black domestics, tobacco workers, garment workers, and others organized strikes and fought for union representation.[54]

Not all unions and economic organizations excluded white women and black women and men. The Knights of Labor, established in 1886, the Industrial Workers of the World, created in 1905, and the Congress of Industrial Organizations, formed in 1938, are noted for encouraging the unionization of millions of black men and black and white women workers. But overall, the record of organized labor on issues of import to black women and men and white women has not been outstanding. Until 1971, the major unions opposed the Equal Rights Amendment; and today, many challenge affirmative action and comparable worth policies. The continued need for black and women's labor organizations suggest that the historic barriers remain to their full participation and rewards in unions. But, it is also important to recognize that the trade unionist approach has many limitations, and first among these is its focus on the individual worker. As a result, the broad issues of poverty and economic inequality are perceived as beyond the purview of most labor activism.

[53]See Jones (n. 22 above); Giddings (n. 20 above); and Davis, *Women, Race and Class* (n. 9 above), for an examination of black women's work roles and labor activism.

[54]See Dolores Janiewski, "Seeking 'a New Day and a New Way': Black Women and Unions in the Southern Tobacco Industry"; and Elizabeth Clark-Lewis, "'This Work Had a End': African-American Domestic Workers in Washington, D.C., 1910–1940," both in Groneman and Norton, eds.

While seeking to ameliorate the worst of industrial society, unionists seldom challenge the economic order of capitalism.

This challenge was left to the Socialist and Communist activists, but this radical critique of the political economy has never been a part of the political mainstream of the United States as it has in other nations. Nevertheless, a small but significant group of activists and intellectuals have advanced radicalism throughout this century.[55] The political Left, in general, supported black women and men and white working women during the Progressive Era. In fact, leading intellectuals, including Emma Goldman, Margaret Sanger, Charlotte Perkins Gilman, Elizabeth Gurley Flynn, Langston Hughes, Paul Robeson, W. E. B. Du Bois, and C. L. R. James saw socialism as the route for liberation. Two black women, Lucy Parsons and Claudia Jones, were among the early labor activists and Socialists of the Old Left. And even Angela Davis, who describes the important role of individual women within the Socialist and Communist parties during the first half of the twentieth century, does not offer us much insight into the general status of black women, besides noting the Socialist party's indifference to blacks, both males and females.[56]

But even within these efforts, there still were gaps in recognizing the needs of black women. In 1900, the Socialist party was founded and immediately began campaigning for women's suffrage and labor rights through its Woman's National Committee. Because it focused on the industrial proletariat, it paid no particular attention to blacks since they were mostly agricultural laborers. Consequently, the party also paid minimal attention to the black women who were not industrially employed. In contrast, members of the Communist party were actively involved in organizing industrial workers, sharecroppers, and the unemployed during the Depression and in championing racial as well as economic justice for blacks.[57] However, the Communist party remained relatively silent on various feminist concerns. Its vigorous defense of the Scottsboro boys and other victims of racial bigotry linked with its call for black self-determination initially attracted numerous blacks to the party in the 1930s and 1940s. Nevertheless, it became increasingly clear that the international Communist party was concerned with the liberation of blacks only as long as those efforts advanced its overall objective of aiding the revolutionary leadership of a European working class. Eventually, the collusion of the American Communist party with racism and sexism dissuaded many blacks and women of the advantages of Soviet-oriented communist activism.

The second surge of anticapitalism was an integral part of the so-called New Left of the 1960s. Sociologist Stanley Aronowitz has described the sixties' radicalism as the movements of a generation, which were not oriented around any particular class or race issue.[58] While this might characterize certain aspects of the radical critique of the liberal society, his interpretation does not account for the ideological and activist history that informed both the black and women's liberation efforts of that decade. In an analysis of the contradictions and dilemmas of the New Left, Peter Clecak described the era as one that lacked a vision of a new society beyond

[55]See Peter Clecak, *Radical Paradoxes: Dilemmas of the American Left: 1945–1970* (New York: Harper & Row, 1973), for an illuminating analysis of the Old and New Left.

[56]Davis, *Women, Race and Class.*

[57]See Vincent Harding, *The Other American Revolution* (Los Angeles and Atlanta: University of California, Los Angeles, Center for Afro-American Studies, and Institute of the Black World, 1980), for discussion of blacks and communist organizing.

[58]Stanley Aronowitz, "When the New Left Was New," in Sayres et al., eds. (n. 36 above), 11–43.

the negation of the present ills of poverty, racism, imperialism, and hegemony. Its apocalyptic perspectives on American society and utopian images of community were founded on a fundamental acceptance of capitalist notions of individualism, personal gain, and personal liberty.[59] By implication, much of the New Left lacked a basic, critical understanding of the dynamics of oppressions as group and systemic processes.

The disillusionment that characterized the New Left movement was compounded by the frustration of its failure to organize the urban poor and racial minorities. The free speech and antiwar activists, Students for a Democratic Society and the Weather Underground (i.e., the weathermen), mistakenly attempted to organize northern urban communities using SNCC's southern mobilization model. At another level, new leftists did not understand that most members of oppressed groups desired a piece of the American Dream, not its destruction. The efforts to create coalitions with civil rights and black nationalist groups were strained and defeated because of the conflicting objectives and tactics. The aims of civil rights groups were integrationist through nonviolent means; and while black militants advocated armed defense or even revolution and adopted a Maoist, anticapitalist program, their separatist orientation made black-white alliances almost impossible. Moreover, while the Left condemned the role of U.S. imperialism in Southeast Asia, it ignored the advance of Western, capitalist interests into the continent of Africa, especially South Africa.

At the same time, women active in the New Left became increasingly frustrated with the theoretical and strategic indifference to the woman question. The sexual politics within the movement subjected women to traditional gender role assignments, sexual manipulation, male leadership and domination, plus a concentration on an essentially male issue, the draft.[60] Once again, invisibility typifies the role of black women in New Left radical politics. Black women responded by incorporating class interests into their race and gender politics. In the founding documents of various black feminist organizations, scathing critiques of the political economy are a cornerstone of the analysis of domination. For example, the *Combahee River Collective Statement* pointedly declared that "the liberation of all oppressed peoples necessitates the destruction of the political-economic systems of capitalism and imperialism, as well as partriarchy. . . . We are not convinced, however, that a socialist revolution that is not also a feminist and anti-racism revolution will guarantee our liberation."[61] This excerpt clearly articulates an understanding of multiple jeopardy and its function in the dominant society and within liberation politics. Out of necessity, black women have addressed both narrow labor and broad economic concerns.

Political theorist Manning Marable has argued that progressive forces must uproot racism and patriarchy in their quest for a socialist democracy through a dedication to equality.[62] Yet a major limitation of both unionism and radical class politics is their monist formulations, wherein economics are exaggerated at the expense of understanding and confronting

---

[59]Clecak.

[60]Heidi Hartmann and Zillah Eisenstein provide theoretical critiques of monist Marxism as an adequate avenue for women's liberation. Both Lydia Sargent and Sara Evans detail the sexual politics on the Left (see Heidi Hartmann, "The Unhappy Marriage of Marxism and Feminism," in Sargent, ed. [n. 44 above]; Eisenstein, "Reform and/or Revolution: Toward a Unified Women's Movement," in Sargent, ed. [n. 44 above], 339–62; Sargent, "New Left Women and Men: The Honeymoon Is Over," in Sargent, ed. [n. 44 above], xi–xxxii; and Evans [n. 9 above]).

[61]See Combahee River Collective, *Combahee River Collective Statement: Black Feminist Organizing in the Seventies and Eighties* (New York: Kitchen Table Press, 1986), 12–13.

[62]Marable (n. 31 above).

other oppressions such as racism and sexism. Despite the historical examples of black women and men and white women as union activists and socialists and the examples of the sporadic concern of organized labor and leftists with race and gender politics, class politics have not provided the solution to black women's domination because they continue to privilege class issues within a white male framework. Given the inability of any single agenda to address the intricate complex of racism, sexism, and classism in black women's lives, black women must develop a political ideology capable of interpreting and resisting that multiple jeopardy.

MULTIPLE CONSCIOUSNESS IN BLACK FEMINIST IDEOLOGY

Gloria Joseph and Jill Lewis have suggested that black women face a dilemma analogous to that of Siamese twins, each of whom have distinct and incompatible interests.[63] Black women cannot, they argue, be wholeheartedly committed and fully active in both the black liberation struggle and the women's liberation movement, because of sexual and racial politics within each respectively. The authors recognize the demands of multiple jeopardy politics and the detrimental effect of neglecting these dual commitments. But what they fail to consider are the multiple and creative ways in which black women address their interdependent concerns of racism, sexism, and classism.

Black women have been feminists since the early 1800s, but our exclusion from the white women's movement and its organizations has led many incorrectly to assume that we were not present in the (white) women's movement because we were not interested in resisting sexism both within and without the black community. What appears recently to be a change in black women's position, from studied indifference to disdain and curiosity to cautious affirmation of the women's movement, may be due to structural changes in relationships between blacks and whites that have made black women "more sensitive to the obstacles of sexism and to the relevance of the women's movement."[64] Black women's apparent greater sensitivity to sexism may be merely the bolder, public articulation of black feminist concerns that have existed for well over a century. In other words, black women did not just become feminists in the 1970s. We did, however, grant more salience to those concerns and become more willing to organize primarily on that basis, creating the Combahee River Collective, the National Black Feminist Organization, and Sapphire Sapphos. Some black women chose to participate in predominantly white, women's movement activities and organizations, while others elected to develop the scholarship and curriculum that became the foundation of black women's studies, while still others founded black feminist journals, presses, and political organizations.[65]

---

[63]Joseph and Lewis (n. 25 above), 38.

[64]Lewis (n. 25 above), 341.

[65]For information on the development of black feminist scholarship and academic programs, see Patricia Bell Scott, "Selective Bibliography on Black Feminism" in Hull et al., eds. (n. 31 above); Black Studies/Women's Studies Faculty Development Project, "Black Studies/Women's Studies: An Overdue Partnership" (Women's Studies, University of Massachusetts–Amherst, mimeograph, 1983); Nancy Conklin et al., "The Culture of Southern Black Women: Approaches and Materials" (Produced and distributed by The University of Alabama Archives of American Minority Cultures and Women's Studies Program, Project on the Culture of Southern Black Women, 1983); the premier issue of *Sage: A Scholarly Journal on Black Women* 1, no. 1 (Spring 1984); and the establishment of Kitchen Table: A Women of Color Press, New York. The Center for Research on Women at Memphis State University, the Women's Research and Resource Center at Spelman College, and the Minority Women's Program at Wellesley College are among the academic centers.

Several studies have considered the relevance of black women's diverse characteristics in understanding our political attitudes; these reports seem fairly inconsistent, if not contradictory.[66] The various findings do suggest that the conditions that bring black women to feminist consciousness are specific to our social and historical experiences. For black women, the circumstances of lower socioeconomic life may encourage political, and particularly feminist, consciousness.[67] This is in contrast to feminist as well as traditional political socialization literature that suggests that more liberal, that is, feminist, attitudes are associated with higher education attainment and class standing. Many of the conditions that middle-class, white feminists have found oppressive are perceived as privileges by black women, especially those with low incomes. For instance, the option not to work outside of the home is a luxury that historically has been denied most black women. The desire to struggle for this option can, in such a context, represent a feminist position, precisely because it constitutes an instance of greater liberty for certain women. It is also important to note, however, that the class differences among black women regarding our feminist consciousness are minimal. Black women's particular history thus is an essential ingredient in shaping our feminist concerns.

Certainly the multifaceted nature of black womanhood would meld diverse ideologies, from race liberation, class liberation, and women's liberation. The basis of our feminist ideology is rooted in our reality. To the extent that the adherents of any one ideology insist on separatist organizational forms, assert the fundamental nature of any one oppression, and demand total cognitive, affective, and behavioral commitment, that ideology and its practitioners exclude black women and the realities of our lives.

A black feminist ideology, first and foremost, thus declares the visibility of black women. It acknowledges the fact that two innate and inerasable traits, being both black and female, constitute our special status in American society. Second, black feminism asserts self-determination as essential. Black women are empowered with the right to interpret our reality and define our objectives. While drawing on a rich tradition of struggle as blacks and as women, we continually establish and reestablish our own priorities. As black women, we decide for ourselves the relative salience of any and all identities and oppressions, and how and the extent to which those features inform our politics. Third, a black feminist ideology fundamentally challenges the interstructure of the oppressions of racism, sexism, and classism both in the dominant society and within movements for liberation. It is in confrontation with multiple jeopardy that black women define and sustain a multiple consciousness essential for our liberation, of which feminist consciousness is an integral part.

---

[66]See Andrew Cherlin and Pamela Waters, "Trends in United States Men's and Women's Sex-Role Attitudes: 1972–1978," *American Sociological Review* 46 (1981): 453–60. See also, Janice Gump, "Comparative Analysis of Black Women's and White Women's Sex-role Attitudes," *Journal of Consulting and Clinical Psychology* 43 (1975): 858–63; and Marjorie Hershey, "Racial Difference in Sex-Role Identities and Sex Stereotyping: Evidence against a Common Assumption," *Social Science Quarterly* 58 (1978): 583–96. For various opinion polls, see "The 1972 Virginia Slims American Women's Opinion Poll," and "The 1974 Virginia Slims American Women's Opinion Poll," conducted by the Roper Organization (Williamstown, Mass.: Roper Public Opinion Research Center, 1974). See Barbara Everitt Bryant, "American Women: Today and Tomorrow," National Commission on the Observance of International Women's Year (Washington, D.C.: Government Printing Office, March 1977). Gloria Steinem, "Exclusive Louis Harris Survey: How Women Live, Vote and Think," *Ms. Magazine* 13 (July 1984): 51–54.

[67]For analyses of the influence of socioeconomic class and race on feminist attitudes, see Willa Mae Hemmons, "The Women's Liberation Movement: Understanding Black Women's Attitudes," in *The Black Woman*, ed. LaFrances Rodgers-Rose (Beverly Hills, Calif.: Sage Publications, 1980), 285–99; and Ransford and Miller (n. 16 above).

Finally, a black feminist ideology presumes an image of black women as powerful, independent subjects. By concentrating on our multiple oppressions, scholarly descriptions have confounded our ability to discover and appreciate the ways in which black women are not victims. Ideological and political choices cannot be assumed to be determined solely by the historical dynamics of racism, sexism, and classism in this society. Although the complexities and ambiguities that merge a consciousness of race, class, and gender oppressions make the emergence and praxis of a multivalent ideology problematical, they also make such a task more necessary if we are to work toward our liberation as blacks, as the economically exploited, and as women.

Department of Sociology
Dartmouth College

THEORIZING RACE, CLASS AND GENDER

The New Scholarship of Black Feminist Intellectuals and Black Women's Labor

ROSE M. BREWER

At the centre of the theorizing about race, class and gender in the USA is a group of Black feminist intellectuals. These are academics, independent scholars and activists who are writing and rethinking the African-American experience from a feminist perspective. In this chapter, I am most concerned with the ideas of those women involved in knowledge production who are situated in the academy: colleges and universities throughout the USA. Their insights are essential to the rethinking which must occur in conceptualizing the African-American experience. Although they are few in number, their recent placement in Women's Studies, Ethnic Studies and traditional disciplines such as sociology, political science, history, English, anthropology, comparative literature and so on, is strategic to the current upsurge in Black feminist scholarship.

What is most important conceptually and analytically in this work is the articulation of multiple oppressions. This polyvocality of multiple social locations is historically missing from analyses of oppression and exploitation in traditional feminism, Black Studies and mainstream academic disciplines. Black feminist thinking is essential to possible paradigm shifts in these fields; for example, in Black Studies to begin explaining the African-American experience through the multiple articulations of race, class and *gender* changes the whole terrain of academic discourse in that area. Black feminist social scientists deconstruct existing frameworks in sociology, history and a range of other disciplines.

In the ensuing discussion I look more carefully at how Black feminist theorizing is central to our rethinking the African-American experience. I examine Black women's labor and African-American class formation to illustrate how race, class and gender in intersection contribute to our understanding of African-American life. I organize the chapter around the following three themes: (1) an examination of the context of recent Black feminist theorizing in the social sciences; (2) a closer analysis of a major proposition of Black feminist thought, "the simultaneity of oppression," given race, class and gender as categories of analyses in the social sciences; and (3) sketching out a reconstructed analysis of Black women's labor and African-American class formation through the lenses of race and gender.

THE SOCIAL CONTEXT OF RECENT BLACK FEMINIST THEORIZING

The theory and practice of Black feminism predates the current period. Even during the first wave of feminism, according to Terborg-Penn (1990), prominent Black feminists combined the fight against sexism with the fight against racism by continuously calling the public's attention to these issues. Turn-of-the-century Black activist Anna Julia Cooper conceived the African-American woman's position thus:

> She is confronted by a woman question and a race problem, and is as yet an unknown or unacknowledged factor in both.
>
> (*A Voice from the South by a Black Woman of the South*, 1892)

Although early-twentieth-century Black suffragettes saw women's rights as essential to relieving social ills, they repeatedly called attention to issues of race. Nonetheless, within the vise of race, African-American women forged a feminist consciousness in the USA. Such women might be called the original Black feminists. Again, the life and work of Anna Julia Cooper is a case in point. Guy-Sheftall and Bell-Scott (1989, 206) point out that Cooper's work, *A Voice from the South by a Black Woman of the South* (1892), "has the distinction of being the first scholarly publication in the area of Black women's studies, though the concept had certainly not emerged during the period."

Yet the gateway to the new Black feminist scholarship of the past twenty years is the civil rights movement and the mainstream feminist movement of the late 1960s and early 1970s. E. Frances White, an activist in the civil rights movement, captures the recent historical context in which contemporary Black feminists are located. She says:

> I remember refusing to leave the discussion at a regional black student society meeting to go help out in the kitchen. The process of alienation from those militant and articulate men had begun for me.
>
> (1984, 9)

White goes on to point out that:

> many of today's most articulate spokeswomen, too, participated in the black student, civil rights, and black nationalist movements. Like their white counterparts, these women felt frustrated by restraints imposed on them by the men with whom they shared the political arena.
>
> (1984, 9)

For Cynthia Washington, an activist in the Student Nonviolent Coordinating Committee (SNCC), this incipient Black feminism is given a different slant. She points out that although Black women's abilities and skills were recognized in the movement, the men categorized the women as something other than female (Echols 1989). Both these positions reflect the historic path of Black feminist development in the second wave of US feminism. White and Washington's interpretations of the movement point to the multiple consciousness which informs Black feminist thinking and struggles. Black feminism is defined as a multiple level engagement (King 1988).

This is strikingly exemplified by the Combahee River Collective. The organization was formed by a group of Black lesbian feminists in the mid-1970s. In the context of murder in Boston, Barbara Smith and a group of other Black women founded the collective. Smith was insistent that the murder of Black women was not only a racial issue. The fact that thirteen Black women were killed cruelly exhibited how sexism and racism intersected in the lives of African-American women. Given this, the collective argued:

> The most general statement of our politics at the present time would be that we are actively committed to struggling against racial, sexual, heterosexual, and class oppression, and see as our particular task the development of an integrated analysis and practice based upon the fact that major systems of oppression create the conditions of our lives. As Black women we see Black feminism as the logical political movement to combat the manifold and simultaneous oppressions that all women of color face.
>
> (Smith 1983, 272)

Importantly, Black feminist theorizing places African-American women at the center of the analyses (Hull et al. 1982; Collins 1986, 1990; King 1988; Dill 1979). By theorizing from the cultural experiences of African-American women, social scientists such as Collins argue epistemologically that experience is crucial to Black women's ways of knowing and being in the world. Thus capturing that cultural experience is essential to a grounded analysis of African-American women's lives. This means analysis predicated on the everyday lives of African-American women. More difficult has been linking the everyday to the structural constraints of institutions and political economy (Brewer 1983, 1989). Indeed, a challenge to Black feminist theory is explicating the interplay between agency and social structure. However, nearly all the recent writing has been about everyday lived experiences. Less successful and visible is the explication of the interrelationship between lives and social structure.

Finally, running through Black feminist analyses is the principle of "the simultaneity of oppression" (Hull et al. 1982). This is the conceptual underpinning of much of recent Black feminist reconceptualization of African-American life. In the following discussion, "the simultaneity of oppression" is examined more carefully and is central to our understanding of Black women's labor and African-American class formation. Furthermore rethinking the social structure of inequality in the context of race, class and gender intersections is crucial to this discussion, using Black women's textile industry work in North Carolina as a case in point.

Race, class and gender: "the simultaneity of oppression"

The conceptual anchor of recent Black feminist theorizing is the understanding of race, class and gender as simultaneous forces. The major propositions of such a stance include:

1. critiquing dichotomous oppositional thinking by employing both/and rather than either/or categorizations
2. allowing for the simultaneity of oppression and struggle, thus
3. eschewing additive analyses: race + class + gender
4. which leads to an understanding of the embeddedness and relationality of race, class and gender and the multiplicative nature of these relationships: race × class × gender
5. reconstructing the lived experiences, historical positioning, cultural perceptions and social construction of Black women who are enmeshed in and whose ideas emerge out of that experience, and
6. developing a feminism rooted in class, culture, gender and race in interaction as its organizing principle.

Importantly, the theorizing about race, class and gender is historicized and contextualized.

Race, class and gender: as categories of analysis

Race has been defined in a number of ways, yet a few powerful conceptualizations are useful to our discussion of Black feminist theory. Recently feminist historian Higginbotham notes:

> Like gender and class, then, race must be seen as a social construction predicated upon the recognition of difference and signifying the simultaneous distinguishing and positioning of groups vis-à-vis one another. More than this, race is a highly contested representation of relations of power between social categories by which individuals are identified and identify themselves.
>
> (1992, 253)

The embeddedness of gender within the context of race is further captured by Higginbotham. She notes that:

> in societies where racial demarcation is endemic to their sociocultural fabric and heritage—to their laws and economy, to their institutionalized

> structures and discourses, and to their epistemologics and everyday customs—gender identity is inextricably linked to and even determined by racial identity. We are talking about the racialization of gender and class.
>
> (1992, 254)

Omi and Winant point out:

> The effort must be made to understand race as an unstable and decentered complex of social meanings constantly being transformed by political struggle.
>
> (1987, 68)

And finally, Barbara Fields conceptualizes race ideologically:

> If race lives on today, it does not live on because we have inherited it from our forebears of the seventeenth century or the eighteenth or nineteenth, but because we continue to create it today.
>
> (1970, 117)

Relatedly, gender as a category of analysis cannot be understood decontextualized from race and class in Black feminist theorizing. Social constructions of Black womanhood and manhood are inextricably linked to racial hierarchy, meaning systems and institutionalization. Indeed, gender takes on meaning and is embedded institutionally in the context of the racial and class order: productive and social reproductive relations of the economy.

Accordingly, class as an economic relationship expressing productive and reproductive relations is a major category of analysis in the notion of the simultaneity of oppression. Yet recent Black feminist writers (hooks 1984; Collins 1990; King 1988) point out the tendency of theorists writing in the class traditions to reduce race and gender to class. Similarly Black feminist economist Rhonda Williams (1985) places changes in the labor market squarely in a race, gender and class framework that cannot be explained through traditional labor/capital analyses.

Yet we can fall into the trap of overdetermination, especially in the case of race as a category of analysis. In fact, Higginbotham (1992) draws our attention to the metalanguage of race in which internal issues of gender and class are subsumed to a unitarian position of African-Americans. Here, class is hidden or misspecified and gender is rendered invisible in this conceptualization of African-American inequality. Indeed, race in the context of the globalization of capitalism makes gender the center of the new working class.

Summary

My purpose in this chapter has been to explicate some of the recent theorizing on race, class and gender by Black feminist thinkers in the academy. This theorizing is further explored in an analysis of Black women's labor and African-American class formation. The labor transformation of Black women has been explicated in terms of economic restructuring and capital mobility, racial formation and gender inequality. It is a process linking Black women in the northeast and midwest to the south and southwest, Asia, Africa and the Caribbean. It is not the tie of poverty to prosperity, but the tie of subordinate status to subordinate status crosscut by internal class differences in all these regions. Because of class, which intersects with race and gender, a sector of Black women is in the upwardly mobile integrated sector of a servicized economy. These are women who are moving out of the fast-growing female service sector made up of clericals into the somewhat slower-growing high technology fields which are male dominated. Even still, the rate of change into high-paying fields has been slow for Black women. In 1970, 1 percent of African-American women were engineers and by 1980 only 7 percent were (Amott and Matthaei 1991). More often Black women professionals are ghettoized in the lowest-paying professional fields. They are poorly represented in engineering, computer science, and other highly skilled fields with high pay. Currie and Skolnick (1984) aptly note that "short of an unprecedented shift in the sex composition of these occupations, their growth (highly paid professionals) seems unlikely to have a very strong effect on the overall distribution of (Black) women in the job hierarchy."

Finally, a discernible number of Black women are subemployed (desire full-time rather than the part-time work they have) or have been marginalized from work altogether (Woody and Malson 1984). This occurs across regions; it is especially evident in northern and southern inner cities and rural areas. About half of all poor female-headed Black families are in the South. Additionally, the bifurcation of Black women's labor plays out a certain logic. Somewhat higher levels of clerical and white-collar service work are being performed by skilled Black women in the northeast, midwest and west while capital mobility has devastated the Black male semi-skilled and unskilled working class in older industrial areas. What is left is a service sector of racial minority women working for low wages. Simultaneously, there is a marginalization of some Black women from work altogether. They depend upon transfer payments, the informal economy of bartering, hustling, exchange, and kinship support.

Even now, the largest category of Black women workers in the USA is clerical and service workers (Simms and Malveaux 1986). The latter is a category encompassing household workers, cleaners, janitors and public service workers, jobs which are extensions of the private household service role. Internationally, there is a broad base of women doing semi-skilled labor in the electronics, computer and other "sunrise" industries which have gone abroad. This is the work, primarily, of the white and Asian working-class female in the internal national women's economy.

Finally, the intersection of race, class and gender, in interplay with economic restructuring, accounts for the internal fractioning and separation of women from one another. Yet, this is not the entire story. Cultural practice, beliefs and ideology also structure female labor. The ideology of what is appropriately Black women's work is played out in the arena of the public social reproduction of labor. Kitchen and cafeteria workers, nurses' aides: these are defined as appropriate jobs for Black women, very much as the domestic labor of a generation ago was defined as "Black women's work." It is only when all these processes are better understood that perspectives on African-American inequality will be more accurate.

Crucially, the Black class structure is made in the context of economic, state restructuring and political struggle, and the recreation of race, and a gender/racial division of labor. These are not unrelated phenomena. The result is a highly complicated positioning of the Black population with some sectors clearly worse off than in the past, and other sectors more securely tied to mainstream institutions. African-American women are at the center of this reconstitution of Black labor and class formation. Most importantly, only in theorizing the complexity of the intersections of race, class and gender can we adequately prepare to struggle for social change in the African-American community.

Conclusions

In theorizing the construction of race, class and gender in intersection, three key themes are apparent. First, gender alone cannot explain the African-American woman's or man's experience. Feminism must reflect in its theory and practice the race and class terrain upon which hierarchy and inequality are built globally and within the USA. Secondly, the simultaneity of these social forces is key. In turn, practice and struggle must be anti-sexist, anti-classist, anti-racist and anti-homophobic.

Finally, the "gender, race, class" dynamic is the major theoretical frame through which gender is incorporated into discussions of the position of Black women. Alone, they are rather sterile categories infused with meaning developed out of many decades of social thought on class and race. In interplay with the concept gender, the paradigm becomes fairly rich (Brewer 1989). It is the simultaneity of these forces which has been identified and theorized by Black feminist thinkers. Preliminary thinking in this direction suggests that any such analyses must be historically based and holistic.

Given the writings of Black feminist thinkers in the social sciences, social scientific analyses embodying race, class and gender are growing. Simms and Malveaux (1986), Dill (1979), Collins (1986), King (1988) and Higginbotham (1992) are among a growing number of Black feminist social scientists. These writers critique parallelist tendencies and oppositional dualistic thinking. The old additive models miss an essential reality, the qualitative difference in the lives of African-American women through the simultaneity of oppression and resistance. Thus we must rethink many of the extant analyses on African-Americans through the lenses of gender, race and class. This is just the beginning phase of the kind of work which must be done for a robust and holistic understanding of African-American life.

Bibliography

Amadiume, Ifi (1988) *Male Daughters, Female Husbands,* London: Zed Books.

Amott, Theresa and Matthaci, Judith (1991) *Race, Gender and Work,* Boston, Mass.: South End Press.

Baron, Harold (1971) "The Demand for Black Labor: Historical Notes on the Political Economy of Racism," *Radical America* (March–April).

Beverly, Creigs C. and Stanback, Howard J. (1986) "The Black Underclass: Theory and Reality," *The Black Scholar* 17: 24–32.

Bluestone, Barry and Harrison, Bennett (1982) *The Deindustrialization of America,* New York: Basic Books.

Bonancich, Edna (1976) "Advanced Capitalism and Black/White Relations," *American Sociological Review* 41: 34–51.

Braverman, Harry (1974) *Labor and Monopoly Capital: The Degradation of Labor in the Twentieth Century,* New York and London: Monthly Review Press.

Brewer, Rose M. (1983) "Black Workers and Corporate Flight." *Third World Socialists* 1: 9–13.

———. (1989) "Black Women and Feminist Sociology: The Emerging Perspective," *American Sociologist* 20 (1): 57–70.

Clavell, Pierre, Forester, John and Goldsmith, William (eds.) (1980) *Urban and Regional Planning in an Age of Austerity,* New York: Pergamon Press.

Collins, Patricia Hill (1986) "Learning from the Outsider Within: The Sociological Significance of Black Feminist Thought," *Social Problems* 33 (6) (December): 14–32.

———. (1989) "Toward a New Vision: Race, Class and Gender as Categories of Analysis and Connection," keynote address, delivered at Integrating Race and Gender into the College Curriculum: A Workshop Sponsored by the Center for Research on Women, Memphis State University, Memphis, TN, May 24, 1989.

———. (1990) *Black Feminist Thought: Knowledge. Consciousness, and the Politics of Empowerment,* Boston, Mass.: Unwin Hyman.

Combahee River Collective (1982) "A Black Feminist Statement," in Hull, Bell-Scott and Smith (1982): 13.

Cooper, Anna Julia (1892) *A Voice from the South by a Black Woman of the South,* Ohio: Aldine.

Currie, Elliott and Skolnick, Jerome H. (1984) *America's Problems,* Boston, Mass.: Little, Brown.

Davis, Angela (1981) *Women, Race and Class,* New York: Random House.

Dill, Bonnie (1979) "The Dialectics of Black Womanhood," *Signs: Journal of Women in Culture and Society* 3: 543–55.

Echols, Alice (1989) *Daring to Be Bad,* Minneapolis, MN: University of Minnesota Press.

Fernandez-Kelly, Maria Patricia (1983) *For We Are Sold,* Albany, NY: State University of New York Press.

Fields, Barbara (1990) "Slavery, Race and the Ideology in the United States of America." *New Left Review*: 181.

Fuentes, Ann and Ehrenreich, Barbara (1983) *Women in the Global Factory,* Boston, Mass.: South End Press.

Glenn, Evelyn Nakano (1985) "Racial Ethnic Women's Labor: The Intersection of Race, Gender and Class Oppression," *Review of Radical Political Economics* 17 (3): 86–108.

Gordon, David, Edwards, Richard and Reich, Michael (1982) *Segmented Work, Divided Workers*, Cambridge: Cambridge University Press.

Gough, Ian (1981) *The Political Economy of the Welfare State*, New York: Macmillan.

Guy-Sheftall, Beverly and Bell-Scott, Patricia (1989), "Black Women's Studies: A View from the Margin," in C. Pearson, J. S. Touchton and D. C. Shavlik (eds) *Educating the Majority: Women Challenge Tradition in Higher Education* New York: Macmillan.

Higginbotham, Evelyn Brooks (1992) "African-American Women's History and the Metalanguage of Race," *Signs: Journal of Women in Culture and Society* 17 (2): 253–4.

hooks, bell (1984) *Feminist Theory: From Margin to Center*, Boston, Mass.: South End Press.

Hull, Gloria T., Bell-Scott, Patricia and Smith, Barbara (1982) *All the Women are White, All the Blacks are Men, But Some of Us are Brave*, Old Westbury, NY: Feminist Press.

Janiewski, Dolores E. (1985) *Sisterhood Denied*, Philadelphia, PA: Temple University Press.

Jones, Jacqueline (1985) *Labor of Love, Labor of Sorrow*, New York: Basic Books.

King, Deborah K. (1988) "Multiple Jeopardy, Multiple Consciousness: The Context of a Black Feminist Ideology," *Signs: Journal of Women in Culture and Society* 14 (1) (August): 42–72.

Leacock, Eleanor and Safa, Helen 1. (1986) *Women's Work: Development and the Division of Work by Gender*, South Hadley, Mass.: Bergin & Garvey.

Lorde, Audre (1983) "Age, Race, Class, and Sex: Women Redefining Difference," in *Sister Outsider, Essays and Speeches*, New York: Crossing Press: 114–23.

Mohanty, Chandra (1991) "Introduction: Cartographies of Struggle. Third World Women and the Politics of Feminism," in Chandra Talpade Mohanty. Ann Russo and Lourdes Torres (eds) *Third World Women and the Politics of Feminism*, Bloomington, IN: Indiana University Press.

Nash, June and Fernandez-Kelly, Maria Patricia (1983) *Women, Men and the International Division of Labor*, Albany, NY: State University of New York Press.

Nash, June and Safa, Helen I. (1976) *Sex and Class in Latin America*, New York: Praeger.

Noyelle, Thierry and Stanback, Thomas M. Jr. (1983) *The Economic Transformation of American Cities*, Totowa, NY: Rowman & Littlefield.

Omi, Michael and Winant, Howard (1987) *Racial Formation in the United States*, New York: Routledge & Kegan Paul.

Perry, David and Watkins, Alfred (1977) *The Rise of Sunbelt Cities*, Beverly Hills, CA: Sage.

Sacks, Karen (1989) "Toward a Unified Theory of Class, Race, and Gender," *American Ethnologist* 16 (3).

Safa, Helen I. (1983) "Women, Production and Reproduction in Industrial Capitalism," in Nash and Fernandez-Kelly (eds).

Sawers, Larry and Tabb, William K. (1984) *Sunbelt/Snowbelt*, New York: Oxford University Press.

Sidel, Ruth (1986) *Women and Children Last*, New York: Viking Press.

Simms, Margaret C. and Malveaux, Julianne M. (eds) (1986) *Slipping Through the Cracks: The Status of Black Women*, New Brunswick, NJ: Transaction Publishers.

Smith, Barbara (ed.) (1983) *Home Girls: A Black Feminist Anthology*, New York: Kitchen Table, Women of Color Press.

Staples, Robert (1991) "The Political Economy of Black Family life," in *The Black Family*, Belmont, CA: Wadsworth.

Terborg-Penn, Rosalyn (1990) "Historical Treatment of Black Women in the Women's Movement," in Darlene Clark Hine (ed.) *Black Women in United States History*, Brooklyn: Carolson Publishing Co.

Vogel, Lise (1983) *Marxism and the Oppression of Women*, New Brunswick, NJ: Rutgers University Press.

Wallace, Phyllis (1974) *Pathways to Work*, Cambridge, Mass.: MIT Press.

———. (1980) *Black Women in the Labor Force*, Cambridge, Mass.: MIT Press.

White, E. Frances (1984) "Listening to the Voices of Black Feminism," *Radical America*: 7–25.

Williams, Rhonda (1985) "Competition, Class Location and Discrimination: Black Workers and the New Growth Dynamic," unpublished paper presented at the Current Economic Revolution in Black America Conference, University of Texas, Austin, Tex.

Wilson, William J. (1980) *The Declining Significance of Race,* Chicago: University of Chicago Press.
———. (1987) *The Truly Disadvantaged,* Chicago: University of Chicago Press.
Woody, Bette and Malson, Michelene (1984) "In Crisis: Low Income Black Employed Women in the U. S. Workplace," Working Paper no. 131, Wellesley College, Center for Research on Women, Wellesley, MA.
Wright, Eric Olin (1985) *Classes,* London: Verso.

Toward a New Vision
Race, Class, and Gender as Categories of Analysis and Connection

PATRICIA HILL COLLINS

The true focus of revolutionary change in never merely the oppressive situations which we seek to escape, but that piece of the oppressor which is planted deep within each of us.

—AUDRE LORDE, *SISTER OUTSIDER,* 123

Audre Lorde's statement raises a troublesome issue for scholars and activists working for social change. While many of us have little difficulty assessing our own victimization within some major system of oppression, whether it be by race, social class, religion, sexual orientation, ethnicity, age or gender, we typically fail to see how our thoughts and actions uphold someone else's subordination. Thus, white feminists routinely point with confidence to their oppression as women but resist seeing how much their white skin privileges them. African-Americans who possess eloquent analyses of racism often persist in viewing poor White women as symbols of white power. The radical left fares little better. "If only people of color and women could see their true class interests," they argue, "class solidarity would eliminate racism and sexism." In essence, each group identifies the type of oppression with which it feels most comfortable as being fundamental and classifies all other types as being of lesser importance.

Oppression is full of such contradictions. Errors in political judgment that we make concerning how we teach our courses, what we tell our children, and which organizations are worthy of our time, talents and financial support flow smoothly from errors in theoretical analysis about the nature of oppression and activism. Once we realize that there are few pure victims or oppressors, and that each one of us derives varying amounts of penalty and privilege from the multiple systems of oppression that frame our lives, then we will be in a position to see the need for new ways of thought and action.

To get at that "piece of the oppressor which is planted deep within each of us," we need at least two things. First, we need new visions of what oppression is, new categories of analysis that are inclusive of race, class, and gender as distinctive yet interlocking structures of oppression. Adhering to a stance of comparing and ranking oppressions—the proverbial, "I'm more oppressed than you"—locks us all into a dangerous dance of competing for attention, resources, and theoretical supremacy. Instead, I suggest that we examine our different experiences within the more fundamental relationship of damnation and subordination. To focus on the particular arrangements that race or class or gender take in our time and place without seeing these structures as sometimes parallel and sometimes interlocking dimensions of the more fundamental relationship of domination and subordination may temporarily ease our consciences. But while such thinking may lead to short term social reforms, it is simply inadequate for the task of bringing about long term social transformation.

While race, class and gender as categories of analysis are essential in helping us understand the structural bases of domination and subordination, new ways of thinking that are not accompanied by new ways of acting offer incomplete prospects for change. To get at that "piece of the oppressor which is planted deep within each of us," we also need to change our daily behavior. Currently, we are all enmeshed in a complex web of problematic relationships that grant our mirror images full human subjectivity while stereotyping and objectifying those most different than ourselves. We often assume that the people we work with, teach, send our children to school with, and sit next to . . . will act and feel in prescribed ways because they belong to given race, social class or gender categories. These judgments by category must be replaced with fully human relationships that transcend the legitimate differences created by race, class and gender as categories of analysis. We require new categories of connection, new visions of what our relationships with one another can be. . . .

[This discussion] addresses this need for new patterns of thought and action. I focus on two basic questions. First, how can we reconceptualize race, class and gender as categories of analysis? Second, how can we transcend the barriers created by our experiences with race, class and gender oppression in order to build the types of coalitions essential for social exchange? To address these questions I contend that we must acquire both new theories of how race, class and gender have shaped the experiences not just of women of color, but of all groups. Moreover, we must see the connections between the categories of analysis and the personal issues in our everyday lives, particularly our scholarship, our teaching and our relationships with our colleagues and students. As Audre Lorde points out, change starts with self, and relationships that we have with those around us must always be the primary site for social change.

How Can We Reconceptualize Race, Class and Gender as Categories of *Analysis?*

To me, we must shift our discourse away from additive analyses of oppression (Spelmen 1982; Collins 1989). Such approaches are typically based on two key premises. First, they depend on either/or, dichotomous thinking. Persons, things and ideas are conceptualized in terms of their opposites. For example, Black/White, man/woman, thought/feeling, and fact/opinion are defined in oppositional terms. Thought and feeling are not seen as two different and interconnected ways of approaching truth that can coexist in scholarship and teaching. Instead, feeling is defined as antithetical in reason, as its opposite. In spite of the fact that we all have "both/and" identities, (I am both a college professor and a mother—I don't stop being a mother when I drop my child off at school, or forget everything I learned while scrubbing the toilet), we persist in trying to classify each other in either/or categories. I live each day as an African-American woman—a race/gender specific experience. And I am not alone. Everyone has a race/gender/class specific identity. Either/or, dichotomous thinking is especially troublesome when applied to theories of oppression because every individual must be classified as being either oppressed or not oppressed. The both/and position of simultaneously being oppressed and oppressor becomes conceptually impossible.

A second premise of additive analyses of oppression is that these dichotomous differences must be ranked. One side of the dichotomy is typically labeled dominant and the other subordinate. Thus, Whites rule Blacks, men are deemed superior to women, and reason is seen as being preferable to emotion. Applying this premise to discussions of oppression leads to the assumption that oppression can be quantified, and that some groups are oppressed more than others. I am frequently asked, "Which has been most oppressive to you, your status as a Black person or your status as a woman?" What I am really being asked to do is divide myself into little boxes and rank my various statuses. If I experience oppression as a both/and phenomenon, why should I analyze it any differently?

Additive analyses of oppression rest squarely on the twin pillars of either/or thinking and the necessity to quantify and rank all relationships in order to know where one stands. Such approaches typically see African-American women as being more oppressed than everyone else because the majority of Black women experience the negative effects of race, class and gender oppression simultaneously. In essence, if you add together separate oppressions, you are left with a grand oppression greater than the sum of its parts.

I am not denying that specific groups experience oppression more harshly than others—lynching is certainly objectively worse than being held up as a sex object. But we must be careful not to confuse this issue of the saliency of one type of oppression in people's lives with a theoretical stance positing the interlocking nature of oppression. Race, class and gender may all structure a situation but may not be equally visible and/or important in people's self-definitions. In certain contexts, such as the antebellum American South and contemporary South America, racial oppression is more visibly salient, while in other contexts, such as Haiti, El Salvador and Nicaragua, social class oppression may be more apparent. For middle class White women, gender may assume experiential primacy unavailable to poor Hispanic women struggling with the ongoing issues of low paid jobs and the frustrations of the welfare bureaucracy. This recognition that one category may have salience over another for a given time and place does not minimize the theoretical importance of assuming that race, class and gender as categories of analysis structure all relationships.

In order to move toward new visions of what oppression is, I think that we need to ask new questions. How are relationships of domination and subordination structured and maintained in the American political economy? How do race, class and gender function as parallel and interlocking systems that shape this basic relationship of domination and subordination? Questions such as these promise to move us away from futile theoretical struggles concerned with ranking oppressions and towards analyses that assume race, class and gender are all present in any given setting, even if one appears more visible and salient than the others. Our task becomes redefined as one of reconceptualizing oppression by uncovering the connections among race, class and gender as categories of analysis.

I. The institutional dimension of oppression

Sandra Harding's contention that gender oppression in structured along three main dimensions—the institutional, the symbolic and the individual—offers a useful model for a more comprehensive analysis encompassing race, class and gender oppression (Harding 1989). Systemic relationships of domination and subordination structured through social institutions such as schools, businesses, hospitals, the work place and government agencies represent the institutional dimension of oppression. Racism, sexism and elitism all have concrete institutional locations. Even though the workings of the institutional dimension of oppression are often obscured with ideologies claiming equality of opportunity, in actuality, race, class and gender place Asian-American women, Native American men, White men, African-American women and other groups in distinct institutional niches with varying degrees of penalty and privilege.

Even though I realize that many . . . would not share this assumption, let us assume that the institutions of American society discriminate, whether by design or by accident. While many of us are familiar with how race, gender and class operate separately to structure inequality, I want to focus on how these three systems interlock in structuring the institutional dimension of oppression. To get at the interlocking nature of race, class and gender, I want you to think about the antebellum plantation as a guiding metaphor for a variety of American social institutions. Even though slavery is typically analyzed as a racist institution, and occasionally as a class institution, I suggest that slavery was a race, class, gender specific institution. Removing any one piece from our analysis diminishes our understanding of the true nature of relations of domination and subordination under slavery.

Slavery was a profoundly patriarchal institution. It rested on the dual tenets of White male authority and White male property, a joining of the political and the economic within the institution of the family. Heterosexism was assumed and all Whites were expected to marry. Control over affluent White women's sexuality remained key to slavery's survival because property was to be passed on to the legitimate heirs of the slave owner. Ensuring affluent White women's virginity and chastity was deeply intertwined with maintenance of property relations.

Under slavery, we see varying levels of institutional protection given to affluent White women, working class and poor White women and enslaved African women. Poor White women enjoyed few of the protections held out to their upper class sisters. Moreover, the devalued status of Black women was key in keeping all White women in their assigned places. Controlling Black women's fertility was also key to the continuation of slavery, for children born to slave mothers themselves were slaves.

African-American women shared the devalued status of chattel with their husbands, fathers and sons. Racism stripped Blacks as a group of legal rights, education and control over their own persons. African-Americans could be whipped, branded, sold, or killed, not because they were poor, or because they were women, but because they were Black. Racism ensured that Blacks would continue to serve Whites and suffer economic exploitation at the hands of all Whites.

So we have a very interesting chain of command on the plantation—the affluent White master as the reigning patriarch, his White wife helpmate to serve him, help him manage his property and bring up his heirs, his faithful servants whose production and reproduction were tied to the requirements of the capitalist political economy and largely propertyless, working class White men and women watching from afar. In essence, the foundations for the contemporary roles of elite White women, poor Black women, working class White men and a series of other groups can be seen in stark relief in this fundamental American social institution. While Blacks experienced the most harsh treatment under slavery, and thus made slavery clearly visible as a racist institution, race, class and gender interlocked in structuring slavery's systemic organization of domination and subordination.

Even today, the plantation remains a compelling metaphor for institutional oppression. Certainly the actual conditions of oppression are not as severe now as they were then. To argue, as some do, that things have not changed all that much denigrates the achievements of those who struggled for social change before us. But the basic relationships among Black men, Black women, elite White women, elite White men, working class White men and working class White women as groups remain essentially intact.

A brief analysis of key American social institutions most controlled by elite White men should convince us of the interlocking nature of race, class and gender in structuring the institutional dimension of oppression. For example, if you are from an American college or university, is your campus a modern plantation? Who controls your university's political economy? Are elite White men over represented among the upper administrators and trustees controlling your university's finances and policies? Are elite White men being joined by growing numbers of elite White women helpmates? What kinds of people are in your classrooms grooming the next generation who will occupy these and other decision-making positions? Who are the support staff that produce the mass mailings, order the supplies, fix the leaky pipes? Do African-Americans, Hispanics or other people of color form the majority of the invisible workers who feed you, wash your dishes, and clean up your offices and libraries after everyone else has gone home?

If your college is anything like mine, you know the answers to these questions. You may be affiliated with an institution that has Hispanic women as vice-presidents for finance, or substantial numbers of Black men among the faculty. If so, you are fortunate. Much more typical are colleges where a modified version of the plantation as a metaphor for the institutional dimension of oppression survives.

2. The symbolic dimension of oppression

Widespread, societally-sanctioned ideologies used to justify relations of domination and subordination comprise the symbolic dimension of oppression. Central to this process is the use of stereotypical or controlling images of diverse race, class and gender groups. In order to assess the power of this dimension of oppression, I want you to make a list, either on paper or in your head, of "masculine" and "feminine" characteristics. If your list is anything like that compiled by most people, it reflects some variation of the following:

Masculine	**Feminine**
aggressive	passive
leader	follower
rational	emotional
strong	weak
intellectual	physical

Not only does this list reflect either/or dichotomous thinking and the need to rank both sides of the dichotomy, but ask yourself exactly which men and women you had in mind when compiling these characteristics. This list applies almost exclusively to middle class White men and women. The allegedly "masculine" qualities that you probably listed are only acceptable when exhibited by elite White men, or when used by Black and Hispanic men against each other or against women of color. Aggressive Black and Hispanic men are seen as dangerous, not powerful, and are often penalized when they exhibit any of the allegedly "masculine" characteristic. Working class and poor White men fare slightly better and are also denied the allegedly "masculine" symbols of leadership, intellectual competence, and human rationality. Women of color and working class and poor White women are also not represented on this list, for they have never had the luxury of being "ladies." What appear to be universal categories representing all men and women instead are unmasked as being applicable to only a small group.

It is important to see how the symbolic images applied to different race, class and gender groups interact in maintaining systems of domination and subordination. If I were to ask you to repeat the same assignment, only this time, by making separate lists for Black men, Black women, Hispanic women and Hispanic men, I suspect that your gender symbolism would be quite different. In comparing all of the lists, you might begin to see the interdependence of symbols applied to all groups. For example, the elevated images of White womanhood need devalued images of Black womanhood in order to maintain credibility.

While the above exercise reveals the interlocking nature of race, class and gender in structuring the symbolic dimension of oppression, part of its importance lies in demonstrating how race, class and gender pervade a wide range of what appears to be universal language. Attending to diversity in our scholarship, in our teaching, and in our daily lives provides a new angle of vision on interpretations of reality thought to be natural, normal and "true." Moreover, viewing images of masculinity and femininity as universal gender symbolism, rather than as symbolic images that are race, class and gender specific, renders the experiences of people of color and of nonprivileged White women and men invisible. One way to dehumanize an individual or group is to deny the reality of their experiences. So when we refuse to deal with race or class because they do not appear to be directly relevant to gender, we are actually becoming part of some one else's problem.

Assuming that everyone is affected differently by the same interlocking set of symbolic images allows us to move forward toward new analyses. Women of color and White women have different relations to White male authority and this difference explains the distinct gender symbolism applied to both groups. Black women encounter controlling images such as the mammy, the matriarch, the mule and the whore, that encourage others to reject us as fully human people. Ironically, the negative nature of these images simultaneously encourages us to reject them. In contrast, White women are offered seductive images, those that promise to reward them for supporting the status quo. And yet seductive images can be equally controlling. Consider, for example, the views of Nancy White, a 73-year old Black woman, concerning images of rejection and seduction:

> My mother used to say that the black woman is the white man's mule and the white woman is his dog. Now, she said that to say this: we do the heavy work and get beat whether we do it well or not. But the white woman is closer to the master and he pats them on the head and lets them sleep in the house, but he ain't gon' treat neither one like he was dealing with a person. (Gwaltney, 148)

Both sets of images stimulate particular political stances. By broadening the analysis beyond the confines of race, we can see the varying levels of rejection and seduction available to each of us due to our race, class and gender identity. Each of us lives with an allotted portion of institutional privilege and penalty, and with varying levels of rejection and seduction inherent in the symbolic images applied to us. This is the context in which we make our choices. Taken together, the institutional and symbolic dimensions of oppression create a structural backdrop against which all of us live our lives.

3. The individual dimension of oppression

Whether we benefit or not, we all live within institutions that reproduce race, class and gender oppression. Even if we never have any contact with members of other race, class and gender groups, we all encounter images of these groups and are exposed to the symbolic meanings attached to those images. On this dimension of oppression, our individual biographies vary tremendously. As a result of our institutional and symbolic statuses, all of our choices become political acts.

Each of us must come to terms with the multiple ways in which race, class and gender as categories of analysis frame our individual biographies. I have lived my entire life as an African-American woman from a working class family and this basic fact has had a profound impact on my personal biography. Imagine how different your life might be if you had been born Black, or White, or poor, or of a different race/class/gender group than the one with which you are most familiar. The institutional treatment you would have received and the symbolic meanings attached to your very existence might differ dramatically from that you now consider to be natural, normal and part of everyday life. You might be the same, but your personal biography might have been quite different.

I believe that each of us carries around the cumulative effect of our lives within multiple structures of oppression. If you want to see how much you have been affected by this whole thing, I ask you one simple question—who are your close friends? Who are the people with whom you can share your hopes, dreams, vulnerabilities, fears and victories? Do they look like you? If they are all the same, circumstance may be the cause. For the first seven years of my life I saw only low income Black people. My friends from those years reflected the composition of my community. But now that I am an adult, can the defense of circumstance explain the patterns of people that I trust as my friends and colleagues? When given other alternatives, if my friends and colleagues reflect the homogeneity of one race, class and gender group, then these categories of analysis have indeed become barriers to connection.

I am not suggesting that people are doomed to follow the paths laid out for them by race, class and gender as categories of analysis. While these three structures certainly frame my opportunity structure, I as an individual always have the choice of accepting things as they are, or trying to change them. As Nikki Giovanni points out, "we've got to live in the real world. If we don't like the world we're living in, change it. And if we can't change it, we change ourselves. We can do something" (Tate 1983, 68). While a piece of the oppressor may be planted deep within each of us, we each have the choice of accepting that piece or challenging it as part of the "true focus of revolutionary change."

HOW CAN WE TRANSCEND THE BARRIERS CREATED BY OUR EXPERIENCES WITH RACE. CLASS AND GENDER OPPRESSION IN ORDER TO BUILD THE TYPES OF COALITIONS ESSENTIAL FOR SOCIAL CHANGE?

Reconceptualizing oppression and seeing the barriers created by race, class and gender as interlocking categories of analysis is a vital first step. But we must transcend these barriers by moving toward race, class and gender as categories of connection, by building relationships and coalitions that will bring about social change. What are some of the issues involved in doing this?

1. Differences in power and privilege

First, we must recognize that our differing experiences with oppression create problems in the relationships among us. Each of us lives within a system that vests us with varying levels of power and privilege. These differences in power, whether structured along axes of race, class, gender, age or sexual orientation, frame our relationships. African-American writer June Jordan describes her discomfort on a Caribbean vacation with Olive, the Black woman who cleaned her room:

> . . . even though both "Olive" and "I" live inside a conflict neither one of us created, and even though both of us therefore hurt inside that conflict, I may be one of the monsters she needs to eliminate from her universe and, in a sense, she may be one of the monsters in mine (1985, 47).

Differences in power constrain our ability to connect with one another, even when we think we are engaged in dialogue across differences. Let me give you an example. One year, the students in my course "Sociology of the Black Community" got into a heated discussion about the reasons for the upsurge of racial incidents on college campuses. Black students complained vehemently about the apathy and resistance they felt most White students expressed about examining their own racism. Mark, a White male student, found their comments particularly unsettling. After claiming that all the Black people he had ever known had expressed no such beliefs to him, he questioned how representative the view points of his fellow students actually were. When pushed further, Mark revealed that he had participated in conversations over the years with the Black domestic worker employed by his family. Since she had never expressed such strong feeling about White racism, Mark was genuinely shocked by class discussions. Ask yourselves whether that domestic worker was in a position to speak freely. Would it have been wise for her to do so in a situation where the power between the two parties was so unequal?

In extreme cases, members of privileged groups can erase the very presence of the less privileged. When I first moved to Cincinnati, my family and I went on a picnic at a local park. Picnicking next to us was a family of White Appalachians. When I went to push my daughter on the swings, several of the children came over. They had missing, yellowed and broken teeth, they wore old clothing and their poverty was evident. I was shocked. Growing up in a large eastern city, I had never seen such awful poverty among Whites. The segregated neighborhoods in which I grew up made White poverty all but invisible. More importantly, the privileges attached to my newly acquired social class position allowed me to ignore and minimize the poverty among Whites that I did encounter. My reactions to those children made me realize how confining phrases such as "well, at least they're not Black," had become for me. In learning to grant human subjectivity to the Black victims of poverty, I had simultaneously learned to demand White victims of poverty. By applying categories of race to the objective conditions confronting me, I was quantifying and ranking oppressions and missing the very real suffering which, in fact, is the real issue.

One common pattern of relationships across differences in power is one that I label "voyeurism." From the perspective of the privileged, the lives of people of color, of the poor, and of women are interesting for their entertainment value. The privileged become voyeurs, passive onlookers who do not relate to the less powerful, but who are interested in seeing how the "different" live. Over the years, I have heard numerous African-American students complain about professors who never call on them except when a so-called Black issue is being discussed. The students' interest in discussing race or qualifications for doing so appear unimportant to the professor's efforts to use Black students' experiences as stories to make the material come alive for the White student audience. Asking Black students to perform on cue and provide a Black experience for their White classmates can be seen as voyeurism at its worst.

Members of subordinate groups do not willingly participate in such exchanges but often do so because members of dominant groups control the institutional and symbolic apparatuses of oppression. Racial/ethnic groups, women, and the poor have never had the luxury of being voyeurs of the lives of the privileged. Our ability to survive in hostile settings has hinged on our ability to learn intricate details about the behavior and world view of the powerful and adjust our behavior accordingly. I need only point to the difference in perception of those men and women in abusive relationships. Where men can view their girlfriends and wives as sex objects, helpmates and a collection of stereotypes categories of voyeurism—women must be attuned to every nuance of their partners' behavior. Are women "naturally" better in relating to people with more power than themselves, or have circumstances mandated that men and women develop different skills?...

Coming from a tradition where most relationships across difference are squarely rooted in relations of domination and subordination, we have much less experience relating to people as different but equal. The classroom is potentially one powerful and safe space where dialogues among individuals of unequal power relationships can occur. The relationship between Mark, the student in my class, and the domestic worker is typical of a whole series of relationships that people have when they relate across differences in power and privilege. The relationship among Mark and his classmates represents the power of the classroom to minimize those differences so that people of different levels of power can use race, class and gender, as categories of analysis in order to generate meaningful dialogues. In this case, the classroom equalized racial difference so that Black students who normally felt silenced spoke out. White students like Mark, generally unaware of how they had been privileged by their whiteness, lost that privilege in the classroom and thus became open to genuine dialogue. . . .

2. Coalitions around common causes

A second issue in building relationships and coalitions essential for social change concerns knowing the real reasons for coalition. Just what brings people together? One powerful catalyst fostering group solidarity is the presence of a common enemy. African-American, Hispanic, Asian-American, and women's studies all share the common intellectual heritage of challenging what passes for certified knowledge in the academy. But politically expedient relationships and coalitions like these are fragile because, as June Jordan points out:

> It occurs to me that much organizational grief could be avoided if people understood that partnership in misery does not necessarily provide for partnership for change. When we get the monsters off our backs all of us may want to run in very different directions (1985, 47).

Sharing a common cause assists individuals and groups in maintaining relationships that transcend their differences. Building effective coalitions involves struggling to hear one another and developing empathy for each other's points of view. The coalitions that I have been involved in that lasted and that worked have been those where commitment to a specific issue mandated collaboration as the best strategy for addressing the issue at hand.

Several years ago, masters degree in hand, I chose to teach in an inner city, parochial school in danger of closing. The money was awful, the conditions were poor, but the need was great. In my job, I had to work with a range of individuals who, on the surface, had very little in common. We had White nuns, Black middle class graduate students, Blacks from the "community," some of whom had been incarcerated and/or were affiliated with a range of federal anti-poverty programs. Parents formed another part of this community, Harvard faculty another, and a few well-meaning White liberals from Colorado were sprinkled in for good measure.

As you might imagine, tension was high. Initially, our differences seemed insurmountable. But as time passed, we found a common bond that we each brought to the school. In spite of profound differences in our personal biographies, differences that in other settings would have hampered our ability to relate to one another, we found that we were all deeply committed to the education of Black children. By learning to value each other's commitment and by recognizing that we each had different skills that were essential to actualizing that commitment, we built an effective coalition around a common cause. Our school was successful, and the children we taught benefited from the diversity we offered them.

. . . None of us alone has a comprehensive vision of how race, class and gender operate as categories of analysis or how they might be used as categories of connection. Our personal biographies offer us partial views. Few of us can manage to study race, class and gender simultaneously. Instead, we each know more about some dimensions of this larger story and less about others. . . . Just as the members of the school had special skills to offer to the task of building the school, we have areas of specialization and expertise, whether scholarly, theoretical, pedagogical or within areas of race, class or gender. We do not all have to do the same thing in the same way. Instead, we must support each other's efforts, realizing that they are all part of the larger enterprise of bringing about social change.

3. Building empathy

A third issue involved in building the types of relationships and coalitions essential for social change concerns the issue of individual accountability. Race, class and gender oppression form the structural backdrop against which we frame our relationship—these are the forces that encourage us to substitute voyeurism . . . for fully human relationships. But while we may not have created this situation, we are each responsible for making individual, personal choices concerning which elements of race, class and gender oppression we will accept and which we will work to change.

One essential component of this accountability involves developing empathy for the experiences of individuals and groups different than ourselves. Empathy begins with taking an interest in the facts of other people's lives, both as individuals and as groups. If you care about me, you should want to know not only the details of my personal biography but a sense of how race, class and gender as categories of analysis created the institutional and symbolic backdrop for my personal biography. How can you hope to assess my character without knowing the details of the circumstances I face?

Moreover, by taking a theoretical stance that we have all been affected by race, class and gender as categories of analysis that have structured our treatment, we open up possibilities for using those same constructs as categories of connection in building empathy. For example, I have a good White woman friend with whom I share common interests and beliefs. But we know that our racial differences have provided us with different experiences. So we talk about them. We do not assume that because I am Black, race has only affected me and not her or that because I am a Black woman, race neutralizes the effect of gender in my life while accepting it in hers. We take those same categories of analysis that have created cleavages in our lives, in this case, categories of race and gender, and use them as categories of connection in building empathy for each other's experiences.

Finding common causes and building empathy is difficult, no matter which side of privilege we inhabit. Building empathy from the dominant side of privilege is difficult, simply because individuals from privileged backgrounds are not encouraged to do so. For example, in order for those of you who are White to develop empathy for the experiences of people of color, you must grapple with how your white skin has privileged you. This is difficult to do, because it not only entails the intellectual process of seeing how whiteness is elevated in institutions and symbols, but it also involves the often painful process of seeing how your whiteness has shaped your personal biography. Intellectual stances against the institutional and symbolic dimensions of racism are generally easier to maintain than sustained self-reflection about how racism has shaped all of our individual biographies. Were and are your fathers, uncles, and grandfathers really more capable than mine, or can their accomplishments be explained in part by the racism members of my family experienced? Did your mothers stand silently by and watch all this happen? More importantly, how have they passed on the benefits of their whiteness to you?

These are difficult questions, and I have tremendous respect for my colleagues and students who are trying to answer them. Since there is no compelling reason to examine the source and meaning of one's own privilege, I know that those who do so have freely chosen this stance. They are making conscious efforts to root out the piece of the oppressor planted within them. To me, they are entitled to the support of people of color in their efforts. Men who declare themselves feminists, members of the middle class who ally themselves with anti-poverty struggles, heterosexuals who support gays and lesbians, are all trying to grow, and their efforts place them far ahead of the majority who never think of engaging in such important struggles.

Building empathy from the subordinate side of privilege is also difficult, but for different reasons. Members of subordinate groups are understandably reluctant to abandon a basic mistrust of members of powerful groups because this basic mistrust has traditionally been central to their survival. As a Black woman, it would be foolish for me to assume that White women, or Black men, or White men or any other group with a history of exploiting African-American women have my best interests at heart. These groups enjoy varying amounts of privilege over me and therefore I must carefully watch them and be prepared for a relation of domination and subordination.

Like the privileged, members of subordinate groups must also work toward replacing judgments by category with new ways of thinking and acting. Refusing to do so stifles prospects for effective coalition and social change. Let me use another example from my own experiences. When I was an undergraduate, I had little time or patience for the theorizing of the privileged. My initial years at a private, elite institution were difficult, not because the coursework was challenging (it was, but that wasn't what distracted me) or because I had to work while my classmates lived on family allowances (I was used to work). The adjustment was difficult because I was surrounded by so many people who took their privilege for granted. Most of them felt entitled to their wealth. That astounded me.

I remember one incident of watching a White woman down the hall in my dormitory try to pick out which sweater to wear. The sweaters were piled up on her bed in all the colors of the rainbow, sweater after sweater. She asked my advice in a way that let me know that choosing a sweater was one of the most important decisions she had to make on a daily basis. Standing knee-deep in her sweaters, I realized how different our lives were. She did not have to worry about maintaining a solid academic average so that she could receive financial aid. Because she was in the majority, she was not treated as a representative of her race. She did not have to consider how her classroom comments or basic existence on campus contributed to the treatment her group would receive. Her allowance protected her from having to work, so she was free to spend her time studying, partying, or in her case, worrying about which sweater to wear. The degree of inequality in our lives and her unquestioned sense of entitlement concerning that inequality offended me. For a while, I categorized all affluent White women as being superficial, arrogant, overly concerned with material possessions, and part of my problem. But had I continued to classify people in this way, I would have missed out on making some very good friends whose discomfort with their inherited or acquired social class privileges pushed them to examine their position.

Since I opened with the words of Audre Lorde it seems appropriate to close with another of her ideas. . . .

> Each of us is called upon to take a stand. So in these days ahead, as we examine ourselves and each other, our works, our fears, our differences, our sisterhood and survivals, I urge you to tackle what is most difficult for us all, self-scrutiny of our complacencies, the idea that since each of us believes she is on the side of right, she need not examine her position (1985).

I urge you to examine your position.

References

Butler, Johnella. 1989. Difficult dialogues. *The women's review of books* 6, no. 5.

Collins, Patricia Hill. 1989. The social construction of black feminist thought. *Signs* (Summer).

Gwaltney, John Langston. 1980. *Drylongso: A Self-portrait of black America.* New York: Vintage.
Harding, Sandra. 1986. *The science question in feminism.* Ithaca, NY: Cornell University Press.
Jordan, June. 1985. *On call: Political essays.* Boston: South End Press.
Lorde, Audre. 1984. *Sister outsider.* Trumansberg, NY: The Crossing Press.
———. 1985. Sisterhood and survival. Keynote address, conference on the Black Woman Writer and the Diaspora, Michigan State University.
Spelman, Elizabeth. 1982. Theories of race and gender: The erasure of black women. *Quest* 5, no. 4:36–62.
Tafe, Claudia, ed. 1983. *Black women writers at work.* New York: Continuum.

Theorizing Difference From Multiracial Feminism

MAXINE BACA ZINN AND BONNIE THORNTON DILL

Women of color have long challenged the hegemony of feminisms constructed primarily around the lives of white middle-class women. Since the late 1960s, U.S. women of color have taken issue with unitary theories of gender. Our critiques grew out of the widespread concern about the exclusion of women of color from feminist scholarship and the misinterpretation of our experiences,[1] and ultimately "out of the very discourses, denying, permitting, and producing difference."[2] Speaking simultaneously from "within and against" *both* women's liberation *and* antiracist movements, we have insisted on the need to challenge systems of domination,[3] not merely as gendered subjects but as women whose lives are affected by our location in multiple hierarchies.

Recently, and largely in response to these challenges, work that links gender to other forms of domination is increasing. In this article, we examine this connection further as well as the ways in which difference and diversity infuse contemporary feminist studies. Our analysis draws on a conceptual framework that we refer to as "multiracial feminism."[4] This perspective is an attempt to go beyond a mere recognition of diversity and difference among women to examine structures of domination, specifically the importance of race in understanding the social construction of gender. Despite the varied concerns and multiple intellectual stances which characterize the feminisms of women of color, they share an emphasis on race as a primary force situating genders differently. It is the centrality of race, of institutionalized racism, and of struggles against racial oppression that link the various feminist perspectives within this framework. Together, they demonstrate that racial meanings offer new theoretical directions for feminist thought.

Tensions in Contemporary Difference Feminism

Objections to the false universalism embedded in the concept "woman" emerged within other discourses as well as those of women of color.[5] Lesbian feminists and postmodern feminists put forth their own versions of what Susan Bordo has called "gender skepticism."[6]

Many thinkers within mainstream feminism have responded to these critiques with

Maxine Baca Zinn and Bonnie Thorton Dill, "Theorizing Difference from Multiracial Feminism" in *Feminist Studies,* Volume 22, Number 2 (Summer 1996): 321–331 by permission of the publisher, *Feminist Studies,* Inc.

efforts to contextualize gender. The search for women's "universal" or "essential" characteristics is being abandoned. By examining gender in the context of other social divisions and perspectives, difference has gradually become important—even problematizing the universal categories of "women" and "men." Sandra Harding expresses the shift best in her claim that "there are no gender relations *per se,* but only gender relations as constructed by and between classes, races, and cultures."[7]

Many feminists now contend that difference occupies center stage as *the* project of women studies today.[8] According to one scholar, "difference has replaced equality as the central concern of feminist theory."[9] Many have welcomed the change, hailing it as a major revitalizing force in U.S. feminist theory.[10] But if *some* priorities within mainstream feminist thought have been refocused by attention to difference, there remains an "uneasy alliance"[11] between women of color and other feminists.

If difference has helped revitalize academic feminisms, it has also "upset the apple cart" and introduced new conflicts into feminist studies.[12] For example, in a recent and widely discussed essay, Jane Rowland Martin argues that the current preoccupation with difference is leading feminism into dangerous traps. She fears that in giving privileged status to a predetermined set of analytic categories (race, ethnicity, and class), "we affirm the existence of nothing but difference." She asks, "How do we know that for us, difference does not turn on being fat, or religious, or in an abusive relationship?"[13]

We, too, see pitfalls in some strands of the difference project. However, our perspectives take their bearings from social relations. Race and class differences are crucial, we argue, not as individual characteristics (such as being fat) but insofar as they are primary organizing principles of a society which locates and positions groups within that society's opportunity structures.

Despite the much-heralded diversity trend within feminist studies, difference is often reduced to mere pluralism: a "live and let live" approach where principles of relativism generate a long list of diversities which begin with gender, class, and race and continue through a range of social structural as well as personal characteristics.[14] Another disturbing pattern, which bell hooks refers to as "the commodification of difference," is the representation of diversity as a form of exotica, "a spice, seasoning that livens up the dull dish that is mainstream white culture."[15] The major limitation of these approaches is the failure to attend to the power relations that accompany difference. Moreover, these approaches ignore the inequalities that cause some characteristics to be seen as "normal" while others are seen as "different" and thus, deviant.

Maria C. Lugones expresses irritation at those feminists who see only the *problem* of difference without recognizing *difference.*[16] Increasingly, we find that difference *is* recognized. But this in no way means that difference occupies a "privileged" theoretical status. Instead of using difference to rethink the category of women, difference is often a euphemism for women who differ from the traditional norm. Even in purporting to accept difference, feminist pluralism often creates a social reality that reverts to universalizing women:

> So much feminist scholarship assumes that when we cut through all of the diversity among women created by differences of racial classification, ethnicity, social class, and sexual orientation, a "universal truth" concerning women and gender lies buried underneath. But if we can face the scary possibility that no such certainty exists and that persisting in such a search will always distort or omit someone's experiences, with what do we replace this old way of thinking? Gender differences and gender politics begin to look very different if there is no essential woman at the core.[17]

What Is Multiracial Feminism?

A new set of feminist theories have emerged from the challenges put forth by women of color. Multiracial feminism is an evolving body of theory and practice informed by wide-ranging intellectual traditions. This framework does not offer a singular or unified feminism but a body of knowledge situating women and men in multiple systems of domination. U.S. multiracial feminism encompasses several emergent perspectives developed primarily by women of color: African Americans, Latinas, Asian Americans, and Native Americans, women whose analyses are shaped by their unique perspectives as "outsiders within"—marginal intellectuals whose social locations provide them with a particular perspective on self and society.[18] Although U.S. women of color represent many races and ethnic backgrounds—with different histories and cultures—our feminisms cohere in their treatment of race as a basic social division, a structure of power, a focus of political struggle, and hence a fundamental force in shaping women's and men's lives.

This evolving intellectual and political perspective uses several controversial terms. While we adopt the label "multiracial," other terms have been used to describe this broad framework. For example, Chela Sandoval refers to "U.S. Third World feminisms,"[19] while other scholars refer to "indigenous feminisms." In their theory text-reader, Alison M. Jagger and Paula M. Rothenberg adopt the label "multicultural feminism."[20]

We use "multiracial" rather than "multicultural" as a way of underscoring race as a power system that interacts with other structured inequalities to shape genders. Within the U.S. context, race, and the system of meanings and ideologies which accompany it, is a fundamental organizing principle of social relationships.[21] Race affects all women and men, although in different ways. Even cultural and group differences among women are produced through interaction within a racially stratified social order. Therefore, although we do not discount the importance of culture, we caution that cultural analytic frameworks that ignore race tend to view women's differences as the product of group-specific values and practices that often result in the marginalization of cultural groups which are then perceived as exotic expressions of a normative center. Our focus on race stresses the social construction of differently situated social groups and their varying degrees of advantage and power. Additionally, this emphasis on race takes on increasing political importance in an era where discourse about race is governed by color-evasive language[22] and a preference for individual rather than group remedies for social inequalities. Our analyses insist upon the primary and pervasive nature of race in contemporary U.S. society while at the same time acknowledging how race both shapes and is shaped by a variety of other social relations.

In the social sciences, multiracial feminism grew out of socialist feminist thinking. Theories about how political economic forces shape women's lives were influential as we began to uncover the social causes of racial ethnic women's subordination. But socialist feminism's concept of capitalist patriarchy, with its focus on women's unpaid (reproductive) labor in the home failed to address racial differences in the organization of reproductive labor. As feminists of color have argued, "reproductive labor has divided along racial as well as gender lines, and the specific characteristics have varied regionally and changed over time as capitalism has reorganized."[23] Despite the limitations of socialist feminism, this body of literature has been especially useful in pursuing questions about the interconnections among systems of domination.[24]

Race and ethnic studies was the other major social scientific source of multiracial feminism. It provided a basis for comparative analyses of groups that are socially and legally subordinated and remain culturally distinct within U.S. society. This includes the systematic discrimination of socially constructed racial groups and their distinctive cultural arrangements. Historically, the categories of African American, Latino, Asian American, and Native American were constructed as both racially and culturally distinct. Each group has a distinctive culture, shares a common heritage, and has developed a common identity within a larger society that subordinates them.[25]

We recognize, of course, certain problems inherent in an uncritical use of the multiracial label. First, the perspective can be hampered by a biracial model in which only African Americans and whites are seen as racial categories and all other groups are viewed through the prism of cultural differences. Latinos and Asians have always occupied distinctive places within the racial hierarchy, and current shifts in the composition of the U.S. population are racializing these groups anew.[26]

A second problem lies in treating multiracial feminism as a single analytical framework, and its principle architects, women of color, as an undifferentiated category. The concepts "multiracial feminism," "racial ethnic women," and "women of color" "homogenize quite different experiences and can falsely universalize experiences across race, ethnicity, sexual orientation, and age."[27] The feminisms created by women of color exhibit a plurality of intellectual and political positions. We speak in many voices, with inconsistencies that are born of our different social locations. Multiracial feminism embodies this plurality and richness. Our intent is not to falsely universalize women of color. Nor do we wish to promote a new racial essentialism in place of the old gender essentialism. Instead, we use these concepts to examine the structures and experiences produced by intersecting forms of race and gender.

It is also essential to acknowledge that race is a shifting and contested category whose meanings construct definitions of all aspects of social life.[28] In the United States it helped define citizenship by excluding everyone who was not a white, male property owner. It defined labor as slave or free, coolie or contract, and family as available only to those men whose marriages were recognized or whose wives could immigrate with them. Additionally, racial meanings are contested both within groups and between them.[29]

Although definitions of race are at once historically and geographically specific, they are also transnational, encompassing diasporic groups and crossing traditional geographic boundaries. Thus, while U.S. multiracial feminism calls attention to the fundamental importance of race, it must also locate the meaning of race within specific national traditions.

THE DISTINGUISHING FEATURES OF MULTIRACIAL FEMINISM

By attending to these problems, multiracial feminism offers a set of analytic premises for thinking about and theorizing gender. The following themes distinguish this branch of feminist inquiry.

First, multiracial feminism asserts that gender is constructed by a range of interlocking inequalities, what Patricia Hill Collins calls a "matrix of domination."[30] The idea of a matrix is that several fundamental systems work with and through each other. People experience race, class, gender, and sexuality differently depending upon their social location in the structures of race, class, gender, and sexuality. For example, people of the same race will experience race differently depending upon their location in the class structure as working class, professional managerial class, or unemployed; in the gender structure as female or male; and in structures of sexuality as heterosexual, homosexual, or bisexual.

Multiracial feminism also examines the simultaneity of systems in shaping women's experience and identity. Race, class, gender, and sexuality are not reducible to individual attributes to be measured and assessed for their separate contribution in explaining given social outcomes, an approach that Elizabeth Spelman calls "popbead metaphysics," where a woman's identity consists of the sum of parts neatly divisible from one another.[31] The matrix of domination seeks to account for the multiple ways that women experience themselves as gendered, raced, classed, and sexualized.

Second, multiracial feminism emphasizes the intersectional nature of hierarchies at all levels of social life. Class, race, gender, and sexuality are components of both social structure and social interaction. Women and men are differently embedded in locations created by these cross-cutting hierarchies. As a result, women and men throughout the social order experience different forms of privilege and subordination, depending on their race, class, gender, and sexuality. In other words, intersecting forms of domination produce *both* oppression *and* opportunity. At the same time that structures of race, class, and gender create disadvantages for women of color, they provide unacknowledged benefits for those who are at the top of these hierarchies-whites, members of the upper classes, and males. Therefore, multiracial feminism applies not only to racial ethnic women but also to women and men of all races, classes, and genders.

Third, multiracial feminism highlights the relational nature of dominance and subordination. Power is the cornerstone of women's differences.[32] This means that women's differences are *connected* in systematic ways.[33] Race is a vital element in the pattern of relations among minority and white women. As Linda Gordon argues, the very meanings of being a white woman in the United States have been affected by the existence of subordinated women of color: "They intersect in conflict and in occasional cooperation, but always in mutual influence."[34]

Fourth, multiracial feminism explores the interplay of social structure and women's agency. Within the constraints of race, class, and gender oppression, women create viable lives for themselves, their families, and their communities. Women of color have resisted and often undermined the forces of power that control them. From acts of quiet dignity and steadfast determination to involvement in revolt and rebellion, women struggle to shape their own lives. Racial oppression has been a common focus of the "dynamic of oppositional agency" of women of color. As Chandra Talpade Mohanty points out, it is the nature and organization of women's opposition which mediates and differentiates the impact of structures of domination.[35]

Fifth, multiracial feminism encompasses wide-ranging methodological approaches, and like other branches of feminist thought, relies on varied theoretical tools as well. Ruth Frankenberg and Lata Mani identify three guiding principles of inclusive feminist inquiry: "building complex analyses, avoiding erasure, specifying location."[36] In the last decade, the opening up of academic feminism has focused attention on social location in the production of knowledge. Most basically, research by and about marginalized women has destabilized what used to be considered as universal categories of gender. Marginalized locations are well suited for grasping social relations that remained obscure from more privileged vantage points. Lived experience, in other words, creates alternative ways of understanding the social world and the experience of different groups of women within it. Racially informed standpoint epistemologies have provided new topics, fresh questions, and new understandings of women and men. Women of color have, as Norma Alarçon argues, asserted ourselves as subjects, using our voices to challenge dominant conceptions of truth.[37]

Sixth, multiracial feminism brings together understandings drawn from the lived experiences of diverse and continuously changing groups of women. Among Asian Americans, Native Americans, Latinas, and Blacks are many different national cultural and ethnic groups. Each one is engaged in the process of testing, refining, and reshaping these broader categories in its own image. Such internal differences heighten awareness of and sensitivity to both commonalities and differences, serving as a constant reminder of the importance of comparative study and maintaining a creative tension between diversity and universalization.

Difference and Transformation

Efforts to make women's studies less partial and less distorted have produced important changes in academic feminism. Inclusive thinking has provided a way to build multiplicity and difference into our analyses. This has led to the discovery that race matters for everyone. White women, too, must be reconceptualized as a category that is multiply defined by race, class, and other differences. As Ruth Frankenberg demonstrates in a study of whiteness among contemporary women, all kinds of social relations, even those that appear neutral, are, in fact, racialized. Frankenberg further complicates the very notion of a unified white identity by introducing issues of Jewish identity.[38] Therefore, the lives of women of color cannot be seen as a *variation* on a more general model of white American womanhood. The model of womanhood that feminist social science once held as "universal" is also a product of race and class.

When we analyze the power relations constituting all social arrangements and shaping women's lives in distinctive ways, we can begin to grapple with core feminist issues about how genders are socially constructed and constructed differently. Women's difference is built into our study of gender. Yet this perspective is quite far removed from the atheoretical pluralism implied in much contemporary thinking about gender.

Multiracial feminism, in our view, focuses not just on differences but also on the way in which differences and domination intersect and are historically and socially constituted. It challenges feminist scholars to go beyond the mere recognition and inclusion of difference to reshape the basic concepts and theories of our disciplines. By attending to women's social location based on race, class, and gender, multiracial feminism seeks to clarify the structural sources of diversity. Ultimately, multiracial feminism forces us to see privilege and subordination as interrelated and to pose such questions as: How do the existences and experiences of all people—women and men, different racial-ethnic groups, and different classes—shape the experiences of each other? How are those relationships defined and enforced through social institutions that are the primary sites for negotiating power within society? How do these differences contribute to the construction of both individual and group identity? Once we acknowledge that all women are affected by the racial order of society, then it becomes clear that the insights of multiracial feminism provide an analytical framework, not solely for understanding the experiences of women of color but for understanding *all* women, and men, as well.

Notes

1. Maxine Baca Zinn, Lynn Weber Cannon, Elizabeth Higginbotham, and Bonnie Thornton Dill, "The Costs of Exclusionary Practices in Women's studies," *Signs* 11 (Winter 1986): 290–303.
2. Chela Sandoval, "U.S. Third World Feminism: The Theory and Method of Oppositional Consciousness in the Postmodern World," *Genders* (Spring 1991): 1–24.
3. Ruth Frankenberg and Lata Mani, "Cross Currents, Crosstalk: Race, 'Postcoloniality,' and the Politics of Location," *Cultural Studies* 7 (May 1993): 292–310.
4. We use the term "multiracial feminism" to convey the multiplicity of racial groups and feminist perspectives.
5. A growing body of work on difference in feminist thought now exists. Although we cannot cite all the current work, the following are representative: Michèle Barrett, "The Concept of Difference," *Feminist Review* 26 (July 1987): 29–42; Christina Crosby, "Dealing with Difference," in *Feminists Theorize the Political,* ed. Judith Butler and Joan W. Scott (New York: Routledge, 1992), 130–43; Elizabeth Fox-Genovese, "Difference, Diversity, and Divisions in an Agenda for the Women's Movement," in *Color, Class, and Country: Experiences of Gender,* ed. Gay Young and Bette J. Dickerson (London: Zed Books, 1994), 232–48; Nancy A. Hewitt, "Compounding Differences," *Feminist Studies* 18 (summer 1992): 313–26; Maria C. Lugones, "On the Logic of Feminist Pluralism," in *Feminist Ethics,* ed. Claudia Card (Lawrence: University of Kansas Press, 1991), 35–44; Rita S. Gallin and Anne Ferguson, "The Plurality of Feminism: Rethinking 'Difference,'" in *The Woman and International Development Annual* (Boulder: Westview Press, 1993), 3: 1–16; and Linda Gordon, "On Difference," *Genders* 10 (spring 1991): 91–111.

6. Susan Bordo, "Feminism, Postmodernism, and Gender Skepticism," in *Feminism/Postmodernism*, ed. Linda J. Nicholson (London: Routledge, 1990), 133–56.
7. Sandra G. Harding, *Whose Science? Whose Knowledge? Thinking from Women's Lives* (Ithaca: Cornell University Press, 1991), 179.
8. Crosby, 131.
9. Fox-Genovese, 232.
10. Faye Ginsberg and Anna Lowenhaupt Tsing, Introduction to *Uncertain Terms, Negotiating Gender in American Culture,* ed. Faye Ginsberg and Anna Lowenhaupt Tsing (Boston: Beacon Press, 1990), 3.
11. Sandoval, 2.
12. Sandra Morgan, "Making Connections: Socialist-Feminist Challenges to Marxist Scholarship," in *Women and a New Academy: Gender and Cultural Contexts,* ed. Jean F. O'Barr (Madison: University of Wisconsin Press, 1989), 149.
13. Jane Rowland Martin, "Methodological Essentialism, False Difference, and Other Dangerous Traps," *Signs* 19 (Spring 1994): 647.
14. Barrett, 32.
15. bell hooks, *Black Looks: Race and Representation* (Boston: South End Press. 1992), 21.
16. Lugones, 35–44.
17. Patricia Hill Collins, Foreword to *Women of Color in U.S. Society,* ed. Maxine Baca Zinn and Bonnie Thornton Dill (Philadelphia: Temple University Press, 1994), xv.
18. Patricia Hill Collins, "Learning from the Outsider Within: The Sociological Significance of Black Feminist Thought," *Social Problems* 33 (December 1986): 514–32.
19. Sandoval, 1.
20. Alison M. Jagger and Paula S. Rothenberg, *Feminist Frameworks: Alternative Theoretical Accounts of the Relations between Women and Men,* 3d ed. (New York: McGraw-Hill, 1993).
21. Michael Omi and Howard Winant, *Racial Formation in the United States: From the 1960s to the 1980s,* 2d ed. (New York: Routledge, 1994).
22. Ruth Frankenberg, *The Social Construction of Whiteness: White Women, Race Matters* (Minneapolis: University of Minnesota Press, 1993).
23. Evelyn Nakano Glenn, "From Servitude to Service Work: Historical Continuities in the Racial Division of Paid Reproductive Labor," *Signs* 18 (Autumn 1992): 3. See also Bonnie Thornton Dill, "Our Mothers' Grief: Racial-Ethnic Women and the Maintenance of Families," *Journal of Family History* 13, no. 4 (1988): 415–31.
24. Morgan, 146.
25. Maxine Baca Zinn and Bonnie Thornton Dill, "Difference and Domination," in *Women of Color in U.S. Society,* 11–12.
26. See Omi and Winant, 53–76, for a discussion of racial formation.
27. Margaret L. Andersen and Patricia Hill Collins, *Race, Class, and Gender: An Anthology* (Belmont, Calif.: Wadsworth, 1992), xvi.
28. Omi and Winant.
29. Nazli Kibria, "Migration and Vietnamese American Women: Remaking Ethnicity," in *Women of Color in U.S. Society,* 247–61.
30. Patricia Hill Collins, *Black Feminist Thought: Knowledge, Consciousness, and the Politics of Empowerment* (Boston: Unwin Hyman, 1990).
31. Elizabeth Spelman, *Inessential Women: Problems of Exclusion in Feminist Thought* (Boston: Beacon Press, 1988), 136.
32. Several discussions of difference make this point. See Baca Zinn and Dill, 10; Gordon, 106; and Lynn Weber, in the "Symposium on West and Fenstermaker's 'Doing Difference,'" *Gender & Society* 9 (August 1995): 515–19.
33. Glenn, 10.
34. Gordon, 106.
35. Chandra Talpade Mohanty, "Cartographies of Struggle: Third World Women and the Politics of Feminism," in *Third World Women and the Politics of Feminism,* ed. Chandra Talpade Mohanty, Ann Russo, and Lourdes Torres (Bloomington: Indiana University Press, 1991), 13.
36. Frankenberg and Mani, 306.
37. Norma Alarçon, "The Theoretical Subject(s) of *This Bridge Called My Back* and Anglo-American Feminism," in *Making Face, Making Soul, Haciendo Caras: Creative and Critical Perspectives by Women of Color,* ed. Gloria Anzaldúa (San Francisco: Aunt Lute, 1990), 356.
38. Frankenberg. See also Evelyn Torton Beck, "The Politics of Jewish Invisibility," *NWSA Journal* (Fall 1988): 93–102.

DOING DIFFERENCE

CANDACE WEST
University of California, Santa Cruz

SARAH FENSTERMAKER
University of California, Santa Barbara

In this article, we advance a new understanding of "difference" as an ongoing interactional accomplishment. Calling on the authors' earlier reconceptualization of gender, they develop the further implications of this perspective for the relationships among gender, race, and class. The authors argue that, despite significant differences in their characteristics and outcomes, gender, race, and class are comparable as mechanisms for producing social inequality.

Few persons think of math as a particularly feminine pursuit. Girls are not supposed to be good at it and women are not supposed to enjoy it. It is interesting, then, that we who do feminist scholarship have relied so heavily on mathematical metaphors to describe the relationships among gender, race, and class.[1] For example, some of us have drawn on basic arithmetic, adding, subtracting, and dividing what we know about race and class to what we already know about gender. Some have relied on multiplication, seeming to calculate the effects of the whole from the combination of different parts. And others have employed geometry, drawing on images of interlocking or intersecting planes and axes.

To be sure, the sophistication of our mathematical metaphors often varies with the apparent complexity of our own experiences. Those of us who, at one point, were able to "forget" race and class in our analyses of gender relations may be more likely to "add" these at a later point. By contrast, those of us who could never forget these dimensions of social life may be more likely to draw on complex geometrical imagery all along; nonetheless, the existence of so many different approaches to the topic seems indicative of the difficulties all of us have experienced in coming to terms with it.

Not surprisingly, proliferation of these approaches has caused considerable confusion in the existing literature. In the same book or article, we may find references to gender, race, and class as "intersecting systems," as "interlocking categories," and as "multiple bases" for oppression. In the same anthology, we may find some chapters that conceive of gender, race, and class as distinct axes and others that conceive of them as concentric ones. The problem is that these alternative formulations have very distinctive, yet unarticulated, theoretical implications. For instance, if we think about gender, race, and class as additive categories, the whole will never be greater (or lesser) than the sum of its parts. By contrast, if we conceive of these as multiples, the result could be larger or smaller than their added sum, depending on where we place the signs.[2] Geometric metaphors further complicate things, since we still need to know where those planes and axes go after they cross the point of intersection (if they are parallel planes and axes, they will never intersect at all).

AUTHORS' NOTE: *We gratefully acknowledge the critical comments and suggestions of John Brown Childs, Adele Clark, Evelyn Nakano Glenn, Herman Gray, Aída Hurtado, Valerie Jenness, Nancy Jurik, Patricia Merriwether, Virginia Olesen, Pamela Roby, Dana Takagi, James R. West, Don H. Zimmerman, Maxine Baca Zinn, the graduate students of UCSB's Sociology 212P (winter 1993), and, especially, Denise Segura. Thanks to Patty Forgie for bibliographic assistance.*

From Candance West and Sarah Fenstermaker, "Doing Difference" *Gender and Society,* Vol. 9, No. 1 February 1995.

Our purpose in this article is not to advance yet another new math but to propose a new way of thinking about the workings of these relations. Elsewhere (Berk 1985; Fenstermaker, West, and Zimmerman 1991; West and Fenstermaker 1993; West and Zimmerman 1987), we offered an ethnomethodologically informed, and, hence, distinctively sociological, conceptualization of gender as a routine, methodical, and ongoing accomplishment. We argued that doing gender involves a complex of perceptual, interactional, and micropolitical activities that cast particular pursuits as expressions of manly and womanly "natures." Rather than conceiving of gender as an individual characteristic, we conceived of it as an emergent property of social situations: both an outcome of and a rationale for various social arrangements and a means of justifying one of the most fundamental divisions of society. We suggested that examining how gender is accomplished could reveal the mechanisms by which power is exercised and inequality is produced.

Our earlier formulation neglected race and class; thus, it is an incomplete framework for understanding social inequality. In this article, we extend our analysis to consider explicitly the relationships among gender, race, and class, and to reconceptualize "difference" as an ongoing interactional accomplishment. We start by summarizing the prevailing critique of much feminist thought as severely constrained by its white middle-class character and preoccupation. Here, we consider how feminist scholarship ends up borrowing from mathematics in the first place. Next, we consider how existing conceptualizations of gender have contributed to the problem, rendering mathematical metaphors the only alternatives. Then, calling on our earlier ethnomethodological conceptualization of gender, we develop the further implications of this perspective for our understanding of race and class. We assert that, while gender, race, and class—what people come to experience as organizing categories of social difference—exhibit vastly different descriptive characteristics and outcomes, they are, nonetheless, comparable as mechanisms for producing social inequality.

White Middle-Class Bias in Feminist Thought

What is it about feminist thinking that makes race and class such difficult concepts to articulate within its own parameters? The most widely agreed upon and disturbing answer to this question is that feminist thought suffers from a white middle-class bias. The privileging of white and middle-class sensibilities in feminist thought results from both who did the theorizing and how they did it. White middle-class women's advantaged viewpoint in a racist and class-bound culture, coupled with the Western tendency to construct the self as distinct from "other," distorts their depictions of reality in predictable directions (Young 1990). The consequences of these distortions have been identified in a variety of places, and analyses of them have enlivened every aspect of feminist scholarship (see, for example, Aptheker 1989; Collins 1990; Davis 1981; Hurtado 1989; Zinn 1990).

For example, bell hooks points out that feminism within the United States has never originated among the women who are most oppressed by sexism, "women who are daily beaten down, mentally, physically, and spiritually—women who are powerless to change their condition in life" (1984, 1). The fact that those most victimized are least likely to question or protest is, according to hooks (1984), a consequence of their victimization. From this perspective, the white middle-class character of most feminist thought stems directly from the identities of those who produce it.

Aída Hurtado notes further the requisite time and resources that are involved in the production of feminist writing: "without financial assistance, few low-income and racial/ethnic students can attend universities; without higher education, few working-class and ethnic/racial intellectuals can become professors" (1989, 838). Given that academics dominate the production of published feminist scholarship, it is not surprising that feminist theory is dominated by white, highly educated women (see also hooks 1981; Joseph and Lewis 1981).

Still others (Collins 1990; Davis 1981; Lorde 1984; Moraga and Anzalduá 1981; Zinn, Cannon, Higginbotham, and Dill 1986) point to the racism and classism of feminist scholars themselves. Maxine Baca Zinn and her colleagues observe that, "despite white, middle-class feminists' frequent expressions of interest and concern over the plight of minority and working-class women, those holding the gatekeeping positions at important feminist journals are as white as are those at any mainstream social science or humanities publication" (1986, 293).

Racism and classism can take a variety of forms. Adrienne Rich contends that, although white (middle-class) feminists may not consciously believe that their race is superior to any other, they are often plagued by a form of "white solipsism"—thinking, imagining, and speaking "as if whiteness described the world," resulting in "a tunnel-vision which simply does not see nonwhite experience or existence as precious or significant, unless in spasmodic, impotent guilt reflexes, which have little or no long-term, continuing usefulness" (1979, 306). White middle-class feminists, therefore, may offer conscientious expressions of concern over "racism-and-classism," believing that they have thereby taken into consideration profound differences in women's experience; simultaneously, they can fail to see those differences at all (Bhavani in press).

There is nothing that prevents any of these dynamics from coexisting and working together. For example, Patricia Hill Collins (1990) argues that the suppression of Black feminist thought stems both from white feminists' racist and classist concerns and from Black women intellectuals' consequent lack of participation in white feminist organizations. Similarly, Cherríe Moraga (1981) argues that the "denial of difference" in feminist organizations derives not only from white middle-class women's failure to "see" it but also from women of color's and working-class women's reluctance to challenge such blindness. Alone and in combination with one another, these sources of bias do much to explain why there has been a general failure to articulate race and class within the parameters of feminist scholarship; however, they do not explain the attraction of mathematical metaphors to right the balance. To understand this development, we must look further at the logic of feminist thought itself.

Mathematical metaphors and feminist thought

Following the earlier suggestion of bell hooks (1981; see also Hull, Scott, and Smith 1982), Elizabeth Spelman contends that, in practice, the term "women" actually functions as a powerful false generic in white feminists' thinking:

> The "problem of difference" for feminist theory has never been a general one about how to weigh the importance of what we have in common against the importance of our differences. To put it that way hides two crucial facts: First, the description of what we have in common "as women" has almost always been a description of white middle-class women. Second, the "difference" of this group of women—that is, their being white and middle-class—has never had to be "brought into" feminist theory. To bring in "difference" is to bring in women who aren't white and middle class. (1988, 4)

She warns that thinking about privilege merely as a characteristic of individuals—rather than as a characteristic of modes of thought—may afford us an understanding of "what privilege feeds but not what sustains it" (1988, 4).

What are the implications of a feminist mode of thought that is so severely limited? The most important one, says Spelman, is the presumption that we can effectively and usefully isolate gender from race and class. To illustrate this point, she draws on many white feminists who develop their analyses of sexism by comparing and contrasting it with "other" forms of oppression. Herein she finds the basis for additive models of gender, race, and class, and "the ampersand problem":

> de Beauvoir tends to talk about comparisons between sex and race, or between sex and class, or between sex and culture . . . comparisons between sexism and racism, between sexism and classism, between sexism and anti-Semitism. In the work of Chodorow and others influenced by her, we observe a readiness to look for links between sexism and other forms of oppression as distinct from sexism. (1988, 115)

Spelman notes that in both cases, attempts to add "other" elements of identity to gender, or "other" forms of oppression to sexism, disguise the race (white) and class (middle) identities of those seen as "women" in the first place. Rich's "white solipsism" comes into play again, and it is impossible to envision how women who are not white and middle class fit into the picture.

Although Spelman (1988) herself does not address mathematical metaphors based on multiplication, we believe that her argument is relevant to understanding how they develop. For example, take Cynthia Fuchs Epstein's (1973) notion of the "positive effect of the multiple negative" on the success of Black professional women. According to Epstein, when the "negative status" of being a woman is combined with the "negative status" of being Black, the result is the "positive status" of Black professional women in the job market. Baca Zinn and her colleagues contend that the very idea of this "multiple negative" having a positive effect "could not have survived the scrutiny of professional Black women or Black women students" (1986, 293). They suggest that only someone who was substantially isolated from Black women and their life experiences could have developed such a theory (and, presumably, only someone similarly situated could have promoted its publication in an established mainstream sociology journal).

Spelman's (1988) analysis highlights the following problem: if we conceive of gender as coherently isolatable from race and class, then there is every reason to assume that the effects of the three variables can be multiplied, with results dependent on the valence (positive or negative) of those multiplied variables; yet, if we grant that gender cannot be coherently isolated from race and class in the way we conceptualize it, then multiplicative metaphors make little sense.

If the effects of "multiple oppression" are not merely additive nor simply multiplicative, what are they? Some scholars have described them as the products of "simultaneous and intersecting systems of relationship and meaning" (Andersen and Collins 1992, xiii; see also Almquist 1989; Collins 1990; Glenn 1985). This description is useful insofar as it offers an accurate characterization of persons who are simultaneously oppressed on the basis of gender, race, and class, in other words, those "at the intersection" of all three systems of domination; however, if we conceive of the basis of oppression as more than membership in a category, then the theoretical implications of this formulation are troubling. For instance, what conclusions shall we draw from potential comparisons between persons who experience oppression on the basis of their race and class (e.g., working-class men of color) and those who are oppressed on the basis of their gender and class (e.g., white working-class women)? Would the "intersection of two systems of meaning in each case be sufficient to predict common bonds among them?" Clearly not, says June Jordan: "When these factors of race, class and gender absolutely collapse is whenever you try to use them as automatic concepts of connection." She goes on to say that, while these concepts may work very well as indexes of "commonly felt conflict," their predictive value when they are used as "elements of connection" is "about as reliable as precipitation probability for the day after the night before the day" (1985, 46).

What conclusions shall we draw from comparisons between persons who are said to suffer oppression "at the intersection" of all three systems and those who suffer in the nexus of only two? Presumably, we will conclude that the latter are "less oppressed" than the former (assuming that each categorical identity set amasses a specific quantity of oppression). Moraga warns, however, that "the danger lies in ranking the oppressions. *The danger lies in failing to acknowledge the specificity of the oppression*" (1981, 29).

Spelman (1988, 123–25) attempts to resolve this difficulty by characterizing sexism, racism, and classism as "interlocking" with one another. Along similar lines, Margaret Andersen and Patricia Hill Collins (1992, xii) describe gender, race, and class as "interlocking categories of experience." The image of interlocking rings comes to mind, linked in such a way that the motion of any one of them is constrained by the others. Certainly, this image is more dynamic than those conveyed by additive, multiplicative, or geometric models: we can see where the rings are joined (and where they are not), as well as how the movement of any one of them would be restricted by the others, but note that this image still depicts the rings as separate parts.

If we try to situate particular persons within this array, the problem with it becomes clear. We can, of course, conceive of the whole as "oppressed people" and of the rings as "those oppressed by gender," "those oppressed by race," and "those oppressed by class" (see Figure 1). This allows us to situate women and men of all races and classes within the areas covered by the circles, save for white middle- and upper-class men, who fall outside them. However, what if we conceive of the whole as "experience"[3] and of the rings as gender, race, and class (see Figure 2)?

Here, we face an illuminating possibility and leave arithmetic behind: no person can experience gender without simultaneously experiencing race and class. As Andersen and Collins put it, "While race, class and gender can be seen as different axes of social structure, individual persons experience them simultaneously" (1992, xxi).[4] It is this simultaneity that has eluded our theoretical treatments and is so difficult to build into our empirical descriptions (for an admirable effort, see Segura 1992). Capturing it compels us to focus on the actual mechanisms that produce social inequality. How do forms of inequality, which we now see are more than the periodic collision of categories, operate together? How do we see that all social exchanges, regardless of the

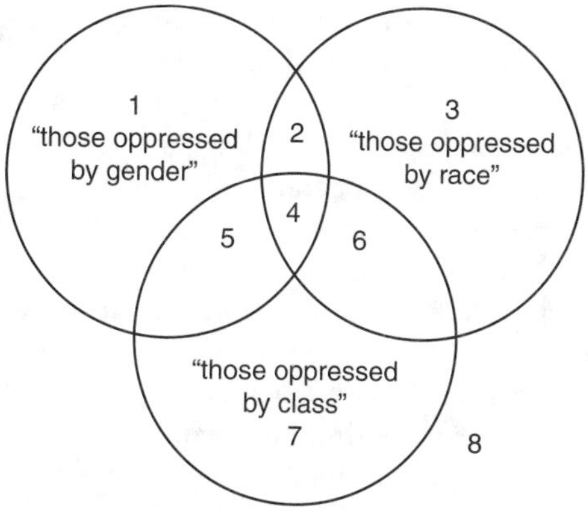

1 "those oppressed by gender"
2
3 "those oppressed by race"
4
5
6
"those oppressed by class" 7
8

FIGURE I ■ Oppressed People

Note: 1 = White upper- and middle-class women; 2 = Upper- and middle-class women of color; 3 = Upper- and middle-class men of color; 4 = Working-class women of color; 5 = White working-class women; 6 = Working-class men of color; 7 = White working-class men; 8 = White upper- and middle-class men. This figure is necessarily oversimplified. For example, upper- and middle-class people are lumped together, neglecting the possibility of significant differences between them.

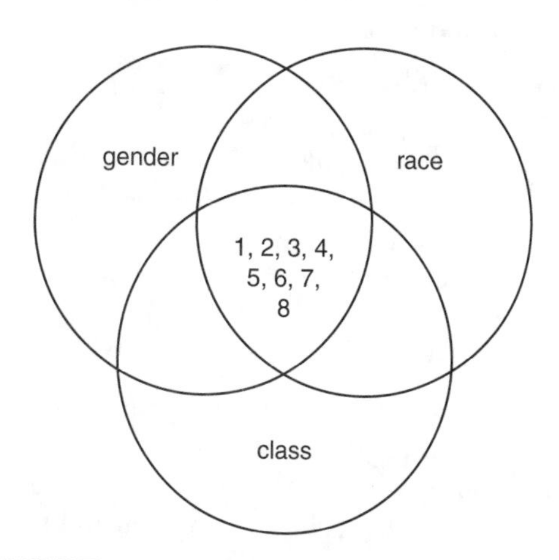

FIGURE 2 ■ Experience

Note: 1 = White upper- and middle-class women; 2 = Upper- and middle-class women of color; 3 = Upper- and middle-class men of color; 4 = Working-class women of color; 5 = White working-class women; 6 = Working-class men of color; 7 = White working-class men; 8 = White upper- and middle-class men. This figure is necessarily oversimplified. For example, upper- and middle-class people are lumped together, neglecting the possibility of significant differences between them.

participants or the outcome, are simultaneously "gendered," "raced," and "classed"?

To address these questions, we first present some earlier attempts to conceptualize gender. Appreciation for the limitations of these efforts, we believe, affords us a way to the second task: reconceptualizing the dynamics of gender, race, and class as they figure simultaneously in human institutions and interaction.

TRADITIONAL CONCEPTUALIZATIONS OF GENDER

To begin, we turn to Arlie Russell Hochschild's "A Review of Sex Roles Research," published in 1973. At that time, there were at least four distinct ways of conceptualizing gender within the burgeoning literature on the topic: (1) as sex differences, (2) as sex roles, (3) in relation to the minority status of women, and (4) in relation to the caste/class status of women. Hochschild observes that each of these conceptualizations led to a different perspective on the behaviors of women and men:

> What is to type 1 a feminine trait such as passivity is to type 2 a role element, to type 3 is a minority characteristic, and to type 4 is a response to powerlessness. Social change might also look somewhat different to each perspective; differences disappear, deviance becomes normal, the minority group assimilates, or power is equalized. (1973, 1013)

Nona Glazer observes a further important difference between the types Hochschild identified, namely, where they located the primary source of inequality between women and men:

> The *sex difference* and [*sex*] *roles* approaches share an emphasis on understanding factors that characterize individuals. These factors may be inherent to each sex or acquired by individuals in the course of socialization. The *minority group* and *caste/class* approaches share an emphasis on factors that are external to individuals, a concern with the structure of social institutions, and with the impact of historical events. (1977, 103)

In retrospect, it is profoundly disturbing to contemplate what the minority group approach and the class/caste approach implied about feminist thinking at the time. For example, Juliet Mitchell launched "Women: The Longest Revolution" with the claim that "[t]he situation of women is different from that of any other social group . . . within the world of men, their position is comparable to that of an oppressed minority" (1966, 11). Obviously, if "women" could be compared to "an oppressed minority," they had to consist of someone other than "oppressed minorities" themselves (cf. Hacker 1951).

Perhaps because of such theoretical problems, feminist scholars have largely abandoned the effort to describe women as a caste, as a class, or as a minority group as a project in its own right (see, for example, Aptheker 1989; Hull, Scott, and Smith 1982). What we have been left with, however, are two prevailing conceptualizations: (1) the sex differences approach and (2) the sex roles approach. And note, while the minority group and caste/class approaches were concerned with factors external to the individual (e.g., the structure of social institutions and the impact of historical events), the approaches that remain emphasize factors that characterize the individual (Glazer 1977).

Arguably, some might call this picture oversimplified. Given the exciting new scholarship that focuses on gender as something that is socially constructed, and something that converges with other inequalities to produce difference among women, have we not moved well beyond "sex differences" and "sex roles"? A close examination of this literature suggests that we have not. For example, Collins contends that

> [w]hile race and gender are both socially constructed categories, constructions of gender *rest on clearer biological criteria* than do constructions of race. Classifying African-Americans into specious racial categories is considerably

> more difficult than noting the *clear biological differences* distinguishing females from males . . . Women do share common experiences, but the experiences are not generally the same type as those affecting racial and ethnic groups. (1990, 27, emphasis added)

Of course, Collins is correct in her claim that women differ considerably from one another with respect to the distinctive histories, geographic origins, and cultures they share with men of their same race and class. The problem, however, is that what unites them as women are the "clear biological criteria distinguishing females from males." Here, Collins reverts to treating gender as a matter of sex differences (i.e., as ultimately traceable to factors inherent to each sex), in spite of her contention that it is socially constructed. Gender becomes conflated with sex, as race might speciously be made equivalent to color.

Consider a further example. Spelman launches her analysis with a discussion of the theoretical necessity of distinguishing sex from gender. She praises de Beauvoir (1953) for her early recognition of the difference between the two and goes on to argue,

> It is one thing to be biologically female, and quite another to be shaped by one's culture into a "woman"—a female with feminine qualities, someone who does the kinds of things "women" not "men" do, someone who has the kinds of thoughts and feelings that make doing these things seem an easy expression of one's feminine nature. (1988, 124)

How, then, does Spelman conceive of the social construction of woman? She not only invokes "sexual roles" to explain this process (1988, 121–23) but also speaks of "racial roles" (1988, 106) that affect the course that the process will take. Despite Spelman's elegant demonstration of how "woman" constitutes a false generic in feminist thought, her analysis takes us back to "sex roles" once again.

Our point here is not to take issue with Collins (1990) or Spelman (1988) in particular; it would be a misreading of our purpose to do so. We cite these works to highlight a more fundamental difficulty facing feminist theory in general: new conceptualizations of the bases of gender inequality still rest on old conceptualizations of gender (West and Fenstermaker 1993, 151). For example, those who rely on a sex differences approach conceive of gender as inhering in the individual, in other words, as the masculinity or femininity of a person. Elsewhere (Fenstermaker, West, and Zimmerman, 1991; West and Fenstermaker 1993; West and Zimmerman 1987), we note that this conceptualization obscures our understanding of how gender can structure distinctive domains of social experience (see also Stacey and Thorne 1985). "Sex differences" are treated as the explanation instead of the analytic point of departure.

Although many scholars who take this approach draw on socialization to account for the internalization of femininity and masculinity, they imply that by about five years of age these differences have become stable characteristics of individuals—much like sex (West and Zimmerman 1987, 126). The careful distinction between sex and gender, therefore, is obliterated, as gender is reduced effectively to sex (Gerson 1985).[5] When the social meanings of sex are rerooted in biology, it becomes virtually impossible to explain variation in gender relations in the context of race and class. We must assume, for example, that the effects of inherent sex differences are either added to or subtracted from those of race and class. We are led to assume, moreover, that sex differences are more fundamental than any other differences that might interest us (see Spelman 1988, 116–19, for a critical examination of this assumption)—unless we also assume that race differences and class differences are biologically based (for refutations of this assumption, see Gossett 1965; Montagu 1975; Omi and Winant 1986; and Stephans 1982).

Those who take a sex roles approach are confounded by similar difficulties, although these may be less apparent at the outset. What is deceptive is role theory's emphasis on the specific social locations that result in particular expectations and actions (Komarovsky 1946, 1992; Linton 1936; Parsons 1951; Parsons and Bales 1955). In this view, the actual enactment of an individual's "sex role" (or, more recently, "gender role") is contingent on the individual's social structural position and the expectations associated with that position. The focus is on gender as a role or status, as it is learned and enacted. In earlier work (Fenstermaker, West, and Zimmerman 1991; West and Fenstermaker 1993; West and Zimmerman 1987), we have noted several problems with this approach, including its inability to specify actions appropriate to particular "sex roles" in advance of their occurrence, and the fact that sex roles are not situated in any particular setting or organizational context (Lopata and Thorne 1978; Thorne 1980). The fact that "sex roles" often serve as "master statuses" (Hughes 1945) makes it hard to account for how variations in situations produce variations in their enactment. Given that gender is potentially omnirelevant to how we organize social life, almost any action could count as an instance of sex role enactment.

The most serious problem with this approach, however, is its inability to address issues of power and inequality (Connell 1985; Lopata and Thorne 1987; Thorne 1980). Conceiving of gender as composed of the "male role" and the "female role" implies a separate-but-equal relationship between the two, one characterized by complementary relations rather than conflict. Elsewhere (Fenstermaker, West, and Zimmerman 1991; West and Fenstermaker 1993; West and Zimmerman 1987), we illustrate this problem with Barrie Thorne and her colleagues' observation that social scientists have not made much use of role theory in their analyses of race and class relations. Concepts such as "race roles" and "class roles" have seemed patently inadequate to account for the dynamics of power and inequality operating in those contexts.

As many scholars have observed, empirical studies of the "female role" and "male role" have generally treated the experiences of white middle-class persons as prototypes, dismissing departures from the prototypical as instances of deviance. This is in large part what has contributed to the charges of white middle-class bias we discussed earlier. It is also what has rendered the sex role approach nearly useless in accounting for the diversity of gender relations across different groups.

Seeking a solution to these difficulties, Joan Acker has advanced the view that gender consists of something else altogether, namely, "patterned, socially produced distinctions between female and male, feminine and masculine . . . [that occur] in the course of participation in work organizations as well as in many other locations and relations" (1992b, 250). The object here is to document the "gendered processes" that sustain "the pervasive ordering of human activities, practices and social structures in terms of differentiations between women and men" (1992a, 567).

We agree fully with the object of this view and note its usefulness in capturing the persistence and ubiquity of gender inequality. Its emphasis on organizational practices restores the concern with "the structure of social institutions and with the impact of historical events" that characterized earlier class/caste approaches, and facilitates the simultaneous documentation of gender, race, and class as basic principles of social organization. We suggest, however, that the popular distinction between "macro" and "micro" levels of analysis reflected in this view makes it possible to empirically describe and explain inequality without fully apprehending the common elements of its daily unfolding. For example, "processes of interaction" are conceptualized apart from the "production of gender divisions," that is, "the overt decisions and procedures that control, segregate, exclude, and construct hierarchies based on gender, and often race" (Acker 1992a, 568). The production of "images, symbols and ideologies that justify, explain, and give legitimacy to institutions" constitutes yet another "process," as do "the [mental] internal processes in which individuals engage as they construct personas that are appropriately gendered for the institutional setting" (Acker 1992a, 568). The analytic "missing link," as we see it, is the mechanism that ties these seemingly diverse processes together, one that could "take into account the constraining impact of entrenched ideas and practices on human agency, but [could] also acknowledge that the system is continually construed in everyday life and that, under certain conditions, individuals resist pressures to conform to the needs of the system" (Essed 1991, 38).

In sum, if we conceive of gender as a matter of biological differences or differential roles, we are forced to think of it as standing apart from and outside other socially relevant, organizing experiences. This prevents us from understanding how gender, race, and class operate simultaneously with one another. It prevents us from seeing how the particular salience of these experiences might vary across interactions. Most important, it gives us virtually no way of adequately addressing the mechanisms that produce power and inequality in social life. Instead, we propose a conceptual mechanism for perceiving the relations between individual and institutional practice, and among forms of domination.

An Ethnomethodological Perspective

Don Zimmerman concisely describes ethnomethodological inquiry as proposing "that the properties of social life which seem objective, factual, and transsituational, are actually managed accomplishments or achievements of local processes" (1978, 11). In brief, the "objective" and "factual" properties of social life attain such status through the situated conduct of societal members. The aim of ethnomethodology is to analyze situated conduct to understand how "objective" properties of social life achieve their status as such.

The goal of this article is not to analyze situated conduct per se but to understand the workings of inequality. We should note that our interest here is not to separate gender, race, and class as social categories but to build a coherent argument for understanding how they work simultaneously. How might an ethnomethodological perspective help with this task? As Marilyn Frye observes,

> For efficient subordination, what's wanted is that the structure not appear to be a cultural artifact kept in place by human decision or custom, but that it appear natural—that it appear to be quite a direct consequence of facts about the beast which are beyond the scope of human manipulation. (1983, 34)

Gender

Within Western societies, we take for granted in everyday life that there are two and only two sexes (Garfinkel 1967, 122). We see this state of affairs as "only natural" insofar as we see persons as "essentially, originally and in the final analysis either 'male' or 'female'" (Garfinkel 1967, 122). When we interact with others, we take for granted that each of us has an "essential" manly or womanly nature—one that derives from our sex and one that can be detected from the "natural signs" we give off (Goffman 1976, 75).

These beliefs constitute the normative conceptions of our culture regarding the properties of normally sexed persons. Such beliefs support the seemingly "objective," "factual," and "transsituational" character of gender in social affairs, and in this sense, we experience them as exogenous (i.e., as outside of us and the particular situation we find ourselves in). Simultaneously, however, the meaning of these beliefs is dependent on the context in which they are invoked—rather than transsituational, as implied by the popular concept of "cognitive consensus" (Zimmerman 1978, 8–9). What is more, because these properties of normally sexed persons are regarded as "only natural," questioning them is tantamount to calling ourselves into question as competent members of society.

Consider how these beliefs operate in the process of sex assignment—the initial classification of persons as either females or males (West and Zimmerman 1987, 131–32). We generally regard this process as a biological determination requiring only a straightforward examination of the "facts of the matter" (cf. the description of sex as an "ascribed status" in many introductory sociology texts). The criteria for sex assignment, however, can vary across cases (e.g., chromosome type before birth or genitalia after birth). They sometimes do and sometimes do not agree with one another (e.g., hermaphrodites), and they show considerable variation across cultures (Kessler and McKenna 1978). Our *moral conviction* that there are two and only two sexes (Garfinkel 1967, 116–18) is what explains the comparative ease of achieving initial sex assignment. This conviction accords females and males the status of unequivocal and "natural" entities, whose social and psychological tendencies can be predicted from their reproductive functions (West and Zimmerman 1987, 127–28). From an ethnomethodological viewpoint, sex is socially and culturally constructed rather than a straightforward statement of the biological "facts."

Now, consider the process of sex categorization—the ongoing identification of persons as girls or boys and women or men in everyday life (West and Zimmerman 1987, 132–34). Sex categorization involves no well-defined set of criteria that must be satisfied to identify someone; rather, it involves treating appearances (e.g., deportment, dress, and bearing) as if they were indicative of underlying states of affairs (e.g., anatomical, hormonal, and chromosomal arrangements). The point worth stressing here is that, while sex category serves as an "indicator" of sex, it does not depend on it. Societal members will "see" a world populated by two and only two sexes, even in public situations that preclude inspection of the physiological "facts." From this perspective, it is important to distinguish sex category from sex assignment and to distinguish both from the "doing" of gender.

Gender, we argue, is a situated accomplishment of societal members, the local management of conduct in relation to normative conceptions of appropriate attitudes and activities for particular sex categories (West and Zimmerman 1987, 134–35). From this perspective, gender is not merely an individual attribute but something that is accomplished in interaction with others. Here, as in our earlier work, we rely on John Heritage's (1984, 136–37) formulation of accountability: the possibility of describing actions, circumstances, and even descriptions of themselves in both serious and consequential ways (e.g., as "unwomanly" or "unmanly"). Heritage points out that members of society routinely characterize activities in ways that take notice of those activities (e.g., naming, describing, blaming, excusing, or merely acknowledging them) and place them in a social framework (i.e., situating them in the context of other activities that are similar or different).

The fact that activities can be described in such ways is what leads to the possibility of conducting them with an eye to how they might be assessed (e.g., as "womanly" or "manly" behaviors). Three important but subtle points are worth emphasizing here. One is that the notion of accountability is relevant not only to activities that conform to prevailing normative conceptions (i.e., activities that are conducted "unremarkably," and, thus, do not warrant more than a passing glance) but also to those activities that deviate. The issue is not deviance or conformity; rather, it is the possible evaluation of action in relation to normative conceptions and the likely consequence of that evaluation for subsequent interaction. The second point worth emphasizing is that the process of rendering some action accountable is an interactional accomplishment. As Heritage explains, accountability permits persons to conduct their activities in relation to their circumstances—in ways that permit others to take those circumstances into account and see those activities for what they are. "[T]he intersubjectivity of actions," therefore, "ultimately rests on a symmetry between the *production* of those actions on the one hand and their *recognition* on the other" (1984, 179)—both in the context of their circumstances.[6] And the third point we must stress is that, while individuals are the ones who do gender, the process of rendering something accountable is both interactional and institutional in character: it is a feature of social relationships, and its idiom derives from the institutional arena in which those relationships come to life. In the United States, for example, when the behaviors of children or teenagers have become the focus of public concern, the Family and Motherhood (as well as individual mothers) have been held accountable to normative conceptions of "essential" femininity (including qualities like nurturance and caring). Gender is obviously much more than a role or an individual characteristic: it is a mechanism whereby situated social action contributes to the reproduction of social structure (West and Fenstermaker 1993, 158).

Womanly and manly natures thusly achieve the status of objective properties of social life (West and Zimmerman 1987). They are rendered natural, normal characteristics of individuals and, at the same time, furnish the tacit legitimation of the distinctive and unequal fates of women and men within the social order. If sex categories are potentially omnirelevant to social life, then persons engaged in virtually any activity may be held accountable for their performance of that activity as women or as men, and their category membership can be used to validate or discredit their other activities. This arrangement provides for countless situations in which persons in a particular sex category can "see" that they are out of place, and if they were not there, their current problems would not exist. It also allows for seeing various features of the existing social order—for example, the division of labor (Berk 1985), the development of gender identities (Cahill 1986), and the subordination of women by men (Fenstermaker, West, and Zimmerman 1991)—as "natural" responses. These things "are the way they are" by virtue of the fact that men are men and women are women—a distinction seen as "natural," as rooted in biology, and as producing fundamental psychological, behavioral, and social consequences.

Through this formulation, we resituate gender, an attribute without clear social origin or referent, in social interaction. This makes it possible to study how gender takes on social import, how it varies in its salience and consequence, and how it operates to produce and maintain power and inequality in social life. Below, we extend this reformulation to race, and then, to class. Through this extension, we are not proposing an equivalence of oppressions. Race is not class, and neither is gender; nevertheless, while race, class, and gender will likely take on different import and will often carry vastly different social consequences in any given social situation, we suggest that how they operate may be productively compared. Here, our focus is on the social mechanics of gender, race, and class, for that is the way we may perceive their simultaneous workings in human affairs.

Race

Within the United States, virtually any social activity presents the possibility of categorizing the participants on the basis of race. Attempts to establish race as a scientific concept have met with little success (Gosset 1965; Montagu 1975; Omi and Winant 1986; Stephans 1982). There are, for example, no biological criteria (e.g., hormonal, chromosomal, or anatomical) that allow physicians to pronounce race assignment at birth, thereby sorting human beings into distinctive races.[7] Since racial categories and their meanings change over time and place, they are, moreover, arbitrary.[8] In everyday life, nevertheless, people can and do sort out themselves and others on the basis of membership in racial categories.

Michael Omi and Howard Winant argue that the "seemingly obvious, 'natural' and 'common sense' qualities" of the existing racial order "themselves testify to the effectiveness of the racial formation process in constructing racial meanings and identities" (1986, 62). Take, for instance, the relatively recent emergence of the category "Asian American." Any scientific theory of race would be hard pressed to explain this in the absence of a well-defined set of criteria for assigning individuals to the category. In relation to ethnicity, furthermore, it makes no sense to aggregate in a single category the distinctive histories, geographic origins, and cultures of Cambodian, Chinese, Filipino, Japanese, Korean, Laotian, Thai, and Vietnamese Americans. Despite important distinctions among these groups, Omi and Winant contend, "the majority of Americans cannot tell the difference" between their members (1986, 24). "Asian American," therefore, affords a means of achieving racial categorization in everyday life.

Of course, competent members of U.S. society share preconceived ideas of what members of particular categories "look like" (Omi and Winant 1986, 62). Remarks such as "Odd, you don't look Asian" testify to underlying notions of what "Asians" ought to look like. The point we wish to stress, however, is that these notions are not supported by any scientific criteria for reliably distinguishing members of different "racial" groups. What is more, even state-mandated criteria (e.g., the proportion of "mixed blood" necessary to legally classify someone as Black)[9] are distinctly different in other Western cultures and have little relevance to the way racial categorization occurs in everyday life. As in the case of sex categorization, appearances are treated as if they were indicative of some underlying state.

Beyond preconceived notions of what members of particular groups look like, Omi and Winant suggest that Americans share preconceived notions of what members of these groups are like. They note, for example, that we are likely to become disoriented "when people do not act 'Black,' 'Latino,' or indeed 'white'" (1986, 62). From our ethnomethodological perspective, what Omi and Winant are describing is the accountability of persons to race category. If we accept their contention that there are prevailing normative conceptions of appropriate attitudes and activities for particular race categories and if we grant Heritage's (1984, 179) claim that accountability allows persons to conduct their activities in relation to their circumstances (in ways that allow others to take those circumstances into account and see those activities for what they are), we can also see race as a situated accomplishment of societal members. From this perspective, race is not simply an individual characteristic or trait but something that is accomplished in interaction with others.

To the extent that race category is omnirelevant (or even verges on this), it follows that persons involved in virtually any action may be held accountable for their performance of that action as members of their race category. As in the case of sex category, race category can be used to justify or discredit other actions; accordingly, virtually any action can be assessed in relation to its race categorical nature. The accomplishment of race (like gender) does not necessarily mean "living up" to normative conceptions of attitudes and activities appropriate to a particular race category; rather, it means engaging in action at the risk of race assessment. Thus, even though individuals are the ones who accomplish race, "the enterprise is fundamentally interactional and institutional in character, for accountability is a feature of social relationships and its idiom is drawn from the institutional arena in which those relationships are enacted" (West and Zimmerman 1987, 137).

The accomplishment of race renders the social arrangements based on race as normal and natural, that is, legitimate ways of organizing social life. In the United States, it can seem "only natural" for counselors charged with guiding high school students in their preparation for college admission to advise Black students against advanced courses in math, chemistry, or physics "because Blacks do not do well" in those areas (Essed 1991, 242). The students may well forgo such courses, given that they "do not need them" and "can get into college without them." However Philomena Essed observes, this ensures that students so advised will enter college at a disadvantage in comparison to classmates and creates the very situation that is believed to exist, namely, that Blacks do not do well in those areas. Small wonder, then, that the proportion of U.S. Black students receiving college degrees remains stuck at 13 percent, despite two decades of affirmative action programs (Essed 1991, 26). Those Black students who are (for whatever reason) adequately prepared for college are held to account for themselves as "deviant" representatives of their race category and, typically, exceptionalized (Essed 1991, 232). With that accomplishment, institutional practice and social order are reaffirmed.

Although the distinction between "macro" and "micro" levels of analysis is popular in the race relations literature too (e.g., in distinguishing "institutional" from "individual" racism or "macro-level" analyses of racialized social structures from "micro-level" analyses of identity formation), we contend that it is ultimately a false distinction. Not only do these "levels" operate continually and reciprocally in "our lived experience, in politics, in culture [and] in economic life" (Omi and Winant 1986, 67), but distinguishing between them "places the individual outside the institutional, thereby severing rules, regulations and procedures from the people who make and enact them" (Essed 1991, 36). We contend that the accountability of persons to race categories is the key to understanding the maintenance of the existing racial order.

Note that there is nothing in this formulation to suggest that race is necessarily accomplished in isolation from gender. To the contrary, if we conceive of both race and gender as situated accomplishments, we can see how individual persons may experience them simultaneously. For instance, Spelman observes that,

> [i]nsofar as she is oppressed by racism in a sexist context and sexism in a racist context, the Black woman's struggle cannot be compartmentalized into two struggles—one as a Black and one as a woman. Indeed, it is difficult to imagine why a Black woman would think of her struggles this way except in the face of demands by white women or by Black men that she do so. (1988, 124)

To the extent that an individual Black woman is held accountable in one situation to her race category, and in another, to her sex category, we can see these as "oppositional" demands for accountability. But note, it is a *Black woman* who is held accountable in both situations.

Contrary to Omi and Winant's (1986, 62) use of hypothetical cases, on any particular occasion of interaction, we are unlikely to become uncomfortable when "people" do not act "Black," "people" do not act "Latino," or when "people" do not act "white." Rather, we are likely to become disconcerted when particular Black *women* do not act like Black *women,* particular Latino *men* do not act like Latino *men,* or particular white *women* do not act like white *women*—in the context that we observe them. Conceiving of race and gender as ongoing accomplishments means we must locate their emergence in social situations, rather than within the individual or some vaguely defined set of role expectations.[10]

Despite many important differences in the histories, traditions, and varying impacts of racial and sexual oppression across particular situations, the mechanism underlying them is the same. To the extent that members of society know their actions are accountable, they will design their actions in relation to how they might be seen and described by others. And to the extent that race category (like sex category) is omnirelevant to social life, it provides others with an ever-available resource for interpreting those actions. In short, inasmuch as our society is divided by "essential" differences between members of different race categories and categorization by race is both relevant and mandated, the accomplishment of race is unavoidable (cf. West and Zimmerman 1987, 137).

For example, many (if not most) Black men in the United States have, at some point in their lives, been stopped on the street or pulled over by police for no apparent reason. Many (if not most) know very well that the ultimate grounds for their being detained is their race and sex category membership. Extreme deference may yield a release with the command to "move on," but at the same time, it legitimates the categorical grounds on which the police (be they Black or white) detained them in the first place. Indignation or outrage (as might befit a white man in similar circumstances) is likely to generate hostility, if not brutality, from the officers on the scene (who may share sharply honed normative conceptions regarding "inherent" violent tendencies among Black men). Their very survival may be contingent on how they conduct themselves in relation to normative conceptions of appropriate attitudes and activities for Black men in these circumstances. Here, we see both the limited rights of citizenship accorded to Black men in U.S. society and the institutional context (in this case, the criminal justice system) in which accountability is called into play.

In sum, the accomplishment of race consists of creating differences among members of different race categories—differences that are neither natural nor biological (cf. West and Zimmerman 1987, 137). Once created, these differences are used to maintain the "essential" distinctiveness of "racial identities" and the institutional arrangements that they support. From this perspective, racial identities are not invariant idealizations of our human natures that are uniformly distributed in society. Nor are normative conceptions of attitudes and activities for one's race category templates for "racial" behaviors. Rather, what is invariant is the notion that members of different "races" *have* essentially different natures, which explain their very unequal positions in our society.[11]

Class

This, too, we propose, is the case with class. Here, we know that even sympathetic readers are apt to balk: gender, yes, is "done," and race, too, is "accomplished," but class? How can we reduce a system that "differentially structures group access to material resources, including economic, political and social resources" (Andersen and Collins 1992, 50) to "a situated accomplishment"? Do we mean to deny the material realities of poverty and privilege? We do not. There is no denying the very different material realities imposed by differing relations under capital; however, we suggest that these realities have little to do with class categorization—and ultimately, with the accountability of persons to class categories—in everyday life.

For example, consider Shellee Colen's description of the significance of maids' uniforms to white middle-class women who employ West Indian immigrant women as child care workers and domestics in New York City. In the words of Judith Thomas, one of the West Indian women Colen interviewed,

> She [the employer] wanted me to wear the uniform. She was really prejudiced. She just wanted that the maid must be identified . . . She used to go to the beach every day with the children. So going to the beach in the sand and the sun and she would have the kids eat ice cream and all that sort of thing . . . I tell you one day when I look at myself, I was so dirty . . . just like I came out from a garbage can. (1986, 57).

At the end of that day, says Colen, Thomas asked her employer's permission to wear jeans to the beach the next time they went, and the employer gave her permission to do so. When she did wear jeans, and the employer's brother came to the beach for a visit, Thomas noted,

> I really believe they had a talk about it, because in the evening, driving back from the beach, she said "Well, Judith, I said you could wear something else to the beach other than the uniform [but] I think you will have to wear the uniform because they're very informal on this beach and they don't know who is guests from who isn't guests." (1986, 57).

Of the women Colen interviewed (in 1985), not one was making more than $225 a week, and Thomas was the only one whose employer was paying for medical insurance. All (including Thomas) were supporting at least two households: their own in New York, and that of their kin back in the West Indies. By any objective social scientific criteria, then, all would be regarded as members of the working-class poor; yet, in the eyes of Thomas's employer (and, apparently, the eyes of others at the beach), Thomas's low wages, long hours, and miserable conditions of employment were insufficient to establish her class category. Without a uniform, she could be mistaken for one of the guests and, hence, not be held accountable as a maid.

There is more to this example, of course, than meets the eye. The employer's claim notwithstanding, it is unlikely that Thomas, tending to white middle-class children who were clearly not her own, would be mistaken for one of the guests at the beach. The blue jeans, however, might be seen as indicating her failure to comply with normative expectations of attitudes and behaviors appropriate to a maid and, worse yet, as belying the competence of her employer (whose authority is confirmed by Thomas displaying herself as a maid). As Evelyn Nakano Glenn notes in another context, "the higher standard of living of one woman is made possible by, and also helps to perpetuate, the other's lower standard of living" (1992, 34).

Admittedly, the normative conceptions that sustain the accountability of persons to class category are somewhat different from those that sustain accountability to sex category and race category. For example, despite earlier attempts to link pauperism with heredity and thereby justify the forced sterilization of poor women in the United States (Rafter 1992), scientists today do not conceive of class in relation to the biological characteristics of a person. There is, moreover, no scientific basis for popular notions of what persons in particular class categories "look like" or "act like." But although the dominant ideology within the United States is no longer based explicitly on Social Darwinism (see, for example, Gossett 1965, 144–75) and although we believe, in theory, that anyone can make it, we as a society still hold certain truths to be self-evident. As Donna Langston observes:

> If hard work were the sole determinant of your ability to support yourself and your family, surely we'd have a different outcome for many in our society. We also, however, believe in luck and on closer examination, it certainly is quite a coincidence that the "unlucky" come from certain race, gender and class backgrounds. In order to perpetuate racist, sexist and classist outcomes, we also have to believe that the current economic distribution is unchangeable, has always existed, and probably exists in this form throughout the known universe, i.e., it's "natural." (1991, 146)

Langston pinpoints the underlying assumptions that sustain our notions about persons in relation to poverty and privilege—assumptions that compete with our contradictory declarations of a meritocratic society, with its readily invoked exemplar, Horatio Alger. For example, if someone is poor, we assume it is because of something *they* did or did not do: they lacked initiative, they were not industrious, they had no ambition, and so forth. If someone is rich, or merely well-off, it must be by virtue of *their own* efforts, talents, and initiative. While these beliefs certainly *look* more mutable than our views of women's and men's "essential" natures or our deep-seated convictions regarding the characteristics of persons in particular race categories, they still rest on the assumption that a person's economic fortunes derive from qualities of the person. Initiative is thus treated as inherent among the haves, and laziness is seen as inherent among the have-nots.[12] Given that initiative is a prerequisite for employment in jobs leading to upward mobility in this society, it is hardly surprising that "the rich get richer and the poor get poorer." As in the case of gender and race, profound historical effects of entrenched institutional practice result, but they unfold one accomplishment at a time.

To be sure, there are "objective" indicators of one's position within the system of distribution that differentially structure our access to resources. It is possible to sort members of society in relation to these indicators, and it is the job of many public agencies (e.g., those administering aid to families with dependent children, health benefits, food stamps, legal aid, and disability benefits) to do such sorting. In the process, public agencies allocate further unequal opportunities with respect to health, welfare, and life chances; however, whatever the criteria employed by these agencies (and these clearly change over time and place), they can be clearly distinguished from the accountability of persons to class categories in everyday life.

As Benjamin DeMott (1990) observes, Americans operate on the basis of a most unusual assumption, namely, that we live in a classless society. On the one hand, our everyday discourse is replete with categorizations of persons by class. DeMott (1990, 1–27) offers numerous examples of television shows, newspaper articles, cartoons, and movies that illustrate how class "will tell" in the most mundane of social doings. On the other hand, we believe that we in the United States are truly unique "in escaping the hierarchies that burden the rest of the developed world" (DeMott 1990, 29). We cannot see the system of distribution that structures our unequal access to resources. Because we cannot see this, the accomplishment of class in everyday life rests on the presumption that everyone is endowed with equal opportunity and, therefore, that real differences in the outcomes we observe must result from individual differences in attributes like intelligence and character.

For example, consider the media's coverage of the trial of Mary Beth Whitehead, the wife of a sanitation worker and surrogate mother of Baby M. As DeMott (1990, 96–101) points out, much of this trial revolved around the question of the kind of woman who would agree to bear and sell her child to someone else. One answer to this question might be "the kind of woman" who learned early in life that poverty engenders obligations of reciprocal sacrifice among people—even sacrifice for those who are not their kin (cf. Stack 1974). Whitehead was one of eight children, raised by a single mother who worked on and off as a beautician. Living in poverty, members of her family had often relied on "poor but generous neighbors" for help and had provided reciprocal assistance when they could. When William and Betsy Stern (a biochemist and a pediatrician) came to her for help, therefore, Whitehead saw them as "seemingly desperate in their childlessness, threatened by a ruinous disease (Mrs. Stern's self-diagnosed multiple sclerosis), [and] as people in trouble, unable to cope without her" (DeMott 1990, 99). Although she would be paid for carrying the pregnancy and although she knew that they were better off financially than she was, Whitehead saw the Sterns as "in need of help" and, hence, could not do otherwise than to provide it. DeMott explains:

> She had seen people turn to others helplessly in distress, had herself been turned to previously; in her world failure to respond was unnatural. Her class experience, together with her own individual nature, made it natural to perceive the helping side of surrogacy as primary and the commercial side as important yet secondary. (1990, 98)

Another answer to the "what kind of woman" question might be Whitehead's lack of education about the technical aspects of artificial insemination (DeMott 1990, 100). A high school dropout, she thought that this procedure allowed clinicians to implant both a man's sperm and a woman's egg in another woman's uterus, thereby making it possible for infertile couples to have their own genetic children. It was not until just before the birth that Whitehead learned she would be the one contributing the egg and, subsequently, would not be bearing their child but her own. Under these circumstances, it would certainly seem "natural" for her to break her contract with the Sterns at the point of learning that it required her to give them her baby.

The media coverage of Whitehead's trial focused neither on class-based understandings of altruism nor on class-associated knowledge of sexual reproduction; rather, it focused on the question of Whitehead's character:

> The answers from a team of expert psychologists were reported in detail. Mrs. Whitehead was described as "impulsive, egocentric, self-dramatic, manipulative and exploitative." One member of the team averred that she suffered from a "schizotypal personality disorder." [Another] gave it as his opinion that the defendant's ailment was a "mixed personality disorder," and that she was "immature, exhibitionistic, and histrionic." . . . [U]nder the circumstances, he did not see that "there were any 'parental rights'"; Mrs. Whitehead was "a surrogate uterus". . . "and not a surrogate mother." (DeMott 1990, 96)

Through these means, "the experts" reduced Whitehead from a woman to a womb, and, therefore, someone with no legitimate claim to the child she had helped to conceive. Simultaneously, they affirmed the right of Betsy Stern to be the mother—even of a child she did not bear. As Whitehead's attorney put it in his summation, "What we are witnessing, and what we can predict will happen, is that one class of Americans will exploit another class. And it will always be the wife of the sanitation worker who must bear the children for the pediatrician" (Whitehead and Schwartz-Nobel 1989, 160, cited in DeMott 1990, 97). The punch line, of course, is that our very practices of invoking "essential differences" between classes support the rigid system of social relations that disparately distributes opportunities and life chances. Without these practices, the "natural" relations under capital might well seem far more malleable.

The accomplishment of class renders the unequal institutional arrangements based on class category accountable as normal and natural, that is, as legitimate ways of organizing social life (cf. West and Zimmerman 1987). Differences between members of particular class categories that are created by this process can then be depicted as fundamental and enduring dispositions.[13] In this light, the institutional arrangements of our society can be seen as responsive to the differences—the social order being merely an accommodation to the natural order.

In any given situation (whether or not that situation can be characterized as face-to-face interaction or as the more "macro" workings of institutions), the simultaneous accomplishments of class, gender, and race will differ in content and outcome. From situation to situation, the salience of the observables relevant to categorization (e.g., dress, interpersonal style, skin color) may seem to eclipse the interactional impact of the simultaneous accomplishment of all three. We maintain, nevertheless, that, just as the mechanism for accomplishment is shared, so, too, is their simultaneous accomplishment ensured.

CONCLUSION: THE PROBLEM OF DIFFERENCE

As we have indicated, mathematical metaphors describing the relations among gender, race, and class have led to considerable confusion in feminist scholarship. As we have also indicated, the conceptualizations of gender that support mathematical metaphors (e.g., "sex differences" and "sex roles") have forced scholars to think of gender as something that stands apart from and outside of race and class in people's lives.

In putting forth this perspective, we hope to advance a new way of thinking about gender, race, and class, namely, as ongoing, methodical, and situated accomplishments. We have tried to demonstrate the usefulness of this perspective for understanding how people experience gender, race, and class simultaneously. We have also tried to illustrate the implications of this perspective for reconceptualizing "the problem of difference" in feminist theory.

What are the implications of our ethnomethodological perspective for an understanding of relations among gender, race, and class? First, and perhaps most important, conceiving of these as ongoing accomplishments means that we cannot determine their relevance to social action apart from the context in which they are accomplished (Fenstermaker, West, and Zimmerman 1991; West and Fenstermaker 1993). While sex category, race category and class category are potentially omnirelevant to social life, individuals inhabit many different identities, and these may be stressed or muted, depending on the situation. For example, consider the following incident described in detail by Patricia Williams, a law professor who, by her own admission, "loves to shop" and is known among her students for her "neat clothes":[14]

> Buzzers are big in New York City. Favored particularly by smaller stores and boutiques, merchants throughout the city have installed them as screening devices to reduce the incidence of robbery: if the face at the door looks desirable, the buzzer is pressed and the door is unlocked. If the face is that of an undesirable, the door stays pressed and the door is locked. I discovered [these buzzers] and their meaning one Saturday in 1986. I was shopping in Soho and saw in a store window a sweater that I wanted to buy for my mother. I pressed my round brown face to the window and my finger to the buzzer, seeking admittance. A narrow-eyed white teenager, wearing running shoes and feasting on bubble gum glared out, evaluating me for signs that would pit me against the limits of his social understanding. After about five minutes, he mouthed "we're closed," and blew pink rubber at me. It was two Saturdays before Christmas, at one o'clock in the afternoon; there were several white people in the store who appeared to be shopping for things for *their* mothers. (1991, 44)

In this incident, says Williams, the issue of undesirability revealed itself as a racial determination. This is true in a comparative sense; for example, it is unlikely that a white woman law professor would have been treated this way by this salesperson and likely that a Latino gang member would have. This is also true in a legal sense; for example, in cases involving discrimination, the law requires potential plaintiffs to specify whether or not they were discriminated against on the basis of sex *or* race or some other criterion. We suggest, however, that sex category and class category, although muted, are hardly irrelevant to Williams's story. Indeed, we contend that one reason readers are apt to find this incident so disturbing is that it did not happen to a Latino gang member but to a Black woman law professor. Our point is not to imply that anyone should be treated this way but to show that one cannot isolate Williams's race category from her sex category or class category and fully understand this situation. We would argue, furthermore, that how class and gender are accomplished in concert with race must be understood through that specific interaction.

A second implication of our perspective is that the accomplishment of race, class, and gender does not require categorical diversity among the participants. To paraphrase Erving Goffman, social situations "do not so much allow for the expression of natural differences as for the production of [those] difference[s themselves]" (1977, 72). Some of the most extreme displays of "essential" womanly and manly natures may occur in settings that are usually reserved for members of a single sex category, such as locker rooms or beauty salons (Gerson 1985). Some of the most dramatic expressions of "definitive" class characteristics may emerge in class-specific contexts (e.g., debutante balls). Situations that involve more than one sex category, race category, and class category may highlight categorical membership and make the accomplishment of gender, race, and class more salient, but they are not necessary to produce these accomplishments in the first place. This point is worth stressing, since existing formulations of relations among gender, race, and class might lead one to conclude that "difference" must be present for categorical membership and, thus, dominance to matter.

A third implication is that, depending on how race, gender, and class are accomplished, what looks to be the same activity may have different meanings for those engaged in it. Consider the long-standing debates among feminists (e.g., Collins 1990; Davis 1971; Dill 1988; Firestone 1970; Friedan 1963; hooks 1984; Hurtado 1989; Zavella 1987) over the significance of mothering and child care in women's lives. For white middle-class women, these activities have often been seen as constitutive of oppression in that they are taken as expressions of their "essential" womanly natures and used to discredit their participation in other activities (e.g., Friedan 1963). For many women of color (and white working-class women), mothering and child care have had (and continue to have) very different meanings. Angela Davis (1971, 7) points out that, in the context of slavery, African American women's efforts to tend to the needs of African American children (not necessarily their own) represented the only labor they performed that could not be directly appropriated by white slave owners. Throughout U.S. history, bell hooks observes,

> Black women have identified work in the context of the family as humanizing labor, work that affirms their identity as women, as human beings showing love and care, the very gestures of humanity white supremacist ideology claimed black people were incapable of expressing. (1984, 133–34)

Looking specifically at American family life in the nineteenth century, Bonnie Thornton Dill (1988) suggests that being a poor or working-class African American woman, a Chinese American woman, or a Mexican American woman meant something very different from being a Euro-American woman. Normative, class-bound conceptions of "woman's nature" at that time included tenderness, piety, and nurturance—qualities that legitimated the confinement of middle-class Euro-American women to the domestic sphere and that promoted such confinement as the goal of working-class and poor immigrant Euro-American families' efforts.

> For racial-ethnic women, however, the notion of separate spheres served to reinforce their subordinate status and became, in effect, another assault. As they increased their work outside the home, they were forced into a productive sphere that was organized for men and "desperate" women who were so unfortunate or immoral that they could not confine their work to the domestic sphere. In the productive sphere, however, they were denied the opportunity to embrace the dominant ideological definition of "good" wife and mother. (Dill 1988, 429)

Fourth and finally, our perspective affords an understanding of the accomplishment of race, gender, or class as constituted in the context of the differential "doings" of the others. Consider, for example, the very dramatic case of the U.S. Senate hearings on Clarence Thomas's nomination to the Supreme Court. Wherever we turned, whether to visual images on a television screen or to the justificatory discourse of print media, we were overwhelmed by the dynamics of gender, race, and class operating in concert with one another. It made a difference to us as viewers (and certainly to his testimony) that Clarence Thomas was a Black *man* and that he was a *Black* man. It also made a difference, particularly to the African American community, that he was a Black man who had been raised in poverty. Each categorical dimension played off the others and off the comparable but quite different categorizations of Anita Hill (a "self-made" Black woman law professor, who had grown up as one of 13 children). Most white women who watched the hearings identified gender and men's dominance as the most salient aspects of them, whether in making sense of the Judiciary Committee's handling of witnesses or understanding the relationship between Hill and Thomas. By contrast, most African American viewers saw racism as the most salient aspect of the hearings, including white men's prurient interest in Black sexuality and the exposure of troubling divisions between Black women and men (Morrison 1992). The point is that how we label such dynamics does not necessarily capture their complex quality. Foreground and background, context, salience, and center shift from interaction to interaction, but all operate interdependently.

Of course, this is only the beginning. Gender, race, and class are only three means (although certainly very powerful ones) of generating difference and dominance in social life.[15] Much more must be done to distinguish other forms of inequality and their workings. Empirical evidence must be brought to bear on the question of variation in the salience of categorical memberships, while still allowing for the simultaneous influence of these memberships on interaction. We suggest that the analysis of situated conduct affords the best prospect for understanding how these "objective" properties of social life achieve their ongoing status as such and, hence, how the most fundamental divisions of our society are legitimated and maintained.

Notes

1. In this article, we use "race" rather than "ethnicity" to capture the commonsensical beliefs of members of our society. As we will show, these beliefs are predicated on the assumption that different "races" can be reliably distinguished from one another.
2. Compare, for example, the very different implications of "Double Jeopardy: To Be Black and Female" (Beale 1970) and "Positive Effects of the Multiple Negative: Explaining the Success of Black Professional Women" (Epstein 1973).
3. In this context, we define "experience" as participation in social systems in which gender, race, and class affect, determine, or otherwise influence behavior.
4. Here, it is important to distinguish an individual's experience of the dynamics of gender, race, and class as they order the daily course of social interaction from that individual's sense of identity as a member of gendered, raced, and classed categories. For example, in any given interaction, a woman who is Latina and a shopkeeper may experience the simultaneous effects of gender, race, and class, yet identify her experience as only "about" race, only "about" gender, or only "about" class.
5. The ambivalence that dogs the logic of social constructionist positions should now be all too familiar to feminist sociologists. If we are true to our pronouncements that social inequalities and the categories they reference (e.g., gender, race, and class) are not rooted in biology, then we may at some point seem to flirt with the notion that they are, therefore, rooted in nothing. For us, biology is not only not destiny but also not the only reality. Gender, race, and class inequalities are firmly rooted in the ever-present realities of individual practice, cultural conventions, and social institutions. That's reality enough, when we ponder the pernicious and pervasive character of racism, sexism, and economic oppression.
6. That persons may be held accountable does not mean that they necessarily will be held accountable in every interaction. Particular interactional outcomes are not the point here; rather, it is the possibility of accountability in any interaction.
7. To maintain vital statistics on race, California, for instance, relies on mothers' and fathers' self-identifications on birth certificates.
8. Omi and Winant (1986, 64–75) provide numerous empirical illustrations, including the first appearance of "white" as a term of self-identification (circa 1680), California's decision to categorize Chinese people as "Indian" (in 1854), and the U.S. Census's creation of the category "Hispanic" (in 1980).
9. Consider Susie Guillory Phipps's unsuccessful suit against the Louisiana Bureau of Vital Records (Omi and Winant 1986, 57). Phipps was classified as "Black" on her birth certificate, in accord with a 1970 Louisiana law stipulating that anyone with at least one-thirty-second "Negro blood" was "Black." Her attorney contended

that designating a race category on a person's birth certificate was unconstitutional and that, in any case, the one-thirty-second criterion was inaccurate. Ultimately, the court upheld Louisiana's state law quantifying "racial identity" and thereby affirmed the legal principle of assigning persons to specific "racial" groups.

10. This would be true if only because outcomes bearing on power and inequality are so different in different situations. Ours is a formulation that is sensitive to variability, that can accommodate, for example, interactions where class privilege and racism seem equally salient, as well as those in which racism interactionally "eclipses" accountability to sex category.
11. As Spelman observes, "The existence of racism does not require that there are races; it requires the belief that there are races" (1988, 208, n. 24).
12. A devil's advocate might argue that gender, race, and class are fundamentally different because they show different degrees of "mutability" or latitude in the violation of expectations in interaction. Although class mobility is possible, one might argue, race mobility is not; or, while sex change operations can be performed, race change operations cannot. In response, we would point out that the very notion that one cannot change one's race—but can change one's sex and manipulate displays of one's class—only throws us back to biology and its reassuring, but only apparent, immutability.
13. Although we as a society believe that some people may "pull themselves up by their bootstraps" and others may "fall from grace," we still cherish the notion that class will reveal itself in a person's fundamental social and psychological character. We commonly regard the self-made man, the welfare mother, and the middle-class housewife as distinct categories of persons, whose attitudes and activities can be predicted on categorical grounds.
14. We include these prefatory comments about shopping and clothes for those readers who, on encountering this description, asked, "What does she look like?" and "What was she wearing?" Those who seek further information will find Williams featured in a recent fashion layout for *Mirabella magazine* (As Smart as They Look 1993).
15. We cannot stress this strongly enough. Gender, race, and class are obviously very salient social accomplishments in social life, because so many features of our cultural institutions and daily discourse are organized to perpetuate the categorical distinctions on which they are based. As Spelman observes, "the more a society has invested in its members' getting the categories right, the more occasions there will be for reinforcing them, and the fewer occasions there will be for questioning them" (1988, 152). On any given occasion of interaction, however, we may also be held accountable to other categorical memberships (e.g., ethnicity, nationality, sexual orientation, place of birth), and, thus, "difference" may then be differentially constituted.

References

Acker, Joan. 1992a. Gendered institutions: From sex roles to gendered institutions. *Contemporary Sociology* 21:565–69.

———. 1992b. Gendering organizational theory. In *Gendering Organizational Theory*, edited by Albert J. Mills and Peta Tancred. London: Sage.

Almquist, Elizabeth. 1989. The experiences of minority women in the United States: Intersections of race, gender, and class. In *Women: A feminist perspective*, edited by Jo Freeman. Mountain View, CA: Mayfield.

Andersen, Margaret L., and Patricia Hill Collins. 1992. Preface to *Race, class and gender*, edited by Margaret L. Andersen and Patricia Hill Collins. Belmont, CA: Wadsworth.

Aptheker, Bettina. 1989. *Tapestries of life: Women's work, women's consciousness, and the meaning of daily experience.* Amberst: University of Massachusetts Press.

As smart as they look. *Mirabella*, June 1993, 100–111.

Beale, Frances. 1970. Double jeopardy: To be Black and female. In *The Black woman: An anthology*, edited by Toni Cade (Bambara). New York: Signet.

Berk, Sarah Fenstermaker. 1985. *The gender factory: The apportionment of work in American households.* New York: Plenum.

Bhavani, Kum-Kum. In press. Talking racism and the editing of women's studies. In *Introducing women's studies*, edited by Diane Richardson and Vicki Robinson. New York: Macmillan.

Cahill, Spencer E. 1986. Childhood socialization as recruitment process: Some lessons from the study of gender development. In *Sociological studies of child development,* edited by Patricia Adler and Peter Adler. Greenwich, CT: JAI.

Colen, Shellee. 1986. "With respect and feelings": Voices of West Indian child care and domestic workers in New York City. In *All American women,* edited by Johnetta B. Cole. New York: Free Press.

Collins, Patricia Hill. 1990. *Black feminist thought.* New York: Routledge.

Connell, R.W. 1985. Theorizing gender. *Sociology* 19:260–72.

Davis, Angela. 1971. The Black woman's role in the community of slaves. *Black Scholar* 3:3–15.

———. 1981. *Women, race and class.* New York: Random House.

de Beauvoir, Simone. 1953. *The second sex.* New York: Knopf.

DeMott, Benjamin. 1990. *The imperial middle: Why Americans can't think straight about class.* New Haven, CT: Yale University Press.

Dill, Bonnie Thornton. 1988. Our mothers' grief: Racial ethnic women and the maintenance of families. *Journal of Family History* 13:415–31.

Epstein, Cynthia Fuchs. 1973. Positive effects of the double negative: Explaining the success of Black professional women. In *Changing women in a changing society,* edited by Joan Huber. Chicago: University of Chicago Press.

Essed, Philomena. 1991. *Understanding everyday racism: An interdisciplinary theory.* Newbury Park, CA: Sage.

Fenstermaker, Sarah, Candace West, and Don H. Zimmerman. 1991. Gender inequality: New conceptual terrain. In *Gender, family and economy: The triple overlap,* edited by Rae Lesser Blumberg. Newbury Park, CA: Sage.

Firestone, Shulamith. 1970. *The dialectic of sex.* New York: Morrow.

Friedan, Betty. 1963. *The feminine mystique.* New York: Dell.

Frye, Marilyn. 1983. *The politics of reality: Essays in feminist theory.* Trumansburg, NY: Crossing Press.

Garfinkel, Harold. 1967. *Studies in ethnomethodology.* Upper Saddle River, NJ: Prentice Hall.

Gerson, Judith. 1985. *The variability and salience of gender: Issues of conceptualization and measurement.* Paper presented at the annual meeting of the American Sociological Association, Washington, DC, August.

Glazer, Nona. 1977. A sociological perspective: Introduction. In *Woman in a man-made world,* edited by Nona Glazer and Helen Youngelson Waehrer. Chicago: Rand McNally.

Glenn, Evelyn Nakano. 1985. Racial ethnic women's labor: The intersection of race, gender and class oppression. *Review of Radical Political Economics* 17:86–108.

———. 1992. From servitude to service work: Historical continuities in the racial division of paid reproductive labor. *Signs: Journal of Women in Culture and Society* 18:1–43.

Goffman, Erving. 1976. Gender display. *Studies in the Anthropology of Visual Communication* 3:69–77.

———. 1977. The arrangement between the sexes. *Theory and Society* 4:301–31.

Gossett, Thomas. 1965. *Race: The history of an idea in America.* New York: Schocken Books.

Hacker, Helen Mayer. 1951. Women as a minority group. *Social Forces* 30:60–69.

Heritage, John. 1984. *Garfinkel and ethnomethodology.* Cambridge, England: Polity.

Hochschild, Arlie Russell. 1973. A review of sex role research. *American Journal of Sociology* 78:1011–29.

hooks, bell. 1981. *Ain't I a woman: Black women and feminism.* Boston: South End.

———. 1984. *From margin to center.* Boston: South End.

Hughes, Everett C. 1945. Dilemmas and contradictions of status. *American Journal of Sociology* 50:353–59.

Hull, Gloria T., Patricia Bell Scott, and Barbara Smith, eds. 1982. *All the women are white, all the Blacks are men, but some of us are brave.* Old Westbury, NY: Feminist Press.

Hurtado, Aída. 1989. Relating to privilege: Seduction and rejection in the subordination of white women and women of color. *Signs: Journal of Women in Culture and Society* 14:833–55.

Jordan, June. 1985. Report from the Bahamas. In *On call: Political essays.* Boston: South End.

Joseph, Gloria, and Jill Lewis, eds. 1981. *Common differences.* Garden City, NY: Anchor.

Kessler, Suzanne J., and Wendy McKenna. 1978. *Gender: An ethnomethodological approach.* New York: Wiley.

Komarovsky, Mirra. 1946. Cultural contradictions and sex roles. *American Journal of Sociology* 52:184–89.

———. 1992. The concept of social role revisited. *Gender & Society* 6:301–12.

Langston, Donna. 1991. Tired of playing monopoly? In *Changing our power: An introduction to women's studies,* 2d ed., edited by Jo Whitehorse Cochran, Donna Langston, and Carolyn Woodward. Dubuque, IA: Kendall-Hunt.

Linton, Ralph. 1936. *The study of man.* New York: Appleton-Century.

Lopata, Helena Z., and Barrie Thorne. 1987. On the term "sex roles." *Signs: Journal of Women in Culture and Society* 3:718–21.

Lorde, Audre. 1984. *Sister outsider.* Trumansburg, NY: Crossing.

Montagu, Ashley, ed. 1975. *Race & IQ.* London: Oxford University Press.

Mitchell, Juliet. 1966. Women: The longest revolution. *New Left Review* 40:11–37.

Moraga, Cherríe. 1981. La güera. In *This bridge called my back: Radical writing by women of color,* edited by Cherríe Moraga and Gloria Anzalduá. New York: Kitchen Table Press.

Moraga, Cherríe, and Gloria Anzaiduá, eds. 1981. *This bridge called my back: Writings by radical women of color.* Watertown, MA: Persephone.

Morrison, Toni, ed. 1992. *Race-ing justice, engendering power: Essays on Anita Hill, Clarence Thomas, and the construction of social reality.* New York: Pantheon.

Omi, Michael, and Howard Winant. 1986. *Racial formation in the United States from the 1960s to the 1980s.* New York: Routledge & Kegan Paul.

Parsons, Talcott. 1951. *The social system.* New York: Free Press.

Parsons, Talcott, and Robert F. Bales. 1955. *Family, socialization and interaction process.* New York: Free Press.

Rafter, Nichole H. 1992. Claims-making and sociocultural context in the first U.S. eugenics campaign. *Social Problems* 39:17–34.

Rich, Adrienne. 1979. Disloyal to civilization: Feminism, racism, gynephobia. In *On lies, secrets, and silence.* New York: Norton.

Segura, Denise A. 1992. Chicanas in white collar jobs: "You have to prove yourself more." *Sociological Perspectives* 35:163–82.

Spelman, Elizabeth V. 1988. *Inessential woman: Problems of exclusion in feminist thought.* Boston: Beacon Press.

Stacey, Judith, and Barrie Thorne. 1985. The missing feminist revolution in sociology. *Social Problems* 32:301–16.

Stack, Carol B. 1974. *All our kin: Strategies for survival in a Black community.* New York: Harper & Row.

Stephans, Nancy. 1982. *The idea of race in science.* Hamden, CT: Archon.

Thorne, Barrie. 1980. Gender . . . How is it best conceptualized? Unpublished manuscript, Department of Sociology, Michigan State University, East Lansing.

West, Candace, and Sarah Fenstermaker, 1993. Power, inequality and the accomplishment of gender: An ethnomethodological view. In *Theory on gender/feminism on theory,* edited by Paula England. New York: Aldine.

West, Candace, and Don H. Zimmerman. 1987. Doing gender. *Gender & Society* 1:125–51.

Williams, Patricia. 1991. *The alchemy of race and rights.* Cambridge, MA: Harvard University Press.

Young, Iris Marion. 1990. Impartiality and the civic public. In *Throwing like a girl and other essays in feminist philosophy.* Bloomington: Indiana University Press.

Zavella, Patricia. 1987. *Women's work and Chicano families: Cannery workers of the Santa Clara Valley.* Ithaca, NY: Cornell University Press.

Zimmerman, Don H. 1978. Ethnomethodology. *American Sociologist* 13:6–15.

Zinn, Maxine Baca. 1990. Family, feminism and race in America. *Gender & Society* 4:68–82.

Zinn, Maxine Baca, Lynn Weber Cannon, Elizabeth Higginbotham, and Bonnie Thornton Dill. 1986. The costs of exclusionary practices in women's studies. *Signs: Journal of Women in Culture and Society* 11:290–303.

Candace West is Professor of Sociology at the University of California, Santa Cruz. Her recent articles focus on different aspects of the problem addressed here: the interactional scaffolding of social structure.

Sarah Fenstermaker is Professor of Sociology and Women's Studies and Associate Dean of the Graduate Division at the University of California, Santa Barbara. Her works have explored the accomplishments of race, class, and gender, and the gendered determinants of the household division of labor. Her current work further articulates the relationship between work and inequality.

Symposium
On West and Fenstermaker's "Doing Difference"

PATRICIA HILL COLLINS
LIONEL A. MALDONADO
DANA Y. TAKAGI
BARRIE THORNE
LYNN WEBER
HOWARD WINANT

PATRICIA HILL COLLINS
University of Cincinnati

REPRINT REQUESTS: *Patricia Hill Collins. Dept. of African-American Studies. ML370. University of Cincinnati, Cincinnati, Ohio 45221.*

How wonderful it would be to possess the insight to see beyond the messy, contemporary politics of race, class, and gender in order to propose "a new way of thinking about the workings of these relations" (West and Fenstermaker 1995, 9). The area of race, class, gender studies struggles with the complex question of how to think about intersections of systems of oppression of race, class, and gender. We clearly need new models that will assist us in seeing how structures of power organized around intersecting relations of race, class, and gender frame the social positions occupied by individuals; work explaining how interlocking systems of oppression produce social locations for us all, where Black men are routinely stopped by the police for no apparent reason, or African American women like Patricia Williams are denied entry to stores where they could spend their hard-earned law professor salaries.

Despite West and Fenstermaker's initial promises to retheorize the intersections of race, class, and gender in a way that transcends the limitations of existing models, a surprising thing happened on the way to the end of their article. One by one, race, gender, and even class were erased. As a result, an article that claims to retheorize the interconnections of race, class, and gender said remarkably little about racism, patriarchy, and capitalism as systems of power. How this happened was impressive. Race and class appeared as gender in drag, each arriving in analytical forms virtually unrecognizable to practitioners of these respective fields. Each made brief appearances, before returning to the safe haven of social constructionist arguments about difference. In the place of the race, class, and gender came a rehashing of social constructionist views of society, a technique of ethnomethodology masquerading as new theory, and—most amazing—the concept of difference used as proxy for the interconnectedness of race, class, and gender itself. The very things the article claimed to reveal it curiously erased, all the while talking about them.

Perhaps articles like "Doing Difference" wouldn't bother me so much if the stakes weren't so high. Since I have long worked in the field of race, class, and gender studies, a quick summary of the field provides a context for evaluating the contributions of this article. For years, scholars in the separate areas of race or

From Patricia Hill Collins, Lionel A. Maldonado, Dana Y. Takagi, Barrie Thome, Lynn Weber, Howard Winant, "Symposium on West and Fenstemaker's 'Doing Difference'" *Gender and Society,* Vol. 9, No. 4, August 1995.

class or gender struggled for the primacy of each as an analytical category explaining inequality. To do this, they diligently chipped away at a social science logic that constructed race, class, and gender as benign attributes that were useful for describing human subjects in research designs, but treated racism, sexism, and class exploitation as variations of other more fundamental processes. More important, race, class, and gender studies each emerged, not in the rarefied atmosphere of academia, but in conjunction with social movements populated by people who had a real stake in understanding and changing inequalities of power resulting from systems of oppression called racism, patriarchy, and class exploitation.

These links between theory and politics meant that, despite their historical differences, all three areas shared certain fundamentals. Each aimed to explain the links between micro level experiences structured along axes of race, class, and gender, with the larger, overarching macro systems. Each reasoned that, if individuals could link their own experiences with oppression on a micro level with the larger macro forces constructing their social position, they could address some of the major social problems of our day.

This commitment to theorizing oppression via these distinctive emphases eventually encountered the limitations of privileging any one system of oppression over others—of patriarchy over class, for example, or white supremacy over homophobia. The very notion of the intersections of race, class, gender as an area worthy of study emerged from the recognition of practitioners of each distinctive theoretical tradition that inequality could not be explained, let alone challenged, via a race-only, class-only, or gender-only framework. No one had all the answers and no one was going to get all of the answers without attention to two things. First, the notion of interlocking oppressions refers to the macro level connections linking systems of oppression such as race, class, and gender. This is the model describing the social structures that create social positions. Second, the notion of intersectionality describes micro level processes—namely, how each individual and group occupies a social position within interlocking structures of oppression described by the metaphor of intersectionality. Together they shape oppression.

At this historical moment we have something very momentous happening—the linking of three historically distinct areas of inquiry with a renewed commitment to theorize connections on multiple levels of social structure. To accomplish this goal, all must support a working hypothesis of equivalency between oppressions that allows us to explore the interconnections among the systems and extract us from the internecine battles of whose oppression is more fundamental. The intent of race, class, gender studies is to push to understand oppression (or in the more polite language of academia. "inequality" or "stratification.")

"Doing Difference" claims the language of inclusivity, but decontextualizes it from the history of race, class, gender studies. It strips the very categories of race, class, and gender of meaning and then recasts the problems of institutional power in the apolitical framework of how we might "do difference."

The authors achieve this intellectual sleight of hand impressively. Consider the order in which they construct the individual discussions of gender, race, and class. Despite criticizing others who use "additive" approaches, in constructing their argument, the authors use this same approach of treating gender as the most fundamental, theoretical category and then "adding" on race and class. They lay out their theoretical argument within a gender-only framework and then generalize this argument to race and class. Note that there are no "experience" examples within the gender category; apparently gender speaks for itself and needs no examples. In contrast, the discussion of race has more "experiences" included, thus providing the unintended but nonetheless unfortunate outcome of constructing people of color as less theoretical and more embodied. Amazingly, the discussion of social class opens with an "experience," foreshadowing an unusual approach to social class. Their treatment of social class remains distinctive because the literature of social class, much more so than that of gender and race, has long been grounded in questions of institutional power. After all, it is hard to discuss global capitalist markets as performances and representations.

By the end of the article, I found little evidence that the authors had really proposed a new way of thinking. Instead, they managed to transform the interlocking systems of oppression of race, class, and gender that produce positions characterized by intersectionality into, as British cultural critic Stuart Hall puts it, "a difference that didn't make any difference at all" (1992, 23).

To recast race, class, gender politics as an issue of postmodernist difference is indicative of some problems of the politics of postmodernist discourse overall. The construct of difference emerges from social constructionist views of self/other where the self is constructed against the difference of the other, but this is not the use of difference we encounter in this article. Social institutions, especially analyses of the institutional bases of power shaping race, class, and gender, are dropped from the analysis, leaving a plethora of postmodernist representations in their wake. Recasting racism, patriarchy, and class exploitation solely in social constructionist terms reduces race, class, and gender to performances, interactions between people embedded in a never ending string of equivalent relations, all containing race, class, and gender in some form, but a chain of equivalences devoid of power relations.

This all leads to the puzzling question of why this is happening. It is one thing to say that manipulating "difference" comprises one effective tactic used by dominant groups to maintain control—this insight is closer to the actual meanings of Williams, Spelman, and myself. It's quite another to wring one's hands about the "problem of difference." laying the groundwork for handling difference as the real problem, instead of the power relations that construct difference.

Since not all social groups appear to find difference to be such a meaningful concept, I'm left wondering who is worried about it? Thinking through the meaning, of difference hasn't much concerned people of color, poor people, and all the other people deemed "different" who disappear from this article. Attention by oppressed groups to the meaning of difference remains firmly rooted in the question of the use to which differences are put in defending unequal power arrangements.

Despite the well-intentioned goal of the authors, "Doing Difference" and similar efforts to infuse race, class, and gender studies with postmodernist notions of difference leave us on dangerously thin ice. What type of oppositional politics emerge from a focus on difference devoid of power? What types of directions emerge from theories stressing representations over institutional structures and social policies as central to race, class, and gender relations? Already, I see far too many students who see resistance to oppression as occurring only in the area of representation, as if thinking about resistance and analyzing representations can substitute for active resistance against institutional power. Quite simply, difference is less a problem for me than racism, class exploitation, and gender oppression. Conceptualizing these systems of oppression as difference obfuscates the power relations and material inequalities that constitute oppression. Doing away with thinking about difference will clarify the real problem.

References

Hall, Stuart. 1992. What is this "Black" in Black popular culture? In *Black popular culture*, edited by Gina Dent and Michele Wallace. Seattle: Bay Press.

West, Candace, and Sarah Fenstermaker. 1995. Doing difference. *Gender & Society* 9:8–37.

Patricia Hill Collins is Professor of African-American Studies and Sociology at the University of Cincinnati. She is the author of Black Feminist Thought: Knowledge, Consciousness and the Politics of Empowerment *and the editor with Margaret Andersen of* Race, Class, Gender. An Anthology.

LIONEL A. MALDONADO
California State University, San Marcos

REPRINT REQUESTS: *Lionel A. Maldonado, Liberal Studies, California State University, San Marcos, San Marcos, CA 92069.*

West and Fenstermaker's (1995) argument is engaging and provocative. They propose extending the use of an ethnomethodological formulation for understanding gender to also include race and class factors. They argue that their approach is a way to understand the social construction of gender, race, and class, and contend that the common distinction between "micro" and "macro" levels of analysis is a false distinction. This point is made in their discussion of "accomplishing" race, but presumably is extended to gender and class. They imply that their formulation is sufficient to understand the processes regarding social inequality, generally, but their argument is not entirely convincing. There are two issues that I believe need to be addressed more fully regarding their social construction of race, class, and gender—the focus on both *social* and *construction.*

First, on the *social* part of this construction. I agree that people make their own history. They do so, however, within the confines of the circumstances and conditions they encounter. For example, Michael Mann (1993) has documented how military, political, and economic conditions of different periods configure the nation-state and influence the experiences of individuals and groups. Out of this context, socially constructed definitions, interpretations, and their rationales are produced. The formulation by West and Fenstermaker shifts our attention from these historical circumstances. The authors' position would be strengthened in more formally acknowledging the constraints imposed by these macro level forces in the social environment.

My second point is that since reality is *constructed,* we need to be clear whose construction is being given attention. West and Fenstermaker's discussion leaves the impression that reality somehow is monolithic. They do this in spite of an early acknowledgment that the feminist movement did not address the needs and conditions of working-class women and women of color, nor did it recruit them; this rendered the movement less than inclusive. Clearly, groups and their members can, and often do, have very different (even diametrically opposed) beliefs about what is "real," "objectively true," "good," and "desirable." Much of this depends on the place each occupies in the social structure. How West and Fenstermaker's conception would accommodate this lack of consensus on social construction is not clear. Good examples on whose ideology wins out in this battle include Andrew Scull (1993) on the treatment of lunacy in Great Britain, George Sanchez (1993) on the development of the Chicano community in Los Angeles, and Paula Giddings (1984) on why Black women were not drawn to the feminist movement of white, middle-class women. West and Fenstermaker's argument would be enriched by consideration of such works.

REFERENCES

Giddings, Paula. 1984. *When and where I enter: The impact of Black women on race and sex in America.* New York: Bantam Books.

Mann, Michael. 1993. *The sources of social power—Vol. II.* New York: Cambridge University Press.

Sanchez, George. 1993. *Becoming Mexican American: Ethnicity, culture, and identity in Chicano Los Angeles, 1900–1945.* New York: Oxford University Press.

Scull, Andrew. 1993. *The most solitary of affliations: Madness and society in Britain*, 1700–1900. New Haven, CT: Yale University Press.

West, Candace, and Sarah Fenstermaker. 1995. Doing difference. *Gender & Society* 9:8–37.

LIONEL A. MALDONADO teaches courses on race/ ethnic identity in American society and on the development and perpetration of ethnic/ racial stratification in the United States. He has also done research on the Chicano community in America. Before joining the faculty at California State University, San Marcos. he was deputy executive officer of the American Sociological Association and director of its Minority Affairs Program.

DANA Y. TAKAGI
University of California, Santa Cruz

REPRINT REQUESTS: *Dana Y. Takagi, Stevenson College. University of California, Santa Cruz. Santa Cruz. CA 95064.*

In *The Ethics of Authenticity*, a pithy book about identity, politics, and modernity, philosopher Charles Taylor (1992) defines three grand malaises of modernity: loss of meaning, loss of ends, and loss of freedoms. Taylor admits these are jumbo-sized themes, and he restricts his discussion to the first malaise—loss of meaning—hoping that others will be persuaded by his analysis and encouraged to take up analysis of the remaining two. Taylor's point is a simple one; namely, that contemporary debates about modernity fail to get to the heart of the problem—an analysis of the moral weightiness of the ideal of authenticity. Indeed, according to Taylor (1992), in spite of the tremendous amount of disagreement between, for example, universalists and relativists, the discussion in toto reveals an "extraordinary inarticulacy" about authenticity, as "one of the constitutive ideals of modern culture" (p. 18).

Like Taylor, West and Fenstermaker are interested in grand malaise. Although they never invoke his discussion, the parallel between their essay and Taylor's book is striking. As if on cue, they pick up Taylor's second grand malaise, "loss of ends," and illustrate how *some* feminist technologies of understanding race, class, and gender are animated by mathematical metaphors—intersections, additivity, and overlapping circles of Venn diagrams. By "loss of ends," Taylor is referring to the "primacy of instrumental reason" in economic, social, and political life. For West and Fenstermaker, arithmetic models, although providing neat diagrams of intersectionality, tend to ignore the socially produced nature of difference.

The problem of mathematics is more than the stammering of language, that is, of fumbling through the list of "inter-" descriptors—intersection, interwoven, interaction, intervening—to grasp the doings of race, class, and gender. The authors quite rightly point out that verbiage about simultaneity is an after-the-fact discussion that says next to nothing about the *mechanisms* that produce inequality.

Their essay, which documents structural and representational aspects of inequality, will I hope be taken as an argument for balance between what is currently seen as interactional consequences and interactional productions. The former should not be confused with the latter; consequences refers to outcomes and "effects," whereas the former constitutes the latter.

Their discussion should not be read, as I fear it might, simply as a plea for a new technology, ethnomethodological vision, for thinking about difference. Approaches to difference must be distinguished from visions of difference. Like technique, approach focuses on apprehending difference. Contrastingly, vision conjures up perspective, utopia, and even that category about which many of us feel ambivalent—science. West and Fenstermaker are offering us the latter, a vision of ethnomethodolgical gains as a means for understanding the mechanisms of doing difference. Their choice of terms, *mechanisms,* is both an appeal [to] and rebuff of science metaphors about society. Mechanisms that are not mechanical refer to situated conduct, interactional accomplishments, and contextually specific interactions.

What is engaging about this essay for me as a sociologist is their move to divide scholarship about difference into metaphors and mechanisms. West and Fenstermaker's notion of mechanisms is not completely at odds with some feminist thinking about difference. Their compelling argument to decenter math metaphors and privilege "situated conduct" is mostly complementary with Haraway's (1991) exposition of situated knowledges and partial perspective, but, whereas Haraway's project is to reclaim and rearticulate notions of science and objectivity for feminist perspectives. West and Fenstermaker appear less sanguine about such a possibility.

If *they* are not keen on math metaphors, then what should we do about the fact that the rest of the world steeps in the language of math, science, and biology? Or put another way, academics are not the only ones who embrace the metaphors of additivity and other mathematical relations. Discourses of science and math, and of instrumental reason, characterize popular understandings of inequality too.

If interactional accomplishments are mechanisms of doing difference, then perhaps the language of mathematics is part of that accomplishment as well.

References

Haraway, Donna J. 1991. Situated knowledges: The science question in feminism and the privilege of partial perspective. In *Simians, cyborgs, and women: The reinvention of nature,* edited by Donna J. Haraway. New York: Routledge.

Taylor, Charles. 1992. *The ethics of authenticity.* Cambridge: Harvard University Press.

West, Candace, and Sarah Fenstermaker. 1995. Doing difference. *Gender & Society* 9:8–37.

Dana Y. Takagi is the author of The Retreat from Race *(Rutgers University Press, 1993) and various essays on race relations. Asian Americans, social problems, affirmative action, and identity politics. She is the kind of constructionist who believes in the existence of facts.*

BARRIE THORNE
University of Southern California

REPRINT REQUESTS: *Barrie Thorne, Department of Sociology. University of Southern California. Los Angeles, CA 90089–2519*

West and Fenstermaker's perceptive discussion of metaphors led me to reflect upon the authors' own imagery for conceptualizing relations among gender, race, and class. Instead of mathematics, West and Fenstermaker evoke the sphere of serious effort or work: "*doing* gender" (race, class); "difference as a *routine, methodical,* and ongoing *accomplishment*"; "the local *management* of conduct in relation to normative conceptions"; race, class, gender as "*mechanisms* for *producing* social inequality" (West and Fenstermaker 1995, 9).

This imagery of daily interaction as a process of production focuses the argument that basic categories of difference and inequality are socially constructed. "Doing gender" is a compelling concept because it jolts the assumption of gender as an innate condition and replaces it with a sense of ongoing process and activity. The process, according to West and Fenstermaker, starts with "normative conceptions," such as "the moral conviction that there are only two sexes" and related assumptions about the "nature" of women and of men. Actors sustain these conceptions through the practice of holding one another accountable as men or women (or Black men or working-class white women). West and Fenstermaker argue that the work of "doing difference"—the repeated act of holding one another accountable to cultural conceptions—is the basic mechanism that connects gender, race, and class.

The upholding of cultural conceptions keeps categories in place, and, turning to the dynamics of racial formation, West and Fenstermaker's framework can help account for the creation and inhabiting of racial categories, but it cannot explain the ways in which racial categories are "transformed and destroyed" (Omi and Winant 1994, 55). Nor does the ethnomethodological approach grapple with historical changes in the organization, meanings, and relationships among gender, race, and class. West and Fenstermaker, like Garfinkel and Goffman, analyze social phenomena with a functionalist tilt, emphasizing the maintenance and reproduction of normative conceptions, but neglecting countervailing processes of resistance, challenge, conflict, and change.

Other contemporary theorists image the construction of gender not as work but as performance and even as parody. Pursuing an insight similar to the one that propels West and Fenstermaker's thinking, the philosopher Judith Butler (1990) writes: "Because there is neither an 'essence' that gender expresses or externalizes nor an objective ideal to which gender aspires, and because gender is not a fact, the various acts of gender create the idea of gender, and without those acts, there would be no gender at all" (p. 140). Butler writes within the tradition of poststructuralism and seems to be unaware of sociological analyses of the construction of gender, which predated her work by more than a decade (Epstein 1994). Like West and Fenstermaker, but with a central emphasis on the heterosexual marking of gender, Butler discusses the routine acts that sustain binary gender categories. Unlike West and Fenstermaker, however, Butler emphasizes possibilities for transgression, looking for ways to "trouble the gender categories that support gender hierarchy and compulsory heterosexuality" (Butler 1990, x).

The dramaturgical approach that feminist sociologists left behind when we discarded the conception of "sex roles" has reappeared in Butler's writings and in the humanities and queer theory more generally. Dramaturgical metaphors seem to fare better in their hands, perhaps because of a shift from reified noun ("role") to verb ("perform") and a cascade of evocative images—masquerade, parody, gender as a fabrication and a persistent impersonation that passes as the real—that provide an engaging counterpoint to the more earnest sociological approach.

But gender extends beyond daily cultural performance, and it will take much more than doing drag and mocking naturalized conceptions to transform it. Gender—and race, class, and compulsory heterosexuality—extend deep into the unconscious and the shaping of emotions (note the cognitive focus of the "doing difference" framework) and outward into social structure and material interests. R. W. Connell (1987), who writes about a "field of gender relations," attends to this scope and insists on a theoretical approach that opens toward history. His reflections on structure and practice and on the organization of gender relations and meanings as a going but contested concern give dynamism to the core argument that gender is a social construction. He and his colleagues (Kessler et al. 1985) lay out a chain of suggestive metaphors when they write that class and gender "abrade, inflame, amplify, twist, negate, dampen, complicate each other" (p. 42). To grasp complex relations among gender, race, class, and sexuality, we need a range of metaphors and theories honed in many sites of analysis. By itself, the construct "doing difference" won't stretch far enough.

References

Butler, Judith. 1990. *Gender trouble: Feminism and the subversion of identity.* New York: Routledge.

Connell, R. W. 1987. *Gender and power*. Stanford, CA: Stanford University Press.

Epstein, Steven. 1994. A queer encounter: Sociology and the study of sexuality. *Sociological Theory* 12:188–202.

Kessler, Sandra, Dean J. Ashenden, R. W. Connell, and Gary W. Dowsett. 1985. Gender relations in secondary schooling. *Sociology of Education* 58:34–48.

Omi, Michael, and Howard Winant. 1994. *Racial formation in the United States: From the 1960s to the 1990s*, 2d ed. New York: Routledge.

West, Candace, and Sarah Fenstermaker. 1995. Doing difference. *Gender & Society* 9:8–37.

Barrie Thorne is Professor of Sociology and Women's Studies at the University of Southern California. She is the author of Gender Play: Girls and Boys in School *and co-editor of* Rethinking the Family: Some Feminist Questions *and* Language, Gender, and Society.

LYNN WEBER
University of Delaware

REPRINT REQUESTS: *Lynn Weber, Department of Sociology University of Delaware New York, DE.*

West and Fenstermaker build an analysis of race, class, and gender from the following foundation: a critique of the metaphors in the emerging scholarship on race, class, and gender; a critique of gender scholarship that ignores race and class; and an ethnomethodological approach, which is not grounded in gender, race, or class analysis. These three building blocks contain the strengths and the weaknesses of their perspective.

Grounded in ethnomethodology, West and Fenstermaker conceptualize race, class, and gender as emergent properties of social situations not reducible to a material or biological essence, and therefore not properties of individuals or some "vaguely defined set of role expectations" (p. 25). They highlight the simultaneity of experience of race, class, and gender by focusing on how they emerge in face-to-face interactions. These are the greatest strengths of their approach: that race, class, and gender are socially constructed simultaneously in interaction and are not reducible to biological or material characteristics of individuals.

Metaphors aside, the fundamental contrast between race, class, and gender scholarship and "doing difference" is that West and Fenstermaker obscure rather than illuminate the mechanisms of power in the production and maintenance of racism, classism, and sexism.

AUTHOR'S NOTE: *I wish to thank Margaret Andersen, Maxine Baca Zinn, Harry Brod, Sarah Jane Brubaker, Elizabeth Higginbotham, and all the members of my graduate seminar on Race, Class, and Gender at the University of Delaware for their helpful insights and critiques of this work.*

For race, class, and gender scholarship, social relations of dominance/control and subordination/resistance are the cornerstones of theory. Because of its exclusive attention on face-to-face interaction, macro social structural processes such as institutional arrangements, community structures, and even family systems are rendered invisible in most observations based on an ethnomethodological analysis. This has several consequences. First, it obscures the freedom from constraints and the access to material resources that frame privileged group members' face-to-face interactions with each other and the control they exert in interactions with oppressed group members. In this way, it subtly reproduces the bias in perspectives that emanate solely from positions of privilege. Second, it conceals the collective involvement, connection, and consciousness of oppressed group members that arise in the struggle for survival within the context of systemic constraints.

A central element of privilege and power is freedom from constraints on material, political, and ideological resources, options, and opportunities. When options are not restricted, face-to-face encounters can take on greater significance in the lives of the participants. For example, in our study of Black and white professional-managerial women, Elizabeth Higginbotham and I asked women to describe any differential treatment or discrimination they experienced at work. Women in female-dominated occupations (teachers, nurses, librarians) talked in detail about structural discrimination against the entire occupation—low wages, lack of respect, and so on. Women in male-dominated occupations (lawyers, professors, business managers) instead talked about face-to-face interactions in the workplace, such as sexist and racist comments, being left out of key work informational networks, and having bosses who did not appreciate their talents. Wages, which were significantly different across these groups, were rarely mentioned by the women in male-dominated occupations. Instead they focused on individual, everyday, face-to-face relationships both to define their problems and to think about solutions (e.g., switch offices, change the way they interacted, and so on). Without attention to macro social structures that enable privilege in ideological and political as well as material/economic domains, we understand less about the processes that are unspoken or not problematic in face-to-face interactions.

From the perspective of subordinate groups, failing to analyze macro social structures and community ties has the effect of producing a static theory of conformity and not a dynamic theory capable of revealing resistance and social change. Race, class, and gender are pervasive social arrangements, and fundamental social structural changes in these arrangements cannot be fully captured in the attitudes and actions of a few unremarkable actors in everyday interactions. When West and Fenstermaker analyze interactions involving dominant and subordinate group members, they can consequently see only the actions of oppressed group actors—whether conforming or resistant—as reinforcing the existing race, class, and gender hierarchy.

Recall the example of the African American man who was stopped by the cop. West and Fenstermaker argue that if he acts passively and accepts the ticket without question, the race, class, and gender hierarchy is reinforced. If he chooses to resist, however, he brings on greater sanctions, and reinforces the ideology about violent Black men that got him stopped in the first place. In that situation, there is no possibility for social change because the forces that could change expectations and behaviors are not always represented in isolated one-on-one interactions. What the Black driver encountered in that situation was more than a set of stereotypes or expectations in another individual's head. He encountered a cop with a gun that he is legitimately authorized to use by his position in a macro political system that preserves the privilege of those in power through the use of force. The approach, as currently conceived, ignores both the material realities in the situation (the gun) and the macro structures that lend force to the police action.

It also hides the connections of African Americans to a community of resistance, because in this situation we can see the driver as having no options only if we assume that he is isolated from others—the tendency when face-to-face interaction is the sole focus of attention. Imagine, instead, that the driver is the '90s version of Rosa Parks, and he is sent down that highway as bait by a consortium of African American civil rights organizations, some of whose representatives are strategically planted with video cams to document unfair police treatment of African American men on the highways. When stopped, the driver might protest and receive harsh treatment, which does not reinforce the status quo, but rather galvanizes the African American community to demand that the officer be fired, the police be monitored for selective enforcement of traffic laws and citizen abuse, the local sheriff be recalled, and so on. This scenario can only happen when we recognize the connection between an individual's collective consciousness, collective action, and macro social structural change.

Besides taking a different stance with respect to power and macro social structures, West and Fenstermaker argue that the mathematical metaphors commonly used in scholarship on race, class, and gender are inadequate and in some ways inaccurate. As West and Fenstermaker note, all of these metaphors imply that race, class, and gender can be isolated from one another in people's lives, a contention that is fairly uniformly rejected by the same authors who employ them (cf. Andersen and Collins 1994; Baca Zinn and Dill 1994; Collins 1990). They also point out that authors sometimes reduce gender, race, or class to a material or biological essence even while asserting that each is socially constructed, as when Collins (1990, 27) suggests that social constructions of gender are based on clearer biological criteria than constructions of race are. By articulating biology as a difference among the dimensions, Collins undercuts the argument that they are socially constructed.

While West and Fenstermaker correctly note the limits of the mathematical metaphors, I think they incorrectly assume that the insights of a race, class, and gender perspective have been seriously restricted by the use of less than perfect metaphors. For example, mathematical metaphors have the most direct relevance to positivist, quantitative research where race, class, and gender are treated as variables in an equation allowed to represent social reality. None of the authors cited here employ that approach and, in fact, are critical of it; furthermore, these authors not only use mathematical metaphors but also many others. Literary images are also quite common: the wall at the end of Brewster Place (Baca Zinn and Dill 1994) or "holding back the ocean with a broom" (Gilkes 1980). The fact that these images do not fully depict the complexities of race, class, and gender in social structural arrangements and lived experience does not inhibit these authors from attempting to do so in the totality of their writing on the subject. In fact, West and Fenstermaker themselves offer no metaphor to illustrate their perspective; instead, they describe the accomplishment of race, class, and gender in social interaction—which is not a metaphor/representation of the thing, but the thing itself—as they see it. They would probably be very hard-pressed to find some other image that would accurately stand for the processes they attempt to describe.

West and Fenstermaker contend that we must analyze gender, race, and class in the *context* in which it is accomplished, and that is precisely what race, class, and gender scholarship does—presents systematic observations of the lives of people of color, women, and the working class. By developing a "doing difference" approach from a critique of race, class, and gender metaphors and ethnomethodology—instead of the systematic observations they call for—they obscure the central dynamics of power relations in the micro and macro structures of oppression.

REFERENCES

Andersen, Margaret, and Patricia Hill Collins. 1994. *Race, class, and gender: An anthology*. 2d ed. Belmont, CA: Wadsworth.

Baca Zinn, Maxine, and Bonnie Thornton Dill. 1994. *Women of color in U.S. society*. Philadelphia: Temple University Press.

Collins, Patricia Hill. 1990. *Black feminist thought: Knowledge, consciousness, and the politics of empowerment*. New York: Routledge.

Gilkes, Cheryl. 1980. "Holding back the ocean with a broom": Black women and community work. In *The Black woman*, ed. La Francis Rodgers-Rose, pp. 217–31. Beverly Hills, CA: Sage.

West, Candace, and Sarah Fenstermaker. 1995. Doing difference. *Gender & Society* 9:8–37.

Lynn Weber is on leave as Director of the Center for Research on Women at the University of Memphis, spending the 1994–96 academic years as Distinguished Visiting Gender Studies Professor in the Department of Sociology at the University of Delaware. Her work focuses on race, class, and gender in the social mobility process and in college and university curriculum transformation. She is co-author of The American Perception of Class *(Temple University Press, 1987) and "Moving Up with Kin and Community: Upward Social Mobility for Black and White Women." published in* Gender & Society.

HOWARD WINANT
Temple University

REPRINT REQUESTS: *Howard Winant, Department of Sociology. Temple University. Philadelphia, PA 19122.*

Candace West and Sarah Fenstermaker (1995) do some marvelous work in their article "Doing Difference." They give us a thoughtful account of the dynamics of gender-, race-, and class-based forms of "difference," which is to say of the dynamics of social inequality and injustice. They also employ ethnomethodology in a creative fashion, producing a wide range of political insights and helping us to reconceptualize some very thorny problems in contemporary U.S. politics.

Their principal achievement is their extension of the ethnomethodological account of difference, almost up to the frontier of a hegemony-oriented analysis. Their account of gender, race, and class as accomplishments, projects from which human agency is never absent, helps explain better than any other approach I know the contradictory character of these dimensions of identity.

By "contradictory character" I mean what Du Bois described nearly a century ago as the "veil" that divided and complicated blackness, the "peculiar sensation" of being "both an American and a Negro." Although he spoke of a racial distinction, his analysis resonates with oppressions of various kinds. "One ever feels his [*sic*] twoness," Du Bois wrote (Du Bois [1903] 1989, 5). Awareness of the distinctive character of Black identity in a white society did not permit any transcendence of the veil, but it did facilitate a survival strategy: one had to divide oneself, to see oneself from both within and without, in order to anticipate and thus withstand the degradation that white supremacy constantly heaped upon its "others."

The contradiction is that to render this survival strategy effective, one has to emulate the oppressor, to think like him, to become him, at least up to a certain point. The Du Boisian analysis explains the "internalized oppression" much denounced by nationalists; more to the point here, it also explains the reproduction of racism as a price of surviving, and of resisting, racism. There are many implications one could draw from such an analysis: Freudian, Marxian, and Foucaultian approaches could all develop further the rich account Du Bois offers. So too can ethnomethodology, in the capable hands of West and Fenstermaker.

What I think is most useful about their work is its ability to stretch the ethnomethodological approach politically. Since Garfinkel, ethnomethodology has understood social relationships in terms of an "experiential technology," a set of tools available to actors to make sense of their interpersonal relations, their "lifeworld" in the Schutzian phrase. I do not think I am exaggerating when I suggest that West and Fenstermaker burst these bounds.

Take this statement:

> While individuals are the ones who do gender, the process of rendering something accountable is both interactional and institutional in character: It is a feature of social relationships, and its idiom derives from the institutional arena in which those relationships come to life. (p. 21)

Or this, immediately following:

> Gender is obviously much more than a role or an individual characteristic: it is a mechanism whereby situated social action contributes to the reproduction of social structure. (p. 21)

This is what I mean by reaching the frontiers of a hegemony-based analysis. As I understand them, West and Fenstermaker argue that there is something generalizable about the production of difference in regular, situated, human interaction. The linguistic regularities (what they call "idiom") through which difference is recognized and the patterned repetition (what they call "mechanism") through which individual characteristics become collectivized produce the divided and unequal social whole. This is a real extension of the traditional ethnomethodological perspective, whose focus was restricted to the generation and confirmation of shared perceptions of interaction. Only if this expanded view of the production of social structure is in place, I suggest, can we begin to talk of the politics of difference.

Yet, is it fully in place? I have spoken of the "frontiers" of a hegemony-based analysis because I think some significant problems persist in West and Fenstermaker's approach. Their account of the institutional dimensions of difference, of the social structures we label gender, race, and class, remains limited. For them, structure is only that which can be shown to be constantly reproduced from moment to moment. It has no ongoing, relatively independent existence.

An important dimension of hegemony is therefore neglected in the ethnomethodological view of difference as situated conduct. In my view, social structure must be understood as dynamic and reciprocal; it is not only a *product* of accreted and repeated subjective action but also *produces* subjects. As an example, consider the commodity form of value. Without necessarily embracing the entire Marxist schema, we can readily see that capitalist classes and their members (as well as most of the other relationships and, consequently, the social roles we take for granted in the postmodern world) would be inconceivable without this structure; yet, it would be difficult to argue that the commodity form exists solely in the ways in which it is presently reproduced. On the contrary, it has a formidable inertia, a historical weight, which is crystallized in innumerable institutions, customs, and laws. It has been engraved in time and space, made into a truly "deep structure"—a past action (Sewell 1992, 25–6). It can produce subjects only because it has acquired its weight, its ubiquity, over epochal stretches of time.

To understand difference in terms of hegemony, then, we must conceive it both as situated conduct that repeats and thus supports systems of power and as a consequence of a pre-existing "structure in dominance" (Hall 1980). Indeed, hegemony is the synthesis of these two "moments" of power: Reproduced by the limited and situated agency of its subjects, it also concedes to them a limited, but real, autonomy. This is a situation that Gramsci described as one of "equilibria in which the interests of the dominant group prevail, but only up to a certain point. . . ." (Gramsci 1971, 182).

This leads me to my final point concerning social change. To theorize difference as I have done so far—as situated conduct plus institutionally conceded autonomy—remains inadequate because neither of these accounts can explain the disruptive, oppositional character of difference. It is striking how both the ethnomethodological and hegemony-based approaches to gender, race, and class argue that these social distinctions are relatively static features of domination and inequality. Whether routinized through "experiential technology" or conceded in limited fashion by the powerful, the agency that "does" difference is conceived as limited and collusive in its own subordination.

Looking at racial difference, for instance: If race consists of "situated conduct" through which actual human subjects necessarily reproduce their subordination, how can large-scale sociopolitical change *ever* occur on racial lines? How was Dr. King able, to pick just one example from a virtually infinite list, to mobilize 6,000 black children(!) to march against the dogs, fire hoses, and truncheons of the Birmingham police one day in 1963? Weren't those children, and their parents, as "situated" as everyone else?

On the other hand, if "structures in dominance" are able to maintain hegemony by judicious concessions of autonomy to the subordinate, how is it that concepts of emancipation, liberation, and freedom have proved so hard to eradicate? The various dimensions of difference—gender-, racial-, and class-based, as well as others—retain an oppositional character that always exceeds the grasp of gestures made to contain it. Even the elimination of inequality (utopian as that might sound at this reactionary political juncture) would not justify the liquidation of difference. The project of self-emancipation, what Du Bois called "the conservation of races," would still await realization. (Once more, I am speaking in the context of racial difference, but I think the insight has wider application.) This work is already visible, prefigured in those aspects of "situated conduct" that do not preserve, but rather subvert, the established "experiential technology" of acquiescence to subordination (Kelley 1994), as well as in counterinstitutions and countercultures of various sorts.

In this respect, difference is not something that one (or many) "do," but rather something that one "is" and many "are." The permanence of difference, situated and structured, but above all oppositional, still points toward freedom.

References

Du Bois, W.E.B. [1903] 1989. *The souls of Black folk.* New York: Penguin.

Gramsci, Antonio. 1971. *Selections from the prison notebooks,* edited by Quintin Hoare and Geoffrey Nowell-Smith. New York: International Publishers.

Hall, Stuart. 1980. Race, articulation, and societies structured in dominance. In *Sociological theories: Race and colonialism.* Paris: UNESCO.

Kelley, Robin D. G. 1994. *Race rebels: Culture, politics, and the Black working class.* New York: Free Press.

Sewell, William H., Jr. 1992. A theory of structure: Duality, agency, and transformation. *American Journal of Sociology* 98 (July):1–29.

West, Candace, and Sarah Fenstermaker. 1995. Doing difference. *Gender & Society* 9:8–37.

Howard Winant teaches sociology and Latin American Studies at Temple University in Philadelphia. He is the co-author (with Michael Omi) of Racial Formation in the United States: From the 1960s to the 1990s *(2d ed. Routledge, 1994); he has also written* Racial Conditions: Politics, Theory, Comparisons *(University of Minnesota Press, 1994) and* Stalemate: Political Economic Origins of Supply-Side Policy *(Praeger, 1988).*

REPLY
(Re)Doing Difference

CANDACE WEST
University of California, Santa Cruz

SARAH FENSTERMAKER
University of California, Santa Barbara

REPRINT REQUESTS: *Candace West, Sociology Board, Stevenson College, University of California, Santa Cruz, CA 95064.*

We are honored to have "Doing Difference" as the subject of this symposium. It is extremely gratifying to have our article read so seriously by Professors Collins, Maldonado, Takagi, Thorne, Weber, and Winant, and to have this opportunity to respond to their remarks. Together, they raise three important concerns to which our reply will be focused. In the space allotted to us, we try to re-articulate the fundamental distinction between process and outcome so crucial to understanding our perspective and then reassess the implications of this distinction for the questions of (a) face-to-face interaction versus structural discrimination; (b) history, institutions, and social structure; and (c) opposition, resistance, and change.

PROCESS VERSUS OUTCOME

Our overarching concern in "Doing Difference" is social inequality, in all its invidious manifestations. We take it as our starting point that the effects of patriarchy, racism, and class oppression have been amply and eloquently demonstrated by the scholars in whose footsteps we follow—and that no one would dispute these. We therefore begin with the assumption that these are well documented (by those who have commented on our article, among others). Our purpose is not to further document the effects of these *outcomes* but, rather, to understand the processes that produce them. In pursuit of this goal, we do not conceptualize difference per se as that which must be overcome: we agree that difference qua difference is not the problem. We believe, however, that a meaningful description of a system in which the bases of inequality *interact* with one another requires attention not only to the troublesome outcomes of the system (e.g., poverty, physical violence, punitive social policies, and so on) but also to the workings of the social relationships that produced those outcomes.

The criticisms raised by our commentators highlight the greatest challenge we faced in writing the article; namely, how to articulate the crucial distinction we advance between the processes and outcomes of social inequality. We tried to clarify this (see West and Fenstermaker 1995) first on page 9: "while gender, race, and class . . . exhibit vastly different descriptive characteristics and outcomes, they are, nonetheless, comparable as mechanisms for producing social inequality." We tried again on page 19: "The goal of this article is not to analyze situated conduct per se but to understand the workings of inequality." And we tried again on page 25: "Despite many important differences in the histories, traditions, and varying impacts of racial and sexual [and class] oppression across particular situations, the

AUTHORS' NOTES: *For their critical comments and suggestions on these ideas, we thank Beltina Aptheker, Valerie Jenness, and Don H. Zimmerman.*

mechanism underlying them is the same." Despite such efforts, the comments of our critics suggest that we have failed to spell out this important distinction adequately and that the implications of our formulation are likely to be misunderstood.

We conceive of gender, race, and class as ongoing interactional accomplishments (i.e., processes) that make patriarchy, racism, and class oppression possible. The accountability of persons to sex category, race category, and class category is, from our perspective, the heart of the matter. By "accountability" we do not mean the act of persons holding one another individually accountable, but the ubiquitous *possibility* of persons being held accountable—of having their actions, their circumstances, and even their descriptions characterized in serious and consequential ways (Heritage 1984, 136–7). Lest we be seen as merely substituting passive for active voice in making this distinction, we reiterate that (a) the notion of accountability pertains to activities that conform to prevailing cultural conceptions as well as to those activities that deviate; (b) the process of rendering some action accountable is an interactional—used in the broadest sense of the term—rather than an individual accomplishment; and, (c) accountability is both interactional and institutional in character (although it is a feature of social relationships, its idiom comes from the institutional arena in which those relationships are brought to life); thus, the agencies involved are institutions as well as individuals engaged in interaction with others.

Face-to-face interaction versus social structural analysis

Given the above distinction between the processes of accomplishing gender, race, and class and the outcomes of those processes (i.e., patriarchy, racism, and class oppression), the question of face-to-face interaction "versus" structural discrimination becomes somewhat mooted. We do not intend to use a postmodern concept of difference as a way to erase or minimize the concrete institutionalization of oppression that exists. This is so because we do not conceive of interaction as standing apart from the production of gender, race, and class divisions but, rather, as integral to the production of those divisions in the first instance (as both "the shadow *and* the substance," in Goffman's terms [1976, 6; italics in original]).

At any given moment, of course, theoretical attention may focus at different levels of concern. As with different lenses of a camera, foreground and background may shift in clarity and salience. So too with a set of theoretical lenses: The role of interaction may momentarily shift the focus from more macro, social structural forms; nevertheless, both are always at work and serve as manifestations of each other. This is why we take issue with Weber (1995), who argues that our perspective is limited by a focus on "a few unremarkable actors in everyday interactions" (p. 501).

To be sure, our analytical perspective on gender, race, and class *is* different from any individual's experience of these dynamics (including our own). As we noted earlier (West and Fenstermaker 1995, 33, n. 4), "a woman who is Latina and a shopkeeper may experience the simultaneous effects of gender, race, and class, yet identify her experience as only 'about' race, only 'about' gender, or only 'about class." When asked to describe any differential treatment or discrimination she experiences at work, this woman might cite the lack of respect accorded to those in her occupation or the racist and/or sexist comments she encounters in her shop, depending on how she sees her experience. Regardless of how she views it, the fact that she can be categorized as a woman, a Latina, *and* a shopkeeper provides the possibility that she may be held accountable for her actions—in ordinary interaction and by the institutional workings of society—as a member of any (or all) of these categories (see Winant's [1995, this issue] discussion of Du Bois). It is this possibility that provides our sense of patriarchy, racism, and class oppression as enduring and pervasive social arrangements.

Here we should note that since accountability is a feature of social relationships (not individuals), participants in any interaction are equally vulnerable to others characterizing their activities in ways that take notice of those activities and place them in a social framework (Heritage 1984, 136–7). For example, the police who stop Black men on the street or pull them over may also be held accountable for *their* actions as members of their sex category, race category, and class category. Indeed, public opinion about the police officers who apprehended and assaulted Rodney King in Los Angeles was shaped largely by public categorization of the officers as white men from suburban, working-class communities outside the city. The explosive reaction to the "not guilty" verdicts in the first trial of these officers leaves little doubt that their actions were seen to support the oppressive practices of the criminal justice system and the existing social order. In short, insofar as sex category, race category, and class category are omnirelevant to social life, no one is immune from being held accountable for their actions as an incumbent of particular categories.

History, Institutions, and Social Structure

With process and outcome distinguished from one another, it should be clear that the accomplishments of gender, race, and class rest on and are situated in history, institutional practices, and social structure, rather than disembodied from people's lives. Of course, the organization and meanings of gender, race, and class change over time, as do relationships among them. By viewing these as accomplishments, however, we can see how situated social action contributes to the reproduction of social structure at any particular sociohistorical moment. The challenge we face—theoretically and empirically—is to describe a system that manifests great interactional variation *but, at the same time,* rests on far more stable structural and historical legacies. Our focus on ever-changing, variously situated social relationships as the sites for the doing of difference does not denude those relationships of the powerful contexts in which they unfold. We argue only that the impact of the forces of social structure and history is realized *in the unfolding of those relationships.*

Take, for example, the remarkable change in the participation of women in public life over the past 50 years. Since 1900, the profile of the U.S. women's workforce has been utterly transformed, from one consisting of primarily young, unmarried, native-born white women or poor women of color, to one virtually indistinguishable from the population of women in general. In the first half of this century, only poor women sought employment after marrying; in the 1950s, mothers with older children joined them; and today most women are employed from the time they first enter the job market until they retire. Despite these radical transformations of the labor force, we consistently find that although work imperatives (e.g., the presence of children and the nature of women's employment outside the home) determine the amount of time that wives spend on household labor, these factors do not have a significant impact on husbands' contributions; moreover, whereas women do the vast majority of the work in U.S. households, most household members (including women) see this as a "fair" arrangement.

Elsewhere (Fenstermaker Berk 1985, 203–4; Fenstermaker, West, and Zimmerman 1991, 297–302; West and Fenstermaker 1993, 162–3) we have argued that the "missing link" in an understanding of these facts is the accomplishment of gender. We suggest that it is difficult to see how people could rationally arrange things as they have for the sole purpose of rationally or efficiently producing household goods and services. The evidence shows that the resolution of who does what in the household is not simply a question of who has more time, whose time is worth more, or is more skilled at the task at hand. Instead, it is resolved by a complex relationship between the structure of work imperatives and the structure of normative conceptions of that work as *gendered,* that is, "only natural" for a woman and not natural for a man. We do not simply contend that household labor is regarded as women's work but, rather, that for a woman to do it and a man not to do it draws on and affirms what people see as the "essential nature" of each. We conclude that it is at the level of the actual practice of gender inequality that economy and family combine to produce both change and continued inequities.

Opposition, resistance, and change

Where is the possibility of people working at various levels of self-consciousness to resist oppression and promote change? Must we, as Thorne (1995) asserts, "[emphasize] the maintenance and reproduction of normative conceptions, but [neglect] countervailing processes of resistance, challenge, conflict, and change" (p. 498)? After all, we have argued that to the extent that sex category, race category, and class category are fundamental criteria for differentiation, the accomplishments of gender, race, and class are unavoidable. This is so because of the social consequences of sex category, race category, and class category membership—the allocation of power in domestic, economic, and political arenas as well as the broad domain of social and institutional relationships; yet, even though gender, race, and class are ubiquitous, they are not identically salient in every set of social relationships in which inequality is done. Here, we believe, is where our formulation differs from the "monolithic" view Maldonado (1995) describes. Contrary to his description, our focus on the process of doing difference (to complement a focus on its outcomes) promotes a clearer perspective on the many moments of resistance that daily play themselves out in social relations. We argue that since difference is "done," there is both activity (including resistance) and agency at its foundation. Indeed, it is likely that resistance is as ubiquitous a feature of the shaping of inequality as is the doing of difference itself. We would agree with Winant (1995) that "the permanence of difference, situated and structured, but above all oppositional, still points toward freedom" (p. 505).

What about lasting social change? For one, we contend that social action that confounds the possibility of differentiating persons according to sex category, race category, and/or class category membership undermines the legitimacy of existing institutional arrangements. Consider, for example, the growing public and scientific interest in the problems associated with race categorization today. As we write this, the *San Jose Mercury News* (among many other newspapers) has published a front page story, announcing that genes do not define race (Alvarado 1995, A1ff) and *Newsweek* has published a cover story on the changing meaning of *Black* as a category (Morganthau 1995, 63ff). Among the highlights of these stories are the public announcements of the facts that, from a genetic standpoint, "race" does not exist (Alvarado 1995, A1) and existing racial classifications do not capture changing demographic realities (Morganthau 1995, 65). Even the U.S. federal government has joined the debate, with the Office of Management and Budget sponsoring a series of public hearings on the topic of revising its statistical categories of race and ethnicity (Lewis 1994, Al). To be sure, none of these sources is proposing that race category be abolished. The consequences, they suggest, would be too dire (e.g., eliminating formulas used to distribute federal aid and to support the Voting Rights Act through districting regulations in congressional elections); however, by raising the untenability of existing "racial categories" as a matter of public debate, they are calling public attention to the question of why we seem so determined to divide humans into mutually exclusive groups to begin with (Begley 1995, 69). Such questioning can not only weaken the accountability of conduct to existing racial categories, but it can also offer the possibility of more widespread loosening of accountability in general (West and Zimmerman 1987, 146).

A second prospect for opposition, resistance, and change lies, of course, in social movements. When individuals are involved in "doing difference" appropriately, they simultaneously sustain, reproduce, and render legitimate the institutional arrangements that are predicated on sex category, race category, and class category (among others). If they fail to "do difference" appropriately, they as individuals—not the institutional arrangements—may be held to account (for their motives, character, and predispositions); however, social movements (e.g., those that oppose patriarchy, racism, and class oppression) can furnish the ideology and impetus to question existing arrangements, and the social support for individual exploration of alternatives to them (West and Zimmerman 1987, 146). Valerie Jenness observes, "many social movements, and certainly . . . 'new social movements' have relied upon the accomplishment of race, class, and gender [and sexuality, for that matter] in exactly the same terms that [our] perspective implies" (personal communication March 4, 1995; see also Taylor and Whittier's [1992] discussion of "collective identities" as a critical resource for mobilizing contemporary social movements). As a result, social movements may call institutions themselves to account for *their* motives, character, and predispositions.

Conclusion

"Doing Difference" is a relatively modest attempt to map the dynamics of gender, race, and class as they unfold in social relations. We intended it to provide, as Takagi (1995) puts it, "an argument for balance between what is currently seen as interactional consequences [on the one hand] and interactional productions [on the other]" (p. 496). We engaged with the general and ongoing project of many scholars to meaningfully link the workings of a system of oppression in order to understand the nature of social domination and possibilities for change. We rejected the notion of a hierarchy of oppressions, and we sought to understand simultaneity as more than a periodic collision of socially determined categories with unpredictable outcomes. Toward this end, we asked how inequalities are produced *together*.

There is a good deal to criticize in this first theoretical statement and much more work is needed to improve on it. We outlined a number of suggestions for further work in the article itself; here, we offer a few more. First, we have not fully articulated how the accomplishment of gender, race, and class actually link the realms of institutional and face-to-face interaction. Second, the dynamics of class inequality, although perhaps not qualitatively different from one another, are different enough in their interaction with other categories to warrant much more investigation. As Bettina Aptheker has noted in response to our article, "'Class' is the most problematic—not because it is not true, but because it is either (apparently) overshadowed by race (most often) or more complicated since it is not necessarily (inherently) immediately identifiable" (personal communication, November 8, 1994). We believe that the question of "inherence" deserves much closer attention, with respect to class as well as other categorical identities, as they operate in confluence with one another. Third, and most important, the ideas we advance in this article must be translated into empirical research. With empirical attention to the mechanisms that produce social inequality, no single theoretical statement will be asked to bear all the weight (and the freight) of the complexity of these social relationships and the politics of studying them; moreover, only in empirical work will Thorne's (1995) call for "a range of metaphors and theories honed in many sites of analysis" (p. 499) make sense.

We agree wholeheartedly with Collins (1995) that there is a great deal at stake: Efforts such as this one have grave consequences for how scholars undertake a collaborative dialogue and for how those who also work directly to end oppression conceive of and realize coalition. Of all the criticisms and praise leveled at our article thus far (prior to publication as well as afterward), however, we would most take issue with the idea that a focus on the socially constructed character of oppression reduces it to "performance" or text, minus the weight of history, torment, struggle, and resistance. A focus on the situated, dynamic, and quintessentially social character of inequality does not deny, dilute, nor erase the very real consequences of domination. To the contrary, it can further clarify how much really *is* at stake.

References

Alvarado, Donna. 1995. Scientist: Race not defined by genes. *San Jose Mercury News,* 20 February, A1ff.

Begley, Sharon. 1995. Three is not enough: Surprising new lessons from the controversial science of race. *Newsweek,* 13 February, 67–9.

Collins, Patricia Hill. 1995. Symposium: On West and Fenstermaker's "Doing Difference," *Gender & Society,* pp. 491–494.

Fenstermaker Berk, Sarah. 1985. *The gender factory: The apportionment of work in American households.* New York: Plenum.

Fenstermaker, Sarah, Candace West, and Don H. Zimmerman. 1991. Gender inequality: New conceptual terrain. In *Gender, family, and economy: The triple overlap,* edited by Rac Lesser Blumberg. Newbury Park, CA: Sage.

Goffman, Erving. 1976. Gender display. *Studies in the Anthropology of Visual Communication* 3:69–77.

Heritage, John. 1984. *Garfinkel and ethnomethodology.* Cambridge, England: Polity Press.

Lewis, Marilyn. 1994. Melting pot ingredients: Oil and water? *San Jose Mercury News,* 14 July, A1ff.

Maldonado, Lionel A. 1995. Symposium: On West and Fenstermaker's "Doing Difference." *Gender & Society,* pp. 494–496.

Morganthau, Tom (with Susan Miller, Gregory Beals, and Regina Elam in New York). 1995. What color is Black? *Newsweek,* 13 February, 63–5.

Takagi, Dana. 1995. Symposium: On West and Fenstermaker's "Doing Difference." *Gender & Society,* pp. 496–497.

Taylor, Verta, and Nancy Whittier. 1992. Collective identities and social movement communities: Lesbian feminist motivation. In *Frontiers in social movement theory,* edited by Aldon D. Morris and Carol McClung Mueller. New Haven, Yale University Press.

Thorne, Barrie. 1995. Symposium: On West and Fenstermaker's "Doing Difference." *Gender & Society,* pp. 497–499.

Weber, Lynn. 1995. Symposium: On West and Fenstermaker's "Doing Difference." *Gender & Society,* pp. 499–503.

West, Candace, and Sarah Fenstermaker. 1993. Power, inequality and the accomplishment of gender: An ethnomethodological view. In *Theory on gender/feminism on theory,* edited by Paula England. New York: Aldine.

———. 1995. Doing difference. *Gender & Society* 9(1):8–37.

West, Candace, and Don H. Zimmerman. 1987. Doing gender. *Gender & Society* 1:125–51.

Winant, Howard. 1995. Symposium: On West and Fenstermaker's "Doing Difference." *Gender & Society,* pp. 503–506.

Candace West is Professor of Sociology at the University of California, Santa Cruz. Her recent articles focus on different aspects of the problem addressed in "Doing Difference": the interactional scaffolding of social structure.

Sarah Fenstermaker is Professor of Sociology and Women's Studies and Associate Dean of the Graduate Division at the University of California, Santa Barbara. Her works have explored the accomplishments of race, class, and gender, and the gendered determinants of the household division of labor. Her current work further articulates the relationship between work and inequality.

PART II

The Methodology of Intersectional Analysis: Qualitative Approaches

INTRODUCTION

One of the goals of intersectional analysis is to gain a more accurate understanding of the processes through which inequality is created and experienced. Collins (1995, 492) notes:

> The very notion of the *intersections* of race, class, gender as an area worthy of study emerged from the recognition of practitioners of each distinctive theoretical tradition that inequality could not be explained, let alone challenged, via a race-only, class-only, or gender-only framework. (italics added)

Realization of this goal, however, depends on the translation of the theory into empirical research. Since we do not know a priori the outcome of the race, gender, and class dynamics in a given situation we must engage in empirical research—both qualitative and quantitative—in a wide variety of areas and situations to determine actual outcomes. To accomplish this we need guidelines for conducting intersectional research; that is, there needs to be a methodology for conducting intersectional research as well as appropriate statistical techniques.[1] What, then, are the methodological guidelines and which statistical techniques are most appropriate for conducting intersectional research?

Currently there are almost no methodological (as opposed to theoretical) guidelines for those attempting to conduct intersectional research (Brod 1999). We might, therefore, begin with the theoretical assumptions and attempt to translate these assumptions into methodological canons or rules. I am assuming that the researcher attempting to conduct intersectional analysis is familiar with the basic methodological strategies for sound research as found in numerous texts on methodology, both qualitative and quantitative. My objective here, therefore, is not to present a general discussion of social science methodology but, rather, to outline the necessary steps for conducting research from the perspective of intersectional theory.

---

[1]A *methodology* can be thought of as a plan to be followed by the researcher, whereas *statistics* refers to the tools for analysis.

SIMULTANEITY

Because *simultaneity* is one of the two major assumptions of the intersectional approach, this may be a good place to start our discussion of intersectional methodology. How can this assumption be translated into methodological guidelines? In the strictest sense simultaneity appears to require that the researcher include all three identities or characteristics—race, gender, and class—in the design, in what we might refer to as the *ideal intersectional model* or the *saturated model*[2] (see Table 1; p. 108). Collins (1993, 560) especially insists on "the theoretical importance of *assuming* that race, class and gender as categories of analysis structure *all relationships* (italics added)." Methodologically this would require that the researcher's sample include blacks and whites (race),[3] males and females (gender), and working-class and middle-class individuals (class);[4] but ideals are often not attainable in the real world of research. This is the case here. There are a number of reasons why this ideal intersectional model may reasonably be modified by the researcher.

Several intersectional theorists suggest that in a given situation all three categories may not be equally important. Collins (1993, 560–61), for instance remarks that "one category may have salience over another for a given time and place." We may expand this to say that one or two categories may be more salient—or more relevant, or even that one category may not exist in a given situation. For instance, if someone is conducting research on pregnant women, then men will be omitted from the design, as well as perhaps nonpregnant women. However, the researcher may include subgroups of race (e.g., blacks, Asians, and/or whites), as well as the subgroups of class (e.g., working class and middle class). Because only one subgroup of gender is of concern, gender is *not* part of the design; that is, gender does not vary and is not entered as one of the independent variables.[5] The researcher may be interested only in, say, which factors influence full-term pregnancies compared with premature births. In such a study the researcher may obtain a random sample of women who were pregnant during the previous year. The *dependent variable* is whether these women experienced a premature birth rather than a full-term birth. Including race and class in the design will make it possible to discover whether the incidence of premature births may be influenced by the circumstances of race and class simultaneously, controlling for other relevant variables. Is this occurrence more prevalent among black or white women (or Latina or Asian), within the working or middle class? Intersectional analysis, however, goes beyond these two dichotomous questions (black *or* white) to focus on women's experience at the *intersection* of race and class. The relevant question then becomes not whether premature births occur more frequently among black women or white women, middle-class women or working-class women but whether they are more prevalent among black working-class women or among white working-class women; among black middle-class women or among

---

[2]By a *saturated model* I mean one in which all social locations are represented in the data; however, the number of social locations depends on the coding of the three variables. When each characteristic—race, gender, and class—is dichotomized 8 intersections result. If, however, there are more than 2 categories for race or class, there will be more than 8 social locations. For example, a $3 \times 2 \times 2$ model yields 12 locations.

[3]Or the researcher might focus on some other group or several groups, such as Latinos or Asians.

[4]Again, one could study any combination of classes.

[5]Still, one often finds that researchers in such instances will write of "race, gender, and class" even though there is variation across only two of the three characteristics. It would be more proper in such cases to focus only on the included groups.

white middle-class women. In this instance, including four locations (e.g., black middle-class women, white middle-class women, black working-class women, and white working-class women)—rather than eight—satisfies the assumption of simultaneity.

This is a very simple research design to illustrate the point that there are instances when the researcher may legitimately omit a *category* of race, gender, or class. In the preceding case, the researcher has no direct interest in the category males, since they do not bear children. From the point of view of social locations, the illustrated research design omits all the social locations in which men are included: black working-class males, white working-class males, black middle-class males, and white middle-class males. The four remaining social locations of concern are African American working-class females, white working-class females, African American middle-class females, and white middle-class females.[6]

The question then becomes whether the incidence of premature births varies across these four groups of women. By including all four locations the researcher gains greater insight into the issue of premature births than if either all women who were pregnant in the previous year or only one group/location such as middle-class white women were included in the analysis. If, for instance, only white middle-class women were included and found to have a certain percentage of premature births, how would the researcher interpret this finding? Is the value low or high? Compared with what? By including the other three groups the researcher can, as a first step, compare the incidence of premature births across the four social locations and gain greater insights into its variation.

The next step may be to begin making educated guesses about the factors influencing variation in the occurrence of premature births across social locations. Do greater economic resources available to middle-class women lead to better prenatal care and therefore fewer premature births? Given similar economic resources, does the incidence vary by race? Do black middle-class and white middle-class women have similar incidences of premature births but lower incidences than both white and black working-class women? The answer to these questions will lead the researcher to draw the conclusion either that race is not a factor once class is taken into consideration or that race plays a role along with class position. That is, the incidence of premature births is conditional on both race and class position, because it varies across the four social locations. Without the inclusion of race and class in the research design, the researcher's ability to gain a better understanding of premature births will be severely limited.

One can think of any number of research questions that may arise in which only two of the three identities are relevant: a study of the decline in working-class unionization (only gender and race vary), the degree of wealth concentration in the upper class (only gender and race can vary), the incidence of breast or prostate cancer (only class and race can vary).

Can the model be further reduced to include only one identity/social location? Suppose the researcher is interested in the upward mobility of only Asian American males. Could such a study be conducted from an intersectional perspective? The answer would appear to be negative. The very essence of intersectional analysis if founded on the premise that experiences and effects vary across race, gender, and class categories. Unless an experience or effect is intrinsically applicable to only one social location, the other relevant locations should be included within the design. In the question of the mobility of Asian American males, relevant comparisons might be Asian American

[6]Of course, the researcher could substitute Asian or Latina women for black or white. Alternatively, Asian and Latina women could also be included. Their inclusion would, of course, create additional social locations.

females, males and females from some other immigrant group such as Latinos, or even white or black males. This discussion leads us to two rules that should be applied in translating the assumption of simultaneity to intersectional research.

Rule 1: Whenever possible and appropriate, all categories of race, gender, and class should be part of the research design; that is, representatives of all eight race/gender/class locations should be included in the researcher's sample:

Black working-class females (B,Wc,F)
White working-class females (W,Wc,F)
Black middle-class females (B,Mc,F)
White middle-class females (W,Mc,F)
Black working-class males (B,Wc,M)
White working-class males (W,Wc,M)
Black middle-class males (B,Mc,M)
White middle-class males (W,Mc,M)

Rule 2: If one of the identities—race, gender, or class—*does not vary,* the research design should include only the other two identities, that is, four social locations instead of all eight.

In such designs the four locations associated with the omitted category (race, gender, or class) will be absent (Table 1, columns A–F). For instance, if race does not vary (columns A and B), the design will include the following locations:

Column A

1. Black working-class females
2. Black middle-class females
3. Black working-class males
4. Black middle-class males

or

Column B

1. White working-class females
2. White middle-class females
3. White working-class males
4. White middle-class males

TABLE I ■ SCHEMA OF SOCIAL LOCATIONS FOR SATURATED AND REDUCED MODELS

	A	B	C	D	E	F
Social locations	Race = B	Race = W	Gender = F	Gender = M	Class = MC	Class = WC
Black middle-class females	B		F		MC	
White middle-class females		W	F		MC	
Black working-class females	B		F			WC
White working-class females		W	F			WC
Black middle-class males	B			M	MC	
White middle-class males		W		M	MC	
Black working-class males	B			M		WC
White working-class males		W		M		WC

Legend: B = black, W = white, F = female, M = male, WC = working class, MC = middle class.

If either gender (columns C and D) or class (columns E and F) does not vary, the design will include the relevant four locations in the appropriate column. These rules apply whether the research is qualitative or quantitative.

Having said this, we cannot ignore real-world constraints, which are generally of two kinds. First, if original data are being collected, the researcher's time and cost of data collection must be taken into consideration. Because both factors are typically limited, either one or both may make it impossible for the researcher to collect data on all eight locations, or if Rule 2 is applicable, even four locations. Second, if, as often happens, the researcher is utilizing existing data and engaging in secondary analysis,[7] the sample may not include individuals in certain locations (e.g., working-class Latina females) or may have insufficient numbers to allow meaningful analysis. In both cases the researcher attempting to conduct intersectional research is limited by a less-than-ideal design. While this often cannot be helped, it should be recognized that from the point of view of intersectional analysis, the research is then flawed. The research may yet have great value but falls short of yielding as much insight as would be possible with a design including all eight (Rule 1) or all four (Rule 2) social locations.

Multiplicative Relationships

The second major assumption suggests that the researcher should go beyond merely including the categories of race, gender, and class in the research design, because these identities are not merely present but are *relatedly* active, or *interactive*. Having noted that "'multiple' refers not only to several simultaneous oppressions but to the multiplicative relationships among them as well," King (1988, 47–48) adds that "the *importance* of any one factor" varies depending on "the particular aspect" of life under consideration or on the "reference groups" being compared (italics added). This suggests that it is not the effects of oppression due to race and class *separately* that are in question but the effects that are generated by the *combination* of the two. As noted in Part 1, Brewer (1993, 16) argues that this combination is not additive but multiplicative: not "race + class + gender" but "race × class × gender." For Zinn and Dill (1996, 326–27): "People experience race, class, gender, and sexuality *differently* depending upon their social location in the structures of race, gender, and sexuality." These statements of intersectional theorists suggest the idea of *variation* of some characteristic, experience, behavior, or effect across social locations, that is, intersections of race, gender, and class.

From a methodological point of view, how can one build the idea of multiplicative relationships, of varying experiences, characteristics, or effects across social locations, into a research design so that these variations can be detected? What further rule is needed? Above I noted that the idea of multiplicative relationships suggests the statistical notion of *interaction*. In the strictest sense, a statistical interaction exists when the effect of an independent variable (x) on a dependent variable (Y) varies across categories of another independent variable (z). For example, it is well established that smoking can lead to lung cancer. But are female smokers as likely to contract lung cancer as male smokers? If both females and males experience the same incidence of lung cancer from smoking equivalent numbers of cigarettes, the relationship between smoking and lung cancer is statistically called a *linear* relationship, relative to men and women smokers. As smoking persists over time, the likelihood of contracting lung cancer also increases, *and* it increases at the *same rate* for females and males. But what if (for some reason) women smokers

[7] *Secondary analysis* is the term used for research utilizing data collected by someone else.

are *more likely* to contract lung cancer for similar amounts of smoking, if women smokers contract lung cancer sooner than men smokers? Such a relationship between smoking and lung cancer for males and females is called a statistical *interaction* (Aiken and West 1991); or we can say that the relationship is multiplicative rather than linear because it varies across groups, in this case females and males.

The example found in Table 2 of King's article (1988) provides another illustration. Although the title of the table is "Multiplicative Effects of Race, Gender, and Class on Income," one can read this table as representing the effect of education on income. From this point of view it is clear that the higher the level of education, the higher the income attained; however, although this general *trend* is true within all four race/gender groups, the actual return on education in income varies by group or social location. White males (R, G) enjoy the highest returns for all levels of education, black males receive higher returns than either black or white females, whereas black and white females have mixed returns depending on the level of education. The effect of education on income is multiplicative or interactive, because it varies by social location. Because the relationship between education and income is multiplicative (a statistical interaction), we cannot accurately predict the income of a college graduate unless we also know the individual's social location. If individuals in all four social locations received the same average return in income for a college degree, the relationship would be additive (linear) rather than multiplicative. This is clearly not the case. But it is not so much that race and gender are themselves experienced differently as it is that the *effect* of education (or the return on education) on income attainment is experienced differently depending on the individual's social location created by the intersections of race and gender.[8]

In the present case the intersections of race and gender create or yield four different groups or social locations: white males, black males, white females, and black females. The members of each group earn different average incomes for the same level of education. The preceding example indicates that the group to which an individual belongs is very consequential. An individual's identity may be black or white, female or male. The combination of male together with white creates the most advantageous social location for those individuals. The combinations black and female, and white and female yield two different locations that are sometimes advantageous, sometimes disadvantageous relative to each other, but both are disadvantageous relative to both white males and black males.

Intersectional theorists suggest that this is generally true, that race, gender, and class are interactive; however, as I argued in Part 1, this assumption is best taken as a hypothesis to be tested through empirical research in a large variety of situations. In the preceding example, using 1979 census data, at the educational level of having earned a bachelor's degree, being black and female offers an income advantage relative to being white and female. This probably would not have been true 10 or 20 years earlier. Is it true today? Only research can provide an answer. The preceding example suggests Rule 3.

Rule 3: In the conduct of intersectional research, the statistical technique utilized should be one that allows the detection of interactions among independent variables.

This rule will have to be modified when we consider qualitative research. For now let us accept the rule in this general form.

---

[8]In Part 3, on quantitative methods, we shall learn that this type of model is represented by three independent variables: race, gender, and the product term race × gender, and the dependent variable income.

Intersectional Analysis in Qualitative Research

At the present historical stage of sociology the discipline places a great deal more emphasis on quantitative than on qualitative research. This is in part because the rules followed in quantitative research yield results that are more generalizable than those applied in qualitative research, and the goal of scientific research is to find generalizable explanations for questions about society. Ideally, in conducting quantitative research one uses relatively large random national samples and robust statistical techniques that optimize generalizations of findings. The questionnaire used for collecting data is usually structured with a few open-ended questions.

Qualitative research, in contrast, typically focuses on relatively small nonrandom samples that are interviewed in-depth using semistructured questionnaires on ethnographic methods, or a combination of the two. Although the questionnaire is structured to cover certain topics, the questions are usually open-ended, allowing the respondents to answer questions at length in their own words. Because the data generated in qualitative research are often not quantifiable, qualitative articles do not use the statistical techniques of quantitative research. Instead, qualitative articles typically rely on the presentation of quotations from interviews and summaries rather than tables with tests of significance. The researcher attempts to "build a case" by presenting the results of carefully analyzed interviews.

I distinguish between qualitative and quantitative articles by the presence or absence of tests of significance. The minimum criterion for an article to be classified as quantitative is the use of measures of association in tables such as chi-square, gammas, or the like. Without tests of significance it is impossible to know whether the relationships found are more than happenstance; and although a positive result from a test of significance does not guarantee a significant relationship, it does increase its likelihood.

What the researcher gains in generalizability through the quantitative approach is balanced by what is lost in gaining insights about the phenomenon. In the preceding example of the effect of education on income we know only that the return on education varies by social location and which locations are advantaged or disadvantaged relative to the others. A great deal more research would be needed to untangle the reasons for these findings. It is not sufficient to speak generally about the advantages and disadvantages of race and gender. What is it about being black or white, male or female that yields these results? What societal structures and processes contribute to these results? It is here that qualitative research can be especially useful by providing in-depth information about relationships and effects. Although the strength of qualitative research is greater insights from collecting more in-depth information, its weakness is its inability to generalize from the small nonrandom samples utilized. Having said this, are the rules to be followed in conducting qualitative research from an intersectional perspective different from those to be followed when conducting quantitative intersectional research?

Rules for qualitative intersectional research

Rules 1 and 2 apply to both qualitative and quantitative research with similar constraints of time and cost. Unlike in quantitative research, however, qualitative researchers typically collect their own data. Growing interest in qualitative research has led to an expanding body of literature on the conduct of qualitative research in sociology (Berg 2001; Denzin and Lincoln 1998a, 1998b). There are two major types of qualitative research. The oldest tradition is that of anthropological ethnographic studies, in which the researcher spends a great deal of time—often years—in a particular location, observing, interviewing, and sometimes participating in social interactions. Although qualitative sociologists sometimes use ethnographic methods, they are more likely to engage in in-depth interviewing using semistructured rather than structured questionnaires. This technique allows the researcher to generate detailed information that still covers a predetermined set of questions or areas of inquiry. The fluidity of the approach allows the interviewer to depart from the questionnaire to pursue ideas that unexpectedly emerge, then to return to the questionnaire.

In quantitative research it is customary to distinguish between the *depedent* variable, an effect or outcome that is the focus of inquiry, and *independent* variables that are believed to be either correlated with or to "cause" the dependent variable. In qualitative research such distinctions are sometimes difficult to make or are not given the same attention as in quantitative research. In the example of the relationship between education and income, income is the effect or dependent variable; education along with race and gender are the independent variables. The researcher seeks to understand how and why income varies, or what factors influence its acquisition, by searching for the "causes" of or influences on income attainment.

The qualitative researcher seldom uses the language of quantitative research and therefore tends not to speak of independent and dependent variables. Nevertheless, as we shall see later, in discussing the qualitative articles in this volume the qualitative researcher often describes the research in language that allows one to distinguish between the dependent and independent factors. Although the qualitative researcher no less than the quantitative researcher is seeking answers to questions, the relationships underlying these questions may not be as easily operationalized as in quantitative research. When the distinction between independent and dependent variables is difficult to make, the qualitative researcher will be well advised to analyze the relationships and questions he or she is attempting to study. In a study of suburbanization, for instance, the question might be: Why do individuals decide to move from the city to suburbs? Here the dependent variable might be the *decision* to move. Rather than hand the respondent a card with a series of options from which to choose, the qualitative researcher will follow the initial question with a series of other questions to discover the reasons for the move. The *reasons* given are the independent variables, the explanations for the move. Because individuals are not always completely aware of the motives for their behavior at a given moment, or may have difficulty recalling the steps in making their decision, the researcher has to probe by sometimes asking numerous questions or by asking the same question in different ways. Hidden in the discussion are the dependent and independent variables of the inquiry, the relationship between reasons or motivation and the decision to move.

Earlier I suggested that in the example used by King (1988) we could view income as the dependent variable, and education, race, and gender as independent or explanatory variables. We are not attempting to explain race, gender, or class but, rather, are seeking to understand how race, gender, and class affect some outcome or how they help explain some aspect of social life, or how some characteristic, behavior, or relationship varies across intersections of race, gender, and class. This is the role of independent variables.

A further distinction needs to be made between *independent* and *control* variables. Although in reality all explanatory variables are independent variables, the researcher may be interested in one particular variable, or in several variables more than others. In attempting to explain income attainment the researcher may be especially concerned about the return to education from income; however, prior research has identified other factors that influence income attainment, such as the age of the individual, length of time on the job, sector of employment (private or public), type of occupation, supervisory status, and region (Landry 1987, 124). Although all these factors influence income, they may nevertheless be of secondary interest to the researcher, included only to ensure that the effect of education has been isolated from other causal factors. These other factors are called *control* variables relative to education. In essence we statistically remove or control for the effects of these other variables to isolate the effect of education after these other effects are accounted for. In qualitative research the distinction between independent and control variables is seldom consciously made by the researcher. Indeed, since in qualitative research it is not possible to statistically manipulate variables, the distinction between independent and control variables becomes almost meaningless, in contrast with quantitative analysis, where the distinction is often necessary. Nevertheless, whether the research is quantitative or qualitative race, gender, and class can serve as either primary independent variables or control variables.

Type I and type II articles

Many researchers in a wide variety of disciplines have attempted to conduct intersectional research. From an examination of a variety of their articles I have identified two general variations or subtypes of intersectional research, which I term Type I and Type II. In Type I, race, gender, and class function as *independent* variables as researchers explore the variation of the dependent variable across social locations created by the intersections of race, gender, and class. In some cases race, gender, and class may be the only independent variables. In other cases there may be additional independent variables that serve as controls. Whether or not there are control variables in the design, in Type I intersectional analysis race, gender, and class are the principal independent variables.

In Type II cases, race, gender, and class are *control* variables, but a special type of control variable serving a function different from the usual function of control variables in quantitative research. In Type II intersectional analysis there is a principal independent variable other than race, gender, and class. For instance, the researcher may want to measure the effect of education on income attainment but also wants to know whether this relationship between education and income varies across social locations created by the intersections of race, gender, and class. It should be noted that in Type II intersectional analysis there may also be other control variables serving the usual function of isolating the effect of the principal independent variable. As we shall observe, both qualitative and quantitative research may fall into either the Type I or the Type II category; however, in qualitative research it is often more difficult to detect this distinction. Additionally, the qualitative researcher cannot statistically manipulate the data. Effects of independent variables are described rather than measured, and variations across social locations are compared with quotations and summaries.

A digression on race, gender, and class

For heuristic reasons I have modeled intersectional analysis with the assumption that race, gender, and class are *dichotomous* variables: a person's race is either black or white; gender is either male or female; and class references middle- or working-class individuals. In reality, neither race nor class is inherently dichotomous. The focus on blacks and whites flows from the origins of the theory: black women in the academy intent on addressing flawed approaches to race and gender that often rendered them invisible. If intersectional research is to reach its full potential, however, it needs to grow beyond its origin. As an approach to social science as well as in other disciplines, conceptualizing race and class as dichotomies is overly restrictive. As noted in Part 1 on the theory of intersectional analysis, race is a social construct that takes on the meaning of a particular society at a given time and place. In the United States race has been defined dichotomously as either black or white. In other societies, such as Brazil, it was pointed out, the approach to race is more nuanced. Further, if one of the objectives of intersectional analysis is to identify and struggle against the oppression of groups within the society, it is necessary to look beyond this narrow American focus on black and white to other groups that are experiencing oppressive treatment and conditions within society. According to a recent *Washington Post* article, the census bureau declared that Hispanics became the "largest minority" in 2000, with 38.8 million, compared with 38.3 million African Americans (Cohn 2003). Statistics on the economic and social conditions of Hispanics—as well as of many other immigrant groups—reveal living conditions that are often appalling, or at least quite inferior to those of white Americans. Many of these groups experience significant discrimination in their everyday lives. Asians, whom some have called the "model minority" (Crystal 1989; Yamanaka and McClelland 1994) include great diversity, from very successful members of the middle class, especially among Chinese, Japanese, and Indian immigrants, to struggling members of more recent immigrants from Vietnam and Cambodia.

By custom social scientists and government reports distinguish between *racial* groups and *ethnics* within the society.[9] These designations are often very useful in differentiating the historical levels of oppression within the United States, oppressions that have been experienced most severely by Native Americans, African Americans, Latinos, and some Asians. Yet, many of those groups referred to as "nonwhite ethnics" experience significant disadvantage and even discrimination today. For these reasons it is appropriate to expand the "race" category beyond the black/white dichotomy to include other minority groups within our society. Some researchers in fact have begun to think in terms of race/ethnic groups, and a number of the articles chosen for this text do, in fact, focus on a variety of race/ethnic groups beyond the black/white dichotomy. Parenthetically it should be noted that researchers in societies other than the United States will want to consider which groups in their own society are oppressed.

The concept of gender—although also socially constructed—is less contested as a dichotomous biological designation. Incidences of hermaphrodites, or transvestites, are generally viewed as exceptions rather than gender categories. Likewise, although gays and lesbians experience significant discrimination in our society because of their sexual orientation, sexual orientation is not a gender category. There are of course other oppressions, discriminations, and disadvantages within our society suffered by the handicapped and the aged, and strong arguments can be made for including these other groups; however, the focus on race, gender, and class is part of the history of the United States, dating to its origin as a republic and even to the Colonial period. Within this history, race/ethnicity, gender, and class oppression stand out for their longevity and persistence. In this text I have chosen to maintain this original focus of intersectional theorists while recognizing that there are significant levels of oppression and disadvantage heaped on other groups. At another level, the focus on race, gender, and class serves as a heuristic model that can be built on and broadened; however, viewed under the empirical lens of quantitative research, the challenge of *simultaneously* analyzing multiple groups beyond the three dichotomies becomes enormous, and sometimes impossible, with our present tools.

Class analysis in the United States has not had a distinguished history. Whether because of the fear of being contaminated by the "communist taint" following the Bolshevik revolution, or because of the belief in the ideology of opportunity and the Horatio Alger (1899; [1872] 1972; [18??] 1974) "rags to riches" myth, or

[9]Foner and Fredrickson (2004) note that the use of these two terms has been confounded by a history of conquest of Native Americans, slavery of Africans, and immigration from Europe, Latin America, and other parts of the world.

because of both, twentieth-century social scientists generally shied away from class analysis. Not so in Europe—nor in nineteenth-century America—when class distinctions marked the experiences of everyday life (Blumin 1989; Ryan 1981). Only recently have we begun, however crudely, to accept the reality of class differences in the United States. An exception was the 2001 PBS special "People Like Us: Social Class in America," which was unusual for its explicit focus on the subject. Class has also surfaced in recent presidential and congressional debates over the beneficiaries of tax cuts. Newspaper reporters now use the term more freely, and President George W. Bush, in the debate over his proposed tax cut, warned about the danger of "class warfare" (Chinni 2003; Dionne 2003).

The concept of class has not fared much better among social scientists in the United States, ranging from declarations in the 1950s that the United States had become a "middle-class society" (Mayer 1956, 1959), to announcements that the concept had become "useless" or "irrelevant" as a tool for analyzing social life (Nisbet 1959). In reality, U.S. social scientists have failed to arrive at a consensus on either the of class definition or its measurement.

Historically there have been two traditions of class analysis, one derived from Karl Marx, the other from Max Weber. Both are considered "grand theorists" who developed explanations of societal change and are routinely covered in theory texts in sociology. It is necessary to distinguish between the *meaning* of the concept and its *measurement.* For both Marx ([1867] 1977) and Weber ([1921] 1968), *class* refers to an individual's position within the economy. On a macro level, both agreed that the major class cleavage within a capitalist society is between those who own property and those who do not, where "property" is primarily the ownership of the corporate and financial assets of society and other sources of vast amounts of wealth. Beyond this point of agreement these two giants of social science diverged. Marx focused on the antagonism between those who own property (variously called "capitalists" or the "bourgeoisie") and those who do not ("workers" or the "proletariat"). Since there were relatively few nonmanual white-collar workers during the period of his writing and because Marx expected the increased exploitation of workers to lead to revolution, he all but ignored white-collar (nonmanual) workers.

Weber, in contrast, incorporated the nonmanual worker in his model of a capitalist society's stratification system. Propertyless workers (both manual and nonmanual) are distinguished by the "kinds of services" (i.e., skills or education) they have to offer when bargaining for a position (occupation) within the labor force (Weber [1921] 1968). Those individuals with similar "situations" (similar occupations) in the labor force form distinct classes. Each group (class) receives similar economic rewards of income, mobility opportunities, job security or lack thereof, and fringe benefits. These *packages* of economic rewards determine their "life chances" or living standard. Thus, education or skill becomes the "coin" an individual uses to trade for a position in the labor force, and that position or occupation provides an income and other economic rewards that enables the individual to provide for his or her needs. Within this Weberian tradition, then, *occupation* became the measure or indicator of an individual's class position (Parkin 1971).

Unfortunately, class analysis in the United States has followed a circuitous path dating to W. Lloyd Warner and Paul S. Hunt and their *Yankee City* (1941) studies and leading eventually to something called "SES" or "socioeconomic status" (Duncan 1961),[10] which is often measured by education, income, or

[10]Duncan was explicit in emphasizing that SES was designed as a measure of occupational prestige rather than as a measure of class.

occupation or some combination of these variables. The result is that rarely do two researchers measure class in the same way. From the perspective of intersection analysis this is a very serious problem that hinders comparability across research articles.

There is yet another problem in the use of class in empirical research: the availability of appropriate data. Within the Weberian tradition, occupation is the most accurate indicator of class position among the propertyless (nonwealthy). Often, however, an existing data set may not contain a good measure of occupation or may omit it altogether. In those cases the best approximation or "proxy" measure of class is education. Education is highly correlated with occupation, since education is the usual credential used to land a job. Empirically it can be shown that entrance to white-collar jobs typically requires some college education, whereas the average manual or unskilled service worker needs only a high school education or less. Thus the dichotomy between college and no college roughly parallels the nonmanual/manual, or white-collar/blue-collar-service dichotomy. Further distinctions can be made in both classes, yielding two or more strata or subdivisions. Within the middle class we can differentiate between the upper and lower middle classes, identified by the occupations of professionals and managers among the former and sales/clerical/technical workers among the latter. Within the working class, divisions into skilled, semiskilled (operatives), and unskilled suggest themselves. Sometimes, a researcher will not have sufficient cases to distinguish beyond the nonmanual/manual divide, between middle class and working class. The upper class typically cannot be reached in surveys or identified in government statistics, although a number of sociologists have conducted focused research on this class (Domhoff 1983). Within the Weberian tradition, then, it is usually sufficient to use a class dichotomy, distinguishing between middle class (white-collar) and working class (blue-collar and unskilled service).

Neo-Marxists theorists and researchers like Erik Olin Wright (1978) define and measure class differently. For them class is a question of capital (property) and authority relationship. Those who own capital and/or have supervisory or managerial authority over others occupy different class positions from those who do not own property and/or do not have authority. It is an approach that coincides with Max Weber's in its emphasis on property relations but differs in its emphasis on authority relations. This neo-Marxist position is also more difficult to translate into research, although some have done so (Wright and Perrone 1977).

Critiquing Qualitative Articles

The following qualitative articles included in this text have been categorized by the number of social locations represented in a particular article. They range from what I call a *fully saturated* model, in which all eight locations are represented, to those that include only two locations. Analyzing these qualitative articles presents a number of challenges. First, although most of the authors include information on their methodology and give the number of cases in each race, gender, and class group, they frequently do not indicate the number of cases in a particular social location. Second, intersectional research still lacks a language and clear strategy for analyzing data from this perspective. This is of course not surprising, given its recency; yet the conduct of empirical research from an intersectional perspective, whether qualitative or quantitative, will progress more rapidly if both a vocabulary and a strategy for analysis become available. Although researchers consciously attempt to perform intersectional analysis, they frequently use the language and approaches that are current in the discipline. Because the intersectional approach to research focuses on social locations rather than on the separate identities of race, gender, or class,

TABLE 2 ■ EXAMPLE OF SATURATED MODEL WITH EIGHT SOCIAL LOCATIONS

	MALES		FEMALES	
Class	White	Black	White	Black
Middle class	WMcM	BMcM	WMcF	BMcF
Working class	WWcM	BWcM	WWcF	BWcF

dependent variables should be compared across these social locations in the case of Type I analysis. In the case of Type II analysis, the relationship between an independent and a dependent variable is examined across social locations. Whatever the case, intersectional analysis needs a vocabulary that facilitates comparisons across social locations. This seems to become especially difficult when, despite the expressed intent to use the intersectional approach, a researcher is more interested in one of the individual identities than the others—more interested in race than in gender, or in gender than in race, for instance. In such cases, authors may analyze race, gender, or class relations individually without ever mentioning social locations. Third, in some instances one or more of the social locations is missing or is represented by too few cases—as a result of the composition of the sample or because sampling was not guided by the objective of including representatives of all relevant social locations. Research from an intersectional perspective requires that the rules of intersectional analysis be *built into* the research design and data collection strategy. Once the data are collected, the relevant social locations may not be present, eliminating effective intersectional analysis.

Tables 2 and 3 provide useful devices for determining the social locations included in a given article. Table 2 presents the saturated model including all eight locations when race is dichotomized into blacks and whites, gender includes females and males, and class is represented by the middle and working classes. In practice, as we shall see, some researchers include other race and/or minority groups, at times intentionally, in other cases as a result of the composition of the group (e.g., a school) studied. Class, likewise, may be defined in different ways by authors, resulting in more than two categories. For heuristic purposes the illustrations in Table 2 uses dichotomies of race and class. Similar tables can be constructed with more categories of racial groups and/or classes.

Table 3 presents three examples that include only four locations each, which result when the research is limited to a single race, gender, or class group. Michael Messner's study of "Masculinities and Athletic Careers," in this section, by definition excludes females and therefore follows column D in Table 1. Likewise, Janet Jacobs's article on teen mothers, "Gender, Race, Class, and the Trend Toward Early Motherhood," includes only teenage girls (column C in Table 1). In both instances the four social

TABLE 3 ■ EXAMPLES OF REDUCED INTERSECTION MODELS WITH FOUR LOCATIONS

	MALES (R × C) RACE			MIDDLE CLASS (R × G) RACE			BLACKS (G × C) GENDER	
Class	Black	White	Gender	Black	White	Class	Males	Females
Middle	BMc	WMc	Males	BM	WM	Middle	McM	McF
Working	BWc	WWc	Females	BF	WF	Working	WcM	WcF

locations are created by the intersection of the race × class categories.[11] Depending on the researcher's approach, the analysis may focus on variations of the dependent variable across the four race × class locations (Type I) or on the variation of the relationship between the independent and dependent variable (e.g., education and income) across the four social locations (Type II). If the focus is on a particular class (columns E and F in Table 1), the four social locations are created by the intersection of race × gender; and for single race groups (columns A and B in Table 1) the gender × class intersections yield the four social locations. Ideally, researchers conducting qualitative intersectional analysis should plan their project to include a sufficient number of cases in each of the intersectional groups represented by the four, eight, or more locations. As we shall see, that is not always the case.

The Saturated Model

Two articles are included in this section. The first article, by Daniel G. Solorzano, "An Exploratory Analysis of the Effects of Race, Class, and Gender on Student and Parental Mobility Aspirations," employs tables showing the raw numbers and percentages for each social location. Because the tables provide only percentages without measures of association, I classify this article as qualitative. Although it is not typical of qualitative articles, it is nevertheless a good example of a saturated model of intersectional analysis. Indeed, it is also a good example of intersectional analysis that goes beyond a dichotomy of class.[12] Since the author divides class into four categories, 16 different social locations are represented. Such distinctions are made possible only by the use of a very large data set that is not typical of qualitative research. I include it here to illustrate the saturated model.

The author appropriately compares across complex rather than simple social locations throughout their analysis. While he sometimes refers to simple social locations ("black eighth graders" or "white students"), most frequently he uses the terminology of complex social locations: "black males," "black females," and "white females." Even in summaries he maintains the focus on complex social locations, as in the following statement on p. 000: "Second, upon controlling for social class, and in all but two cases (middle-high-SES female and high-SES male) Blacks display higher expectations than do Whites [in the same social locations]."

---

[11]Of course, if race and/or class are defined with more categories, the schema will yield more than four social locations.

[12]The use of SES, socioeconomic status, as a measure of class is common in educational research and also is found in other areas of sociological research. The measure is typically created by some combination of education, occupation, and income.

This article also provides a good example of two other important issues in intersectional analysis: How many social locations should be compared, and how should they be compared? My position is that the number and manner of comparisons should be guided by the researcher's purpose. In the present article the author appears to be interested in all social locations, and he studies them effectively by comparing race/gender groups across the four levels of their class measure. "Third, in all but one SES quartile (high-SES Black) both Black and White parents held higher expectations for their daughters than they did for their sons (p. 000)." Since this statement refers to Table 3, it is clear that he is comparing parents in multiple race × gender × class social locations.

The second article in this group, "Policing Boundaries: Race, Class, and Gender in Cartagena, Colombia," by Joel Streicker, is concerned with boundaries. Streicker is concerned with the way intersectional boundaries themselves are fluid in the Santa Ana neighborhood of Cartagena. This article presents a good example of what intersectional theorists refer to as the mutual construction of race, gender, and class identities. Streicker focuses especially on the contested definition of race. Unlike in the United States, residents of Santa Ana have at least four different racial designations whose meanings interact with class position and even gender. They are "blanco" (white), "claro" (fair, light), "moreno" (brown), and "negro" (black). The "decisive criterion" for membership in one of these groups, Streicker observes, "is often behavioral rather than phenotypical" (p. 137). Thus *blanco* is a term reserved for individual's of the dominant class, regardless of their skin color, hair type, or facial features; and a poor person is considered *claro* rather than blanco, even if the poor person has physical characteristics associated with the category blanco. Thus class and race identities are mutually constructed rather than being fixed markings. Furthermore, gender norms influence definitions of both class and race, as Streicker notes: "I show that notions of gender are central to the meaning of class and race: for santaneros, an important means of establishing an individual's class and race identity is to measure that persons' actions against standards of gender conduct" (p. 132). Although the neighborhood studied is a poor working-class neighborhood, residents of Santa Ana nevertheless make further class distinctions within their community, as well as recognize a wealthy class within the city.

This is an ethnographic study of a neighborhood of undisclosed dimensions. Given the four racial designations ("blanco," "claro," "Moreno," and "Negro"), three class categories ("la clase media," "los pobres," "la clase baja"—"la clase alta" is referred to but does not form part of the neighborhood studied), and two genders, there are potentially 24 social locations. It is impossible to clearly identify the size of these categories using an ethnographic approach in a neighborhood with limited formal interviews (in the present study, 78). Further, identifying those who occupy a particular social location is problematized by the fluidity of the categories of race and class. In one instance, Streicker recounts his conversation with "two teenaged girls who considered themselves morenas" (p. 137) as they discussed one of the girl's boyfriend whom the other classified as "negro." This fluidity is especially striking in the following statement by a young woman: "I'm *clara* [fair], but I'd be *blanca* if I had money. You can be *moreno* [brown], but if you've got money then you're *blanco*" (p. 137). In addition to wealth, however, class designation is influenced by behavior, with the label "negro" attached to anyone who behaves in a socially disapproved of manner.

In this article, respondents are frequently not identified by complex social locations but by a simple gender location. The study, therefore, is primarily enlightening as a very insightful study of the fluid social construction of the categories race and class and the mutual social construction of class, race, and gender. Finally, because the study is concerned with community-level dynamics in the construction of race, class, and gender it is a type of messo analysis.

An Exploratory Analysis of the Effects of Race, Class, and Gender on Student and Parent Mobility Aspirations

DANIEL G. SOLORZANO
Graduate School of Education, University of California–Los Angeles

At any given point in the educational and occupational pipeline, using most measures of educational and occupational outcome, Blacks do not fare as well as Whites (Farley & Allen, 1989; Jaynes & Williams, 1989; Reid, 1982). For instance, in 1988, at the upper end of the educational pipeline, 11.3% of Black females and 11.2% of Black males attained at least four years of college. In contrast, 17.3% of White females and 24.9% of White males had reached such attainment levels (U.S. Bureau of the Census, 1990). Occupationally, 17.5% of Black females and 13.3% of Black males held managerial or professional occupations, while 26.3% of White females and 26.6% of While males held similar occupations (U.S. Bureau of Labor Statistics, 1989).

One theoretical model used to explain racial differences in educational and occupational attainment is the "cultural deficit" or "culture of poverty" model (also referred to recently as the "cultural underclass" model) (see Baca Zinn, 1989; Inniss & Feagin, 1990; Mincy, Sawhill, & Wolf, 1990). The cultural deficit model contends that Black cultural values, as transmitted through the family and specifically the parents, are dysfunctional, and therefore the reason for Blacks' low educational and later occupational attainment (Banfield, 1970; Moynihan, 1965; Sowell, 1981; see Lewis, 1968 and Wilson, 1987). It further postulates that Blacks do not place a high value on education as a vehicle of upward mobility. Social scientists who use the cultural deficit model focus on racial/ethnic background as one predictor of educational and occupational aspirations. Accordingly, Blacks possess deficient values (as measured by their lower aspirations) that place little emphasis on education, which in turn explains why they do not do well in school. For instance, Ogbu (1983, 1988, 1990a, 1990b) explains how "involuntary" racial minorities (i.e., Blacks and Chicanos) reinforce their own inequality through a cultural frame of reference which ensures failure. As he argues, these involuntary minorities "do not have the expectations of a better future that characterize immigrant minorities" (1990b, p. 47). Moreover, they "have not developed a widespread effort optimism or a strong cultural ethic of hard work and perseverance in the pursuit of education" (1990b, p. 53).

The cultural deficit view of minority inequality has become the social scientific norm even though little empirical evidence exists to support many of its claims (Baca Zinn, 1989; Ginsburg, 1986; Keddie, 1973; Neisser, 1986; Persell, 1977; Tienda, 1981; Valentine, 1968; Wilson, 1987). However, claims that the cultural deficit model has been debunked and is no longer widely used seem premature. The 1980s witnessed a revival of this model under the rubric of theories about the "underclass" to explain low minority attainment (Baca Zinn, 1989). One need only examine the journalistic literature on the underclass (Auletta, 1982; Gershman, 1980; Hamill, 1988; Lemann, 1986a, 1986b) along with the scholarly works of Murray (1984), Sowell (1981), and Steele (1990) to review contemporary versions of the cultural deficit model. As Persell (1977) notes, other public and private statements made in teacher lounges, college classrooms, and educational board rooms suggest that the cultural deficit model continues to be widely used (either explicitly or implicitly) to explain the low attainment of Black students.

A major criticism of the cultural deficit model is that it focuses on individual and group characteristics and avoids institutional or social structural factors, thereby shifting the responsibility for educational and occupational attainment away from the school and onto family and student background characteristics (Ryan, 1971; Steinberg, 1989; Valentine, 1968). It also assumes that students attend schools of equal quality and receive equal treatment in their schools. Thus, the cultural deficit model does not examine or account for the effect of such school factors as ability grouping, tracking, teacher/student interactions, or educational resources on minority educational attainment.

This exploratory study focuses on the cultural deficit model in an attempt to determine whether it indeed disentangles the effects of race, social class, and gender on student and parent aspirations and expectations. The following questions are posed:

1. Do racial and gender differences exist in the educational and occupational aspirations/expectations of Black and White students and their parents?
2. Do these racial and gender differences exist once social class is controlled?

The cultural deficit model hypothesizes that because Blacks place less value on education and upward mobility, they therefore have lower aspirations/expectations than have Whites, even when social class is controlled. If the model is robust, then the relationship between racial group membership and aspirations/expectations should be maintained regardless of social class. However, if the relationship breaks down as social class is controlled, then one must conclude that the model has some weaknesses.

METHODOLOGY

Sample

Baseline data for this exploratory study are drawn from the eighth grade cohort of the National Educational Longitudinal Survey of 1988 (NELS:88). This nationwide study was sponsored by the U.S. Department of Education's National Center for Education Statistics. The NELS:88 survey design covered a two-stage, stratified national probability sample. About 24,599 eighth graders, enrolled in 1,052 public and private high schools across the nation, participated in the 1988 base-year survey, which examined the school-related experiences and accomplishments of eighth grade students, their parents, and their teachers, along with information on their schools. In the NELS:88 design, the student is the basic unit of analysis. That study's parent survey, intended to supplement the student data set, covers related areas and was administered to 22,651 parents.[1]

The analyses reported herein are based on Black and White eighth grade students who participated in the initial NELS:88 survey. The sample sizes for the student and parent cohorts are reported in the tables.

Operational definitions

Racial Group Membership was constructed from a self-report question in the survey on racial background. The two racial groups of concern were Blacks and Whites.

Socioeconomic Status (SES) was constructed from father's occupation, father's education, mother's education, family income, and material items in the household. This variable was created by National Center for Education Statistics staff. The SES composite score was disaggregated into four quartiles: low, low-middle, high-middle, and high (Ingels et al., 1989a, 1989b).

[1]A more complete description of the student and parent data is found in the data user's guides (Ingels et al., 1989a, 1989b) and the base-year sample design report (Spencer, Frankel, Ingels, Rasinski, & Tourangeau, 1990).

Student Educational Aspiration was constructed from student self-reports in response to the question, "As things stand now, how far in school do you think you will get?" The responses were coded "> (greater than) College Aspiration" if the students indicated that they aspired to at least attend college.

Perceived Mother's Educational Aspiration was constructed from student responses to the question, "How far in school do you think your mother wants you to get?" The responses were coded "> College Aspiration" if the students indicated that they believed their mothers aspired for them to at least attend college.

Actual Parent's Educational Expectation was constructed from parent responses to the question, "How far in school do you expect your child to go?" The responses were coded "> College Expectation" if the parents indicated they expected their children to at least attend college.

Student Occupational Expectation was constructed from student responses to the question, "What kind of work do you expect to be doing when you are 30 years old?" The responses were coded "professional" if students answered (1) business or managerial professional, or (2) science or engineering professional. Responses were coded "mid-level" if they answered (1) craftsperson or operator; (2) farmer or farm manager; (3) military, police, or security officer; (4) small business or service entrepreneur; or (5) technical worker. They were coded "low-level" if students answered (1) housewife/homemaker; (2) laborer or farmworker; (3) salesperson, clerical, or office worker; or (4) service worker.

Procedures

Using descriptive cross-tabular techniques, this exploratory study began by comparing overall educational aspirations and occupational expectations for Black and White female and male students without controlling for social class. Next, the study controlled for race, social class, and gender by separately comparing (using cross-tabular techniques) the educational aspirations and occupational expectations of Black and White female and male students at each SES quartile. Identical analysis procedures were applied to the data from the parent survey.

Results

Student's educational aspirations

Despite the differences in educational attainment cited earlier, Table 1 shows that in 1988, before controlling for social class, 82.4% of Black females and 80.2% of Black males aspired to attend college after high school. In contrast, 83.5% of White females and 78.6% of White males held such aspiration. However, when social class was controlled, Black eighth graders evidenced higher educational aspirations than did White students. For example, at the lowest SES quartile, 73.0% of Black female and 70.9% of Black male students aspired to attend college, while 58.5% of White females and 48.9% of White males held such aspirations. This pattern continues at each quartile except the highest and then only for females, whereupon Black females were found to have slightly lower aspirations than have White females. Additionally, at every quartile except the highest, Black females indicated higher educational aspirations than did Black males. White females indicated higher aspirations at every quartile compared to their male counterparts.

At least four patterns emerge upon analysis of the data. First, regardless of racial group, student educational aspirations rise as their SES rises. Second, when social class is controlled, and in all but the highest SES quartiles, Black female and male students have higher aspirations than have Whites. Third, in all but one SES quartile (high-SES Blacks), both Black and White females have higher aspirations than have their male counterparts. Fourth, regardless of racial group, a significant differnce exists between actual educational attainment (as measured by census data) and student educational aspirations; however, this gap is much greater for Blacks than it is for Whites.

TABLE 1 STUDENTS' COLLEGE ASPIRATIONS[1] OF THE NATIONAL EDUCATION LONGITUDINAL SURVEY OF 1988, EIGHTH GRADE STUDENTS BY RACE/ETHNICITY, SOCIOECONOMIC STATUS,[2] AND SEX (PERCENTAGES)

		Socioeconomic quartiles			
	Overall	Low	Low–middle	Middle–high	High
BLACK					
Female					
College aspirations (%)	82.4	73.0	84.6	93.0	93.8
Total (*N*)	1,502	629	408	287	178
Male					
College aspirations (%)	80.2	70.9	80.2	88.4	96.3
Total (*N*)	1,424	573	378	285	188
WHITE					
Female					
College aspirations (%)	83.5	58.5	77.8	88.0	96.8
Total (*N*)	8,061	1,356	1,927	2,100	2,678
Male					
College aspirations (%)	78.6	48.9	68.2	82.6	94.9
Total (*N*)	8,036	1,238	1,824	2,088	2,886

NOTES: [1]Students' College Aspirations = Students' responses to the question, "As things stand now, how far in school do you think you will get?" The responses were coded "> College Aspiration" if the students indicated they would at least attend college.
[2]Socioeconomic Status = Variable constructed from father's occupation, father's education, mother's education, family income, and material items in the household; it was broken down into four quartiles.
SOURCE: Ingels, S. et al. (1989b). *National Educational Longitudinal Study of 1988: Student component data file user's manual.*

Perceived mother's educational aspirations

Table 2 shows that, before controlling for social class, 89.3% of Black females and 86.9% of Black males in the NELS:88 cohort perceived that their mothers wanted them to attend college after high school. In contrast, 90.1% of White females and 87.1% of White males indicated similar maternal aspirations. Yet, when social class was controlled, Black eighth graders' perceptions of their mothers' educational aspirations for them exceeded the perceptions of White students. For example, at the lowest SES quartile, 85.9% of Black female and 78.8% of Black male students perceived that their mothers wanted them to attend college. Among Whites, 72.7% of females and 66.7% of males indicated such perceptions. At each SES quartile, Black male students perceived their mothers as having higher aspirations for them than did White males. The pattern differs for Black female students, who perceived high maternal aspirations for their educational attainment at the two lowest quartiles, similar aspirations at the third quartile, and lower aspirations at the highest quartile. Black female students also indicated higher perceived maternal aspirations than did Black male students in the two lowest quartiles, while Black males perceived higher maternal aspirations in the two highest quartiles. For White students, females indicated higher perceived maternal aspirations in all of the SES quartiles.

Five patterns emerge from the data shown in Table 2. First, regardless of racial group, perceived mothers' educational aspirations rise as SES rises. Second, when controlling for social class and in all but one SES quartile (middle/high), Black females and males hold higher perceived maternal aspirations than do Whites. Third, in the two lowest quartiles for Blacks and in all quartiles for

TABLE 2 ■ Perceived Mothers' College Aspirations[1] for the National Education Longitudinal Survey of 1988, Eighth Grade Students by Race/Ethnicity, Socioeconomic Status,[2] and Sex (Percentages)

		Socioeconomic quartiles			
	Overall	Low	Low–middle	Middle–high	High
BLACK					
Daughter					
College aspirations (%)	89.3	85.9	88.6	92.5	96.8
Total (*N*)	1,303	533	359	254	157
Son					
College aspirations (%)	86.9	78.8	87.4	94.0	98.1
Total (*N*)	1,184	458	317	248	161
WHITE					
Daughter					
College aspirations (%)	90.1	72.7	86.3	92.8	98.6
Total (*N*)	7,254	1,149	1,691	1,907	2,507
Son					
College aspirations (%)	87.1	66.7	80.1	89.7	97.1
Tota (*N*)	7,168	1,039	1,576	1,859	2,694

NOTES: [1]Mothers' College Aspirations = Students' responses to the question, "How far in school do you think your mother wants you to get?" The responses were coded "> College Aspiration" if the student indicated their mothers wanted them to at least attend college.

[2]Socioeconomic Status = Variable constructed from father's occupation, father's education, mother's education, family income, and material items in the household; it was broken down into four quartiles.

SOURCE: Ingels, S. et al. (1989b). *National Educational Longitudinal Study of 1988: Student component data file user's manual.*

Whites, females perceive that their mothers have higher aspirations for them than do their male counterparts. Fourth, regardless of racial group, student perceptions of their mother's aspirations exceed their own aspirations (compare with Table 1). Fifth, regardless of racial group, significant differences exist between the actual educational attainment of the group (as measured by census data) and student perceptions of their mothers' aspirations. This gap is much greater for Blacks than for Whites.

Parent's actual educational expectations for their children

Table 3 shows that, before controlling for social class, 79.2% of Black parents in the NELS:88 sample expected their daughters to attend college after high school, while 76.5% held similar expectations for their sons. In contrast, 81.9% and 78.1% of White parents held college aspirations for their daughters and sons, respectively. When social class was controlled, Black parents in each of the SES quartiles indicated slightly higher or similar expectations for their daughters and sons compared to White parents and both Black and White parents held slightly higher expectations for their daughters than they did for their sons. For example, at the lowest SES quartile, Black parents had college expectations for 66.8% of their daughters and 64.4% of their sons, while White parents had similar expectations for 58.1% of their daughters and 50.3% of their sons.

Five patterns emerge from the data shown in Table 3. First, regardless of racial group, parents' educational expectations rise as their SES rises. Second, when controlling for social class, Black

TABLE 3 PARENTS' COLLEGE EXPECTATIONS[1] FOR THE NATIONAL EDUCATION LONGITUDINAL SURVEY OF 1988, EIGHTH GRADE STUDENTS BY RACE/ETHNICITY, SOCIOECONOMIC STATUS,[2] AND SEX (PERCENTAGES)

		Socioeconomic quartiles			
	Overall	Low	Low–middle	Middle–high	High
BLACK					
Daughter					
College expectations (%)	79.2	66.8	83.5	91.8	94.1
Total (*N*)	1,405	590	395	268	152
Son					
College expectations (%)	76.5	64.4	80.6	83.8	97.0
Total (*N*)	1,334	556	351	259	168
WHITE					
Daughter					
College expectations (%)	81.9	58.1	75.1	85.7	95.7
Total (*N*)	7,891	1,319	1,896	2,071	2,605
Son					
College expectations (%)	78.1	50.3	67.2	80.8	94.9
Total (*N*)	7,931	1,196	1,800	2,099	2,836

NOTES: [1]Parents' College Expectations = Parents' responses to the question, "How far in school do you expect your eighth grader to go?" The responses were coded "> College Expectation" if the parents expected their child to at least attend college.
[2]Socioeconomic Status = Variable constructed from father's occupation, father's education, mother's education, family income, and material items in the household; it was broken down into four quartiles.

SOURCE: National Educational Longitudinal Study of 1988: Parent component data file user's manual. Ingels, S. et al. (1989a).

parents indicate mostly higher expectations than do White parents. Third, in all but one SES quartile (high-SES Black) both Black and White parents held higher expectations for their daughters than they did for their sons. Fourth, regardless of racial group, student perceptions of their mothers' aspirations were higher than their parents' actual expectations (compare with Table 2). Fifth, regardless of racial group, a significant difference was found between the actual educational attainment of the group (as measured by census data) and the parent's educational expectations for their children. Once more, this gap is much greater for Blacks than for Whites.

Student's occupational expectations

Government data show that, when compared to Whites, Blacks are less likely to be employed in high-status occupations. For instance, in 1988, 26.3% of White females and 26.6% of White males had attained high-status professional occupations. In contrast, only 17.5% of Black females and 13.3% of Black males had attained such occupations (U.S. Bureau of Labor Statistics, 1989). Table 4 shows that despite the overall low occupational attainment of Blacks, before controlling for social class 54% of Black female and 38.9% of Black male eighth grade students expected to attain professional occupational status by age 30. Among White students, 58.1% of females and 42.8% of males held such expectations. When social class was controlled, Black eighth graders were shown to have higher occupational expectations than White students. For example, at the lowest SES quartile, 44.6% of Black female and 30.8% of Black male students expected to hold a professional position by the time they were 30 years old; yet only 39.1% of White female and 20.4%

TABLE 4 ■ STUDENTS' OCCUPATIONAL EXPECTATIONS[1] OF THE NATIONAL EDUCATION LONGITUDINAL SURVEY OF 1988, EIGHTH GRADE STUDENTS BY RACE/ETHNICITY, SOCIOECONOMIC STATUS,[2] AND SEX (PERCENTAGES)

	Overall	Socioeconomic quartiles			
		Low	Low–middle	Middle–high	High
BLACK					
Female					
Professional occupation (%)	54.0	44.6	54.4	58.0	76.2
Mid-level occupation	26.1	29.2	27.2	24.1	17.0
Low-level occupation	19.9	26.2	18.4	17.9	6.8
Total %	100.0	100.0	100.0	100.0	100.0
N	1,123	455	309	212	147
Male					
Professional occupation (%)	38.9	30.8	40.7	45.2	57.1
Mid-level occupation	51.1	60.2	52.2	48.2	40.0
Low-level occupation	6.9	9.0	7.1	6.5	2.9
Total %	99.9	100.0	100.0	99.9	100.0
N	918	357	253	168	140
WHITE					
Female					
Professional occupation (%)	58.1	39.1	52.3	60.2	69.8
Mid-level occupation	19.2	23.1	20.5	19.8	16.0
Low-level occupation	22.6	37.8	27.1	20.0	14.2
Total %	99.9	100.0	99.9	100.0	100.0
N	5,718	929	1,378	1,470	1,941
Male					
Professional occupation (%)	42.8	20.4	27.7	40.5	61.3
Mid-level occupation	51.4	70.5	65.8	53.4	34.8
Low-level occupation	5.7	9.1	6.4	6.1	3.9
Total %	99.9	100.0	99.9	100.0	100.0
N	5,657	800	1,241	1,449	2,167

NOTES: [1]Students' Occupational Expectations = Students' responses to the question, "What kind of work do you expect to be doing when you are 30 years old?" The responses were coded "Professional" if they answered (1) business or managerial professional, or (2) science or engineering professional. They were coded "Mid-Level" if they answered (1) craftsperson or operator; (2) farmer or farm manager; (3) military, police, or security officer; (4) business or service entrepreneur, or (5) technical worker. They were coded "Low-Level" if they answered (1) housewife/homemaker; (2) laborer or farmworker; (3) salesperson, clerical, or office worker; or (4) service worker. [2]Socioeconomic Status = Variable constructed from father's occupation, father's education, mother's education, family income, and material items in the household; it was broken down into four quartiles.

SOURCE: Ingels, S. et al, (1989b). *National Educational Longitudinal Study of 1988: Student component data file user's manual.*

of White males had such expectations. At the second quartile both Black females and males had slightly higher expectations than Whites. At the third quartile Black males and White females had the highest expectations, while at the highest SES quartile Black females and White males had the higher expectations.

At least four patterns emerge from the data presented in Table 4. First, regardless of racial group, student occupational expectations rise as their SES rises. Second, upon controlling for social class, and in all but two cases (middle-high-SES female and high-SES male) Blacks display higher expectations than do Whites. Third, in all the SES quartiles both Black and White females have higher occupational expectations than have their male counterparts. Fourth, regardless of racial group, a significant gap exists between the actual occupational attainment of the group (as measured by census data) and student occupational expectations.

Discussion

Are there racial and gender differences in the educational and occupational aspirations/expectations of Black and White students and their parents? The answer to this question is "yes." Overall, White females and males and their parents have higher educational and occupational aspirations/expectations than have Black females and males and their parents. However, once social class is controlled, mixed patterns appear of racial and gender differences in educational and occupational aspirations/expectations between Black and White students and their parents: Black females and males have higher educational aspirations in the lowest SES quartiles compared to White females and males. At the highest quartiles Black females and males have higher aspirations/expectations in some quartiles, the same in others, and lower in still others. Overall, the data obtained from this exploratory study seem to challenge the prevailing attitude that Black students and their parents do not value education, at least when educational values are measured by the traditional construct of educational and occupational aspirations and expectations.

For both Black female and male students, high aspirations have clearly become a necessary but not sufficient condition for later attainment. The cultural deficit model predicts higher attainment for those with higher aspirations, yet Blacks apparently do not receive equivalent educational attainment returns for their high aspirations investment. The finding that Blacks have higher aspirations than do Whites in virtually every SES quartile challenges the validity of the cultural deficit model, which predicts that Black students' educational aspirations should not exceed those of Whites in any social strata. At those quartiles in which Blacks hold higher aspirations than Whites, some evidence exists to challenge the cultural deficit model. At the one quartile in which White females hold slightly higher aspirations, the deficit model is partially confirmed. However, the model did not predict that Black students would have higher aspirations in all other social strata. At the two least SES quartiles, data which show that Blacks have higher occupational expectations than do Whites also challenges the cultural deficit model. However, at the third and fourth quartiles, the data are mixed. The model did not predict that Blacks would have higher expectations in any of the social strata. Therefore, another theoretical model must be used to explain this finding.

According to Kirk and Goon (1975), much of the cultural deficit research places its emphasis on the degree of Black/White difference in outcome measures (i.e., aspirations), using Whites as the norm. The present study used Whites as the aspirational norm, yet they apparently did less well than Blacks. What, then, would be the effect of using minority groups as the norm? How would researchers then explain differences in aspirations and expectations? The findings of this exploratory study thus raise questions regarding the validity and reliability of the cultural deficit theory as well as the use of group norms.

Were the cultural deficit model a robust one, then the Blacks in the present study would have reported receiving the same educational and occupational returns on their higher educational aspirations and occupational expectations investment. Clearly, however, this is not the case, as the findings, census, and employment data confirm. Indeed, the finding of a high educational aspiration–low educational attainment mismatch raises the issue of the effects of unfulfilled dreams on both the individual and society. As Coleman et al. (1966) argue, high Black educational aspirations, because they deviate so much from actual rates of high school completion and college going, indicate a "lack of realism in aspiration" (p. 280). Current social mobility research offers little information on the effect of the high educational aspiration–low educational attainment mismatch of Black students and parents. However, Carnoy and Levin (1985) attribute such quality control problems as job dissatisfaction, lower worker productivity, high employee turnover, and alcohol and drug abuse to the aspirations-employment mismatch at the work site.

Although one might argue that an educational and occupational aspiration-attainment mismatch can have similar negative outcomes for students at the school site, what actually happens when there are no realistic opportunities for such high aspirations? Are these high aspirations "cooled out" as these students make their way through the educational and occupational pipeline, and if so, how? Further research must be conducted to examine these issues.

Conclusion

High aspirations may be a necessary but insufficient condition for later attainment, yet the search for the sufficient condition may lead researchers back to the school context. For instance, the present study's finding of high Black aspirations challenges the cultural deficit model and allows one to shift the theoretical and conceptual focus from family background and cultural factors to school characteristics and processes. These data reported herein also challenge the underclass model, which argues that people who live in persistent poverty or impoverished neighborhoods and who exhibit dysfunctional behaviors do so because of a tangle of pathologies not unlike those described by the cultural deficit and culture of poverty models. Further, by empirically showing that Black students and their parents aspire to be occupationally successful, these data challenge Ogbu's notion that involuntary minorities do not have a cultural frame of reference that encourages success. The more appropriate question thus appears to be: Are Black students and their parents given an equal opportunity to reach those aspirations?

If the cultural deficit model has served as a theoretical rationale for the cultural rehabilitation of racial/ethnic minorities and the poor, then debunking the model should provide a theoretical rationale for refocusing on structural and institutional factors to explain low Black educational attainment. Although earlier school-effects studies have shown differing environments to have minimal effects on individual outcomes (see Kerckhoff, 1984), some of the effective and accelerated schools research (Edmonds, 1979, 1982,1984,1986; Levine, 1986,1987a, 1987b, 1989) has shown just the opposite; that is, the quality of the school *does* make a difference.

Refocusing on and redefining the school context allows the researcher to challenge the assumption that Black and White students attend schools of equal quality. By challenging this assumption, researchers can then redefine and analyze the effect of segregated, overcrowded, and underfinanced schools; school staffing, curriculum, and tracking patterns; and teacher expectations and interaction patterns on the educational achievement and attainment of Black students. Some research suggests that these characteristics are related to the educational attainment of minority students (Baron, Tom, & Cooper, 1985; Espinoza, 1986; Oakes, 1985). By examining the school context, researchers can observe how schools reproduce minority social inequality. They can also examine how minority students resist the schools' mechanisms of control (MacLeod, 1987; McLaren, 1989). Further research is clearly needed in this area as well.

This line of research can also lead to another related research direction. As argued earlier in this article, moving away from the individual and home context to the school context is an important direction for future research. However, if one starts from the assumption that minority parents and students value educational achievement and if this strength is the basis for intervention, then the cultural continuities rather than cultural deficit approach might be the more likely model by which to improve the achievement of minority students. The cultural continuities model examines the home for cultural activities that are compatible with school achievement; it then adapts these culturally compatible activities for classroom use (Goldenberg, 1987; Reese, Goldenberg, Loucky, & Gallimore, 1989; Tharp, 1989; Weisner, Gallimore, & Jordan, 1988; see also Clark, 1983). This model has shown some promising research and intervention directions.

The success of minority student intervention programs at each point in the educational pipeline challenges both the cultural deficit and cultural underclass models and provides powerful evidence that the barriers inhibiting minority participation and success in education are social and therefore subject to policy action. Continued research, focusing on school structure and process, that links successful home/school practices, identifies successful school programs, and takes advantage of high minority student and parent aspirations and expectations, is critical to support the educational and occupational mobility of these groups.

References

Auletta, K. (1982). *The underclass.* New York: Random House.

Baca Zinn, M. (1989). Family, race, and poverty in the eighties. *Signs: Journal of Women in Culture and Society, 14;* 856–874.

Banfield, E. (1970). *The unheavenly city* (2nd ed.). Boston: Little, Brown.

Baron, R., Tom, D. & Cooper, H. (1985). Social class, race and teacher expectations. In J. B. Dusek, (Ed.), *Teacher expectancies* (pp. 251–269) Hillsdale, NJ: Lawrence Erlbaum Associates.

Brandt, R. (1982). On school improvement: A conversation with Ronald Edmonds. *Educational Leadership, 40;* 13–15.

Carnoy, M., & Levin, H. (1985). *Schooling and work in the democratic state.* Stanford, CA: Stanford University Press.

Clark, R. (1983). *Family life and school achievement: Why poor Black children succeed or fail.* Chicago: The University of Chicago Press.

Coleman, J. E., Campbell, D., Hobson, J., McPartland, A., Mood, F., Weinfeld, R., & York, R. (1966). *Equality of educational opportunity.* Washington, DC: U.S. Government Printing Office.

Edmonds, R. (1979). Effective schools for the urban poor. *Educational Leadership, 37;* 15–24.

Edmonds, R. (1984). School effects and teacher effects. *Social Policy, 15;* 37–39.

Edmonds, R. (1986). Characteristics of effective schools. In U. Neisser, (Ed.), *The school achievement of minority children: New perspectives.* Hillsdale, NJ: Lawrence Erlbaum Associates.

Espinoza, R. (1986). *Myths: Educational myths regarding education as the great equalizer.* Unpublished manuscript prepared for the Tomas Rivera Center for Policy Studies.

Farley, R., & Allen, W. (1989). *The color line and the quality of life in America.* New York: Oxford University Press.

Gershman, C. (1980, October 5). A matter of class. *New York Times Magazine,* pp. 92–105.

Ginsburg, H. (1986). The myth of the deprived child: New thoughts on poor children. In U. Neisser, (Ed.), *The school achievement of minority children: New perspectives.* Hillsdale, NJ: Lawrence Erlbaum Associates.

Goldenberg, C. (1987). Low income Hispanic parents' contributions to their first-grade children's word-recognition skills. *Anthropology and Educational Quarterly, 18;* 149–179.

Hamill, P. (1988, July). America's Black underclass: Can it be saved? *Readers Digest,* p. 105.

Ingels, S., Abraham, S., Rasinski, K., Karr, B., Spencer, B., & Frankel, M. (1989a). *National Educational Longitudinal Study of 1988, Base year: Parent component data file user's manual.* Washington, DC: National Center for Education Statistics.

Ingels, S., Abraham, S., Rasinski, K., Karr, B., Spencer, B., & Frankel, M. (1989b). *National Educational Longitudinal Study of 1988, Base year: Student component data file user's manual.* Washington, DC: National Center for Education Statistics.

Inniss, L., & Feagin, J. (1989). The Black 'underclass' ideology in race relations analysis. *Social Justice,* 16; 13–34.

Jaynes, G., & Williams, R. (1989). *A common destiny: Blacks and American society.* Washington, DC: National Academy Press.

Keddie, N. (1973). *The myth of cultural deprivation,* Baltimore, MD: Penguin.

Kerckhoff, A. (1984). The current state of social mobility research. *The Sociological Quarterly, 25;* 139–153.

Kirk, D., & Goon, S. (1975). Desegregation and the cultural deficit model: An examination of the literature. *Review of Educational Research, 45;* 599–611.

Lemann, N. (1986a, June). The origins of the underclass: Part 1. *The Atlantic Monthly,* pp. 31–55.

Lemann, N. (1986b, July). The origins of the underclass: Part 2. *The Atlantic Monthly,* pp. 54–68.

Levin, H. (1986). *Educational reform for disadvantaged students: An emerging crises.* West Haven, CT: National Educational Association.

Levin, H. (1987a). Accelerated schools for disadvantaged students. *Educational Leadership, 44;* 19–21.

Levin, H. (1987b). New schools for the disadvantaged. *Teacher Education Quarterly, 14;* 60–83.

Levin, H. (1989). Accelerated schools: A new strategy for at-risk students. *Indiana Policy Bulletin, 6;* 1–6.

Lewis, O. (1968). The culture of poverty. In D. Moynihan, (Ed.), *On understanding poverty: Perspectives from the social sciences.* New York: Basic Books.

MacLeod, J. (1987). *Ain't no makin it: Leveled aspirations in a low-income neighborhood.* Boulder, CO: Westview.

McLaren, P. (1989). *Life in schools: An introduction to critical pedagogy in the foundations of education.* New York: Longman.

Mincy, R., Sawhill, I., & Wolf, D. (1990). The underclass: Definition and measurement. *Science, 248,* 450–453.

Moynihan, D. (1965). *The Negro family: The case for national action.* Washington; DC: U.S. Government Printing Office.

Murray, C. (1984). *Losing ground: American social policy, 1950–1980.* New York: Basic Books.

Neisser, U. (1986). New answers to an old question. In U. Neisser, (Ed.), *The school achievement of minority children: New perspectives.* Hillsdale, NJ: Lawrence Erlbaum Associates.

Oakes, J. (1985). *Keeping track: How schools structure inequality.* New Haven, CT: Yale University Press.

Ogbu, J. (1983). Minority status and schooling in plural societies. *Comparative Education Review,* 27; 168–190.

Ogbu, J. (1988a). Class stratification, racial stratification, and schooling. In L. Weis (Ed.), *Class, race, and gender in American education.* Albany, NY: State University of New York Press.

Ogbu, J. (1990a). Minority status and literacy in comparative perspective. *Daedalus, 119;* 141–168.

Ogbu, J. (1990b). Minority education in comparative perspective. *Journal of Negro Education, 59;* 45–57.

Persell, C. (1977). *Education and inequality: The roots and results of stratification in America's schools.* New York: Free Press.

Reese, L., Goldenberg, C., Loucky, J., & Gallimore, R. (1989, November). *Ecocultural context, cultural activity, and emergent literacy: Sources of variation in home literacy experiences of Spanish-speaking children.* Unpublished manuscript presented at the annual meeting of the American Anthropological Association.

Reid, J. (1982). Black America in the 1980's. *Population Bulletin, 37;* 1–38.

Ryan, W. (1971). *Blaming the victim.* New York: Random House.

Sowell, T. (1981). *Ethnic America: A history.* New York: Basic Books.

Spencer, B., Frankel, M., Ingels, M., Rasinski, S., & Tourangeau, R. (1990). *NELS:88 base year sample design report.* Washington, DC: National Center for Education Statistics.

Steele, S. (1990). *The content of our character: A new view of race in America.* New York: St. Martin's Press.

Steinberg, S. (1989). *The ethnic myth: Race, ethnicity, and class in America.* Boston: Beacon Press.

Tharp, R. (1989). Psychocultural variables and constant effects on teaching and learning in the schools. *American Psychologist, 44;* 1–10.

Tienda, M. (1981). The Mexican population. In A. H. Hawley & S. M. Mazie, (Eds.), *Nonmetropolitan America in transition.* Chapel Hill, NC: University of North Carolina Press.

United States Bureau of the Census, (1990). *Statistical abstract of the United States: 1990.* (110th ed.), Washington, DC: U.S. Government Printing office.

United States Bureau of Labor Statistics. (1989). *Employment and earnings* (Vol. 36, No. 1). Washington, DC: U.S. Government Printing Office.

Valentine, C. (1968). *Culture and poverty: Critique and counter-proposals.* Chicago: University of Chicago Press.

Weisner, T., Gallimore, R., & Jordan, C. (1988). Unpacking cultural effects on classroom learning: Native Hawaiian peer assistance and child-generated activity. *Anthropology and Education Quarterly, 19;* 327–353.

Wilson, W. (1987). *The truly disadvantaged: The inner city, the underclass, and public policy.* Chicago: University of Chicago Press.

Policing Boundaries

Race, Class, and Gender in Cartagena, Colombia

JOEL STREICKER
Brandeis University

In this article I examine the connections among class, race, and gender in the everyday discourse of *santaneros,*[1] popular class residents of the neighborhood of Santa Ana in Cartagena, a city on Colombia's Caribbean coast. Most santaneros, like most other *cartageneros,* perceive little racial prejudice or discrimination in Cartagena; this view is common in many parts of Afro-Spanish America (Benitez Rojo 1984; Casal 1979; Rout 1976; Wright 1990).[2] Instead, the dominant view in Cartagena holds that class is the most salient social division, and thus santaneros' everyday discourse on inequality and social identity focuses on class. Here, however, I argue that it is precisely in the process of forging their class identity that santaneros discriminate racially.

I show that santaneros' discourse about class encodes racial concepts that are seldom explicitly articulated or discussed in everyday life. As an unacknowledged but pervasive language of race, class discourse promotes racism while enabling santaneros to believe that little or no racial prejudice or discrimination exists in Cartagena. These people, who do not think of themselves as racially prejudiced or discriminatory, and most of whom North Americans would consider black, by and large identify blackness with acts that contradict normative popular class identity. Ironically, a class identity that the poor see as providing strength and dignity in opposition to ruling class values also enforces racial hierarchy. At the same time, disparaging blackness in this way has the effect of discrediting what might be considered an incipient expression of pride in blackness and African-identified culture.

I also contend that santaneros use racial concepts as a language for talking about class and gender. Although the work of scholars such as Verena Martinez-Alier (1989[1974]) has been important in examining race and class in Afro-Spanish America, these writers treat race primarily as a symbol of class relations. In contrast, my analysis suggests that race is not reducible to other categories, even though it also symbolizes class standing and gender attributes. In particular, I hold that blackness acts as a source of naturalized meanings for describing and stigmatizing people who are said to transgress class and gender norms. As other analysts have observed (Bourdieu 1977; Connell 1987; Stolcke 1981), naturalizing inequalities is a powerful means of representing them as legitimate or even inevitable. At the same time, however, santaneros also see blackness, and race in general, as socially constructed.

Analysis of everyday discourse among the poor of Cartagena, Colombia, reveals the mutual construction of race, class, and gender identities. Discourse on class and gender encodes racially discriminatory concepts, identifying blackness with acts that contradict normative class and gender identities. This article shows how the interlocking meanings of race, class, and gender enforce the status quo of men's, nonblacks', and elders' authority within the popular class. [race, class, gender, symbolic analysis of difference and inequality, Afro-Spanish America]

My analysis seeks to advance our understanding of racial dynamics in Afro-Spanish America by examining the intersection of race with other social identities such as class. It thus builds on the strengths of previous works dealing with race and class in the region (Schubert 1981; Wade 1985; Whitten 1986[1974]) while arguing more forcefully for the importance of gender in constructing race and class identities. In particular, I show that notions of gender are central to the meaning of class and race: for santaneros, an important means of establishing an individual's class and race identity is to measure that person's actions against standards of gender conduct. In so doing, I demonstrate the fruitfulness of the feminist insight that any given social identity is formed within a web of diverse social relationships rather than principally in the domain that folk and social scientific theories assign to its production (for example, gender as produced in the family, class in economic relations) (Ginsburg and Tsing 1990; M. Rosaldo 1980; Sacks 1989; Yanagisako and Collier 1987). Moreover, just as we must understand that santaneros construct their notions of class and race in oppostion to alternative notions, so must we also recognize the relational character of efforts to legitimate gender conceptions: santaneros form and assert images of normative masculinity in relation to competing notions of masculinity as well as in opposition to femininity, while the converse holds for femininity. This perspective permits a more nuanced account of gender than is possible in works that either present masculinity as stable and homogeneous or ignore it altogether.

Furthermore, I argue that the dominant representation of class, gender, and race among santaneros tends to support the authority of men, and especially of older men, within the popular class. Given the specific ways in which race connects with gender and class identities in Santa Ana, racial discrimination aids men (particularly older men) in representing as general what are in fact sectional interests. While hardly new, this strategy of domination has recently been the focus of a number of sociocultural analyses (Asad 1990; Dominguez 1989; Fraser and Nicholson 1990; Moraga and Anzaldua 1981; Mosse 1985; Pratt 1984; R. Rosaldo 1989; Joan Scott 1988; Wittig 1980).

A word on the vocabulary of class—both mine and that of santaneros—is appropriate here. "Popular class" is a term borrowed from the Latin American political vocabulary (*clase popular,* sometimes in the plural form: *clases populares*) and broadly includes peasants, proletarians, and the urban poor, the latter two categories partially, though not always wholly, synonymous. The popular class occupies society's most subordinate social, economic, and political positions (Cotler 1989; Galin, et al. 1986; Lancaster 1988a, 28–32). As we shall see, in santaneros' usage, "class" (*clase*) incorporates both social and economic stratification, combining notions of wealth, status, social honor, and other criteria of rank. I will use the term "class" in the same way.

I will also collectively call the santaneros the "popular class" in order to suggest the subordinate social, economic, and political standing that they attribute to themselves. Where "popular class" usually suggests "the lowest class," however, santaneros often distinguish themselves from "the lower class" (*la clase baja*) below them. Thus, santaneros call themselves the "middle class" (*la clase media*), "the poor" (*los pobres*), "the people" (*el pueblo*) or, less frequently, *la clase baja,* all but the last being conceptually opposed to both la clase baja and "the rich" (*los ricos*) or "the upper class" (*la clase alta*). As being black is considered tantamount to being de clase baja (lower class), employing this notion of blackness creates pressure for santaneros to conform to class norms. As we shall see, the dominant notion of class identity among santaneros invokes gender norms, the violation of which tends to define the violator as black. Thus, the interrelation of class and gender norms helps construct blackness as the inferior category par excellence.

Class and Gender Identity in Santa Ana

"Respectable" santaneros (*los respetables, los que respetan, los de respeto*) support the class, gender, and race identities dominant in Santa Ana. In these people's view, the pursuit of self-interest at the expense of respect and solidarity is a major reason for what they see as the collapse of a formerly orderly social world. Self-interested action is evidence of "corruption" (*descorrompimiento, corrupción*), causing "disorder" (*desorden*) because it disrupts the exchange of obligations between subordinates and superordinates upon which order—class, gender, and age hierarchies—was based.

Questions of class identity are particularly acute for santaneros right now. Cartagena, a city of about one million people on Colombia's Caribbean coast, has undergone wrenching economic change in the past 20 years. Once a sleepy port, Cartagena now boasts a major petrochemical complex (Nichols 1973) and depends heavily on international tourism (Lemaitre 1983; Strassman 1982). The traditional commercial and cattle-ranching bourgeoisie has expanded into industry, running its varied enterprises along much more clearly capitalist lines than previously. Money from the marijuana and cocaine trades has also been funneled into the construction of expensive hotels and tourist enterprises; luxury apartments have sprung up to cater to a mixture of old elites and the new class whose wealth derives from the drug trade. At the same time, poor neighborhoods proliferate beyond the capacity of the city's already over-taxed public services network. Male unemployment and sub-employment have risen, women have increasingly sought work outside the home, and most people contend that real wages have declined.[3]

Most santaneros (especially older ones) talk of these changes as having undermined their formerly cordial and beneficial relationships with the rich. As employers of artisans and domestic servants, the wealthy purportedly paid good wages and, just as important, could be counted on to help economically in a crisis or to intervene with authorities on behalf of workers. Over and above strictly economic concerns, *patrones* (bosses) felt bound to employees by sentimental ties. In turn, workers (so the story goes) served the same *patrón* for years, linked by a sense of loyalty and affection. In short, most people claim that in the old days the wealthy placed meeting their economic and social obligations to the poor above narrow self-interest. These people consider fulfilling obligations a sign of being motivated by sentiment, solidarity, and respect.

In contrast, they say, today the rich have forsaken these paternalistic relations and instead seek only personal advantage. Santaneros use this image of the past to construct a class identity that contrasts the desire of the poor to help others, and to fulfill obligations to others, with the pursuit of individual gain by the rich. The poor see themselves as feeling (*condoliente*[4]), solidary (*solidario*), and respecting (*respetan*), and the rich as self-interested (*interesado*) and unfeeling (*indoliente*). As Rosa, a middle-aged housewife who used to work as a domestic servant, put it,

> The rich don't sympathize with the poor any more. A poor person sympathizes [*conduele*] with another poor person. You yourself are the one who patches things together with another poor person because . . . now the rich don't want you to work, now the rich don't want you to study, so that everyone will be in slavery—we've got slavery. So how does a poor person get by? With help from another poor person.

Or, she added, by stealing. Note that the selfishness of the rich causes division, not only between rich and poor, but among the poor themselves; santaneros are understandably more concerned about crime among the poor than about crime against the rich. Santaneros claim that the pursuit of self-interest by the rich extends to all domains of social life, including work, religious sentiment and practice, politics, celebration of the city's Independence and patron saint's day fiestas, marital decisions, and conjugal and filial relations.

The theme of self-interest is also central to santaneros' concepts of gender. Acts that contravene dominant definitions of manhood and womanhood violate popular class identity. According to "respectable" santaneros (that is, those who support this identity), self-interest also motivates young popular class men and women to challenge established gender ideals. The respectable sharply criticize young men who do not fulfill their obligations to support spouses and children and to help parents. Young men's selfishness generates discord, reversing the flow of traditional economic obligations: parents support their grown sons and women support their husbands. As Antonio, an older man, said,

> We [men] worked when we were little, selling kerosene, candy, and other things in the street. And what we earned was to buy rice, coconut, butter, for our parents. Now, if a young man works, he doesn't give anything to his parents, he spends the money on drugs or he eats it up. Before, one gave to one's parents, now one expects one's parents to give to one. . . . We've always first met our obligations to our women and children, whereas these young men would rather drink or take drugs than support their families.

Popular class masculine self-image exalts men's enjoyment of sensuous experience—drinking, dancing, sexual conquests—but only after a man has met his obligations to his family and to others (friends or creditors, for example) may he legitimately pursue enjoyment. Neither younger men nor wealthy men participate in this ideal, say respectable santaneros: younger men renege on commitments to their families, while the wealthy refuse to recognize any obligations to the poor and at the same time are insufficiently manly to resist their wives' attempts to curtail their enjoyment.

Young women who flout feminine ideals—particularly ideals of remaining virgins until, and monogamous within, marriage or common-law union, and avoiding male arenas and male activities—are said to act out of self-interest and to cause division. These women enter into sporadic or stable sexual relationships with men, purportedly in order to satisfy their sexual desires or in exchange for economic support, rather than out of "love" (*amor*). "Love" in this context means that a woman's courtship and marriage decisions are overseen by parents and are based on the latter's assessment of the man's character as well as of that of his family. According to the respectable, young women who pursue sex or money create conflict between themselves and their parents and lose reputation in the community's eyes.

The respectable at times blame young people's disrespect and lack of solidarity on the self-interest of the rich. As Antonio put it, "The crisis today is the fault of the rich, because for them money is the only thing that matters. . . . The rich are guilty—they oblige people to become thieves. Corruption comes from the top and works its way down [*La corrupción viene de arriba para abajo*]." At other times, however, some respectable people (like Antonio) lay the blame for young popular class people's transgression of proper behavior squarely on the young people themselves, without invoking mitigating factors. "The world today is corrupt [*descorrompido*] because young people don't respect," one older woman said. "The children hit the mother, the father—one doesn't know who's the mother, who's the father, who's the child."[5]

What the respectable lament, in part, is that challenges to this order are supposedly more acute than in the past, and that they are increasingly difficult to contain. We should also keep in mind that the challenges threaten to keep older men from enjoying the authority that they thought would be rightfully theirs with age, as the reference to children hitting parents indicates. This is one reason why older men's talk so notably revolves around the theme of self-interest and respectability. Older people in general most actively promote the notion that respectability characterized both class and gender behavior in the old days. Because older people grew up during that mythical time, they can convincingly represent themselves as respectable while claiming that relatively few young people today have achieved this status. I would also stress, however, that most younger respectable people share their elders' view of the past.

At the same time, the notions of respect and solidarity so central to popular class identity are most easily realized by men, especially by older men. The acts that are publicly recognized as solidary are those that are considered the men's province and, fittingly, take place in the street, the preeminent male space. Such acts include labor exchange in house building and repair, sharing of information on employment and entrepeneurial opportunities, loans, reciprocity in drinking, contributing ingredients and labor to the cooking of improvised soups as part of drinking bouts, and the rivalry and camaraderie of sports and board games.

In contrast, respectable women concern themselves primarily with domestic duties, avoiding male spaces and activities. Respectable santaneros charge that a woman who willingly strays beyond the physical and social constraints of the household destroys the delicate ties of obligation between herself and her husband, parents, and children. "Women in (or of) the street," as in the common phrase, are variously accused of neglecting their duties, gossiping, performing witchcraft, and stealing other women's husbands, all of which challenge social order by defying male authority and violating norms for women's conduct. For example, one young woman noted with disapproval that women use witchcraft "to dominate [*dominar*] the man, to make it so the woman can be with a lot of men, go to dances, and leave the man at home like an old rag." (Indeed, the respectable may consider that a woman "*in* the street" passes into the category of a "woman *of* the street," meaning a "whore," if they suspect her of illicit sexual relations.) In respecting, women isolate themselves from the spaces and activities in which the respectable recognize solidarity as being primarily constructed, thereby reinforcing their circumscription to the domestic realm in a dependent relation to men (husbands, fathers, grown sons).

Women's gatherings in the street are rare and socially disapproved. Of course, women do get together informally, for example, while making purchases at the neighborhood stores. This is an important means for women to talk among themselves without giving the appearance of meeting for meeting's sake, as women go to the store in the line of domestic duty. Yet these encounters are not recognized as acts constructing solidarity, since women feel the need to mask the sociality of the occasion with the justification of domestic necessity. Failure to do so would open them to charges of gossiping. The dominant definition of the situation excludes even these acts of women's sharing (if only conversation) from the conceptual domain of solidarity. Indeed, women's actions that verge on gossip are seen to threaten solidarity. The same concerns motivate respectable women to avoid spending much time in other women's homes. Women commonly say that they only go to someone else's house when there is a *novedad,* something noteworthy, like an illness or a death, implying that women normally do not visit one another's homes.

Restrictions on women's movements and injunctions against their gathering reduce the opportunities for women to share food or drink. While women are never supposed to share alcohol like men, the Holy Week tradition of preparing desserts for neighbors does provide a chance for women to share food. Ironically, this publicly sanctioned act of women's food-sharing is fraught with danger: many santaneros (including women) claim that they accept but do not eat female neighbors' desserts for fear that the desserts bear witchcraft material.

Younger men are also disadvantaged in this system as it is held that they are, in general, self-interested and disrespectful, not solidary. The respectable partly attribute this alleged stance to the susceptibility of younger men to the ideology of self-interest advanced by the wealthy. At the same time, the respectable also recognize that younger men have less opportunity to realize solidarity because their economic situation is by and large more precarious than older men's as a result of recent economic crises; this makes it more difficult for them to participate as equals in solidary relations. In sum, popular class emphasis on what santaneros recognize as solidarity, sentiment, and respect privileges men's interests over women's, and older men's over younger men's, as in each case the dominant group is in a better position to embody or realize these characteristics. Enforcing class norms therefore also effectively shores up men's (and, in particular, older men's) authority.

As we will see, one who breaks with dominant notions of gender not only violates class identity but is considered to be—or to be like—a "black" (*un negro*), a "lower-class person" (*una persona de clase baja*), or a "*champetudo*" (see ensuing discussion). Respectable people's use of these three labels is one means of countering what they feel is an assault on a supposedly harmonious social order: to avoid being considered a bad man or woman, or a lower-class person, one must act like a non-*negro*. Likewise, to avoid being called "*negro,*" which most santaneros consider a stigma, one must adhere to gender norms, which are simultaneously class norms.

Before dealing in detail with race and its connection with class and gender, it is important to discuss briefly the fieldwork situation. Although I eventually met and interacted with a wide range of santaneros, my best friends and informants tended to be older men who considered themselves respectable. Most men and women, of all ages, regard the prevailing sexual division of labor and space as desirable, and their sense of propriety, their "respectability" as men and women, rests on upholding this division. This social and spatial segregation is intended to make it difficult for men outside the household to gain access to the household's women, and in general I found it effectively enforced. Though in some cases I feel that I managed to break down or elude this barrier quite well, especially where I was close to the male household head or where an older woman headed the household, in many others my presence was always somewhat awkward for all concerned.[6] Thus my field experience was skewed toward men: I was more easily included in male activities, I talked informally with men more than with women, and 44 of the 78 formal interviews I conducted were with men (17 individuals) as opposed to 30 interviews with 20 women.

Respectable people draw a sharp distinction between themselves and the disreputable, stigmatizing the latter in discourse that seems intended to keep the weaker within their own ranks from defecting. As it became increasingly clear to me during fieldwork that the issue of "respect" (*respeto*) was so crucial to understanding respectable santaneros' views of recent changes and current conflicts both within their class and vis-à-vis the dominant class, I decided that to seek disreputable friends and informants would jeopardize my standing with the respectable people with whom I had initially aligned myself. For example, had I begun talking with *viciosos* (drug users), the respectable would have been reluctant to accept me since they have staked their reputation on excluding and opposing viciosos and other disreputable people. Most cartageneros are aware of drug use among young North Americans, often blaming Colombia's drug problems on North American consumers' demands. Some santaneros, claiming to have witnessed drug use by North American tourists in Cartagena, tell lurid tales that reinforce the image of *gringos* as viciosos. For santaneros, at least initially and probably enduringly, my fair skin, education, and relative wealth made me much closer to the city's elite than to mainly darker-skinned and less educated popular class men. Given the popular view of both gringos and the young rich as viciosos, I was doubly prone to be seen as a potential if not actual vicioso. In light of this, I steered clear of viciosos. Similarly, I avoided associating with champetudos (most of who are also considered viciosos). Thus I met few people who considered themselves beyond the pale of respectability, though I was friendly with a number whom others regarded as borderline cases.

I consider the problem of access to women and the disreputable to have been less a limitation on "data collection" than an inevitable part of the positioning within fieldwork and, consequently, writing that confronts all social analysts (Abu-Lughod 1986; Clifford and Marcus 1986; Kondo 1990; R. Rosaldo 1989). I was subject to the same social pressures as others resident in Santa Ana, though to a lesser degree, and this obliged me to choose how I wanted others to view me. My account thus reflects, even as it analyzes, the social vision of respectable santaneros. In the conclusion I deal briefly with the consequences of this fact.

Race in Cartagena

Cartagena was a major slave entrepôt and the capital of a slave-holding province until emancipation in 1852 (Meisel Roca 1980). Sexual relations among Spaniards, Africans, and Indians produced a large population of mixed descent that, in turn, generated a complex system of social stratification based on ancestry, skin color, wealth, degree of "education" (*educación,* that is, "knowing how to act"), and slave versus free status for African-descended people (Juan and Ulloa 1978[1735], 40–42; Posada 1920[1883], 334–344). Today, the vast majority of cartageneros are (from a North American perspective) of noticeable African descent (Solaun and Kronus 1973).[7]

In Cartagena, the term "*blanco,*" white, seems originally to have referred to any Spaniard or person descended exclusively from Spaniards (Juan and Ulloa 1978[1735]; Posada 1920[1883]). By the beginning of the 20th century, however, "*blanco*" came to mean only a member of the dominant class. While this class was comprised mainly of light-skinned people of exclusively Spanish descent, some wealthy, darker-skinned individuals, particularly the illegitimate sons of *blanco* men with non-*blanca* women, had entered the dominant class and thus were labelled "*blancos.*" Older santaneros still sometimes refer to the rich as "*blancos*" and to the poor as "*negros.*" Younger people seldom use "*blanco*" and "*negro*" in this way, as class terms.

Most santaneros agree that "*blancos*" refers only to dominant class people, no matter their skin color, hair type, or facial features. By the same token, santaneros call a poor person "*claro*" (fair, light), rather than "*blanco,*" even if that person's skin color and other physical characteristics are typically "*blanco.*" As one young woman put it, "I'm *clara* [fair], but I'd be *blanca* if I had money. You can be *moreno* [brown], but if you've got money then you're *blanco.*"

"*Moreno*" is a category between *claro* and *negro*. (Other categories exist, but they are less frequently used than those discussed here.[8]) Morenos are said to have lighter skin, straighter hair, thinner noses and lips, and higher cheekbones than *negros*. However, the decisive criterion is often behavioral rather than phenotypical: people called moreno rather than *negro* are considered to act more in accord with class and gender norms. For example, during a conversation with two teenaged girls who considered themselves morenas, the topic of boyfriends came up. Lupe teased her cousin about having a *negro* boyfriend. The cousin bridled, disputing the charge. Lupe sat back in her chair and sighed, "I want to have a really white son [*un hijo blanquito*], with straight hair and blue eyes." "You'll have a fat, *negro* one with kinky hair," her cousin laughed. I asked them why people have such a quarrel with *negros*. "It's not that we have any quarrel," Lupe said, "but have you realized how they are? They walk around all disorderly [*desordenados*], they talk like this," and here she shouted, her voice "thick" (*gruesa,* or what North Americans might call "rude"), "and they're vulgar [*son vulgares*]. They don't sweet talk the girls in a good way, they . . ." She stopped. She and her cousin looked at each other and laughed. "They're *vulgar,*" Lupe said, leaving the content of their vulgarity to my imagination. Given the negative connotations of being considered *negro,* it is not surprising that nearly all santaneros self-identify as moreno or claro—even (or especially) those whose physical characteristics are, for santaneros, typically "*negro*."

Yet santaneros do not use race terms often. I believe that they are reluctant to use race terms in part because the terms carry a heavy emotional charge, as indicated above and as will become clearer below. This is consistent with santaneros' denial of racial discrimination in Cartagena. Nearly all santaneros claim that the poor do not discriminate racially, a sentiment that embodies santaneros' self-image as solidary. At the same time, most people argue that societywide discrimination is based on class rather than race, though nearly all agree that the elite informally bars blacks from the Navy and from residence in the city's wealthiest sector. Note that santaneros here again portray the wealthy as divisive.[9]

Santaneros also seem to avoid describing each other as *negro,* a tendency consistent with santaneros' self-definition as solidary. A person may have physically *negro* traits, and may be poor, but, unless known to "act like a *negro*" (or unless the speaker wants to imply this), that person will usually be called moreno. A brief consideration of the context of the conversation among Lupe, her cousin, and me, reveals something of the practical effect of explicit racial discourse, illustrating the reasons for its strategic though infrequent intervention in daily life.

Before our conversation, the three of us were sitting with Lupe's mother, Dalia, and her grandmother, Cándida, in the latter's yard when Aurelio arrived. Aurelio is a *carretillero,* a man who travels from neighborhood to neighborhood selling fruit and vegetables from a hand-drawn cart. While bantering with Cándida, Aurelio declared in jest that he was going to set up house (that is, enter into common-law union)[10] with Lupe. Cándida and the others laughed. "No way!" Cándida exclaimed. "Why would she set up house with you, you're so black!" "Never with a *negro,*" added Lupe. "If I came home with a *negro* my dad would kill me." It is important to point out that the women's negative evaluation of Aurelio's blackness also surely included his lowly occupation. Carretilleros are generally held to be the least educated, most vulgar men, and the job itself involves hard labor and meager earnings. Parents often admonish their sons about the necessity of studying so that they will not remain ignorant (*ignorantes*) and have to become carretilleros, while warning daughters that if they do not study or are otherwise disrespectful they will be fit only to marry carretilleros. In this case, Lupe's mother and grandmother clearly intended to reinforce the lesson—already stressed by her father—that she should not set up house with or marry a *negro*. Lupe's subsequent comments to her cousin and me indicate that she apparently accepts the lesson.[11] Thus, the older women mobilized a racial discourse in order to discourage Lupe from even contemplating a match that they deemed inappropriate at least in part on class grounds (that is, Aurelio's poverty and low social standing); Lupe's father is a small-time building contractor and her mother is a nurse.

In part, the women's disparagement of Aurelio's blackness also rested on the assumption that to be *negro* is to be ugly. As noted, santaneros generally avoid discussing blackness and claim not to discriminate racially. Indeed, santaneros can avoid using explicitly racial terms because their language contains an implicit racial hierarchy, with *negros* on the lowest rung. In particular, santaneros' descriptions of beauty define whiteness as pretty in opposition to blackness as ugly, all without recourse to explicitly racial terms. In most of the Spanish-speaking world (including Cartagena), *simpático* means "genial, likeable, nice"; it does not refer to physical appearance. In Cartagena, however, simpático also means "good-looking." Cartageneros' use of simpático in these two senses indicates that what is considered pleasing to another person is one's physical appearance. Moreover, in Cartagena to be simpático means to have features associated with Europeans or *blancos:* a straight nose, thin lips, and high cheekbones. For cartageneros, an ugly person has a flat nose, thick lips, and low cheekbones, all features that santaneros associate with African or *negro* ancestry. In Cartagena, *maluco* is the most commonly used word for "ugly." In most of the Spanish-speaking world, including Cartagena, maluco also means "slightly sick" or "indisposed" and sometimes connotes a feeling of regret or mild shame for having disappointed or upset someone. Thus to be ugly in Cartagena is to be more *negro* than *blanco,* and to feel slightly sick or ashamed. To be good-looking is to be more *blanco* than *negro,* and to be pleasing to others.

Another pair of terms describe the same opposition. The features of *una persona simpática* are also said to be "*finas*" (fine). "Fine" in cartagenero Spanish also refers to "refinement" or "exquisiteness." In contrast, the features of *una persona maluca* are "*ordinarias*" (ordinary), having the sense of "common," "coarse," "vulgar." These two terms for physical appearance also encode a covert color/class component because the rich/whites are associated with both physical and spiritual refinement (the latter understood as "greater culture"), while the poor and *negros* are said to be more "common" in both aspects. Thus the language of physical appearance in Cartagena exalts European/*blanco* standards of taste while denigrating those of non-European origin.[12]

La champeta

More crucial, santaneros discriminate racially by using the terms "*champetudo*" and "*clase baja*" (lower class) as euphemisms for "*negro.*" Santaneros use all three labels to refer to people who violate dominant gender and class ideals.

La música champeta or *champetuda* (a pejorative form of the word *champeta*) is African and African-influenced dance music from the non-Spanish-speaking Caribbean and even North America. This music began arriving in Cartagena in the 1960s and is currently popular among poor youth. Non-Spanish lyrics (commonly thought to be "African") and a good dance beat are the main criteria for calling a song champeta.[13] The music gets its name from the "champeta," a Bowie-shaped kitchen knife about a foot long. Cartageneros named the music "champeta" because those who dance to it are reputed to fight frequently at dances, and the easily concealed champeta was (and is) a favorite dance floor weapon. I say "easily concealed" because male champetudos typically dress in baggy pants and shirts—a style the respectable consider "outlandish" (*estrafalario*), "scandalous" (*escandaloso*), and "disorderly" (*desordenado*).

Dances featuring champeta are said to attract blacks. The respectable hold that champeta dancers transgress gender ideals. Young men reportedly drink to excess, use drugs, and provoke bloody fights, all of which, the respectable allege, indicates that they pursue self-interest at the expense of respect. The respectable complain that young men waste money on these disreputable and dangerous entertainments instead of supporting their spouses and children and helping elderly or indigent parents. Moreover, the frequent fights at the dances are viewed as proof of these men's divisiveness.

Young women who attend these dances are accused of sexual promiscuity. First, the music and the dance steps are said to be sexually provocative. As one young man told me, "Take a look and see if that's dancing or if it's something else," the "something else" being "making love with your clothes on." Second, the presence of alcohol and drugs is thought to lead women to premarital or extramarital sex, which most respectable santaneros consider morally reprehensible for women. Finally, women's reputations suffer by their being present at these dances because they enter a male space without the protection of parents or brothers; these dances are considered part of the street, which is the quintessentially male space. Women who attend the dances, and who therefore are supposedly promiscuous, are thought to act out of self-interest—the desire for sex—instead of "respect" (that is, concern for their standing as reputable women). Typical is the following remark by a young man: "Those women are plebeian, bandits [*bandidas,* a euphemism for "whores"]—no decent woman would go to one of those dances." Indeed, the respectable claim that some *champetudas* (women who dance to la música champeta) commit the worst offense of which a woman is capable: neglecting her children.

Some respectable people equate *negros* with champetudos (both male and female). Most santaneros, however, simply describe *negros* and champetudos in identical terms, implying an equivalence between the two. A young friend of mine, Rogelio, who considered himself moreno and respectable, illustrated how santaneros equate "*negros*" and "champetudos" in describing *negros:* "They dress scandalously [*escandalosos*], they wear a red shirt, blue pants, green shoes. And they dance all disorderly [*desordenados*]—they *are* disorderly. And they talk 'thick' [*grueso*]. They're vulgar, champetudo. The moreno dances cool because he carries the rhythm in his blood, but when a *negro* comes and dances, shit, you know there's going to be a fight."

The respectable male and female champetudos' actions repudiate the respect upon which social order, and thus men's and elders' authority, is based. At the same time, anyone who violates gender norms may now be branded "champetudo," regardless of whether the violation in question involves dancing to champeta. Thus, a young man who is irresponsible toward his family is called champetudo, while a woman who others think spends too much time in the street or in men's company, or who is otherwise "disrespectful," is called champetuda. For example, when Rosa's daughter-in-law Gloria insulted her, Rosa called Gloria a champetuda, impugning her reputation by implying that only a champetuda would be so disrespectful as to insult her mother-in-law. In short, violating dominant conceptions of proper manhood and womanhood is to act like a champetudo, which in turn is to act like a *negro*. Class and gender attributes are central to the definition of blackness. Labeling all these transgressors "champetudos" is one way of repelling the perceived attack on social order, since the label evokes powerfully stigmatizing racial terms without explicitly specifying them.

Such stigmatizing has tangible effects. Many young women try to avoid being called champetudas by staying away from champeta dances, thereby ensuring that they spend little time in the street, and by otherwise fulfilling the role of dutiful daughter or wife. The respectable are particularly sensitive to the implications that champetuda behavior can have for daughters, arguing that champetudas' actions ultimately prevent them from keeping their spouses. Indeed, calling Gloria a champetuda was part of Rosa's and her husband's strategy for persuading their son to break up with Gloria. Similarly, parents attempt to discourage champetudo tendencies in sons by spending much time and energy criticizing champetudo music, dance, and behavioral dispositions. Thus, the respectable use the fear of being labeled "champetudo" to induce conformity to dominant gender, class, and, thus, race identities.

I would also point out that calling the music "champeta," and the disrespectable and disorderly "champetudos," underlines the notion that champetudos are *not* solidary with their classmates, but are instead divisive: the words "champeta" and "champetudo" draw attention to the knife (*la champeta*), which is a metonym for violence. Classifying the music as "African" also links blackness to violence and divisiveness and so suggests that blackness contradicts popular class identity. In turn, blackness and being champetudo are strongly identified because santaneros consider champeta to be "African" music.

Ironically, the assault of the respectable on the champetudo phenomenon discredits an apparently budding Afro-Colombian cultural movement. In a context in which blackness and African heritage are consistently belittled, champetudos defiantly celebrate "African" music. In contrast, the city's white elite derives its musical and dance tastes largely from white Anglo-American rock. English in Cartagena is the language of cultural cachet and economic dominance, a link with the desired world of hipness to which many young cartageneros aspire, but to which only the wealthy have access, through such resources as vacations in Miami, bilingual schools, and secondary studies in the United States.[14]

Champetudo music confounds the cultural and linguistic hierarchy, proclaiming that what is *really* cool is "African" and thus unintelligible to the elite—but not to the champetudos, who sing the champeta tunes phonetically. (In a fitting irony, some of the tunes they "sing" are in English.) Respectable santaneros occupy a cultural middle ground, preferring regional Spanish-language musical varieties such as *vallenato* and *salsa*. In putting down the champetudos, then, the respectable attempt to neutralize a cultural force that champions "Africanness," blackness, in opposition to European, white standards of taste. (The elite, in different ways, also directly opposes the champetudos.) Indeed, for respectable popular class people the champetudo phenomenon, with its alternative vision of gender, work, generational relations, and culture, represents a bid to redefine popular class identity in terms much "blacker" or more African-identified than the respectable find palatable. The dominant way of defining popular class identity, then, excludes those who would exalt blackness. Again, it is worth stressing that this notion of popular class identity, like the gender and race concepts underwriting it, reinforces the authority of men over women and of older men over younger men.

The lower class

Santaneros also use the same qualities that stigmatize *negros* and champetudos to construct a "lower class" beneath their own class. Thus I heard desperately poor people talk of themselves as "middle class" while calling "lower class" others who were better off economically but who did not act from respect. For example, a young woman who considers herself morena and middle class claimed that the poor are not necessarily "lower class." In contrast to the "middle class," the "lower class" is *cochina* (dirty, piggish), *puerca* (again, dirty, piggish), and *desordenado* (disorderly). The example she cited—lower class women's failure to maintain clean, orderly homes—implies that these women do not do their housework because they are outside the home, meddling in other people's affairs, perhaps being unfaithful to their spouses, or using witchcraft ("piggish," puerca, implies both uncleanliness and the use of witchcraft). Abandoning domestic duties and entering the world of the street are considered actions based on self-interest, creating discord between spouses and between neighbors. In one act, then, these women show themselves to fail both as women and as "middle class" people: they are labeled "bad" women and "de clase baja."

Others more directly describe "lower-class" people as disorderly and quarrelsome (*peleoneros, problematico*), often citing the champetudos as a prime example. The president of the neighborhood council, a man in his early 70s, told me that when la música champeta first arrived in Cartagena it was greeted with enthusiasm by "low class people": "The majority of the people who went to those [champetudo] dances were very low class guys [*tipos de muy baja clase*]. . . . That attracts very low class people. So fights started, deaths, stabbings."[15] To anticipate my argument below, I quote a young man on the same subject: "La champeta began as music for lower class people [*de clase baja*] . . . and it continues to be [in the eyes of the rich and of respectable santaneros alike] the music of the low [*del bajo*], the poor person [*el pobretón*], those without culture [*sin cultura*]."

Class, gender, and racial identities are based on the opposition of respect, solidarity, and sentiment to/self-interest and divisiveness. Thus, when santaneros invoke any one identity, they necessarily evoke the others. To label people *"de clase baja," "champetudos,"* or *"negros"*—nearly synonymous terms—is a way of calling them violators of normative class and gender identities alike and of repelling the challenge that violators' actions represents to the status quo of male (and especially older male) domination of popular class life.

Race: symbol of class or irreducible category?

In arguing that class, gender, and racial identities are mutually constructed, have I reduced race to a symbol of class difference, as Verena Martinez-Alier ([1974]1989) did for 19th-century Cuba? Or is there a core meaning to race, something irreducible to other categories such as gender and class? These two positions are in fact not mutually exclusive. Martinez-Alier maintained that race discourse both masked and implied class differences, as a slaveholding elite tried to preserve the association between blackness and servile labor. I have demonstrated the converse, namely, that talk about class implies racial difference.[16] Nevertheless, as in Cuba, the negative qualities that santaneros generally consider inherent to *negros* partially serve to justify class domination. Because lower class people share the same characteristics as *negros,* for lower class people these characteristics acquire an aura of immutability that defines—and helps maintain—their subordinate position. At the same time, santaneros associate blackness with allegedly inherent characteristics that manifest themselves in certain types of action. From their persective, race is not reducible to other categories.

What I am arguing is that santaneros naturalize difference: santaneros see *negros,* champetudos, and la clase baja as naturally rather than culturally determined: their actions flow from (and are expressed in) their physical makeup. This notion of the natural as determining the three overlapping identities is also opposed to the cultural in another way: *incultura,* lack of culture, is imputed to *negros,* champetudos, and the lower class, while *cultura* is held as the hallmark of respectability—of people who are middle (or upper) class, moreno (or claro or *blanco*), and not champetudos. "Culture" here means knowing how to act appropriately.

For santaneros, what distinguishes the cultural from the natural is the capacity to control one's desires, channeling them toward the collective good. Those with the most cultura, those who know how to act, receive recognition as such because they are seen to act out of solidarity, sentiment, or respect—that is, out of obligations toward others—rather than out of self-interest.[17] *Negro,* champetudo, and lower class men have certain characteristics that the respectable admire and that are part of the popular class male self-image, such as physical strength and sexual potency. Like their female counterparts, however, these men's putative inability to harness their desires to serve others and thus produce social order gives the respectable license to consider them naturally determined and to consider them ignorant of the correct ways to act.

The use of animal images to portray blacks is an especially important means for santaneros to deploy this contrast between culture and nature. This practice is most evident when discussing *palenqueros,* who occupy the very bottom of the social hierarchy in Cartagena. Palenqueros are natives of the village of el Palenque de San Basilio, a settlement founded by runaway slaves in the 17th century. Long isolated from the outside world in an inaccessible area only 70 kilometers from Cartagena, the palenqueros developed a Bantu-Iberian creole language (called *palenquero*), still spoken by older palenqueros, and they retain certain practices, especially in funerals and marriages, that distinguish them from the surrounding coastal culture (Arrazola 1970; Friedemann [1979]1987; Friedemann and Patino 1983). Cartagena has a large palenquero community, part of which lives on the edge of Santa Ana; the neighborhood also has a fair number of palenqueros residing in its less desirable, hilly sections. Santaneros seem more comfortable in talking about palenqueros as blacks than about non-palenqueros as blacks, probably because palenqueros are ethnically distinct, thus lessening the risk of offending interlocutors sensitive to being considered *negros*. At the same time, for santaneros, palenqueros are the archetypal *negros:* blackness is defined in terms of approximation to the palenquero pole of the racial spectrum.[18]

My friend Rogelio, who described *negros* in the same terms as champetudos, provided a good example of the "animalization" or "naturalization" of palenqueros. Rogelio likened palenqueros to donkeys:

> They eat a ton, whole pots of rice with cassava and plantain and potato [the latter three are foods said to confer physical strength and sexual potency]. But they also work more, they're like donkeys. Even the women, they carry those basins of bananas on their heads [to sell], and those things are heavy. And the men are well-endowed, they've got big pricks; the women are also voluminous. That's why you don't see a palenquero take up with a woman from here, because he'd do her a lot of damage.

Palenqueros' physical excesses mark them as being closer to the animal than to the human world. Because they exaggerate masculine qualities (sexual potency, work capacity, healthy appetite), male palenqueros are perceived as dangerous (their huge sexual organs do damage to non-palenquera women) and thus are banished to the animal kingdom, where they may be both admired and despised but in any case not treated as equals. Indeed, santaneros condemn palenqueros for their purported stupidity ("donkey" is also commonly used as a synonym for "stupid"), ignorance, lack of culture, laziness, and violence, claiming that palenquero youths are particularly disrespectful toward parents and irresponsible toward spouses.[19]

Palenquero youths are also held to be champetudos. Aside from the negative characteristics we have already seen associated with champetudos, I should point out that people also use animal imagery to talk of champetudos in general. Thus, one young man who liked champeta but who did not consider himself a champetudo complained that people "want to put [the champetudo] down as if he were a dog, they want to put one down on the ground [for being] an uncultured guy," and potentially a *ratero* (thief, from the word "rat").

Respectable santaneros also use animal metaphors to vilify poor people who renege on the obligations of class solidarity and respect for gender norms. For instance, the respectable delighted in the downfall of a poor man who struck it rich and then abandoned his poor friends, claiming that he "died like a dog" in poverty and isolation. And, as I have mentioned, women who neglect their domestic obligations are labelled *puercas*, pigs, while sexually promiscuous women are frequently called *perras*, female dogs, a synonym for "whores."[20]

The stress on animal qualities highlights the body, including the body's packaging. Discourse on what I will call "the low"—that is, on *negros*, champetudos, and the lower class—is about physicality, about presence and appearance. This is evident in descriptions of genital size and the "coarseness" (*lo ordinario*) of blacks' bodies and faces, as well as in portrayals of blacks and champetudos as "disorderly" (*desordenados*) in appearance, uncombed and unkempt, "extravagant" (*extravagantes*) or "outlandish" (*estrafalarios*) in dress, wearing baggy clothes to accommodate weapons that proclaim their aggressive disposition. For the male champetudo, baggy clothing is a sartorial reminder of the bellicose origins of his very name. His female partner equals him in (supposedly) exhibiting her intentions in her dress: she is said to sport sexually provocative clothing, her very presence disordering the spatial and social boundaries of female propriety. Indeed, by the semiotics of their bodies and dress, the effect, if not the intent, of "the low" is to disorder the gender and class discourses dominant within the popular class.

Dance is at the center of discourse on "the low." Here, again, respectable santaneros associate the exaltation of the body and sexuality in dance by "the low" with sexual impropriety, and thus with moral and social disorder. This link has deep roots in Cartagena; throughout the colonial period, church officials were scandalized by the "lascivious" dances that popular class people held (Bensusan 1984). The threat from disorderly, dark lower class bodies and sexuality is grave enough for respectable people to equate them with social and moral chaos, while banishing these bodies' owners to the lowest level of the social hierarchy.

The physicality of "the low's" is accentuated by their reputed inarticulateness. As Antonio claimed, "people of low culture don't understand things with words but with violent deeds. . . . They swell with pride when they take that determination to say certain barbarities to others who don't deserve it because they lack culture, they don't have the facility with words to convince a person of this or that and so they do everything by force, they say very ugly words to goad you to get on their level." The opposite of physical force or rude words is verbal ability. Knowing "how to express oneself" is considered an admirable quality, one that demonstrates cultura.[21]

Most santaneros arrange the universe of capable speakers in a hierarchy. Not surprisingly, santaneros believe that the rich are better able to express themselves verbally than are the poor, while poor men stand above poor women. For instance, Antonio discouraged me from interviewing his common-law wife by claiming that "she doesn't know how to express herself." Though his real reasons may have been different (perhaps she would have expressed herself only too well), it is telling that he seized upon what he probably assumed was my acquired knowledge of this hierarchy of speakers. Santaneros say that compared with cartageneros, and with coastal dwellers in general, the *cachacos* (light-skinned inhabitants of Colombia's interior) speak "better Spanish," that is, they are able to express themselves more clearly. The Spanish themselves occupy a higher position, while English speakers as a whole sit at the top of the heap as the possessors of what santaneros call a "more developed culture."

We have seen that some santaneros hold *negros,* like the poor, to be less articulate than other people: they talk "thickly" (*grueso*) (or have "thick," coarse voices) and are vulgar in speech. *Negros* are thus located below the poor in general in the linguistic hierarchy. Palenqueros are considered to be at the lowest end of the scale, both for speaking "poor" Spanish ("*hablan mal el español*"), as santaneros have it, and for speaking palenquero, which santaneros tellingly label "African."[22] The linguistic peculiarities of champeta music further align the champetudos with the inarticulate: champeta songs are unintelligible to nearly all cartageneros since the words are not in Spanish but in "African." Most respectable santaneros, particularly older ones, complain that no one can even understand the words to the champeta songs. What really irritates the respectable, I think, is that la champeta extols inarticulateness (or an alternative articulateness) by deliberately seizing on songs whose words are unintelligible, and thus announces dance, with its sexual connotations, as the songs' motivation. To like champeta is, in a sense, to drop any pretense to an interest in lyrics and, instead, to exalt body movement for its own sake or as an incitement to sex. To celebrate the body and disdain verbal intelligibility is to carry popular class masculine self-image to an unacceptable extreme that the respectable handle by dehumanizing the offenders, symbolically locking them away in an inferior social status—"the natural," "the animal," "the uncultured," "the low." Women's celebration of the body and sexuality sparks a similar reaction: champetuda women are considered *perras,* female dogs, that is, "whores." Again, the champetudos' uncultured, animal-like, gender- and class-transgressing qualities are coded as black because (among other things) champeta is considered "African" music.

Blackness appears as the supreme category of "naturalness" in Cartagena because of the historical stereotype of Africans as bearers of a less-developed culture and as therefore driven by their passions rather than by considerations of social good (Friedemann 1984, 512–15).

A recent incident dramatizes the persistence of this association. A newspaper reporter described the common people's participation in the main parade of the city's independence festivities in 1988 as "a demonstration of the worst lack of culture and lack of respect . . . putting us at the level of some African tribe or at the lowest rung of the stone age," as something certainly not characteristic of "civilized places" (*El Universal* 1988b, 6).[23]

In this sense, race is irreducible: origins or physical traits are thought to cause certain behaviors. African origin and blackness are equated with the uncultured, the barely human. At the same time, blackness also symbolizes class standing, not because of its association with slavery (as Martinez-Alier demonstrated for 19th-century Cuba), but because blackness acts as the source of naturalized meanings for describing the champetudos and la clase baja, providing the language in which to cast them as uncultured animals and thus implying that they are naturally suited to occupy their low social position.

Nonetheless, while santaneros endow blackness with essential, inherited characteristics, my analysis shows that they also acknowledge that it is socially constructed (at least for non-palenqueros): blackness depends to a large degree on what one does, not what one is. Yet being called *negro* on the basis of what one does tends to slide into being considered *negro* on the basis of what one is. This occurs precisely because respectable santaneros see the behavioral aspects of blackness as naturally rather than socially determined. For the respectable, what makes an act typical of blackness is that it is evidence of motivation by self-interest rather than by the social good, by one's innate passions rather than by socially approved norms. It is an act more typical of an animal than a human, of those closer to nature than of those closer to culture.

Conclusion

Much recent academic literature has argued that analysts, political actors, and ordinary citizens have often minimized the racial discrimination against blacks in Spanish America by privileging the class dimension of blacks' oppression (Moore 1988; Wade 1985; Whitten [1974]1986; Wright 1990). To understand this racial discrimination, I suggest we must examine the sustaining dynamics of racism in these societies as well as the content of the racial categories themselves. To do this means looking not only at larger economic and political inequalities based on race but also at how race intersects with other social identities, particularly class and gender, in everyday life. The nonconflictual surface impression of race relations that scholars of the area have often noted (Rout 1976; Solaun and Kronus 1973; Wade 1989) demands that we look for racial politics in novel areas. As I have shown, assertions of an oppositional popular class identity are also statements about gender and racial identity. In other words, race is embedded in class and gender discourse. We have found race (and gender) where others see only class.

Thus, the kind of symbolic analysis attempted here can help to expose otherwise opaque connections among different dimensions of inequality. In particular, close attention to everyday discourse reveals how language embodies the normative ordering of social relations and identities. Santaneros' language suggests that the interdependence of class, race, and gender identities and inequalities relies crucially on the naturalization of difference, a powerful means for immobilizing social arrangements and individual subjectivities (Bourdieu 1977; Connell 1987, 85–87; Stolcke 1981).

As feminist scholars have recently pointed out (Cinsburg and Tsing 1990; M. Rosaldo 1980; Sacks 1989; Yanagisako and Collier 1987), this endeavor necessitates viewing the creation of any given social identity as occurring through relationships in diverse areas of life, not merely in those arenas that folk and academic wisdom have privileged as the production site for that identity. Thus, for example, we have seen that santaneros will call a woman "lower class" rather than "middle class," not because of her wealth or her relation to the means of production alone, but because of gender-linked qualities such as her reputation for being a responsible housekeeper and a sexually faithful spouse. In much the same way, race is partially determined by conformity to class and gender norms. In Cartagena, the connections between race, class, and gender cannot be ignored: popular class people's use of racial terms relies on and enforces normative class and gender identities, just as those who assert an oppositional class identity and advocate gender norms supporting it thereby reinforce the notion that to be *negro* is to be socially inferior.

I have also shown that understanding gender involves an examination of both masculinity and femininity and of how people think about and enact masculinity in relation to femininity and to competing masculinities; the converse, of course, holds for femininity. Thus, the notion of masculinity at the center of normative popular class identity is constructed not only in opposition to femininity but also in opposition to competing masculinities—namely, those of *negros*, champetudos, and lower class men, and that of rich men (who are more "feminine" because they are self-interested and because their wives restrict their enjoyment of drinking, dancing, and sexual conquests). In this way, the analysis avoids the tendency of some literature either to ignore masculinity or, what amounts to the same thing, to assume that it is stable and homogeneous. Moreover, I have pointed out that a generational dimension is crucial to how people form their class and gender identities: older santaneros have succeeded in convincing others that their conceptions of the past should serve as the measure for the notions of respectability and solidarity at the heart of these identities, notions that those labeled "*negro*," "champetudo," and "lower class" challenge.

In this way, the particular configuration of class, gender, and race depicted here supports ways of being that tend to legitimate older people's authority, particularly that of older men, as well as of men in general. As I have argued, privileging this particular form of popular class identity also underwrites men's authority over women by isolating them socially and maintaining the expectation that women be dependent on men. Like certain nationalist (Asad 1990; Dominguez 1989; Mosse 1985; R. Rosaldo 1989), working class (Joan Scott 1988), feminist (Moraga and Anzaldua 1981; Pratt 1984), and philosophical (Fraser and Nicholson 1990; Wittig 1980) discourses that represent sectional interests as general ones, santaneros' discourse of class identity subordinates part of the group it purports to represent, namely, women and anyone who challenges gender norms or who celebrates blackness. To paraphrase James Scott (1985), if the success of a system of domination can be measured by the degree to which members of the subordinate classes exploit and oppress one another, the system in Cartagena works admirably. We have seen that the system's racial dimension is crucial to its operation.

The success of the strategy of the respectable, whether conscious or not, to meet challenges from "the low," and thus to preserve their own position, relies partly on their ability to define the standards and boundaries of class, race, and gender identities. One important means of achieving this is by excluding the voices of "the low" from debate as much as possible while roundly condemning their actions. The respectable attempt to force "the low" into silence by proscribing contact with them. Of course, social isolation cannot be completely effective because these people remain sons and daughters, siblings, and neighbors. The price of fraternizing too much with these rebels and outcasts, however, is steep in a community in which personal identity is tightly linked to perceptions of the character of those with whom one socializes. "The low" therefore have fewer opportunities to present their case, and little chance of getting a sympathetic hearing when they do. The success of this containment strategy is also evident from the absence of these people's voices in the present article: by allowing the respectable to exert pressure on me, I conducted fieldwork mainly among the respectable and have thus presented *their* case largely without challenge. Imputing a contestatory impulse to the champetudos' actions does not remedy the exclusion of their views or of those of other disreputable groups. I hope, however, that my account of the injustices of this situation will somewhat compensate for the silence it has created.

NOTES

Acknowledgments. The fieldwork on which this article is based was carried out from October 1988 through March 1990 with support from the National Science Foundation (BSN 8812808). I would like to thank Deb Amory, Evie Blackwood, Don Brenneis, George Collier, Jane Collier, Ethan Goldings, Ted Hardy, Bill Maurer, Laura Nelson, and the *American Ethnologist's* anonymous reviewers for their comments and encouragement.

1. Throughout this paper I use *santaneros* and other Spanish masculine plural nouns to include both men and women. Use of the masculine singular noun will refer exclusively to men (or the masculine), while both the plural and singular feminine nouns will refer to women (or the feminine). Santaneros' names in the article are pseudonyms, as is "Santa Ana" itself.
2. Even some authors who clearly recognize the existence of racism virtually efface race relations by placing class struggle at the center of analysis (for example, Taussig 1980). Much recent work on Afro-Hispanic America deals almost exclusively with race (Friedemann and Arocha 1987; Moore 1988). Exceptions to these trends include works that take race as their primary focus while also treating it as part of a structure of inequality featuring class (Taussig 1987; Wade 1985, 1989; Whitten 1986[1974]).
3. Women's participation in the workforce rose from 26 percent in 1951 (DANE 1956) to 42 percent in 1988 (DANE 1988). Figures on male unemployment and subemployment are shown in Table 1. Berry (1980) shows that real wages for working class and self-employed people declined in the early 1970s. Urrutia (1985) argues that real wages as a whole rose in the late 1970s, though he concedes that they probably declined for the poor in the first half of the 1980s. The nation's largest labor federation, the Central Unitaria de Trabajadores, claims that purchasing

TABLE I ■ UNEMPLOYMENT AND SUBEMPLOYMENT IN CARTAGENA, 1973–88

	Male unemployment	Total unemployment	Male subemployment	Total subemployment
1973[a]	9.7%	15.6%	—	—
1983[b]	7.0%	12.7%	8.5%	8.7%
1988[c]	9.8%	13.3%	18.1%	15.7%

SOURCES: a = DANE 1973
b = DANE 1983
c = DANE 1988

power for working class Colombians declined 8 percent between 1986 and the end of 1988 (*Latin American Weekly Reports* 1988 5). (Other sources contend that during the 1980s, real wages increased slightly, or that their evolution has not been unidirectional. See, for example, Reyes Posada 1988.)

4. *Condoliente* comes from the verb *condoler*, meaning, literally, "to feel pain, hurt with." While it functions like the English "to sympathize," condoler has a stronger connotation of urgency and suffering because *doler* means "to feel pain, hurt."
5. Whether a respectable person blames the rich or young popular class people for the failures of these two groups depends largely on the context of discourse. These people's judgments are usually harsher when discussing a concrete case involving a young person more closely associated with the discussants' social circle. Conversely, the respectable tend to emphasize more strongly the larger political and economic determinants of young people's inappropriate actions when talking of young people or of political economy in more abstract terms.
6. It is worth pointing out that the restrictions are aimed at preventing relations between heterosexuals and/or heterosexual relations. Had I been perceived as gay, I might have had more contact with women, since gay men—being above suspicion of sexual interest in women—seem to enjoy freer access to women of other households. Local notions of male homosexuality are consistent with the literature on other Latin American societies (cf. Alonso and Koreck 1989; Lancaster 1988b).
7. There are no official census data on race in Colombia today; the government stopped including racial classifications in censuses after 1918 (Smith 1966), most probably in order to avoid the embarrassing (from an elite perspective) quantification of the country's non-European heritage (Arocha 1984; Pineda Camacho 1984: 206–211). This is not unusual in Latin America (Andrews 1991; Rout 1976).
8. These terms include *triqueño* ("wheat-colored"), *acanelado* ("cinnamon-colored"), *indio* ("Indian"), and *chino* ("Chinese"). I heard the first term used only once, the second slightly more often. The last two terms are synonyms and are almost exclusively used to refer to someone with straight hair, or to refer to the hair itself. The few people flatly called indios are indigenous people who have recently settled or currently live in Cartagena, such as the few indians from the Putumayo region who sell saints' portraits, sorcery counters, and love potions downtown and in the market. People with *pelo indio* (Indian hair) are subsumed under the other major categories: *claro, moreno*, and (less often) *negro.* In a 1973 study, Solaun and Kronus (1973:165) noted 62 different color terms used by people of different classes.

   I never heard anyone apply the term *mulato* or *mulata* to a person; the terms were frequently used in Cartagena, at least during the colonial era, and are still current throughout Spanish America. Interestingly, cartageneros call a type of large, brown bird common to the city *Mariamulata*, "Maria mulata." I believe that the bird probably gained this name both because of its light chocolate coloring and because of its presence in large numbers. While the "mulata" part of the name may allude to the color of the bird, it may also call attention to the bird's ubiquity, much as does "Maria," a very popular name in Cartagena. This reflects or reinforces the notion that those of intermediate color, being neither *blanco* nor *negro*, form the largest sector of the population. The bird's unspectacular appearance, which contrasts with the dazzling plumage of the wild birds that many cartageneros trap and cage, may also have influenced the choice of a name that connects color, judgments of physical beauty and ugliness, and social status. As we will see, santaneros associate beauty with *blancos'* physical features and ugliness with those of the *negro;* the moreno comes somewhere in between.
9. Santaneros rightly view the Navy as the branch of the armed forces most removed from combat. Santaneros believe that being barred from entering the Navy prevents *negros* from making a decent living in the service branch that affords the greatest physical safety (it seldom combats the guerrilla groups) and that is least oppressive to the poor (it is seldom involved in human rights abuses or in forced recruiting). This contrast between rich and poor regarding combat is made sharper by the fact that in Cartagena the

Navy shares a base with the Marines, the service branch that most poor cartageneros are obliged to enter and that suffers high combat casualties.

I should also point out that talk about society-wide racial discrimination usually emerged in casual conversation rather than in response to my direct questioning. This suggests that santaneros are conscious of more racial discrimination than they are disposed to acknowledge (at least to outsiders and at least in formal discussion of race).

10. *Comprometerse con,* literally, "commit himself with," Lupe.
11. Incidentally, Cándida also said, "I'm *negra,* but not like you," suggesting behavioral if not physical superiority vis-à-vis Aurelio.
12. The superiority of light skin is enacted each year during the National Beauty Contest held in Cartagena. The contestants, mainly from upper or upper-middle class families, are light-skinned, considerably more so than the majority of the residents of the departments they represent. Just before the independence festivities under whose auspices the National Beauty Contest takes place, the city holds its Popular Beauty Contest. The Popular Beauty Contest showcases morenas and *negras* from the city's poor and middle-class neighborhoods. Once an important event in the city's independence celebration, government and upper-class neglect in recent years has subordinated the status of the popular contest to that of the national one; the former is now a low-budget imitation of the latter. The popular contest's inferior status dramatizes the inferior race and class status of its participants. For the poor, new, self-interested attitudes on the part of the rich are evident in their promoting the National Beauty Contest and gradually marginalizing the events of the independence celebration—events that encourage popular participation: the notoriety and tourism attendant on the content enhances the prestige and wealth of the rich, as hosts to illustrious visitors and as organizers of this high-profile event and as owners of hotels and related tourist enterprises.
13. Paul Simon's song "I Know What I Know," from the *Graceland* album, was a popular champeta song in Cartagena in 1988. Cartageneros called it "The Turkey" because the female chorus sounded to them like a turkey gobbling. Because most champeta songs are pirated, arriving in Cartagena unencumbered by such niceties as liner notes, cartageneros invent their own names for songs.
14. English is spoken on Colombia's Caribbean islands of San Andres and Providencia, which at one time were British possessions. Despite being a short flight from Cartagena, the islands are perceived by the city's upper class as inferior culturally to both mainland Colombia and the United States, not least because the islands' "natives," descendants of African slaves, are *negros.* Indeed, most cartageneros do not consider the isleños' language to be English, but rather *patois,* a "dialect" inferior to English.
15. This man noted proudly that the council, composed of other (mostly older) men, had avoided bloodshed at Santa Ana's annual patron saint's day celebration by hiring a brass band rather than a disk jockey with a sound system. Most sound systems prominently feature champeta music in their repertoire and consequently attract "low class" and champetudo people. Brass bands attract mainly older people because their repertoire is based on songs native to the coastal region, the majority of which were hits before most champetudos were born.
16. Although origins and/or physical features were the primary markers of status during the initial colonial years, by the early 19th century the calculus of social classification also included wealth, occupation, level of "education" (*educación*—manners, knowing how to act), and legal status (slave versus free) (Posada 1920[1883] 334–343).
17. Curiously, santaneros consider the rich "cultured" (*cultos, de mucha cultura*) even though the latter renege on their obligations to the poor. I believe that the polysemy of the term "cultura" enables santaneros to remain untroubled by this seeming contradiction. Santaneros conceive of the rich as cultured because they are well-educated; they possess *una gran cultura,* as the phrase there goes. At the same time, the rich are held to be more cultured than the poor in the sense of being polite, knowing how to act effortlessly in most social situations. In the view of one older man, a staunch critic of the exploitativeness of the wealthy, even when the rich "discriminate" (on the basis of wealth and culture, not race, as he clarified) they do so "diplomatically."
18. Norman Whitten and Grace Schubert, working in the predominantly *negro* lowland town of San

Lorenzo, reported in the late 1960s and early 1970s, respectively, that transplanted highland *blancos* similarly de-humanized *negros*, also sometimes likening them to animals (Schubert 1981 572–577; Whitten 1986[1974] 192). Schubert's account suggests that most *negros* implicitly accepted the assertion that *blancos* are "more civilized" (*más civilizados*) than *negros*, despite the fact that most *negros* also explicitly reject the devaluation of blackness and the putative superiority of whiteness.

19. Michael Taussig's (1987) recent work on shamanism traces out this ambivalence—the mixture of fear, hate, and imputation of supranormal powers—toward colonized inferiors. Insofar as santaneros talk of non-palenquero *negros* in similar terms, this case suggests that such ambivalence can also exist when the inferior group is not a colonial or ethnic minority.
20. Cachacos, light-skinned natives of Colombia's interior departments, considered by cartageneros to be selfish, heartless, and hypocritical, are put down in a similar way in a popular saying: "There are three ungrateful animals: the cat, the pigeon, and the cachaco."
21. In the official story of the early 17th-century founding of Cartagena's Convent of La Popa, dedicated to la Virgen de la Candelaria, the colored masses' inarticulateness appears as a sign of their impiety. On the hill of La Popa, directly behind Santa Ana, a group of Indians worshipped the devil in the form of a goat. At the end of the "demonic ceremony" those present "danced a *dans macabre* [*sic*], at the end of which the Indians fell, exhausted with fatigue, in a confused mob, setting the place athunder with weird shouts and coarse monosyllables" (Delgado 1972[1972] 47). Under la Virgen de la Candelaria's injunction, the intrepid priest Fray Alonso de la Cruz Paredes expelled the Indians from la Popa in 1608 and constructed a church in la Virgen's honor. Of course, knowing the "word of God" constituted, and continues to constitute, the priesthood's primary claim to authority. This may be one reason that popular class anticlericalism centers on the disparity between priests' words and deeds.
22. Non-palenqueros' disparagement of the palenquero language has caused many young palenqueros residing outside Palenque to abandon the language altogether. Palenquero and non-palenquero intellectuals, as well as ordinary palenqueros, told me that, because of such stigmatization, most palenqueros born and raised outside Palenque today refuse to speak or even to learn palenquero.
23. The independence celebration is the highlight of Cartagena's festival season, providing popular entertainment and a chance for the city—as host to Colombia's National Beauty Contest—to represent itself to a domestic and international audience in attendance or watching on television. Given Cartagena's economic dependence on tourism, the city's display of cultura during the festivities is crucial to its image as a desirable tourist destination. Hence the heated debates in the local press and among the populace at large after the 1988 celebration, when rumors circulated that the National Beauty Contest organizers were threatening to move the contest site from Cartagena in 1990 if the public in 1989 was as disorderly as it had been the previous year.

Another journalist linked the "disorder" of recent parades to the uncontrollable passions of the champetudos. He saw the celebration in former years as

> an admirable expression of public-spiritedness . . . representing the friendly behavior of the entire participating community, founded on respect, social integration [of class, not race], decency, solidarity, and good manners, with which healthy coexistence—which is nothing more than the exercise of freedom up to the point at which the rights of others begin—is guaranteed. Contrary to those who think that the *fiestas* grant them the faculty to do whatever they please, in open stupidity constituting libertinism, the cause of so many outrages and misfortunes. And, precisely, to this is due the bitter experiences of the last few years, hurricane gusts of disorder and confusion, favorable to looting, destruction, and assaults on physical integrity and modesty. A reflection of a depressing spectacle, not apt for decent people but for the "*champe*" [champeta] multitudes of every condition, who converge with morbid hunger upon the banquet of their debauchery and frustrations, leaving in their clumsy actions the miserable imprint of a sickening vulgarity. [*El Universal* 1988a: 4]

References

Abu-Lughod, Lila 1986 Veiled Sentiments: Honor and Poetry in Bedouin Society. Berkeley: University of California Press.

Alonso, Ana M., and Maria Teresa Korek 1989 Silences: "Hispanics," AIDS, and Sexual Practices. Differences 1(1):1–24.

Andrews, George Reid 1991 Blacks and Whites in Sâo Paulo, Brazil, 1888–1988. Madison: University of Wisconsin Press.

Arocha, Jaime 1984 Antropologia en la historia de Colombia: Una vision. (Anthropology in the History of Colombia: One Vision.) *In* Un siglo de investigacion Social: Antropologia en Colombia. (A Century of Social Investigation: Anthropology in Colombia.) Jaime Arocha and Nina S. de Friedemann, eds. Pp. 27–130. Bogotá: Etno.

Arrazola, Roberto 1970 Palenque: Primero pueblo libre de America. (Palenque: America's First Free Town.) Cartagena: Ediciones Hernandez.

Asad, Talal 1990 Multiculturalism and British Identity in the Wake of the Rushdie Affair. Politics and Society 18(4): 455–480.

Benitez Rojo, Antonio 1984 La cultura Caribeña en Cuba: Continuidad versus ruptura. (Caribbean Culture in Cuba: Continuity versus Rupture.) Cuban Studies/Estudios Cubanos 14(1):1–15.

Bensusan, Guy 1984 Cartagena's Fandango Politics. Studies in Latin American Popular Culture 3:127–134.

Berry, R. Albert 1980 The Effects of Inflation on Income Distribution in Colombia; Some Hypotheses and a Framework for Analysis. *In* Economic Policy and Income Distribution in Colombia. R. Albert Berry and Ronald Soligo, eds. Pp. 113–133. Boulder, CO: Westview Press.

Bourdieu, Pierre 1977 Outline of a Theory of Practice. Cambridge: Cambridge University Press.

Casal, Lourdes 1979 Race Relations in Contemporary Cuba. *In* The Position of Blacks in Brazilian and Cuban Society. Pp. 11–27. London: Minority Rights Group.

Clifford, James, and George E. Marcus, eds. 1986 Writing Culture: The Poetics and Politics of Ethnography. Berkeley: University of California Press.

Connell, Robert W. 1987 Gender and Power: Society, the Person and Sexual Politics. Stanford, CA: Stanford University Press.

Cotler, Julio, ed. 1989 Clases populates, crisis y democracia en America Latina. (Popular Classes, Crisis, and Democracy in Latin America.) Lima, Peru: Instituto de Estudios Peruanos.

Delgado, Camilo S. 1972[1912] Historias y leyendas de Cartagena, 1. Bogotá: Ministerio de Educacion Nacional, Instituto Colombiano de Cultura.

Departmento Administrativo Nacional de Estadistica (DANE) 1956 Censo de poblacion de 1951. (1951 Population Census.) Bogotá: Imprenta Nacional.

———. 1973 XIV Censo nacional de poblacion y III de vivienda (Departamento de Bolivar). (Fourteenth National Population Census and Third National Housing Census.) Bogotá: DANE.

———. 1983 Encuesta nacional, etapa 41 (Septiembre). (National Survey, 41st Stage [September].) Bogotá: DANE. Microfilm.

———. 1988 Encuesta nacional, etapa 31 (Septiembre). (National Survey, 31st Stage [September].) Bogotá: DANE. Microfilm.

Dominguez, Virginia R. 1989 People as Subject, People as Object: Selfhood and Peoplehood in Contemporary Israel. Madison: University of Wisconsin Press.

Fraser, Nancy, and Linda J. Nicholson 1990 Social Criticism without Philosophy: An Encounter between Feminism and Postmodernism. In Feminism/Postmodernism. Linda J. Nicholson, ed. Pp. 19–38. New York: Routledge.

Friedemann, Nina S. de 1984 Estudios de negros en la antropologia Colombiana. *In* Un Siglo de Investigacion Social: Antropologia en Colombia. Jaime Arocha and Nina S. de Friedemann, eds. Pp. 507–572. Bogotá: Etno.

———. 1987[1979] Ma Ngombe: guerreros y ganaderos en Palenque. (Ma Ngombe: Warrior and Cattle Ranchers in Palenque.) Bogotá: Carlos Valencia.

Friedemann, Nina S. de, and Jaime Arocha 1987 De sol a sol: Genesis, transformacion y presencia de los negros en Colombia. (From Sunrise to Sunset: Genesis, Transformation, and Presence of the Blacks in Colombia.) Bogotá: Planeta.

Friedemann, Nina S., and Carlos Patino Rossel 1983 Lengua y sociedad en el Palenque de San Basilio. (Language and Society in Palenque de San Basilio.) Bogotá: Instituto Caro y Cuervo.

Galin, Pedro, Julio Carrion, and Oscar Castillo 1986 Asalariados y clases populares en Lima. (Salary Workers and Popular Classes in Lima.) Lima, Peru: Instituto de Estudios Peruanos.

Ginsburg, Faye, and Anna Lowenhaupt Tsing 1990 Uncertain Terms: Negotiating Gender in American Culture. Boston: Beacon.

Juan, Jorge, and Antonio de Ulloa 1978 [1735] Relacion historica del viaje a la America Meridional. (Historical Narrative of the Trip to Southern America.) Madrid: Fundacion Universitaria Espanola.

Kondo, Dorinne K 1990 Crafting Selves: Power, Gender, and Discourses of Identity in a Japanese Workplace. Chicago: University of Chicago Press.

Lancaster, Roger 1988a Thanks to God and the Revolution: Popular Religion and Class Consciousness in the New Nicaragua. New York: Columbia University Press.

1988b Subject Honor and Object Shame: The Construction of Male Homosexuality and Stigma in Nicaragua. Ethnology 27(2): 111–126.

Latin American Weekly Reports 1988 Siege Rules Used to Quash Strike. November 10 (WR-88-44).

Lemaitre, Eduardo 1983 Historia general de Cartagena. Tomo IV: La republica. (General History of Colombia. Vol. 4: The Republic.) Bogotá Banco de la Republica.

Martinez-Alier, Verena 1989 [1974] Marriage, Class and Colour in Nineteenth-Century Cuba: A Study of Racial Attitudes and Sexual Values in a Slave Society. Ann Arbor: University of Michigan Press.

Meisel Roca, Adolfo 1980 Esclavitud, mestizaje y haciendas en la provincia de Cartagena: 1533–1851. (Slavery, Race Mixture, and Haciendas in the Province of Cartagena.) Desarrollo y Sociedad 4:228–277.

Moore, Carlos 1988 Castro, the Blacks, and Africa. Los Angeles: Center for Afro-American Studies, UCLA.

Moraga, Cherie, and Gloria Anzaldua, eds. 1981 This Bridge Called My Back: Writings by Radical Women of Color. Watertown, NY: Persephone.

Mosse, George L. 1985 Nationalism and Sexuality: Middle-Class Morality and Sexual Norms in Modern Europe. Madison: University of Wisconsin Press.

Nichols, Theodore E. 1973 Tres puertos de Colombia: Estudio sobre el desarrollo de Cartagena, Santa Maria Barranquilla. (Three Ports of Colombia: A Study of the evelopment of Cartagena, Santa Maria and Barranquilla.) Bogotá: Biblioteca Banco Popular.

Pineda Camacho, Roberto 1984 La reivindicacion del indio en el pensamiento social Colombiano (1850–1950). In Un Siglo de Investigacion Social: Antropologia en Colombia. Jaime Arocha and Nina S. de Friedemann, eds. Pp. 197–252. Bogotá: Etno.

Posada Gutierrez, Joaquin 1920 [1883]. Memorias historico-politicas, 2. (Historical-Political Memoirs, 2.) Madrid: Editorial America.

Pratt, Minnie 1984 Identity: Skin Blood Heart. *In* Yours in Struggle: Three Feminist Perspectives on Anti-Semitism and Racism. Elly Bulkin, Minnie Bruce Pratt, and Barbara Smith, eds. Pp. 9–63. New York: Long Haul Press.

Reyes Posada, Alvaro 1988 Evolucion de la distribucion del ingreso en Colombia. (Evolution of the Distribution of Income in Colombia.) *Desarrollo y Sociedad* 21:37–52.

Rosaldo, Michelle Zimbalist 1980 The Use and Abuse of Anthropology: Reflections on Feminism and Cross-Cultural Understanding. Signs: Journal of Women in Culture and Society 5(3):389–417.

Rosaldo, Renato 1989 Culture and Truth: The Remaking of Social Analysis. Boston: Beacon.

Rout, Leslie B., Jr. 1976 The African Experience in Spanish America: 1502 to the Present. New York: Cambridge University Press.

Sacks, Karen Brodkin 1989 Toward a Unified Theory of Class, Race, and Gender. American Ethnologist 16(3):534–550.

Schubert, Grace 1981 To Be Black Is Offensive: Racist Attitudes in San Lorenzo. In Cultural Transformations and Ethnicity in Modern Ecuador. Norman Whitten jr., ed. Urbana: University of Illinois Press.

Scott, James 1985 Weapons of the Weak: Everyday Forms of Peasant Resistance. New Haven, CT: Yale University Press.

Scott, Joan W. 1988 Women in the Making of the English Working Class. In Gender and the Politics of History. Pp. 68–90. New York: Columbia University Press.

Smith, T. Lynn 1966 The Racial Composition of the Population of Colombia. Journal of Interamerican Studies 8(2):213–235.

Solaun, Dis Mauricio, and Sidney Kronus 1973 Discrimination without Violence: Miscegenation and Racial Conflict in Latin America. New York: John Wiley & Sons.

Stolcke, Verena 1981 Women's Labours: The Naturalisation of Social Inequality and Women's Subordination. *In* Of Marriage and the Market: Women's Subordination Internationally and its Lessons. Kate Young, Carol Wolkowitz, and Roslyn McCullagh, eds. Pp. 159–177. London: Routledge & Kegan Paul.

Strassmann, W. Paul 1982 The Transformation of Urban Housing: The Experience of Upgrading in Cartagena. Baltimore: Johns Hopkins.

Taussig, Michael 1980 The Devil and Commodity Fetishism in South America. Chapel Hill: University of North Carolina Press.

———. 1987 Shamanism, Colonialism, and the Wild Man: A Study in Terror and Healing. Chicago: University of Chicago Press.

El Universal (Cartagena) 1988a Historia del reinado. (History of the Pageant.) November 11:20.

———. 1988b Las tristes fiestas. (Sad Fiestas.) December 12:6.

Urrutia, Miguel 1985 Winners and Losers in Colombia's Economic Growth of the 1970s. New York: Oxford University Press.

Wade, Peter 1985 Race and Class: The Case of South America Blacks. Ethnic and Racial Studies 8(2):233–249.

———. 1989 Black Culture and Social Inequality in Colombia. Tunbridge Wells, England: Institute for Cultural Research Monograph Series No. 28.

Whitten, Norman E., Jr. 1986 [1974] Black Frontiersmen: Afro-Hispanic Culture of Ecuador and Colombia. Prospect Heights, IL: Waveland Press.

Wittig, Monique 1980 The Straight Mind. Feminist Issues 1(1):101–111.

Wright, Winthrop 1990 Cafe con Leche: Race, Class, and National image in Venezuela. Austin: University of Texas Press.

Yanagisako, Sylvia Junko, and Jane Fishburne Collier 1987 Toward a Unified Analysis of Gender and Kinship. *In* Gender and Kinship: Essays Toward a Unified Analysis. Jane Fishburne Collier and Sylvia Junko Yanagisako, eds. Stanford, CA: Stanford University Press.

submitted April 2, 1992
revised version submitted July 8, 1992
revised version submitted February 10, 1993
accepted March 3, 1993

Intersectional Analysis with Four Social Locations

As discussed previously, a researcher may focus on a single racial, gender, or class category to the exclusion of the others, yielding four rather than eight social locations, constructed from the intersection of the other two identities. In the article by Janet L. Jacobs, "Gender, Race, Class, and the Trend Toward Early Motherhood," the focus is on 45 teenage mothers: 25 African Americans and 20 Latinas. The resulting four social locations from the race × class intersection are African American middle-class girls, Latina middle-class girls, African American working-class girls, and Latina working-class girls (column C in Table 1; p. 108). As unemployed youth, these girls have not yet achieved their own class position; their class is therefore identical with that of their parents. Although we know the racial composition and the percentage of the girls who are working class (80%) and middle class (20%), the author does not provide the race × class distribution. Without this information we cannot know the precise size of each of the four social locations, although we might assume that all four are represented in the sample.

Jacobs is primarily interested in the relationship among several independent variables—family structure, need for autonomy, and need for attachment—and the dependent variable teen motherhood. Race and class are control variables. Examining these relationships *across* the four social locations becomes an exercise in intersectional analysis. For example, does the effect of the need for autonomy on pregnancy and motherhood among these girls vary between Latina and black middle-class and working-class girls? It is not sufficient to compare African American with Latina girls. Such comparisons are racial comparisons and are not complex social locations in the intersectional sense. Properly specifying complex social locations in articles of this type should include the second identity. In this case it is class. The multiplicative assumption suggests that comparisons should be made here across social locations formed from the intersections of race × class.

This article has many features of effective intersectional analysis. One feature that is not always present in articles informed by the intersectional approach is the explicit connection between the micro and higher levels. Jacobs makes this connection with the macro level when she comments on "the strain in mother-daughter relationships that originate out of race and class oppression" experienced by the mother (p. 158). In this way the relationships studied are, to use Rose Brewer's (1993) language, "contextualized." Another example of intersectional analysis is the comment that "integrating a class analysis with the gender interpretation reveals that, among the working poor and poverty level respondents, independence is primarily sought from mothers who, contending with race and class oppression, seek to protect their daughters from similar struggles by restricting their social lives in a family that is already strained by economic hardship" (p. 165). Missing, however, are explicit comparisons with middle-class African American and Latina girls. While the race of the respondent is typically given, the class identity is not.

The article would be improved by providing more information on the social locations (numbers of teen mothers in each location) and more explicit analysis of the relationship between independent and dependent variables across these social locations. A negative finding might indicate that the relationship was not multiplicative, but this would not negate the usefulness of intersectional analysis. A negative finding may be as important as a positive one in providing insights about the relationships studied. In this article, however, there is the suggestion that the relationships may be multiplicative, from the comment by Jacobs: "Motherhood thus becomes a choice to save one's self, often within a social environment that, because of economic and race oppression, offered few other alternatives for self-development," (p. 161, italics added). The primary motivation of girls "to save one's self" is conditioned by "economic [class] and race oppression." What remains missing is a comparison across class locations.[13]

Greater specificity about social locations is provided in Michael A. Messner's article, "Masculinities and Athletic Careers." In this article on the formation of masculine identities sufficient information on the race × class distribution is provided to allow the construction of a table of the four locations.

	RACE	
Class	Black	White
Middle	1	9
Working	15	5

One obvious limitation is the presence of only one individual in the social location black middle-class males. Messner notes: "Fifteen of the sixteen

[13]Given the topic studied, it may be that there were not enough middle-class girls in the sample to be analyzed.

come from poor or working-class families, while the majority (9 of 14) of the white men had come from middle-class or professional families" (p. 169). As a consequence, Messner focuses his analysis primarily on two social locations, white middle-class males ("high status") and black working-class males ("low status"). The two Latino males in the sample are not given much attention. The "low status" group actually comprises both black and white males from working-class origins. It appears that no difference is found in their use of sports to construct their masculine identities, whereas analysis of the high-status group of white males of middle-class origin is of necessity silent on race differences of males of that class origin. In this analysis class emerges as the dominant factor shaping males' use of sports in the construction of their masculine identities; working-class males (black and white) rely more on sports than middle-class males. In his analysis of those middle-class white males who choose not to pursue professional sports careers, Messner comments:

> How and why do they make this early assessment and choice to shift from sports and toward educational and profession goals? The white, middle-class institutional context, with its emphasis on education and income, makes it clear to them that choices exist and that the pursuit of an athletic career is not a particularly good choice to make" (p. 171).

What we do not learn, because of the lack of black middle-class males in the sample, is whether both black and white males from middle-class backgrounds make similar choices. We do learn that males from working-class backgrounds—both black and white—are similarly influenced by minimal class resources in their decisions to seek a career in professional sports. From the analysis in this article, then, race does not appear to play a different role among those from a working-class background beyond the cultural variation indicated by the "cool pose" of black males. Therefore the relationship between sports and identity is *not* multiplicative between African American and white working-class males but *is* multiplicative across middle-class and working-class white and black males' social locations. The inclusion of more black or Latino males from middle-class origins would have allowed analysis of the fourth social location, to determine whether males from black middle-class origins use sports differently than do males from white middle-class origins. Unless a study is designed purposefully to include sufficient cases in each location, the researcher may discover at the analysis stage that a particular social location has too few cases for meaningful intersectional analysis of that location.

Gender, Race, Class, and the Trend Toward Early Motherhood

A Feminist Analysis of Teen Mothers in Contemporary Society

JANET L. JACOBS

Contemporary research on teen pregnancy has primarily focused on the increasing number of teen mothers among African American and Latina adolescents (Darabi and Ortiz 1987; Pittman and Adams 1988). These studies, which provide diverse explanations for

From Janet L. Jacobs, "Gender, Race, and Class, And The Trend Toward Early Motherhood: A Feminist Analysis of Teen Mothers in Contemporary Society" *Journal of Contemporary Ethnography*, Vol. 22, No. 4, January 1994.

explanations for the rise of early motherhood among teenaged women, attribute this phenomenon to family structure (Hogan and Kitagawa 1985), limited economic opportunities (Geronimus 1987; Staples 1985), and cultural values of ethnically diverse communities (Ladner 1972; Staples 1985). As such, the study of teen pregnancy has been framed within a sociocultural paradigm that emphasizes the importance of race and class in the analysis of early motherhood. What is missing from the extensive literature on this social trend is the impact of gender on adolescent girls who become pregnant and choose to single parent, an approach that examines the intersection of race, class, and gender in the study of teenage sexuality and pregnancy.

Not since the publication of Ladner's (1972) *Tomorrow's Tomorrow* more than 20 years ago has the research on adolescent motherhood considered the relationship between early parenting and growing up female in the African American community. With the continual growth of this phenomena and its expansion to young Latina adolescents as well, a contemporary analysis is now needed to further the understanding that Ladner's research brought to the early study of teen mothers. The objective of this research therefore is to offer a feminist approach to the study of teen pregnancy and single parenting, an approach that, as Nathanson (1991) points out, "has been conspicuously absent" from the discourse on adolescent sexuality in contemporary culture (p. 220).

Existing studies of teen pregnancy have focused on two dimensions of this phenomenon: the initiation of sexual intimacy in adolescence and the decision to single parent once a pregnancy is discovered (Furstenberg, Lincoln, and Menken 1981; Furstenberg and Brooks-Gunn 1987). Primarily quantitative in orientation, these studies have neglected to fully explore the relationship between female adolescence and the trend toward early motherhood within a social framework that addresses the dynamics of race, class, and gender. This research offers such an analysis through a qualitative study of adolescent mothers.

The findings of this research highlight the complex relationship between female adolescence, family structure, and social location. Thus the research reveals that sexuality, pregnancy, and motherhood in adolescence is contextualized by the developmental needs of autonomy and attachment. First, the path toward early motherhood begins with the initiation of sexual intimacy as a step toward gaining autonomy from parental control, a desire for separation that is informed by race and class. Second, the choice to mother among teenage girls who become pregnant resolves the conflicting needs of autonomy and attachment that characterize adolescent development, a resolution that, like the initiation of sexual intimacy, emerges out of the social location of the teen mother. Each of these findings is elaborated more fully below.

Methodology and Sample Characteristics

I conducted this study between 1989 and 1991 at a regional high school for teen mothers in the Denver metropolitan area. The school can accommodate 120 students and maintains four nurseries for children up to 2 years of age. The research involved participant observation and in-depth interviews with 45 teen mothers attending the school. The participant observation took place in the classrooms and nurseries during school hours. The interviews were conducted on the school premises in an office that had been set aside for the research. I selected respondents at random from the school population and included them in the study on a voluntary basis. The interviews lasted from 1 to 2 hours and were taped and then transcribed. I used a semistructured open-ended interview schedule to obtain information on sexual behavior, attitudes toward pregnancy and mothering, relationships with peers and male partners, and data on family of origin. In addition, I obtained demographic information about the participants from school records.

The ages of the participants ranged from 14 to 19 years, with a mean age of 16. Twenty of the respondents were Latina and 25 were of African American descent. Twenty-four (54%) of the respondents were raised in single-parent households; 18 were headed by mothers and 6 by fathers. Twenty-one (46%) of the respondents were raised in two-parent families; 10 included both biological parents and 11 included a stepfather. Eighty percent of the sample were from poor and working-class backgrounds; the remaining 20% were from middle-class families.

Among the poor respondents ($n = 15$), all of the families were headed by single women, 5 of whom supported their children and grandchildren with welfare payments. Of the working-class respondents ($n = 20$), 4 were single mothers, 5 were single fathers, and 11 were dual-income families. All of the middle-class respondents ($n = 10$) were raised in dual-income, two-parent households. Two-thirds of the teen mothers resided with their families of origin, and 11 of the respondents had an older sister who was also a teen mother. The majority (92%) of the teens in the sample had one child at the time of the interview. The others had two children.

Although the sample population represented diversity in family structure and class backgrounds, the sample was limited by including only those adolescents who chose to complete their education while mothering young children. Thus the findings reflect the experience of a range of teen mothers whose education had not been disrupted by pregnancy, childbirth, and parenting.

Sexual Intimacy and the Quest for Independence

Theories of adolescent development stress the importance of separation and individuation as crucial to the establishment of an autonomous adult self (Miller 1986). Until the past decade, research on adolescence assumed that men and women proceeded through similar stages of development and that autonomy could be understood using the male model of psychosocial development. More recently, the scholarship on gender and personality (Chodorow 1978; Gilligan 1982; Jordan 1984) established that, as in all other areas of social life, adolescent development is gendered, and thus teenage girls seek to establish their independent identity within a framework of social relations that balances the need for autonomy with the need for connection and attachment. In this regard, Stern (1990) has written,

> Adolescent girls represent the embodiment of a fascinating paradox. Although theories of adolescence describe a time of separation, individuation, and autonomy seeking, theorists of female development have observed that for women, the importance of strong relationships does not abate. In other words, theory tells us that by virtue of being female, adolescent girls especially value their connection; whereas by virtue of being adolescent, they are attending particularly to their separation.

Such competing needs among adolescents are manifested in social behaviors that challenge parental restrictions on social life and sexuality while engaging in sexual intimacy through which continuing needs for attachment are sought. Prior studies (DeLameter and MacCorquodale 1979; Nathanson 1991) of sexual behavior among college and noncollege youth found that premarital relations is a significant step in becoming independent from parents, leading Nathanson (1991) to conclude that "Male as well as female sexuality in adolescence represents an assertion of adult status—of maturity and independence of parental control—by individuals socially defined as children" (p. 208).

Among the respondents in this study, 35 teen mothers (70%) reported that opposition to parental restrictions on social life created tensions that were resolved through a form of defiance that resulted in the initiation of sexual intimacy with male peers. This finding is consistent with an earlier study of teen pregnancy in which Cohen and Friedman (1975) found that "parents who are uneasy, anxious and threatened when confronted with sexual matters are the most vulnerable to the potent weapon of sexual activity" (p. 16). Despite these findings in White middle-class populations, they have rarely been used to explain pregnancy among Black teenagers, although Ladner (1972) found similar patterns of behavior in her research:

> Girls who engaged in premarital sex were more inclined to be critical of parental controls and to feel that adults did not understand the needs and problems of adolescents. The fact that they engaged in premarital sex was a strong indication of defiance, because they frequently acted against parental desires—parents did not encourage premarital relations owing to the problems involved. (pp. 203–4)

In the majority of cases reported here, the teenager's social life was carried out through secrecy and nondisclosure, which included sneaking out and withholding information about social and sexual relationships. One teen mother described the conflict in this way:

> Well, my mom used to try and keep me from going out. She was really strict, and my friends and I, we used to sneak around, and I think that's the worst thing to do, is try to keep a child from it.

The effects of race and class oppression on autonomy

The conflicts over autonomy and independence that predominate in single-parent households differ from those that characterize two-parent families. Of the respondents raised by mothers in single-headed households ($n = 19$), the tensions surrounding separation and sexual intimacy were contextualized by the strain in mother-daughter relationships that originate out of race and class oppression. Single mothers who were themselves teen parents were often portrayed as the most restrictive, as the following account from a 15-year-old African American respondent illustrates:

> My mom was 3 months pregnant when she got married. She was 17. She'd say stuff like "I don't want my kids to turn out the way I did, get pregnant at a young age," so she tried to discourage us. I was not supposed to date until I was 16, but I could double date at 15. Last year they knew I was seeing Bobby. I just told my mom we were friends. I don't know how I did it, but I did. I snuck out at night all the time. I climbed out my bedroom window. It's ground level. We'd always wait until 10:30 and then my sister and I would crawl out and stay out until 3.

A follow-up study of Black adolescent mothers conducted by Furstenberg, Brooks-Gunn, and Morgan (1987) confirmed that women who were teen mothers are indeed concerned about the sexuality of their children and will often encourage the use of contraception. Among the respondents interviewed here, the teenaged girls reported that a greater emphasis was placed on restrictions around dating than on contraceptive practices. This is an important finding in light of the research that attributes the rise in teen pregnancy to single-headed households in which mothers fail to adequately supervise their daughters (Hogan and Kitagawa 1985). Such an approach, which originates out of the deviant family interpretation of African American home life (Moynihan 1965), assumes that such supervision must be lacking because the daughter becomes pregnant, an "after the fact" analysis, as pointed out by Bumpass and McLanahan (1989). The perspective offered here challenges such assumptions, suggesting that teen pregnancy might better be understood as an outcome of conflicting needs of autonomy and attachment, especially within those families where parental restrictions create strain with the teenaged daughter.

The familial tensions reported by the respondents have a class component as well, in that restrictions over social life were often tied to responsibilities for housework and childcare in homes where mothers worked long hours to provide for the family. Under these conditions, teenaged daughters sought freedom and independence through social relations outside the home that were often prohibited, as the following account of a 16-year-old Latina mother suggests:

> My mom worked at night and came home. I guess she was tired and she would just make me do everything. I got stuck babysitting and doing the housework. I would get mad and take off, and then I could never talk on the phone or go outside.

As the control over sexuality became a focus of mother-daughter relations, such control was impacted by the multiple roles that mothers assumed as income producer, childcare provider, and household manager. As these women sought to protect their daughters from similar hardships, conflicts emerged, and it was not uncommon for the teen parents to express a longing for a more nurturing relationship with their mothers. Collins (1990) discussed this aspect of mother-daughter relationships in African American families:

> Black women's efforts to provide a physical and psychic base for their children can affect mothering styles and the emotional intensity of Black mother-daughter relationships. . . . For far too many Black mothers, the demands of providing for children in interlocking systems of oppression are sometimes so demanding that they have neither the time nor the patience for affection. And yet most Black daughters love and admire their mothers and are convinced that their mothers truly love them. (p. 127)

The adolescent daughter, seeking the maternal affection that may be unavailable to her, experiences her mother as overly protective, rigid, and unreasonable. In turning to heterosexual intimacy, she obtains the freedom from parental control through an alternative relationship of attachment and connection.

Conflicts over autonomy in two-parent families

In comparison with the female single-headed households, in those families where two parents resided ($n = 21$), issues of autonomy tended to center around morality and cultural values rather than protection from hardship and oppression. Thus religion often played an important role in legitimizing parental control over teenage daughters. Here, an 18-year-old respondent whose parents were active in the Black church describes the impact on her life:

> I wasn't using birth control. I was afraid that my parents would find it and I would get in trouble for having sex. They were very strict and never wanted anybody to have sex or go out. My mom was always telling me not to have sex, especially when my sister got pregnant a year before I did. She said, "Don't have sex because it's fornication and it's sin." She said, "Wait until you get married," but I was already having sex. She was real ashamed of me when I got pregnant.

Among the Latina population, the traditional values of the church and family often come into conflict with the sexual norms of teenage social life in North America. As such, the rise in teen pregnancy among Mexican Americans has been correlated with assimilation (Darabi and Ortiz 1987). For these adolescents, independence is defined in terms of the values and behaviors associated with the assimilated reference group. A good example is an 18-year-old mother whose parents immigrated from Guatemala. As she entered adolescence, the culture conflict with her family resulted in misunderstanding and a fear of disclosure:

> In Guatemala it's real strict. The way my mom grew up, she was like "Little Miss Goody." Like with parties, I'd be leaving at 10 o'clock at night and she'd be like, "When I was growing up I had to be home at 7." I used to go to church and everything, but now I'm into everything else.

> My mom's more into church than we are. When we were growing up, we never really talked about boys to my mom because we kept it a secret. We thought she would disapprove. I wanted her to talk about sex, then maybe I could have heard about the pill and I wouldn't have gotten pregnant.

Further, teen mothers from two-parent families reported a greater incidence of family violence, including battering, child abuse, and incest. In these cases, 9 of which involved physical abuse by fathers and 12 of which involved sexual abuse by fathers, stepfathers, or other family members, the conflicts surrounding autonomy were compounded by feelings of betrayal and abandonment that were, for the most part, directed at mothers who were perceived both as nonprotective and nonnurturing. A case in point is that of a 15-year-old African American respondent whose stepfather repeatedly abused her. Here she describes how this violence affected her relationship with her mother:

> I think she didn't want to know about his hitting us all the time. He's an alcoholic and he emotionally abuses her all the time. We thought if she looked hard enough she'd begin to know. When he liked to give us whippings and things we had to be naked and when he gets drunk he gets too cozy. When I tell my mom, because I just told her about it, just a couple of months ago, she said it was just because he was drunk. That was always her excuse. Everything that goes on is because he's drunk.

Thus, in those families where violence informed the life of the adolescent daughter, the desire for autonomy became infused with a need for alternative forms of connection that became a source of protection as well as nurturance. As such, 1 respondent reported that "whenever my boyfriend is there, it's fine, but if my dad ever got mad when he wasn't there, I'd be scared." In addition, for the sexually abused adolescent, a relationship with a male peer became a means for separation and independence from the perpetrator.

Sexual Intimacy, Motherhood, and the Need for Attachment

As this analysis has thus far suggested, sexual intimacy for adolescent girls developed in accordance with a need for autonomy. This path to independence was contextualized by the connection to a male partner who represented a new source of attachment in the life of the young woman. Salzman (1990) has described this aspect of female adolescent behavior as trading sex "in return for the promise of attachment" (p. 36). Sexuality thus became a basis for emotional exchange early in the life of the female adolescent. Accordingly, less than 20% ($n = 8$) of the respondents reported that sexual relations were a source of gratification. Rather, the most frequent response with regard to the experience of sexual intercourse was that "it was tolerable." Although 14 girls (28%) indicated that they had been coerced or pressured into engaging in sex with their boyfriends, the majority expressed a willingness to become sexually intimate as means to affirm the relationship with a male partner. A 17-year-old respondent described her attitude toward sexual relations:

> The first time it was painful, but afterwards it was okay. It's not something that's going to change my personality or anything, but it makes me feel loved from him because he's not the kind of guy that likes to show it all the time, so whenever he does, it surprises me.

In this regard, the teenage girls who became young mothers were not unlike other female adolescents who negotiated the terrain of sexuality and emotional connection within an adolescent culture in which attachment to boys was sustained through sexual intimacy. One obvious outcome of such forms of attachment, as Chilman (1977) has pointed out, is an unintended pregnancy. In keeping with national studies, the vast majority of teen mothers in this study did not intend to become pregnant but nonetheless did not use contraception effectively. Similar to other research in this area (Baldwin 1983; Dembo and Lundell, 1979; Levinson 1986; Lieberman 1981; Nathanson, 1991; Zelnik, Kantner, and Ford 1981), the teen mothers reported that they did not use contraception for a variety of reasons, including lack of availability, negligence, unpreparedness, misinformation, and pressure from boyfriends.[1] Faced with the dilemma of an unwanted pregnancy, the choice to mother became a further manifestation of the conflicting needs for attachment and autonomy in adolescence.

The findings of this research strongly support a perspective on teen pregnancy that emphasizes the significance of attachment in the young mother's decision to continue a pregnancy and raise a child (Zongker 1977). As such, the young women in this study expressed strong feelings against abortion and adoption, as the knowledge of pregnancy engendered a sense of responsibility to a baby that, for the adolescent girl, was already an infant in need of protection and nurturing. Perhaps the most poignant example of this response is illustrated by the case of a 17-year-old African American respondent who chose to continue a pregnancy that resulted from repeated assaults by her stepfather. Here, she explains her decision to mother the child:

> I'm very against abortion. I have all these friends that have had abortions, but I don't believe in it. I was considering adoption, but I decided to go ahead and keep the baby because it wasn't the baby's fault what I had to go through. If I let the baby be adopted, I would always be worried something's happening to her. And I can't see myself abandoning her like that. I don't care what the circumstances are, you just don't abandon your child on somebody else.

The responsibility that the young women felt toward the potential life within them is consistent with the ethic of responsibility that, according to Gilligan (1982), characterizes female development, as morality is shaped by relationships to others. The dilemma of an unwanted pregnancy was therefore resolved with the choice to mother, demonstrating, in Gilligan's view, that an ethic of responsibility lies at "the center of a woman's moral concern, anchoring the self in a world of relationships and giving rise to activities of care" (Gilligan 1982, 132). Further, the choice to mother among teenaged girls whose lives were informed by the strain of race and class oppression, contained an element of care of self as well as care of other, in that the nurturing and caretaking they wished to give their children was that which they desired for themselves. This identificatory aspect of teen pregnancy, to which Gilligan has referred as well, often results in adolescents assuming responsibility for themselves in a new way, especially in those cases where gang violence and drug abuse inform the social relations of the adolescent culture. As one 16-year-old Latina respondent described this transformation,

> When I got pregnant I was living on the streets at the time. I had dropped out of school and I was kicked out of my house because I'd come home drunk or high or just not come home at all. And Hernando was in a gang—that's the baby's father. I was in the girls' gang and we were always getting into fights. But everything changed when I found out I was pregnant. I was walking with Hemando and this car pulls up and they start shooting. I was screaming, "No more, no more!" I told him after that, I won't see him unless he quits the gangs. And my parents let me move back in and I quit smoking and drinking.

Motherhood thus becomes a choice to save one's self, often within a social environment that, because of economic and race oppression, offered few other alternatives for self-development. This perspective is perhaps another way of explaining the relationship between poverty, racism, and the trend toward early motherhood.

In the violence and economic strain that permeates the impoverished adolescent community, mothering was a life-affirming choice for young girls who idealized their children as the hope for themselves and a future generation for which they felt responsible.

Within this relational framework, educational goals became tied to providing a better life for the children, as evidenced by recent research on teen pregnancy and high school completion. These studies, reported by Geronimus (1987) and Knubel (1990), indicate that teen mothers are just as likely to complete high school as are their childless classmates, in spite of the difficulties they encountered as they struggled to mother, attend school, and, in many cases, work to support their children (Held 1981). The motivation to complete school can, in part, be understood in terms of the mothers' attachment to the children and the ethic of responsibility that such attachment engendered. The sample population of high school teen mothers interviewed for this study affirmed that in choosing to stay in school the young women believed they were making a choice not only for themselves but, more important, for the children they would mother or who they had already begun to parent. The data show that these young women in particular had high aspirations for themselves, as the following quote from an African American high school junior suggests:

> I want to work in a profession. You know I have to be in school, even though it's hard. Mothering is kind of hard. I want to take up computer science. I'm working on that. I tell myself it's all for her [the baby]. Taking welfare ain't my business, not my pride. I hate welfare and I say no, no, no. I know I'm going to better myself, and it makes me feel good to know I can do that.

Aspirations such as these often led to success in later life. In this regard, Furstenberg, Brooks-Gunn, and Morgan (1987) found that teen mothers who remained in school during their pregnancy and after the birth of their child were more likely to become self-supporting as adults.

Parenthood as a Path toward Autonomy and Adulthood

Ladner's (1972) research established that motherhood provides a transition to adulthood among Black teenagers because of the shift in status that parenthood signifies:

> The adolescent Black girl who becomes pregnant out of wedlock changed her self conceptions from one who was approaching maturity to one who had attained the status of womanhood. In a similar manner, individuals with whom she associated changed their conceptions of her to fit the same role. (p. 215)

Accordingly, a number of respondents spoke of improved relationships with their mothers who now treated them less like children and more like adults, as the following account suggests:

> It's gotten better since I had the baby because now we can talk about babies where before it was like we're not going to say anything to each other, you know, about certain things like sex or something. Before I had her [the baby], she would say, "Why are you asking me this?" Now, she just tells me and I tell her.

At the same time that the birth of a child may change the status of the daughter, the research reported here also reveals that the disclosure of a pregnancy may initially lead to further conflicts over autonomy, particularly when there is disagreement over whether to continue or terminate the pregnancy. With the growth in teenage motherhood among poor Black families, intergenerational conflicts are becoming increasingly frequent as many grandmothers, still in their childbearing years, are caring both for their own children and for their daughters' (Ladner and Gourdine 1984). The reports of the teen mothers in this study indicate that one response to this phenomenon was parental pressure to have an abortion. This trend is illustrated by a 17-year-old respondent who described this altercation with her mother:

> My mother tried to talk to me, to tell me to "please get an abortion, you can't have this baby." But I was going to have it, period. I don't care what anybody said. . . . My mom took me to the doctor, and when I get down there come to find out I'm supposed to be getting an abortion and she didn't tell me nothing about it. And I looked at the nurse and I said, "No, we're not terminating this baby," I just wanted to have it. Not because it was his or anything. I just wanted to.

A number of Latina respondents reported similar parental pressure to terminate the pregnancy. In one case, a Latina respondent disclosed that her parents "begged" her to have an abortion rather than dishonor the family:

> They gave me two choices. I could stay home and have an abortion or leave and have the baby. I took the second choice because I didn't want to kill my baby and I just couldn't consider adoption—that would have been even harder than an abortion.

In another account, a Latina adolescent, 14 years of age, reported that she, too, defied her parents in continuing the pregnancy:

> The doctor came in and told me I was pregnant, and that's when I got scared. I told him, "Don't tell my mother," and he says, "It will be better than you telling her on your own." So I let him tell her. She called my dad and after that we walked over to my aunt's house. They were convincing me to have an abortion, and my dad kept saying, "I'll pay for her, I'll do anything for you not to have this baby." I just got so mad. I told them to stay away from me. I told them I hated them and they can't make me have an abortion.

Further, the autonomy issues that developed over the continuation of the pregnancy were not always resolved with the birth of the child. Not all families, as Ladner (1972) has pointed out, remove restrictions on the teen mother's social life once she becomes a parent. Such restrictions continue to be a source of tension, as indicated by one young mother who moved out of her mother's house soon after her child was born:

> At first I was living with my mother. But we were fighting all the time. My parents are divorced, so I moved in with my dad. I like living with him better because I can basically do anything I want. My mom would never let me spend the night at my boyfriend's house because she is just that way. She wanted me to get to know him better and thought I was still too young. But my dad lets me spend the night at his house. He doesn't care.

Following the birth of a child, tensions in the family also arose over parenting as the young mothers sought to establish their independence within the framework of motherhood. In the following account, a 15-year-old respondent discusses this continuing problem with her mother:

> My mother—well, she's too helpful. It's always, "I've got Sheena, give her here. She's crying, I don't want to hear her crying. Give her here." And I say, "No, would you let me take care of her? I'm her momma." And then she goes on to tell me what I should do. She's definitely trying to control what's going on here. If I had a choice, I wouldn't have moved back home with my baby.

The desire for autonomy as represented by a desire to separate from parents was, in some cases, also manifested in the teen mothers' changing attitude toward their relationships to the children's fathers. Although this relationship originally provided an alternative source of attachment, pregnancy and childbearing more often than not changed the nature of sexual and emotional intimacy between the young mother and father. As the responsibility of pregnancy and child rearing fell primarily to the teenaged girl, the respondents expressed a disillusionment with male intimacy and a realization that they could not depend on male partners to take care of them or their children.

In this regard, one third of the adolescents reported that the fathers abandoned them once the pregnancy was confirmed, often denying paternity and engaging in new relationships. For these girls, the pain of separation from the relationships was especially acute, particularly in those cases where another girl became pregnant by the same boy. A case in point is that of a 17-year-old African American mother with a 10-month-old daughter. Here, she describes a difficult separation from her child's father:

> You know, he said he wanted the baby and everything. And I believed everything he told me. Like we were going to get married, and if he saw a baby, he'd say, "That's how our baby is going to look. It's going to have all nice clothes." He tell me, "Linda, don't get an abortion, we're going to be together forever." Now he never comes around anymore. Sometimes, I read back over his notes and letters to me. And when I look at her [the baby], it's like that's him. I want to be with him. I think maybe he'll one day come around again, but I'm not sure I'm going to take him back. I seen him at the mall a couple of days ago. He just looked at her and then turned his head. Sometimes, I get depressed because I don't have him anymore.

For other respondents who remained involved with the baby's father throughout the pregnancy and the first year of the child's life, the conflicting needs of autonomy and attachment were often expressed as ambivalence over the future of the relationship. In the case of one young Latina mother of a year-old baby, concerns over marriage developed as her boyfriend became possessive and abusive:

> I wanted to end the relationship first because he was really jealous and possessive of me and I wasn't free enough. Everything was about me and the baby, and he thought in his mind the only way he could keep me was getting me pregnant again, and I didn't want that so we broke up.

Another respondent, an African American teenager with a year-old child, similarly discussed her concerns over marriage:

> We are trying to get married, but we're not too sure. He has a job and he's trying to get an apartment by himself, but I don't know. When you get married I think you have to stay at home and I don't want to stay at home. I want to work. I want to get out and see the world and have a job and support my child. Later on I may want to marry but not now.

Finally, a third respondent, an 18-year-old mother whose daughter was a year and a half old at the time of the interview, also spoke of her reservations about marriage:

> It's hard because I think I would like to live with him just to see if I could take it. Because I don't know, I think it's more me than him. I think he wants it more than I do. He's really nice to me, but I don't think I'm ready for marriage right now or even later, not for a long time.

Accounts such as these illustrate the extent to which autonomy is desired as the mother-child dyad provides an emotional attachment that replaces the dependency on male intimacy. This analysis, framed within a feminist perspective on developmental needs, suggests that the choice to single parent may be made even under those circumstances when marriage is a possibility. Such an interpretation offers a departure from an exclusively race and class analysis that attributes low marriage rates among teen parents primarily to high unemployment among young Black males (Johnson and Sum 1987). This viewpoint assumes a preference for marriage among teen mothers, which remains unrealized because of economic deprivation. Although economic oppression may influence attitudes toward marriage for both the young mother and adolescent father, the research presented here suggests that adolescent girls envision a more dependent future for themselves as the desire for autonomy is impacted by the realities of parenting and undependable or controlling emotional attachments.

Conclusion

This analysis of teen pregnancy raises significant questions regarding the diversity of factors that may be used to explain a phenomenon as complex as early mothering. Placing gender at the center of the analysis provides a framework for understanding the way in which gender, race, and class interact to create a trend in single parenting that results in much hardship for the young mother as she struggles to care for herself and her child while passing through the stages that characterize female adolescence in male-dominant culture. In this regard, the case studies reveal a pattern of social behavior that links sexual intimacy and motherhood with a desire for autonomy, which is contextualized by a continuing need for attachment, a need that is first met through heterosexual relationships and then through connection to the child.

Further, integrating a class analysis with the gendered interpretation reveals that, among the working poor and poverty-level respondents, independence is primarily sought from mothers who, contending with race and class oppression, seek to protect their daughters from similar struggles by restricting their social lives in a family that is already strained by economic hardship. Conflictual mother-daughter relationships may therefore contribute to the desire for alternative attachments that are realized through heterosexual intimacy and mothering.

Such a perspective, although representing the reality of tensions that pervade the lives of young mothers, may reinforce the tendency toward mother-blame that already pervades the literature on adolescent pregnancy and family structure. Thus it is important to stress the significance of social oppression on mother-daughter relationships in the analysis of poverty and the trend toward single parenting. This approach, rather than a replication of previous research, recognizes that the dynamics surrounding maternal attachment and separation are influenced by a social environment of inequality that exacerbates the tensions associated with adolescent development.

The conclusions of this study therefore support the views articulated by Chilman (1977) and others (Patten 1981; Furstenberg, Brooks-Gunn, and Morgan 1987) who have maintained that the prevention of early adolescent pregnancy involves more than the availability of family planning services and low-cost and safe abortions. In addition, policies and programs are needed that recognize the importance of adolescent development among teenaged girls who are at risk for early motherhood. In particular, prevention programs might be aimed at developing alternative paths to achieving autonomy, including a greater emphasis on education and career goals. Furstenberg, Brooks-Gunn, and Morgan (1987), in fact, have specifically recommended that remedial education programs be provided for those teenaged girls whose unsuccessful school performance place them at risk for early childbearing. This perspective suggests that as adolescent development is contextualized by race and class, the expansion of educational and employment opportunities for young women of color can influence a pattern of development wherein the quest for autonomy has become linked to early motherhood because of the absence of other options for attaining adult status.

Note

1. Baldwin (1983) has reported that among sexually active teenagers 24% use contraception regularly and 42% on an irregular basis. With regard to race differences, she reported that Black adolescents were less likely to have ever used a contraceptive but that Black and White adolescents were equally likely to use contraceptives regularly if they began a contraceptive method at first intercourse.

References

Baldwin, Wendy. 1983. Trends in adolescent contraception, pregnancy, and childbearing. In *Premature adolescent pregnancy and parenthood,* ed. Elizabeth R. McAnalney, 3–19. New York: Gruen & Stration.

Bolton, Frank G. 1980. *The pregnant adolescent.* Beverly Hills, CA: Sage.

Bumpass, Larry, and Sara McLanahan. 1989. Unmarried motherhood: Recent trends, composition, and Black-White differences. *Demography* 26 (2): 279.

Chilman, Catherine. 1977. Some policy and program implications of an overview of research concerning adolescent sexuality. Paper presented at the annual conference of the National Council on Family Relations, San Diego.

Chodorow, Nancy. 1978. *The reproduction of mothering: Psychoanalysis and the sociology of gender.* Berkeley and Los Angeles: University of California Press.

Cohen, M. W., and S. B. Friedman. 1975. Nonsexual motivation of adolescent sexual behavior. *Medical Aspects of Human Sexuality* 9:8–31.

Collins, Patricia Hill. 1990. *Black feminist thought: Knowledge, consciousness, and the politics of empowerment.* Boston: Unwin Hyman.

Darabl, Katherine, and Vilma Ortiz. 1987. Childbearing among young Latino women in the United States. *American Journal of Public Health* 77:25–28.

DeLameter, J., and M. MacCorquodale. 1979. *Premarital sexuality: Attitudes, relationships, behaviors.* Madison: University of Wisconsin Press.

Dembo, Myron H., and Beverly Lundell. 1979. Factors affecting adolescent contraception practices: Implication for sex education. *Adolescence* 14:657–63.

Furstenberg, Frank F., Jr., and Jeanne Brooks-Gunn. 1987. Teenage childbearing: Causes, consequences, and remedies. In *Applications of social science to clinical medicine and health policy,* ed. Linda H. Aiken and David Mechanic, 307–34. New Brunswick, NJ: Rutgers University Press.

Furstenberg, Frank F., Jr., Jeanne Brooks-Gunn, and S. Phillip Morgan. 1987. *Adolescent mothers in later life.* New York: Cambridge University Press.

Furstenberg, Frank F., Jr., Richard Lincoln, and Jane Menken, eds. 1981. *Teenage sexuality, pregnancy and childbearing.* Philadelphia: University of Pennsylvania Press.

Geronimus, Ariene T. 1987. On teenage childbearing and neonatal mortality in the United States. *Population and Development Review* 13:245–79.

Gilligan, Carol. 1982. *In a different voice.* Cambridge, MA: Harvard University Press.

Held, Linda. 1981. Self-esteem and social network of the young pregnant teenager. *Adolescence* 16 (64): 904–12.

Hogan, Dennis P., and Evelyn M. Kitagawa. 1985. The impact of social status, family structure, and neighborhood on the fertility of black adolescents. *American Journal of Sociology* 90:825–53.

Johnson, Clift, and Andrew Sum. 1987. *Declining earnings of young men: Their relation to poverty, teen pregnancy, and family formation.* Washington, DC: Children's Defense Fund Adolescent Pregnancy Prevention Clearinghouse.

Jordan, Judith. 1984. Empathy and self-boundaries. Work in progress. Wellesley, MA: Stone Center Working Paper Series.

Knubel, Fred. 1990. Untitled paper presented at the annual meeting of the American Association for the Advancement of Science, New Orleans.

Ladner, Joyce A. 1972. *Tomorrow's tomorrow.* New York: Anchor Books.

Ladner, Joyce A., and Ruby M. Gourdine. 1984. Intergenerational teenage motherhood: Some preliminary findings. *SAGE: A Scholarly Journal on Black Women* 1:22–24.

Levinson, Ruth Andrea. 1986. Contraceptive self-efficacy: A perspective on teenage girls' contraceptive behavior. *Journal of Sex Research* 22:347–69.

Lieberman, Janet Joseph. 1981. Loss of control as related to birth control: Knowledge, attitudes and practices. *Adolescence* 16:1–21.

Miller, Jean Baker. 1986. *Toward a new psychology of women.* Boston: Beacon.

Moynihan, D. P. 1965. *The Negro family: The case for national action.* Washington, DC: U.S. Department of Labor, Office of Policy Planning and Research.

Nathanson, Constance. 1991. *Dangerous passages: The social control of sexuality in women's adolescence.* Philadelphia: Temple University Press.

Patten, Marie. 1981. Self concept and self esteem: Factors in adolescent pregnancy. *Adolescence* 16 (64): 764–77.

Pittman, Karen, and Gina Adams. 1988. *Teenage pregnancy: An advocate's guide to the numbers*. Washington, DC: Children's Defense Fund Adolescent Pregnancy Prevention Clearing House.

Salzman, Judith P. 1990. Save the world, save myself. In *Making connections: The relational worlds of adolescent girls at Emma Willard School*, ed. Carol Gilligan, Nona Plyors, and Trudy J. Hanmer, 110–45. Cambridge, MA: Harvard University Press.

Staples, Robert. 1985. Changes in Black family structure: The conflict between family ideology and structural conditions. *Journal of Marriage and the Family* 47:1005–13.

Stem, Lori. 1990. Conceptions of separation and connection in female adolescents. In *Making connections. The relational worlds of adolescent girls at Emma Willard School*, ed. Carol Gilligan, Nona Plyors, and Trudy J. Hanmer, 73–87. Cambridge, MA: Harvard University Press.

Zeinik, Melvin, John F. Kantner, and Kathleen Ford. 1981. *Sex and pregnancy in adolescence*. Beverly Hills, CA: Sage.

Zongker, Calvin. 1977. The self concept of pregnant adolescent girls. *Adolescence* 12 (48): 477–88.

JANET L. JACOBS is Assistant Professor of Women's Studies at the University of Colorado, Boulder. She is author of Divine Disenchantment: Deconverting from New Religions *(Indiana University Press, 1989). Her published articles include "Reassessing Mother Blame in Incest,"* Signs *(1990), and "Effects of Ritual Healing among Female Victims of Abuse,"* Sociological Analysis *(1989). Her most recent work,* Victimized Daughters: Incest and the Development of the Female Self, *is forthcoming from Routledge.*

Masculinities and Athletic Careers

MICHAEL A. MESSNER

The growth of women's studies and feminist gender studies has in recent years led to the emergence of a new men's studies (Brod 1987; Kimmel 1987). But just as feminist perspectives on women have been justifiably criticized for falsely universalizing the lives and issues of white middle-class U.S. women (Baca Zinn, Cannon, Higginbotham, and Dill 1986; hooks 1984), so, too, men's studies has tended to focus on the lives of relatively privileged men. As Brod (1983–1984) points out in an insightful critique of the middle-class basis and bias of the men's movement, if men's studies is to be relevant to minority and working-class men, less emphasis must be placed on personal lifestyle transformations and more emphasis must be placed on developing a structural critique of social institutions. Although some institutional analysis has begun in men's studies, very little critical scrutiny has been focused on that very masculine institution, organized sports (Messner 1985; Sabo 1985; Sabo and Runfola 1980). Not only is the institution of sports an ideal place to study men and masculinity, careful analysis would make it impossible to ignore the realities of race and class differences.

AUTHOR'S NOTE: Parts of this work were presented as papers at the American Sociological Association Annual Meeting in Chicago, in August 1987, and at the North American Society for the Sociology of Sport Annual Meeting in Edmonton, Alberta, in November 1987. I thank Maxine Baca Zinn, Bob Blauner, Bob Dunn, Pierrette Hondagmen-Sotelo, Carol Jacklin, Michael Kimmel, Judith Lorber, Don Sabo, Barrie Thorne, and Carol Warren for constructive comments on earlier versions of this work.

In the early 1970s, Edwards (1971, 1973) debunked the myth that the predominance of blacks in sports to which they have access signaled as end to institutionalized racism. It is now widely accepted in sport sociology that social institutions such as the media, education, the economy, and (a more recent and controversial addition to the list) the black family itself all serve to systematically channel disproportionately large numbers of young black men into football, basketball, boxing, and baseball, where they are subsequently "stacked" into low-prestige and high-risk positions, exploited for their skills, and, finally, when their bodies are used up, excreted from organized athletics at a young age with no transferable skills with which to compete in the labor market (Edwards 1984; Eitzen and Purdy 1986; Eitzen and Yetman 1977).

While there are racial differences in involvement in sports, class, ago and educational differences seem more significant. Rudman's (1986) initial analysis revealed profound differences between whites' and blacks' orientations to sports. Blacks were found to be more likely than whites to view sports favorably, to incorporate sports into their daily lives, and to be affected by the outcome of sporting events. However, when age, education, and social class were factored into the analysis, Rudman found that race did not explain whites' and blacks' different orientations. Blacks' affinity for sports is best explained by their tendency to be clustered disproportionately in lower-income groups.

The 1980s ushered in what Wellman (1986, 43) calls "new political linguistics of race," which emphasize cultural rather than structural causes (and solutions) to the problems faced by black communities. The advocates of the cultural perspective believe that the high value placed on sports by black communities has led to the development of unrealistic hopes in millions of black youths. They appeal to family and community to bolster other choices based upon a more rational assessment of "reality." Visible black role models in many other professions now exist, they say, and there is ample evidence which proves that sports careers are, at best, a bad gamble.

Critics of the cultural perspective have condemned it as conservative and victim blaming. But it can also be seen as a response to the view of black athletes as little more than unreflexive dupes of an all-powerful system, which ignores the importance of agency. Gruneau (1983) has argued that sports must be examined within a theory that views human beings as active subjects who are operating within historically constituted structural constraints. Gruneau's reflexive theory rejects the simplistic views of sports as either a realm of absolute oppression or an arena of absolute freedom and spontaneity. Instead, he argues, it is necessary to construct an understanding of how and why participants themselves actively make choices and construct and define meaning and a sense of identity within the institutions that they find themselves.

None of these perspectives consider the ways that gender shapes men's definitions of meaning and choices. Within the sociology of sport, gender as a process that interacts with race and class is usually ignored or taken for granted—except when it is *women* athletes who are being studied. Sociologists who are attempting to come to grips with the experiences of black men in general, and in organized sports in particular, have almost exclusively focused their analytic attention on the variable "black," while uncritically taking "men" as a given. Hare and Hare (1984), for example, view masculinity as a biologically determined tendency to act as a provider and protector that is thwarted for black men by socioeconomic and racist obstacles. Staples (1982) does view masculinity largely as a socially produced script, but he accepts this script as a given, preferring to focus on black men's blocked access to male role fulfillment. These perspectives on masculinity fail to show how the male role itself, as it interacts with a constricted structure of opportunity, can contribute to locking black men into destructive relationships and lifestyles (Franklin 1984; Majors 1986).

This chapter will examine the relationships among male identity, race and social class by listening to the voices of former athletes. I will first briefly describe my research. Then I will discuss the similarities and differences in the choices and experiences of men from different racial and social class backgrounds. Together, these choices and experiences help to construct what Connell (1987) calls "the gender order." Organized sports, it will be suggested, is a practice through which men's separation from and power over women is embodied and naturalized at the same time that hegemonic (white, heterosexual, professional-class) masculinity is clearly differentiated from marginalized and subordinated masculinities.

Description of research

Between 1983 and 1985, I conducted thirty open-ended, in-depth interviews with male former athletes. My purpose was to add a critical understanding of male gender identity to Levinson's (1978) conception of the "individual lifecourse"—specifically, to discover how masculinity develops and changes as a man interacts with the socially constructed world of organized sports. Most of the men I interviewed had played the U.S. "major sports"—football, basketball, baseball, track. At the time of the interview, each had been retired from playing organized sports for at least five years. Their ages ranged from twenty-one to forty-eight, with the median, thirty-three. Fourteen were black, fourteen were white, and two were Hispanic. Fifteen of the sixteen black and Hispanic men had come from poor or working-class families, while the majority (9 of 14) of the white men had come from middle-class or professional families. Twelve had played organized sports through high school, eleven through college, and seven had been professional athletes. All had at some time in their lives based their identities largely on their roles as athletes and could therefore be said to have had athletic careers.

Male identity and organized sports

Earlier studies of masculinity and sports argued that sports socializes boys to be men (Lever 1976; Schafer 1975). Here, boys learn cultural values and behaviors, such as competition, toughness, and winning at all costs, that are culturally valued aspects of masculinity. While offering important insights, these early studies of masculinity and sports suffered from the limiting assumptions of a gender-role theory that seems to assume that boys come to their first athletic experience as blank slates onto which the values of masculinity are imprinted. This perspective oversimplifies a complex reality. In fact, young boys bring an already gendered identity to their first sports experiences, an identity that is struggling to work through the developmental task of individuation (Chodorow 1978; Gilligan 1982). Yet as Benjamin (1988) has argued, individuation is accomplished, paradoxically, only through relationships with other people in the social world. So, although the major task of masculinity is the development of a "positional identity" that clarifies the boundaries between self and other, this separation must be accomplished through some form of connection with others. For the men in my study, the rule-bound structure of organized sports became a context in which they struggled to construct a masculine positional identity.

All of the men in this study described the emotional salience of their earliest experiences in sports in terms of relationships with other males. It was not winning and victories that seemed important at first; it was something "fun" to do with fathers, older brothers or uncles, and eventually with same-aged peers. As a man from a white, middle-class family said, "the most important thing was just being out there with the rest of the guys—being friends." A thirty-two-year-old man from a poor Chicano family, whose mother had died when he was nine years old put it more succinctly:

> What I think sports did for me is it brought me into kind of an instant family. By being on a Little League team, or even just playing with kids in the neighborhood, it brought what I really wanted, which was some kind of closeness.

Though sports participation may have initially promised "some kind of closeness," by the ages of nine or ten, the less skilled boys were already becoming alienated from—or weeded out of—the highly competitive and hierarchical system of organized sports. Those who did experience some early successes received recognition from adult males (especially fathers and older brothers) and held higher status among peers. As a result, they began to pour more and more of their energies into athletic participation. It was only after they learned that they would get recognition from other people for being a good athlete—indeed, that this attention was contingent upon being a winner—that performance and winning (the dominant values of organized sports) became-extremely important. For some, this created pressures that served to lessen or eliminate the fun of athletic participation (Messner 1987a, 1987b).

While feminist psychoanalytic and developmental theories of masculinity are helpful in explaining boys' early attraction to and motivations in organized sports, the imperatives of core gender identity do not fully determine the contours and directions of the life course. As Rubin (1985) and Levinson (1978) have pointed out, an understanding of the lives of men must take into account the processual nature of male identity as it unfolds through interaction between the internal (psychological ambivalences) and the external (social, historical, and institutional) contexts.

To examine the impact of the social contexts, I divided my sample into two comparison groups. In the first group were ten men from higher-status backgrounds, primarily white, middle-class, and professional families. In the second group were twenty men from lower-status backgrounds, primarily minority, poor, and working-class families. While my data offered evidence for the similarity of experiences and motivations of men from poor backgrounds, independent of race. I also found anecdotal evidence of a racial dynamic that operates independently of social class. However, my sample was not large enough to separate race and class, and so I have combined them to make two status groups.

In discussing these two groups, I will focus mainly on the high school years. During this crucial period, the athletic role may become a master status for young man, and he is beginning to make assessments and choices about his future. It is here that many young men make a major commitment to—or begin to back away from—athletic careers.

Men from higher-status backgrounds

The boyhood dream of one day becoming a professional athlete—a dream shared by nearly all the men interviewed in this study—is rarely realized. The sports world is extremely hierarchical. The pyramid of sports careers narrows very rapidly as one climbs from high school, to college, to professional levels of competition (Edwards 1984; Harris and Ritzen 1978; Hill and Lowe 1978). In fact, the chances of attaining professional status in sports are approximately 4/100,000 for a white man, 2/100,000 for a black man, and 3/1,000,000 for a Hispanic man in the United States (Leonard and Reyman 1988). For many young athletes their dream ends early when coaches inform them that they are not big enough, strong enough, fast enough, or skilled enough to compete at the higher levels. But six of the higher-status men I interviewed did not wait for coaches to weed them out. They made conscious decisions in high school or in college to shift their attentions elsewhere—usually toward educational and career goals. Their decision not to pursue an athletic career appeared to them in retrospect to be a rational decision based on the growing knowledge of how very slim their chances were to be successful in the sports world. For instance, a twenty-eight-year-old white graduate student said:

> By junior high I started to realize that I was a good player—maybe even one of the best in my community—but I realized that there were all these people all over the country and how few will get to play pro sports. By high school, I still dreamed of being a pro—I was a serious athlete, I played hard—but I knew it wasn't heading anywhere. I wasn't going to play pro ball.

A thirty-two-year-old white athletic director at a small private college had been a successful college baseball player. Despite considerable attention from professional scouts, he had decided to forgo a shot at a baseball career and to enter graduate school to pursue a teaching credential. As he explained this decision:

> At the time I think I saw baseball as pissing in the wind, really. I was married, I was twenty-two years old with a kid. I didn't want to spend four or five years in the minors with a family. And I could see I wasn't a superstar; so it wasn't really worth it. So I went to grad school. I thought that would be better for me.

Perhaps most striking was the story of a high school student body president and top-notch student who was also "Mr. Everything" in sports. He was named captain of his basketball, baseball, and football teams and achieved All-League honors in each sport. This young white man from a middle-class family received attention from the press and praise from his community and peers for his athletic accomplishments. as well as several offers of athletic scholarships from universities. But by the time he completed high school, he had already decided to quit playing organized sports. As he said:

> I think in my own mind I kind of downgraded the stardom thing. I thought that was small potatoes. And sure, that's nice in high school and all that, but on a broad scale, I didn't think it amounted to all that much. So I decided that my goal's to be a dentist, as soon as I can.

In his sophomore year of college, the basketball coach nearly persuaded him to go out for the team, but eventually he decided against it:

> I thought, so what if I can spend two years playing basketball? I'm not going to be a basketball player forever and I might jeopardize my chances of getting into dental school if I play.

He finished college in three years, completed dental school, and now in his mid-thirties, is again the epitome of the successful American man, a professional with a family, a home, and a membership in the local country club.

How and why do so many successful male athletes from higher status backgrounds come to view sports careers as "pissing in the wind" or as "small potatoes"? How and why do they make this early assessment and choice to shift from sports and toward educational and professional goals? The white, middle-class institutional context, with its emphasis on education and income, makes it clear to them that choices exist and that the pursuit of an athletic career is not a particularly good choice to make. Where the young male once found sports to be a convenient institution within which to construct masculine-status, the post adolescent and young adult men from a higher-status background simply transfers these same strivings to other institutional contexts—education and careers.

For the higher-status men who had chosen to shift from athletic careers, sports remained important on two levels. First, having been a successful high school or college athlete enhances one's adult status among other men in the community—but only as a badge of masculinity that is *added* to his professional status. In fact, several men in professions chose to be interviewed in their offices, where they publicly displayed the trophies and plaques that attested to their earlier athletic accomplishments. Their high school and college athletic careers may have appeared to them as "small potatoes," but many successful men speak of their earlier status as athletes as having "opened doors" for them in their present professions and in community affairs. Similarly, Farr's (1988) research on "Good Old Boys Sociability Groups" shows how sports, as part of the glue of masculine culture, continues to facilitate "dominance bonding" among privileged men long after active sports careers end. The college-educated, career-successful men in Farr's study rarely express overtly sexist, racist, or classist attitudes; in fact, in their relationships with women, they "often engage in expressive intimacies" and "make fun of exaggerated 'machismo'" (p. 276). But though they outwardly conform more to what Pieck (1982) calls "the modern male role," their informal relationships within their sociability groups, in effect, affirm their own gender and class status by constructing and clarifying the boundaries between themselves and women and lower-status men. This dominance bonding is based largely upon ritual forms of sociability (camaraderie, competition), "the superiority of which was first affirmed in the exclusionary play activities of young boys in groups" (Farr 1988, 265).

In addition to contributing to dominance bonding among higher-status adult men, sports remains salient in terms of the ideology of gender relations. Most men continued to watch, talk about, and identify with sports long after their own disengagement from athletic careers. Sports as a mediated spectacle provides an important context in which traditional conceptions of masculine superiority—conceptions recently contested by women—are shored up. As a thirty-two-year-old white professional-class man said of one of the most feared professional football players today:

> A woman can do the same job as I can do—maybe even be my boss. But I'll be *damned* if she can go out on the football field and take a hit from Ronnie Lott.

Violent sports as spectacle provide linkages among men in the project of the domination of women, while at the same time helping to construct and clarify differences among various masculinities. The preceding statement is a clear identification with Ronnie Lott *as a man,* and the basis of the identification is the violent male body. As Connell (1987, 85) argues, sports is an important organizing institution for the embodiment of masculinity. Here, men's power over women becomes naturalized and linked to the social distribution of violence. Sports, as a practice, suppresses natural (sex) similarities, constructs differences, and then, largely through the media, weaves a structure of symbol and interpretation around these differences that naturalizes them (Hargreaves 1986, 112). It is also significant that the man who made the statement about Ronnie Lott was quite aware that he (and perhaps 99 percent of the rest of the U.S. male population) was probably as incapable as most women of taking a "hit" from someone like Lott and living to tell of it. For middle-class men, the "tough guys" of the culture industry—the Rambos, the Ronnie Lotts who are fearsome "hitters," who "play hurt"—are the heroes who "prove" that "we men" are superior to women. At the same time, they play the role of the "primitive other," against whom higher status men define themselves as "modern" and "civilized."

Sports, then, is important from boyhood through aduthood for men from higher-status background. But it is significant that by adolescence and early adulthood, most of these young men have concluded that sports *careers* are not for them. Their middle-class cultural environment encourages them to decide to shift their masculine strivings in more "rational" directions: education and nonsports careers. Yet their previous sports participation continues to be very important to them in terms of constructing and validating their status within privileged male peer groups and within their chosen professional careers. And organized sports, as a public spectacle, is a crucial locus around which ideologies of male superiority over women, as well as higher-status men's superiority over lower-status men, are constructed and naturalized.

Men from lower-status backgrounds

For the lower-status young men in this study, success in sports was not an added proof of masculinity; it was often their only hope of achieving public masculine status. A thirty-four-year-old black bus driver who had been a star athlete in three sports in high school had neither the grades nor the money to attend college, so he accepted an offer from the U.S. Marine Corps to play on their baseball team. He ended up in Vietnam, where a grenade blew four fingers off his pitching hand. In retrospect, he believed that his youthful focus on sports stardom and his concomitant lack of effort in academics made sense:

> You can go anywhere with athletics—you don't have to have brains. I mean, I didn't feel like I was gonna go out there and be a computer expert, or something that was gonna make a lot of money. The only thing I could do and live comfortably would be to play sports—just to get a contract—doesn't matter if you play second or third team in the pros, you're gonna make big bucks. That's all I wanted, a confirmed livelihood at the end of my ventures, and the only way I could do it would be through sports. So I tried. It failed, but that's what I tried.

Similar, and even more tragic, is the story of a thirty-four-year-old black man who is now serving a life term in prison. After a career-ending knee injury at the age of twenty abruptly ended what had appeared to be a certain road to professional football fame and fortune, he decided that he "could still be rich and famous" by robbing a bank. During his high school and college years, he said, he was nearly illiterate:

> I'd hardly ever go to classes and they'd give me Cs. My coaches taught some of the classes. And I felt, "So what? They *owe* me that! I'm an *athlete*!" I thought that was what I was born to do—to play sports—and everybody understood that.

Are lower-status boys and young men simply duped into putting all their eggs into one basket? My research suggested that there was more than "hope for the future" operating here. There were also immediate psychological reasons that they chose to pursue athletic careers. By the high school years, class and ethnic inequalities had become glaringly obvious, especially for those who attended socioeconomically heterogeneous schools. Cars, nice clothes, and other signs of status were often unavailable to these young men, and this contributed to a situation in which sports took on an expanded importance for them in terms of constructing masculine identities and status. A white, thirty-six-year-old man from a poor, single-parent family who later played professional baseball had been acutely aware of his low-class status in his high school:

> I had one pair of jeans, and I wore them every day. I was always afraid of what people thought of me—that this guy doesn't have anything, that he's wearing the same Levi's all the time, he's having to work in the cafeteria for his lunch. What's going on? I think that's what made me so shy. . . . But boy, when I got into sports, I let it all hang out—[laughs]—and maybe that's why I became so good, because I was frustrated, and when I got into that element, they gave me my uniform in football, basketball, and baseball, and I didn't have to worry about how I looked, because then it was *me* who was coming out, and not my clothes or whatever. And I think that was the drive.

Similarly, a forty-one-year-old black man who had a twenty-year professional football career described his insecurities as one of the few poor blacks in a mostly white, middle-class school and his belief that sports was the one arena in which he could be judged solely on his merit:

> I came from a very poor family, and I was very sensitive about that in those days. When people would say things like "Look at him—he has dirty pants on," I'd think about it for a week. [But] I'd put my pants on and I'd go out on the football field with the intention that I'm gonna do a job. And if that calls on me to hurt you, I'm gonna do it. It's a simple as that. I demand respect just like everybody else.

Respect, was what I heard over and over when talking with the men from lower-status backgrounds, especially black men. I interpret this type of respect to be a crystallization of the masculine quest for recognition through public achievement, unfolding within a system of structured constraints due to class and race inequities. The institutional context of education (sometimes with the collusion of teachers and coaches) and the constructed structure of opportunity in the economy made the pursuit of athletic careers appear to be the most rational choice to these young men.

The same is not true of young lower-status women. Dunkle (1985) points out that from junior high school through adulthood, young black men are far more likely to place high value on sports than are young black women, who are more likely to value academic achievement. There appears to be a gender dynamic operating in adolescent male peer groups that contributes toward their valuing sports more highly than education. Franklin (1986, 161) has argued that many of the normative values of the black male peer group (little respect for nonaggressive solutions to disputes, contempt for nonmaterial culture) contribute to the constriction of black men's views of desirable social positions, especially through education. In my study, a forty-two-year-old black man who did succeed in beating the odds by using his athletic scholarship to get a college degree and eventually becoming a successful professional said:

> By junior high, you either got identified as an athlete, a thug, or bookworm. It's very important to be seen as somebody who's capable in some area. And you *don't* want to be identified as a bookworm. I was very good with books, but I was kind of covert about it. I was a closet bookworm. But with sports, I was *somebody;* so I worked very hard at it.

For most young men from lower-status backgrounds, the poor quality of their schools, the attitudes of teachers and coaches, as well as the antieducation environment within their own male peer groups, made it extremely unlikely that they would be able to succeed as students. Sports, therefore, became *the* arena in which they attempted to "show their stuff." For these lower-status men, as Baca Zinn (1982) and Majors (1986) argued in their respective studies of Chicano men and black men, when institutional resources that signify masculine status and control are absent, physical presence, personal style, and expressiveness take on increase importance. What Majors (1986, 6) calls "cool pose" is black men's expressive, often aggressive, assertion of masculinity. This self-assertion often takes place within a social context in which the young man is quite aware of existing social inequities. As the black bus driver, referred to earlier, said of his high school years:

> See, the rich people use their money to do what they want to do. I use my ability. If you wanted to be around me, if you wanted to learn something about sports, I'd teach you. But you're gonna take me to lunch. You're gonna let me use your car. See what I'm saying? In high school I'd go where I wanted to go. I didn't have to be educated. I was well-respected. I'd go somewhere, and they'd say, "Hey, that's Mitch Harris.[1] yeah, that's a bad son of a bitch!"

Majors (1986) argues that although "cool pose" represents a creative survival technique within a hostile environment, the most likely long term effect of this masculine posturing is educational and occupational dead ends. As a result, we can conclude, lower-status men's personal and peer-group responses to a constricted structure of opportunity—responses that are rooted, in part, in the developmental insecurities and ambivalences of masculinity—serve to lock many of these young men into limiting activities such as sports.

Summary and Conclusions

This research has suggested that within a social context that is stratified by social class and by race, the choice to pursue—or not to pursue—an athletic career is explicable as an individual's rational assessment of the available means to achieve a respected masculine identity. For nearly all of the men from lower-status backgrounds, the status and respect that they received through sports was temporary—it did not translate into upward mobility. Nonetheless, a strategy of discouraging young black boys and men from involvement in sports is probably doomed to fail, since it ignores the continued existence of structural constraints. Despite the increased number of black role models in nonsports professions, employment opportunities for young black males have actually deteriorated in the 1980s (Wilson and Neckerman 1986), and nonathletic opportunities in higher education have also declined. While blacks constitute 14 percent of the college-aged (18–24 years) U.S. population, as a proportion of students in four-year colleges and universities, they have dropped to 8 percent. In contrast, by 1985, black men constituted 49 percent of all college basketball players and 61 percent of basketball players in institutions that grant athletic scholarships (Berghorn et al., 1988). For young black men, then, organized sports appears to be more likely to get them to college than their own efforts in nonathletic activities.

But it would be a mistake to conclude that we simply need to breed socioeconomic conditions that make it possible for poor and minority men to mimic the "rational choices" of white, middle-class men. If we are to build an appropriate understanding of the lives of all men, we must critically analyze white middle-class masculinity, rather than uncritically taking it as a normative standard. To fail to do this would be to ignore the ways in which organized sports serves to construct and legitimate gender differences and inequalities among men and women.

Feminist scholars have demonstrated that organized sports gives men from all backgrounds a means of status enhancement that is not available to young women. Sports thus serve the interests of all men in helping to construct and legitimize their control of public life and their domination of women (Bryson 1987; Hall 1987; Theberge 1987). Yet concrete studies are suggesting that men's experiences within sports are not all of a piece. Brian Pronger's (1990) research suggests that gay men approach sports differently than straight men do, with a sense of "irony." And my research suggests that although sports are important for men from both higher- and lower-status backgrounds, there are crucial differences. In fact, it appears that the meaning that most men give to their athletic strivings has more to do with competing for status among men than it has to do with proving superiority over women. How can we explain this seeming contradiction between the feminist claim that sports links all men in the domination of women and the research findings that different groups of men relate to sports in very different ways?

The answer to this question lies in developing a means of conceptualizing the interrelationships between varying forms of domination and subordination. Marxist scholars of sports often falsely collapse everything into a class analysis; radical feminists often see gender domination as universally fundamental. Concrete examinations of sports, however, reveal complex and multilayered systems of inequality: racial, class, gender, sexual preference, and age dynamics are all salient features of the athletic context. In examining this reality, Connell's (1987) concept of the "gender order" is useful. The gender order is a dynamic process that is constantly in a state of play. Moving beyond static gender-role theory and reductionist concepts of patriarchy that view men as an undifferentiated group which oppresses women, Connell argues that at any given historical moment, there are competing masculinities—some hegemonic, some marginalized, some stigmatized. Hegemonic masculinity (that definition of masculinity which is culturally ascendant) is constructed in relation to various subordinated masculinities as well as in relation to femininities. The project of male domination of women may tie all men together but men share very unequally in the fruits of this domination.

These are key insights in examining the contemporary meaning of sports. Utilizing the concept of the gender order, we can begin to conceptualize how hierarchies of race, class, age, and sexual preference among men help to construct and legitimize men's overall power and privilege over women. And how, for some black, working-class, or gay men, the false promise of sharing in the fruits of hegemonic masculinity often ties them into their marginalized and subordinate statuses within hierarchies of intermale dominance. For instance, black men's development of what Majors (1986) calls "cool pose" within sports can be interpreted as an example of creative resistance to one form of social domination (racism); yet it also demonstrates the limits of an agency that adopts other forms of social domination (masculinity) as its vehicle. As Majors (1990) points out:

> Cool pose demonstrates black males' potential to transcend oppressive conditions in order to express themselves *as men.* [Yet] it ultimately does not put black males in a position to live and work in more egalitarian ways with women, nor does it directly challenge male hierarchies.

Indeed, as Connell's (1990) analysis of an Australian "Iron Man" shows, the commercially successful, publicly acclaimed athlete may embody all that is valued in present cultural conceptions of hegemonic masculinity—physical strength, commercial success, supposed heterosexual virility. Yet higher-status men, while they admire the public image of the successful athlete, may also look down on him as a narrow, even atavistic, example of masculinity. For these higher-status men, their earlier sports successes are often status enhancing and serve to link them with other men in ways that continue to exclude women. Their decisions not to pursue athletic careers are equally important signs of their status vis-à-vis other men. Future examinations of the contemporary meaning and importance of sports to men might take as a fruitful point of departure that athletic participation, and sports as public spectacle serve to provide linkages among men in the project of the domination of women, while at the same time helping to construct and clarify differences and hierarchies among various masculinities.

Note

1. "Mitch Harris" is a pseudonym.

References

Baca Zinn, M. 1982. Chicano men and masculinity. *Journal of Ethnic Studies* 10:29–44.

Baca Zinn, M., L. Weber Cannon, E. Higginbotham, and B. Thornton Dill. 1986. The costs of exclusionary practices in women's studies. *Signs: Journal of Women in Culture and Society* 11:290–303.

Benjamin, J. 1988. *The bonds of love: Psychoanalysis, feminism, and the problem of domination.* New York: Pantheon.

Berghorn, F. J. et al. 1988. Racial participation in men's and women's intercollegiate basketball: Continuity and change, 1958–1985. *Sociology of Sport Journal* 5:107–24.

Brod, H. 1983–84. Work clothes and leisure suits: The class basis and bias of the men's movement. *M: Gentle Men for Gender Justice* 11:10–12, 38–40.

Brod, H., ed 1987. *The making of masculinities: The new men's studies.* Winchester, MA: Alien & Unwin.

Bryson, L. 1987. Sport and the maintenance of masculine hegemony. *Women's Studies International Forum* 10:349–60.

Chodorow, N. 1978. *The reproduction of mothering.* Berkeley: University of California Press.

Connell, R. W. 1987. *Gender and power.* Stanford, CA: Stanford University Press.

———. 1990. An Iron Man: The body and some contradictions of hegemonic masculinity. In *Sport, men, and the gender order: Critical feminist perspectives.* ed. M. A. Messner and D. S. Sabo. Champaign IL: Human Kinetics.

Dunkle, M. 1985. Minority and low-income girls and young women in athletics. *Equal Pay* 5 (Spring–Summer): 12–13.

Edwards, H. 1971. The myth of the racially superior athlete. *The Black Scholar* 3 (November).

———. 1973. *The sociology of sport,* Homewood, IL: Dorsey.

———. 1984. The collegiate athletic arms race: Origins and implications of the Rule 480 controversy. *Journal of Sport and Social Issues* 8:4–22.

Eitzen, D. S., and D. A. Purdy. 1986. The academic preparation and achievement of black and white college athletes. *Journal of Sport and Social Issues* 10:15–29.

Eitzen, D. S., and N. B. Yetman. 1977. Immune from racism? *Civil Rights Digest* 9:3–13.

Farr, K. A. 1988. Dominance bonding through the good old boys sociability group. *Sex Roles* 18:259–77.

Franklin, C. W. II. 1984. *The changing definition of masculinity.* New York: Plenum.

———. 1986. Surviving the institutional decimation of black males: Causes, consequences, and intervention. In *The making of masculinities: The new men's studies,* edited by H. Brod. Winchester, MA: Allen & Unwin.

Gilligan, C. 1982. *In a different voice: Psychological theory and women's development.* Cambridge, MA: Harvard University Press.

Greneau, R. 1983. *Class, sports, and social development.* Amherst: University of Massachusetts Press.

Hall, M. A., ed 1987. The gendering of sport, leisure, and physical education. *Women's Studies International Forum* 10:361–474.

Hare, N., and J. Hare, 1984. *The endangered black family: Coping with the unisexualization and coming extinction of the black race.* San Francisco, CA: Black Think Tank.

Hargreaves, J. A. 1986. Where's the virtue? Where's the grace? A discussion of the social production of gender through sport. *Theory, Culture and Society* 3:109–21.

Harris, D. S., and D. S. Eitzen. 1978. The consequences or failure in sport. *Urban life* 7:177–88.

Hill, P., and B. Lowe. 1978. The inevitable metathesis of the retiring athlete. *International Review of Sport Sociology* 9:5–29.

hooks, b. 1984. *Feminist theory: From margin to center.* Boston: South End Press.

Kimmel, M. S., ed. 1987. *Changing men: New directions in research on men and masculinity.* Newbury Park, CA: Sage.

Leonard, W. M. II, and J. M. Reyman. 1988. The odds of attaining professional athlete status: Refining the computations. *Sociology of Sport Journal* 5:162–69.

Lever, J. 1976. Sex differences in the games children play. *Social Problems* 23:478–87.

Levinson, D. J. 1978. *The seasons of a man's life.* New York: Ballantine.

Majors, R. 1986. Cool pose: The proud signature of black survival. *Changing men: Issues in gender, sex, and politics* 17:5–6.

———. 1990. Cool pose: Black masculinity in sports. In *Sport, men, and the gender order: Critical feminist perspectives,* ed. M. A. Messner and D. S. Saho. Champaign, IL: Human Kinetics.

Messner, M. 1985. The changing meaning of male identity in the lifecourse of the athlete. *Arena Review* 9:31–60.

———. 1987a. The meaning of success: The athletic experience and the development of male identity. In *The Making of masculinities: The new men's studies,* ed. H. Brod. Winchester, MA: Allen & Unwin.

———. 1987b. The life of a man's seasons: Male identity in the lifecourse of the athlete. In *Changing men: New directions in research an men and masculinity,* ed. M. S. Kimmel. Newbury Park, CA: Sage.

Pleck, J. H. 1982. *The myth of masculinity.* Cambridge: MIT Press.

Pronger, B. 1990. Gay jocks: A phenomenology of gay men in athletics. In *Sport, men and the gender order: Critical feminist perspectives.* ed. M. A. Messner and D. S. Sabo. Champaign, IL: Human Kinetics.

Rubin, L. B. 1985. *Just friends: The role of friendship in our lives.* New York: Harper & Row.

Rudman, W. J. 1986. The sport mystique in black culture. *Sociology of Sport Journal* 3:305–19.

Sabo, D. 1985. Sport, patriarchy, and male identity: New questions about men and sport. *Arena Review* 9:1–30.

Sabo, D., and R. Runfola, eds. 1980. *Jock: Sports and male identity.* Upper Saddle River, NJ: Prentice Hall.

Schafer, W. E. 1975. Sport and male sex role socialization. *Sport Sociology Bulletin* 4:47–54.

Staples, R. 1982. *Black masculinity.* San Francisco, CA: Black Scholar Press.

Theberge, N. 1987. Sport and women's empowerment. *Women's Studies International Forum* 10:387–93.

Wellman, D. 1986. The new political linguistics of race. *Socialist Review* 87/88:43–62.

Wilson, W. J., and K. M. Neckerman, 1986. Poverty and family structure: The widening gap between evidence and public policy issues. In *Fighting poverty,* ed. S. H. Danzinger and D. H. Weinberg. Cambridge, MA: Harvard University Press.

Intersectional Analysis with Two Social Locations

In this section I include one article with only two social locations. Although two locations alone do not satisfy the optimum requirements of intersectional analysis, it will be instructive to explore the reasons for such limitation of social locations and to learn what information can still be gained. This article is a study of the "ways of knowing" of black and white working-class women, "Working-Class Women's Ways of Knowing: Effects of Gender, Race, and Class," by Wendy Luttrell. It is unique among the articles included in this text in that, although focusing exclusively on women, it compares across race rather than within race. From a data collection point of view, it may be more difficult to obtain a sample of women across race than across class within the same race. The author accomplished this by gaining access to two different schools in which adult women attend adult basic education programs. The researcher was able to do so because of her previous experience as a teacher in these schools. It is the absence of middle-class women of either race that results in just two locations. In this case, therefore, inclusion of the two missing locations—black middle-class women and white middle-class women—would have required either a different design or an expansion of the one used. Rather than resulting from a "mishap" in the data collection, as was the case in several other articles reviewed, the two locations emerged out of a conscious design. It would, of course, have been desirable—from an intersectional analysis point of view—for the researcher to have expanded her design to include black and white middle-class women. Such an expansion would have required considerably more time and perhaps also expense that may not have been available.

What do we learn from the inclusion of just two social locations? The author's comparisons of these working-class women in *multiple* social locations—defined by and differentiated by race—makes this an example of intersectional analysis. This is not a comparison of black with white women generically, or of just working-class women, but a comparison of black working- class and white working-class women. It is this intersection of race and class—even though class does not vary—that adds an intersectional dimension to this study. Throughout, the author compares and contrasts the ways of knowing of women in these two social locations, and we learn a great deal about working-class women and about racial differences among working-class women. The focus on working-class women is especially welcome, since there is so little research on the working class. Luttrell comments on both similarities and differences across these two social locations. On differences she writes:

> Women do not experience their exclusion in the same way, however, their daily experiences of maintaining a household, raising children, and sharing a life with men vary according to race and class and create different imperatives for women's ways of knowing (p. 188).

Or again: "Black women . . . claim knowledge not only through gender, but through racial identity and relations" (p. 190). At the same time Luttrell notes: "White and black working-class women are drawn to common sense and intuition because both forms of knowledge allow for subjectivity between the knower and the known, rest in women themselves (not in higher authorities), and are experienced directly in the world (not through abstractions)" (p. 188).

A special section focuses on racial differences between these working-class women's ideas of intelligence and knowing by reporting their own words. These quotes identified by race are very effective in these comparisons and appear in other parts of the article. In some instances, however, the race of the respondent is not given, leaving the reader to guess her identity. The article would have been further strengthened by providing racial identification for all quotes.

WORKING-CLASS WOMEN'S WAYS OF KNOWING

Effects of Gender, Race, and Class

WENDY LUTTRELL
Duke University

ADDRESS. *All correspondence to Dr. Wendy Luttrell, Sociology Department, Duke University, Durham, North Carolina 27706.*

This article describes and analyzes how black and white working-class women define and claim knowledge. It is based on participant observation in classrooms and in-depth interviews outside school with women attending adult basic education programs. The women's perspectives challenge feminist analyses that have identified a single or universal mode of knowing for women; instead, they speak to complex gender, racial, and class relations of power that shape how they think about learning and knowing. Their claims to knowledge simultaneously accept and reject dominant social relations and create paradoxical situations for the women as they pursue adult basic education.

Well, I'm not schoolwise, but I'm streetwise and motherwise and housewifewise. I think there are two kinds of intelligence—streetwise and schoolwise. I don't know much facts about things I learned in school, but I know a lot about life on the streets. I guess I someday might be schoolwise if I stick to it long enough. But what I have now, what I know already, nobody can take away.

–Doreen

You don't need an education to be smart. I know people who can read and write and do their figures. They are smart but they just never finished school. Like me and my husband. We've learned a lot along the road—in that school of hard knocks. We've got what you call common sense.

–Beatrice

The two women just quoted come from distinctly different cultural backgrounds. Doreen, a student in a community-based adult education program, was born and raised in a white, ethnic working-class community in a northeastern city; she characterized her early school experiences as "uncomfortable" and explained that she could not wait until the day she could quit and go to work in the local box factory. Beatrice, a student in a workplace-based adult

---

This article is a revised version of a paper presented at the 1988 Annual Meetings of the American Sociological Association. The author would like to thank Jean O'Barr for her encouragement and Martha Dimes Toher, Rachel Rosenfeld, Robert Shreefter, Jean Stockard, John Wilson, and Julia Wrigley for their perceptive comments on earlier versions. The author is also indebted to the women who participated in the study (whose names have been changed to protect confidentiality) for their patience, openness, and critical insights.

education program, was born and raised on a farm in the southeast; she described going to school as a luxury—something she could do only on rainy days, along with all the other black children she knew who worked for white farmers. Despite their differences, these women share some similar ideas about knowledge and a common framework for evaluating their claims to knowledge. They both distinguish between knowledge produced in school or in textbooks by authorities and knowledge produced through experience. They also have some similar ideas about their "commonsense" capabilities to take care of others. Their ways of knowing are embedded in community, family, and work relationships and cannot be judged by dominant academic standards. Most important, their commonsense knowledge cannot be dismissed, minimized, or "taken away."

This article describes and analyzes how black and white working-class women define and claim knowledge. It is based on participant observation in classrooms and in-depth interviews outside school with 30 women who enrolled in adult basic education programs. The article argues that although these women's conceptions about knowledge overlap, they are not the same and can be traced to differences in their lives. Both the similar and contrasting meanings that the women attached to their knowledge provide us with unique lenses through which to examine the development of gender, race, and class identities and consciousness.

The article begins with a brief discussion of the relevant literature and a description of the research methodology. It then examines the women's shared views of intelligence and common sense, exploring the conflicting working-class interests and values that are promoted through these self-perceptions. This section is followed by a description of hidden gender asymmetries and inequalities in working-class women's ways of knowing and how these asymmetries surface differently for black and white working-class women. The article ends with a discussion of how dominant ideologies of knowledge undermine women's collective identities, claims to knowledge, and power and the consequences for the adult education of working-class women.

Relevant Literature

Although the literature has not specifically addressed working-class women's ways of knowing, several bodies of theoretical and empirical scholarship framed my study. First are ethnographic accounts that describe the schooling process as an arena of struggle in which dominant and subordinate cultures, values, and knowledge collide, producing both resistance to and compliance with dominant social relationships (Apple and Weiss 1983; Connell et al. 1982; Eisenhart and Holland 1983; Fuller 1980; Gaskell 1985; Holland and Eisenhart 1988, in press; McRobbie 1978; Valli 1983; Willis 1977). These accounts form the basis of a critical theory of education in their focus on the experiences of teenagers and young adults in secondary, vocational, or postsecondary education but do not address the issues that adults face when returning to school. This literature argues that working-class girls prepare for their future identities as wives, mothers, and workers through school. However, the women I interviewed seek to change their lives as women through education; their identities are already firmly embedded in cultural, community, family, and work relationships, yet their desire to expand, perfect, or contradict the work they do as women underlies their participation in school. An understanding of how they think they learn and know enables us to appreciate better how people negotiate external constraints and internal meanings in and outside school.

A second body of literature addresses the subjective experiences of adult learners. What is strikingly absent is a critical theory of adult learning that analyzes the production of meanings and class, racial, and gender identities through resistance to imposed knowledge and adult education practices. Although Freire (1970, 1972, 1973, 1978) outlined such a theoretical approach in his work on adult literacy, he minimized gender issues.

Only a handful of researchers have approached the issue of women's adult basic education or literacy practices from a critical perspective, exploring the dilemmas and double binds that working-class women face as they pursue an education (Luttrell 1984; McLaren 1985; Rockhill 1987). Their accounts suggest that working-class women feel a deep conflict between self and others, placing their needs last either by choice or force. Therefore, if learning is to engage working-class women, it must be presented not only as an individual self-development process but as one that is rooted in family and community relationships (Luttrell 1984). In her study of Hispanic women learners, Rockhill (1987) argued that women participate in literacy education as part of the work of the family—a way to serve their children and husbands better and to comply with the dominant values of the middle class, femininity, and Anglo ethnocentrism—but that women's participation in school also challenges Hispanic patriarchal family relations by threatening men's power and control. Despite her compelling analysis of what Hispanic women must risk to become literate and what is at stake when they are denied this basic right, Rockhill did not address the effects of those social, cultural, and political realities on how women learn and understand the world.

This is not to say that feminist questions have not surfaced in research on adult education. Some researchers have examined women's and men's differential access to adult education (McLaren 1981; Scott 1980), and others have explored the psychological, social, and economic impact of education on women's lives (Robinson, Paul, and Smith 1973, 1978). Although scholars generally agree that women's self-perceptions may improve as a result of adult education, some have found women's economic and occupational gains to be negligible (Lovell 1980; McLaren 1985). Still others have focused on the content and pedagogy of adult education courses, suggesting that women's lives and concerns are being minimized or neglected by adult education theory and practice, which further promote unequal gender relations (Hootsman 1980; Thompson 1983). But overall, the field has not provided a comprehensive approach to the understanding of power relations and resistance in women's learning and knowing.

Relevant to this issue is the burgeoning, yet controversial, feminist scholarship about "women's ways of knowing" (Belenky et al. 1986; Chodorow 1978; Gilligan 1982; Keller 1978, 1982), which is the third body of literature to frame my study. The literature claims that through unconscious psychodynamic processes, cognitive development, and gender-role socialization, women develop propensities toward self and knowing that are less linear, separate, and hierarchical than are men's. It also suggests that women's more continuous and connected sense of self-knowledge is embedded in their social relationships and sustained and reproduced by patriarchal Western conceptions of rationality. Both men and women internalize these concepts of rationality and knowledge that falsely dichotomize emotion and thought, objectivity and subjectivity, mind and body, masculinity and femininity (Bordo 1986; Fee 1983; Rose 1983; Smith 1979). Yet, although patriarchal impositions on knowledge may be said to exist, not all women experience them in the same way. Despite the call of feminist scholars for a more comprehensive discussion of differences among women and an examination of the construction of gender in specific historical and social contexts (Dill 1983; Jaggar 1983; Rosaldo 1980; Stack 1986; Thorne 1986), we still know little about the multiple meanings that women attach to the knowledge they have or are seeking and its relationship to the concrete conditions of their lives.

Finally, to understand the cultural and political significance of working-class women's ways of knowing, I drew on Thompson's (1963) analysis of class, culture, and consciousness as ways of living within certain relationships of power. These relationships are formed and change when people articulate and identify their class interests, capabilities, or concerns as being common to others like themselves and against those whose interests are different from (and usually opposed to) theirs. Applying Thompson's framework, I examined how black and white working-class women define their knowledge and capabilities in this way. Cognitive processes are usually understood as individual or psychological, not as part of class, racial, or gender culture and consciousness. Yet, a focus on women's claims to knowledge can help expand the parameters for explaining how consciousness develops in the context of political struggle.

Methodology

The findings reported in this article are from a study of the educational experiences and perceptions of black and white working-class women attending two programs: an urban, northeastern, community-based program serving a white ethnic working-class population and an adult basic education program serving predominantly black maintenance and housekeeping employees of a southeastern university. I chose these programs because they provide a unique access to working-class women learners. The community-based program, with its emphasis on supportive services for women, particularly day care, has made it possible for white working-class women, who otherwise would not have had or considered the opportunity, to continue their education. The workplace literacy program, with its four-hour-a-week work-release arrangement, makes adult education accessible to people whose family responsibilities and transportation problems seriously limit their participation in classes held at night. Both programs attract students who do not feel comfortable in middle-class educational settings, such as high schools or community colleges. In the classroom observations and in-depth interviews, the black women identified their workplace and the white women identified the local settlement house in which the program is housed as hospitable sites for adult learning.

I was first involved in both programs as an adult educator, teaching classes, training teachers, and developing learner-centered curriculum materials. Later, I returned to the programs to conduct research. I informed the women in each program that I was studying working-class women's experiences with and perceptions of education. I collected data in classrooms at different levels of instruction (zero to fourth-grade reading level, fifth- to eighth-grade reading level) preparatory classes for the high school equivalency examination, and community-college preparatory classes) and conducted unstructured interviews with over 200 women. I took notes openly during observations and the initial unstructured interviews. Field notes included descriptions of conversations before, during, and after classes. Notes from the unstructured interviews and classroom observations were coded on a variety of dimensions that emerged as persistent themes, including past school experiences, past and present family experiences and relations, self-concept and self-esteem, educational values, and future aspirations. These themes became the focus of the in-depth interviews.

I selected 15 women from each program to interview in depth. The stratified, selective samples represent the basic demographic profile of women in each community: their marital status, occupation, income, educational level, and religion. The samples also reflect the basic profile of women in each program: their age; past attendance and type of school; number of children living at home; and participation in a classroom, program, or community (active and inactive).

The 15 white women who were interviewed all grew up in a tightly knit, ethnic working-class urban community (mostly Polish and Irish) that has suffered from industrial relocation, inadequate social services, and neglect by officials for the past two decades. Like the subjects of other studies of white working-class communities (Kohn 1977; Rubin 1976), the majority of adults in this neighborhood drop out of or have no education beyond high school, are employed in skilled or semiskilled occupations, are paid an hourly wage, and experience periodic unemployment. All the women attended neighborhood schools (two-thirds attended public school and one-third attended Catholic schools) and since then have moved in and out of the work force as clerical workers, factory workers, waitresses, or hospital or teachers' aides. Two women were displaced homemakers when the study began in 1980.

The black working-class women all grew up in southern rural communities and attended segregated schools. Their work histories are more homogeneous than the white women's in that they all work as housekeepers on the university campus, and some have done so for as many as 20 years. More than half have done domestic work in white people's homes either full time or to supplement their incomes, and most picked cotton or tended tobacco during their youth. Some women have split their work between service and farm labor in an effort to hold onto the land—a practice that is common among southern black working-class people (Stack and Hall 1982). Even though these women reside in different neighborhoods near the university, they share a common heritage in and identity with black rural communities.

The women in both groups shared one basic characteristic: all were mothers, aged 25–50, with children still living at home. The two groups differed, however, in which stage of the life cycle they were in, income, and marital history. Thus, black women of the same age as white women tended to be grandmothers and to have older children or grandchildren living at home. In addition, the family incomes of the white women were higher than those of the black women. And more white women were married at the time of the interviews; the proportion of never-married women with children was higher among black women than among white women, but the same number of black women and white women had dropped out of school because they were pregnant.

The final interviews took place in the women's homes, lasted from two to four hours, and were repeated over the course of a year. In the first interview, I asked each woman to tell me what she remembered about being in school—to describe what she liked and disliked and what kind of student she had been. As part of these accounts, the women also talked about their early work and family experiences. In the second interviews, I asked the women to talk about their current school experiences and what caused them to participate and to evaluate themselves as learners now. These discussions led to an exploration of the women's concepts of intelligence and knowledge. Although I had not included questions about intelligence or common sense in the original guide for the in-depth interviews, each woman inevitably brought up the issue of intelligence in response to the question, "How would you describe yourself as a student?" Definitions of intelligence and common sense, who possesses them, and how they are acquired focused the women's reflections about their capacities as learners. In the final interviews, I followed up on earlier discussions, asking the women to clarify their life histories or to respond to my interpretations of their experiences. This last interview was especially important for me because as a white middle-class researcher, I felt hesitant to interpret experiences that were so vastly different from my own.

The interviews were tape recorded and then transcribed. The interviews with the white working-class women were analyzed and written up as part of my doctoral dissertation (Luttrell 1984) before I began interviewing black women to deepen and expand my understanding and analysis of working-class women's ways of knowing. In analyzing all the interviews, I tried to balance between identifying persistent themes across the interviews and treating each woman's narrative as a unique text. Translating working-class women's ways with words into sociological analysis is problematic, but as other feminist researchers have argued, it is also the task at hand (McRobbie 1982; Oakley 1981; Smith 1987).

Intelligence and Common Sense

Individually, the women expressed diverse and wide-ranging definitions of intelligence, but as a whole, they distinguished between intelligence and common sense. Common sense was most often described as a category of "smarts" attained outside school—a form of knowledge that stems from experience and is judged by people's ability to cope with everyday problems in the everyday world:

> Jim considers himself stupid. He's very good at what he does at his job, but he was never good in school. He has a kind of streetsmarts—he's the commonsense type. I don't know, I'm not sure that intelligence can be measured.
>
> Intelligence is knowing how to use what you know—it's knowing how to do things. I think being intelligent means coping with things in life. Even people with high IQs or with college degrees don't know how to do the simplest, everyday things or cope with everyday problems— that takes *real* intelligence; it takes common sense.

"Real intelligence," or common sense, is a highly valued capacity that flourishes outside school. It is not measured by what school authorities teach you, but by what you can teach yourself or what you learn in the "school of hard knocks":

> My brother is very intelligent—he's self-educated, not school educated. He reads a lot and has taught himself how to play musical instruments. I consider him one of the most intelligent people I know.
>
> My father is *really* intelligent. He loves to read everything and is interested in all sorts of things. He graduated high school, but he did really lousy. But he's by far one of the most intelligent people around and what he knows he taught himself.

The women usually contrasted common sense with school intelligence and indicated that common sense can be ruined by too much education or formal schooling:

> I don't think that intelligence has anything to do with schooling. Schools only make you know more. Education is not a sign of intelligence. But people who are well schooled always seem intelligent. I suppose they might not be any more intelligent than me. My husband has this idea that people with a lot of schooling don't have common sense. It is like the more schooling you have, the less common sense you have.
>
> I used to beg my mother to let me go to school. She would say, "girl, you have no common sense." Or when I would want to read instead of doing my chores she would say, "You're never going to learn anything like that—you've got to have common sense in this world."

Common sense has been characterized as a cultural form of knowledge, a way to apprehend the world as familiar and knowable, and as concrete knowledge to inform action (Fingeret 1983a, 1983b; Geertz 1983). The women's definitions of common sense confirm these characterizations by identifying the knowledge that grows out of people's lived experiences. For these women, common sense is accessible; it requires no specialized training or credentials.

Common sense is a way of assessing or judging the truth on the basis of what people have seen and know to be true. The black women especially believed that you can assess the truth more reliably if you know the person or if the person is known by someone within the community. As Barbara said:

> The people I know have common sense. Like my grandmother. She knows a lot because she's seen

> a lot. She's seen it all and I believe what she says because she's been there. Like she knows about slavery, she didn't read about it, like all of us young folk.

In addition to its cultural base, common sense is also a class-based form of knowledge—a way that the women distinguished themselves from "professionals" and identified themselves as working class:

INTERVIEWER: So who do you consider to be intelligent?

DEBRA: I don't know. I know a lot of people who are very intelligent but they are fruity; I wouldn't want to be one. I have common sense. Maybe I have more intelligence than I'm aware of in some areas, but I am not an academic, learned person, and I don't think I'll ever be. I'm not the professional type. I can work with those kind of intelligent people, but I don't want to be like them.

DOTTIE: I have just never thought about average people like myself being intelligent. People like me have common sense.

According to these women, common sense is not simply an individual characteristic or possession; it reflects working-class capabilities. Common sense affirms and validates working-class experiences and is a way to identify oneself with others who share problems and potentials, creating common bonds and a sense of community. This affirmation came across most strongly in the interviews when the women described how they solved everyday problems through common sense. To them, common sense means relying on family and friends who "know the ropes" to help you learn how to negotiate bureaucracies (schools, welfare agencies, and hospitals) and seeking advice from people who can be trusted, not because they are professional experts, but because they share the same problems. The claim of common sense recognizes and validates working-class solutions, despite the power of scientific knowledge. Common sense supports working-class judgments about what is relevant to everyday life and assessments about what one social historian referred to as "really useful knowledge" in educational practice (Johnson 1979).

Unlike common sense, which is easily defined and acquired through daily life experiences as part of working-class cultures, intelligence, which is acquired through schooling, cannot be so clearly defined and is in potential conflict with working-class cultures. For example, the women thought that although schoolwise intelligence can enhance one's life, it can also interfere with one's ability to meet the demands of working-class existence; they suggested that the *more* schooling one has, the *less* common sense she is likely to have. Similarly, "real intelligence" that is gleaned from books that people teach themselves to read can benefit working-class life, but schoolwise intelligence that is gleaned from textbooks or school authorities can come in conflict with working-class, especially black working-class, experiences and values.

By distinguishing between common sense and schoolwise intelligence, the women came to believe that a certain type of intelligence, rather than class, separates people and that intelligence, rather than class, determines a person's place in the social structure:

> Intelligence has to do with how people accept life, how life comes to them, and how they deal with it. My boys don't use their intelligence. I don't use half my intelligence. If I did, why would I be here?

The women's shared notions of intelligence embraced the dominant ideology of meritocracy in a capitalist society: people's class position is not fixed but is determined by their individual efforts and ambitions:

> There are a few people who make it. They are the ones that are blessed or that has intelligence. The rest of us just have to make do.
>
> The important point is that the system is not working. People's mobility is very limited. People really need education to get out of their

> ruts. The system keeps people in their place, in their class. You need intelligence to get out of your place.

When I responded, "I know a lot of intelligent people living here," one woman replied:

> Yeah, but if they were more ambitious, like me—what I'm trying to do here is use my intelligence—then at least they'd have half a chance of getting out of their ruts.

The ideology of intelligence is a filter through which these women think about and express themselves as adult learners, denying the actual experience and knowledge they have in their everyday lives. The dichotomy they make between intelligence and common sense reflects the disjuncture between the world they know and experience directly and the dominant ideas and images that are fabricated externally, provide a way to understand the everyday world, and serve as a means of social control (Smith 1987). For this reason, although working-class women can claim commonsense knowledge, they are distanced from their intellectual capacities, as is Mary:

> When I was in grade school, one of my teachers said I was smart, so they put me in the advanced class. Now I didn't think of myself as smart until the teacher pointed it out. I would say I have common sense, but then maybe I am smart, maybe I'm intelligent, and I don't know it. But it's been my common sense that has gotten me by in life—how I get along with people—not my grades in school. You can bet on that.

In the end, the women accepted class stratification and relations of domination through the false dichotomy of common sense and intelligence and through class-based notions of "real intelligence."

GENDER-BASED KNOWLEDGE

When the women discussed commonsense knowledge and how it is gained, they revealed their belief that common sense is not a genderless concept. Instead, they indicated that men's claims to knowledge are superior to women's and affirmed the idea that men are more powerful by virtue of their knowledge, not the privilege they have as men. However, the pattern of this gender asymmetry and its impact on each group of women was not the same and thus requires a careful examination.

When talking about people they knew who were intelligent, the white working-class women gave only men as their examples. Although they described their mothers, aunts, or sisters as having common sense, they saw only certain aspects of common sense as "real intelligence"—those that are associated with men's work and their activities.

These differences are most evident in the women's distinction between mental and manual work and ways of knowing. Throughout the interviews, the white working-class women reiterated that intelligence is required to do manual work:

> The most intelligent person I know is my brother—he can fix anything. And when you get right down to it, what's more important than being able to make things work? Not everybody can do that, you know.
>
> Now just because we're going to school and getting educated, we shouldn't forget that people, like my husband, who work with their hands are just as important as college professors and just as smart.

But when the white working-class women defined manual ways of knowing as "real intelligence," they always referred to skilled manual work performed by *men*, not to the manual work required of women in factory jobs. Similarly, they equated men's physical common sense—the ability to work with their hands—with "real intelligence," never discussing women's ability to work with their hands, as in sewing.

In the same spirit, the women also equated men's self-learned activities, such as reading and playing a musical instrument, with intelligence, ignoring the wide range of activities that women teach themselves, including reading and helping children with homework. Instead, the white working-class women described themselves as "housewifewise," "motherwise," "good problem solvers," or "always balancing a lot of things, if that counts." They associated commonsense abilities with activities in the family or the community and considered them trivial.

Not only did the white women value men's common sense more than their own, they described the different ways that working-class men and women acquire common sense. White working-class men learn common sense that translates into "real intelligence" through a set of collective, work-related experiences, including apprenticeships, as sons or employees, or as participants in vocational training programs that teach them what might be called "craft" knowledge. This "craft" knowledge—the ability to work with one's hands and muscles—belongs to the work group; it is not individualized as a character trait and cannot be learned from books. It also identifies one as masculine, capable of performing traditionally sex-stereotyped manly tasks. Men acquire this masculinity and "craft" knowledge not by nature or instinct, but through some public, collective experience. In contrast, working-class women acquire common sense naturally, as intuition. They describe this knowledge as simply a part of being a woman. As Anne explained:

> There are lots of things I know—what you might call woman's intuition or mother's intuition. Taking care of a child with a chronic disease teaches you this. You can begin to predict what the doctors are going to tell you and then you go home and deal with it on your own. That's just common sense; in the end, you do what you have to do as a mother.

For women, common sense stems from relational activities that are embedded in the care of and affiliation with others. They do not recognize these activities as learned but associate them with feelings and intuition. Women's common sense comes in flashes, precipitated by an event such as childbirth or divorce. It can also develop over the years, as women evaluate their ability to cope with extenuating circumstances. The learning process is invisible because this intuitive knowledge is individualized and personal. It is not collective or public, even though it identifies women as feminine and able to fulfill sex-stereotyped roles as mothers and wives, and is seen as affective rather than cognitive. As Cheryl explained:

> Common sense is a feeling, really. Like being a mother. You do things that seem right at the time. Nobody ever tells you to do this or do that. Although my sister, she just had a baby, drives me crazy always calling me up, saying, "What do I do?" You'd think she would have a little more common sense than that.

The black working-class women also located their commonsense knowledge in a variety of caretaking and domestic skills done for the benefit of others. Like the white working-class women, they referred to their common sense as intuitive and stemming from feelings and most often focused on the common sense that it takes to raise children:

INTERVIEWER: Where did you get the common sense you have to raise your children?

LOTS: I was born with it. Now I didn't always use it, like with my boys, but then I was young and running all the time. But you get older, you experience things, you know what's right to do for them and what they need. You're their mother and you stay close to them; you can just feel it.

The women's classification of their knowledge as "affective," not "cognitive"; as "intuitive," not "learned"; or as "feelings," not "thoughts" all reflect an acceptance of dominant conceptions of knowledge and ultimately diminish women's power. Feminist critics of dominant conceptions of knowledge have challenged these ideological dimensions of women's ways of knowing (Rose 1983; Smith, 1979). They have argued that just as the nature of women's domestic work makes it impossible to distinguish what is "love" from what is "labor," the nature of women's knowledge makes it impossible to distinguish what is emotional from what is objective or rational. They also noted that the false dichotomy between emotional versus objective labor promotes relations of authority and the domination of men (who are exempt from personal service work) over women (who perform unpaid domestic work as part of their gender role); this false dichotomy is translated into a distinction between feelings and thoughts. Women are then falsely associated with feelings, while men are falsely associated with thoughts (Fee 1983).

Because society does not view women as sources of official, legitimate, or rational knowledge (nor do women), the women who were interviewed associated their commonsense knowledge with feelings and intuitions. As class relations shape attitudes toward schoolwise versus commonsense knowledge, gender relations influence attitudes toward rational versus intuitive knowledge, thus constraining societal expectations of women's intellectual capabilities.

White and black working-class women are drawn to common sense and intuition because both forms of knowledge allow for subjectivity between the knower and the known, rest in women themselves (not in higher authorities), and are experienced directly in the world (not through abstractions). But both classifications (common sense and intuition) place women in less powerful positions vis-à-vis men (both black and white) and white middle-class professionals (men and women). And they do so not simply because women are fooled or seduced into believing in the ideological split between feelings and rationality, the false dichotomy of mental and manual work, or the promise of meritocracy, but because the real nature of women's knowledge and power is hidden from view and excluded from thought.

How race makes a difference

Women do not experience their exclusion in the same way, however; their daily experiences of maintaining a household, raising children, and sharing a life with men vary according to race and class and create different imperatives for women's ways of knowing. Race affects how women claim knowledge, which is reflected in how the black women differentiated common sense from "real intelligence." First, they did not make the same distinctions between mental and manual ways of knowing or emphasize the intelligence required to do manual work perhaps because black men have historically had limited access to the "crafts." Instead, they viewed common sense, most often referred to as "motherwit," as encompassing everything from solving family disputes to overcoming natural disasters. It was not uncommon for black women to identify both men and women relatives who possess commonsense capabilities that stem from keeping families together. As Lois said:

> I got my common sense from my momma and daddy. They worked real hard to keep us, and they would always be there to help anyones that needed it.

Second, unlike white women, black women did claim "real intelligence" for themselves and their experiences in doing domestic, caretaking work. This "real intelligence" is based on their ability to work hard and get the material things they and their children need and want, with or without the support of a man:

> I got a sister I think she is smart, real intelligent. All of them is smart, but this one is special and she do the same kind of work I do but she's smart. She can hold onto money better than anyone. It look like anything she want she can get it. She bought her a car, this was in the 60s. Then after that she bought her a trailer. She don't buy that many cars, but anytime she or her childrens need something, she can go and get it. But she has a husband that help her, not like my other sisters or me. Her husband is nice to her and both of them working. But even that, it takes a lot of intelligence.
>
> I would say my sister is the most intelligent person I know. She knows how to get what she wants and she has done it on her own, her kids

and working; she ain't never been on welfare or nothing.

Black women are central in keeping black families together—swapping resources and child care and adapting to adverse economic constraints through extended kin networking and mutual support (Jones 1985; Ladner 1972; Stack 1974). As a result, their work as women is also the work of black survival and, therefore, is not as easily diminished or trivialized as that of the white women.

The ability to deal with racism—another type of "real intelligence"—is also something black women learn through doing domestic work in the service of others.

KATE: I'll tell you what takes real intelligence—dealing with people's ignorance. One day, I was at the department store, you know, maybe it was Belk's. I was getting on the escalator and there was this little white boy pointing at me saying to his daddy, "look there at that nigger." Now you should have seen the look on his daddy's face; he looked scared, like I was going to start a race riot or something. He pushed this boy along trying to get out of my way fast. But I know children and they don't mean what they say. He was just saying what he hears at home. But people are ignorant, and it takes real intelligence to know that it's not that little boy's fault.

INTERVIEWER: And how did you get that kind of intelligence?

KATE: Oh, well, you live and learn. You see a lot and watch people. It's a feeling you have to have because not all white people are the same. I sure know that cause I worked for different ones, you know, taking care of their children, and I've seen different things.

This "real intelligence" is acquired by virtue of being a black woman in a white world. It is also a knowledge that black women share equally with black men. It is collective, learned through extended-kin relations, and practiced in daily interactions with white people.

Class-based concepts of intelligence and common sense pit experience against schooling and working-class people against middle-class people; race-based concepts of "ignorance" and "real intelligence" pit whites against blacks. But the invisible gender-based concept that pits collectivity against individuality and autonomy against dependence is the basis for unequal power relations between working-class men and women. The craft knowledge of white working-class men, like scientific knowledge, which is acquired through collective experience and consensual agreement on what constitutes a "fact," is seen as more legitimate and therefore more powerful in the hierarchy of knowledge. White working-class women's knowledge, which is acquired through individual or private experience, seems to provide no basis for consensual agreement to legitimate the "facts" of caretaking. The particulars of meeting individual needs make it impossible to universalize this knowledge and thus make women's collective claims to the knowledge of relationships unthinkable. Therefore, women's knowledge and power are structurally excluded from thought. Similarly, because intuitive common sense comes from domestic responsibilities that are not recognized as work, it appears that white working-class women do not initiate their knowledge but must be receptive when it comes; thus, the actual hard work, mastery, and collective nature of their activities in acquiring knowledge are concealed. It also appears that white working-class men seek autonomy through their knowledge and that white working-class women preserve relationships through theirs; this false notion undermines women's claims to authority or power.

Black women, however, claim knowledge not only through gender, but through racial identity and relations. Their intuitions and claims to the knowledge of relationships are part of a collective identity as black women. This knowledge is a particular, not a universal, kind in that one must be black to have real knowledge about the world of white people, who are often "ignorant" (prejudiced). Both black men and black women collect and disseminate their knowledge within extended-kin and community relationships and through hard manual work. The result is that black women are not distanced from their knowledge and power. The daily reminder of their collective identity as working-class blacks mitigates the daily reminder of their individual identity as women.

Knowledge: Paradox or Power?

The women's images, concepts, knowledge, and ways of knowing must be seen as integral to the practice of power. To understand how claims to knowledge become empowering, one can apply Thompson's (1963) analysis of how class identities and interests get defined in opposition to ruling-class interests and see that when women define and claim their knowledge, they articulate class and race relations the most clearly. All the women acquire common sense in opposition to middle-class professional people, and black women acquire "real intelligence" in opposition to white people. This "real intelligence" poses whites, who lack the knowledge of racism or who behave in racist ways, as "ignorant"—regardless of their education, status, income, or power—against blacks who "know better." In the struggle to maintain dignity and self-respect in a world that judges people according to white middle-class standards, the "real intelligence" and knowledge of blacks and the common sense of working-class people suggests the possibility of collective autonomy and power. However, women's claims to motherwise common sense do not suggest their collective autonomy and power because women's knowledge is not acquired as a group in opposition to men, but, appears to be individually intuited. Thus, the gender conflicts that exist are made invisible.

At the same time, black and white working-class women express these gender conflicts differently. White working-class women express a gender conflict when they talk about going to school to be "better" in relation to their husbands:

> I'm coming back to school to show my husband that he isn't the only one in the family who can carry on an intelligent conversation.
>
> I can't wait to wave my diploma in his face and say, "Listen here, I know what I'm talking about."

They also acknowledge a conflict when they identify the catalyst for enrolling in school as their separation or divorce. Ironically, white working-class women seek school knowledge to empower themselves. Since it is clear that their intuitive commonsense knowledge is valued less than is men's learned common sense, they turn to school knowledge to legitimate their opinions, voices, and needs—to be "better" in relation to their children, family members, and jobs.

Pursuing schoolwise knowledge puts white working-class women in a paradoxical situation and creates in them considerable ambivalence. Schooling puts a strain on working-class women's ties with the working-class culture—a culture that values commonsense knowledge and working-class men's "real intelligence" more than it does book learning and mental work. Yet schooling is perceived as one of the few avenues by which working-class women can achieve upward mobility. Consequently, working-class women must seek legitimation from the same source that undermines their knowledge and sense of identity (as women and as part of the working class). Nevertheless, working-class women's access to school learning and to white-collar jobs gives them an edge in the balance of power. If their common sense is inevitably valued less than is the common sense of husbands, brothers, or fathers, having schoolwise *and* motherwise intelligence is perhaps their only chance. In the end, white working-class women embrace the dominant concepts of knowledge because doing so not only promises them class mobility but gives them their sole legitimate form of power vis-à-vis working-class men.

Black working-class women express this gender conflict differently. Although they do not embrace the dominant white male value of knowledge, they attribute black men's power to black men's superior knowledge. In addition to all the many skills that black men have developed to survive, the black women mentioned that black men's "real intelligence" is getting black women to "take leave of their senses." Black men have the ability to convince black women to do the very things they have sworn they will not do. Thus, black women see black men's knowledge as the power to dominate black women and black women's lack of intelligence or common sense as their willingness to accept domination:

> I lose my common sense when it comes to men. I don't know how it happens. They're just so smart getting you to listen to them and what they want. I should have learned that lesson by now, but I haven't—it's just plain stupidity on my part.
>
> There's lots of kinds of intelligence. It's not so easy to say. And sometimes I have it and sometimes I don't, you know the commonsense type. I can get myself into some trouble when I don't. I sure need more, but not the kind we get here in school. I mean John, you know, he can get me to do just what he wants, just like that. And that takes real intelligence, it takes something to get me to do things I know's not good for me.

In the end, unequal gender relations are concealed through the women's notion that men's power lies in their intelligence or knowledge and not in their culturally sanctioned license to dominate women in many ways, including sexually.

The paradox for black working-class women vis-à-vis adult education is complex, reflecting the multiple layers of their oppression in American society. Although black working-class women do not seem to need schoolwise knowledge to legitimate their power within black communities, they do need ways to balance and legitimate their power with black men and with white men and women. They have been denied entrance to the pathways to legitimation with whites, however, through their systematic exclusion from schooling and jobs that provide the social and economic resources for upward mobility. So black women may appear less ambivalent about their ways of knowing and less willing to embrace dominant white middle-class values of knowledge, but the arenas in which their knowledge, intelligence, and common sense can be developed and disseminated have been severely limited.

In addition to this discrimination, some "scientific studies" have suggested that blacks are genetically inferior to whites in intelligence; these studies have had devastating effects on public educational policy and practice with regard to blacks, warping the expectations of both blacks and whites about what black people can achieve. Another erroneous finding that educators commonly believe is that black women are genetically more intelligent than are black men (Reid 1975). In this context, black women's claims to schoolwise intelligence are problematic and may be destructive to the relationships of black men and women. Furthermore, although there has been a parallel system of black education, which historically has provided for the development of black identities, interests, and knowledge (Giddings 1984), black working-class women have not always been its beneficiaries.

That black women's pursuit of adult education is embedded in all these contexts necessarily casts schoolwise intelligence and book learning in a vastly different light for them than for white working-class women. White working-class women's antagonism toward schoolwise intelligence is grounded in their class consciousness, but black women's conflict stems from their "dual consciousness"—of being black and working class. Although the ways in which these multiple constraints are manifested in classroom learning are beyond the scope of this article, it should be emphasized that, ultimately, black women's claim to "real intelligence" cannot be easily translated into perceptions of academic skill or competence.

Conclusion

The differences between white and black working-class women's claims to knowledge reveal that women do not have a common understanding of their gender identities and knowledge. But what they *do* have in common is the organization of knowledge as a social relation that ultimately is successful in diminishing their power as they experience the world. To understand women's exclusion requires an examination of the similarities and differences in the objective conditions of women's lives, as well as an analysis of how ideologies of knowledge shape women's perceptions and claims to knowledge. Since women do not all experience the work of being a woman in the same way, it is impossible to identify a single mode of knowing. To understand why certain forms of knowledge appear more amenable to women, we must look more closely at the ethnic-, class-, and race-specific nature of women's experiences, as well as the values that are promoted in each context.

In the end, the paradox and the challenge of education for all women under patriarchy are to confront the balance of power as they pursue new and different kinds of knowledge. What is important to emphasize, however, is the *ideological nature* of the knowledge women seek. The universality and rationality of schoolwise knowledge conceal its opposite: that credentials and instrumental reason are not answers to asymmetrical and unequal social relationships. If women are to *claim* rather than simply *receive* an education—an act that "can literally mean the difference between life and death" (Rich 1979, p. 232), we feminists, sociologists, and educators must be prepared to untangle both the ideologies and objective conditions in women's lives that render our work, knowledge, and power invisible.

References

Apple, M. W., and L. Weiss. 1983. "Ideology and Practice in Schooling" Pp. 3–33. In *Ideology and Practice in Schooling,* edited by L. Weiss. Philadelphia: Temple University Press.

Belenky, M. F., B. M. Clinchy, N. R. Goldberger, and J. M. Tarule. 1986. *Women's Ways of Knowing: The Development of Self, Voice and Mind.* New York: Basic Books.

Bordo, S. 1986. "The Cartesian Masculinization of Thought." *Signs: Journal of Women in Culture and Society* 11(3):439–456.

Chodorow, N. 1978. *The Reproduction of Mothering: Psychoanalysis and the Sociology of Gender.* Berkeley: University of California Press.

Connell, R. W., D. J. Ashenden, S. Kessler, G. W. Dowsett. 1982. *Making the Difference: Schools, Families and Social Division.* London, England: George Allen & Unwin.

Dill, B. T. 1983. "On the Hem of Life: Race, Class and Prospects for Sisterhood." In *Class, Race and Sex: The Dynamics of Control,* edited by A. Swerdlow and H. Lessinger. Boston: G. K. Hall & Co.

Eisenhart, M., and D. Holland. 1983. "Learning Gender from Peers: The Role of Peer Groups in the Cultural Transmission of Gender." *Human Organization* 42(4):321–332.

Fee, E. 1983. "Women's Nature and Scientific Objectivity." In *Women's Nature: Rationalizations of Inequality,* edited by M. Lowe and R. Hubbard. New York: Pergamon Press.

Fingeret, A. 1983a. "Common Sense and Book Learning: Cultural Clash?" *Lifelong Learning: the Adult Years* 6(8).

———. 1983b. "Social Network: A New Perspective on Independence and Illiterate Adults." *Adult Education Quarterly* 33(3):133–146.

Freire, P. 1970. *Pedagogy of the Oppressed.* New York: Seabury Press.

———. 1972. *Cultural Action for Freedom.* Harmondsworth, England: Penguin Books.

———. 1973. *Education for Critical Consciousness.* New York: Continuum.

———. 1978. *Pedagogy-in-Process.* New York: Continuum.

Fuller, M. 1980. "Black Girls in a London Comprehensive School." In *Schooling for Women's Work,* edited by R. Deem. London, England: Routledge & Kegan Paul.

Gaskell, J. 1985. "Course Enrollment in the High School: The Perspective of Working-Class Females." *Sociology of Education* 58:48–57.

Geertz. C. 1983. *Local Knowledge: Further Essays in Interpretive Anthropology.* New York: Basic Books.

Giddings, P. 1984. *When and Where I Enter: The Impact of Black Women on Race and Sex in America.* New York: William Morrow & Co.

Gilligan, C. 1982. *In a Different Voice: Psychological Theory and Women's Development.* Cambridge, MA: Harvard University Press.

Holland, D., and M. Eisenhart. 1988. "Moments of Discontent: University Women and the Gender Status Quo." *Anthropology and Education Quarterly* 19:115–138.

———. In press a. "On the Absence of Women's Gangs in Two Southern Universities. In *Women in the South,* edited by H. Mathews, Athens: University of Georgia Press.

———. In press b. "Women's Ways of Going to School: Cultural Reproduction of Women's Identities as Workers." In *Class, Race and Gender in U.S. Education,* edited by L. Weiss. Buffalo: State University of New York Press.

Hootsman, H. M. 1980. "Educational and Employment Opportunities for Women: Main Issues in Adult Education in Europe." *Convergence.* 13(1–2):79–89.

Jaggar, A. 1983. *Feminist Politics and Human Nature.* Totowa, NJ: Rowman & Allenheld.

Johnson, R. 1979. "'Really Useful Knowledge': Radical Education and Working-Class Culture, 1790–1848." In *Working Class Culture: Studies in History and Theory,* edited by J. Clarke, C. Critcher, and R. Johnson. New York: St. Martin's Press.

Jones, J. 1985. *Labor of Love, Labor of Sorrow: Black Women, Work, and the Family from Slavery to the Present.* New York: Basic Books.

Keller, E. F. 1978. "Gender and Science." *Psychoanalysis and Contemporary Thought* 1:409–433.

———. 1982. "Feminism and Science." *Signs* 7(3):589–602.

Kohn, M. 1977. *Class and Conformity.* Chicago: University of Chicago Press.

Ladner, J. 1972. *Tomorrow's Tomorrow: The Black Woman.* Garden City, NY: Doubleday Anchor Press.

Lovell, A. 1980. "Fresh Horizons: The Aspirations and Problems of Intending Mature Students." *Feminist Review* 6:93–104.

Luttrell, W. 1984. "The Getting of Knowledge: A Study of Working-Class Women and Education." Unpublished Ph.D. dissertation, University of California at Santa Cruz.

McLaren, A. T. 1981. "Women in Adult Education: The Neglected Majority." *International Journal of Women's Studies* 4(2):245–258.

———. 1985. *Ambitions and Realizations: Women in Adult Education.* London, England: Peter Owen.

McRobbie, A. 1978. "Working Class Girls and the Culture of Femininity." Pp. 96–108 in *Women Take Issue: Aspects of Women's Subordination,* edited by Women Studies Group CCCS. London, England: Hutchinson.

———. 1982. "The Politics of Feminist Research: Between Talk, Text and Action." *Feminist Review* 12:46–57.

Oakley, A. 1981. "Interviewing Women: A Contradiction in Terms." In *Doing Feminist Research,* edited by H. Roberts. London, England: Routledge & Kegan Paul.

Reid, I. 1975. "Science, Politics, and Race." *Signs: Journal of Women in Culture and Society* 1(2):397–422.

Rich, A. 1979. "Claiming an Education." In *On Lies, Secrets and Silence.* New York: W. W. Norton & Co.

Robinson, J., S. Paul, and G. Smith. 1973. *Project Second Start: A Study of the Experience of a Group of Low-Income Women in Adult Programs at Brooklyn College.* New York: John Hay Whitney Foundation.

———. 1978. *Second Start Revisited.* New York: John Hay Whitney Foundation.

Rockhill, K. 1987. "Literacy as Threat/Desire: Longing to Be Somebody," Pp. 315–333 in *Women and Education: A Canadian Perspective,* edited by J. Gaskell and A. T. McLaren. Calgary, Alberta, Canada: Detselig Enterprises Ltd.

Rosaldo, M. 1980. "The Use and Abuse of Anthropology." *Signs* 8:389–417.

Rose, H. 1983. "Hand, Brain, and Heart: A Feminist Epistemology for the Natural Sciences." *Signs: Journal of Women in Culture and Society* 9(1):73–90.

Rubin, L. B. 1976. *Worlds of Pain: Life in the Working-Class Family.* New York: Basic Books.

Scott, N. A. 1980. *Returning Women Students: A Review of Research and Descriptive Studies.* Washington, DC: National Association for Women Deans, Administrators, and Counselors.

Smith, D. 1979. "A Sociology for Women." In *The Prison of Sex: Essays in the Sociology of Knowledge,* edited by J. Sherman and E. Beck. Madison: University of Wisconsin Press.

———. 1987. *The Everyday World As Problematic: A Feminist Sociology.* Boston: Northeastern University Press.

Stack, C. 1974. *All Our Kin: Strategies for Survival in the Black Community.* New York: Random House.

———. 1986. "The Culture of Gender: Women and Men of Color." *Signs: Journal of Women in Culture and Society* 11(2):321–324.

Stack, C., and R. Hall. 1982. *Holding on to the Land and the Lord: Kinship, Ritual, Land Tenure and Social Policy in the Rural South.* Athens: University of Georgia Press.

Thompson, E. P. 1963. *The Making of the English Working-Class.* New York: Vintage Books.

Thompson, J. 1983. *Learning Liberation: Women's Responses to Men's Education.* London, England: Croom Helm.

Thorne, B. 1986. "Girls and Boys Together, But Mostly Apart: Gender Arrangements in Elementary Schools." Pp. 167–184 in *Relationships and Development,* edited by W. Hartup and Z. Rubin. Hillsdale, NJ: Lawrence Erlbaum Associates.

Valli, L. 1983. "Becoming Clerical Workers: Business Education and the Culture of Feminity." Pp. 213–234 in *Ideology and Practice in Schooling,* edited by M. Apple and L. Weiss. Philadelphia: Temple University Press.

Willis, P. 1977. *Learning to Labor: How Working-Class Kids Get Working-Class Jobs.* New York: Columbia University Press.

Intersectional Analysis in Historical Studies

Intersectional research need not be confined to the present, as a number of historical studies demonstrate. One can distinguish a number of different types of historical studies that have consequences for the manner in which intersectional analysis is incorporated. Historical studies using primary documents offer the possibility of conducting quantitative research, or at least of identifying the individuals who are in a given social location. Obtaining a saturated model may be challenging given the need to identify a sufficient number of individuals whose race, gender, and class position are known from the records. Although this may be difficult in many cases, it should by no means be impossible. Intersectional analysis with three or four social locations is probably easier to accomplish because of the difficulty just mentioned.

Often, however, historical studies are conducted by nonhistorians or by historians using secondary data. These data may come from the studies of other historians who have analyzed and drawn conclusions from their research on primary data. In these cases it may not be possible to identify social locations as such, or the number of individuals within social locations. A third type of historical analysis focuses primarily on institutions or on whole societies. These are, properly speaking, studies at the messo or macro level and therefore are concerned not with social locations but with policies or norms. These policies or norms are analyzed for their racist, patriarchal, or classist effects. This is intersectional analysis that explores the interlocking systems of oppression at their origin (societal or macro level) or in their daily functioning at the institutional (messo) level of societies.

The article by M. Deborah Bialeschki and Kathryn Lynn Walbert, "'You Have to Have Some Fun to Go Along with Your Work': The Interplay of Race, Class, Gender, and Leisure in the Industrial New South," presents historical analysis of the leisure activities of black and white working-class women between 1910 and 1940. They rely on primary sources, interviews conducted by researchers in an oral history project between 1976 and 1980. Although the authors did not participate in the original project, the data remain primary nonetheless; and their use by the authors is a case of "secondary analysis" of primary data. These primary data—interviews with women who had worked in textile mills and tobacco factories between 1910 and 1940—provide an immediate source for analyzing the leisure activities of these black and white working-class women.

Although the primary objective of the authors is to study the leisure activities of these women, they make comparisons with black and white male employment and earnings to provide context. "Race as well as gender," they note, "dictated the jobs available and their environments" (p. 201). Men obtained better jobs and higher pay in the textile mills and tobacco factories, even though women were the majority of workers in these industries. Among women workers, white working-class women constituted the primary work force in textile mills, whereas black working-class women made up the labor force in the less desirable tobacco factories. Since mill and tobacco factory owners provided housing and recreational activities to white women workers but not to black women, "African American women tobacco workers had more limited opportunities for leisure than their White counterparts in the textile mills" (p. 205). The authors compare opportunities for work and income across the intersections of race and gender within the working class of that period and locality and compare leisure and recreational activities across race within gender (women) and class (working class) groups. Thus, although the authors do not provide counts of the number of individuals in each social location, they do make comparisons across these locations and provide copious quotes from women who had occupied them. The result is an example of historical intersectional analysis using primary data.

"You Have to Have Some Fun to go Along with Your Work"

The Interplay of Race, Class, Gender, and Leisure in the Industrial New South

M. DEBORAH BIALESCHKI
Leisure Studies and Recreation Administration, University of North Carolina—Chapel Hill

KATHRYN LYNN WALBERT
Department of History, University of North Carolina—Chapel Hill

The author may be contacted at: CB #3185 Evergreen, University of North Carolina-Chapel Hill, Chapel Hill, NC 27599-3185.

The purpose of this paper is to explore the leisure experiences of Southern women textile and tobacco workers from 1910 to 1940 as a way to analyze the meaning of recreation to working-class Southerners and the role of leisure in the development of communities of workers. Important differences in recreation and leisure opportunities for Black and White working class women became clear in the analysis. While White women textile worker's

Thanks are extended to Kimberly Pearce for her readings of the manuscript. Acknowledgment is also extended to the Southern Oral History Program for the use of the interviews housed in the Southern Historical Collection, Manuscript Department, University of North Carolina at Chapel Hill.

"You Have to Have Some Fun to go Along With Your Work: The Interplay of Race, Class, Gender, and Leisure in the Industrial New South" by M. Deborah Bialeschki and Kathryn Lynn Walbert *Journal of Leisure Research*, Vol. 30, No. 1, 79–100. © 1998. Reprinted by permission.

recreation was relatively politically uncharged, perhaps posing only a minor challenge to employers' intentions, African American women tobacco workers transformed recreation and leisure experiences into a vehicle for social change based on race and class issues. White workers seemed to have used leisure for its own sake, perhaps gaining some sense of solidarity with one another in the process, while in the Black community, leisure was almost always entwined with struggles for fair treatment in the work place or a political voice.

Keywords

Race, class, gender, historical analysis, labor movements

Introduction

Textile and tobacco communities, symbols of the transformation of the Southern economy from a rural to an industrial basis, have proven rich subjects for the study of industrialization, trade unionism, and, perhaps most critically, the reinforcement of race, class, and gender hierarchies in the New South (Janiewski 1985; Korstad 1987; Peiss 1986). While careful study of working-class experience has revealed that forces such as federal policy and economic transformation shaped working people's lives and communities, few leisure researchers or historians have considered the role that leisure has played in the creation of social identity (Cross 1990; Fischer 1994; Stokowski 1990). In fact, the paucity of historical study focused on leisure could reflect the degree to which leisure scholars and historians have failed to look to each other to illuminate their work and intellectual contributions (Burton and Jackson 1989). The purpose of this paper is to explore the leisure experiences of Southern women textile and tobacco workers from 1910 to 1940 as a way to analyze the meaning of recreation to working-class Southerners and the role of leisure in the development of communities of workers. By refocusing the historical lens toward a concept of social leisure, we hope to demonstrate the critical need for a leisure-based perspective on history as well as a historical perspective on leisure.

Background

Following the Civil War, distinctions in Southern culture and traditions began to emerge. These distinctions essentially separated the slave South (the "Old") from the Southern society that resulted from Reconstruction (the "New" South) (Ayers 1992; Tindall 1967; Woodward 1951). Ayers (1992) described this time in the following way:

> The era was crucial in the history of the region and of the nation, a time when Southerners of both races confronted the aftermath of emancipation and the reassertion of control by White Southerners. The Southern economy went through wrenching change; politics witnessed desperate conflict; Blacks and Whites redefined their relationships to one another; farmers launched the largest electoral revolt in American history. Other, more hopeful, things marked these years as well, for they saw the birth of the blues and jazz, the rapid spread of vibrant new denominations, an efflorescence of literature. (p. vii)

The New South faced a staggering economic crisis. Without slave labor upon which the area had relied for so long, how could the South reestablish its economy and compete with the industrial North? The South needed to transform the entire system of labor relations and at the same time, alter the race relations that existed with slavery. The post-Reconstruction years seemed ripe for dramatic change. The New South's economic salvation lay in textiles and tobacco. Somewhat ironically, these two industries largely *reinforced* rather than revolutionized the hierarchies of race, class, and gender inherent in the Old South.

Mills and factories sprang up across the South beginning in the 1870s and continued to multiply until the Great Depression. For example, many mill owners, like Alexander Chatham, owned large plantations prior to the war and amassed a huge fortune from the slave-based agricultural economy. Chatham purchased a small cotton mill on a bend in the Yadkin River in North Carolina in 1877 with a business partner, Thomas Lenoir Gwyn. Over the next fifty years, Chatham built that small concern into the Chatham Manufacturing Company, which became a powerful force in the textile industry in both Winston-Salem and Elkin, North Carolina, well into the twentieth century (Town of Elkin, 1989). Chatham's example indicates the transition from master of slaves to mill operator often proved an easy one.

Ambitious owners were aided by a widespread impulse to create Southern industrial success. Politicians, bankers, ministers, and other community leaders used their influence to pave the way for mill and factory men to open plants in their towns and invited them into partnerships for the new Southern dream of textile and tobacco capitalism. Railroads and the improved transportation networks of the late nineteenth century pushed the process along, and the growing demands of industrial cities provided an unprecedented market for Southern-milled cloth and tobacco products (Hall et al. 1987). Owners had the capital, the community support, the technology, and the market to build the textile and tobacco industries. Their final need was labor.

The South had remained a predominantly agricultural region long after many yeoman farmers of the New England countryside had traded their ploughshares for the industrial timeclock. Even into the 1920s, most Southern states had populations that were at least two-thirds rural (Kirby 1987). Southerners were used to earning their living from the land and setting their own hours. The transition to factory work did not come easily for Southern workers. The appeal of factory work at the local mill did not pull the majority of workers to the mills and factories; rather they were pushed in that direction by larger, more impersonal economic forces such as the boll weevil attacks and the collapse of farm prices in the 1920s, the Great Depression, and the mechanization of farming (Hall et al. 1987; Janiewski 1985; Kirby 1987).

As the economic crisis deepened, rural people sought out the surrounding towns and cities for work. Janiewski (1985) suggested that intensity and the direction of the flow depended on the prices paid for tobacco and cotton, the cost of land, the level of indebtedness among farmers, and the economic opportunities available. Since agriculture rewarded female labor less than male, these expendable young women were more likely to turn to factory work as a source of income. There they evolved into industrial workers in a complex procedure that reconstructed racial, gender, and class relationships within the factory, the household, and the surrounding community (Janiewski 1985).

Southern employers often influenced the migrants by actively soliciting particular types of workers for certain kinds of jobs. North Carolina census data from 1910 to 1930 illustrate this trend. For example, the 1920 data show that White women were dominant in textile factories (laborers = 92%, operatives = 99%) while Black women were concentrated in the tobacco factories (laborers = 79%, operatives = 71%) (U.S. Dept. of Commerce 1923, pp. 987–89). The work opportunities were more plentiful in textiles, so the percentage also demonstrates greater access to employment for the White women.

As indicated by the census data (U.S. Dept. of Commerce 1914, 1923, 1933) and other research (Hall et al. 1987; Janiewski 1985; Kirby 1987; Wood 1986), Southern women formed the backbone of the initial labor force as many families tried to maintain a farm in the countryside with men staying at home to tend the land while women ventured to the mill to bring home much-needed income. Even after most mill families gave up all but a small garden plot and perhaps a cow and sent all eligible workers into the mills, women's predominance made them central members of the labor force. These women were not only balancing full-time occupations as paid workers but were also fulfilling roles as housewives and mothers.

With this background in mind, the stage is set to explore the way gender and race became instrumental in establishing social identities within the mill and factory towns. By examining leisure from these women's perspectives, we begin to understand better the role of leisure in reshaping their worlds, developing class consciousness, and building social constructions of community institutions.

Methodology

While historians have explored a number of influences such as welfare capitalism on the formation of working-class communities, few have deeply considered the role that leisure has played in the creation of social identity. Too often, historians focused on cultural meanings or social power relations that emerged from leisure experiences rather than the intrinsic meanings of those experiences. Even those historians who considered leisure in their analyses often failed to take into account the findings of leisure scholars when considering the choices historical actors made or the meanings those actors found in leisure (Hall et al. 1987; Janiewski 1985; Kasson 1978; Korstad 1987, Peiss 1986; Rosenzweig 1983).

Leisure scholars, on the other hand, have addressed the importance of leisure to the building of communities and social identity but seldom within a historical context. Cross (1990) provided a broad social history of leisure but focused on a generalized perspective of leisure activity. While useful as an overview, Cross does not delve into historical foundations of leisure related to factors such as race and class, nor does the book address the complexities of social identities. Recent studies (Stokowski 1990; Stokowski and Lee 1991; Wynne 1990) indicated leisure had an important part to play in the building of social networks and communities, but they have seldom branched out beyond present-day sources for data. For example, Stokowski offered new methods of social network analysis for leisure scholarship. However, her prescriptions for accurate data collection involved surveys or interviews where the researcher carefully controlled both the questions asked and the interpretive methods used while working with currently active leisure participants. Such an approach is certainly useful, but nonetheless, limited. Contemporary social network analyses rule out many historical sources in which the leisure participants might be deceased, the interviews conducted or narratives produced have different research agendas in mind, or incomplete collectible materials are used. For the most part, the accepted methods of leisure research have failed to consider ways in which less controllable historical sources might be used as data for leisure studies. Thus, the two disciplines of history and leisure studies each note the conclusions about the nature and meaning of leisure as suggested by their own methodologies and data sources without venturing into one another's terrain.

Unfortunately, the two disciplines of history and leisure studies have not yet entered into meaningful conversation. A survey of active leisure scholars indicated that while 60.8% of respondents thought that historical scholarship made minor contributions to the development of leisure and recreation research, only 6.3% believed major contributions had resulted (Burton and Jackson 1989). The study went on to conclude that while recreation and leisure studies are perceived to have developed on several disciplinary fronts, some fields such as history, have made little, if any, impact. This perception reflects the paucity of historical study focused on leisure, the degree to which leisure scholars have failed to look to historians to illuminate their work, or, most likely, a combination of the two perceptions as neither group has turned to the other for intellectual contributions. This paper is an attempt to provide such an interdisciplinary perspective on the leisure experiences of Southern women textile and tobacco workers.

This research used traditional historical methodology as the basis for data collection and interpretation. The main technique used for the primary sources in this research paper was oral history. Oral histories can fill some of the many gaps that exist in our knowledge of women and allow researchers to create some of the sources we lack (Nasstrom 1992). These oral histories bring visibility to women often overlooked in traditional written histories as well as capture the memories of women whose cultures favor oral ways of preserving their heritage. Many of the oral history interviews used in this study were undertaken with the aim of recovering previously hidden histories and charting new interpretations of southern women's lives (Nasstrom, 1992). As suggested by Nasstrom:

> Oral history begins with the spoken word, generated in a conversation between interviewer and interviewee. In the process of telling their stories, informants define their own identities and suggest the meaning of their lives. (p. vii)

Researchers who use oral histories must consider how time may alter memories. As a general rule, however, recurrent processes and routines of daily life are better remembered than singular events (Nasstrom 1992). The promise of these Southern oral histories lies in the challenges they present to existing historical interpretations, particularly related to women's factory work as described from a primarily northeastern perspective. "As they define their connections to the past, southern women resist their marginalization in the historical record and encourage us to do likewise" (Nasstrom 1992, p. ix).

The primary data sources for this research paper were oral histories from the Piedmont Industrialization Project (Series H) held by the Southern Oral History Program Collection at the University of North Carolina at Chapel Hill. Oral history interviews were conducted with approximately 300 individuals as a way to focus on the lives of working class men and women in the South. Of these interviews, approximately 150 were with Southern women who worked in textile mills and tobacco factories from 1910 to 1940. The interviews were completed between 1976 and 1980 with a focus on the physical and social changes that accompanied the arrival of the industrial revolution in the piedmont South. While recreation and leisure was not a focus of the original study, an examination of the interview data uncovered *an acknowledgment* of the role of recreation and leisure in the women's work and private lives. After initially screening for interviews that addressed issues related to recreation and leisure, 50 tapes and transcriptions of women workers were analyzed with the purpose of discovering ways in which women talked about the importance of recreation and leisure in their lives.

Major emergent themes were identified and corroborated by both researchers during the analysis and interpretation of the data. A modified constant comparison was used to maximize credibility through comparison of groups and data (Glaser and Strauss 1967; Henderson 1991). This technique allows the researcher to compare different data sets, literature, and different groups. As is true for all historical analyses, the emergent themes were analyzed and interpreted within the context of multiple secondary sources. These processes were instrumental to understanding the ways in which gender, race, and class operated within work and leisure experiences of working women in the Industrial New South.

Findings

The work setting for women

Tobacco factories and textile mills often grew up alongside one another and came out of similar social and economic trends. Born of the post–Civil War need to revitalize the Southern economy, both laid their foundations squarely on the region's agricultural background and drew their labor force from the increasingly harsh realities of late-nineteenth and early-twentieth-century subsistence and tenant farming. Textiles and tobacco both relied on traditional Southern notions of racial and gender hierarchies to distribute jobs, set pay scales, and divide workers based on their differences (Janiewski 1985; Kirby 1987; Newby 1989). Most importantly for the purposes of this study, both industries relied strongly on the workers most overlooked—women.

While many women worked in the same factories as their fathers, husbands, or sons, they did not do the same kind of work within the mill nor were they compensated equally (Newby 1989). White women found many work opportunities, but those jobs were firmly rooted in the prevailing gender system. While White men were often assigned high-paying skilled jobs involving heavy physical work or some sort of authority, women found themselves doing repetitive low-skill jobs on machines. As described by one woman textile worker:

> They just had the women's jobs and the men's jobs. The men's jobs were for a heavier or stronger person and all. That's the way it was divided up. The spinning room downstairs was mostly women. They had boy doffers and some help like that, and the winding. Of course, they had a boy bring us bobbins and put them in our trough, we called it, for us to wind and like that.
>
> (Louise Jones)

These work patterns fit neatly into employers' assumptions that women would not mind the lack of intellectual stimulation and that they would be temporary workers who would not warrant the long-term investment required for more skilled training (Hall et al. 1987; Kirby 1987).

Wages matched the employers' assumptions about the value of sex-typed jobs and the workers who filled them. White women often received wages on a "piece" basis in the spinning or weaving rooms, being paid by the amount produced rather than by the hour or by the week, making their wages far less dependable than men's wages. For example, in an interview with Alice Evitt who was a spinner in the textile mills, she described how she earned twenty-five cents per day as a twelve-year-old girl in the mills and, by 1915 when she married, she earned $1.44 per day. In contrast, Martin Lowe began making $1.00 per day at Poe Mill in Greenville, North Carolina, in 1912 and within a few years was making $2.25 per day grinding cards. While White women had a rare opportunity to be gainfully employed in the textile industry, the options for their employment and their wages still firmly reflected traditional gender ideals and role expectations (Wood 1986).

The heavily mechanized textile industry drew almost exclusively White women into its labor force to run its expensive machinery (e.g., U.S. Dept. of Commerce 1914, 1923, 1933). Only a few Black women were ever employed by the mills, and they worked primarily as cleaning women (Hall et al. 1987; Newby 1989). However, the tobacco factories were a different situation. Tobacco processing relied on hot, dusty handwork that was both repetitive and physically taxing, so the work appealed to few people. Not surprisingly, this work was reserved for African Americans, especially Black women since this group was perceived as lowest on the Southern social ladder (Janiewski 1985). Kirby (1987) described the Black migration to tobacco towns in this way:

> Migrants settled into crowded, established Black neighborhoods, where there was little or no room for gardens, livestock, or the other requisites of living at home. The warehouses and factories employed men and women of both races and rigorously discriminated against Blacks. They might load boxes or baskets of tobacco, sweep floors, sort tobacco, or work as "stemmers," performing the dirty, tedious task of stripping leaves from stems at the beginning of the manufacturing process. (p. 288)

The tobacco industry had its cleaner jobs, such as machine operation in the cigarette plant or the supervision of other workers, but those jobs went to White workers (primarily men) who were paid better wages for their efforts. Black men, in contrast, moved tobacco and worked in the casing and cutting departments where the work required heavy lifting and often posed risks to personal safety. African American women tended to work in stemming, stripping the leaves from the stems of goldleaf tobacco by hand and were paid by quantity rather than an hourly or annual wage (Kirby 1987; Korstad 1987).

The work settings of the textile mills and tobacco factories provide an ideal illustration of the dismantling of the structures erected by Reconstruction Radicals after the Civil War to protect the civil and other rights of Black people (Newby 1989). The mill owners replaced the protective structures with an elaborate system of White supremacy that rested on the cornerstones of segregation and disfranchisement. "The system incorporated rigid barriers of social separation between the races, and a spreading segmentation of labor markets that reserved more and more jobs exclusively for Whites or Blacks. The social and political aspects of this system were written into [Jim Crow] law in the quarter century after 1890" (Newby 1989, p. 463).

As illustrated by the preceding descriptions, the work settings for White and Black women were different from the beginning. Race as well as gender dictated the jobs available and their environments. Nevertheless, while the women in the mills and factories performed demanding and dangerous jobs for poor compensation, they formed the backbone of their respective industries (Hall et al. 1987; Janiewski 1985). Their initial willingness to come off the farms before their husbands and brothers and enter the industrial economy meant that they enjoyed a firm foothold in the factory and mill settings. Thus, these women workers who were considered less valuable than men for farm labor became the critical component to production in the burgeoning textile and tobacco industries.

Recreation in the new south textile communities

The White women textile workers had little trouble finding recreational activities in the mill towns of the South. Along with the mill housing, health care, educational programs, stores, and insurance that welfare capitalists offered in an effort to secure worker loyalty, many mills sponsored recreational activities for their workers. These mill-sponsored recreation programs included bands, parties, and sports teams. Louise Jones, one of several women who talked about athletic teams sponsored by the company, mentioned "they had real good ball teams here then. And ooh, I used to go and just holler my head off." Myrtle Cleveland recalled that the mill "would have street cars to come, and they would take all the children on a picnic . . . on some Fourth of Julys, they would have an all-day outing and give away prizes and things." Alice Hardin also recalled that "if I got a band together and wanted to play at something or other, why, they'd usually give you a little something." Another woman millhand, Pauline Griffith, recalled that the mill sponsored a picnic "every Fourth of July—they'd have a big to-do over there with firecrackers. They'd have a greasy pig and baseball game over there." She also remembered:

> (The mill) used to have a playground, they called it, up here in the mill yard. And they had swings. They had different things, you know, to enjoy. And they would have things up there, you know, for the people to go and be amused and enjoy.

Tessie Dyer and Mamie Shue both recalled attending a cooking club sponsored by the mill:

> We'd (the club) meet every Tuesday night or every Thursday night, so we'd used to meet on Thursday night. We was asked to cook [the band] a supper, so we did. They had one that they were going to ask to eat supper with the band boys that night. I never will forget that.

> They called my name out, and I just almost fell in the floor!
>
> (Tessie Beatrice Helms Dyer)

> The mill, they would sponsor it. And they had a house back down—built way back here, and had it fixed up for that. And we'd go down there, they'd teach us to cook. And we'd have dances down there . . . We just went for the fun of it. We didn't care nothing about cooking . . . But we had a good time.
>
> (Mamie Shue)

As a part of the welfare capitalist traditional, mill owners hoped these inexpensive recreational activities would instill in their workers a sense of loyalty and pride in the company, and would translate into increased profits and decreased labor troubles. However, there was no evidence that the women workers saw it that way. Instead, they took from the opportunities the intrinsic value that they could and ignored the remainder of the message (Hall et al. 1987).

Even when attending events not sponsored by companies, the interview data supported the idea that White mill women often participated in leisure activities together, most notably at church. Church was an important outlet for not only Christian teachings and charity, but also recreation. Churches, like other activities and institutions, were often company-sponsored, and mill workers were strongly encouraged to attend. Myrtle Cleveland remembered, "Every time the doors opened, we were there. We were brought up in the church." Pauline Griffith recalled that after work, she would teach Bible classes, "seven 'til nine. I had forty juniors myself. I gave out more certificates. Over half the Bible school was in my class." Several other women talked about the importance of church activities:

> We finally organized a class, you know, later on in years, the young ladies, the girls and married women had a class . . . And I mean maybe there was seven or eight members of that class, you know, all the same age, and we were really close together. And we loved our Sunday school and our Sunday school class and our Sunday school teacher and all, always. We loved going to church . . . And sometimes the different churches would gather at one church for a song festival to carry dinner and have a dinner on the grounds. And our church would go to picnics sometimes. I know we went to Raleigh one time. We had to go by train.
>
> (Louise Rigsbee Jones)

> We didn't have any recreation, only what the church put out, because we wasn't allowed to go just anywhere. Some people may not have been as strict on their children, but my father and them did. Anything the church had to do, parties and all, we got to go to, but we wasn't allowed to go to dances.
>
> (Mary Thompson)

Church work for many mill women served as an outlet for religious expression and as a form of leisure. The emphasis that the women placed on the *people* in their congregations and the group activities seemed to indicate a social form of leisure that enabled workers to enjoy one another's company outside work. While the church may have served a recreational purpose, it did not serve a politically active one (e.g. Hall et al. 1987). Due to the fact that many ministers and churches were wholly funded by the mill owners, they both stood to lose if workers began to organize along class lines for social change. Alice Hardin remembered that the mill "helped build the church and give them the land it's built on."

Outside church, women textile workers found other ways of spending their free time. Some, like Alice Hardin, devoted that time to their children. She recalled going to the PTA:

> I was in the grammar schools. I helped out in them all the time. I was grade mother, and if I could help the teachers any way, I did, and I went with them on parties with the children and

> helped with them, and the PTAs and everything. I was always there.

Some White women workers also found recreation and leisure in the home and during home-centered social occasions such as playing music or quilting. Ethel Marshall Faucette recalled, "sometimes half a dozen different families might gather to sing and listen to music at one worker's house." Louise Jones described the importance of visiting neighbors at home:

> People always got along good together here, and they thought well of one another because there were good people here most of the time. And we would all visit one another. They worked all day; they visited more at night. We called it going and staying till bedtime with neighbors.

The social element of leisure that was evident in church work was also clear here. Women, more so than men, chose to use their leisure time in their children's schools or in home-centered activities. While these leisure activities may have had some intrinsic value, they also provided a specific benefit to the family and reinforced gender roles.

These women textile workers may have had more opportunities to participate in their own recreation and leisure pursuits because of a common practice of hiring African American domestic workers to help out in the home and with the children (e.g., Janiewski 1985; Kirby 1987). Black women comprised more than 86% of all domestic workers (U.S. Dept. of Commerce 1923), and White women mill workers often made sufficient weekly cash to hire Black women to do their washing and provide childcare while they worked or engaged in other activities (Kirby 1987). Janiewski (1985) suggested one possible insight for this phenomenon:

> The household supplied one of the few acceptable areas for encounters between women of different races: the Black maid or washerwoman relieved her female White employer (possibly a wage-earner like herself but better paid) from some burdens of housework. White women thus shared the privilege of exploiting Black labor. (pp. 128–129)

Myrtle Cleveland recalled that her mother, who also worked in the mills, "always had a colored person do the washing." Several of the women interviewed talked about the help of Black women domestic workers with household chores:

> We had a colored woman that done the wash. Well, we'd pay her the last of the week. And sometimes momma pay her when she done it, so she wouldn't have to come back. They had a big wash place right down here at this old poplar tree. Maybe there'd be five or six colored people down there washing clothes.
>
> (Ethel Faucette)

> Well, here in this area domestics have always been Black, because there never were any Whites . . . We didn't have one that stayed all that long a time. We had the cook that stayed at home all the time. Then we had a laundry woman or washerwoman as she was called then. We'd have to take the laundry to her and go get it. She lived over in what we called the Negro section.
>
> (Grace Moore Maynard)

Many of the women also talked about the importance of Black women's help with childcare:

> Old Aunt Mary Hemphill. She was a Black lady. I never will forget that old soul. She was just like one of the family. She stayed with me all during the children's small years, and after they got up big enough to look after theirself, why, she quit, she got so old. She looked after all the children, done the washing and ironing, cooking, cleaning the house, and never charged me but five dollars a week the whole time. You know, they're kind of close-mouthed about theirselves and all their generations. But she was a fine old Black lady, I'm telling you.
>
> (Ada Mac Mosely Wilson)

> But I know when Mama was working she had a colored lady to stay with us, and she stayed nights. And then when I went to work (on the night shift), I had a colored girl to stay with my children, and she stayed nights, too. She had a baby, and she wanted to know what she could do with the baby. I said, 'Bring it on with you.' I needed somebody to stay, and she stayed nights. She'd go home on weekends. She'd be there in the mornings to start fixing the breakfast and all. That was before I went on the first shift . . . I think about some people talking about colored people doing this and doing that and the other. Well, why did they used to. . . . They trusted them with the most precious thing in the world, with their children.
>
> (Stella Foust Carden)

With the help of these part-time domestic workers, many of the White women were able to maintain their jobs at the mills without neglecting family and household responsibilities. Black women domestic workers indirectly as well as directly freed White women to pursue their own work and leisure interests as well as be involved in community volunteer and social events. An obvious function of racial hierarchy, working-class White women enjoyed the socially accepted luxury of hired help from women in the Black community.

When women got together for social activities, they were likely employees of only one particular mill. As most White women workers lived in mill housing, the opportunities for friendships and activities outside the worker community were extremely limited. The women lived in the mill villages, worked in the mills, and developed ties with other women based on shared experiences. Kinship found in the mill towns is evidenced in this quote:

> You grew up here and you knew everybody. It had its bad points. We didn't make too much money. I know my father didn't. But like I said, it was kind of one big family, and we all hung together and survived.
>
> (Hoyle McCorkle)

Women workers also managed to interject their own ideas about leisure into the workplace. They recalled trying to make the job more fun by playing practical jokes or having time to visit with the other women workers. The following quotes illustrate these ideas:

> We was just playing like, and we was all young, right in there. You have to have some fun as you go along with your work, to make it interesting.
>
> (Pauline Griffith)

> Sometimes they'd get under the spinnin' frame and reach under there and get a-hold of somebody's dress and jerk 'em. Make 'em think the machine'd had 'em. They'd do that. Try to scare them. But they was good. They didn't mean no harm—havin' fun. Sometimes there at Concord, back then, they'd play Black Jack . . . We'd get to our spinnin', get all our ends up, and all our stuff done on the frames. We'd go out there and play . . . Then we'd have to jump up and run and catch up with our work, and go back and play a little more.
>
> (Alice Parker Evitt)

> Yes, it was noisy, but we learned to talk. And when you're used to the noise, you can understand better. Somebody going in wasn't used to it, you'd have to talk louder to them. We'd have to talk louder than just natural talking . . . Yes, we had the privilege of speaking to anyone in there if we wanted to. If we were on up through the spinning room, we could stop and speak to different ones that were working up there if we wanted to, just so it didn't affect our work . . . I think that's one reason people liked to work there, even though they didn't pay as good wages here as they did in some other places.
>
> (Louise Jones)

Several women recalled that they also would sing on the job:

> Yeah, they'd sing, but you couldn't hear 'em [because of the machines]. You knowed they was doing something, you'd see their mouth

> working . . . [T]hey'd sing sacred songs and they would sing jazz.
>
> (Ethel Faucette)

> People used to sing all the time . . . I used to sing all the time. When I was working, I'd just sit there and just sing, sing . . . at work we'd sing by ourself, because we couldn't hardly sing together, not any job. But just sit there and sing and work.
>
> (Mary Thompson)

Just as their refusal to accept the welfare capitalist message of mill recreation indicated the women's insistence on a leisure meaning of their own, the singing and socializing on the job stated their demand that some of the company's time should also be their own to be used as *they* saw fit.

In summary, the White women managed to find time for leisure activities at work, after hours, or on days off despite the long hours worked in the textile mills. Their activities often reflected family-oriented values and were seldom outside the social paradigm. White women in the mills had the opportunity to participate more than they would have in other contexts due to the labor of hired African American domestic help. Mill managers hoped that recreation activities would encourage company loyalty and create a docile, easily controlled workforce. However, the women seemed to choose to focus on the intrinsic, not extrinsic, values of their activities. They took away cherished memories of friendships and enjoyment. By experiencing leisure in this company-dominated setting, women managed to meld their recreation, work, family, interpersonal, and religious lives. Leisure experience became a relief from work but was almost entirely constructed through a workplace context.

Recreation in the new south tobacco communities

African American women tobacco workers had more limited opportunities for leisure than their White counterparts in the textile mills. One of the largest factors was the residential segregation that marked the estrangement between the two racial groups. Black and White workers shared no common meeting places such as churches, schools, clubhouses, parks, or athletic facilities (Janiewski 1985, p. 140). Their jobs paid less than textile jobs or the tobacco jobs held by their White coworkers and often left them in desperate economic straits that required them to take on additional employment to make ends meet (Janiewski 1985; Wood 1986). Moreover, White tobacco factory owners felt no compulsion to offer services, including recreation services, to their African American employees. While the owners had a vested interest in maintaining the loyalty of White workers in order to keep a happy, stable labor force that reinforced cross-class ties of the New South White dominance, they had no such reason to cater to their Black workforce. Hallie Caesar, a stemmer for R.J. Reynolds and Liggett Myers recalled that "Liggett Myers didn't do too much for the people—no more than work them and pay them."

Unlike White textile mill workers, tobacco employees did not generally live in housing owned by their companies, probably due to the large numbers of African American workers whom Southern industrialists were disinclined to assist (Korstad 1987; Newby 1989). The lack of close living quarters, however, did not mean that Black women tobacco workers found no sense of community amongst themselves. The bond of poverty created cohesion among many neighborhoods, sometimes extending across the color line, but usually stopping at the borders of segregated housing areas. Margaret Turner, a worker for American Tobacco, recalled:

> We lived as neighbors. We knew everybody in the community, all the way up the street, everybody. Every house, you could say 'Well, this family lives here; this family lives here.'

In tobacco towns like Durham and Winston-Salem, most residents of Black communities were employees of one of the factories although not always the same one. Margaret Turner stated, "most of the people that lived in the community where I lived worked in the tobacco factories. That was the only thing that a Black person had to turn to." Dora Scott Miller recalled that in her Durham community "quite a few was employed in tobacco," but there were also "people working out"—maids and other types of domestic workers. These neighborhoods provided a source of friendship and community among the residents regardless of their residents' source of employment.

Black women frequently found themselves to be the most abused members in the tobacco factories. Margaret Holmes Turner recalled that "the White people were nice to you, because they knew what you come for, and they felt that you was their servant. They used you that way." Similarly, Dora Scott Miller, a butt machine worker at Liggett Myers, remembered one foreman who would "get on top of that machine and watch you, see if you was workin' all right and holler down and curse . . . That's what we had to undergo." Ruby Jones commented that "the foremen didn't respect you unless you done their dirty work or went with them." Annie Mack Barbee subtly referred to the fact that Black women were frequently subjected to unwanted sexual advances or sexual humor in the workplace in this quote:

> They'd laugh and play them old nasty jokes and here they go. And I would never laugh. Someone'd say you so solemn. I said 'I'm up here to work.'

Despite their working and living conditions, Black women managed to find their own recreation on the job as well as in their communities. Working together in hot, dusty stemmeries, African American women forged fast friendships on the job. Blanche Scott, a stemmer, recalled:

> We would have a lot of fun together. We tried to keep it so the bossman couldn't see it, but we just got along nice together. We formed a little club. Just like your birthday's in one month, maybe in December, when your birthday come, all of us that worked together, we'd go in and give so much money to you. Either we'd take the money and go and buy you a gift. It would make you feel very good.

Dora Scott Miller remembered when workers had problems in the home, they could turn to their network of coworkers for support: "we always did that. We'd always visit each other, and we had very close communication with each other like that." Spending time on the job celebrating birthdays or chatting with friends surely helped to alleviate the boredom and weariness associated with a long day of stemming tobacco. In the absence of company-sponsored social activities, such informal moments set aside for leisure surely made a tremendous difference in the quality of life on the job.

Music played a critical role in the leisure experiences of African American women tobacco workers, both on the job and outside the work place. Hallie Caesar remembered:

> We would sing every day in the factory. Sometimes they would sing in the morning when they was working, and they'd sing in the evening while they was working . . . contests were held among the different lines—they'd just sing . . . Everybody would join in the singing. It was all Christian music and they didn't sing blues.

Black women workers also sang on their lunch break outside the cafeteria. Company officials frequently encouraged these activities. Caesar remembered that "The foremen loved the singing. They'd gather around and listen" to the Christian music workers sang.

In his recent research on music in New South Atlanta, Campbell (1995) suggested that Whites frequently listened to the music of African Americans at various music festivals, revivals, and other occasions. While they may have commented favorably on a variety of Black music, their primary interest was in the singing of spirituals and traditional hymns representative of songs sung by slaves prior to emancipation. By showing such obvious preference for music associated with African Americans' enslaved past, Whites consciously or subconsciously sought to reaffirm their role as "master" and reaffirm White dominance in the context of freedom (Campbell 1995). For African American musicians, this music obviously had different, less power-laden meanings, and workers' interest in music (both spiritual and secular) often carried over outside the White-dominated workplace, as families listened to quartet records and choirs and heard music at church.

Within the African American community, inexpensive forms of recreation spontaneously sprang up on the weekends and after working hours. Excluded from recreational services offered to Whites and with little money for entertainment, Black women and men workers formed what Korstad (1987) termed a "separate and meaningful world" where their recreational and spiritual needs could be met. Margaret Turner remembered that in Durham in the 1920s and 1930s:

> [W]e did have people that drank a lot during that time, and they would get dressed up on Saturday night and go out. They'd come down the street singing the blues and different things like that. They were going to see the girls. They just had a good time. But they were nice people.

Occasionally, people would get together at one of the few Black-owned movie theaters where they wouldn't have to sit in a balcony or they organized baseball teams in the neighborhood. While tobacco workers exercised great creativity and initiative in developing these informal networks for social activities, they could not, ultimately, watch a film from the main floor of the best White-owned theaters in town, could not eat in many Southern restaurants, and could not hope that their interest in sport might one day lead to a professional contract (Hall et al. 1987). Their opportunities for leisure activities as individuals were, at best, circumscribed by the racial dynamics of the New South.

As it did for economics, politics, and other arenas of social life, the African American church formed the backbone of Black women workers' leisure experiences (e.g., Henderson et al. 1996; Higginbotham 1993). Unlike textile communities where the group of people gathered for leisure activities was almost entirely composed of workers from a single company who lived, worked, and prayed together, African Americans frequently participated in leisure activities in race- and class-based, but not company-specific, groups at church. With few public or private recreation facilities and virtually no company-sponsored activities available, the church was the natural location for recreational activities that required complex organization or involved large numbers of people. For example, the African American neighborhood in Winston-Salem known as "Monkey Bottom," had no public recreational facilities, and beer gardens formed the only commercial form of entertainment. The community did, however, boast 35 Black churches (Korstad 1987). The choirs, picnics, Bible and self-help classes, and the fellowship of Christianity offered at church were more appealing ways for Black women to spend their time rather than go downtown where they were denied a seat at the local lunch counter or refused service in a retail shop. As stated by Margaret Holmes Turner:

> (the church) was the only place we could go and feel free, free at home . . . We'd shine up those shoes and get everything ready to dress up and go to church.

In the churches, Black women could not only relax and enjoy themselves but could also do so in an environment in which they would not be subject to the racist realities of the larger community. The church became a center for a wide variety of activities and activism, but importantly, the church became a vehicle for pride in the African American community.

For these African American women, recreation and leisure perhaps most strongly represented something that Whites could *not* appropriate. African Americans could be denied access to higher education, good jobs, and the power of the ballot box, but they could not be denied the meanings they derived from their own communities' spiritual and recreational activities. The institutions within the Black community provided strong ties upon which to build group identity. Not only did these bonds arise from poverty, but they were strengthened with shared experiences of racism, segregation, and religion and were solidified through the social interactions in recreation and leisure experiences.

Union organizing in the new south

Efforts to organize and promote unions were also linked to the recreation and leisure lives of the women in the mills and factories. A closer look at the early organizing activities showed the involvement of women as well as ties to their leisure. Organizing efforts often centered on existing social structures such as the church or social activities as a way to gain entry and establish trust. While unionization largely failed in the New South, the following description of organizing efforts illustrates interesting relationships between race, gender and leisure.

The textile and tobacco industries experienced crises in labor relations in the first half of the twentieth century. The textile industry was wracked by strikes in 1929 and 1934 in response to employers' desires to speed up work while decreasing wages. The strikes, though, were not universal and many workers stayed out of what they perceived to be trouble caused by outsiders. Pauline Griffith remembered that a bunch of strangers came in to organize a union at Judson Mills and that "it was a bunch that really meant business . . . They were really rough." Many women textile workers believed that the mill owners had their best interests at heart and were hesitant to oppose them in hopes that their loyalty might be rewarded later on. Ultimately, the textile unions failed to deliver on their promises and workers wound up suffering defeat for their efforts (Hall et al. 1987).

Trade unionism in the tobacco industry was often more militant and widespread. While White workers might have been skeptical of outsiders, Black workers had little reason to trust the White "insiders" with power in their workplaces and had nothing to lose by listening to national union or government agents (Korstad 1987). Southern activists and national or international union leaders provided tobacco workers with a wealth of experience, strategies for union success, and intellectual tools to help them enact change. These leaders were welcomed with open arms by the African American community.

As tobacco unionism swept the South, Black women often stepped forward into leadership roles. As workers with the most complaints of poor treatment, low wages, and disrespect, African American women had the least to lose from unionization and made natural union leaders (Korstad 1987). While men held some of the most powerful positions in the unions, women served as shop stewards and organizers, playing an instrumental role in the trade union movement.

Initially, the unions relied on the leadership, songs, prayers, and associations of the Black church in their efforts to organize tobacco workers. Margaret Turner remarked that an all-Black union at American Tobacco was beneficial to workers and mentioned that "we dressed up like we were going to church"—a connection symbolic of the seriousness with which workers approached their unionism and the meaning it had for them. When union groups got together, they frequently started with a religious song or a prayer. At R.J. Reynolds in Winston-Salem, the union theme song became "Do Lord, Remember Me," and the hymn was frequently led by Theodosia Simpson, church leader and union organizer. Velma Hopkins, a Reynolds worker and union member, recalled that "We always started off with a song and a prayer. We had a real prayer meeting going because we had some good Christian women on the committee."

Union organizers also drew upon the recognition within the Black community of the value of recreation facilities and opportunities often provided to the White mill workers. Local 22 at R.J. Reynolds provided a good example of this concern when Mabel Jessup wrote to the Winston-Salem Journal and argued:

> As for the . . . recreational centers, we deserve them. Have not the colored people of Winston-Salem helped to make R.J. Tobacco Reynolds Company the great manufacturing plant that it is today? Have not many of our people worked long hours for low wages, and for many years before R.J. Reynolds Tobacco Company used their money for any such humanitarian purpose? (Korstad 1987, p. 127)

Workers struck for higher wages, better benefits, and decent treatment in the workplace, but it is significant that among their demands was a plea for construction of recreational facilities for Black working-class communities. Interestingly, Whites responded to Black trade unionism with threats to what few recreational facilities the African American community did have. One advertisement (Korstad 1987, p. 151) cautioned union members:

> The Hospitals, the Schools, the Churches, the playgrounds, the Health Department, and the recreational facilities, the best in the entire South, are not the result of any trading—not the result of any demands . . . Will this growth continue? . . . It's up to you.

The unions not only recognized the importance of leisure in their demands, but their leaders also realized the importance of recreational activities to recruitment and morale, perhaps learning that lesson from the African American churches with which they worked. The union hall served as a supplement to the church in a number of ways including offering voter registration services, educational programs, and self-help classes as well as a recreational center. The library stocked not only labor journals and books on Black history but also novels, biographies, and poetry in an attempt to make the union a place where employees would want to spend their free time after a long day's work (Korstad 1987). At R.J. Reynolds, organizers made records available that combined the inspiration of Negro spirituals with the message of the Congress of Industrial Organizations (CIO), enabling the union to reach workers who were not literate and bridge the sacred world of the church and the secular world of the union.

Union leaders brought in outside performers to further draw upon workers' love of musical entertainment. Paul Robeson, a famous African American entertainer, sang for the union in June of 1947 in an effort to raise awareness and foster support (Korstad 1987). While White foremen may have loved to hear African American workers sing spirituals that harkened back to the days of slaves and masters, Robeson tried to elevate Black culture and place the spirituals on the same cultural plane as the classical works he also sang. Korstad argued that the use of music drew people into the union who, while they felt right at home singing in a church choir, might have been hesitant to speak up at a union meeting. By superimposing class consciousness and trade unionism over a musical tradition that was a large part of the recreational and spiritual life of many workers and by celebrating that tradition as a superior cultural form, the union in Winston-Salem managed to craft a particularly powerful movement.

Interestingly, unions also relied on union hall recreation to draw in the support of the White workers. A predominantly Black union in Winston-Salem sponsored segregated social activities, a recreational center, and dances for White workers (Korstad 1987). African American workers realized their dues were used to pay for non-dues-paying Whites to enjoy these activities, but they were willing to accept that for the purposes of gaining White support for their movement. By relying on established networks for social change and taking on some of the church's roles as educator, political voice, and leisure provider for the Black community, unions engaged African American support. Later, with the help of segregated dances and the provision of a recreational space, the unions gained a foothold in the White community as well (Korstad 1987).

Effects of union activities

Although the union at R.J. Reynolds was ultimately disbanded and unions in other factories failed due to mechanization of factories, accusations of communism, or the vigilance of White opposition, some gains were won. While Whites continued to make every effort to squelch Black political and economic power, the White community began to take more seriously the race relations problems that plagued their communities. For example, one of the first cases of Whites' new attitude of philanthropy toward the African American community was the construction of a new YMCA-YWCA in 1948 in Winstson-Salem with R.J. Reynolds company money (Korstad 1987). Whites were concerned about juvenile delinquency and the need for moderate Black leaders with whom they could work in future years, and so they had a vested interest in such a facility, while African Americans knew that Black youth needed more outlets for recreation and social interaction. That both the White and Black communities saw this recreation center as a real need, although for very different reasons, attested to the importance of recreation and leisure to leaders of both races. Through recreation, they expected youth would avoid trouble, develop leadership skills, and have a more wholesome transition to young adulthood. Moreover, the fact that the company saw this center as important enough to use as a potential bargaining chip further emphasized the centrality of recreation to the community and its sense of identity.

The leisure community of women tobacco workers was based primarily on race and class and was bound by racial uplift and spiritual life as leisure services also became entwined with church and union work. While tobacco workers shared recreational experiences among themselves, they also sang, danced, and participated in other activities with members of their congregations who did not stem brightleaf for a living, but rather held other jobs in the working class. For all of these African Americans, recreation and leisure perhaps most strongly represented the meanings that they derived from their own communities' spiritual and social sense of identity.

That African Americans, and particularly African American women tobacco workers, chose to layer their leisure experiences with religious, political, or union activism is not surprising. Their time was stretched to the limit by long hours in the factory, possibly a second job, housekeeping, and children who needed care. Dora Scott Miller recalled that by the time she got home, her husband had usually cooked dinner, but she still had to do housework:

> [M]aybe I had to wash. Didn't have but a scrubboard, no washing machine and no washerette to go to. I went on that scrubboard and wash my clothes, hang them out.

Blanche Scott remembered working at Liggett Myers, going to beauty school in the evenings, and continuing her work at Mount Vernon Baptist Church, commenting that "with the help of the Lord, I've got along just fine. You have to put God in the front, you can't do nothing without him." In both the Black churches and the unions, the women workers were often the base of support and exerted key leadership capabilities that included the importance of recreation to quality of life issues.

Conclusion

Important differences in recreation and leisure opportunities for Black and White working class women became clear in the analysis. While White women's recreation was relatively politically uncharged, perhaps posing only a minor challenge to employers' intentions, African American women transformed recreation and leisure experiences into a vehicle for social change based on race and class issues. In textile mill villages, White women had a more limited variety of leisure services made available to them than did their husbands or brothers, and the activities in which they participated were mostly directed toward social activities with family and friends. In the Black community, however, leisure services in a formal sense were often nonexistent outside the church and the union, both of which relied heavily on women's leadership. Therefore, because of women's influence, the activities made available through the church and union were likely to serve the leisure needs of women tobacco workers as well as the men. While White workers seemed to have used leisure for its own sake, perhaps gaining some sense of solidarity with one another in the process, in the Black community leisure was almost always entwined with struggles for fair treatment in the work place, better education, a political voice, or a sense of identity.

Through these experiences, women in both industries managed to make leisure experiences a battleground on which wars over social hierarchies were waged. Although the women textile workers may have enjoyed the company games and social opportunities, recreational activities were not accepted as Trojan horses for management's ideas about absolute company loyalty and maintenance of a docile work force. Moreover, when tobacco unions used recreation based on traditional forms of African American leisure to gather support from Black workers, they mounted a direct challenge to not only class but also racial hierarchies. Women, as primary speakers and organizers, challenged gender conventions that dictated women's submersion in the private sphere.

Union dances and company bands may seem marginal on the surface, but the importance of these activities were clearly wrapped up in the meanings of community and individual identity. By acknowledging how workers used leisure, either for its own sake or for some type of social good such as racial uplift, we gain a sharper understanding of the priorities of individuals and communities; we learn about the integration of work and leisure in a way that we otherwise cannot detect. We also begin to understand the role that leisure has in specific historical moments. Whether it be on the ballfields or dance floors or in the churches or union halls, leisure played a critical role in working-class identity and challenged the social hierarchies centered on subordination to the White male ruling class. Looking at leisure with historical specificity allows us to better understand the interplay between leisure meaning and larger social circumstances of race, class, and gender. As today's recreation professionals struggle to meet the needs of all members of their communities, some of the answers may come from a better understanding of the roots of social injustices due to race, gender, and class issues. Just as recreation served as a focal point for quality of life in the communities of textile and tobacco workers in the past, we may need to once again recognize the significance and power of recreation to bring about social change needed today.

By analyzing the experiences of women textile and tobacco workers at a particular historical moment, we can draw conclusions to further both disciplines of leisure studies and history. First, one might conclude from the use of leisure as a means to another end that leisure does not have to be intrinsic to be individually fulfilling or valuable. Leisure can be relational not only in the interpersonal sense of textile community suppers but on a larger level of race, class, and gender as participants assign meaning to activities based on the history of their communities or choose to include and exclude individuals on the basis of demographic categories. Finally, leisure can reflect social hierarchies as well as challenge them. Recreation, on the surface, may seem far less dangerous to the social order than political movements or unions, but when layered with broader community needs, can be a similarly effective tool for institution-building and social change. Collaborative efforts between historians and leisure studies researchers are imperative if we are to build a body of knowledge inclusive of the many voices from our past. Ultimately, perhaps the greatest contribution is the recognition of the critical need for a leisure-based perspective on history and a historical foundation for leisure. Historical perspectives will situate much of our understandings of recreation and leisure within historical contexts that not only establish links to our past but provide credibility to the importance of recreation and leisure in the development of social identities. Historical studies focused on emergent social concepts such as race, gender, and class will establish a foundation from which our present-day assumptions about recreation and leisure can be examined and expanded. These broader understandings should, in turn, create new models for the future and directions needed for social change efforts by recreation and leisure professionals.

References

Ayers, E. L. (1992). *The promise of the New South: Life after reconstruction*. New York: Oxford University Press.

Burton, T. L., & Jackson, E. L. (1989). Leisure research and the social sciences: An exploratory study of active researchers. *Leisure Studies, 8* 270.

Campbell, G. (1995). *"My own kind of people": Grand opera, old time fiddling and the creation of Whiteness in Atlanta, 1910–1925*. Unpublished seminar paper, University of North Carolina at Chapel Hill.

Cross, G. (1990). *A social history of leisure since 1600*. State College, PA: Venture Publishing, Inc.

Fischer, C. S. (1994). Change in leisure activities, 1890–1940. *Journal of Social History, 27, 453–475.*

Glaser, B. G., & Strauss, A. L. (1967). *The discovery of grounded theory: Strategies for qualitative research*. Chicago, IL: Aldine Publishing, Co.

Hall, J.-D., Leloudis, J., Korstad, R., Murphy, M., Jones, L. A., & Daly, C. P. (1987). *Like-a family: The making of a Southern cotton mill world*. Chapel Hill. NC University of North Carolina Press.

Henderson, K. A. (1991). *Dimensions of choice: A qualitative approach to recreation, parks, and leisure research*. College Park, PA: Venture Publishing, Inc.

Henderson, K. A., Bialeschki, M. D., Shaw, S. M., & Freysinger, V. J. (1996). *Both gains and gaps: Feminist perspectives on women's leisure*. State College, PA: Venture Publishing, Inc.

Higginbotham, E. B. (1993). *Righteous discontent: The women's movement in the Black Baptist Church 1880–1929*. Cambridge, MA: Harvard University Press.

Janiewski, D. E. (1985). *Sisterhood denied: Race, gender, and class in a New South community*. Philadelphia: Temple University Press.

Kasson, J. F. (1978). *Amusing the million: Coney Island at the turn of the century*. New York: Hill and Wang.

Kirby, J. T. (1987). *Rural worlds lost: The American South, 1920–1960*. Baton Rouge: Louisiana State University Press.

Korstad, R. R. (1987). *Daybreak of freedom: Tobacco worker and the CIO Winston-Salem, North Carolina 1943–1950*. Unpublished dissertation, University of North Carolina Chapel Hill.

Nasstrom, K. L. (Ed.). (1992). *Women's voices in the Southern Oral History Program Collection*. Chapel Hill, NC: University of North Carolina.

Newby, I. A. (1989). *Plain folks in the New South: Social change and cultural persistence, 1880–1915*. Baton Rouge: Louisiana State University Press.

Peiss, K. (1986). *Cheap amusements: Working women and leisure in turn-of-the-century New York*. Philadelphia: Temple University Press.

Rosenzweig, R. (1983). *Eight hours for what we will: Workers and leisure in an industrial city, 1870–1920*. New York: Cambridge University Press.

Stokowski, P. (1990). Extending the social groups model: Social network analysis in recreation research. *Leisure Sciences, 12*, 254–255.

Stokowski, P. A., & Lee, R. G. (1991). The influence of social network ties on recreation and leisure: An exploratory study, *Journal of Leisure Research, 22*(2):95–113.

Tindall, G. B. (1967). *The emergence of the New South, 1913–1945*. Baton Rouge: Louisiana State University Press.

Town of Elkin Joint Committee for the Collection of Historical Information (1989). *Elkin 1889–1989: A centennial history*. Charlotte, NC: The Delmar Company.

U.S. Department of Commerce, Bureau of the Census. (1914). *Thirteenth census of the United States taken in the year 1910, Volume IV*. Washington: Government Printing Office.

U.S. Department of Commerce, Bureau of the Census. (1923). *Fourteenth census of the United States taken in the year 1920, Volume IV*. Washington: Government Printing Office.

U.S. Department of Commerce, Bureau of the Census. (1933). *Fifteenth census of the United States taken in the year 1930, Volume IV*. Washington: Government Printing Office.

Wood, P. J. (1986). *Southern capitalism: The political economy of North Carolina, 1880–1980*. Durham, NC: Duke University Press.

Woodward, C. V. (1951). *Origins of the New South, 1877–1913*. Baton Rouge: Louisiana State University Press.

Wynne, D. (1990). Leisure, lifestyle, and the construction of social position, *Leisure Studies, 9*, 21–34.

Summary

In this part I have attempted to provide some guidelines for those wishing to utilize intersectional perspective in their research. Although this approach has existed for more than a decade in the theoretical writings of black feminist scholars, the methodology of intersectional analysis is yet to be developed. This and the following part on quantitative methods for intersectional analysis are intended as a contribution to the methodology. A number of rules were suggested to serve as guides in developing a research design that incorporates the intersectional assumption of *simultaneity* as well as guides for testing the *multiplicative* assumption. Distinctions were made between qualitative and quantitative approaches, and examples of qualitative articles using the intersectional approach were presented and briefly critiqued. Although the objective was to focus on the methodology rather than on the substance of these articles, these articles cover a very wide variety of substantive issues, demonstrating the wide appeal and applicability of the intersectional approach. In the next part will discuss methodological issues for utilizing intersectional analysis in quantitative research, with special attention to testing the multiplicative assumption.

References

Aiken, Leona S., and Stephen G. West. 1991. *Multiple regression: Testing and interpreting interactions*. Newbury Park, CA: Sage.

Alger Jr., Horatio. [1872] 1972. *Strive and succeed: or, The progress of Walter Conrad*. Philadelphia: Porter & Coates.

———. 1899. *Mark Mason's victory: The trials and triumphs of a telegraph boy*. New York: A. L. Burt.

———. [18??] 1974: *Making his way; or, Frank Courtney's struggle upward*. New York: Arno Press.

Berg, Bruce L. 2001, 4th ed. *Qualitative research methods for the social sciences*. Boston: Allyn and Bacon.

Brewer, Rose M. 1993. Theorizing race, class, and gender: The new scholarship of black feminist intellectuals and black women's labor. In *Theorizing black feminisms: The visionary pragmatism of black women,* ed. Stalie M. James and Abena P. A. Busia, 13–30. London: Routledge.

Blumin, Stuart M. 1989. *The emergence of the middle class: Social experience in the American city, 1760–1900.* New York: Cambridge University Press.

Brod, Rodney L. 1999. Logistic regression modeling of race, gender, and class: Illustrated by gender bias in wages. In *ASA Resource Materials for Teaching,* 81–93. Washington, D.C.

Chinni, Dante. 2003. Crying "class warfare." *Christian Science Monitor,* September 23.

Cohn, D'Vera. 2003. Hispanics declared largest minority: Blacks overtaken in census update. *Washington Post,* June 19.

Collins, Patricia Hill. 1993. Toward a new vision: Race, class, and gender as categories of analysis and connection. *Race, Sex, & Class* 1, no. 1 (Fall): 557–71.

———. 1995. "Symposium on West and Fenstermaker's 'Doing Difference.'" *Gender & Society* 9, no. 4 (August): 491–94.

———. 1998. "Some group matters: Intersectionality, situated standpoints, and black feminist thought." Chap. 6 in *Fighting words: Black women and the search for justice,* 201–28 Minneapolis: University of Minnesota Press.

Crystal, David. 1989. Asian Americans and the myth of the model minority. *Social Casework* 70 (September): 405–13.

Denzin, Norman K., and Yvonna S. Lincoln, eds. 1998a. *Collecting and interpreting qualitative materials.* Thousand Oaks, CA.: Sage.

———. 1998b. *Strategies of qualitative inquiry.* Thousand Oaks, CA: Sage.

Dionne, Jr., E. J. 2003. Bush: Tax cut criticism is "class warfare." *Washington Post,* January 7.

Domhoff, G. William. 1983. *Who rules America now?: A view for the '80s.* Upper Saddle River, NJ: Prentice Hall.

Duncan, Otis Dudley. 1961. "A socio-economic index for all occupations. In *Occupations and social status,* ed. Albert J. Reiss, 109–38 New York: Free Press.

Foner, Nancy, and George M. Fredrickson, eds. 2004. *Not just black and white: Historical and contemporary perspectives on immigration, race, and ethnicity in the United States.* New York: Russell Sage Foundation.

Landry, Bart. 1987. *The new black middle class.* Berkeley: University of California Press.

Karl Marx. [1867] 1977. *Capital.* Vol. 1. New York: Vintage.

King, Deborah K. 1988. Multiple jeopardy, multiple consciousness: The context of a black feminist ideology. *Signs: Journal of Women in Culture and Society* 14 (no. 1) 88–111.

Mayer, Kurt. 1956. Recent changes in the class structure of the United States. *Transactions of the Third World Congress of Sociology,* vol. 3.

———. 1959. Diminishing class differentials in the United States. *Kyklos* 12: 605–28.

Nisbet, Robert. 1959. The decline of social class. *Pacific Sociological Review* 2 (Spring): 11–17.

Parkin, Frank. 1971. *Class inequality and political order.* New York: Praeger.

PBS. *People like us: Social class in America.* 2001. New York: The Center for New American Media.

Ryan, Mary. 1981. *Cradle of the middle class: The family in Oneida County, New York: 1790–1865.* New York: Cambridge.

Warner, W. Lloyd, and Paul S. Lunt. 1941. *The social life of a modern community.* New Haven, CT: Yale University Press.

Weber, Max. 1968 [1921]. The distribution of power within the political community: Class, status, party. In *Economy and Society,* trans. G. Roth and C. Wittich, 926–40. New York: Bedminster Press.

Wright, Erik Olin. 1978. Varieties of Marxist conceptions of class structure. Unpublished paper, Institute for Research on Poverty. Univ. of Wisconsin–Madison.

Wright, Erik Olin, and Luia Perrone. 1977. Marxist class categories and income inequality. *American Sociological Review* 42: 32–55.

Yamanaka, Deiko, and Kent McClelland. 1994. "Earning the model-minority image: Diverse strategies of economic adaptation by Asian-American women." *Ethnic and Racial Studies* 17 (January): 79–114.

Zinn, Maxine Baca, and Bonnie Thornton Dill. 1996. Theorizing difference from multiracial feminism. *Feminist Studies* 22, no. 2 (Summer): 321–31.

PART III

The Methodology of Intersectional Analysis: Quantitative Approaches

INTRODUCTION

Intersectional analysis using quantitative approaches assumes that Rules 1, 2, and 3, as defined in Part 2, are followed. According to Rule 1, the saturated model with all eight social locations represented is optimal. If the research question focuses on only one category of race, gender, or class (e.g., women gymnasts), then only the four social locations resulting from the intersection of the other two identities are present (Rule 2). These two rules address the assumption of *simultaneity.* It is Rule 3 that requires special attention in quantitative intersectional analysis.

According to Rule 3, when intersectional research is conducted, the statistical technique utilized should allow for the detection of *interactions.* Statistical interactions, I have argued, are what is meant by *multiplicative relationships* in intersectional research. An interaction exists when the effect of an independent variable (x) on a dependent variable (Y) is *conditional* on the values of a second independent variable (z). For instance, we expect education to influence the income an individual receives, an effect that can be measured as the increase in income received for each additional year of education completed. From an intersectional analytic point of view, however, such a finding is incomplete. We would also like to know if individuals in different social locations receive the same return in income for each additional year of education. Do blacks or females obtain the same return as whites or males? Do white females with a college degree earn more than, the same as, or less than black females with a college degree? If individuals in different social locations receive the same income for each additional year of education, there is no interaction, and the relationship is not multiplicative. If whites receive higher income than blacks for the same education, or white middle-class women earn less than comparably educated black middle-class women, then there is an interaction or a multiplicative effect. The amount of income gained from one's education varies across social locations.

Whether the multiplicative assumption holds in a particular case is an *empirical question.* The multiplicative assumption, therefore, should be viewed as a hypothesis to be tested in each individual case, rather than as a given. Quantitative statistical techniques such as multiple regression are well suited for testing the presence and significance of the multiplicative hypothesis.

This does not mean that qualitative researchers cannot uncover the presence of interactions. Indeed, careful and insightful qualitative analysis can suggest that relationships between independent and dependent variables vary across categories of race, gender, or class; however, such multiplicative relationships cannot be subjected to rigorous tests of significance.[1] Testing for the presence and significance of interactions (multiplicative relationships) is not only possible with quantitative statistical techniques but necessary for sound quantitative intersectional analysis.

The Basic Approach

The most common and basic quantitative statistical approach to detecting and measuring interaction effects is *multiple regression.* In most quantitative studies, the researcher wishes to explain an outcome or an effect. Because humans are complex beings embedded in multiple groups and organizations, engaged in myriad actions, the researcher needs tools that will aid in untangling the complexity of social life. Multiple regression was designed with that purpose in mind. This statistical approach enables the researcher to identify a large number of factors that are believed to have some influence on the outcome, effect, or condition of interest. Whether the researcher is attempting to understand income attainment, educational attainment, premarital pregnancy, full-term births, or delinquency, there are likely to be multiple influences or causes. Discovering these causes (independent variables) is in part a matter of educated guesses and exploratory research. In this sense, the research enterprise is a *cumulative* process in which each researcher builds on the efforts of others. Each researcher brings to her or his undertaking the results learned from the past and the new insights present in the given project. It is hoped that together they will lead to new findings or insights that will serve as a foundation on which others will build. Although a number of statistical techniques can be used to test for interactions, such as analysis of variance, logistic regression, and ordinary least squares multiple regression, the last type of analysis is the most common. It is the most basic approach to multiple regression and the technique most likely to be taught at both the undergraduate and graduate levels. For this reason almost all the quantitative articles included in this text employ ordinary least squares multiple regression analysis.

To illustrate this process we shall return to the example of income attainment, but first, let us think in terms of what I call *simple* versus *complex* social locations. Race, gender, and class all represent *simple* social locations. In our society we often think of an individual as being black *or* white, female *or* male, and sometimes as belonging to the working class or the middle class *or* the upper class. Since the 1960s a great deal of attention has also been paid to the poor, and more recently to the underclass. For example, during the 2000 presidential elections Al Gore criticized George W. Bush for proposing a tax cut that Gore claimed would benefit the upper class while claiming that his own proposal would better serve the middle-class worker.

---

[1]Since researchers normally analyze samples rather than data from entire populations, it is possible that a given sample may not be representative of the population from which it is derived. Hence the relationships found in that sample will also not be representative of those within the population. Tests of significance are statistical operations used to evaluate the degree to which relationships found in a sample could have occurred by chance.

Thus, black or white; male or female; rich, poor, or middle class have become meaningful social distinctions of everyday life. Yet, as we have seen, an individual is not a member of a race *or* of a particular gender *or* of an individual class. We carry around with us all three characteristics, and while we are not always conscious of this, there certainly are times when we confront an individual as a member of a gender *and* a race *and* a class. This individual is a working-class white (or Latino, or Native American) male on a construction site, or an upper middle-class black male attempting to hail a taxi downtown. It may at first appear difficult to wrap our minds around all three characteristics simultaneously, but that is exactly what we do in the nanosecond of perception in the half-conscious periphery of our minds. I refer to situations in which two or three of these identities are recognized as *complex* social locations.

Although our ultimate goal is to understand complex social locations, we begin with simple locations by asking the question: Is income attainment the same for Asians as for whites, for females as for males, or for a working-class individual as for someone in the middle class? Here we think of the simple locations—race, gender, or class—as independent variables and income as the dependent variable. We then ask whether income varies across these simple locations, or phrased slightly differently, we ask: Do race, gender, and class matter in income attainment? Do men earn more than women, or do middle-class individuals earn more than those in the working class? For purposes of illustration we shall conceptualize each of these simple locations as a dichotomy. Race is black (Latino, Asian) or white, gender is male or female, and class refers to middle class and working class. We can model this relationship with a multiple regression equation with race, gender, and class as independent variables (endnote i). We can further simplify this example by dropping race and class, creating an equation with one independent variable—gender—and income as the dependent variable (endnote ii). Because gender is dichotomous, a solution to this question will tell us whether the average income of males or of females is greater. This is the same as comparing the mean incomes for males and females. Results would reveal the well-established fact that women earn on average about 74 percent of what men earn.[2]

In most cases, however, the researcher is interested in a substantive issue and is attempting to measure the effects of a number of independent variables that either have been shown to affect the dependent variable or are assumed to do so. Because past research has demonstrated that education influences income attainment, a researcher will include education as one of the principal independent variables. Indeed, the researcher may be primarily interested in the effect of education on income; but since other factors influence income attainment, such as age, work experience, and supervisory status, multiple regression offers a powerful tool for developing a model that allows the researcher to measure the effect of education on income while "controlling" for these other variables. To simplify the example let us add only education to the model (endnote iii).

Such a model (along with other relevant control variables) is common in sociological research. Gender and/or race are frequently added as "main effect" variables because of the general knowledge that the return in income for education differs by gender and race. As before, income is the dependent variable, and gender and education are independent variables.

[2]The value of the ratio of female to male income varies by the characteristics of those being compared. The ratio is smallest among young college-educated males and females.

Earlier I noted that we can think of education as a "cause" of income. The more years of education an individual has, the higher the income she or he is likely to earn. The statistical solution to this simplified model will reveal the gains in income for a year increase in education, net of the effect of gender. It should be noted, however, that education and gender can serve as either independent or control variables. Neither is inherently one or the other; the classification depends on the point of view or intent of the researcher. When education is chosen as the independent variable, then the model measures the returns in income to education, holding gender constant. If gender is the independent variable, then the model measures the difference in the average incomes of males and females, holding education constant. This is rather straightforward. No mystery here.

Simple social locations

From an intersectional point of view, if education is the independent variable, the question becomes a Type II problem: the researcher wants to determine whether the relationship between education and income is the same for males and females. Gender then can be thought of as a simple location; however, the question cannot be answered using equation [3.3] (endnote iii), because equation [3.3] assumes a *linear* relationship. It is assumed that the income return to education is the same for males and females. Since we suspect that this is not the case, we need a different model to test for the existence of a *nonlinear* relationship. As explained in Part 2, to test the assumption that the effect of education differs across categories of gender—is different for males and females—an *interaction* or *product* term, created by multiplying one variable by another, must be added to the equation. In the present case we multiply education by gender to give a nonlinear model (endnote iv) [3.4]. Or course, we could just as easily have used race or class instead of gender.

How does the addition of the interaction term help us determine whether the income gains from education vary across the simple locations of females and males? The term enables us to test our hypothesis that we really cannot know the true effect of education on income without also knowing whether the individual is female or male. This is what intersectional theorists refer to as a *multiplicative relationship.* If the interaction term is statistically significant (i.e., not likely to have happened by chance), we then know that the effect of education on income is different for males and females. In the language of intersectional analysis we can say that the effect of education on income attainment varies across the simple locations of gender (endnote v).

Let us carry this exercise further by adding the additional simple social location represented by race and removing the education × gender interaction term. We now have a linear model with three independent variables: education, gender, and race (endnote vi). It is important to understand that linear models such as this one allow the researcher to measure the effect of a *single* independent variable while holding all others constant. For instance, the researcher can determine the effect of race on income, net of the effects of education and gender. Because race is dichotomous, the result would give the mean income of blacks and whites, after the effects of education and race have been taken into consideration. Conversely, the researcher can focus on the effect of gender, net of the effects of education and race, and likewise for the effect of education.

To determine whether the effect of education varies by race as well as by gender, we must add a second interaction term between education and race to the model (endnote vii). This transforms the expression once again into a nonlinear model with interaction terms education × race and education × gender. We are now assuming that the effect of education on income is not the same across categories of race *or* gender. Rather, we are hypothesizing that the effect of education on income is conditional on the simple social locations of race and gender. If the interaction terms are statistically significant, we can conclude that the relationship between education and income varies across these two simple social locations. Males and females as well as blacks and whites with a college degree, for instance, will all earn different incomes on average. The same test can be performed for class by adding the simple location of class and its interaction term with education to the equation (endnote viii).

Complex social locations

Thus far we have explored multiplicative relationships involving what I call simple social locations, the difference between two identities: black or white, male or female, middle class or working class.[3] Although these results are informative, they are limited. Knowing that blacks and whites receive unequal income for the same education leaves us ignorant of differences by race *and* gender. Do black *women* and white *women* receive different income returns? Do black *men* and white *men* receive different returns? Likewise for gender, knowing that males and females receive unequal incomes for the same education leaves us in the dark about the returns on education for *black* men compared with *white* men, or *black* women compared with *white* women. Of course, we cannot really abstract from an individual's race or gender or class. These characteristics are a given. Rather, the income gained from education probably varies by an individual's race *as well as* gender and class. To test this hypothesis, that the effect of education on income varies across the complex social locations of race, gender, *and* class, we must introduce what is called a *higher-order interaction* term. We first consider the case in which only two of the three identities vary: race and gender.

Type I cases

In Type I cases, race and gender are the independent variables, with all other independent variables serving as controls. In the present example there is only one control variable, education. To determine whether income varies across the four social locations we need introduce only one interaction term: race × gender (endnote ix). This term yields four social locations, which can be illustrated by a 2 × 2 table, with each cell representing a single complex social location formed by the intersection of race and gender: black males, white males, black females, and white females.

	RACE	
GENDER	Black	White
Males	BM	WM
Females	BF	WF

The solution to this problem involves comparisons of the four groups at selected education levels and when properly worked out allows the researcher to determine whether there are significant differences in income among the four social locations (endnote x).

Type II cases

In Type II cases, education is the principal independent variable, and race and gender become control variables. As noted previously, these are a special type of control variable in RGC analysis. This model focuses on the relationship between education and income. But rather than holding race and gender constant, that is measuring the effect of education on income net of the effects of race and gender, the researcher wants to test the null hypothesis that there is *no* difference in the effect of education on income across the four social locations.

[3]Testing for interactions, however, is not a new analytical approach, although Aiken and West (1991) suggest that it is underutilized, given the types of variables social scientists study.

There are several ways to model this problem, the most direct of which is to use second- and third-order interaction terms[4]: education × race, education × gender, race × gender, and education × race × gender (endnote xi). Although this model is straightforward statistically, third-order interaction terms are notoriously difficult to interpret. As a consequence, researchers often adopt the strategy of combining interaction terms with subgroup analysis.

In the present case, with race and gender (but not class) in the model, subgroup analysis requires running a model with a first-order interaction term of education × gender separately for blacks and whites (endnote xii) (or conversely for males and females). The education × gender interaction term combined with the black and white subgroups is equivalent to a third-order interaction term of education × gender × race. Having calculated the coefficients of the interaction term for the black and white subgroups, the researcher uses a *t*-test to determine if these coefficients are significantly different from each other.[5] If the *t*-test comparing two coefficients for a particular social location (e.g., black college-educated males and white college-educated males) is significant, it can be concluded that the relationship of education and income for these two social locations is multiplicative; therefore, the researcher cannot determine the true relationship of education and income for black and white college-educated males without using an intersectional approach.[6] If, however, a *t*-test is not significant, the researcher concludes that the relationship is not interactive (multiplicative). Several examples of this approach are included in the articles in this text.[7]

The saturated model

An intersectional model with race, gender, and class becomes more complicated. Again, the statistical expression for this model is straightforward, but its solution almost defies interpretation (endnote xiii). As a result, the researcher must again resort to subgroup comparisons with *t*-tests of the difference of coefficients across subgroups. Because race, gender, and class are in this model predicting income from education, it is a saturated model, as described in Part 2. A saturated model with the three dichotomous variables—race, gender, and class—contains eight social locations. Again, if this is a Type II analysis with education as the principal independent variable, and race, gender, and class as controls, the researcher uses one interaction term with the model run on each subgroup. Unlike the preceding example, with only race and gender, which had two subgroups

[4]Second-order interactions contain two terms (e.g., race × gender); third-order interactions contain three terms (e.g., race × gender × class).

[5]There are actually two steps to this process, as noted in endnote v. There are a number of *t*-tests available for accomplishing this; see, for instance, Hardy (1993, 51–52) and Paternoster and Mazerolle (1994). The only drawback to using this approach is that these *t*-tests must be calculated by hand.

[6]In cases where one of the variables of the interaction term is continuous (e.g., education), potentially there is a social location for each year of education; that is, we could compare black and white males and females at each year of education. These calculations not only would be excessively tedious but would result in data overload that would be difficult to summarize. In such cases the researcher can choose to make comparisons at educational levels of substantive interest (e.g., high school, college, postgraduate). When points on the scale lack intrinsic meaning (e.g., income), as in the case of education, it is customary to use the mean plus points one standard deviation above and below the mean (Aiken and West 1991, 12–14).

[7]See, for instance, the last four articles in this text.

(social locations), the saturated model requires four.

This problem can be solved by creating a model with one interaction term (e.g., education × gender) and four subgroups formed from the intersection of race × class: black middle class, white middle class, black working class, and white working class (endnote xiv). Of course, any one of the three identities can be used in the interaction term with appropriate changes in the subgroups. Again, this is equivalent to calculating the four-way interaction term education × race × gender × class needed to develop all eight intersectional groups. From an intersectional perspective the researcher wants to know whether there are differences in the income return on education across the eight social locations. Which social locations receive greater income for their education? Which locations receive less? The answer to these questions can be determined only by statistically comparing the income return on education for individuals in different social locations. As before, after running the model with one interaction term by the four subgroups the researcher uses, *t*-tests to determine whether the four subgroups differ significantly from one another for each gender at specific educational levels.

Some Issues and Statistical Problems

How many comparisons?

Although the strategy of subgroup comparisons solves the problem of interpreting higher-order interaction terms, it raises the question: How many *t*-test comparisons should be made? I have argued that both simultaneity and multiplicative relationships are assumptions or hypotheses that must be tested. When using subgroup analysis the multiplicative assumption is tested by calculating *t*-tests for the interaction coefficients to determine whether individual coefficients are significant and whether these coefficients are significantly different from one another. In the case of four subgroups above (e.g., black middle-class, white middle-class, black working-class, and white working-class) the researcher wants to know whether the interaction term education × gender is significant for *each* of the four race × class subgroups. Table 1 presents one example of this problem using education at the high school level.[8] Column A represents the regression equation[9] containing the education × gender interaction term calculated for each of the four subgroups in columns B–E, which yields eight unique social locations. In practice, the coefficients for the interaction terms for each of the four complex social locations are first examined for significance.

Testing for significant interactions is only the first step, however. The more important question (from an intersectional point of view) is whether the relationship between education and income varies for individuals in different social locations. Do working-class Asian females with a high school education earn the same income as working-class white females with a high school education? Do working-class Asian males with a high school diploma earn the same as working-class white males with the same education? If they do, then the relationship between education and income is not multiplicative. If they do not earn the same income, then the relationship is multiplicative

[8] As noted earlier, since education is a continuous variable, it is necessary to select specific education levels for comparison.

[9] In this model, education is the principal independent variable, with race, gender, and class the control variables, and education × gender the interaction term.

TABLE I ■ SOCIAL LOCATIONS FOR OLS REGRESSION OF INCOME ON EDUCATION CONTROLLING FOR RACE, GENDER, AND CLASS

A Education × gender	B Asian middle class	C White middle class	D Asian working class	E White working class
HS/Male	HS Asian Mc Male	HS White Mc Male	HS Asian Wc Male	HS White Wc Male
HS/Female	HS Asian Mc Female	HS White Mc Female	HS Asian Wc Female	HS White Wc Female

Legend: HS = high school, Mc = middle class, Wc = working class

(interactive). This second step—making comparisons across social locations—is accomplished by using *t*-tests.

Selection of comparisons

But which comparisons should be made? Which locations receive greater income returns to education? Which locations receive less? Potentially, one could compare each of the eight social locations with every other social location. Although, this is physically possible (but extremely tedious), it may not be substantively desirable or meaningful. Furthermore, there is the danger that calculating a large number of *t*-tests will yield some significant ones by chance (a Type 1 error). The larger the number of *t*-tests run, the greater this likelihood.

Rather than attempting to make all possible comparisons, the researcher should be guided by some particular interest or theory. In the present example, a researcher may be interested in comparisons across race but within the same gender and class: Asian middle-class males with white middle-class males, and Asian middle-class females with white middle-class females. Another researcher may want to study comparisons across class but within the same race and gender: Asian working-class females with Asian middle-class females, and white working-class females with white middle-class females. The important point here is that intersectional analysis does not trump decisions guided by relevant theory and the specific interest of the researcher. Intersectional analysis requires only that the comparisons involve complex social locations. At the same time, a researcher who chooses to ignore some of the possible comparisons should explain the reasons for this omission, noting that because they are left unexplored, nothing can be concluded about them. A fuller picture is left for future research or for the research of other scholars. Determining how many comparisons to make depends on personal judgment and on the state of research on the topic being explored.

Sample size

There are also technical issues that make using quantitative methods in intersectional analysis a challenge. One is the consideration of sample size. Discovering significant relationships in a data set is related in part to sample size. The use of interaction terms further divides the existing cases into "cells" corresponding to the number of groups representing social locations. Even four social locations severely reduce the numbers in each group. A small number of cases in a particular cell or cells makes it difficult to detect significance even when it exists. The problem becomes an inherent difficulty in quantitative intersectional analysis because it requires data on minority groups. A random sample of the population will ordinarily contain representative samples of minority subgroups in their proportion of the total U.S. population. Given that blacks, Latinos, and Asians are 12.3, 12.5, and 3.6 percent[10] of the U.S. population respectively, one would expect to have 123 blacks, 125 Latinos, and 36 Asians in a sample of 1000. Such a sample would contain only a negligible number of Native Americans. Some large national studies oversample subgroups that are a small percentage of the population. But even when using data that have oversampled minority groups, the number of individuals in particular social locations can be very small. A rule of thumb is that there should be at least 20 individuals in each "cell" (here read social location). Researchers often find themselves with fewer cases even when using data with oversampled subgroups. For instance, how many Latina and black middle-class women would one find in a national sample of 1000? Employing only one interaction term with subgroup analysis reduces the severity of the problem but does not eliminate it.

Multicollinearity

Another pesky problem is one statisticians call *multicollinearity,* which occurs when independent variables "overlap" considerably (Agresti and Finlay 1997, 541–43). The result is an inflation of the standard errors of the implicated variables and nonsignificance. Because interaction terms are highly correlated with the individual variables that make up the interaction term, multicollinearity must typically be considered in intersectional research. Fortunately, the statistical packages commonly used by researchers (SPSS and SAS) allow the researcher to test for the problem, although solving it may not be easy.

Critiquing Quantitative Articles

The following articles have been grouped according to the authors' strategies for analyzing intersections of race, gender, and class asnd by the number of social locations represented. Strategies include the use of interaction terms alone, subgroup analysis alone, or a combination of the two. Because ordinary least-squares (OLS) regression is the statistical technique most widely used in sociology, I tried to find articles that principally rely on this approach. Given the dearth of good quantitative studies using the intersectional approach, this was not altogether possible. A number of the articles use logistic regression, a version of multiple regression employed when the dependent variable is dichotomous rather than interval; however, my decision to rely primarily on articles using OLS regression is not to suggest that OLS is superior to other techniques. Rodney Brod (1999) has written convincingly on the use of logistic regression in intersectional analysis. Analysis of variance (ANOVA) is still another possible approach to analyzing interactions.

In some of the following articles, the authors consciously link their research to intersectional theory; others do not. Many have some version of race, gender, and/or class in the title. It is hoped that the 15 articles included in this part will be sufficient to provide useful models of quantitative intersectional analysis. In my comments I try to touch on some of the principal strengths and weakness of the articles from the viewpoint of the intersectional approach, not on the substantive issues themselves. Otherwise strong articles may nevertheless manifest methodological weaknesses from an intersectional perspective. These articles have all passed the test of the peer review process, but not necessarily from an intersectional point of view. With the exception of articles in the journal *Race, Gender & Class,* articles submitted to journals are not likely to be evaluated from the intersectional perspective. It is hoped that this text will provide useful guidelines with which to critique articles from an intersectional perspective.

[10]According to the 2000 census there is an additional .06 percent of individuals among African Americans and Asians respectively, who checked another race/ethnic identity along with African American or Asian.

Quantitative Studies with Four Locations: Separate Group Analysis

I include two articles in this group. The first article, by Hogan and Perrucci, explores racial and gender gaps in U.S. employment and retirement income. These authors are particularly interested in learning whether there are significant interaction effects between two of their independent variables, self-employment and marital status, with race and gender. The authors run their models for three different dependent variables using four different subgroups: black males, white males, black females, and white females. The results clearly suggest interactions with self-employment and marital status (as well as with several other independent variables). At one point Hogan and Perrucci conclude: "Marriage does not predict lower employment earnings for white males but only for white females (and less reliably for black females)" (p. 238). Comparing the coefficients for self-employment or marriage across the four groups is equivalent to using a third-order interaction term: marriage × race × gender. As noted previously, third-order interaction terms are very difficult to interpret. Analysis using the four social locations achieves the same goal with more clearly interpretable results.

The authors, however, do not use *t*-tests to assess whether the differences in specific coefficients (e.g., marriage) across subgroups are significant. Instead, they employ an *F*-test for each equation (subgroup). Although many of the comparisons of coefficients suggest significant differences among these subgroups, as Hardy (1993) suggests, without *t*-tests one cannot be certain that these results did not occur by accident.

Another common problem that limits this study is sample size. The authors acknowledge this when they point out that "21 percent of white males but only 12 percent of black males were self-employed in their longest held job. Comparable figures for females were only 7 percent for whites and 5 percent for blacks (n = 16)" (p. 236). The already small samples of black males (325) and black females (328) are drastically reduced in individual subgroups associated with particular independent variables. By contrast, there are 3589 white males and 2801 white females. The small subsamples of black males and females force the authors to qualify their findings with such expressions as "less reliably, for black females" or in referring to the coefficient for core-sector employment, to remark "but is much less reliable (larger standard error) for blacks" (p. 238). As noted earlier, sample size is often a problem that plagues the use of interaction terms. Although class, as measured by neo-Marxist class categories developed by Wright and Perrone (1977), is included in the models, it is not the principal independent variable and receives only passing mention. For all practical purposes, therefore, this is a study of the effects of self-employment and marriage on various forms of income across four race by gender social locations.

In "Gender and Race Differences in the Predictors of Daily Health Practices among Older Adults," Gallant and Dorn conclude that "examining older adults' health behaviors by race and gender leads to a fuller understanding of these behaviors" (p. 249). The behaviors referred to are physical activity, weight maintenance, smoking, alcohol consumption, and sleep patterns. Rather than focusing on a single independent variable, along with a number of controls, and the variation of its effect on the dependent variables by race and gender, the authors investigate 19 different independent variables and measure the fit of the model (R^2) and the patterns of prediction across subgroups. They conclude: "Differences in both the amount of variance explained and the significant predictors that emerged are evident across health behaviors and across population subgroups" (p. 253). Using hierarchical stepwise multiple regression they determine variations in the pattern of predictors among their four subgroups: black females, black males, white females, and white males (Tables 2 through 6; pp. 254–256). For instance, they find that although cigarette smoking is influenced by age in all groups, other influences differ by gender and still others by gender and race. Variation in predictors of BMI (body mass index) across social locations was summarized as follows:

> As Table 3 (p. 254) illustrates, for males, only BMI at Wave 1 is predictive of BMI at Wave 2. For females, a few other factors emerged as predictors of BMI. White females who have greater education and who have fewer depressive symptoms are more likely to have a BMI in the ideal range. Older black females and those who have fewer chronic conditions are more likely to have a BMI in the ideal range. (p. 254)

The preceding paragraph is notable in a number of ways. There is no difference in the pattern of predictors of BMI among males (i.e., there is no interaction across these two social locations). Therefore, black and white males can be collapsed into the simple location "males." This is not the case for women. The patterns of variables predicting BMI is different for black females and white females. This relationship is therefore interactive or multiplicative. Such findings support the notion that the multiplicative assumption is indeed a hypothesis that must be tested in each case. In the present one it is found to be present among black and white females, but not between black and white males.

Producing and Reproducing Class and Status Differences
*Racial and Gender Gaps in U.S. Employment and Retirement Income**

RICHARD HOGAN
Purdue University

CAROLYN C. PERRUCCI
Purdue University

Direct correspondence to Richard Hogan, Sociology and Anthropology, 1365 Stone Hall, Purdue University. West Lafayette, Indiana 47907-1365, E-mail: hoganr@sri.soc.purdue.edu

Recent research indicates that between 1970 and 1990 the racial gap in employment income increased (Cancio, Evans, and Maume 1996), while the gender gap decreased (Wellington 1994). We find a parallel pattern in retirement income for the cohort that retired in 1980–1981. The racial gap is greater in retirement than it was in employment, while the gender gap is smaller. Regression analyses specify the qualitatively different ways in which racial and gender inequality are produced in employment and reproduced in retirement. Focusing on how self-employment and marital status interact with race and gender in predicting income, we explain how the redistributive effects of Social Security, pensions, and assets contribute to the enduring racial gap (and, perhaps, to the declining gender gap).

The production and reproduction of racial and gender inequality occur on two increasingly separate fronts—at work and at home. Quite apart from its effects on the distinctive and often conflicting struggles for racial and gender equality (Davis 1983; Kraditor 1981), the alienation of life and work and, particularly, the decline of family proprietorship, beginning in the nineteenth century, undermined the long-term financial security of middle class (or, more generally, "average") U.S. families (Kulikoff 1989). Nevertheless, extant studies of racial and gender inequality have tended to ignore the importance of "traditional" middle class strategies, notably, marriage and self-employment, for accumulating income-producing assets (Carr 1996 is exceptional in this regard). Instead, the literature has focused on the competition for wages, salaries, and pension benefits without considering income-producing assets (or wealth—see Oliver and Shapiro 1995; Smith 1995 for analyses of racial differences in wealth). These income-producing assets are, however, the most tangible form of inherited or accumulated wealth and the clearest indicator of class position. Wealth, in the form of income-producing assets, reproduces itself in the form of industrial, financial, or commercial capital. It also facilitates the accumulation of human capital (in professional credentials and managerial experience) and provides the security for high-risk investments, including self-employment. Finally, it provides financial security for self, spouse, and children in retirement and for generations to come.

In the analysis that follows, racial and gender inequality in employment and retirement, will be analyzed, using a national sample of persons who began receiving Social Security Old Age benefits in 1980–1981 (Maxfield 1983). The analysis will indicate the extent of racial and gender inequality in previous employment income (from longest held job) and in current (1982) retirement income from Social Security,

---

*The authors wish to thank Jill Quadagno and Stan DeViney for their advice and assistance.

Richard Hogan and Carolyn C. Perrucci. "Producing and Reproducing Class and Status Differences: Racial and Gender Gaps in US Employment and Income" *Social Problems*, Vol. 45, No. 4 (November 1998): 528–549.

pensions, and asset earnings. We use human capital, occupational status, industrial sector, and class measures in ordinary least squares (OLS) regression models to predict employment and each type of retirement income for white males, white females, black males, and black females. We pay particular attention to the ways in which marital status and self-employment interact with race and gender in predicting earnings from employment and each source of retirement income.

Based on these analyses, it appears that the "traditional" path to financial security, associated with marriage and self-employment, continues to provide a means for reproducing wealth and class privilege. It appears, however, that this path is open only to whites. Also, at least for this cohort, marriage seems to be an important path to long-term financial security (in retirement) despite its limitations in the short-term (in employment). For this cohort of 1980–1981 retirees, the short-term costs and long-term advantages of marriage are particularly pronounced for women, especially for white women.

RACE VERSUS GENDER EARNINGS GAPS

The best available evidence suggests that the racial gap in per-capita income, after substantial decline between 1959 and 1969, has ceased to decline (since 1979) and has, if anything increased modestly between 1979 and 1984 (Jaynes and Williams 1989:274, 295). The gender gap, on the other hand, after remaining more or less constant between 1959 and 1969 (Jaynes and Williams 1989:295), declined somewhat between 1969 and 1979 (Reskin and Roos 1990:83).

How much gap and how much increase or decrease varies according to the definition and operationalization of the "gap." Figures vary dramatically depending on the base selected for comparison. The "racial gap" within gender, for example, is much smaller for women than it is for men, particularly since 1969 (Cancio, Evans and Maume 1996:550; Jaynes and Williams 1989:295). Nevertheless, comparing white men and women (Wellington 1993, 1994) or white and black men (Hogan, Kim and Perrucci 1997) generally produces race and gender gaps that are substantially smaller than the gap between white men and black women (Cancio, Evans and Maume 1996:550). Equally important, the base year chosen for comparison is critical. White females earned 59 percent of white male earnings in 1939, 44 percent in 1959 and 1969, 45 percent in 1979 and 51 percent in 1984. During this same period (1939 to 1984) the "racial gap" declined dramatically. Black males earned 44 percent of white male earnings in 1939 and 65 percent in 1984; black female earnings increased from 24 percent to 50 percent of white male earnings during this (1939 to 1984) period (all of these figures were calculated from data reported by Jaynes and Williams 1989:295).

One thing is clear. There are "substantially different processes by which the black-white and male-female wage gaps are generated" (Tomaskovic-Devey 1993:123). Generally, human capital (education and experience) accounts for more of the racial gap, while industry, firm, and occupational segregation accounts for more of the gender gap (Tomaskovic-Devey 1993:122–123). Women tend to be "ghettoized" in "female" work, segregated within occupation across industry, and within industry-occupation across specialty/task or firm. "As was true a century ago, women and men still rarely work side by side on the same jobs" (Reskin and Roos 1990:306). In fact, the "limited progress" toward "earnings equity" within those occupations that are increasingly available to women is "mostly through an erosion of men's real earnings during the 1970s" (Reskin and Roos 1990:306–307). In fact, the declining gender gap in annual mean earnings between 1979 and 1984 is due largely to the fact that white and black male earnings declined more rapidly (to 89 percent and 87 percent of 1979 earnings, in constant [1984] dollars) than white and black female earnings, which declined to 99 percent and 98 percent of 1979 earnings (calculated from data in Jaynes and Williams 1989:295).

In this context, the recently published findings of change between 1976 and 1985 in the relative importance of discrimination versus experience (based on decomposition of the race and gender wage gaps for 1976 and 1985) can be interpreted.

Cancio, Evans, and Maume (1996:551) report. "The role of discrimination increased as the explanation for the growing wage gap between White men and Blacks." This "discrimination effect" explains why black men suffered more than white men as men faced unemployment or declining wages/salaries during the "downsizing" or "downturn" period. At the same time, the authors note, "Almost the entire wage gap (98%) between highly educated Black women and White men is accounted for by differences in worker quality (the nondiscrimination component" [1996:551]). Thus, we find highly educated black women (and, as we shall see, white women as well) taking entry-level jobs, replacing more highly paid male workers and, most probably, being supervised by the most senior (and most "trained") white males, who managed to retain their relatively privileged positions and earnings.

This scenario also fits recent findings on the declining gender gap that compares white males and females. Wellington (1994:847) reports that "the net penalty for being female (the coefficient on the dummy variable for sex) decreased [1976–1985] . . . [but] differences in types of experiences [and] firm-specific human capital . . . and particularly years of training have a greater impact on wages than that of general human capital."

Taken together, the results of these two studies (using the same panel data to compare the racial and gender gaps of 1976 and 1985) suggest that white and black women were "integrating" occupations and industries where male earnings were declining and where only the most senior white males were able to retain their relatively privileged positions and earnings. The result is a small decrease in the gender gap at the expense of a marginal increase in the racial gap. Ultimately, however, the ordinal ranking of average annual earnings remains the same. In 1984, white males earned, on average, $20,457, compared to $13,218 for black males, $10,354 for white females, and $10,252 for black females (Jaynes and Williams 1989:295).

Racial and Gender Gaps in Retirement

The best available data on racial and gender gaps in retirement income indicate that among persons who began receiving Social Security Old Age benefits in 1980–1981, total annual retirement income for blacks was 54 percent of white income (53 percent if one excludes public assistance; calculated from Ozawa and Kim 1989 345). Estimates of the racial gap for future retirement cohorts (all sources of retirement income for persons aged 51 to 61 in 1992) suggest that the racial gap will increase (for the preretirement cohort, it is predicted that blacks will claim only 46 percent of white retirement income, once this cohort reaches retirement age; Smith 1995:S179). Women in the 1980–1981 retirement cohort report somewhere between 70 percent (see Table 1, below) and 81 percent (calculated from DeViney and Solomon 1995:89) of total male retirement income (excluding public assistance).[1] Based on available evidence it is difficult to predict whether the gender gap in

[1]DeViney and Solomon (1995:87) note that their sample provides a rather conservative estimate of female/male retirement income (81%), since they include only women who claim Social Security benefits based on their own career employment earnings. Including women who receive 50 percent of their spouse's benefits, in lieu of their own benefits, provides a more realistic estimate of the gender gap. Using this sample, women report 70 percent of male retirement income (see Table 1).

retirement income will increase or decrease in subsequent cohorts, since that would depend upon marital and employment trends (Gustman, Mitchell and Steinmeier 1996:S68; Moon and Juster 1995:S146–147). Nevertheless, appropriate disclaimers about the effects of using different bases for comparison notwithstanding, it seems that the racial gap in retirement income is substantially greater than the gender gap for those who retired in 1980 to 1981.

As was the case with employment earnings gaps, the components of the racial and gender gaps in retirement income are qualitatively different. The gender gap in retirement earnings is largely a function of the gap in pension earnings. Single females report 91 percent of Social Security and 93 percent of "other" income (from sources other than Social Security, pensions, and public assistance) reported by single males in the 1980–1981 retirement cohort. These same women report only 68 percent of single male pension income. Blacks claim only 68 percent of white Social Security and 54 percent of white pension income, but the biggest gap is in "other" income, where blacks claim only 36 percent of white earnings (calculated from Ozawa and Kim 1989 345). Projections for future retirement cohorts estimate that blacks will continue to narrow the gap in Social Security and pension earnings (claiming 75 percent and 60 percent, respectively), but the gap in "other" income is likely to grow. Black/ white "net worth" (assets minus debts) is projected to decline to 27 percent for those in the (aged 51 to 61) preretirement cohort (Smith 1995:S179).

The biggest gap in Social Security earnings, however, is between unmarried and married households, with the unmarried claiming only 53 percent of married Social Security income. Furthermore, the unmarried claim only 55 percent of married pension, and 60 percent of married "other," income, suggesting, on balance, that the "marital gap" is considerably greater than the gender gap and not far behind (within two or three percentage points) the racial gap (calculated from Ozawa and Kim 1989:345). It appears, however, that marital status interacts with gender, which further complicates efforts to distinguish the racial and gender gaps.

As complex as the analysis of earnings gaps might be, the analysis of retirement income gaps is, if anything, even more complex. Employment earnings tend to predict retirement income, but variables that predict the former do not always predict the latter. O'Rand (1986:657) argues that benefits (including retirement pensions) are part of the "hidden payroll," a relatively independent component of "compensation," which, together with earnings, "stratify the workplace into occupational markets."

O'Rand (1986:668) reports significant differences in the effects of race, gender, human capital, occupation, and industry in predicting employment earnings versus benefits. Some but not all of these findings have been reproduced in analyses using the New Beneficiaries data (Maxfield 1983), a representative sample of persons who began receiving Social Security Old Age benefits in 1980–1981. DeViney (1995) used these data to predict receipt of private (non-Social Security) pensions and found, as did O'Rand (1986), no significant race effect but (unlike O'Rand) significant gender and education effects. He also found that pensions are more likely in "core" (large-scale corporate or public) industrial sectors, less likely for women in "competitive" occupations (O'Rand's occupational market distinction), but more likely for women in "female" occupations. Marriage increases the probability of pensions for men but decreases the probability for women. The widowed (male and female) are more likely, but persons with children less likely, to receive pensions.

The effects of "core" sector employment and the interactive effects of gender and marriage are not surprising. It is difficult to disentangle the effects of occupation ("market" or "female") since DeViney (1995), like O'Rand (1986), does not control for the effect of employment earnings, and thereby assumes the independence of earnings and pensions as components of "compensation packages" (O'Rand

1986). Nevertheless, the literature generally confirms the gender and marriage effects that DeViney (1995) reports.

Quadagno (1988 542) reviews this literature, indicating that women are less likely to receive pensions, in part due to marriage and child-bearing responsibilities that result in irregular employment. She also indicates, however, that some women in "female" occupations (notably, the Ladies Garment Workers) were able to secure pension rules that accommodated their "irregular work histories" by virtue of their unionization (the ILGWU, which is compared to the UAW, a predominantly "male" union; Quadagno 1988 554). The counterintuitive effect of "female" occupation may be due in part to the unmeasured effect of "female" union.

More generally, the relatively large gender gap and the relatively small racial gap in private pension benefits is particularly striking in comparison to Social Security retirement income. Ozawa and Kim (1989) focus on the redistributive effects of Social Security, private pensions, and public assistance, comparing married couples to single individuals, single males to females, whites to blacks and other nonwhites, and managerial-professionals to nonprofessionals. On balance, these data suggest, first, that public assistance has trivial effects on the racial gap in retirement income and virtually no effect on any of the other gaps. Second, Social Security redistributes from single to married, to a lesser extent from single women to single men, to a considerable extent from whites to blacks, and from-professional-managerial workers to less privileged workers. Third, private pensions increase the gap between single men and women (by five percentage points) and between managerial-professional and other workers (by two percentage points).

Meyer (1996) offers a more extensive and much more critical analysis of the redistributive nature of Social Security benefits, focusing on the "noncontributory" benefits received by spouses and widows, which "are most advantageous to middle-class and upper-middle-class married White women who have never contributed to the system" (1996 449). O'Rand (1996 26) concurs, reporting, "The U.S. Social Security System systematically favors 'traditional' married couples (husband-worker, wife-nonworker) over single individuals and dual-career couples in the calculation and distribution of retirement benefits."

The redistributive effects of Social Security are, obviously, subject to diverging interpretations. It is clear that those who need the money the least receive the most, but it is also true that those who need it the most really need whatever they can get (Hogan, Kim and Perrucci 1997). More important than the redistributive effects of Social Security, however, is the incredible racial gap in "other" retirement income.

"Other" income reported in Ozawa and Kim (as "pretransfer income," [1989:345]) is a residual category including all that is not Social Security, pension, or public assistance. Recent research (Oliver and Shapiro 1995) suggests that a large part of the racial gap in this "other" income is due to the sizable racial gap in wealth. In 1984, black per-capita wealth (total assets minus debts) equaled only 21 percent of white wealth (Jaynes and Williams 1989 274). In a 1988 survey black households reported 25 percent of white wealth (mean assets minus debts [Oliver and Shapiro 1995:86]). Preliminary analysis of the preretirement cohort (aged 51 to 61 in 1992) estimates average black household wealth at 27 percent of white wealth (Smith 1995:S179). Thus with appropriate cautions regarding the comparability of samples and measures, it appears that the racial gap in wealth may be declining but the decline is slow and the gap remains substantial. In fact, the 1988 racial gap in "net financial assets" (wealth minus home and vehicle equity), which is closer to our concept of "income-producing assets," is even greater, with black households reporting only 11 percent of white "net financial assets" (Oliver and Shapiro 1995:86). Thus we should expect the racial gap in retirement earnings (or income) from assets to be even greater than the racial gap in wealth.

Clearly, racial segregation and discriminatory mortgage practices undermine the accumulation of black wealth, in the form of housing equity (Farley and Frey 1994; Massey, Gross and Shibuya 1994; Oliver and Shapiro 1995:136–152). This is a critical factor in the racial gap in wealth, since most (75%) of black wealth is invested in real estate (compared to 53% for whites [Jaynes and Williams 1989:274]).[2] Generally, blacks lack income-producing assets which, for whites, provide financial security in retirement and, ultimately, a legacy for future generations (Hogan, Kim and Perrucci 1997).

Why blacks have been unable to accumulate assets has been the subject of considerable debate in research comparing the experience of immigrant and black proprietorship (Bates 1996; Greene 1996; Johnson 1996; Light 1996; Portes 1996). Recent research has indicated that immigrants continue to use family proprietorships not simply as a stop-gap means to survive but as a means for accumulating wealth (Portes 1996:46). One explanation for the success of the immigrant proprietor is savings, and some studies have focused on cultural differences in savings (Light 1996:67–68). More pertinent to the problem of racial versus ethnic accumulation, however, is recent research that focuses on the family as a source of labor as well as capital. Sanders and Nee (1996:235) report, "our experiences in the field suggest that the family is often the main social organization supporting the establishment and operation of a small business." Thus the recipe for immigrant accumulation combines self-employment with the exploitation of family labor and the appropriation of whatever surplus (savings) family members might be able to generate.

Since 1960 there has been increase in black self-employment, with the entrance of younger, more highly educated blacks, especially in business services, finance, insurance, real estate, transportation, communication, and wholesaling. Only since 1980, however, has average black self-employment earnings begun to compare favorably to black wage and salary earnings. In 1985, the racial gap in self-employment earnings still exceeded (by two percentage points) the racial gap in employment earnings (Jaynes and Williams 1989:314–315).

Generally, self-employment yields higher income, on average, than wage or salaried employment, but the rate of return per hour of labor invested is subject to debate (Bates 1996).[3] Portes and Zhou (1996: 223) report that the net effect of self-employment on 1979 earnings (raw scores) was positive and significant for Cuban, Chinese, Japanese, and Korean immigrants, and for whites. The effect for blacks, although positive, was much smaller and statistically insignificant, suggesting that self-employment does not provide a viable alternative to wage labor for U.S. blacks. Furthermore,

---

[2]Oliver and Shapiro (1995:106) report that 63 percent of black and 43 percent of white wealth is invested in owner-occupied housing. Blacks and whites may have been diversifying their investments between 1984 and 1988, but there is some reason to believe that the 1988 SIPP survey underestimated assets. If this is true, this "estimation bias" should, perhaps, encourage caution in the interpretation of these SIPP 1988 data (cf. Moon and Juster 1995:S153, S156).

[3]Portes and Zhou (1996) explain how self-employment tends to produce higher income but lower income per hour. Consequently, the net effect of self-employment (as in the data reported below) is frequently negative, even though the gross effect (without controlling for other variables) is generally positive. As Portes and Zhou (1996) indicate, unlogged income measures tend to yield positive net effects of self-employment on earnings due to the positive outliers. This may also explain why Wright and Perrone (1977) found that self-employment interacted with educational credentials in predicting higher income for self-employed persons with greater credentials. Although not reported here, this same interaction effect was found in these data, when using unlogged income measures (cf. Hogan, Kim and Perrucci 1997).

Bates' (1996:31) analysis of immigrant versus black-owned business in the U.S. indicates that even in more recent years (firms formed between 1979 and 1987), black-owned businesses report substantially less capital, income (sales), and (not surprisingly) higher rates of demise. Clearly, blacks are less successful in accumulating assets through the exploitation of family labor by combining self-employment and marriage in the traditional family proprietorship that continues to provide immigrants with an alternative to wage labor.

Oliver and Shapiro (1995:151–169) offer evidence to suggest that inheritance may be the critical factor in explaining the enduring racial gap in financial assets (or wealth). Their data suggest that inheritance is more important for blacks than for whites. The black children of "upper white-collar" parents report substantially greater median net worth (assets minus debts) and are the only black households to report non-zero median "net financial assets" ("net worth" minus home and vehicle equity). For whites, there appears to be no consistent pattern and fairly limited variance in net worth by parents' occupation. The lack of "inheritance of class/occupational status" effect among whites might be attributed to the use of occupational status as a proxy for class, but the fact that even working class whites were able to capitalize on the housing boom of the post World War II era might also explain the interactive effects of race and "inheritance." This interpretation is consistent with the finding that, even for whites, the children of "lower working class" parents report extremely limited financial assets (Oliver and Shapiro 1995:162). These "lower working class" whites might have accumulated housing equity that they could bequeath to their children, but otherwise they (like black members of their "class") generally lacked income-producing assets (or capital).

More direct evidence of the effect of inheritance is provided in preliminary analysis of the preretirement cohort (aged 51 to 61 in 1992). Multivariate analysis indicates substantial effects of "value of inheritance" received from parents in predicting net worth (Smith 1995:S174, S182). "For every dollar of inheritance received, total net worth increases by 36 cents" (Smith 1995:S174). The racial gap in inherited wealth is enormous, however, with 34 percent of white and only 11 percent of black households reporting inheritance of parental wealth. Furthermore, the value of black inheritance (for the fortunate 11 percent who report inheritance) is only 58 percent of the average white inheritance (Smith 1995 S175). The compounded (multiplicative) effects of racial differences in probability (.343 versus .105) and value ($148,578 versus $85,598) of inheritance produce a substantial racial gap in inherited wealth. Black households, based on this measure, report only 18 percent of white inheritance.

While blacks (and black men in particular) may lack the family support (labor and wealth) that facilitates self-employment, it appears that family status may be facilitating, in some sense, self-employment for women, particularly white women. Of course, for women, family status is a double-edged sword. Husbands and children are, on balance, more of a demand on women's labor than a supply of family labor that might be exploited in self-employment (Presser 1994; South and Spitze 1994:340–345). As Carr (1996 47) explains, "It appears that self-employment . . . is a strategy for women to circumvent the constraints that their child-care needs may place on their traditional wage labor force participation. At the same time, self-employment is not an option readily available to all women. Personal resources, such as education and the financial security of having a spouse, appear to be prerequisites for women to select this flexible work strategy."

Thus, it appears that self-employment and marriage, which combine in family proprietorship to constitute the traditional path to financial security, interact with race and gender in the production and reproduction of the racial and gender gaps in employment earnings and in retirement income. If we seek to understand the lack of cumulative progress in the struggle for racial and gender equality, we should consider the experience of those who worked during the boom period of the post World War II era and who reaped the benefits of the Equal Opportunity legislation of the 1960s. In considering their experiences, we should not ignore their human capital and their progress in competition for managerial and professional positions, or for wage-labor in the privileged "core" industrial sector. We should, however, also look at the effects of self-employment and marriage if we wish to understand why white women and black men don't seem to be making the steady progress toward racial and gender equality that the immigrant experience might suggest. In this analysis we should also take care not to lose sight of black women, whose relative gains in this period may hold the key to understanding change in both the racial and gender gaps.

THE DATA

The New Beneficiary Survey (Maxfield 1983) collected structured interviews from a national, representative sample, drawn from the Social Security Administration's Master Beneficiary Record of nondeceased, noninstitutionalized persons who began receiving Social Security benefits in 1980–1981 (N = 9,520). Social Security coverage grew from 76 percent of the 1954 labor force to include almost all workers (94%) by 1977 (DeViney and O'Rand 1988). Thus, this sample represents most workers who retired in 1980–1981. We have focused on previously employed and currently (1982) retired workers, including only persons who claimed at least some earnings from their longest held job (held for at least twelve months) and who also claimed at least some earnings from Social Security Old Age pensions (Ekerdt and DeViney 1990).

Employment earnings and employment experience were coded for individuals, in a series of questions concerning employment since 1951 (or the year when the respondent turned twenty-one, whichever was later). For most respondents, their first job was their longest job. Detailed employment information was coded, however, beginning with the respondent's most recent job, for up to three jobs, including the longest job. If the most recent or last job was also the longest job the questions were not repeated for longest job. In no case were the detailed questions asked for more than three jobs, and in most cases there is only one set of responses. We followed the skip pattern in the questionnaire to capture the missing data for longest job, which was, in most cases, first job, last job, or both.

Independent variables that represent status include race (white = 1; black = 0), gender (male = 1), marital status (currently married = 1), marital history (ever married = 1), and occupational status (using Duncan's SEI). Human capital is measured by educational credentials, following the coding used by Wright and Perrone (1977),[4] and by years of tenure at longest held job. We also included hours worked per week and weeks worked per year. Industrial sector (which is also a proxy for firm size and unionization, variables not included in these data) is coded (core = 1; periphery = 0), using, in general, Beck, Horan, and Tolbert's (1978) classification. Class is measured with two dummy variables: Self-employed (coded "1") and Managerial-Professional (coded "1")—Worker is the excluded category. Self-employment is based on the respondent's report. Managerial-professional was coded from the detailed occupational code (occupations coded 1–199 were coded ["1"] managerial-professional if and only if the respondent was not self-employed in that job).

[4]Educational credentials is coded (0–6) to represent years of education in the following manner: "0" = 0–7 years. "1" = 8 years, "2" = 9–11 years, "3" = 12 years, "4" = 13–15 years, "5" = 16 years, and "6" = 17 or more years.

Thus, we have an extremely broad class of self-employed persons (including carpenters and physicians) and an extremely narrow class of managerial-professionals (excluding supervisorial workers who did not have managerial and professional titles [cf. Wright and Perrone 1977:34–35]). Nevertheless, by distinguishing the self-employed from the employed managerial-professional workers, and comparing each to "other" workers, we approximate, albeit crudely, Wright and Perrone's (1977) class categories. Since we do not have data on firm size or on supervisorial duties, this is as close as we can come, with these data, to approximating the Marxist class category measures currently in use (Western and Wright 1994).

The dependent variables are employment earnings (in 1967 dollars) and annual retirement income (in 1982 dollars) from each of three sources: Social Security, public or private pensions, and asset income from money market accounts, certificates of deposit, all savers certificates, savings accounts, interest-bearing checking accounts, credit union accounts, bonds, mutual funds, stocks, rents, trusts, estates, royalties, IRA or Keogh, insurance, or annuities. Retirement income from each source was reported for the three months preceding the interview, so these figures were multiplied by four to provide estimates of annual income.

For the Ordinary Least Squares (OLS) regression models, we logged each of the income measures except for Social Security income. Employment, asset, and (to a lesser extent) pension income distributions were highly skewed, due largely to the positive outliers. Consequently, OLS models predicting logged employment and asset income fit the data substantially better than models predicting raw scores (there was little difference in the logged and unlogged models in predicting pension earnings). In contrast, Social Security income approached the normal distribution (as confirmed upon inspection of the histograms). In addition, the OLS model predicting Social Security income yielded a substantially better fit (higher adjusted R-square) when predicting raw (rather than logged) income.

In computing the racial and gender "earnings gaps" (reported below), however, we used raw (unlogged) scores in constant (1982) dollars (for employment and retirement income), so that the figures would be more meaningful to the reader. These raw scores (reported in Table 1) indicate the extent to which the distribution of income is skewed. Social Security is the only earnings variable where the mean is consistently larger than the standard deviation (for whites, it is more than twice as large). Converting preretirement employment income into 1982 dollars tends to exaggerate the earnings of these individuals (for white males, from $17,648 in 1967 dollars to $48,925 in 1982 dollars) but it does not affect the size of the race or gender gaps and it does provide a common metric for employment and retirement earnings, which clearly indicates the general tendency for people (regardless of race or gender) to earn substantially less in retirement than they did in employment.

Income Gaps

Table 1 displays mean income (and standard deviation), converted into 1982 dollars, from employment (preretirement), from Social Security, pensions, assets, and total retirement income (Social Security + pension + asset income) for white males, white females, black males, and black females. For each of the last three subsamples, average income is presented as a percent of white male income. For present purposes, the inverse of (one minus) this percentage is interpreted as the racial or gender gap.

As seen in Table 1, white female employment income constitutes only 50 percent of white male income (the gender gap is 1 – 50 or 50%). Black males report, on average, slightly more, but still only 56 percent of white male income (the racial gap is 44%). Black females claim, on average, substantially less, indicating a compounded race and gender gap of 64 percent. Not surprisingly, the race and, particularly,

TABLE 1 ■ MEAN AND STANDARD DEVIATION OF INCOME IN 1982 DOLLARS FROM EMPLOYMENT (INCOME), SOCIAL SECURITY (SS), PENSIONS, ASSETS, AND TOTAL RETIREMENT INCOME (TOTAL: SUM OF SS + PENSION + ASSETS) FOR WHITE MALES, WHITE FEMALES, BLACK MALES, AND BLACK FEMALES (WITH PERCENT (%) OF WHITE MALE INCOME, FOR EACH OF THE LAST THREE SUBSAMPLES, INDICATED IN PARENTHESES)

	White males		White females			Black males			Black females		
	Mean	Std dev	Mean	Std dev	(%)	Mean	Std dev	(%)	Mean	Std dev	(%)
Income	$48,925	50,354	$24,317	18,236	(50)	$27,356	18,821	(56)	$17,707	13,163	(36)
SS	$8,510	3,500	$7,321	3,586	(86)	$5,946	3,048	(70)	$5,495	3,195	(65)
Pension	$4,049	7,701	$1,506	3,222	(37)	$2,466	4,529	(61)	$1,365	3,239	(34)
Assets	$5,139	13,819	$3,597	11,917	(70)	$457	1,598	(9)	$342	1,038	(7)
Total	$17,697	17,359	$12,424	13,370	(70)	$ 8,869	5,946	(50)	$7,202	5,193	(41)
N		3589		2801			325			328	

the gender gaps are substantially lower for Social Security income. The gender gap (white females) is only 14 percent, while the racial gap (black males) falls to 30 percent, and even the compound race and gender gap (black females) is only 35 percent. The redistributive effects of Social Security, particular for women, are apparent. As indicated in Table 1, this is as close to racial and gender equality as these income figures ever get.

Not surprising, the gender gap in pension income is much greater than the racial gap. Black males claim 61 percent of white male income, while white and black females claim only 37 percent and 34 percent (respectively). The most striking contrasts, however, are in asset income, where white females claim 70 percent of white male income yet blacks claim less than 10 percent. Thus, despite the fact that black males fare somewhat better in employment income, white females fare far better in total retirement income, claiming 70 percent of white male income, while black males claim 50 percent and black females only 41 percent.

For white females, the gender gap in retirement income is less than the gap in employment income, despite the considerable gap in pension income, because of the relatively narrow gap in asset and, especially, Social Security income. For black males, the retirement income gap is greater than the employment income gap, despite the redistributive effects of Social Security, because of the incredible racial gap in asset income. Black females actually fare better in retirement, but only because their employment income was, on average, so low that the boost from Social Security more than compensated for the tremendous gap in asset income.

It is also worth noting, however, that black females do relatively better in pension income, suggesting that, in this case at least, the compounded racial and gender gap is much less pronounced than it was in employment. Relative to their extremely low employment income, black women seem to suffer less than white women from the burden of gender in the competition for pension income, although, in absolute terms, they continue to claim the least. Nevertheless, unlike black males who actually do better in comparison to white males in pension as opposed to employment income, the pension income gap (66%), for black females, is slightly greater than the employment income gap (64%), suggesting, once again that black women experience both racial and gender barriers and thus tend to suffer the greatest income inequality.

In the Social Security market, black females enjoy the relative advantage of gender; in pensions, they have the relative advantage of race. In both cases, however, they seem to suffer disadvantages that outweigh their minimal gains. Furthermore, the compounded barriers of race and gender in employment and asset income are sufficiently great to maintain black females at the most disadvantaged position in retirement as well as in employment. If they do somewhat better in retirement than they did in employment it is only because they were so dramatically disadvantaged in the employment market.

It is, perhaps, also worth repeating that the respondents included in this analysis all claimed Old Age Social Security benefits. Thus, the most impoverished respondents (who received only public assistance) are not included in these data. The poorest persons (particularly the poorest women and, presumably, many black women) are not included in this analysis. It is quite reasonable to assume that the "true" nature of the racial and gender gap in retirement earnings is considerably greater than these data suggest. The small (one percentage point) decline in the racial gap in total retirement income, associated with public assistance (see discussion of Ozawa and Kim 1989, above), may constitute a significant effect for black women living in poverty (even if the effect appears to us to be statistically insignificant).

Nevertheless, these data are useful in providing a baseline for evaluating how Social Security redistributes earnings, particularly for white women, how pensions redistribute earnings, particularly for men, and how assets continue to distinguish whites from blacks, thus contributing a substantial amount of retirement income for the privileged classes, in general, and for whites in particular. These data confirm the findings of previous research (Hogan, Kim, and Perrucci 1997; Kim and Perrucci 1994), suggesting that the accumulation (or inheritance) of income producing assets is a major component of the process of reproducing not only class but racial inequality. These data also indicate the relative poverty of the retired (as compared to the employed).

Predicting Income

Table 2 presents the results of an OLS regression model, estimated separately for white males, white females, black males, and black females, in which human capital, industrial sector, current marital status, marital history, and "Marxist" class categories (following the early work of Wright and Perrone 1977) predict logged employment income from respondent's longest held job. Not surprisingly, when the model is estimated for the entire sample, all of the variables prove to be significant predictors of employment income, collectively accounting for about 42 percent of the variance. All effects are positive except for self-employment and marriage. Otherwise, human capital, core-sector employment, and managerial-professional position all predict higher earnings (results not shown but available from authors on request).

When run separately for white males, white females, black males, and black females, the model produces considerable variation in the size and significance of coefficients. In some cases, these differences can be attributed to the subsample size (black subsamples are considerably smaller, i.e., N < 350) or the lack of variance in some predictors within particular subsamples. For example, although 19 percent of white males and females were employed in managerial or professional occupations, only 14 percent of black females and 5 percent of black males (n = 16) occupied similar positions. In a similar vein, 21 percent of white males but only 12 percent of black males were self-employed in their longest held job. Comparable figures for females were only 7 percent for whites and 5 percent for blacks (n = 16). Thus, it appears that racial barriers to managerial and professional positions (particularly for males) and gender barriers to self-employment (for black and white women) may be responsible for

TABLE 2 ■ PREDICTING LOGGED EMPLOYMENT INCOME FOR WHITE MALES, WHITE FEMALES, BLACK MALES, AND BLACK FEMALES

	White males			White females			Black males			Black females		
Predictor	b	(se)	beta	b	(se)	beta	b	(se)	beta	b	(se)	beta
Education	.074****	(.009)	.149	.115****	(.011)	.195	.103***	(.030)	.184	.036	(.027)	.069
Status	.006****	(.001)	.167	.004****	(.001)	.112	.001	(.003)	.022	.009***	(.002)	.280
Hrs/wk	.009****	(.001)	.155	.020****	(.001)	.286	−.001	(.004)	−.01	.024****	(.003)	.344
Wks/yr	.024****	(.002)	.185	.030****	(.002)	.263	.038****	(.007)	.296	.027****	(.005)	.229
Years/job	.019****	(.001)	.239	.021****	(.001)	.245	.013**	(.005)	.133	.007*	(.004)	.087
Sector	.226****	(.026)	.131	.197****	(.027)	.114	.433****	(.093)	.232	.247*	(.096)	.113
Mgr-prof	.137***	(.038)	.065	.156***	(.043)	.071	.018	(.249)	.004	.174	(.165)	.069
Self-empl	−.178****	(.034)	−.087	−.407****	(.051)	−.125	−.575***	(.150)	−.204	−.562**	(.172)	−.138
Married	.030	(.040)	.012	−.158****	(.027)	−.093	−.152	(.103)	−.076	−.185*	(.078)	−.103
Ever-mar	.280***	(.072)	.064	.199****	(.049)	.066	.295	(.187)	.082	−.006	(.132)	−.002
Constant	6.37			5.51			6.24			5.85		
	N = 3589			N = 2801			N = 325			N = 328		
	F = 140.99****			F = 188.25****			F = 14.20****			F = 27.62****		
	Adjusted R^2 = .28			Adjusted R^2 = .40			Adjusted R^2 = .29			Adjusted R^2 = .45		

*p < .05 **p < .01 ***p < .001 ****p < .0001

some of the apparent differences in the size and significance of main effects.

These differences notwithstanding, it is apparent that the effects of class and marital status differ significantly by race and gender. The effect of managerial or professional position is significant only for whites, while the effect of core sector employment is, if anything, greater for blacks, particularly black men, but is much less reliable (larger standard error) for blacks. Consequently, the effect of sector is only marginally significant ($p < .05$) for black women.

More central to current concerns, the "disadvantage" of self-employment and marriage is significantly less pronounced among white males. Here again, the negative effects are larger for women and for blacks but the reliability of these coefficients is much smaller for blacks. The relatively larger standard errors produce less significant effects of self-employment, particularly for black females (based on a very small but highly diverse population of sixteen self-employed women) and produce insignificant effects of marriage for black males.

In any case, the effects of marriage and marital history (ever married) are much more striking for whites. *Marriage does not predict lower employment earnings for white males but only for white females (and, less reliably, for black females). On the other hand, former marriage predicts higher employment earnings for white men and women but not for blacks (although the effect is large for black males it is highly unreliable). Thus, on balance, it is fair to say that the disadvantages of self-employment and marriage are much greater for women and blacks.*

Table 3 displays the results of OLS models predicting Social Security earnings. The model is the same as in Table 2 (above) except that the dependent variable is Social Security earnings (unlogged, since the distribution approximates the normal curve) and that logged employment earnings is included in Table 3, to control for the effects of the other variables in predicting employment income, which is, of course, an excellent predictor of retirement income (regardless of source).

Because we are controlling for the effect of employment earnings from longest held job, effects that were highly significant in predicting employment income are frequently less significant here, or, in some cases, the effect has been reversed (the sign of the coefficient has changed). In particular, some human capital measures, particularly hours worked per week, predict lower Social Security earnings (significantly lower for white males). Recall, however, that after controlling for employment income the negative effect of hours per week indicates lower Social Security earnings for persons who were earning less per hour than others with comparable incomes. Similarly, the negative effects of class indicate lower earnings than others with comparable education, work experience, and employment earnings. In estimating this model for the total sample, it appeared that persons who achieved more educational credentials, who worked more years at longest job, and who earned higher incomes earn more Social Security in retirement. Furthermore, married persons (married when they began receiving Social Security), whites, and females all earn more Social Security than non-married persons, blacks, or males with similar employment preparation and experience (results not shown but available from authors).

Estimating this model separately, however, for each of the subsamples (as in Table 2), yields considerable variation in the size and significance of these effects, as seen in Table 3. Most important, for present purposes, is the effect of self-employment and marriage. As was the case with employment income, *the negative effects of self-employment on Social Security earnings are much smaller and much more reliable for white males. In fact, the negative effects are much larger but also much less reliable for blacks, being largest and marginally significant ($p < .05$) for black males, smaller but more significant ($p < .01$) for white females, quite large but insignificant for black females, and quite small and insignificant*

TABLE 3 ■ PREDICTING SOCIAL SECURITY INCOME FOR WHITE MALES, WHITE FEMALES, BLACK MALES, AND BLACK FEMALES

	White males			White females			Black males			Black females		
Predictor	b	(se)	beta	b	(se)	beta	b	(se)	beta	b	(se)	beta
Education	89.35*	(39.29)	.042	89.84	(50.27)	.036	78.52	(109.97)	.043	222.29*	(108.54)	.119
Status	24.10****	(3.08)	.159	12.99***	(3.43)	.084	−6.22	(9.33)	−.044	7.53	(9.24)	.063
Hrs/wk	−17.96****	(3.87)	−.076	−8.92	(5.14)	−.031	13.64	(14.72)	.049	14.34	(13.44)	.056
Wks/yr	−15.27	(9.12)	−.028	2.99	(8.49)	.006	−27.63	(24.67)	−.066	14.37	(20.77)	.034
Years/job	27.52****	(5.42)	.082	65.26****	(6.35)	.183	36.63*	(16.63)	.118	27.09	(14.36)	.088
Sector	−79.76	(120.88)	−.011	31.50	(125.25)	.004	−106.68	(344.33)	−.017	339.84	(338.76)	.043
Mgr-prof	−707.39***	(171.49)	−.080	−81.26	(199.36)	−.009	530.64	(893.28)	.038	640.44	(660.32)	.070
Self-empl	−241.21	(153.21)	−.028	−620.35**	(239.07)	−.045	−1085.57*	(551.28)	−.117	−845.25	(698.25)	−.057
Married	2101.61****	(183.05)	.204	3416.91****	(125.41)	.474	1009.18**	(371.97)	.155	2989.97****	(314.77)	.458
Ever-mar	500.09	(327.18)	.027	454.06*	(225.62)	.035	536.72	(672.42)	.045	−84.66	(527.86)	−.008
Income	828.54****	(76.14)	.196	900.99****	(87.81)	.213	974.54****	(202.46)	.297	653.64**	(224.47)	.180
Constant	−2242.39			−4726.21			−3625.58			−3626.75		
	N = 3589			N = 2801			N = 325			N = 328		
	F = 64.17****			F = 100.67****			F = 6.17****			F = 15.83****		
	Adjusted R^2 = .16			Adjusted R^2 = .28			Adjusted R^2 = .15			Adjusted R^2 = .33		

*p < .05 **p < .01 ***p < .001 ****p < .0001

for white males. Marriage, on the other hand, predicts significantly higher earnings for whites males and, particularly, for white and black females. Marriage has smaller, less reliable, but still significant ($p < .05$) effects for black males, predicting, as for others, higher income for married respondents. Generally, however, the effects of marriage are larger and more reliable for females and for whites.

Table 4 presents results of the OLS model predicting logged pension earnings, using the same variables as were used to predict Social Security earnings. Generally, even when estimated for the total sample, the model produces distinctively different effects in predicting pension earnings (as compared to Social Security). Although education and job tenure (years on job) predict higher pension earnings, while self-employment predicts lower earnings (as was the case with Social Security earnings), occupational status is insignificant, industrial sector is highly significant (predicting higher pension earnings), hours per week and managerial-professional position predict less significant but opposite effects (as compared to the Social Security model). Not surprisingly, full-time, managerial-professional workers and, to a greater extent, core-sector employees claim higher pension earnings. More important for present purposes and quite unlike the prediction of Social Security earnings, unmarried respondents and men claim higher pension earnings, but there is no significant difference (net of the effects of employment preparation and experience) between blacks and whites (results not shown but available from authors).

Table 4 specifies the nature of these effects by presenting the results of separate OLS estimates for each of our subsamples (as in Tables 2 and 3). As indicated in Table 4, *the negative effect of self-employment is both larger and more reliable (smaller standard error) for white men.* The effect is comparably large for black men, but it is somewhat less reliable (although still highly significant: $p < .0001$). Generally, the effects are smaller for women, particularly black women, but the reliability of these effects is more problematic (being insignificant for black women). Of course, since so few ($n = 16$) of these women were self-employed, it is understandable that the effects should be less reliable.

The effect of marriage is much more clear-cut. *Marriage predicts somewhat higher pension earnings for men and substantially lower earnings for women, but this is only true for whites.* For blacks, the marriage penalty is insignificant (for males and females), and there is no evidence of a marriage bonus for black males (although the standard error is so large that it is difficult to draw any conclusion other than that the effects, positive or negative, are insignificant).

Table 5 displays the results of estimating logged asset earnings, using the same variables used to predict Social Security and logged pension earnings. When estimating this model for the entire sample, the pattern of net effects is similar to the pattern displayed in predicting Social Security earnings, except that the net effect of self-employment is positive. As might be expected, *the self-employed, while claiming less employment, Social Security, and pension earnings than persons with comparable background and experience, claim higher asset earnings.* Beyond this, as was the case in Social Security earnings, married persons, whites, and women claim higher asset earnings (results not shown but available from authors).

When estimating separate OLS equations for each of our subsamples, as indicated in Table 5, the effect of race is clear. Except for education, which is moderately significant for black males and females, none of the variables is significant in predicting logged asset earnings for blacks. There is, in fact, so little variance in asset earnings among blacks (see Table 1) that these models are only marginally significant (and, in fact, insignificant for males) in predicting black asset earnings (logged or otherwise—results for unlogged models not shown).

For whites, education, occupational status and experience, class, marital status, and employment income all predict higher asset earnings.

TABLE 4 ■ PREDICTING LOGGED PENSION INCOME FOR WHITE MALES, WHITE FEMALES, BLACK MALES, AND BLACK FEMALES

	White males			White females			Black males			Black females		
Predictor	b	(se)	beta	b	(se)	beta	b	(se)	beta	b	(se)	beta
Education	.327****	(.045)	.126	.237****	(.056)	.088	.380**	(.137)	.152	.157	(.133)	.072
Status	−.008*	(.004)	−.042	−.002	(.004)	−.014	.019	(.012)	.098	.005	(.011)	.037
Hrs/wk	.005	(.004)	.016	.010	(.006)	.033	.040*	(.018)	.107	−.021	(.016)	−.070
Wks/yr	.016	(.011)	.024	−.041****	(.009)	−.079	.012	(.031)	.021	−.038	(.025)	−.077
Years/job	.049****	(.006)	.120	.070****	(.007)	.183	.117****	(.021)	.280	.060****	(.018)	.168
Sector	1.501****	(.140)	.167	.717****	(.140)	.091	1.24**	(.429)	.149	.823	(.475)	.088
Mgr-prof	−.024	(.199)	−.002	.673**	(.223)	.068	−.238	(1.11)	−.012	.620	(.807)	.058
Self-empl	−3.869****	(.177)	−.364	−2.08****	(.267)	−.141	−3.158****	(.687)	−.252	−1.33	(.853)	−.077
Married	.537*	(.212)	.042	−.703****	(.140)	−.091	−.106	(.463)	−.012	−.108	(.384)	−.014
Ever-mar	.337	(.379)	.015	−.046	(.252)	−.003	.806	(.838)	.050	.727	(.645)	.055
Income	.606****	(.088)	.117	1.07****	(.098)	.235	.459	(.252)	.103	1.79****	(.274)	.420
Constant	−4.92			−6.41			−7.73			−12.34		
	N = 3589			N = 2801			N = 325			N = 328		
	F = 114.09****			F = 73.55****			F = 12.51****			F = 12.10****		
	Adjusted R^2 = .26			Adjusted R^2 = .22			Adjusted R^2 = .28			Adjusted R^2 = .27		

*p < .05 **p < .01 ***p < .001 ****p < .0001

TABLE 5 ■ PREDICTING LOGGED ASSET INCOME FOR WHITE MALES, WHITE FEMALES, BLACK MALES, AND BLACK FEMALES

	White males			White females			Black males			Black females		
Predictor	b	(se)	beta	b	(se)	beta	b	(se)	beta	b	(se)	beta
Education	.419****	(.034)	.252	.482****	(.048)	.221	.243*	(.112)	.139	.230*	(.117)	.136
Status	.018****	(.003)	.134	.013***	(.003)	.097	.011	(.010)	.085	.008	(.009)	.077
Hrs/wk	−.011***	(.003)	−.054	−.023****	(.005)	−.091	.013	(.015)	.050	.003	(.014)	.012
Wks/yr	.008	(.008)	.016	−.014	(.008)	−.033	−.013	(.025)	−.033	−.001	(.022)	−.002
Years/job	.049****	(.005)	.165	.023***	(.006)	.074	.015	(.017)	.052	−.009	(.015)	−.032
Sector	−.293**	(.104)	−.045	.335**	(.120)	.053	.380	(.351)	.065	.264	(.418)	.037
Mgr−prof	−.005	(.147)	−.001	−.613**	(.191)	−.077	−.294	(.912)	−.022	.333	(.710)	.040
Self−empl	.404**	(.131)	.053	.502*	(.229)	.042	.300	(.563)	.034	−1.07	(.750)	−.080
Married	.833****	(.157)	.092	1.01****	(.120)	.161	.254	(.380)	.041	.453	(.338)	.077
Ever−mar	−.488	(.280)	−.030	−.222	(.216)	−.020	−.544	(.686)	−.048	.258	(.567)	.025
Income	.514****	(.065)	.138	.423****	(.084)	.115	.078	(.207)	.025	.186	(.241)	.057
Constant	−2.06			.876			.718			−.363		
	N = 3589			N = 2801			N = 325			N = 328		
	F = 88.57****			F = 37.40****			F = 1.56			F = 2.75**		
	Adjusted R^2 = .21			Adjusted R^2 = .13			Adjusted R^2 = .02			Adjusted R^2 = .06		

*p < .05 **p < .01 ***p < .001 ****p < .0001

There are some interesting gender differences (among whites). For example, sector interacts with gender (for whites), with "core" sector employment predicting higher earnings for women and lower earnings for men. Similarly, managerial-professional employment predicts significantly lower asset earnings only for white women. Less surprising and more pertinent for present purposes, self-employment and marital status predict higher earnings for white men and women, although the effect of self-employment is more reliable and more significant for men. The effect of marriage, on the other hand, is, if anything, larger and more reliable for white women.

What is most important here, however, is the fact that *self-employment and marriage are associated with higher asset earnings for both men and women but only for whites.* Attempting to tease out the causal relations in employment or marital status, as they relate to asset earnings, is particularly difficult. If we could reconstruct not only employment and marital history but also the history of asset accumulation, we might be able to estimate these effects. In these data, we can only conclude that there is a relationship between marital and employment history and asset accumulation. Asset accumulation, obviously, is causally prior to asset earnings, but the relationship between accumulation and employment/marital status is, quite probably, reciprocal.

Self-employment, for example, requires assets, particularly if self-employment is to be remunerative. If nothing else, the carpenter must own her tools. At the same time, self-employment may be a source of asset accumulation, assuming that the business grows. The same, of course, is true of marriage. Marriage costs time and money. In fact, the cost of sustaining a marriage is far greater than the initial cost of the license and the wedding. At the same time, however, marriage may be a source of wealth, for either partner. While this marriage bonus may be available to rich and poor alike, it is not clear that the wealthy marry the poor very often or that they are able, in those exceptional cases, to take their family wealth with them into such a marriage. It seems more likely that family wealth is reproduced through self-employment opportunities and marriage opportunities that tend to be associated with class and racial privilege and exclusion.

Discussion

Clearly, class, race, and gender inequality are produced and reproduced through life and work, throughout the life course. As indicated in Table 1, employment income is distributed unequally across race and gender. Furthermore, while income is redistributed in various retirement packages, considerable racial and gender inequality remains. Each source of retirement income is redistributive. Social Security redistributes in favor of married persons, particularly white women. Pensions redistribute from married white women to married white men and from women to men, more generally. Assets redistribute income from single to married, from white men to white women, and from blacks (particularly from black men) to whites.

Consequently, women, particularly married women, tend to do relatively better in retirement than they did in employment (at least, that was true for this cohort, who retired in 1980–1981). Blacks, on the other hand, and black males in particular, tend to do better in employment. In that regard, we may offer two general conclusions about racial and gender inequality for this 1980–1981 retirement cohort. *First, the gender gap was greater in employment than it is in retirement, while the racial gap is greater in retirement.* Thus, racial inequality has increased across the life course of these 1980–1981 retirees. Although racial inequality in employment earnings may have been greater when they entered the labor force than it was when they left it, for these individuals, the income gap increased between employment and retirement. In that regard, a lifetime of struggle against racial inequality ultimately brought these retirees back to a level of racial inequality that they had, it appears, reduced in employment. This may, in fact, help us to understand why racial inequality endures. It is reproduced across generations, as the children and grandchildren of these retirees experience the costs/benefits of white affluence in the legacy of the retiring generation.

The second general conclusion is that racial and gender inequality are distinctive additive effects. White women benefit from their whiteness but suffer from their womanhood. Black men benefit and suffer in distinctive but parallel fashion. Black women, consequently suffer on both accounts. Their white female or black male counterparts continue to fight from a position of strength to overcome their disadvantaged position. The latter groups claim the benefits of either race (particularly in the patriarchal protection of marriage, and its institutional support in Social Security, which supports white women) or gender (particularly in its privileged corporate or public sector salary and pension bonuses, which benefit black men). Black women, on the other hand, suffer the most and earn the least, in each of the income markets, despite whatever benefits the married black woman or managerial-professional black woman might gain. Race and gender are distinctive additive effects that constitute the black female as the truly disadvantaged status.

As a practical matter, the data presented above suggest the need to specify what has come to be conventional wisdom regarding the effects of marriage and self-employment in predicting employment and retirement income. Briefly stated, conventional wisdom is that marriage is good for men but bad for women (Bernard 1972; Perrucci 1978), while self-employment is uniformly bad, being associated with small-scale enterprises in competitive markets, characterized by low rates of profit and high rates of business failure (Bates 1996; cf. Portes and Zhou 1996; and note 3 [above] for a revisionist approach). Like most elements of conventional wisdom, these are not entirely mistaken and are, perhaps, on balance, more right than wrong. Nevertheless, both are overgeneralizations rooted in analyses that focus on the educational and employment experience of whites. If one focuses only on wage-earning whites and analyzes only their employment income and their employment-related retirement benefits (or pensions), conventional wisdom is supported. Once one expands the analysis to include black workers, Social Security pensions, and white wealth, however, the picture becomes much more complex and the need to qualify conventional wisdom becomes increasingly apparent.

With regard to marriage, the data presented here suggest that the effect of marriage is much more significant for whites. White men who were (or once were) married report higher income from employment and from all sources of retirement income. For white women, marriage is associated with decreased employment income and decreased pension earnings in retirement. Nevertheless, the increased Social Security income (which all married respondents seem to enjoy) and the additional benefits of increased asset earnings (which accrue only to whites) produce, on balance, greater retirement income for married white women. Thus, for whites, we should modify conventional wisdom as follows. Marriage seems to be an unqualified benefit for white males, in predicting higher employment and retirement income. For white females, it appears to be a double-edged sword. Marriage tends to limit white female labor force participation (thus earnings and pensions) but tends to contribute to long-term financial security (due to increased Social Security and asset earnings).

For blacks, the effects of marriage on income are much less significant, in general, largely because blacks lack real wealth (income-producing assets) which tends to be acquired and accumulated through marriage. Thus, a substantial component of the marriage bonus is not available for blacks. Married black males and females do report higher Social Security income (as do married whites), and married black women (like married white women) do report significantly lower employment earnings. Nevertheless, the significance of the marriage penalty for black women is considerably less than for their white counterparts, being marginally significant in predicting employment earnings ($p < .05$—see Table 2) and insignificant in predicting pension earnings (see Table 4). Generally then, although we could say that marriage seems to be an unconditional benefit for black men and a double-edged sword for black women, both costs and benefits are much more limited. Suffice it to say that for purposes of predicting financial security (or income), marriage is much less significant for blacks than it is for whites.

The effects of self-employment on income are, in some ways, more straightforward. Once again, if we focus on employment income and employment-related retirement benefits, self-employment predicts lower earnings. In this case, the effects seem to be fairly consistent across race and gender. In all four subsamples, self-employment predicts lower employment income. It predicts lower pension income for all but black females (only 16 black females were self-employed, which may explain the lack of significant effects). It also predicts lower Social Security earnings for self-employed white women ($n = 206$) and black men ($n = 40$). Nevertheless, self-employment predicts higher asset earnings in retirement for white men and women, thereby suggesting that, like marriage, self-employment may be something of a double-edged sword.

The challenge in analyzing the effects of self-employment is to tease out the components of class position that distinguish the entrepreneurial worker (or craft worker), the shopkeeper, and the capitalist. One problem with these data (as noted by at least one anonymous reviewer) is that the self-employed includes qualitatively different classes, ranging from persons who do odd jobs or provide child care to physicians, lawyers, and corporate capitalists. Theoretically, these class positions could be distinguished by the size of the firm (data not available here) and by the supervisorial responsibilities of the respondent. Those who do not employ and supervise (directly or indirectly) more employees than the number of family members in the average contemporary family would not be considered capitalists. Beyond that minimum, firm size would predict higher profits for capitalists (and higher wages for workers). Unfortunately, we are not able to apply this coding scheme to these data. Neither are we able to distinguish managerial workers by supervisorial status or professional workers by "credentials." Unfortunately, in these data (as in much of available survey data), we are limited to occupational titles to distinguish "managerial and professional" workers. Consequently, this "class" measure proved to be of limited importance, indicating mixed effects for whites and no significant effects for blacks (only 16 black males and 46 black females reported managerial or professional occupational titles).

We were somewhat more successful in crudely distinguishing industrial sector, which, in these data, represents firm size and unionization, critical variables which are not otherwise available in these data (or in many comparable surveys). Here, however, it appears that even this crude measure captures at least some of the effect of privileged employment (or investment) opportunities. For all four subsamples, sector predicted higher employment earnings. It predicted higher pension earnings for black men and white women. Also, somewhat surprisingly, it predicted higher asset earnings for white women (employed in public or core industrial sector) but lower asset earnings for comparably located white males. The apparent interaction of gender and sector in predicting assets (for whites) is, it appears, the product of a more complex set of higher-order interactions.[5]

[5]Regression models including the interactive effects of marital status, industrial sector, and employment status (along with all of the other variables included in the regressions reported above) specified the negative effect of sector in predicting asset income for white males. Results of these and other analyses referenced in the text are available from the authors upon request.

Data limitations notwithstanding, we are able to specify, to some extent, the nature of racial and gender inequality in this 1980–1981 retirement cohort. Much of the previous research has attempted to disentangle the effects of "human capital" versus "discrimination" (Cancio, Evans, and Maume 1996; Wellington 1994). Generally, racial and gender differences are specified, first, in employment preparation (education), then in employment experience (occupation, hours/week and weeks/year, industrial sector), and finally in accumulated advantage (years of experience in occupation and industrial sector). Once all these effects have been estimated and controlled, any residual racial or gender differences in earnings are attributed to discrimination.

Viewed in these terms, of the various "problems" facing blacks and women, "human capital" seems the most confusing and least promising explanation for the gender and racial gaps identified in these data. In this cohort, women report higher education and men (especially white men) report higher occupational prestige. Thus, after controlling for education and occupation, more racial than gender inequality is explained, because the highly educated women are not getting the high status jobs. Why women who are under-employed are going to school, or, alternatively, why black men with better employment opportunities are not going to school, is not clear, and "human capital" or rational choice theories offer limited insights on these issues.

Particularly for white women, work experience and availability for continuous full-time employment specify male of the gender gap than do measures of human capital. Married white and black women in this 1980–1981 retirement cohort generally worked fewer hours per week than comparable single women. The differences are not substantial, but when combined with the fact that married men, particularly married white men in core industrial sectors, tended to work more hours per week, these findings indicate (crudely) the burden of marriage for women. Much more striking, however, are the accumulated costs of marriage for white women. If we consider years in occupation, occupational status, industrial sector, and managerial or professional status, (for longest held preretirement job) as indicators of accumulated advantage, married white women suffer (relative to single white women) on all measures, while married black males, black females, and white males all do better than their unmarried counterparts. In this sense, the marriage penalty for white women (in this cohort at least) is the accumulated disadvantage in competition for the best jobs (high status managerial and professional occupations in public or "core" industrial sectors).

The problem for blacks in this 1980–1981 retirement cohort seems to be access to education and occupational opportunities, particularly high status (managerial and professional) positions in core industrial sectors, where blacks, particularly black males, are decidedly under-represented. Clearly, black and white women and black men earned higher employment income and, on balance, higher retirement incomes, when they worked in the core sector. The problem, of course, was that while 64 percent of white males worked in the "core," only 54 percent of black males, 40 percent of white females, and 20 percent of black females worked in "core" industries. While high-paying industrial jobs were opening up for black males in this cohort, the opportunities for white and particularly black females were much more limited.

References

Bates, Timothy 1996 "Why are firms owned by Asian immigrants lagging behind black-owned businesses?" National Journal of Sociology 102:27–43.

Beck, E.M., Patrick Horan, and Charles M. Tolbert 1978 "Stratification in a dual economy: A sectoral model of earnings determination." American Sociological Review 43:704–720.

Bernard, Jessie 1972 The Future of Marriage. New York: World Publishing.

Cancio, A. Silvia. T. David Evans, and David J. Maume, Jr. 1996 "Reconsidering the declining significance of race: Racial differences in early career wages." American Sociological Review 61:541–556.

Carr, Deborah 1996 "Two paths to self-employment: Women's and men's self-employment in the United States, 1980." Work and Occupations 23:26–53.

Davis, Angela Y. 1983. Women, Race and Class. New York: Vintage.

DeViney, Stanley 1995 "Life course, private pension, and financial well-being." American Behavioral Scientist 39:172–185.

DeViney, Stanley, and Angela M. O'Rand 1988 "Gender-cohort succession and retirement among older men and women, 1951–1984." Sociological Quarterly 29:525–540.

DeViney, Stanley, and Jennifer Crew Solomon 1995 "Gender differences in retirement income: A comparison of theoretical explanations." Journal of Women and Aging 7:83–100.

Ekerdt, David J., and Stanley DeViney 1990 "On defining persons as retired." Journal of Aging Studies 3:211–229.

Farley, Reynolds, and William H. Frey 1994 "Changes in the segregation of whites from blacks during the 1980s: Small steps toward a more integrated society." American Sociological Review 59:23–45.

Greene, Patricia G. 1996 "Comment: A call for conceptual clarity." National Journal of Sociology 102:49–55.

Gustman, Alan L., Olivia S. Mitchell, and Thomas L. Steinmeier 1995 "Retirement measures in the health and retirement study." Journal of Human Resources 30:S57-S83.

Hogan, Richard, Meesook Kim, and Carolyn C. Perrucci 1997 "Racial inequality in men's employment and retirement earnings." Sociological Quarterly 38:431–438.

Jaynes, Gerald David, and Robin M. Williams, Jr. 1989 A Common Destiny: Blacks and American Society. Washington D.C.: National Academy Press.

Johnson, Margaret A. 1996 "Comment: Understanding differences between Asian immigrants and African-Americans: Issues of conceptualization and measurement." National Journal of Sociology 102:57–64.

Kim, Meesook, and Carolyn C. Perrucci 1994 "Race and income: A comparison of employment and retirement income determination processes." International Journal of Contemporary Sociology 31:235–252.

Kraditor, Aileen 1981 The Ideas of the Woman Suffrage Movement, 1890–1920. New York: W.W. Norton.

Kulikoff, Allan 1989 "The transition to capitalism in rural America." William and Mary Quarterly (3rd series) 46:120–144.

Light, Ivan 1996 "Comment: Reply to Timothy Bates." National Journal of Sociology 102:65–71.

Massey, Douglas S., Andrew B. Gross, and Kumiko Shibuya 1994 "Migration, segregation, and the geographic concentration of poverty." American Sociological Review 59:425–445.

Maxfield, Linda D. 1983 "The 1982 new beneficiary survey: An introduction." Social Security Bulletin 46:3–11.

Meyer, Madonna Harrington 1996 "Making claims as workers and wives: The distribution of Social Security benefits." American Sociological Review 61:449–465.

Moon, Marilyn, and F. Thomas Juster 1995 "Economic status measures in the health and retirement study." Journal of Human Resources 30:S138-S157.

Oliver, Melvin L., and Thomas M. Shapiro 1995 Black Wealth/White Wealth: A New Perspective on Racial Inequality. New York: Routledge.

O'Rand, Angela 1986 "The hidden payroll: Employee benefits and the structure of workplace inequality." Sociological Forum 1:657–683.

———. 1996 "Women and retirement in the U.S." In Women and Work: A Handbook, eds, Paula J. Dubeck and Kathryn Borman, 25–27. New York: Garland Publishing.

Ozawa, Martha N., and Toc Sung Kim 1989 "Distributive effects of Social Security and pension benefits." Social Service Review 63:335–358.

Perrucci, Carolyn C. 1978 "Income attainment of college graduates: A comparison of employed women and men." Sociology and Social Research 62:361–386.

Portes, Alejandro 1996 "Comment: A dissenting view: Pitfalls on focusing on relative returns to ethnic enterprise." National Journal of Sociology 102:45–47.

Portes, Alejandro, and Min Zhou 1996 "Self-employment and the earnings of immigrants." American Sociological Review 61:219–230.

Presser, Harriet B. 1994 "Employment schedules among dual-earner spouses and the division of household labor by gender." American Sociological Review 59:348–364.
Quadagno, Jill 1988 "Women's access to pensions and the structure of eligibility rules: Systems of production and reproduction." Sociological Quarterly 29:541–558.
Reskin, Barbara F., and Patricia A. Roos 1990 Job Queues, Gender Queues: Explaining Women's Inroads Into Male Occupations. Philadelphia: Temple University Press.
Sanders, Jimy M., and Victor Nee 1996 "Social capital, human capital, and immigrant self-employment." American Sociological Review 61:231–249.
Smith, James P. 1995 "Racial and ethnic differences in wealth in the health and retirement study." Journal of Human Resources 30(Supplement): S158–S183.
South, Scott J., and Glenna Spitze 1994 "Housework in marital and non-marital households." American Sociological Review 59:327–347.
Tomaskovic-Devey, Donald 1993 Gender and Racial Inequality at Work: The Sources and Consequences of Job Segregation. Ithaca, New York: ILR Press.
Wellington, Alison J. 1993 "Changes in the male/female wage gap, 1976–85." Journal of Human Resources 28:383–411.
———. 1994 "Accounting for the male/female wage gap among whites: 1976 and 1985." American Sociological Review 59:839–848.
Western, Mark, and Erik Olin Wright 1994 "The permeability of class boundaries to intergenerational mobility among men in the United States, Canada, Norway, and Sweden." American Sociological Review 59:606–629.
Wright, Erik Olin, and Luca Peronno 1977 "Marxist class categories and income inequality." American Sociological Review 42:32–55.

Gender and Race Differences in the Predictors of Daily Health Practices among Older Adults

MARY P. GALLANT AND GAIL P. DORN
Department of Health Policy, Management and Behavior, School of Public Health, University at Albany, State University of New York, One University Place, Rensselaer, NY 12144-3456, USA

Abstract

Preventive health behaviors are crucial for older adults' well-being. This study examined the factors that influence the practice of positive daily health behaviors over time in a sample of older adults ($N = 1266$) and investigated whether explanatory factors differ by health behavior, gender or race. Physical activity, weight maintenance, smoking, alcohol consumption and sleep patterns were examined as dependent variables. Independent variables included demographic characteristics, baseline health behavior, health status variables, psychological factors and social network characteristics. Results indicate that age and health status are important predictors of preventive health behaviors. However, the factors that predict preventive health behaviors vary by behavior, gender and race. The independent variables included in this study were most successful in explaining cigarette smoking

Mary P. Gallant and Gail P. Dom, "Gender and race differences in the predictors of daily health practices among older adults" *Health Education Research,* Vol. 16, No. 1: 21–31.

and weight maintenance, and least successful in explaining amount of sleep. In addition, results suggest that social network variables are particularly influential for women's health behaviors, while health status is more influential among men. Greater education predicts better health behaviors among whites, while formal social integration seems particularly important for the health behaviors of older black women. These results indicate that examining older adults' health behaviors by race and gender leads to a fuller understanding of these behaviors.

INTRODUCTION

Recently, increased attention has been paid to the importance of self-care to the health and well-being of older adults. One important component of self-care includes preventive health practices—those routine, day-to-day behaviors undertaken to promote health and prevent illness. Over the last 30 years, much evidence has accumulated linking these health practices with long-term health outcomes. Among the general population, both physical health status and mortality have been related to the following health behaviors: exercise and physical activity, sleep patterns, maintaining a regular meal schedule, proper nutrition, eating breakfast, cigarette smoking, alcohol consumption, and maintaining appropriate body weight (Belloc and Breslow, 1972; Wingard *et al.*, 1982; Berkman and Breslow, 1983; McIntosh *et al.*, 1989). This relationship between health practices and health status exists among older adults as well. Breslow and Breslow (Breslow and Breslow, 1993) found that older adults with poor health practices experienced 50% greater disability and mortality over a 10-year period than those with a pattern of good health practices. Similarly, health promotion activities, such as exercise and good nutrition, have been related to older adults' functional health (Duffy and MacDonald, 1990), and impaired function in older women has been linked to obesity, smoking and physical inactivity (Ensrud *et al.*, 1994).

Several studies have attempted to understand the predictors of good health practices among older adults. For example, Brown and McCreedy (Brown and McCreedy, 1986) examined 386 individuals aged 55 and older, and discovered that females tended to have better health behaviors than males. Among females, socioeconomic status was most predictive of health behaviors, while among males, marital status was most predictive. Dean (Dean, 1989), in a study of 465 people over 45, also found that being female predicted better health behaviors. In addition, social network and social support variables were influential in men's health behaviors. Among 2303 Medicare recipients, Potts *et al.* (Potts *et al.*, 1992) found that women, individuals with stronger social support networks and those endorsing more health-promotive beliefs engaged in more positive health behaviors. Finally, Rakowski *et al.* (Rakowski *et al.*, 1987) reported that gender and a supportive family environment consistently predicted good health practices.

In addition, similar studies have examined the predictors of preventive health behaviors among middle-aged and younger adults (Langlie, 1977; Hibbard, 1988; Antonucci *et al.*, 1990; Palank, 1991; Stoller and Pollow, 1994). Taken together, these studies suggest that greater education, stronger internal health locus of control, being married, being white, higher socioeconomic status, stronger social support networks and female gender are all predictive of better preventive health behaviors.

Unfortunately, although these studies have been informative, most explain only a small amount of the variance in health behaviors and thus we still know relatively little about what factors influence the performance of these behaviors among older adults. This low predictive power may be due, at least in part, to two factors. First, health habits are usually combined into one summary dependent variable. Although this is intuitively appealing, especially since these health behaviors appear to have an additive effect on health outcomes (Belloc and Breslow, 1972), in reality these behaviors generally do not correlate very highly with one another (Rakowski *et at.*, 1987). Therefore, it is likely that they may be influenced by different predictive factors.

Second, little attention has been paid to the possibility of gender and race differences in the predictors of these behaviors. The prevalence of these behaviors has been shown to differ by gender and race, so it is possible that the predictors of these behaviors may be different as well or that the predictors may differ in relative strength. A brief review of the literature concerning gender and race differences in health practices follows.

Several studies have documented better health behaviors among women (Brown and McCreedy, 1986; Rakowski *et al.*, 1987; Dean, 1989; Antonucci *et al.*, 1990; Potts *et al.*, 1992; Stoller and Pollow, 1994). Studies that have examined predictors of health behaviors within genders have found that for women, higher socioeconomic status, older age, greater education, being married, experiencing fewer negative life events, having a more supportive social network and attending church are predictive of better health behaviors (Gottlieb and Green, 1984; Brown and McCreedy, 1986). Among men, higher education, being married, experiencing fewer negative life events, having a more supportive social network and attending church are predictive (Gottlieb and Green, 1984; Brown and McCreedy, 1986; Dean, 1989; Antonucci *et al.*, 1990; Ungemack, 1994).

There is far less research pertaining to the influence of race on health practices, primarily because non-white individuals are not well represented in most study samples. In fact, the lack of knowledge about all types of self-care practices among minority elders has been identified as a serious gap in the self-care literature (Davis and Wykle, 1998). Among the available literature examining older adults' preventive self-care practices, being white is associated with greater preventive health behaviors (Kart and Engler, 1994) and with more positive assessments of capacity for self-care (Kart and Dunkle, 1989).

This study was conducted to examine the following research questions:

1. What factors influence the practice of positive daily health behaviors in older adults over time?
2. Does this differ according to health behavior?
3. Do these explanatory factors differ by gender?
4. Do these factors differ by race?

Physical activity, maintaining appropriate body weight, smoking, alcohol consumption and sleep patterns were examined as dependent variables. Independent variables included demographic characteristics, baseline health behavior, health status variables, psychological factors and social network characteristics.

Methods

Sample

This study uses data from the Americans' Changing Lives (ACL) longitudinal panel survey (House, 1997). The ACL survey was conducted in 1986 and 1989 with a multistage stratified area probability design. The sample included residents of all US households, age 25 years or older, and excluded residents of Alaska and Hawaii, military bases, group quarters, and institutions. In Wave 1, 3617 persons were interviewed in their homes, with a response rate of 68%. The response rate for Wave 2 was 79%, yielding a sample size of 2867. Older adults and black Americans were oversampled at twice the rate of those under age 60 and whites.

The present study examined only that portion of the ACL sample that responded in both Wave 1 and Wave 2, and who were at least 60 years of age at Wave 1. The final sample included 1266 persons, divided into four groups: 112 black males, 284 white males, 251 black females and 619 white females. Mean age was 69 years for black males, 68 years for white males, 69 years for black females and 70 years for white females.

Measures

Independent variables included demographic characteristics, baseline health behavior health status variables, psychological factors and social network variables. Five dependent variables were examined. These included physical activity, weight maintenance, smoking, alcohol consumption and sleep. All independent variables were measured at Wave 1, while all dependent variables were measured at Wave 2. The variables were measured as follows.

Demographics *Age*, measured in years, was computed from the respondent's birth date. *Education* was determined by asking the participant to indicate the highest degree they obtained. Responses were categorized into one of the following six categories: 0–8, 9–11, 12, 13–15, 16 or 17 or more years. *Income* represents total household income for the previous 12 months, recoded into 10 categories (<$5K, $5–9K, $10–14K, $15–19K, $20–24K, $25–29K, $30–39K, $40–59K, $60–79K and $80K+). *Marital status* was dichotomously coded with 1 indicating married and 0 assigned to not married.

Health status *Self-rated physical health* was assessed by asking respondents to characterize their health as poor, fair, good, very good or excellent. Respondents were also asked to indicate whether or not they had any of the following chronic health problems during the last 12 months: arthritis or rheumatism, lung disease, hypertension, heart attack, diabetes, cancer, foot problems, stroke, broken bones, or urine beyond control. These items were summed to create a measure of *number of chronic conditions*. A *functional health index* was created with items measuring the amount of difficulty the respondent has in bathing, climbing stairs, walking and doing heavy housework. The resulting index ranged from 1 = worst functional health (i.e. most severe functional impairment) to 4 = best functional health (i.e. no functional impairment).

Psychological factors Six items were used to create a measure of *mastery*. These items were "I take a positive attitude toward myself," "I can do just about anything I really set my mind to do," "At times I think I am no good at all," "All in all, I am inclined to feel that I am a failure," "Sometimes I feel that I am being pushed around in life" and "There is really no way I can solve the problems I have." Response choices for all six items ranged from strongly agree to strongly disagree on a four-point scale. Items were recoded so that higher scores reflected greater levels of competence. These items were summed to create a mastery measure with a possible range of 6–24. The α reliability for this scale was 0.65.

Respondents were also asked to indicate whether or not they had experienced any of the following events in the past 3 years: death of a spouse, death of a child, death of a parent, death of a close friend or relative, divorce, assault, involuntary job loss, burglary and any other upsetting event. These nine events were dichotomously coded and summed to obtain a measure of *stressful life events* with a potential range of 0–9.

Depressive symptoms were measured with the Iowa form for the Center for Epidemiologic Studies Depression Scale (CES-D) (Radloff, 1977; Kohout *et al.*, 1993). The Iowa form is an 11-item version of the CES-D that taps the same underlying dimensions as the original 20-item scale (depressed affect, positive affect, somatic complaints and interpersonal problems). Items ask how often respondents experienced each depressive symptom during the past week. Response choices include hardly ever or never, some of the time and much or most of the time. Items were summed to create a measure of depressive symptoms with a range of 0–22. Previous research indicates an α reliability of 0.76 for this short version, which is comparable with the original scale (α = 0.80). The α reliability in this sample was 0.80.

Social factors Several indicators of social support were included in this study. The item How often does someone remind you to do things which will help you stay healthy, such as getting enough sleep or exercise, or taking medications? was used as an indicator of *health behavior-specific support*. The original responses of often, sometimes, rarely and never, were recoded into a new dichotomous variable in which 1 = often or sometimes and 0 = rarely or never.

Informal social integration was measured with two items which asked how often the respondent (1) talks on the telephone with friends, neighbors, or relatives and (2) gets together with friends, neighbors, or relatives. Response categories included more than once a day, once a day, 2–3 times a week about once a week, less than once a week, and never. Responses to these two items were summed. Similarly, *formal social integration* was measured with two items that asked how often the respondent (1) attended meetings or programs of groups, clubs or organizations that they belong to and (2) attended religious services.

General social support was indicated with a summary measure combining measures of support received from a spouse, children, and friends or relatives. For each source of support, respondents were asked How much does your _____ make you feel loved and cared for? and How much is _____ willing to listen when you need to talk about your worries or problems? Response choices for these items ranged from a great deal to not at all on a five-point scale. These six items were summed to reflect general social support. The α reliability for this scale was 0.67.

Health behaviors Five health behaviors were assessed at both Waves 1 and 2. *Alcohol consumption* was indicated by two items that, in combination, estimated the number of drinks in the last month. These items were "During the last month, on how many days did you drink beer, wine or liquor?" and "On days that you drink, how many cans of beer, glasses of wine or drinks of liquor do you usually have?" A *physical activity* index was created by asking respondents how often they engage in the following activities: work in the garden or yard, participate in active sports or exercise and take walks. A four-point response scale ranged from often to never. If the respondent reported *smoking* cigarettes, they were asked, On the average, how many cigarettes or packs do you usually smoke in a day (1 pack = 20 cigarettes)? *Hours of sleep* were assessed with the item, How many hours of sleep do you usually get in a 24-h period, including naps? An ordinal variable was created with 1 assigned to less than 6 or more than 9 h of sleep each day, 2 assigned to 6 or 9 h of sleep each day, and 3 assigned to 7 or 8 h of sleep each day. *Body mass index (BMI)* was used to indicate weight maintenance. Respondents were classified into five gender-specific categories of BMI as follows: underweight (lowest 5% of cases), low normal (next lowest 25%), mid-normal (middle 30%), high normal (next to highest 25%), and overweight (highest 15%). These categories were then combined into a three-category ordinal scale which included underweight or overweight, low normal and high normal, and mid-normal. Corresponding Wave 1 health behavior variables were used as control variables in the analyses.

Data analyses

Hierarchical multiple linear regression analyses involving stepwise selection were used to predict the number of drinks last month, physical activity, number of cigarettes smoked each day, BMI, and hours of sleep among the four race and sex groups separately. For all analyses, independent variables were entered in blocks, to assess the influence of each set of predictors over and above the influence of previous variables. Thus, respondent demographic characteristics (age, education, marital status, and income) were entered first. Block 2 consisted of Wave 1 health behavior. Next, health status variables were entered (self-rated health, number of chronic conditions, and functional health), followed by the psychological factors (stress,

TABLE I ■ MEANS (STANDARD DEVIATIONS) FOR ALL INDEPENDENT VARIABLES

Variable	Black females (n = 251)	Black males (n = 112)	White females (n = 619)	White males (n = 284)
Age	69.4 (7.0)	69.1 (7.1)	69.9 (6.9)	68.1 (7.1)
Education	2.0 (1.2)	1.8 (1.2)	2.8 (1.3)	2.9 (1.5)
Marital status	0.3 (0.5)	0.5 (0.5)	0.5 (0.5)	0.7 (0.4)
Income	2.2 (1.6)	2.8 (2.0)	3.8 (2.4)	4.9 (2.5)
Wave I smoking (cigarettes/day)	1.6 (5.2)	5.2 (9.2)	2.9 (7.5)	4.9 (10.5)
Wave I BMI	1.8 (0.7)	2.0 (0.8)	2.1 (0.7)	2.1 (0.7)
Wave I physical activity	6.8 (2.4)	7.2 (2.3)	7.8 (2.6)	8.8 (2.5)
Wave I alcohol consumption	2.0 (8.0)	16.1 (41.9)	5.8 (16.0)	20.5 (45.7)
Wave I sleep	2.1 (0.8)	2.3 (0.8)	2.5 (0.7)	2.5 (0.8)
Self-rated health	3.0 (1.1)	3.1 (1.2)	3.3 (1.1)	3.4 (1.1)
Functional health	3.2 (1.1)	3.3 (1.0)	3.4 (0.9)	3.6 (0.9)
No. of chronic conditions	2.5 (1.3)	2.1 (1.4)	2.0 (1.3)	1.5 (1.4)
Mastery	19.0 (3.6)	19.8 (3.7)	20.0 (3.2)	20.2 (3.4)
Depressive symptoms	5.5 (4.0)	4.5 (4.4)	4.1 (3.4)	3.5 (3.7)
Stressful life events	0.8 (0.8)	0.8 (0.8)	0.8 (0.8)	0.8 (0.8)
Support	13.0 (5.2)	14.4 (6.1)	15.3 (5.1)	16.2 (5.6)
Reminder	3.3 (1.1)	3.0 (1.2)	3.2 (1.1)	3.1 (1.1)
Informal social integration	8.7 (2.5)	7.6 (2.5)	9.6 (2.1)	8.4 (2.4)
Formal social integration	7.4 (3.1)	6.9 (2.9)	6.7 (3.0)	6.2 (3.0)

depressive symptoms, mastery). Finally, the social support variables were entered. Within each block, stepwise selection was used to determine significant predictors. The 95% significance level was used as a cut-off for statistically significant results.

RESULTS

Table 1 presents means and standard deviations for all study variables by population subgroup.

Results of the multivariate regression analyses are presented in Tables 2–6. Differences in both the amount of variance explained and the significant predictors that emerged are evident across health behaviors and across population subgroups.

With respect to percent variance explained, cigarette smoking is the dependent variable best predicted by the set of independent variables used in these analyses, with the R^2 ranging from 0.37 for black males to 0.63 for white females. For all groups, number of cigarettes smoked per day was best predicted by cigarette smoking at Wave 1, which accounted for the vast majority of variance explained. Also significant across all age groups was age, with older individuals smoking fewer cigarettes. Results indicate that health status influences smoking among males, while among females, social network characteristics influence smoking behavior. White males with more chronic conditions smoke fewer cigarettes and black males with better self-rated health smoke more. White females who have someone who reminds them to take care of their health tend to smoke more, while black females who report greater amounts of informal social integration smoke fewer cigarettes.

TABLE 2 ■ HIERARCHICAL STEPWISE MULTIPLE REGRESSION ANALYSIS OF FACTORS PREDICTING CIGARETTE SMOKING FOR EACH RACE/GENDER GROUP

Race/gender group	*n*	Order of entry	β[a]	Total R^2	Incremental R^2	*P* value
Black female	251	Age	−0.17	0.03	0.03	0.006
		Wave I cigarette smoking	0.75	0.59	0.56	0.000
		Formal social integration	−0.08	0.60	0.01	0.044
Black male	112	Age	−0.21	0.04	0.04	0.029
		Wave I cigarette smoking	0.55	0.34	0.30	0.000
		Self-rated health	0.18	0.37	0.03	0.024
White female	619	Age	−0.26	0.07	0.07	0.000
		Wave I cigarette smoking	0.78	0.62	0.55	0.000
		Reminder	0.06	0.63	0.01	0.022
White male	284	Age	−0.15	0.02	0.02	0.010
		Wave I cigarette smoking	0.71	0.50	0.48	0.000
		No. of chronic conditions	−0.11	0.51	0.01	0.012

[a]β at entry.

BMI, used as an indicator of weight maintenance behavior, was also fairly well explained by the current set of predictors, with percent variance explained ranging from 39 to 51%. As Table 3 illustrates, for males, only BMI at Wave 1 is predictive of BMI at Wave 2. For females, a few other factors emerge as predictors of BMI. White females who have greater education and who have fewer depressive symptoms are more likely to have a BMI in the ideal range. Older black females and those who have fewer chronic conditions are more likely to have a BMI in the ideal range.

The percent variance explained in physical activity ranged from 29 to 51% (see Table 4) and the greatest number of significant predictors emerged for this health behavior. For both black and white females, older age and lower income predicted less physical activity, while greater education predicted more physical activity for white males and females. Again, for all population subgroups, physical activity at

TABLE 3 ■ HIERARCHICAL STEPWISE MULTIPLE REGRESSION ANALYSIS OF FACTORS PREDICTING BMI FOR EACH RACE/GENDER GROUP

Race/gender group	*n*	Order of entry	β[a]	Total R^2	Incremental R^2	*P* value
Black female	251	Age	0.21	0.04	0.04	0.001
		Wave I BMI	0.67	0.49	0.44	0.000
		No. chronic conditions	−0.11	0.50	0.01	0.017
Black male	112	Wave I BMI	0.62	0.39	0.39	0.000
White female	619	Education	0.14	0.02	0.02	0.000
		Wave I BMI	0.70	0.51	0.49	0.000
		Depressive symptoms	−0.08	0.51	0.01	0.005
White male	284	Wave I BMI	0.71	0.51	0.51	0.000

[a]β at entry.

TABLE 4 HIERARCHICAL STEPWISE MULTIPLE REGRESSION ANALYSIS OF FACTORS PREDICTING PHYSICAL ACTIVITY FOR EACH RACE/GENDER GROUP

Race/gender group	*n*	Order of entry	β[a]	Total R^2	Incremental R^2	*P* value
Black female	251	Income	0.25	0.07	0.07	0.000
		Age	−0.18	0.09	0.03	0.006
		Wave I physical activity	0.42	0.27	0.18	0.000
		No. chronic conditions	−0.14	0.29	0.02	0.014
		Formal social integration	0.14	0.31	0.02	0.016
Black male	112	Wave I physical activity	0.47	0.22	0.22	0.000
		Functional health	0.29	0.29	0.07	0.001
White female	619	Age	−0.36	0.13	0.13	0.000
		Income	0.18	0.16	0.03	0.000
		Education	0.12	0.17	0.01	0.006
		Wave I physical activity	0.59	0.49	0.32	0.000
		Functional health	0.12	0.50	0.01	0.000
		Self-rated health	0.08	0.50	0.00	0.026
		Social support	0.09	0.51	0.01	0.006
White male	284	Education	0.21	0.04	0.04	0.001
		Wave I physical activity	0.60	0.38	0.33	0.000
		Self-rated health	0.17	0.40	0.02	0.001
		Reminder	−0.11	0.41	0.01	0.026

[a]β at entry.

Wave 1 was a strong influence on Wave 2 health behavior. Health status also emerged as a significant influence on physical activity, particularly for black males. Among both black males and white females, better functional health predicted greater physical activity; for black males this variable accounted for an additional 7% explained variance. White males and females who reported better self-rated health had greater levels of physical activity, as did black females who reported fewer chronic conditions. Finally, social network variables emerged as significant, but weak, predictors of physical activity for all groups except black males. White males who had someone to remind them to take care of their health were less likely to be physically active, while white females with greater levels of general social support and black females who reported greater formal social integration were more likely to be physically active.

Alcohol consumption was only moderately well explained by this model, with R^2 values ranging from 0.21 to 0.30 (see Table 5). As with all the other dependent variables, alcohol consumption at Wave 1 was the strongest independent variable across all population subgroups. Among whites, greater education predicted greater alcohol consumption, while among males, being married predicted lower alcohol consumption. In addition, older white females were less likely to consume alcohol. For black males, self-rated health influenced alcohol consumption, with those individuals reporting better health more likely to consume more alcohol. On the other hand, psychological factors emerged as weak, but significant predictors for both white males and females. White males with

TABLE 5 ■ HIERARCHICAL STEPWISE MULTIPLE REGRESSION ANALYSIS OF FACTORS PREDICTING ALCOHOL CONSUMPTION FOR EACH RACE/GENDER GROUP

Race/gender group	*n*	Order of entry	β[a]	Total R^2	Incremental R^2	*P* value
Black female	251	Income	0.16	0.03	0.03	0.011
		Wave I alcohol consumption	0.41	0.19	0.17	0.000
		Formal social integration	−0.12	0.21	0.01	0.038
Black male	112	Marital status	−0.25	0.06	0.06	0.007
		Wave I alcohol consumption	0.39	0.21	0.14	0.000
		Self-rated health	0.24	0.26	0.05	0.006
White female	619	Education	0.14	0.02	0.02	0.000
		Age	−0.10	0.03	0.01	0.016
		Wave I alcohol consumption	0.51	0.28	0.25	0.000
		Stressful life events	0.11	0.30	0.01	0.002
White male	284	Education	0.18	0.03	0.03	0.003
		Marital status	−0.15	0.05	0.02	0.015
		Wave I alcohol consumption	0.48	0.28	0.23	0.000
		Mastery	0.14	0.30	0.02	0.010

[a]β at entry.

greater mastery scores and white females with more stressful life events had greater alcohol consumption. Among black females, formal social integration again emerged as a significant predictor of health behavior, with those individuals who were more socially integrated reporting less alcohol consumption.

Sleep was the health behavior that was least well predicted by the present set of independent variables, with percent variance explained ranging from 4 to 21% (see Table 6). Again, across all groups, hours of sleep at Wave 1 was the best predictor of sleep at Wave 2. Demographic characteristics predicted sleep among white

TABLE 6 ■ HIERARCHICAL STEPWISE MULTIPLE REGRESSION ANALYSIS OF FACTORS PREDICTING HOURS OF SLEEP FOR EACH RACE/GENDER GROUP

Race/gender group	*n*	Order of entry	β[a]	Total R^2	Incremental R^2	*P* value
Black female	251	Wave I sleep	0.13	0.02	0.02	0.037
		Functional health	0.14	0.04	0.02	0.033
Black male	112	Wave I sleep	0.26	0.07	0.07	0.006
White female	619	Income	0.13	0.02	0.02	0.001
		Wave I sleep	0.33	0.13	0.11	0.000
		Functional health	0.09	0.14	0.01	0.017
White male	284	Age	−0.17	0.03	0.03	0.005
		Wave I sleep	0.40	0.19	0.16	0.000
		No. chronic conditions	−0.16	0.21	0.03	0.004

[a]β at entry.

males and females, with younger males and females with greater income reporting better sleep habits. Health status variables predicted hours of sleep for all subgroups except black males. White males with more chronic conditions were more likely to report less than ideal sleep habits, while for females, both black and white, better functional health predicted more ideal sleep. Psychological factors and social network characteristics did not emerge as significant predictors of hours of sleep for any of the subgroups.

Discussion

The prediction of daily preventive health practices

As these results indicate, the predictive model tested in these analyses, which included demographics, baseline health behavior, health status variables, psychological factors and social network characteristics, was moderately successful in predicting the practice of daily preventive health behaviors. The overall success of the model, as well as which individual predictors attained significance, varied markedly by health behavior and by race/gender subgroup. This lends support to the notion that to more fully understand older adults' health practices, we need to examine them individually as well as within race and gender groups.

For each of the five health behaviors examined here, the corresponding health behavior at Wave 1 was, not surprisingly, the strongest predictor of behavior at follow-up, explaining from 2 to 56% of the variance at Wave 2. While this reflects a fair amount of stability in these behaviors over time, the large amount of variance left unexplained by baseline behavior in most of these analyses indicates a significant potential for change in these routine behaviors among the older adult population.

The strength of baseline health behavior in predicting follow-up behavior varied significantly across behaviors. Cigarette smoking and BMI had the most variance accounted for by baseline behavior, indicating that cigarette smoking and weight maintenance are relatively stable behaviors over time. This finding is not surprising in light of the fact that these behaviors are among the most difficult to change. Hours of sleep, on the other hand, was least well predicted by baseline sleep and was least well predicted overall.

Other than baseline health behavior, no other variables emerged as strong predictors of all five health practices, but looking across all analyses, some predictors emerged as more influential than others. Age attained significance in at least one group for every behavior examined, reflecting that older individuals exhibit better health practices. This supports findings found in some previous literature (Gottlieb and Green, 1984; Prohaska et al. 1985; Hibbard, 1988). The conclusions to be drawn from this finding are uncertain, however. It may be that as individuals age, they make positive changes in their health practices. Equally likely is a selection effect. That is, individuals with good health practices are more likely to survive to older ages and, thus, good health practices are better represented among older individuals. Health status variables also emerged as significant predictors, especially for physical activity and sleep. This makes intuitive sense, as many health problems common to older adults may directly interfere with one's ability to be physically active and to get a good night's sleep. However, inasmuch as being active and well-rested contribute to other positive health outcomes, these findings indicate that older adults with impaired functional health or with a greater number of chronic conditions, for example, represent an at-risk population with a special need for intervention.

Interestingly, physical activity emerged as the behavior with the most number of different significant predictors and sleep the least. This underscores the fact that physical activity is a complex behavior that is responsive to many influential factors, thus making it a challenge for intervention.

Differences by gender

Interesting gender differences emerged in these analyses. For two behaviors, cigarette smoking and weight maintenance, the predictive model employed in these analyses explained more variance for females than males. In addition, cigarette smoking was significantly influenced by social network characteristics for women only and by health status variables for men only. In fact, throughout these analyses, social network variables emerged as more important for women than men in general. This indicates that women may perform many of these health behaviors within a social context, and this has important implications for the nature and location of intervention efforts. Formal social integration demonstrated a special importance for black women, particularly for smoking, physical activity and alcohol consumption. Formal social settings, such as religious groups, clubs and other organizations, may be especially appropriate intervention settings for this segment of the population. Finally, although marital status has been previously shown to be influential in men's health behaviors (Brown and McCreedy 1986), in this study being married was predictive only of less alcohol consumption for men.

Differences by race

Fewer conclusions can be drawn in terms of differences by race. Overall, the model explained more variation for whites than blacks, although this may be due to sample size effects. The model was particularly poor in explaining black males' smoking and weight maintenance behavior, indicating an area for further research. The only other race difference that emerged here was that greater education predicted more physical activity and less alcohol consumption among whites, as compared to blacks.

The present study has several limitations. The analyses reported here were limited by the constraints on the choice of independent and dependent variables that are inherent in secondary data analysis. The preventive health behaviors were all represented by single-item measures, when in reality multiple-item indicators may better reflect these complex behaviors. Preventive health behaviors may be better explained if the selection of predictors could be based on more theoretical considerations. The Health Belief Model and Social Cognitive Theory seem particularly well suited to serve as guides for the prediction of these behaviors. For example, it would be instructive to include measures of perceived benefits and barriers, self-efficacy and outcome expectations as predictors in future research. In addition, the 3-year time frame between waves of data collection in this study may not represent the most meaningful time lag for the investigation of influences on preventive health behaviors among older adults. Finally, it must be recognized that the data used in these analyses are a decade old, and the important influences on preventive practices may be different for current and future cohorts of older adults. Despite these limitations, however, the differences that emerged among the four race–gender subgroups provide an intriguing indication that the influential forces on preventive health behaviors may vary to a considerable degree for men and women, and for blacks and whites. At the very least, intervention efforts that target older adults' health behaviors may need to be tailored to the racial and gender makeup of the target population.

The overall low amount of variance explained in these analyses reaffirms the notion that we still have significant progress to make in terms of understanding older adults' preventive health behaviors. In general, efforts to understand these types of health behaviors have concentrated on the role of individual factors in determining behavior. Future research would do well to also take a broader focus that includes a look upstream for broader social and environmental influences that shape older adults' behavior by enhancing or restricting opportunities to behave in health promotive ways.

Acknowledgments

We thank Michelle van Ryn for her helpful comments on an earlier draft of this manuscript. This research was supported by a Faculty Research Awards Program grant from the University at Albany to M. P. G.

References

Antonucci, T. C., Akiyama, H. and Adelmann, P. K. (1990) Health behaviors and social roles among mature men and women. *Journal of Aging and Health,* **2,** 3–14.

Belloc, N. B. and Breslow, L. (1972) Relationship of physical health status and health practices. *Preventive Medicine,* **1,** 409–421.

Berkman, L. F. and Breslow, L. (1983) *Health and Ways of Living: The Alameda County Study.* Oxford University Press, New York.

Breslow, L. and Breslow, N. (1993) Health practices and disability: some evidence from Alameda County. *Preventive Medicine,* **22,** 86–95.

Brown, J. S. and McCreedy, M. (1986) The hale elderly: health behavior and its correlates. *Research in Nursing and Health,* **9,** 317–329.

Davis, L. and Wykle, M. L. (1998) Self-care in minority and ethnic populations: the experience of older black Americans. In Ory, M. G. and DeFriese, G. H. (eds), *Self-Care in Laser Life.* Springer, New York, pp. 170–179.

Dean, K. (1989) Self-care components of lifestyles: the importance of gender, attitudes and the social situation. Social Science and Medicine, **29,** 137–152.

Duffy, M. E. and MacDonald, E. (1990) Determinants of functional health of older persons. *The Gerontologist,* **30,** 503–509.

Ensrud, K. E., Nevitt, M. C. Yunis, C., Cauley, J. A., Seeley, D. G., Fox, K. M. and Cummings, S. R. (1994) Correlates of impaired function in older women. *Journal of the American Geriatric Society,* **42,** 481–489.

Gottlieb, N. H. and Green, L. W. (1984) Life events, social network, life-style, and health: an analysis of the 1979 National Survey of Personal Health Practices and Consequences. *Health Education Quarterly,* **11,** 91–105.

Hibbard, J. H. (1988) Age, social ties and health behaviors: an exploratory study. *Health Education Research,* **3,** 131–139.

House, J. S. (1997) *Americans' Changing Lives: Waves I and II, 1986 and 1989* [Computer file]. ICPSR Version. University of Michigan, Survey Research Center, Ann Arbor, MI [Producer]. Inter-university Consortium for Political and Social Research, Ann Arbor, MI [Distributor].

Kart, C. S. and Dunkle, R. E. (1989) Assessing capacity for self-care among the aged. *Journal of Aging and Health,* **1,** 430–450.

Kart, C. S. and Engler, C. A. (1994) Predisposition to self-health care: who does what for themselves and why? *Journal of Gerontology,* **49,** S301–308.

Langlie, J. K. (1977) Social networks, health beliefs, and preventive health behavior. *Journal of Health and Social Behavior,* **18,** 244–260.

Mclntosh, W. A., Shifflet, P. A. and Picou, J. S. (1989) Social support, stressful events, strain, dietary intake, and the elderly. *Medical Care,* **27,** 140–153.

Palank, C. L. (1991) Determinants of health-promotive behavior. *Nursing Clinics of North America,* **26,** 815–832.

Potts, M. K., Hurwicz, M.-L., Goldstein, M. S. and Berkanovic, E. (1992) Social support, health-promotive beliefs, and preventive health behaviors among the elderly. *Journal of Applied Gerontology,* **11,** 425–440.

Prohaska, T. R., Leventhal, E. A., Leventhal, H. and Keller, M. L. (1985) Health practices and illness cognition in young, middle aged, and elderly adults. *Journal of Gerontology,* **40,** 569–578.

Rakowski, W., Julius, M., Hickey, T. and Halter, J. B. (1987) Correlates of preventive health behavior in late life. *Research on Aging,* **9,** 331–355.

Stoller, E. P. and Pollow, R. (1994) Factors affecting the frequency of health enhancing behaviors by the elderly. *Public Health Reports,* **109,** 377–387.

Ungernack, J. A. (1994) Patterns of personal health practice: men and women in the United States. *American Journal of Preventive Medicine,* **10,** 38–44.

Wingard, D. L., Berkman, L. F. and Brand, R. J. (1982) A multivariate analysis of health-related practices: a nine-year mortality follow-up of the Alameda County Study. *American Journal of Epidemiology,* **116,** 765–775.

Received on January 31, 2000; accepted on April 17, 2000

Quantitative Studies with Four Locations: Interaction Analysis

The single article in this section, by Ostrove, Feldman, and Adler (1999), investigates factors affecting self-reported health and depression in older Americans. Interestingly, gender and age serve as control variables while the authors' focus on the effects of race and socioeconomic status (SES, which we can take as a rough measure of class) on physical and mental health. Interaction terms are formed with race and four separate SES measures: education, employment status, household income, and wealth. Whereas Ostrove et al. find that race and SES variables are significantly related to both dependent variables, they do not find significant race × class interactions. They conclude: "Overall, our results suggest that SES—including as assessed by a more comprehensive and less traditional indicator, wealth—is operating quite similarly for African-Americans and whites in predicting self-reported physical health" (p. 271). The authors observed similar findings for the association of race and SES with depression. Since the samples are sizable, it appears that the multiplicative assumption was not realized in this study.

Relations among Socioeconomic Status Indicators and Health for African-Americans and Whites

JOAN M. OSTROVE
Program in Health Psychology, University of California, San Francisco, USA

PAMELA FELDMAN
Department of Psychology, Carnegie Mellon University, USA

NANCY E. ADLER
Program in Health Psychology, University of California, San Francisco, USA

JOAN M. OSTROVE, PhD., *completed this research while she was research assistant with the MacArthur Network on Socioeconomic Status and Health at the University of California, San Francisco, and is currently an assistant professor at Macalester College in St Paul, MN, USA.*

PAMELA FELDMAN, PhD., *completed this research while she was a postdoctoral fellow at Carnegie Mellon University. She is currently a researcher at University College in London.*

NANCY E. ADLER, PhD., *is Professor of Medical Psychology and Director of the Center for Health and Community at the University of California, San Francisco.*

ACKNOWLEDGEMENTS. *The research reported in this article was supported by the John D. and Catherine T. MacArthur Foundation Network on Socioeconomic Status and Health, and by two National Institutes of Health Training Grants, MH19391 T32 (supporting Ostrove) and MH19953 T32 (supporting Feldman). We would like to thank David Williams for his encouragement of this project, Jeanne Tschann for statistical consultation, and three anonymous reviewers for their useful comments. We are grateful to the staff at the Inter-university Consortium for Political and Social Research (ICPSR) at the University of Michigan's Institute for Social Research, and in particular to Dave Howell at the Health and Retirement Survey, for assistance with accessing the archived data used in this project.*

COMPETING INTERESTS: *None declared.*

ADDRESS. *Correspondence should be directed to:*
JOAN M. OSTROVE, *Department of Psychology, Macalester College, 1600 Grand Avenue, St Paul, MN 55105 USA. Tel. 651-696-6464; Fax: 651-696-6430; e-mail:* ostrove@macalester.edu

ABSTRACT

This investigation explored the relationship of socioeconomic status (SES) to physical and mental health in two nationally representative samples of whites and African-Americans. We examined the interrelations among SES variables and assessed their contribution to health for the two racial groups. Throughout, we assessed the contribution of a less traditional indicator of SES—wealth—in the SES–health relationship. As we expected, African-Americans had lower levels of education, household income, and wealth than whites. Unexpectedly, however, the strength of the interrelationships among the three SES indicators did not differ for African-Americans and whites. In addition, we found that SES operated to affect health in a very similar fashion for African-Americans and whites. We found that wealth, in addition to more traditional indicators of SES (education and household income), made a unique and significant contribution to explaining both physical and mental health. Examining relations of different SES indicators to health across groups is critical to eliminating persistent social inequalities in health.

KEYWORDS

ethicity, health, race, SES, wealth

A graded relation has been established between socioeconomic status (SES) and health; as SES levels increase, rates of physical morbidity and mortality decrease (for reviews, see Adler et al., 1994; Feinstein, 1993; Marmot, Kogevinas, & Elston, 1987; Williams & Collins, 1995). SES also shows a linear association with mental health (e.g. Dohrenwend & Dohrenwend, 1969; for a recent review, see Brown & Adler, 1998). Although this association has been demonstrated in many countries and across time, the nature of the association may not be the same in different populations even within the United States. Increasing attention is being paid to the ways in which race interacts with SES to affect both physical and mental health (see e.g. Kessler & Neighbors, 1986; Ren & Amick, 1996; Williams, Takeuchi, & Adair, 1992; Williams, Yu, Jackson, & Anderson, 1997). The work on SES, race, and health has raised important questions about the differential meaning of SES for different racial groups (see e.g. Anderson & Armstead, 1995; Kaufman, Cooper, & McGee, 1997; Williams & Collins, 1995).

Various indicators of SES may not show as strong an association with one another for members of ethnic minorities (Smith, 1985). In addition, higher SES appears to confer fewer health benefits for members of ethnic minorities in the U.S. (e.g. Ren & Amick, 1996), while other research suggests that 'marginal increases in socioeconomic status generally have larger positive effects on the health of Blacks than on the health of Whites' (Schoenbaum & Waidmann, 1997, p. 71).

Researchers have conceptualized and measured SES in a number of ways (for a comprehensive review of measurement issues related to social class in general and for implications related to health, see Krieger, Williams, & Moss, 1997). The most commonly used indicators of SES are income, education, and occupation (Liberatos, Link, & Kelsey, 1988). Although occupation is a major component of SES and is consistently related to health outcomes (e.g. Marmot et al., 1991; Susser, Watson, & Hopper, 1985; Townsend, Davidson, & Whitehead, 1988), it can only be assessed among people who are in the paid labor force. Income is also consistently related to health and is a good indicator of immediately available resources that can be assessed at both the individual and the household level (see Kaufman, Long, Liao, Cooper, & McGee, 1998, for further discussion of the merits of income-based measures of SES). However, income is volatile. For example, Duncan (1988) estimated that approximately one-third of the population experienced at least a 50 percent drop in their income-to-needs ratio over the course of an 11-year period. Education is a more stable indicator of SES, and is usually established fairly early in life. Education is an important indicator in that it can contribute to both occupational and income attainment. Despite the wide use of these three indicators and their generally robust relationship to health, it has been suggested that additional measures of SES are needed better to understand persistent social inequalities in health (Williams & Collins, 1995; Williams et al., 1997).

Assessment of wealth, or net worth, has been suggested as an additional and potentially more comprehensive measure of SES than income (e.g. Oliver & Shapiro, 1995). Wealth is generally more stable than income and may provide a better measure of the resources available to an individual or household. Wealth provides greater access to life opportunities, a financial buffer during times of hardship, and is a way of passing SES onto the next generation (Oliver & Shapiro, 1995). Thus, it is a more comprehensive measure of command over resources than income and education. Most studies of SES and health have not incorporated this indicator (for a recent exception, see Schoenbaum & Waidmann, 1997), although other less traditional indicators associated with wealth such as car or home ownership are increasingly employed (e.g. Davey Smith, Shipley, & Rose, 1990).

Wide disparities in the overall level and distribution of economic resources exist between African-Americans and whites in the United States (Oliver & Shapiro, 1995). Furthermore, at the same levels of education and in similar occupations, African-Americans tend to experience poorer economic returns than whites. It has been argued that institutionalized racism and other forms of discrimination produce unequal returns in the form of income and occupational status at a given level of education for African-Americans and whites (Lillie-Blanton & Laveist, 1996). Although we expect SES variables to be related to one another for both whites and African-Americans, the inequality in returns may translate into weaker correlations for African-Americans than for whites (Smith 1985; see Ostrove & Adler, 1998, for a discussion of these issues with respect to gender).

Even greater disparities between whites and African-Americans are found in levels of wealth at different levels of education and of income due, among other reasons, to a history of discrimination in housing and banking practices in the U.S. (Oliver & Shapiro, 1995). African-Americans with the same incomes as whites are likely to have accumulated less wealth (Oliver &

Shapiro, 1995). They are less likely to have inherited resources and are also more likely to have a larger extended network of people who are dependent on their income.

Given that broad social conditions limit economic returns on SES, African-Americans may also not benefit equally in terms of attaining better physical health as their SES levels rise (Anderson & Armstead, 1995). Data indicate that even at higher educational levels, compared to whites, African-Americans experience poorer physical health outcomes such as high rates of infant mortality and low birthweight infants (Williams & Collins, 1995). Researchers in the area of SES, race, and health have suggested that the indicators of SES may have differential meaning across racial groups (Anderson and Armstead, 1995; Williams & Collins, 1995) and that it is particularly important to assess the interaction of SES and race in predicting health. Ren and Amick (1996) recently found that at low levels of education there were no racial differences in self-reported health, but at high levels of education African-Americans and Latinos were more likely to report poorer health than whites. A different pattern emerged with respect to income, such that at low levels of income African-Americans and Latinos reported poorer health than whites, but at high income levels only Latinos reported poorer health than whites. Kaufman and his colleagues (1997, 1998) stress the importance of understanding how SES and race interact, rather than using analytic methods that control for SES in studies of black–white differences in mortality. They have devised statistical models that demonstrate that blacks 'encounter a given mortality level sooner in age than whites, but also appear to derive less protection from higher income' (Kaufman et al., 1998, p. 152).

There may also be differential returns on SES in mental health outcomes for African-Americans and whites. For example, Kessler and Neighbors (1986) found that across eight extensive epidemiological studies of psychological distress there were no overall race differences in psychological distress, but there was an interaction of race and SES such that levels of psychological distress were more pronounced among low-income blacks than among low-income whites. These findings were replicated in a subsequent epidemiological study (Ulbrich, Warheit, & Zimmerman, 1989). In examining the relation between rates of psychiatric disorders (as distinct from psychological distress), SES, and race, Williams et al. (1992) found that SES was inversely related to psychiatric disorders among both whites and blacks. The relationship, however, was stronger among white males than among black males, such that lower-SES white men had higher rates of psychiatric disorders than their black counterparts. Among women, the situation was slightly different, and lower-SES black women had higher rates of substance abuse than lower-SES white women. Thus the interaction between race and SES in mental health outcomes may depend on whether distress or psychiatric disorders are being considered and may also vary across gender and type of disorder.

Much of the work that has generated interest in examining SES by race interactions in predicting health has focused on explaining persistent black–white differences in physical and (to a less consistent degree) mental health. Although our focus is slightly different—understanding whether the patterning of SES–health relationships is similar for whites and African-Americans using a variety of SES indicators—we rely on similar conceptual and analytic strategies in doing this research. Both literatures suggest that two questions are central to examining race differences in the association of SES and health: (1) are SES indicators similarly related to one another in different racial groups; and (2) are specific indicators of SES (e.g. education, income, and wealth) differentially related to health among members of different racial groups?

In this investigation, we use data from two national surveys with large subsamples of African-Americans and whites to examine the meaning of traditional (education, employment status, and income) and less traditional (wealth) SES indicators and their relation to health in each racial group. This investigation has several purposes. First, we examine racial differences in levels of education, income, and wealth. We predict that African-Americans will have lower levels of each. Second, we examine whether there are racial differences in the strength of the correlations between education and income, between education and wealth, and between income and wealth. We expect that these indicators will be positively related to one another within each racial group, but that, given differential economic returns on education, the associations will be weaker among African-Americans than among whites. Third, we examine whether there are differential returns on these indicators for the health of whites and African-Americans by assessing the relationships of education, employment status, income, and wealth to both physical and mental health. Because of the social conditions that limit economic returns on SES for African-Americans as compared to whites, we expect that the more traditional SES indicators of education and income will not produce as strong connections with health for the former group as they would for the latter. However, we speculate that because it is a more comprehensive measure of SES, wealth may be similarly related to health for both African-Americans and whites.

Method

This study used data from two nationally representative surveys of adults in the United States, the Americans' Changing Lives survey (House et al., 1990; 1994) and the Health and Retirement Survey (see Juster & Suzman, 1995).

Study descriptions

Americans' Changing Lives (ACL) The ACL survey is a national longitudinal panel survey of African-American and white non-institutionalized adults that was designed to investigate adult activities and social relationships, and adaptation to life events and stress. The first wave of data collection in 1986 used a multistage stratified area probability sampling strategy, with oversampling of African-Americans and those over 60 years of age, and obtained responses from 3617 people. In 1989, contact with all original respondents was attempted, and 2867 individuals completed that questionnaire. The questionnaire covered interpersonal relationships, activities and life events, health care and retirement, and psychological well-being. Measures of particular interest for the current study included SES measures, physical health, and depressive symptoms.

The data were weighted to adjust for variations in probabilities of selection and in response rates, making the data representative of the US population. In order to use data from a time period closest to that of the other survey (described below), the current study included participants from the second (1989) wave (weighted $n = 2568$; 47 percent male) who had data available for all of our variables of interest and were either African-American (weighted $n = 290$, 11 percent) or white (weighted $n = 2278$, 89 percent). Participants ranged in age from 27 to 98 years (mean = 49).

Health and Retirement Survey (HRS) The HRS is a national panel survey of non-institutionalized adults between the ages of 51 and 61 years (in 1992) and their spouses. The data for the current study are from the original wave of data collection from 1992, in which over 7600 households were sampled, yielding interviews with over 12,600 people. Since the study was intended to interview people before they had actually retired, most of the sample participants were in the paid labor force (approximately 70 percent of men and 60 percent of women), though approximately 20 percent of the men and 6 percent of the women were already retired. The study used a multistage area probability sample design and oversampled for African-Americans, Latino/as, and residents of Florida. Participants answered questions about their families, retirement plans, expectations for the future, work and work history. Measures assessed that were of particular interest for this study included SES indicators, physical health, and depressive symptoms.

The data were weighted to adjust for unequal selection probabilities, and for geographic and race group differences in response rates, creating a nationally representative sample. The current study included 6032 participants (53 percent male) who had data available for all of our variables of interest and were either African-American (weighted n = 725, 12 percent) or white (weighted n = 5307, 88 percent). Participants ranged in age from 51 to 61 years (mean = 56).

Although both surveys used national samples, and the mean age is similar, the age structure differs between the two surveys. The ACL included persons between the ages of 25 and 98 years, while the HRS limited eligibility to those between the ages of 51 and 61 years. Differences between these samples in the relations between SES indicators and health may reflect the life-span patterning of the SES–health gradient. The gradient tends to be strongest among middle-aged individuals with a flattening out (either due to selection or stabilizing of resources) among adults over the age of 65 (see Williams & Collins, 1995, for a discussion). Because the ACL has both more younger adults and more older adults, where the SES–health gradient is weaker, we would expect a smaller association of the SES indicators and health in this sample than in the HRS sample. Because of the association between age and the SES–health gradient, and because of the differences in age structure in the two samples used in this study, we controlled for age in all analyses.

Measures

Race In both surveys, respondents were asked to choose among racial/ethnic categories with which they primarily identified. We limited the participants in for this project to those who responded white or Caucasian or African-American or black.

Employment status In both surveys, participants' occupations were coded according to US census codes. We considered participants who had a numeric code other than 0 (which indicated homemakers, retired persons, students, etc.) and/or who indicated directly that they were in the paid labor force to be employed. Sixty-seven percent of ACL participants and 59 percent of HRS participants were in the paid labor force.

Education In both the ACL and the HRS studies, participants were asked the highest grade of school or year of college they completed between 0 and 17; any number higher than 17 was coded as 17. We created a four-level education variable to capture the meaningful distinctions in educational attainment: (1) *less than high school*; (2) *high school graduation*; (3) *some college*; and (4) *college graduation or more*. In the ACL, the average educational level was 2.42 (SD = 1.06). In the HRS, it was 2.40 (SD = 1.07).

Household income In the ACL study, participants were asked: 'If you include [all] sources,[1] your and your spouse's earnings what would your income for the last 12 months (before taxes) add up to?' They were provided with 10 categories in which to place their household income: (1) *under $5000;* (2) *$5001–10,000*; (3) *$10,001–15,000*; (4) *$15,001–20,000*; (5) *$20,001–25,000*; (6) *$25,001–30,000*; (7) *$30,001–40,000*; (8) *$40,001–60,000*; (9) *$60,001–80,000*; and (10) *over $80,001*. The average household income level for the ACL sample was 5.93 (SD = 2.67).

In HRS, household income was computed from a number of questions concerning sources of income, each of which was answered with an actual monetary value. The imputed variable was the sum of the following: (1) earnings, unemployment or workers' compensation; (2) pensions and annuities; (3) social security income (SSI) or welfare; (4) capital income (which included income from a business, gross rent, interest/dividend income, and trust/royalty income); (5) disability income; (6) other income received by the respondent (e.g. from alimony or child support); and (7) income of other household members. In order to maximize measurement similarity between the ACL and the HRS, we created the same 10-category variable as was used in the ACL study described above. The sample average was 6.60 (SD = 2.70).

Wealth In the ACL study, participants were asked: If you needed money quickly and cashed in all bank accounts, investments, and real estate, how much would this amount to? Participants were provided with seven categories in which to place their estimated assets. The distribution of this variable was skewed, so we collapsed categories to create a four category variable: (1) *less than $10,000*; (2) *$10,000–20,000*; (3) *$20,000–50,000*; and (4) *more than $50,000*. The sample average was 2.28 (SD = 1.27).

In the HRS study, wealth was computed by adding two variables: housing equity (minus mortgage) and non-housing equity (from the value of vehicles, bank accounts, liquid assets, minus all debts). Because the continuous data generated from this assessment of wealth were highly skewed, and because we had increments at higher levels of wealth available in HRS that we did not have in ACL, we placed all of these values into one of eight categories: (1) *less than $0*; (2)*$1–10,000*; (3) *$10,001–20,000*; (4) *$20,001–50,000*; (5) *$50,001–100,000*; (6) *$100,001–200,000*; (7) *$200,001–500,000*; and (8) *more than $500,001*. The sample mean was 5.10 (SD = 2.08).[2]

Physical health In both the ACL and the HRS studies, participants were asked to rate their overall health on a five-point scale, ranging from (1) *poor* to (5) *excellent*. The average health rating in the ACL study was 3.54 (SD = 1.01); in HRS it was 3.47 (SD = 1.21). One-item, global self-assessments of health have been demonstrated to be good predictors of mortality in a number of studies even when known biomedical risks are controlled for (see e.g. Idler & Angel, 1990; Idler & Benyamini, 1997; Kaplan & Camacho, 1983; Mossey & Shapiro, 1982) and these assessments are highly correlated with other measures of health (Cunny & Perri, 1991).

Depressive symptoms The 11-item version of the Center for Epidemiological Studies Depression Scale (CES-D; Radloff, 1977) was available in both the ACL and HRS studies. The CES-D is a reliable and valid measure of depressive symptoms for use in the general population (Radloff, 1977). In the ACL study it had an alpha reliability of .83 and a mean of 1.36 (SD = .33). In HRS, the alpha was .85 and the average score was 1.46 (SD = .43).

Results

Race differences in SES

In both studies, there were significant differences between African-Americans and whites on all SES variables, such that whites had higher levels of education, income, and wealth than African-Americans (see Table 1). There were no differences, however, between African-Americans and whites on employment status, with similar percentages of people in each racial group employed in the paid labor force. In addition, in both studies, at each level of education, whites had significantly higher levels of income and wealth than African-Americans (data not shown).

Race differences in intercorrelations among SES variables

We examined the intercorrelations among SES indicators separately by racial group. In both studies, SES variables were moderately to highly intercorrelated and, contrary to our expectations, the strength of these correlations did not generally differ by race (see Table 2). Education showed an equally strong association with both income and wealth for African-Americans as for whites. The only difference was found in HRS, where the relation between wealth and household income was significantly stronger among whites than among African-Americans.

TABLE 1 ■ RACE DIFFERENCES IN MEANS OF SES IN THE ACL AND HRS STUDIES

	African-American	White	*t*
ACL study			
Education	2.04 (1.04)	2.46 (1.06)	6.48*
Income	4.56 (2.80)	6.11 (2.60)	8.93*
Wealth	1.71 (1.08)	2.36 (1.27)	9.44*
Employment status (percent employed)	67%	66%	χ^2 (1) = 0.33, NS
HRS study			
Education	1.99 (1.02)	2.45 (1.06)	11.23*
Income	5.20 (2.86)	6.79 (2.62)	14.17*
Wealth	3.49 (2.05)	5.32 (1.99)	22.60*
Employment status (percent employed)	55%	59%	χ^2 (1) = 4.07 NS

NOTE. Because of the large sample size, we used $*p < .01$ as our criterion for statistical significance.

TABLE 2 ■ INTERCORRELATIONS AMONG SES VARIABLES[a]

	White	African-American	Difference between correlations
Americans' Changing Lives	(Weighted $n = 2278$)	(Weighted $n = 290$)	
Wealth and income	.56*	.46*	2.15
Wealth and education	.33*	.34*	−0.36
Income and education	.43*	.48*	−1.05
Health and Retirement Survey	(Weighted $n = 5307$)	(Weighted $n = 725$)	
Wealth and income	.50*	.57*	−2.48*
Wealth and education	.33*	.37*	−1.15
Income and education	.40*	.41*	−0.30

[a]Age is partialled out of all correlations.
$*p < .01$.

The association of SES indicators with physical and mental health

Based on the associations among age, gender, race, the SES measures, and physical and mental health[3] (see Table 3), we conducted the following multivariate analyses to predict first physical and then mental health in each sample.

Multivariate analyses predicting physical health In all models, we controlled for the contribution of age and gender to health in the first step. We entered race in the second step and the SES indicator(s) in the third step. In the fourth step, we entered the race by SES indicator(s) interaction term(s). We began by fitting individual regression models entering each of the SES indicators alone in the third step and their interaction with race in the fourth step. Next, we fit a simultaneous regression model, entering all four SES indicators together in the third step and all the interactions of SES by race in the fourth step. This model provided a test of the independent association of each SES indicator, as well as the interaction of race with each indicator, with self-reported health independent of the remaining indicators and interactions. The results are presented in Table 4.

TABLE 3 ■ CORRELATIONS AMONG VARIABLES IN REGRESSIONS

	1	2	3	4	5	6	7	8	9
1. Age	1.00	.04*	−.01	−.06*	−.10*	.07*	−.13*	−.02	−.08*
2. Gender	.07*	1.00	.08*	−.15*	−.26*	−.16*	−.05*	.14*	−.08*
3. Race	−.02	.01	1.00	−.14*	−.19*	−.29*	−.03	.10*	−.17*
4. Education	−.37*	−.10*	−.13*	1.00	.42*	.36*	.12*	−.21*	.31*
5. Income	−.37*	−.17*	−.17*	−.53*	1.00	.53*	.26*	−.31*	.35*
6. Wealth	.19*	−.07*	−.18*	.24*	.45*	1.00	.01	−.30*	.35*
7. Employment	−.51*	−.22*	−.01	.33*	.42*	−.01	1.00	−.19*	.25*
8. CES-depression	.04	.06*	.13*	−.19*	−.25*	−.20*	−.15*	1.00	−.44*
9. Self-reported health	−.27*	−.08*	−.08*	.27*	.26*	.08*	.28*	−.39*	1.00

NOTE. ACL correlation coefficients are printed in bold, below the diagonal.

*$p < .01$.

TABLE 4 ■ INDIVIDUAL AND SIMULTANEOUS REGRESSION MODELS PREDICTING SELF-REPORTED HEALTH

	Americans' Changing Lives		Health and Retirement Survey	
	Individual model Bs	Simultaneous model Bs	Individual model Bs	Simultaneous model Bs
Step 1				
Age	−.29*	−.29*	−.09*	−.09*
Gender[a]	−.05*	−.05*	−.08*	−.08*
Step 2				
Race[b]	−.07*	−.07*	−.16*	−.16*
Step 3				
Education	.18*	.12*	.34*	.19*
Employment status	.23*	.19*	.23*	.20*
Household income	.19*	.06	.39*	.13*
Wealth	.12*	.04	.38*	.25*
Step 4				
Race * education	.00	−.03	.01	.01
Race * employment status	.06	.03	.07*	.04
Race * household income	.04	.05	.01	.00
Race * wealth	.02	−.01	−.01	−.03
Overall R^2	.09* to .12*	.14*	.10* to .14*	.22*

NOTE. All continuous independent variables are standardized. Unstandardized betas are reported for these variables; standardized betas are reported for categorical variables.

[a]Gender is dummy coded, 0 = male, 1 = female.

[b]Race is dummy coded, 0 = white, 1 = African-American.

*$p < .01$.

Age, gender, and health In both studies, the control variables were predictive of health, such that older people and women reported worse health than younger people and men.

Individual models of race, SES, and health In both studies, race was significantly associated with health such that African-Americans reported worse health than whites. In both studies, each SES indicator was a significant predictor of health, such that higher levels of education, income, and wealth, and being in the paid labor force, were associated with better health. There was only one significant interaction of race by SES, in HRS. Post hoc analyses in which we performed separate regressions for whites and African-Americans revealed that employment status was more strongly related to health for African-Americans ($B = .38, p < .01$) than for whites ($B = .22, p < .01$).

Simultaneous models of SES and health In both studies, education and employment status were significant predictors of health when all four SES indicators were entered simultaneously into the model. In the HRS study, income and wealth also had unique associations with health. In the ACL study, however, income and wealth did not predict health when employment status and education were considered.[4] There were no interaction effects of race and any SES indicator in either survey.

Multivariate analyses predicting depressive symptoms

We followed the same procedure described above for predicting overall self-rated health to predict depressive symptoms. Results are presented in Table 5.

Age, gender, and depressive symptoms In both studies, gender was a significant predictor of depression, such that women reported higher levels of depressive symptoms than men. Age was unrelated to depressive symptoms in both studies.

Individual models of race, SES and depressive symptoms In both studies, race was significantly associated with depression such that African-Americans reported more depressive symptoms than whites. In both studies, each SES indicator was a significant predictor of depression, such that lower levels of education, income, and wealth, and not being in the paid labor force were associated with higher depressive symptoms scores. In the ACL study, there were no significant interactions of race by any SES indicator. In the HRS study, there was an interaction effect of race by employment status. Post hoc analyses in which we performed separate regressions for whites and African-Americans revealed that employment status was more strongly related to depressive symptoms for African-Americans ($B = -.28, p < .01$) than for whites ($B = -.17, p < .01$).

Simultaneous models of SES indicators and depressive symptoms In both studies, education, employment status, income, and wealth were all significant predictors of depressive symptoms when all four SES indicators were entered simultaneously into the model. There were no interaction effects of race and any SES indicator in either study.

Discussion

This investigation accomplished three main goals. We explored the meaning of SES indicators among nationally representative samples of whites and African-Americans. We also examined whether SES indicators operated similarly for whites and African-Americans in predicting both physical and mental health. In all analyses, we assessed the contribution of a less traditional indicator of SES—wealth—to the SES–health relationship.

As expected, African-Americans had lower levels of education, household income, and wealth than whites. Unexpectedly, however, the strength of the interrelationships among the three SES indicators did not differ for African-Americans and whites. Although we did find

TABLE 5 ■ INDIVIDUAL AND SIMULTANEOUS REGRESSION MODELS PREDICTING DEPRESSION

	Americans' Changing Lives		Health and Retirement Survey	
	Individual model Bs	Simultaneous model Bs	Individual model Bs	Simultaneous model Bs
Step 1				
Age	.03	.03	−.01	−.01
Gender[a]	.08*	.08*	.14*	.14*
Step 2				
Race[b]	.13*	.13*	.09*	.09*
Step 3				
Education	−.16*	−.07*	−.08*	−.03*
Employment status	−.17*	−.14*	−.19*	−.15*
Household income	−.25*	−.10*	−.12*	−.05*
Wealth	−.18*	−.08*	−.12*	−.08*
Step 4				
Race * education	−.01	.01	−.03	−.02
Race * employment status	−.03	.01	−.08*	−.03
Race * household income	−.02	−.03	−.03	−.01
Race * wealth	−.03	−.02	−.01	.02
Overall R^2	.04* to .08*	.09*	.06* to .10*	.15*

NOTE. All continuous independent variables are standardized. Unstandardized betas are reported for these variables; standardized betas are reported for categorical variables.

[a]Gender is dummy coded, 0 = male, 1 = female.

[b]Race is dummy coded, 0 = white, 1 = African-American.

*$p < .01$.

that at any given level of education, African-Americans had significantly less income and less wealth than whites, the strength of the association between education and income and between education and wealth was not different for the two groups. This suggests that while there are differential rates of return on education for African-Americans and whites, these are not reflected in how the variables operate with respect to one another *within* racial groups. For African-Americans as well as for whites, more education is associated with higher income and greater wealth.

We did find a significant difference by race in the association between wealth and income, but this difference was not consistent in the two studies. In HRS, which had a sample that included only those between the ages of 51 and 61 years, there was a stronger relationship between wealth and income among African-Americans than among whites, contrary to our prediction; this was not the case in ACL. Although this could be a function of the different age structures of the samples, when we limited the analyses to those aged 51 to 61 in ACL there was still no significant race difference in the strength of the correlation between wealth and income for African-Americans (r = .61) compared to whites (r = .49), although the pattern of difference is now in the same direction as in HRS. It is perhaps safest to assume no systematic pattern in the association between wealth and income for the two racial groups, although it may be worth pursuing further investigation into the ways in which income is associated with wealth among African-American and white individuals at later midlife, a time of maximum accumulation of wealth.

In examining the role of SES in predicting physical health for African-Americans and whites, we found that both race and SES—variously defined—made significant independent contributions to health. Specifically, African-Americans reported worse overall health than whites. Education and employment status were consistently and independently related to health after the health effects of race were taken into account. When it was measured in a more differentiated manner (in the HRS study; see also note 4) wealth also made a contribution to health independent of the two more traditional indicators of SES, education and household income. Importantly, however, it did not supersede the effects of income or education, suggesting that it is an important addition to, but not a sufficient substitution for, these other variables in understanding the SES–health relationship.

Previous work has emphasized the importance of looking at interactions between race and SES in predicting physical health (e.g. Ren & Amick, 1996), which we did in this investigation. Although we expected that income and education would be stronger predictors of health among whites than among African-Americans, we found no such interaction effects in the current study. Employment status was differentially related to health for African-Americans and whites in the individual model in HRS, but not in ACL or in any of the simultaneous models, leaving us reluctant to overinterpret this interaction. Overall, our results suggest that SES—including as assessed by a more comprehensive and less traditional indicator, wealth—is operating quite similarly for African-Americans and whites in predicting self-reported physical health.

We also assessed the relationship of race and SES to mental health, and found that both race and SES were related to depressive symptoms in very similar ways as they were to physical health. However, in contrast to the results for physical health, income and wealth were significant predictors in *all* models for *both* studies, as were education and employment status. Consistent with our findings regarding physical health, there were no race by SES interactions in the simultaneous models, suggesting that the SES indicators were operating in similar ways with respect to depressive symptoms for both whites and African-Americans.

Virtually all of the previous work that examined interactions of SES and race in predicting health has focused on explaining race differences in physical and mental health, rather than on understanding whether or not the SES–health gradient is similar for different racial groups. In the studies in which the focus was on race differences (e.g., Kaufman et al., 1998; Kessler & Neighbors, 1986; Ren & Amick, 1996; Williams et al., 1992), interactions of SES and health were evident, if not consistent, suggesting that SES explained some, but not all, of the race differences in health, and that race differences in health were differentially evident at different socioeconomic levels. In the current study, we did not find any interaction of race with SES, using four different indicators of SES. We could argue then, that SES seems to be equally important in affecting the health of both African-Americans and whites, at least in the domains of self-assessed physical and emotional health examined here. It is also possible that if we examined the relations among SES, race, and health using procedures in which we compared across every SES category to examine race by SES interactions, we might have found interactions similar to those found by the researchers mentioned above. However, one of the strengths of our project that mitigated against doing such a category-by-category analysis is that we were able to take account of a number of different SES measures simultaneously.

We found some evidence for the age patterning of the SES–health gradient, in which the relation between SES and health is strongest among people at midlife: the association between SES and health was stronger in HRS (ages 51 to 61) than it was in ACL. Although it substantially reduced the sample size, we checked on the reliability of this effect by assessing it among those aged 51 to 61 in ACL. First, we found that the SES measures accounted for more variability in physical and mental health in this age group, supporting the notion that these relations are strongest among people at midlife. Restricting the ACL sample in this way increased the relationship of income, employment status, and wealth to health (arguably the time of maximum assets in individuals' lives), but weakened the relationship between education and health. The same pattern of findings was obtained for depressive symptoms, suggesting that SES has important implications for both physical and mental health during midlife.

There are, of course, a number of limitations of this investigation. We paid very little attention to gender in these analyses, even though we took account of its contribution to health in our analyses (for recent analyses of gender, SES, and health, see Arber, 1997; Ostrove & Adler, 1998). Although it would have been ideal to include interactions of race, gender, and SES in our analyses, such examinations significantly reduce statistical power. Even greater sample sizes than the rather substantial ones available to us here, including those of racial groups other than whites and African-Americans, would be required to address adequately the ways in which race and gender both interact with socioeconomic status to affect health. In order best to understand SES and health, it is important to include as many different groups of people—with their common and divergent social, cultural, economic, educational, and psychological experiences—as possible in our analyses. This will also prove most helpful for developing effective strategies for eliminating persistent social inequalities in health.

Notes

1. In a previous question, participants were prompted about different sources of income besides salary. These included the following: (1) rent/interest/dividends/mutual funds; (2) social security; (3) veterans' benefits/retirement/pension; (4) unemployment/disability/workers' compensation; (5) alimony or child support; (6) SSI, ADC, AFDC or other welfare or public assistance; (7) food stamps; and (8) other sources.
2. Overall, the HRS respondents had somewhat higher levels of income and wealth than the ACL participants. Both higher income and greater wealth among the HRS participants may be due to the fact that the HRS has a greater proportion of respondents in high-earning years, while the ACL has both younger and older people whose earnings are likely to be lower.
3. Note that the associations between each SES indicator and health are stronger among HRS participants than among ACL participants. This is consistent with the age patterning of the SES–health gradient, since the HRS participants are all middle-aged while the ACL has both younger and older adults, where the gradient is generally weaker. To evaluate this, we reanalyzed the zero-order correlations between each of the SES variables and self-reported health among the 51- to 61-year-olds in ACL ($n = 373$). Consistent with the age patterning of the SES–health gradient, the association between wealth and health was considerably stronger in this age group ($r = .17$ compared with $r = .08$). However, the association between income and health was unchanged ($r = .23$ compared with $r = .26$), and the association between employment and health was similar ($r = .29$ compared with $r = .28$). The association between education and health was weaker among 51- to 61-year-olds than in the whole sample ($r = .10$ compared with $r = .27$).
4. Since the assets measure in the ACL study was not as comprehensive as that found in the HRS study, we also examined home ownership as an additional indicator of wealth. When we added home ownership to the regression models, it did not make a significant contribution to explaining health but it was significantly associated with depression. There were no interaction effects of home ownership by race in either health or depression.

References

Adler, N. E., Boyce, T., Chesney, M. A., Cohen, S., Folkman, S., Kahn, R. L., & Syme, S. L. (1994). Socioeconomic status and health: The challenge of the gradient. *American Psychologist, 49,* 15–24.

Anderson, N. B., & Armstead, C. A. (1995). Toward understanding the association of socioeconomic status and health: A new challenge for the biopsychosocial approach. *Psychosomatic Medicine, 57,* 213–225.

Arber, S. (1997). Comparing inequalities in women's and men's health: Britain in the 1990s. *Social Science and Medicine, 44,* 773–787.

Brown, H. D., & Adler, N. E. (1998). Socioeconomic status. In H. S. Friedman (Ed.) *Encyclopedia of mental health, vol. I* (pp. 555–561). San Diego: Academic Press.

Carroll, D., & Davey Smith, G. (1997). Health and socioeconomic position. *Journal of Health Psychology, 2,* 275–282.

Cunny, K. A., & Perri, M. III (1991). Single-item vs. multiple-item measures of health-related quality of life. *Psychological Reports, 69,* 127–130.

Davey Smith, G., Shipley, M. J., & Rose, G. (1990). The magnitude and causes of socioeconomic differentials in mortality: Further evidence from the Whitehall study. *Journal of Epidemiology and Community Health, 44,* 265–270.

Dohrenwend, B., & Dohrenwend, B. (1969). *Social status and psychological disorder: A causal inquiry.* New York: Wiley.

Duncan, G. (1988). The volatility of family income over the life course. In P. Bates, D. Featherman & R. Lerner (Eds.) *Life span development and behavior* (pp. 317–358). Hillsdale, NJ: Lawrence Erlbaum Associates.

Feinstein, J. S. (1993). The relationship between socioeconomic status and health: A review of the literature. *Milbank Quarterly, 71,* 279–322.

House, J. S., Kessler, R. C., Herzog, A. R., Mero, R. P., Kinney, A. M., & Breslow, M. (1990). Age, socioeconomic status, and health. *Millbank Quarterly, 68,* 383–411.

House, J. S., Lepkowski, J. M., Kinney, A. M., Mero, R. P., Kessler, R. C., & Herzog, A. R. (1994). The social stratification of aging and health. *Journal of Health and Social Behavior, 35,* 213–234.

Idler, E. L., & Angel, R. J. (1990). Self-rated health and mortality in the NHANES-I epidemiologic follow-up study. *American Journal of Public Health, 80,* 446–452.

Idler, E. L., & Benyamini, Y. (1997). Self-rated health and mortality: A review of twenty-seven community studies. *Journal of Health and Social Behavior, 38,* 21–37.

Juster, F. T., & Suzman, R. (1995). An overview of the health and retirement study. *Journal of Human Resources, 30,* S7–S56.

Kaplan, G. A., & Camacho, T. (1983). Perceived health and mortality: A nine-year follow-up of the Human Population Laboratory cohort. *American Journal of Epidemiology, 117,* 292–304.

Kaufman, J. S., Cooper, R. S., & McGee, D. L. (1997). Socioeconomic status and health in blacks and whites: The problem of residual confounding and the resiliency of race. *Epidemiology, 8,* 621–628.

Kaufman, J. S., Long, A. E., Liao, Y., Cooper, R. S., & McGee, D. L. (1998). The relation between income and mortality in U.S. blacks and whites. *Epidemiology, 9,* 147–155.

Kessler, R. C., & Neighbors, H. W. (1988). A new perspective on the relationships among race, social class, and psychological distress. *Journal of Health and Social Behavior, 27,* 107–115.

Krieger, N., Williams, D. R., & Moss, N. E. (1997). Measuring social class in US public health research: Concepts, methodologies, and guidelines. *Annual Review of Public Health, 18,* 341–378.

Liberatos, P., Link, B. G., & Kelsey, J. L. (1988). The measurement of social class in epidemiology. *Epidemiologic Reviews, 10,* 87–121.

Lillie-Blanton, M., & Laveist, T. (1996). Race/ethnicity, the social environment, and health. *Social Science and Medicine, 43,* 83–91.

Marmot, M. G., Davey Smith, G., Standfeld, D., Patel, C., North, F., Head, J., White, I., Brunner, E., & Feeney, A. (1991). Health inequalities among British civil servants: The Whitehall II study. *Lancet, 337,* 1387–1393.

Marmot, M. G., Kogevinas, M., & Elston, M. A. (1987). Social/economic status and disease. *Annual Review of Public Health, 8,* 111–135.

Mossey, J. M., & Shapiro, E. (1982). Self-rated health: A predictor of mortality among the elderly. *American Journal of Public Health, 72,* 800–808.

Oliver, M. L., & Shapiro, T. M. (1995). *Black wealth, white wealth.* New York: Routledge.

Ostrove, J. M., & Adler, N. E. (1998). The relationship of socioeconomic status, labor force participation, and health among men and women. *Journal of Health Psychology, 3,* 451–463.

Radloff, L. (1977). The CES-D scale: A self-report depression scale for research in the general population. *Applied Statistical Measurement, 1,* 385–401.

Ren, X. S., & Amick, B. C. (1996). Racial and ethnic disparities in self-assessed health status: Evidence from the National Survey of Families and Households. *Ethnicity and Health, 1,* 293–303.

Schoenbaum, M., & Waidmann, T. (1997). Race, socioeconomic status, and health: Accounting for race differences in health. *Journal of Gerontology, 52B,* 61–73.

Smith, A. W. (1985). Social class and racial cleavages on major social indicators. *Research in Race and Ethnic Relations, 4,* 33–65.

Susser, M., Watson, W., & Hopper, K. (1985). *Sociology in medicine.* Oxford: Oxford University Press.

Townsend, P., Davidson, N., & Whitehead, M. (1988). *Inequalities in health.* London: Penguin.

Ulbrich, P. M., Warheit, G. J., & Zimmerman, R. S. (1989). Race, socioeconomic status, and psychological distress: An examination of differential vulnerability. *Journal of Health and Social Behavior, 30,* 131–146.

Williams, D. R., & Collins, C. (1995). U.S. socioeconomic and racial differentials in health: Patterns and explanations. *Annual Review of Sociology, 21,* 349–386.

Williams, D. R., Takeuchi, D. T., & Adair, R. K. (1992). Socioeconomic status and psychiatric disorder among blacks and whites. *Social Forces, 71,* 179–194.

Williams, D. R., Yu, Y., Jackson, J. S., & Anderson, N. (1997). Racial differences in physical and mental health. *Journal of Health Psychology, 2,* 335–351.

Quantitative Studies with Four Locations: Interactions Combined with Separate Group Analysis

The three articles in this section all utilize some combination of interaction terms with subgroup analysis. In "Predictors of Fear of Criminal Victimization at School Among Adolescents," May and Dunaway search for the predictors of fear among a sample of 742 high school students. Specifically, they want to learn whether these predictors are different from those that raise fear among adults. Of these 742 students in grades 10 to 12, 316 are black and 426 white; 425 are females and 317 males. But the authors do not give the frequencies for the intersectional groups black females, white females, black males, and white males.

They find that gender and race, "two of the strongest predictors for adult fear of crime, have non-significant associations with fear of crime among adolescents" (p. 282). To test for possible interactions, May and Dunaway add a race × gender interaction term to their model (Table 3; p. 283). The significant interaction term reveals that females are more fearful of crime than males. Further exploration, running separate analyses for females and males, uncovers additional interactions. These include the finding that black males are more fearful of crime than white males and that "prior victimization experience and perceived safety at school were found to significantly affect female adolescent fear but not male adolescent fear" (p. 284). The latter finding is for simple social locations (female versus male), whereas the former for black males compared with white males reveals an interaction across a complex social location (race and gender).

This article contains most of the ingredients for effective interaction analysis. Interactions are analyzed both through interaction terms within models and through separate group analysis. Both approaches yield positive results; however, separate group analysis yields more than the use of interaction terms. In part this may be due to the relatively small sample size of 742 students, for it is likely that when the sample was parceled out among multiple cells, a number of them were too small to detect relationships. This would especially be true for the class variable, because although the race and gender variables are fairly evenly split, the class variable is highly skewed, with 16.3 percent poor and 87.3 percent nonpoor. Not only is this lopsided split statistically problematic, the 16.3 percent (120) of cases spread over multiple social locations no doubt resulted in a number of very small cells. This flaw is a function of the available data rather than the author's approach, however. As in the case of the Hogan and Perrucci (1998) article, *F*-tests are used without *t*-tests for individual coefficients across subgroups. Although this is a shortcoming, the article clearly demonstrates the advantages to be gained from an intersectional approach. Without the analysis of interactions and subgroups, much would have been missed.

In the article by Adler, Koelweijn-Strattner, and Lengermann, the authors do appear to have consciously set out to use the intersectional approach. In part 2, on the use of qualitative methods, I suggested that, often, researchers will have one principal independent variable. Both this article and the previous one demonstrate that at times researchers may have equal interest in several independent variables. The present article focuses on the effects of "human capital, work authority, and marital status" (p. 292) on the incomes of black and white female and male chemists. In cases such as this one, conducting intersectional analysis with interaction terms becomes very difficult if not impossible. The number of interaction terms needed in a model containing race, gender, and two or three independent variables would probably result in such high multicollinearity that the model would be unreliable.

Adler et al. use several strategies to test for interactions across social locations. First, they examine the interaction of gender in a combined model (black and white males and females) with all independent variables and calculate *t*-tests for the differences between men and women (Table 2; p. 295). Because race is not significant in Table 2, the results show differences only across the simple social locations of women and men. Table 3 presents four complex social locations of black women, white women, black men, and white men. *T*-tests of interactions shown in this table are from comparisons across race: black women with white women, and black men with white men, resulting from the authors' choice to run interaction terms for two combined models, one for all women and one for all men with race interactions.

Very few interactions are found to be significant: two gender interactions and one race interaction among women. The authors acknowledge that this may be due in part to the small numbers of black men (167) and black women (51). Another approach would be simply to conduct the analysis in Table 3 for the four race × gender social locations with *F*-tests for each social location and *t*-tests for the coefficients across social locations. Again, this article is a good example of the utility of the intersectional approach for uncovering nuances that would have been lost using more traditional analysis without interactions.

"Race, Gender, and Attitudes toward Gender Stratification," by Emily Kane, explores the "degree of agreement between men and women in their attitudes toward gender stratification" (p. 302). Three areas of gender stratification are explored as dependent variables: work-related gender attitudes, home-related gender attitudes, and attitudes toward gender-related social action. This is a Type I analysis, since race and gender are the principal independent variables with controls for education, age, marital status, presence of children, class, employment status, and income. Kane hypothesizes that the gap in attitudes toward gender stratification is smaller among blacks than among whites and therefore searches for significant race × gender interactions. At the bivariate level she compares the mean attitude scores for each of the four social locations, testing for the significance of difference of means. In Table 2 (p. 308) she presents the results of her multivariate models for the effect of race and gender on the three dependent variables net of the effects of the seven control variables.

Both univariate and multivariate analyses support her hypothesis that views on gender stratification are more congruent among black males and females than among white males and females. In Table 2 she finds a significant interaction at the $p \leq .05$ level for work-related gender attitudes but only a $p \leq .10$ significance level for home-related gender attitudes and attitudes toward gender-related social action. She speculates that the significance level might have been higher had the number of blacks in the sample (62 black men and 80 black women) been larger. Kane summarizes her findings by noting:

> The results of these analyses suggest that race and gender intersect in shaping gender ideologies, and disagreement between the sexes in their attitudes toward gender stratification is greater among whites than among blacks. In addition, the greater agreement evident among black respondents tends to represent a shared *critical* interpretation of greater inequality. (p. 309)

Predictors of Fear of Criminal Victimization at School Among Adolescents

DAVID C. MAY
Indiana University—Purdue University Fort Wayne, Fort Wayne, Indiana, USA

R. GREGORY DUNAWAY
Mississippi State University, Mississippi State, Mississippi, USA

ADDRESS. *Correspondence to:*
DAVID C. MAY, *Indiana University—Purdue University Fort Wayne, School of Public and Environmental Affairs, 2101 Coliseum Boulevard East, Fort Wayne, IN 46805, USA. E-mail: mayd@ipfw.edu.*

Adolescent crime at school, as well as adolescent fear of crime at school, have increasingly become serious social problems. Although many studies have been conducted examining the predictors of fear of crime among adults in various settings, fear of criminal victimization among adolescents at school has been

Appreciation is extended to the Mississippi Crime and Justice Research Unit at the Social Science Research Center, Mississippi State University, for access to the data used in this study. These data were collected under a grant to the Social Science Research Center by the Division of Public Safety Planning, Mississippi Department of Public Safety.

practically ignored. Using a representative sample of 742 high school students from a southeastern state, this study examined the predictors of adolescent fear of crime at school in an attempt to determine whether they are similar to predictors of adult fear of crime. Results indicate that, although the predictors of fear among adolescents are, in many cases, similar to those of adults, there are important differences. As expected, youths with lower levels of perceived safety at school and youths who perceive their neighborhoods as exhibiting signs of incivility were more likely to be fearful of criminal victimization at school Interestingly, however, there were important differences between adolescents and adults regarding the effects of race, gender, and victimization experience and fear of crime. The results from this study indicate that the effects of race and victimization experience on fear of crime vary by gender: Namely, Black males were more fearful than White males, and female victims of crime were more fearful than females who had not been victimized by crime. This study suggests that the phenomena that underlie fear of crime among adults are somewhat different than those of adolescents.

In 1998, the United States witnessed horrific shootings at schools across the country. Despite recent reports that the crime rate has slightly decreased (Federal Bureau of investigation 1999), crimes such as these continue to create an impression among the general public that violence is rampant. Thus, in the face of statistics showing that violent crime rates are receding from previous highs, Americans are increasingly wary and, in many cases, continue to be fearful of crime and violence.

Part of this wariness and fear may be attributable to the fact that the crime rate, although decreasing slightly overall, continued until very recently to rise among adolescents (Maguire and Pastore 1996). Further, in 1986, firearms became the second leading cause of death among youths aged 15 to 19 (Fingerhut, Ingram, and Feldman 1992) and are now the leading cause of death for Blacks and Hispanics (both male and female) and the second leading cause of death for Whites in that same age group (Federal Interagency Forum on Child and Family Statistics 1998).

The growth of criminal activity and violence among youth is particularly pronounced in places where youth spend much of their time—the school. Recent homicides in Colorado, Oregon, Virginia, Mississippi, Kentucky, Arkansas, and Pennsylvania schools are unsettling, yet obviously not isolated incidents and appear to be increasing (Arndt 1995). Kachur and his associates (1996), examining school-associated deaths between 1992 and 1994, uncovered 85 deaths resulting from interpersonal violence. Furthermore, it appears that the problem of school violence, and particularly the problem of weapons at school that aggravate the violence, is not going away. Of high school students, 18.3 percent admitted that they have carried a weapon of some sort to school in the past 30 days; 5.9 percent indicated that the weapon was a firearm (Kann et al. 1998). Additionally, almost 1 in 25 students (4.2 percent) was victimized by a violent crime at school in 1995, an increase of over 20 percent since 1989 (Chandler et al. 1998).

Given the likelihood of being exposed to crime and violence at school—both directly and indirectly—it is somewhat surprising that little attention has been paid to understanding the extent to which youth fear crime, particularly in the school environment, and what factors contribute to such fears. In an extensive review of the fear-of-crime literature, Hale (1996) noted that children and adolescents have generally been neglected by fear-of-crime researchers and advocated that fear of criminal victimization among these groups be an "... important research priority" (Hale 1996, 100).

With the recent media attention dedicated to violent crime and its implications on the school setting, it is crucial that social scientists examine the impact that violent crime has had on adolescents, particularly in the places where they spend most of their time—schools. Thus, the purpose of this study was to examine determinants of fear of criminal victimization among adolescents at school to determine if the predictors of fear of criminal victimization (gender, race, etc.) among adolescents are the same as those among adults.

Adult fear of crime

Research ascertaining the extent and the determinants of fear of crime has become a substantial area of study within the field of criminology. In fact, studies examining fear of crime date back more than three decades. Some scholars have even argued that fear of crime is a more severe problem than crime itself (Clemente and Kleiman 1976). Since its inception, the General Social Survey has asked respondents, "Is there any area right around here—that is, within a mile—where you would be afraid to walk alone at night?" In 1994, 47 percent of respondents answered yes, the highest percentage responding affirmatively since 1983 (Maguire and Pastore 1996, 151). Even though there is some controversy over whether this question is a valid measure of fear of crime (see Ferraro 1995), Americans are experiencing heightened anxiety about their personal safety. This concern about safety and potential criminal victimization has dramatically affected the lives of many people. Fearful individuals may not travel at night or may avoid certain areas that they consider "dangerous," and they may engage in myriad other avoidance behaviors and adaptive strategies (see Hale 1996 and Ferraro 1995 for review). Further, fear of crime may contribute to a host of negative psychological states (Hale 1996).

In addition to the research examining consequences of fear of crime, a large body of research has also examined its predictors. In the 30 years that have passed since fear-of-crime research emerged (Baumer 1978; Clemente and Kleiman 1976, 1977; Garofalo 1979), several variables have consistently been found to be associated with fear of crime among adults.

There are a number of individual level variables that are associated with fear of crime among adults. Numerous studies have consistently indicated that females, non-whites (particularly African Americans and Hispanics), individuals with lower levels of income and education, and urban residents are more likely to experience fear of crime (Baumer 1985; Chiricos, Hogan, and Gertz 1997; Ferraro 1995; Hale 1996; LaGrange and Ferraro 1989; LaGrange, Ferraro, and Supancic 1992; Parker 1988; Parker and Ray 1990; Parker et al. 1993; Thompson, Bankston, and St. Pierre 1989; Warr 1984, 1990; Will and McGrath 1995). Furthermore, there is evidence to suggest that victimization experience and a greater perception of risk of victimization are positively related to fear of crime (Arthur 1992; Chiricos et al. 1997; Ferraro 1995; Hale 1996; Parker and Ray 1990; Thompson et al. 1989).

In recent years, research interest has moved away from individual background factors of fear to more structural-level predictors. The most significant of these is perceived neighborhood incivility. LaGrange, Ferraro, and Supancic (1992) defined incivilities as "low-level breaches of community standards that signal an erosion of conventionally accepted norms and values" (p. 312). Nearly all the studies examining community characteristics and fear of crime have reported a significant positive relationship between incivility and fear of crime (Bursik and Grasmick 1993; Covington and Taylor 1991; Taylor and Covington 1993; Will and McGrath 1995). Some researchers have argued, however, that incivilities indirectly affect fear of crime through elevated perceived risk of criminal victimization (Ferraro 1995; LaGrange et al. 1992; Rountree and Land 1996).

Adolescent fear of crime

Despite the abundance of research examining fear of crime among adults, there has been scant attention paid to examining fear of crime among adolescents. Given research on adult fear of crime that has argued that fear of crime is heightened when individuals perceive themselves to be more vulnerable and likely to be victimized, it is plausible that adolescents might realistically assess their chances of being victimized by crime as being greater and would subsequently experience higher levels of fear of crime than their adult counterparts (Ferraro 1995; Parker 1988).

Nevertheless, the large majority of studies examining adolescent fear of criminal victimization, and particularly adolescent fear of criminal victimization at school, are descriptive, indicating that many students are fearful of being victimized by crime at school but failing to provide explanations for this fear. Approximately 30 percent of junior high students and 22 percent of senior high students were at least sometimes afraid another student would hurt them at school (Parents Resource Institute for Drug Education 1996), and 7 percent of eighth graders reported staying home from school during the previous month out of fear of crime (National Education Goals Panel 1993). Further, 22 percent of students in Grades 3–12 reported that because of violence or the threat of violence at school, they were less eager to attend school (Metropolitan Life 1993).

In addition, it appears that levels of fear of criminal victimization at school are increasing. The proportion of students who "... sometimes or most of the time feared they were going to be attacked or harmed at school" increased 50 percent between 1989 and 1995 and the percentage of students who "... avoided one or more places at school for fear of their own safety" increased 80 percent during the same time period (Kaufman et al. 1998, vii).

Although previous studies have examined the extent of adolescent fear of criminal victimization at school, there has been virtually no research on the determinants of adolescent fear. A review of the literature yielded three published works on the topic (see Hepburn and Monti 1979; Parker and Onyekwuluje 1992; and Wayne and Rubel 1982). The studies conducted by Wayne and Rubel (1982) and Hepburn and Monti (1979) purported to measure fear of crime among students; however, both studies are somewhat dated and include measures of fear of crime that may not be considered conceptually appropriate (see Ferraro and LaGrange 1987; Ferraro 1995).

The remaining study by Parker and Onyekwuluje (1992), though limited, is still the most pertinent to this area. Using a small, urban, and racially homogeneous sample, Parker and Onyekwuluje (1992) determined that none of the demographic variables (i.e., gender, income status, and education) examined in the analysis had a statistically significant effect on fear of crime among adolescents. Clearly, the lack of statistical significance may be due, at least partly, to a small sample size (112 respondents), as well as a lack of variation on some key causal variables. Thus, it is difficult to make definitive statements about juvenile fear of crime on the basis of this study.

In this study, we sought to address this void in the literature. Using a large and representative youth sample, we examined an array of factors that have been found to be related to adult fear of crime. Anticipated determinants include demographic, contextual, and experiential characteristics of adolescents. In the absence of previous research on adolescent fear of crime, we hypothesize that the factors that affect adult fear of crime will be similar for juveniles.

METHOD

The sample

Our sample consisted of 742 public high school students (Grades 10–12). The respondents were part of the 1997 Mississippi High School Youth Survey, conducted by the Mississippi Crime and Justice Research Unit at the Social Science Research Center at Mississippi State University. The data were gathered from schools randomly selected within four geographically distinct areas of the state. Students were administered a survey consisting of items relating to their experiences and attitudes with crime (e.g., criminal victimization and fear of criminal victimization). Of the students eligible to participate in the study, our response rate was 88.6 percent.[1] In general, the sample's demographic characteristics are representative of the adolescent population within the state of Mississippi.

Dependent variable

Fear of criminal victimization at school

Within the literature on fear of crime, a serious debate has been documented regarding how to operationalize the concept of fear of crime. Early measures of fear of crime were critiqued either for being too general or for not distinguishing between one's actual fear of crime and the perception of risk of being victimized by crime (see Ferraro and LaGrange 1987). Ferraro (1995) and Warr (1984) suggested that the most appropriate measures of fear of crime are indices composed of questions asking respondents whether they are fearful or afraid of various scenarios. We thus used a multi-item scale of fear that taps fear of crime in and around the school environment. Students were asked to what extent they agreed or disagreed (coded 6 = *strongly agree,* 5 = *agree,* 4 = *somewhat agree,* 3 = *somewhat disagree,* 2 = *disagree,* and 1 = *strongly disagree*) with the following statements: "I am afraid to go to school because I might become a victim of crime," "I am afraid to stay late after school because I might become a victim of crime," "I am afraid to attend school events (i.e., football games, dances, etc.) because of fights," and "There are places at school where I am afraid to go (i.e., bathroom, cafeteria, gym, etc.) because I might become a victim of crime." We conducted item analysis on the index and used Cronbach's alpha to determine its reliability. The construct demonstrated an internal reliability of .708.

Independent variables

Race or ethnic origin

The respondent's race or ethnic origin was determined by the question "How do you describe yourself?" As over 97 percent of the sample consisted of White or African American respondents, only they were included in the study. Race/ethnicity was coded as African American (1) and White (0). There were 316 (42.6 percent) Blacks and 426 (57.4 percent) Whites in the sample.

Gender

Gender was determined by the question "What is your sex?" Males were coded 1 and females were coded 0. There were 425 females (57.3 percent) and 317 males (42.7 percent) in the sample.

Economic status

The measurement of social class or economic status among adolescents is a controversial issue. Adult fear-of-crime research typically measures socioeconomic status through individual income or education. Given that adolescents do not have income in the same way as would reflect socioeconomic status for adults and that education among adolescents does not vary greatly, adolescent class cannot be directly measured for adolescents. Additionally, adolescent reporting of parental/family income is often unreliable. Braithwaite (1981) contended that defining economic status, particularly among adolescents, should be ascertained by distinguishing between those who fall below the absolute poverty line and those who are above it. Adolescents are generally knowledgeable about whether their family is at or below the poverty line because they are familiar with the receipt of public assistance funds. Consequently, following

[1]To be eligible to be administered the survey, students under the age of 18 had to provide a parental consent form indicating that their parent approved of the child's participation in the study. Of students in the schools, 64.8 percent returned parental consent forms. The response rate was also affected by students who were absent on the day of the survey administration, as well as those who chose not to participate.

Brownfield's (1986) measure, economic status was determined by the question "In the past year, has your family received some form of public assistance (such as WIC, AFDC/welfare, or food stamps)?" There were 121 respondents (16.3 percent) in the sample who responded affirmatively to this question. Those respondents who responded affirmatively were coded 1, and their counterparts who did not respond affirmatively were coded 0.[2]

Grade

Respondent's grade was determined by the question "What grade are you currently in?" Tenth graders were coded 1, 11th graders were coded 2, and 12th graders were coded 3. There were 264 10th graders (36.1 percent), 229 11th graders (31.3 percent), and 239 12th graders (32.7 percent).

Criminal victimization at school

The variable victimization experience was obtained by determining if respondents had ever "had someone threaten to hurt me at school." In those studies where victimization experience exhibited an association with fear of criminal victimization among adults (Arthur 1992; Thompson et al. 1989), victimization by violent crime typically has a stronger association with fear of criminal victimization than victimization by other types of crime. Forty-one percent of the sample (306 respondents) answered that someone had threatened to hurt them at school. Those who answered affirmatively were coded 1, and those who responded negatively were coded 0.

Perceived safety at school

Recently, fear-of-crime researchers have determined that those individuals who perceive themselves to be most at risk are also the most fearful (see Ferraro 1995 for discussion). As we included no indicators that measured perceived risk adequately, we were not able to directly examine this relationship. Instead, borrowing from Williams, Dingh, and Singh (1996), we used a proxy to measure perceived risk. Williams et al. (1996), in their study of defensive adaptations to fear of crime, suggested that overall perceptions about safety and security affected one's level of fear. Thus, we used a perceptual measure assessing adolescents' level of safety in school. The variable perceived safety at school was obtained by examining responses to the statement "I feel safe from crime at my school." The student was given a choice between six Likert-scale responses ranging from *strongly disagree* (coded 6) to *strongly agree* (coded 1). Those who scored high on the variable thus perceived the school environment to be a less secure environment.

Perceived neighborhood incivility

The exogenous variable perceived neighborhood incivility was obtained by constructing an index that used responses to statements concerning how the respondent viewed their neighborhood. Students were asked to what extent they agreed or disagreed (coded *strongly agree* = 6; *agree* = 5; *somewhat agree* = 4; *somewhat disagree* = 3; *disagree* = 2; and *strongly disagree* = 1) with the following statements: "My neighborhood is noisy and the streets always seem to have litter on them," "There are gangs in my neighborhood," "There are drug dealers in my neighborhood," "I feel safe from crime in my neighborhood," and "My neighborhood is getting worse and worse all the time." We conducted item analysis on the index and used Cronbach's alpha to determine its reliability. The construct demonstrated an internal reliability of .825.

Table 1 presents the percentage distributions for the dichotomous variables and the means and standard deviations for the categorical variables and scales used in this study.

---

[2]We also used father's education as a proxy measure for economic status. As the association between father's education level and fear of crime was nonsignificant, we chose to use receipt of public assistance instead.

TABLE 1 ■ TABLE OF MEANS AND STANDARD DEVIATIONS FOR ADOLESCENT SAMPLE

Variable	
Independent	
Race (%)	
Black	42.6
White	57.4
Gender (%)	
Male	42.7
Female	57.3
Grade (%)	
10th	35.6
11th	30.9
12th	32.2
Economic status (%)	
Yes	16.3
No	87.3
Victimization experience	
Yes	41.2
No	58.4
Perceived safety at school	
m	3.16
SD	1.44
Perceived incivility	
m	13.24
SD	6.41
Dependent	
Fear of criminal victimization	
m	7.72
SD	3.43

STATISTICAL METHOD

We examined multivariate models in which adolescent fear of crime was regressed on several independent variables, including race, gender, grade, economic status, victimization experience, perceived neighborhood incivility, and perceived safety at school.[3] As several of the variables in question (perceived safety, perceived neighborhood incivility, and fear of criminal victimization) have been demonstrated to have associations with both race and gender, we used race–gender subgroup mean substitution to allow continuity in sample size across models.

The results of the linear regression model regressing adolescent fear on the independent variables are presented in Table 2. The model explained 17.7 percent of the variation in fear of criminal victimization at school. Perceived neighborhood incivility emerged as the best predictor for adolescent fear of crime, as those who perceived their neighborhoods as exhibiting signs of incivility were more likely to be fearful than those youth who did not have that same perception ($\beta = 0.247, p < .001$). Perceived safety at school was the next best predictor of adolescent fear of criminal victimization at school, as those youths who perceived school as an unsafe environment were more likely to be fearful than those youth who did not have the same perception ($\beta = 0.241, p < .001$). Further, students in lower grades were significantly more fearful than those students in higher grades ($\beta = -0.099, p < .01$). Contrary to research examining fear of crime among adults, gender, race, economic status, and victimization experience did not have a statistically significant effect on adolescent fear of crime at school. Thus, it appears at first glance that the dynamics driving fear of crime among adolescents may be somewhat different than those driving fear of crime among adults.

The results presented in Table 2 indicate that gender and race, two of the strongest predictors for adult fear of crime, have nonsignificant associations with fear of crime among adolescents. As indicated by previous adult fear-of-crime research, race and gender also tend to be associated

[3]Adolescent fear of crime at school was also regressed on a number of community contextual variables (i.e., percentage poor, percentage Black, school size, and median income). As none of the variables had a statistically significant effect on adolescent fear of crime at school, they are not included in the models in this study.

TABLE 2 IMPACT OF PERCEIVED SAFETY AT SCHOOL ON ADOLESCENT FEAR OF CRIME CONTROLLING FOR PRIOR CRIMINAL VICTIMIZATION, PERCEIVED NEIGHBORHOOD INCIVILITY, AND SELECTED BACKGROUND VARIABLES

Variable	B	*SE*	β	*t*
Black	.334	.272	.048	.221
Male	−.236	.236	−.034	.318
Poor	−.325	.333	−.035	.328
Grade	−.415	.141	−.099	.003
Perceived neighborhood incivility	.132	.021	.247	.000
Victimization experience	.374	.236	.054	.113
Perceived safety at school	.573	.083	.241	.000
Constant	4.830	.472		.000

NOTE. $N = 742$, $F(7,734) = 22.577$, $p < .001$; $R^2 = .177$.

with both neighborhood incivility and perceived risk (see Ferraro 1995). Consequently, the lack of a significant association between race or gender and adolescent fear of crime may be the result of an interaction between these variables and some of the other predictor variables. To check for possible interaction effects, we computed a number of product terms and analyzed them as to their impact on fear of crime. Though not presented here, the results revealed that there were no statistically significant interaction effects between either race or gender with economic status, respondent's grade, victimization experience, perceived neighborhood incivility, or perceived safety at school.

The analysis did, however, reveal a statistically significant interaction effect between race and gender. The results of the linear regression model regressing adolescent fear of crime on perceived safety at school, perceived neighborhood incivility, the demographic variables, and the product term representing the interaction between race and gender are presented in Table 3. With the addition of the product term to the model, the explained variation in fear of crime

TABLE 3 IMPACT OF GENDER–RACE INTERACTION ON ADOLESCENT FEAR OF CRIME CONTROLLING FOR PERCEIVED SAFETY AT SCHOOL, PRIOR VICTIMIZATION EXPERIENCE, PERCEIVED NEIGHBORHOOD INCIVILITY, AND SELECTED BACKGROUND VARIABLES

Variable	B	*SE*	β	*t*
Black	−.122	.335	−.018	.716
Male	−.692	.306	−.100	.024
Poor	−.245	.334	−.026	.462
Grade	−.423	.141	−.101	.003
Perceived neighborhood incivility	.127	.021	.238	.000
Victimization experience	.394	.235	.056	.094
Perceived safety at school	.577	.083	.242	.000
Race × Gender interaction term	1.101	.473	.123	.020
Constant	5.071	.482		.000

NOTE. $N = 742$, $F(8,733) = 20.549$, $p < .001$; $R^2 = .183$.

among the adolescents in this sample increased to 18.3 percent. Perceived safety at school became the best predictor of fear of crime, as those who perceived their schools to be unsafe environments continued to be significantly more likely to be fearful than those youth who did not have that same perception ($\beta = 0.242$, $p < .001$). Those adolescents who perceived their neighborhoods as exhibiting signs of incivility continued to be significantly more fearful of crime than those adolescents who did not ($\beta = 0.238$, $p < .001$), whereas youths from lower grades remained significantly more fearful than their counterparts from higher grades ($\beta = 0.101$, $p < .01$). With the addition of the product term to the model, the effect of gender ($\beta = -0.100$, $p < .05$) became statistically significant, with females more likely to be fearful.

To further explore the interaction between race and gender, we analyzed separate models for males and females. Table 4 includes the effects of the predictor variables for both male and female adolescent fear of crime. With regard to race, it appears that the race effect is only significant for male adolescent fear of crime. Specifically, Black males are more fearful than White males. Additionally the analysis revealed varying effects between predictors of male and female fear of crime at school. Specifically, males in lower grades were significantly more likely to be fearful, whereas the effect of grade on fear of criminal victimization at school was not statistically significant for females. Additionally, prior victimization experience and perceived safety at school were found to significantly affect female adolescent fear but not male adolescent fear. Neighborhood incivility continued to be a significant predictor of both male and female adolescent fear of crime.

Discussion

Fear of crime, as a research topic, has enjoyed a high level of interest among criminologists and criminal justice policy analysts and practitioners.

TABLE 4 ■ Impact of Perceived Safety at School, Prior Victimization, Perceived Neighborhood Incivility, and Selected Background Variables on Adolescent Fear of Crime by Gender

Variable	B	*SE*	β	*t*
Black	−.212	.346	−.030	.542
Poor	−.026	.409	−.003	.949
Grade	−.169	.185	−.040	.362
Perceived incivility	.113	.028	.203	.000
Victimization experience	.623	.310	.087	.045
Perceived safety at school	.877	.109	.364	.000
Constant	3.692	.603		.000
Black	1.096	.427	.161	.011
Poor	−.512	.561	−.049	.360
Grade	−.764	.212	−.189	.000
Perceived incivility	.134	.032	.263	.000
Victimization experience	.042	.351	.006	.906
Perceived safety at school	.174	.125	.074	.164
Constant	6.331	.699		.000

NOTE. For females, $N = 425$. $F(6,418) = 20.711$, $p < .001$, $R^2 = .229$.
For males, $N = 317$, $F(6,316) = 11.071$, $p < .001$, $R^2 = .176$.

Although much is known regarding patterns and trends of fear of crime, as well as the correlates of individual fear of crime, the vast majority of research on fear of crime has focused on adult populations. Thus, despite this plethora of research, very little is known about fear of crime among adolescents. We find this a peculiar omission in the literature given that youth are much more likely to actually experience crime through participation, victimization, and observation.

The purpose of this study was to partially address this void in the literature by examining factors that may be linked to adolescent fear of crime. Guided by research on the determinants of adult fear of crime, we examined the effect of a set of factors on adolescent fear, including both background and experiential and perceptual measures. Using a large and representative sample of Mississippi youth, we assessed the impact of selected background and perceptual variables on fear of crime among adolescents.

Our findings suggest that there is a great deal of similarity in the determinants that affect both adult and adolescent fear of crime. Specifically, adolescents who perceive their immediate community environment as exhibiting signs of incivility are likely to have higher levels of fear. Further, adolescent fear of crime was positively affected by perceived safety at school—a proxy for perceived risk of victimization. Both neighborhood incivility and perceived risk have been consistently shown to affect adult fear of crime (see Ferraro 1995 for review). Additionally, when controlling for a gender-race interaction, females were found more likely to be fearful of crime. Typically, research on adult fear of crime has found that females have greater levels of fear.

On the other hand, actual criminal victimization, a significant predictor for adult fear of crime in many studies, was found not to demonstrate a significant effect on adolescent fear of crime in the pooled sample. Also, unlike previous research on fear of crime, socioeconomic status was not found to affect adolescent fear. This finding may, as intimated earlier, be more of a result of how juvenile economic status was measured rather than a unique attribute of juvenile fear of crime. Finally, the variable of grade in school was found to be inversely related to fear of crime. In other words, adolescents were less likely to fear crime as they matriculated through high school.

Our research also suggests that male and female adolescent fear is influenced differently. The effect of race operates differently for males and females. We find that African American male adolescents were more fearful of crime at school. On the other hand, no race effect was witnessed for females. This study also uncovered that although previous victimization experience was not significant in the pooled sample, it did have a statistically significant impact on female fear of crime. Further, perception of safety was found to be an important factor in predicting female, but not male, fear of crime.

The differential effects of victimization and safety by gender may be a result of a specific type of crime that is both feared and experienced more by females. In fact, some have argued that the specific fear of rape by women is the dominant factor that explains gender differences for fear of crime (Ferraro 1995; Warr 1990). Though our measures of both fear of crime and victimization experience did not specifically ask about sexual assault, it is possible that women may be taking into account that particular offense.

Ferraro (1995) suggested that the effect of victimization by crime may be different for females than for males. Female victims of crime, no matter what type of criminal victimization they are exposed to, may realize that criminal victimization makes them particularly vulnerable to rape. Whether women are victims of rape or some other crime, this victimization often forces women to realize that they are particularly vulnerable to sexual assault, a vulnerability not often faced by male victims of crime. According to Gordon and Riger (1989) and Ferraro (1995), this shadow of sexual assault may cause particular emotional damage for female crime victims that often endures for years. This emotional damage resulting from victimization by crime may cause female victims to have subsequently greater levels of fear of crime and to react to that fear in different ways; Thompson, Bankston, and St. Pierre (1991) demonstrated that, among adult females, victims of crime are more likely to own handguns than their nonvictim counterparts. Although this study failed to examine gun possession among females, it is quite possible that the emotional turmoil caused by victimization among adult females is similar among adolescents, thus explaining the differential effect of victimization by gender in this study.

Generally, our overall findings suggest that factors that affect adult fear of crime are also important for adolescent fear. Further, these initial results do tend to lend support to the social vulnerability thesis, which argues that those who are regularly exposed to the threat of criminal victimization suffer severe social consequences, one of which is a heightened level of fear of crime (Rohe and Burby 1988). Those who perceive school as an unsafe environment and perceive their neighborhood as a potentially dangerous environment may experience a heightened sense of vulnerability, and, in turn, this vulnerability may translate to higher levels of fear. Moreover, previous work has suggested that women view themselves as more vulnerable to victimization (see Ferraro 1995 for review). Our finding that Black males are more likely to be fearful of crime is consistent with actual victimization patterns that indicate that young Black males have the highest rate of criminal victimization (U.S. Department of Justice 1996). Further, the effects of grade also support the social vulnerability argument. Here, presumably, younger adolescents have higher levels of fear. Clearly, it can be argued that younger adolescents may perceive themselves as being more vulnerable to a number of victimizations, from minor hazing by upperclassmen to more serious victimization.

We began this study by noting that relatively little is known about the factors that contribute to adolescent fear of crime. This study has intimated that fear of crime, whether adolescent or adult, shares many of the same predictors. Still, this study was based on data that may not be generalizable to adolescent populations outside of the state of Mississippi. Therefore, additional studies on adolescent fear should seek to replicate these findings. In addition, other factors that affect adolescent fear of crime must be examined. Our models only accounted for a modest amount of variation in adolescent fear. Given that our study concentrated on school fear, as well as experiences within the school context, it would, perhaps, be useful to examine victimization experiences and safety perceptions in a larger context. Fear of crime within school is only one dimension of overall adolescent fear. Thus, fear of crime in other environments is likely to affect specific fears. Further, attention needs to be paid to the cultural context of adolescents and its relationship to fear of crime. Popular culture and media directed specifically at adolescents often contains violent content that may raise fears about being victimized. Finally, fear-of-crime research in general may want to consider a life-course approach in order to understand when fear of crime develops in individuals and whether fear of crime is constant across one's life span.

References

Arndt, Randolph C. 1995. *School Violence in America's Cities.* Washington, DC: National League of Cities.

Arthur, John A. 1992. "Criminal Victimization, Fear of Crime, and Handgun Ownership Among Blacks: Evidence from National Survey Data." *American Journal of Criminal Justice* 16(2):121–141.

Baumer, Terry L. 1978. "Research on Fear of Crime in the United States." *Victimology* 3(3,4):254–64.

———. 1985. "Testing a General Model of Fear of Crime: Data from a National Sample." *Journal of Research in Crime and Delinquency* 22(3):239–55.

Braithwaite, John. 1981. "The Myth of Social Class and Criminology Reconsidered." *American Sociological Review* 46:36–57.

Brownfield, David. 1986. "Social Class and Violent Behavior." *Criminology* 24:421–37.

Bursik, Robert J., Jr., and Harold G. Grasmick. 1993. *Neighborhoods and Crime: The Dimensions of*

Effective Community Control New York: Lexington Books.

Chandler, Kathryn A., Christopher D. Chapman, Michael R. Rand, and Bruce M. Taylor. 1998. *Students' Reports of School Crime: 1989 and 1995.* (NCES 98-241/NCJ-169607), Washington, DC: U.S. Departments of Education and Justice.

Chiricos, Ted, Michael Hogan, and Marc Gertz. 1997. "Racial Composition of Neighborhood and Fear of Crime." *Criminology* 35(1):107–31.

Clemente, Frank and Michael Kleiman. 1976. "Fear of Crime among the Aged." *The Gerontologist* 16(3):207–10.

———. 1977. "Fear of Crime in the United States: A Multivariate Analysis." *Social Forces* 56(2):519–31.

Covington, Jeanette and Ralph B. Taylor. 1991. "Fear of Crime in Urban Residential Neighborhoods: Implications of Between- and Within-Neighborhood Sources for Current Models." *Sociological Quarterly* 32(2):231–49.

Federal Bureau of Investigation. 1999. *Crime in the United States—1998.* Washington, DC: U.S. Department of Justice.

Federal Interagency Forum on Child and Family Statistics. 1998. *America's Children: Key National Indicators of Well-Being.* Washington, DC: U.S. Government Printing Office.

Ferraro, Kenneth F. 1995. *Fear of Crime: Interpreting Victimization Risk.* Albany: State University of New York Press.

Ferraro, Kenneth and Randy LaGrange. 1987. "The Measurement of Fear of Crime." *Sociological Inquiry* 57(1):70–101.

Fingerhut, Lois A., Deborah D. Ingram, and Jacob J. Feldman. 1992. "Firearm and Nonfirearm Homicides among Persons 15 Through 19 Years of Age." *Journal of the American Medical Association* 267(22):3048–53.

Garofalo, James. 1979. "Victimization and the Fear of Crime." *Journal of Research in Crime and Delinquency* 16(1):80–97.

Gordon, Margaret T. and Stephanie Riger. 1989. *The Female Fear.* New York: Free Press.

Hale, Chris. 1996. "Fear of Crime: A Review of the Literature." *International Review of Victimology* 4:79–150.

Hepbum, John R. and Daniel J. Monti. 1979. "Victimization, Fear of Crime, and Adaptive Responses among High School Students." Pp. 121–32 in *Perspectives on Victimology.* Beverly Hills, CA: Sage.

Kachur, S. Patrick, Gail M. Stennies, Kenneth E. Powell, William Modzeleski, Ronald Stephens, Rosemary Murphy, Marcie-Jo Kresnow, David Sleet, and Richard Lowry. 1996. "School-Associated Violent Deaths in the United States, 1992 to 1994." *Journal of the American Medical Association* 275(22):1729–33.

Kann, Laura, Steven A. Kinchen, Barbara I. Williams, James G. Ross, Richard Lowry, Carl V. Hill, Jo Anne Grunbaum, Pamela S. Blumson, Janet L. Collins, and Lloyd J. Kolbe. 1998. "Youth Risk Behavior Surveillance—United States, 1997." *Morbidity and Mortality Weekly Report* 47(SS-3).

Kaufman, Phillip, Xianglei Chen, Susan P. Choy, Kathryn A. Chandler, Christopher D. Chapman, Michael Rand, and Cheryl Ringel. 1998. *Indicators of School Crime and Safety,* 1998. NCES 98-251/NCJ-172215, Washington, DC: U.S. Departments of Education and Justice.

LaGrange, Randy L. and Kenneth F. Ferraro, 1989. "Assessing Age and Gender Differences in Perceived Risk and Fear of Crime." *Criminology* 27(4):697–719.

LaGrange, Randy L., Kenneth F. Ferraro, and Michael Supancic. 1992. "Perceived Risk and Fear of Crime: Role of Social and Physical Incivilities." *Journal of Research in Crime and Delinquency* 29(3):311–34.

Maguire, Kathleen and Ann L. Pastore, eds. 1996. *Sourcebook of Criminal Justice Statistics, 1994.* Washington, DC: U.S. Department of Justice, Bureau of Justice Statistics.

Metropolitan Life. 1993. *Survey of the American Teacher, 1993: Violence in America's Public Schools.* New York: Louis Harris and Associates.

National Education Goals Panel. 1993. *The National Education Goals Report, 1993.* Washington, DC: National Education Goals Panel.

Parents Resource Institute for Drug Education. 1996. *1995–96 National Summary, Grades 6–12.* Atlanta, GA: Author.

Parker, Keith D. 1988. "Black-White Differences in Perceptions of Fear of Crime." *The Journal of Social Psychology* 128(4):487–98.

Parker, Keith D. and Anne B. Onyekwuluje. 1992. "The Influence of Demographic and Economic Factors on Fear of Crime Among African-Americans." *The Western Journal of Black Studies* 16(3):132–40.

Parker, Keith D. and Melvin C. Ray. 1990. "Fear of Crime: An Assessment of Related Factors." *Sociological Spectrum* 10:29–40.

Parker, Keith D., Barbara J. McMorris, Earl Smith, and Komanduri S. Murty. 1993. "Fear of Crime and the Likelihood of Victimization: A Bi-Ethnic Comparison." *The Journal of Social Psychology* 133(5):723–32.

Rohe, William M. and Raymond J. Burby. 1988. "Fear of Crime in Public Housing."*Environment and Behavior* 20(6):700–20.

Rountree, Pamela Wilcox and Kenneth C. Land. 1996. "Perceived Risk Versus Fear of Crime: Empirical Evidence of Conceptually Distinct Reactions in Survey Data." *Social Forces* 74(4):1353–76.

Taylor, Ralph B. and Jeanette Covington. 1993. "Community Structural Change and Fear of Crime." *Social Problem's* 40(3):374–94.

Thompson, Carol Y. William B. Bankston, and Roberta St. Pierre. 1989. "Parity and Disparity among Three Measures of Fear of Crime: A Research Note." *Deviant Behavior* 13:373–89.

———. 1991. "Single Female–Headed Households, Handgun Possession, and the Fear of Rape." *Sociological Spectrum* 11(3):231–44.

U.S. Department of Justice. 1996. *Criminal Victimization in the United States, 1994.* Bulletin NCJ-158022, Washington, DC: U.S. Department of Justice, Bureau of Justice Statistics.

Warr, Mark. 1984. "Fear of Victimization: Why Are Women and the Elderly More Afraid?" *Social Science Quarterly* 65:681–702.

———. 1990. "Dangerous Situations: Social Context and Fear of Victimization." *Social Forces* 68(3): 891–907.

Wayne, Ivor and Robert J. Rubel. 1982. "Student Fear in Secondary Schools." *Urban Review* 14(3):197–237.

Will, Jeffry A. and John H. McGrath III. 1995. "Crime, Neighborhood Perceptions, and the Underclass: The Relationship Between Fear of Crime and Class Position." *Journal of Criminal Justice* 23(2):163–76.

Williams, J. Sherwood, B. Krishna Dingh, and Betsy B. Singh. 1996. "Urban Youth, Fear of Crime, and Resulting Defensive Actions." *Adolescence* 29(114):323–31.

The Intersection of Race and Gender Among Chemists

*Assessing the Impact of Double Minority Status on Income**

MARINA A. ADLER
University of Maryland Baltimore County

GIJSBERTA J. KOELEWIJN-STRATTNER
MACRO International Inc.

JOSEPH J. LENGERMANN
University of Maryland College Park

This study assesses the income attainment of African American women relative to that of three race/gender groups (white women, African American men, white men) among industrial chemists, using the

*Earlier versions of this paper were presented at the annual meetings of the American Sociological Association in 1991 and the Southwestern Sociological Association in 1993. We thank the American Chemical Society for the use of the 1985 Survey of Members' Salary and Employment Status. We appreciate the assistance of Janet Hunt, Joan Kahn, Stanley Presser, Reeve Vanneman, Julie Ann Weeks and several anonymous reviewers. The Computer Science Center at the University of Maryland provided funds and facilities for the analysis. Please address all correspondence to Marina A. Adler, Department of Sociology, University of Maryland Baltimore County, Baltimore, MD 21228-5398.

"The Intersection of Race and Gender Among Chemists: Assessing the Impact of Double Minority Status on Income" by Marina A. Adler, Gijsberta J. Koelewijn-Strattner, and Joseph J. Lengemann *Sociological Focus,* Vol. 28, No. 3, August 1995: 245–259.

American Chemical Society (ACS) member survey. Regression models including education, professional work experience, work authority and marital status predict the annual income of the four race/gender groups. The findings indicate that in this sample of chemists, African American women earn on average less than white women, black men and white men. The main disadvantage experienced by black women relates to income returns to authority: compared with white men, African American women (and women in general) continue to receive significantly less income for authority positions. In addition, within the ACS membership, gender seems to be a larger "liability" for income attainment than race, and being married is more advantageous to men than to women.

Despite civil rights efforts and affirmative action programs, race and gender inequality remain evident in American labor market statistics in general and in the professions in particular. In 1990, 11.2 percent of all African American[1] female workers and 15.6 percent of all white female workers were employed in "professional specialties" (Ries and Stone 1992). Blacks continue to be marginalized in the elite professions (Collins 1989; Cappell 1990) and men in power positions still outearn their female counterparts (Reskin and Ross 1992). While the overall rate of growth of women in the professions was slower than their increase in the total labor force, the number of black female professionals grew faster because of their originally small numbers (Sokoloff 1988, 1992). Despite these increases in numbers, however, Higginbotham (1987) found evidence of continued racial segregation among professional women. Census data also reflect that the gains made by women in male-dominated professions, such as law, medicine, chemistry, engineering and pharmacy, have been overestimated and that African American women remain particularly under-represented in these professions (Sokoloff 1988, 1992). Sokoloff (1988, 1992) used an "Index of Representation" to demonstrate that of all four race/gender groups, the proportion of black women in male-dominated professions relative to their numbers in the labor force has improved the least between 1960 and 1980. Even in 1990, only 8 percent of all engineers were women in general and only 0.1 percent were black women (Ries and Stone 1992).

Black female professionals face barriers related to hiring and promotion practices in "white-defined" institutions (Greene 1991; Essed 1992; Merritt and Reskin 1992). In addition to these proportional and job-advancement disadvantages, black professional women may also experience income disadvantages. One way to estimate black women's status in white male-dominated professions is to focus on earnings differences by gender and race within a particular field, such as chemistry. In doing so, our study evaluates the applicability of two previously used concepts, i.e., "double jeopardy" (or double bind) and "double negative" (or two-for-one), in explaining race- and gender-related income variation among industrial chemists. These approaches provide conflicting arguments and evidence regarding the effect of double minority status on black women's position in the economy. Specifically, this study assesses the income attainment of black women compared with that of white women and with that of men in a relatively homogenous group of professionals, i.e., chemists.

According to Sokoloff's (1988) definition, chemistry remains a male-dominated profession because it consists of fewer than 20 percent women. Data from the American Chemical Society (ACS) allow us to assess the combined effects of race and gender on the financial rewards of non-academic chemists. The selection of one particular male-dominated profession (membership of the ACS) for the present analysis controls for the effects of any unique cultures that are established within the various professions. While research exists on minority women in law, medicine and sociology (Epstein 1973; Kulis and Miller 1988; Merritt and Reskin 1992) or professions in general (Sokoloff 1988, 1992), in-depth studies of minority women in the natural sciences are still quite rare, mainly due to their low numbers in these occupations (Collins and Matyas 1985; Sokoloff 1988, 1992). Little is known about women and minority scientists working outside of academia. The American Chemical Society's data offer a unique opportunity to examine industrial scientists rather than academics. This is of particular relevance since about 80 percent of the full-time employed ACS members work in industry and the variation of incomes is greater among industrial chemists than among academics (ACS 1986).

FRAMEWORKS FOR THE EFFECTS OF DOUBLE MINORITY STATUS

Most researchers agree that African American women as a group tend to be concentrated near the bottom of the American reward structure: their average earnings are below those of white women, black men and white men (Wallace 1980; King 1988; Almquist 1989). It is possible that the combination of two ascribed statuses (being both black and female) accounts for the disadvantaged position of African American women in the workplace. The terms "double jeopardy" (Beale 1970) and "double bind" (Anderson 1988; Almquist 1989) describe the disadvantages black women face in the labor market based on their double minority status (King 1988). This view has been applied, implicitly or explicitly, to explain the status of black women at all occupational levels, including professional occupations.

The literature on labor markets and occupations, studies about white male-dominated professions and research on the social context of the workplace contain extensive empirical evidence for the double jeopardy argument. Thus, Cotton (1988) argues that African American women are undervalued in the labor market, although this may be attributed more to their gender than to their race. Other researchers, using varying criteria and studying different occupational groups (Lorber 1984a; Andersen 1988; Sokoloff 1988, 1992; Almquist 1989; McIlwee and Robinson 1992; Merritt and Reskin 1992), show that black professional women suffer from the same effects of discrimination, based on race and gender, as black women in other occupations.

While it is assumed that the reward structure of science occupations is based on universal standards and norms, recent literature suggests that careers are greatly influenced by organizational dynamics (Bielby 1991). Hence, Fox (1991) points out that in corporations, white men are the dominant group both in terms of organizational culture and numbers. Empirical findings consistent with the "double jeopardy view" indicate that once a woman or a black person enters a white male-dominated profession, s/he faces barriers, such as exclusion from the informal structure of the profession (Reskin 1980; Blackwell 1981; Lorber 1984a; McIlwee and Robinson 1992). The so-called "old boys' network" in general, and in non-traditional occupations in particular, encourages a culture of white-male styles of interaction, which reflects gender-based power relations within organizations (McIlwee and Robinson 1992). Cappell (1990) and Collins (1989) extend this argument at the structural level and demonstrate that race-based power relations are maintained for lawyers and corporate managers. Collins (1989) points out that affirmative action and civil rights pressures have not led to the assimilation of blacks in the professions, but rather have "created a highly visible but economically vulnerable black elite" (1989, p. 317), whose attainment occurs within race-conscious systems. Consequently, since women and blacks do not "fit" into the cultural setting of a white male-dominated professional environment, they encounter problems in advancing in their careers (Blackwell 1981). It is reasonable to expect that the double minority status of black women may make them especially vulnerable within white male-defined institutional cultures (see Essed 1992).

The distinct but related "tokenism" approach advanced by Kanter (1977a) stresses the importance of the numerical size of various groups within the work organization. Research indicates that minority attainment is partly an outcome of the social context of the workplace and that underrepresentation in majority-dominated groups impinges on professional advancement. Specifically, several researchers demonstrate that it is possible for women and minorities to do better when they are not handicapped by low numbers. Thus, higher representation of African Americans on the university faculty seems related to better minority student performance in the sciences (Garrison 1987), and blacks attending predominantly black universities tend to be academically more successful than black students attending predominantly white institutions (Berryman 1983).

Although Kanter (1977b) tested her tokenism theory exclusively on white women, her theory may apply to the case of black women professionals because double minority status may increase the likelihood that a person will be a numeric minority in a professional setting. Greene (1990) has applied the tokenism concept to African American female law professors and found that the combination of race and gender in the social context of the workplace affects a black professional women's career adversely. Consequently, "token status" and double minority status often coincide and both may create disadvantages for the individual vis-à-vis the racial and numeric majority.

Both Kanter's theory of tokenism and the notion of double jeopardy would lead us to speculate that minority women face even more difficulties than white women or black men in white male-dominated professions, such as chemistry. The conceptual arguments and evidence suggesting that black women tend to be hired at lower entry levels and are less likely to advance to the higher echelons of professions than other race/gender groups lead us to expect that African American female chemists will earn less than white women, African American males and white male chemists.

In contrast to the double jeopardy argument, the "double negative view" (Epstein 1973) has received less attention by researchers since the 1970s, but seems to remain common in popular discourse. This view directly contradicts the double jeopardy idea by suggesting that African American professional women can benefit from their joint ascribed status (Epstein 1973). Black women's assumed advantage at work is attributed to their greater visibility relative to other groups. Consequently, contrary to Kanter's theory of tokenism, Epstein argues that in the social context of the workplace, their high visibility (as "tokens") and their low perceived threat result in advantages for black female professionals. In addition, black women's double minority status becomes a positive factor for their career development because they face fewer barriers in a male-dominated profession than white women. In her controversial study of black professionals, Epstein (1973) explains that this assumed advantage arises from the higher market price black women can exact based on their uniqueness or rarity. In terms of the organizational dynamics emphasized by Epstein, double minority status results in certain kinds of advantages while simultaneously decreasing some of the disadvantages often experienced by white women. For example, African American women are less likely to be perceived as challenging to the traditional lifestyle of white male professionals and they are less likely to be seen as sex objects.

It has also been suggested that employers, under pressure by affirmative action legislation, are inclined to hire African American women in order to fill two "quotas" (minorities and women) with one person (see Sokoloff 1992). Therefore, black women could also be promoted faster to higher authority positions in organizations than white women, thereby attaining higher incomes.

However, these arguments have been criticized as the "fallacy of double advantage" because they remain unsupported by empirical evidence (Sokoloff 1992; McGuire and Reskin 1993). Research suggests that women and racial minorities are able to translate higher authority and autonomy on the job into higher monetary rewards, albeit not necessarily at the same rate as white men (Kluegel 1978; Roos 1981; Adler 1990; McGuire and Reskin 1993). While Reskin and Ross (1992) show that among all groups of managers, authority generally increases wages, Adler (1993) and Spaeth (1985) demonstrate that sex differences in access to authority persist. Thus, women, especially minority women, may have less access to authority and/or gain lower income returns for authority than white men. McGuire and Reskin's recent research on the income and authority attainment of employees helps to "dispel the myth that Black women benefit from their dual-minority status" (1993, p. 500). Their results show that African American women gained lower payoff for their human capital and authority.

In addition to the assumed positive effect of organizational dynamics, various demographic factors are often cited by supporters of the double negative hypothesis. African American women are less likely to be married than white women and if married, they tend to have husbands who are similarly disadvantaged by race discrimination in education, job mobility and salary. Reskin (1980) argues that societal norms regard white married women as more committed to their families than to their jobs. This "cultural mandate," as Lorber (1984b) puts it, influences the perception of employers and co-workers. Although white women are taking increasingly less time off to raise a family (Presser 1989), black women have historically had more continuous careers (Wallace 1980) and have taken less time off to raise children than white women (Malson 1983). Assuming that career commitment pays off equally for all women, black women should earn higher incomes than white women.

Apart from not having parity in terms of population share or labor force participation rates in the professions, an income gap persists between black women and the other groups in chemistry (ACS 1986). Given the fact that careers are influenced by organizational dynamics, which in turn are affected by the dominance of white males in the high-prestige professions, we would expect white male chemists' income to be higher than that of white and black women. We follow McGuire and Reskin's (1993) strategy of using white males as the standard of comparison to assess the degree of disadvantage. An explanation of the income gap has to take into account possible differences in human capital (education and experience), authority position and marital status. Based on the reviewed frameworks and previous research, we expect men in the male-dominated profession of chemistry to be rewarded more for their human capital and authority position than women, regardless of race. More importantly, although some arguments in the literature suggest the contrary, we expect that, relative to white men, African American female industrial chemists will attain lower monetary gains based on their human capital, work authority and marital status.

DATA, VARIABLES AND METHODS

This study is based on data from the ACS's 1985 Comprehensive Salary and Employment Status Survey (ACS 1986). The target population of this survey consists of all non-student ACS members with a U.S. address who were under age 70 and not retired at the time of the survey. The total ACS membership in 1985 was 134,019. Of those, 86,609 members met the eligibility criteria of the survey. The response rate for the Comprehensive Salary and Employment Status Survey was 49.2 percent. The complete data set consists of 38,906 white and black respondents, 32,918 (84.6 percent) of whom are white males, 344 (.9 percent) African American males, 5,535 (14.2 percent) white females and 109 (.3 percent) African American females. Although the minority sample size is small, it is representative of the total ACS membership, which consists exclusively of professional chemists. The literature suggests that women and minorities are less likely to join professional organizations (Lorber 1984b) and thus, the ACS membership and survey respondent distribution may underestimate the proportion of minorities relative to the total universe of chemists.[2] One may further speculate that those with lower earnings are less likely to belong to professional organizations. While this should affect all race/gender groups, the fact that they are ACS members and responded to the survey could inflate the incomes of minorities in the sample relative to those of minority chemists in general. The final sample used in this analysis is limited to U.S. natives who are employed full-time, are between the ages of 18 and 65 and are non-academic chemists. These restrictions and the listwise deletion of missing data reduce the sample size for all race/gender groups to 18,438 white men, 167 black men, 2,814 white women and 51 black women.[3]

The dependent variable in this analysis is income, which is a continuous variable and is measured as the combination of the base annual salary from the respondent's principal job and any supplemental income from the main employer. Authority at work is operationalized in two ways: The question "Do you have the authority to influence the pay of others?" (1 = yes; 0 = no) assesses the authority to pay and the response to "Do you have the authority to hire, transfer, or remove other employees?" measures the authority to hire (1 = yes; 0 = no).[4] The dummies for gender and race are male (0 = female; 1 = male) and white (0 = black; 1 = white). The analysis will control for individual differences in education and professional and marital experience. Thus, Master's and Bachelor's are dummy variables, indicating whether the respondent's highest degree attained is a B.S, an M.S or a Ph.D. (the omitted comparison category). Professional work experience is measured as the number of years of professional work experience since receiving the B.S. degree, including postdoctoral study. Since there is some evidence in the literature suggesting that the experience of marriage may affect male chemists' and female chemists' careers differently (Reskin, 1980), marital status (ever married = 1; never married = 0) is also included in the analysis.

Both descriptive and multivariate techniques were used to assess the status of non-academic chemists. In order to compare the race/gender groups with respect to the dependent and independent variables in the multivariate models, the descriptive analysis determines bivariate differences via Chi-square and T-tests. Subsequently, Ordinary Least Squares (OLS) regression models by gender and then for each race/gender group estimate the combined effects of the independent variables on income.

Results

Table 1 compares means, standard deviations and percentages for the variables of interest among all four race and gender groups. Differences among the groups are determined by T-tests for continuous variables and by Chi-square tests for categorical variables. Table 1 shows that with regard to the variables of interest, ACS chemists exhibit race/gender patterns similar to those found among Americans in general. On average, male chemists have higher incomes, more authority at work and more professional experience and are more likely to have a Ph.D. than females. Furthermore, men are more likely to be married than women. While white men also exhibit significantly higher average income, more authority to pay, more professional experience and higher educational degrees than black men, no significant racial differences were observed among women. African American female chemists have on average work experience, average income, authority and education similar to their white counterparts. Overall, the race differences among female chemists are much less pronounced than those among male chemists and the gender differences are generally larger

TABLE I ■ MEANS, STANDARD DEVIATIONS AND PERCENTAGES OF SELECTED VARIABLES FOR THE SAMPLE OF NON-ACADEMIC CHEMISTS BY GENDER AND RACE USED IN THE MULTIVARIATE ANALYSES

	Black women	White women	p[a]	White men	Black men	p[b]
Annual income ($)	34,043[c] (13,591)[d]	34,288 (13,528)	NS	48,267 (20,010)	45,088 (17,221)	.05
Professional experience (years)	10.86 (8.14)	10.18 (8.90)	NS	18.06 11.12)	16.58 (9.77)	.01
% authority to hire	20	22	NS	39	32	NS
% authority to pay	31	29	NS	54	46	.05
% ever married	61	69	NS	89	88	NS
% B.S. is highest degree	57	49	NS	30	38	.01
% M.S. is highest degree	26	26	NS	21	25	NS
% Ph.D. is highest degree	17	25	NS	49	37	.001
N	51	2,814		18,438	167	

[a]Significance level of the difference between black women and white women based on t-test (continuous variables) or chi-square test (categorical variables).
[b]Significance level of the difference between black men and white men based on t-test (continuous variables) or chi-square test (categorical variables).
[c]Mean
[d]Standard deviation

than the race differences. In addition, the gender differences within the race groups vary: the gender gap in all variables is much smaller among African Americans than among whites.

The pay gap between white men and the three disadvantaged groups of chemists, expressed as the percentage of the respective groups' income relative to white males' income (computed from the means in Table 1), echoes that which is observed in the general population: While African American and white women earn about 71 percent of white male income, black men receive about 93 percent of white male income. White men clearly had the most professional work experience (about 18 years), compared with about 11 years for black women, 10 years for white women and 17 years for black men. While 39 percent of the white men have the authority to hire, only 20 percent of the African-American women, 22 percent of the white women and 32 percent of the black men have hiring authority. Similarly, while 54 percent of white men have pay authority, only 31 percent of black women, 29 percent of white women and 46 percent of black men have the authority to pay. With respect to qualifications and experience, women also rank lower than men. Only 17 percent of black women, 25 percent of white women and 37 percent of black men hold a Ph.D., compared with 49 percent of the white men. It seems that the recent entry of women into chemistry is responsible for the lower levels of work experience in the field. Nevertheless, the female chemists in this sample are less likely to be married, an indication that women who are pursuing careers in non-traditional fields may preclude or postpone marriage.

The descriptive analysis reveals that women chemists, both black and white, clearly earn less than white male chemists. However, it is important to examine whether the income gap is due to differential returns to human capital (qualifications) and other worker characteristics.[5]

In order to assess the independent effects of these characteristics on income, OLS regression analyses were completed in several steps. First, separate regressions for women and men are presented in Table 2. Second, to test whether any differences were observed in the coefficients predicting female and male chemists' income attainment, a combined multiple regression analysis with gender and gender interactions with all independent variables was performed. Instead of presenting the resulting coefficients for this combined model, the T-scores presented in Table 2 (right column) refer to the T-tests associated with the multiplicative terms of gender with each independent variable.

Table 2 shows that a Doctoral degree (as opposed to a Bachelor's or Master's degree), more professional experience and the authority to influence pay and to hire enhance the income of female and male chemists significantly. In addition, it becomes clear that race does not affect the income of either gender group. The T-test results for the gender interactions show

TABLE 2 ■ Ordinary Least Squares Regression Coefficients of a Model Predicting Income by Gender[a]

	Women		Men		
	b	Beta	b	Beta	T-test[b]
Race	−362 (1497)[c]	−.004	229 (1296)	.001	.28
Master's	−7654*** (565)	−.25	−8755*** (326)	−.18	−1.21
Bachelor's	−12048*** (507)	−.44	−13334*** (292)	−.30	−1.58
Professional experience	546*** (23)	.36	598*** (12)	.33	1.41
Ever married	685 (438)	.02	3431*** (422)	.05	3.56***
Authority to pay	4792*** (631)	.16	6199*** (334)	.15	1.41
Authority to hire	1477* (685)	.05	4213*** (336)	.10	2.52*
Constant	34706		35121		
R-square	.39***		.31***		
N	2,755		18,097		

[a]Non-academics only

[b]T-test for differences between men and women (interaction)

[c]Standard error

*$p < .05$

**$p < .01$

***$p < .001$

that both the gender-authority to hire interaction and the gender-married interaction are statistically significant. That indicates that men gain more income from having authority to hire and from ever having been married than do women. While both genders' incomes benefit from pay authority equally, men gain more income from hiring authority than women. Overall, fewer professionals have the authority to hire (20–39 percent, see Table 1) than the authority to pay (29–54 percent), which signifies (by its rarity) that hiring authority may be associated with a higher position in industrial chemistry. Being "ever married" has a significant positive effect on the income of male ACS chemists but not on that of females. Marriage may enhance men's but not women's ability to devote themselves to career advancement (income attainment). The descriptive comparison showed male chemists, regardless of race, to be more likely to be married than female chemists. Those female chemists who choose both career and marriage do not benefit monetarily. The models explain 31 percent of the variation in income for men and 39 percent for women.

In order to test how the four race and gender groups differ in their income attainment, the same strategy as in Table 2 was followed to produce Table 3. Four separate OLS regressions race-gender groups were generated, and the resulting coefficients are presented. Another regression was performed for the total sample of women (not shown) and the first column of T-values in Table 3 refers to the interaction

TABLE 3 ■ Ordinary Least Squares Regression Coefficients (Unstandardized) of a Model Predicting Income by Race-Gender Group[a]

	Black women	White women	White men	Black men	T-test[b]	T-test[c]
	b	b	b	b		
Master's	−10069	−7732***	−8773***	−9943***	.69	.66
	(5695)	(558)	(320)	(2777)		
Bachelor's	−11975*	−12074***	−13344***	−12308***	.20	.55
	(4899)	(501)	(288)	(2520)		
Professional experience	739**	544***	603***	361**	−.74	1.46
	(255)	23	(12)	(116)		
Ever married	−2024	637	3358***	8083*	.57	−.57
	(3750)	(434)	(413)	(3348)		
Authority to pay	−6286	4975***	6231***	3538	2.29*	.18
	(5818)	(623)	(328)	(2778)		
Authority to hire	6746	1529*	4073***	10506***	−.90	−1.32
	(6911)	(677)	(330)	(2802)		
Constant	37268	34407	35323	34044		
R-square	.30	.39	.32	.41		
Adjusted R-square	.21	.39	.32	.38		
N	51	2.814	18.438	167		

[a]Non-academics only

[b]T-test for differences between black women and white women (interactions)

[c]T-test for differences between black men and white men (interactions)

*$p < .05$

**$p < .01$

***$p < .001$

terms of race with all independent variables among women. The regression for the total male sample produced the second column of T-scores.

When focussing on the results for the two female regressions, Table 3 demonstrates that lacking a Ph.D. affects the income attainment of both groups negatively. The Master's coefficient for black women is statistically significant at $p < .10$. There is no significant difference in the effects of educational degree on income between black and white women (T-tests for "white-Master's" and "white-Bachelor's" are not significant). Professional experience has an equally positive influence on the income of both groups of women. Having authority to influence pay and to hire have significant positive effects on white women's income, but not on black women's income. In fact, the "white-authority to pay" interaction is statistically significant among women, indicating that white women benefit more monetarily from this authority than African American women. The coefficient for the black female sample is negative and one reason for the lack of significance of the relatively large black female coefficients may be the small sample size ($N = 51$), which tends to increase the standard error.

Table 3 also contains the coefficients for the male samples. The patterns for white and African American men are similar in terms of educational attainment and professional experience and echo those found among the women. The effects are positive and no race interactions are observed between black and white men regarding the magnitude of the effects on income. Elaborating the results in Table 2, the experience of marriage enhances both groups of men's earnings equally. The authority to influence pay and to hire has a positive effect on salary for white men. Contrary to the authority to hire, authority to influence pay did not noticeably influence black men's earnings. Nevertheless, as the T-values demonstrate, no race interactions were detected in these effects. The model explains larger amounts of variation in the income attainment of African American men (38 percent), white women (39 percent) and white men (32 percent) than in that of African American women (21 percent).

Discussion

This analysis has focussed on gender and race differences in income among chemists employed in non-academic settings. The results suggest that (a) black women are clearly disadvantaged vis-à-vis white men and that (b) black women chemists are generally not very different in transforming their human capital (education and work experience) into income from their white female counterparts. Nevertheless, the monetary benefits associated with pay authority are larger for white women than for African American women in chemistry, which is evidence supporting the "double jeopardy" view. In other words, even when black women enter positions granting them pay authority, they do not achieve the same financial rewards as white women, or men. White and black women have equally low access to both pay and hiring authority. Since fewer chemists have hiring authority than pay authority, hiring authority may occur at the higher echelons of the organizational hierarchy than pay authority. Once they gain hiring authority, neither group of women is able to benefit monetarily from it to the same extent as men. Thus, gender discrimination prevents black women (just like white women) from gaining access to authority in the same way as men; race discrimination prevents black women from transforming authority to influence pay into income to the same extent as white women; and gender discrimination prevents women of both races from turning hiring authority into income like men. Unlike black women, black men get rewarded for hiring authority like white men. This may indicate that black men are being "rewarded" for their gender (for being similar to white men), rather than black women being "punished" for their race (being different from white women).

This study shows that gender is more important than race to understanding income attainment among chemists. Within the ACS membership, gender clearly is a larger "liability" for income attainment than race. The ACS data contain unequivable evidence of the existence of a large gender income gap among chemists: Women earn between 75 percent and 82 percent of men's income in industry (ACS 1986). Since chemistry is a male-dominated profession, one may speculate that the greater the gender gap, the less the likelihood of the dominant group to "defend their turf" through additional discriminatory practices based on race (see McIlwee and Robinson 1992). The race discrimination against black males may be somewhat reduced by their integration in the "male culture" of the male-dominated occupation, whereas women pose a larger threat in numbers and potential forces of change to this bastion of "male power."

An interesting finding relates to the intersection of employment and family in terms of marital experience and industrial chemists' income attainment. Although marital status does not reduce black or white women's income, men seem actually to benefit financially from the experience of marriage. It could be that in the crucial career making years, women may fall behind at the same time that men are moving ahead (Zuckerman and Cole 1975). Considering the historically less intermittent work careers of African American women, one may expect that their attainment pattern would resemble that of men more than that of white women. Other research confirms that women's higher participation in household maintenance and childrearing explains the lack of professional benefit from marriage (Reskin 1980; Vanek 1980). The perception that women have family obligations affecting their job performance may impinge on their career advancement and their rewards attainment, disregarding race. At the same time, the male "breadwinner" stereotype may reinforce men's income advantage in the professions.

Although black women are by virtue of being female disadvantaged vis-à-vis men, their race presents an additional barrier to their salary attainment in chemistry only with respect to pay authority. However, the combination of being both black and female is definitely not an asset to income attainment. Consequently, this analysis provides more support for the double jeopardy framework than for the double negative view. However, it is possible that African American women experience their double minority status in some situations as double jeopardy and in others as double negative, while in some instances both forces may operate simultaneously. While for some black women professionals being black and female may be a liability, for others this combined status might be an asset. Unfortunately, assessing these complex dynamics for black women is beyond the scope of our analysis. Therefore, it is reasonable to call for a new, more refined approach to provide a better understanding of the status of minority women in chemistry and in other white male-dominated professions. Additional studies based on more representative samples of professionals are needed, particularly in light of recent increase in the number of women in the sciences. It would be of value to investigate to what extent women are able to penetrate the higher echelons of the profession and to assess the interaction of race and gender as women become more established in managerial positions. Future research has to qualitatively assess the organizational, occupational and job task-specific circumstances under which these dynamics are shaped. McIlwee and Robinson's (1992) power analytic framework serves as a starting point because it shows that not race or gender per se, but employer characteristics, employee position and capacity within a profession, as well as the gender composition and culture of work groups, can affect the opportunity structure.

To confirm and expand the results of our research, future studies should attempt to replicate similar analyses in different professions. It is possible that less male-dominated professions incur larger costs for black women relative to white women than more male-dominated professions. White males may fear possible loss of prestige associated with the "intrusion" of white females (larger numbers) more than that of black men and black women. Hence, one could ask whether within white female-dominated occupations race becomes more important because white women fear possible loss of prestige associated with the "intrusion" of black women (larger numbers) more than that of white men or black men. In other words, double minority status may become even more of a liability within female-dominated than within male-dominated professions. Although she did not focus on race, Williams (1995) found that in the nursing profession, men are readily accepted because they serve to increase the occupational prestige. In fact, male nurses were tracked into more "masculine" specialties, which enhanced their income and prestige. This is contradictory to patterns for women in male-dominated professions, who tend to be tracked into more "feminine" specialties, which are usually associated with lower pay and less prestige (Williams 1995).

While the ACS data did not offer conclusive support for a particular theoretical framework, it has generated some new hypotheses and directions for future research. Like previous research in this area, some of the limitations relate to matching available indicators with hypotheses. Research aimed at constructing a new perspective should also incorporate personal interviews with black professional women to assess how they perceive themselves vis-à-vis white women and black and white men. Essed's (1992) work on black women's experiences with racism while working in settings defined by white culture is an excellent start. The women's adjustment to norms and conditions of "white-defined institutional life" are vividly reflected in Essed's interviews detailing "routine" encounters with racism. Nevertheless, integrating the effects of race and gender into a perspective on professional status is complicated by many factors, such as historical differences, socialization patterns, socio-economic structures, the division of household tasks, quality of doctoral training and career interruptions. It is only after the inclusion of these factors that social science can present women in general and African American women in particular with a coherent approach that will enable them to better understand which avenues are available to enter and advance careers in the white male-dominated professions.

Notes

1. In this paper we will use the terms "African American" and "black" interchangeably.
2. ACS statisticians assured as that the proportion of blacks and women in the sample is representative of the membership.
3. Due to the large sample size of the white male sample, analyses were also performed on a random sample of white males ($N = 2{,}000$). We did not find significant differences between the results using the smaller sample of white males and the original sample. In order to reduce the effects of sampling error we report only the findings of the total sample. We can be reasonably sure that the final results are not excessively biased by the large male sample size. Among the 18–65 year old respondents who worked full-time and had data on all other variables in the analysis (28,248 white men, 4,822 white women, 283 black men, and 86 black women) 20 percent (713) white women, 27 percent (61) black men and 20 percent (4,670) white men were later excluded because they were academics.
4. The correlation coefficient (r) between the two authority indicators is 0.66; the analysis was also performed using a combined index, which proved to be a less powerful predictor of income than the separate estimates. Furthermore, the use of two separate variables allows us to capture any qualitative differences between the authority to influence pay and hiring.
5. The combined regression analysis for all race/gender groups (not shown) has demonstrated that gender has a significant independent effect on income. Therefore, separate estimates for women and men are presented in Table 2.

Marina Adler is an Assistant Professor of Sociology at the University of Maryland Baltimore County. Her research areas include gender and race inequality, cross-national work and family issues and the welfare state. She is currently studying the resurgence of xenophobia in Europe and the effects of German unification on East German women's lives.

Gijsberta Koelewijn-Strattner worked as a research analyst with MACRO International Inc. where she was involved with a large-scale government project examining rent control issues. She currently resides in Jakarta. Indonesia, where she works with various Dutch volunteer organizations on programs aimed to improve the lives of women and the poor in Jakarta.

Joseph Lengermann is an Associate Professor and Associate Chair in the Department of Sociology at the University of Maryland College Park. His primary areas of interest include the sociology of work and the sociology of health. Specific current interests focus on health promotion programs in the workplace. He is involved in several education projects concerning the impact of HIV/AIDS in the workplace, both in the Washington, DC area and in Rio de Janeiro, Brazil.

REFERENCES

Adler, Marina A. 1990. *Gender, Income and Power in the Workplace*. Unpublished Doctoral Dissertation. University of Maryland, College Park, MD.

———. 1993. "Gender Differences in Job Autonomy: The Consequences of Occupational Segregation and Authority Position." *The Sociological Quarterly* 34:449–465.

Almquist, Elizabeth M. 1989. "The Experiences of Minority Women in the United States: Intersections of Race, Gender and Class." Pp. 414–445 in *Women: A Feminist Perspective,* edited by Jo Freeman. Mountain View, CA: Mayfield.

American Chemical Society. 1986. "Women Chemists 1985: A Supplementary Report to the ACS's 1985 Survey of Members' Salary and Employment." Washington, DC: ACS Distribution Office.

Andersen, Margaret L. 1988. *Thinking about Women: Sociological Perspectives on Sex and Gender*. New York: MacMillan Co.

Beale, Francia. 1970. "Double Jeopardy: To be Black and Female." Pp. 90–100 in *The Black Woman: An Anthology,* edited by Toni Cade. New York: Mentor Books.

Berryman, Sue E. 1983. *Who Will Do Science: Trends and Their Causes in Minority and Female Representation Among Holder of Advanced Degrees in Science and Mathematics.* New York: Rockefeller Foundation.

Bielby, William T. 1991. "Sex Differences in Careers: Is Science a Special Case?" Pp. 171–187 in *The Outer Circle. Women in the Scientific Community,* edited by Harriet Zackarman, Jonathan R. Cole and John T. Bruer. New York: W.W. Norton & Company.

Blackwell, James E. 1981. *Mainstreaming Outsiders: The Production of Black Professionals.* Bayside: General Hall.

Cappell, Charles L. 1990. "The Status of Black Lawyers." *Work and Occupations* 17:100–121.

Collins, M. and Martha L. Matyas. 1985. "Minority Women: Conquering both Sexism and Racism." Pp. 102–123 in *Women in Science: A Report from the Field,* edited by Jane Kahle. London: Falmar Press.

Collins, Sharon M. 1989. "The Marginalization of Black Executives." *Social Problems* 36:317–331

Cotton, Jeremiah. 1988. "Discrimination and Favoritism in the U.S. Labor Market: The Cost to a Wage Earner of Being Female and White and the Benefit of Being Male and White," *American Journal of Economics* 47:15–28.

Epsteien, Cynthia F. 1973. "Positive Effects of the Multiple Negative: Explaining the Success of Black Professional Women." *American Journal of Sociology* 78:912–935.

Essed, Philomena. 1992. *Understanding Everyday Racism.* Newbury Park, CA: Sage.

Fox, Mary Frank. 1991. "Gender, Environmental Milieu and Productivity in Science." Pp. 188–204 in *The Outer. Circle. Women in the Scientific Community,* edited by Harriet Zuckermen, Jonathan R. Cole and John T. Bruer, New York: W. W. Norton & Company.

Garrison, Howard H. 1987. "Undergraduate Science and Engineering Education for Blacks." Pp.

39–65 in *Minorities: Their Underrepresentation and Career Differentials in Science and Engineering*, Proceedings of a Workshop, edited by Linda S. Dix. Washington, DC: National Academy Press.

Greene, Linda S. 1990. "Tokens, Role Models, and Pedagogical Politics: Lamentations of an African American Female Law Professor." *Berkeley Women's Law Journal* 6:81.

Higginbotham, Elizabeth. 1987, "Employment for Black Professional Women in the Twentieth Century," Pp. 73–91 in *Ingredients for Women's Employment Policy*, edited by Christine Bose and Glenna Spitze, Albany, NY: State University of New York Press.

Kanter, Rosabeth Moss. 1977a. "Numbers: Minorities and Majorities." Pp. 206–242 in *Men and Women of the Corporation*. New York: Basic Books.

———. 1977b. "Some Effects of Proportions on Group Life: Skewed Ratios and Responses to Token Women." *American Journal of Sociology* 84:965–990.

King, Deborah, K. 1988. "Multiple Jeopardy, Multiple Consciousness: The Context of a Black Feminist Ideology." *Signs* 14:42–72.

Kluegel, James, R. 1978. "The Causes and Cost of Racial Exclusion from Job Authority." *American Sociological Review* 43:285–301.

Kulis, Stephen and Karen A. Miller. 1988. "Are Minority Women Sociologists in Double Jeopardy?" *The American Sociologist* 19:323–339.

Lorber, Judith. 1984a. *Women Physicians: Careers, Status and Power*. New York: Tavistock.

———. 1984b. "Trust, Loyalty, and the Place of Women in the Informal Organization of Work," Pp. 370–377 in *Women: A Feminist Perspective*, edited by Jo Freeman, Palo Alto, CA: Mayfield Publishing.

Malson, Micheline Ridley. 1983. "Black Families and Childrearing Support Networks." In *Research in the Interweave of Social Roles: Jobs and Families*. Vol. 3. Greenwich, CT: JAI Press.

McGuire, Gail M. and Barbara Reskin. 1993. "Authority Hierarchies at Work: The Impacts of Race and Sex." *Gender and Society* 7:487–506.

Mcllwee, Judith S. and J. Gregg Robinson. 1992. *Women in Engineering: Gender, Power and Workplace Culture*. Albany, NY: State University of New York Press.

Merritu, Deborah J. and Barbara F. Raskin. 1992. "The Double Minority: Empirical Evidence of a Double Standard in Law School Hiring of Minority Women." *Southern California Law Review* 65:2,299–3,359.

Merritt, Deborah J., Barbara F. Reskin and Michelle Fondell. 1993. "Family, Place and Career: The Gender Paradox in Law School Hiring." *Wisconsin Law Review* 395–463.

Presser, Harriet, S. 1989. "Can We Make Time for Children? The Economy, Work Schedules and Childcare." *Demography* 26:545–561.

Reskin, Barbara, F. 1960. *Sex Differences in the Professional Life Chances of Chemists*, New York: Arno Press.

Reskin, Barbara, F. and Catherine Ross. 1992. "Jobs, Authority, and Earnings among Managers." *Work and Occupations* 19:342–365.

Ries, Pauia and Anne J. Stone, eds. 1992. *The American Woman 1992–1993*. New York: W.W. Norton & Co.

Roos, Patricia. 1981. "Sexual Stratification in the Workplace: Male-Female Differences in Economic Returns to Occupation." *Social Science Research* 10:195–324.

Sokoloff, Natalie, J. 1988. "Evaluating Gains and Losses by Black and White Women and Men in the Professions, 1960–1980." *Social Problems* 35:36–53.

Sokoloff, Netalie, J. 1992. *Black Women and White Women in the Professions: Occupational Segregation by Race and Gender*, 1960–1980. New York: Routledge.

Spaeth, Joe. 1985. "Job Power and Earnings." *American Sociological Review* 50:503–617.

Vanek, Joann. 1980. "Time Spent in Housework." Pp. 82–90 in *The Economics of Women and Work*, edited by Alice H. Amsden. New York: St. Martin Press.

Wallace, Phyllis A. 1980. *Black Women in the Labor Force*. Cambridge, MA: M.I.T. Press.

Williams, Christine L. 1995. "Hidden Advantages for Men in Nursing." *Nursing Administration Quarterly* 19:63.

Zuckerman, Harriet, and Jonathan R. Cole. 1975. "Women in American Science." *Minerva* 13:82–102.

RACE, GENDER, AND ATTITUDES TOWARD GENDER STRATIFICATION*

EMILY W. KANE
University of Wisconsin

This paper addresses the intersection of race and gender in contemporary American society by exploring how one aspect of gender relations, the degree of agreement between men and women in their attitudes toward gender stratification, varies between blacks and whites. Both black men and black women tend to express more criticism in their gender-related attitudes than whites, and the level of agreement between the sexes is greater for blacks. I interpret this greater agreement in the context of the resistance to racial inequality, levels of exposure to gender inequality, and the degree of interdependence between the sexes among blacks. I consider the implications of my results for understanding how race and gender interact in shaping attitudes toward gender inequality and how men's social dominance and women's dependence influence the degree of agreement between men and women in their criticism of gender stratification.

Race and gender are two of the main dimensions of social stratification in contemporary American society, and the intersection of these dimensions is an essential topic of inquiry for scholars interested in stratification. That intersection can be explored by investigating how one form of stratification is conditioned by the other. In this paper I address how an important aspect of gender relations, the degree of similarity in men's and women's attitudes toward gender stratification, varies across racial groups. It might seem reasonable to expect that dominant and subordinate groups would develop very different attitudes toward inequality, but a relative lack of disagreement between these groups is one of the most notable attributes of gender stratification.[1] Whereas the importance of such agreement in class relations has been debated at length (see, for example, Abercrombie, Hill, and Turner 1980; Gramsci 1971; Marcuse 1964), agreement between the parties involved in gender inequality has received far less consideration.

I contend that men's and women's attitudes toward gender stratification are shaped by a number of factors that vary across individuals and groups, including men's social dominance and women's dependence on men, exposure to salient inequalities, and both group and individual interests. Men's social dominance and women's dependence play a role in shaping gender attitudes by discouraging criticism of the gendered status quo and thus drawing together men's and women's attitudes. The intersection of racial and gender inequalities creates unique structural positions for black women, black men, white women, and white

*This is a revised version of a paper presented at the 1989 meetings of the American Sociological Association, held in San Francisco. This research was funded by a grant from the University of Wisconsin's Graduate School Research Committee. I am grateful to Laura Sanchez for research assistance and to Judith Seltzer, Ann Shola Orloff, Pamela Oliver, Cora Marrett, and Mary Jackman for comments on drafts of this manuscript. I also appreciate the helpful suggestions offered by the anonymous reviewers and the editors.

[1]Although some previous attitudinal research suggested a gender difference in gender-role attitudes (for example, Thornton, Alwin, and Camburn 1983), most studies concluded that men and women tend to hold relatively similar beliefs about gender inequality (Cherlin and Walters 1981; Gurin, Miller, and Gurin 1980; Klein 1984; Kluegel and Smith 1986; Martin et al. 1980; Quarm 1983; Simon and Landis 1989).

"Race, Gender, and Attitudes Toward Gender Stratification" by Emily W. Kane *Social Psychology Quarterly*, 1992, Vol. 55, No. 3, 311–320.

men. Investigating the degree to which these structural positions translate into varying gender attitudes, and especially whether they translate into varying levels of agreement between the sexes by race, allows me to explore my contention about the forces shaping men's and women's interpretations of gender stratification and the forces shaping agreement. In addition, this exploration offers an opportunity to address variations in the character of gender relations across racial groups: in view of the high degree of racial segregation that continues to pervade American life, gender relations are experienced to some extent within racial groups.

I will argue that unique conditions in the history and the contemporary context of gender relations among blacks and whites in the United States foster greater criticism of gender inequality and greater agreement between the sexes among black Americans than among white Americans. To probe gender differences in blacks' and whites' attitudes toward gender stratification, I use public opinion data. A great deal of public opinion research focusing on gender relations emphasizes role-related attitudes (i.e., attitudes about what activities are appropriate for men and for women), and these studies provide a useful point of departure. The analysis of attitudes toward gender roles alone, however, does not capture the full extent of attitudes about gender inequality, and my analyses reveal that an emphasis on roles is especially problematic for studying how race shapes gender attitudes. Therefore I investigate roles along with a broad array of other topics, including attitudes reflecting constructs more commonly addressed in the literature on racial attitudes, but equally relevant to understanding attitudes toward gender as a stratified intergroup relationship. Focusing on a broader array of attitudes toward gender stratification allows me to treat these attitudes as elements of the ideology surrounding a relationship of inequality.[2] Although I do not contend that the attitudes and beliefs I have measured *constitute* a gender ideology, I conceptualize them as *expressions* of such an ideology in that they are indicators of the interpretations surrounding gender inequality as a social phenomenon.

Expectations regarding agreement

I have argued that attitudes toward gender stratification are shaped by men's dominance and women's dependence, as well as by interests and exposure to gender inequalities. Given that contention, I do not expect to find large gender differences in attitudes. Yet previous research on racial variations in the nature of gender relations and family arrangements offers reasons to expect an even greater degree of agreement between the sexes among blacks than among whites. Black women's greater labor force participation and economic independence (Almquist 1979; Farley and Allen 1987; Sorenson and McLanahan 1987), their history of more equal roles in family decision making (Gutman 1976; Hill 1971; King 1975; Staples 1971), and their special outsider status (Collins 1986, 1989) may allow them greater freedom than white women to develop a critical interpretation of the status quo in gender relations. Previous research on racial variations in women's gender-role attitudes supports this expectation, generally documenting more critical attitudes among black women than among white women (Dugger 1988; Macke, Hudis, and Larrick 1978). Yet in exploring the degree to which agreement between the sexes varies within racial groups, one highlights a qualitatively different aspect of the intersection of race and gender in shaping gender-related attitudes. More important to this

[2]For the purposes of this inquiry, the ideology surrounding this intergroup relationship at the social level is of interest; possibly a different pattern of disagreement between the sexes would be evident if gender issues were framed on an interpersonal rather than a social level.

issue of agreement is whether black men also will offer the criticism expected among black women; there are several reasons to believe that they will.

First, greater sensitivity to oppression in general among black men (relative to white men) may encourage them to interpret gender inequality critically. Second, conflict between men and women over gender inequality within the black community may be muted by shared resistance to racial inequality, especially because racial oppression tends to have greater salience (Gurin, et al. 1980). Third, black women's greater labor force participation not only increases their own exposure to occupational gender inequalities but increases black men's exposure as well. All of these factors may lead to less distinct, and more critical or more egalitarian, attitudes toward gender stratification among black men and women than among their white counterparts.[3]

In addition, Collins (1990) characterizes black men's and women's labor force experience as one of "higher-paying yet less secure work for Black men as contrasted with lower-paying, more plentiful work for Black women" (p. 59). These qualitatively distinct patterns of labor market disadvantage may create a greater degree of interdependence among black men and women in contrast to white women's greater degree of nonreciprocal economic dependence on white men (Sorenson and McLanahan 1987). Collins's (1990) analysis of the character of black women's family activities also suggests this kind of interdependence between men and women, an interdependence in the task of resisting racial inequality. According to Collins, some scholarship on labor within extended families "suggests that Black women see their unpaid domestic work more as a form of resistance to oppression than as a form of exploitation by men" (p. 44; see also Davis 1983). If shared resistance to racial inequality in fact encourages criticism and agreement between black men and women in their attitudes toward gender stratification, this situation should be especially evident for attitudes toward group-related social action (such as attitudes toward collective action by women and attitudes toward policy efforts targeting women as a group, both of which I address here).

Conflicting conclusions emerge from the few previous studies that make any reference to agreement between the sexes within racial groups. Although Ransford and Miller (1983) emphasize racial differences within gender groups, their analysis of role-related gender issues also suggests that black men are more traditional than black women, and more traditional than whites of either gender. In their opinion, the traditional gender-role attitudes evident among the black men in their study show that black men rely more strongly on male privilege as a source of status than do white men, who can rely on their racial privilege as well. The authors suggest that because of the combination of white supremacy and male domination evident in racial discrimination, the movement for black rights "has for some become tantamount to the need for greater male control and leadership in general" (p. 49). In contrast, Fulenwider's (1980) analysis of a broader array of gender-related attitudes documents that in some respects, black men express more of what she calls "feminist" attitudes than black women. White men and white women express more similar attitudes, which tend to be less "feminist" than those of black men.

These competing findings stem from the different attitudinal domains addressed in the two studies; Fulenwider (1980) incorporates measures relevant to gender-related social action that are similar to some of those included in my analyses. Addressing a wider array of gender-

[3]Many of these racial differences are measured at the aggregate level and obviously do not affect every black and every white individual, but they may define a difference in cultural environment that affects most members of each group, especially in view of the high degree of racial segregation evident in the United States.

related attitudes, however, allows a test of the implications of Ransford and Miller's (1983) argument about black men's gender attitudes. I expect that expanding beyond role-related attitude items will reveal a more critical orientation toward gender inequality among black men and therefore greater agreement between the sexes among blacks.

DATA AND METHODS

The data for this research are drawn from a public opinion survey administered to a probability sample of adults in the United States (N = 1,750).[4] Between September 1990 and June 1991,[5] a telephone survey was conducted by the Letters and Science Survey Center at the University of Wisconsin, Madison. To explore men's and women's gender ideologies I use a set of 10 attitude items to address a variety of aspects of gender stratification (the appendix provides the text of each item). Two items focus on gender-role orientations, which traditionally have been central to research on gender attitudes. These items address the discrepancy between preferred and perceived roles at home and at work. The other eight items are designed to tap issues that have been central to the study of intergroup attitudes more generally, but they are equally applicable to understanding attitudes toward gender as a stratified intergroup relationship. One pair of these items addresses satisfaction with the influence afforded to men and to women as groups. Another two items measure beliefs about the origins of gender stratification, contrasting natural with social explanations for inequalities at home and in employment. The next two items are relevant to attitudes toward collective action by women; both of these items contrast individual with collective strategies for changing the position of American women. Finally, two items measure policy orientations, tapping satisfaction with existing governmental efforts to encourage equality of opportunity in occupations and to provide day care for working parents.

Factor analyses show that these 10 items form three factors with clear substantive content.[6] The first factor includes the two items that refer specifically to work-related issues: the occupational roles item and beliefs about the origins of gender stratification in employment. This factor also includes the items on men's and women's social influence. Although these two questions do not refer specifically to influence in employment or in the "public" sphere, the fact that they share their factor location with work-related items suggests that respondents may be focusing on work-related influence. The second factor includes the two items on home-related inequality, one on domestic roles and the other addressing beliefs about the origins of women's homemaking abilities. Finally, the third factor includes attitudes toward collective action and policy orientations. All four of the items that load on this factor refer to whether social action should be taken in response to gender inequalities.

I combine the items loading on each of the three factors to form a summary measure of attitudes within that domain. Each summary index is constructed by identifying the response categories that represent criticism of the gendered status quo (these are documented in the appendix). Each index is a count of the number of critical responses offered by an individual across the item that load on a given factor; higher scores indicate greater criticism. For

[4]The sample is drawn from a continuous national survey, designed such that the accumulation of interviews over several months constitutes a probability sample of currently working telephone numbers in the continental United States over that period. One adult was selected at random from each contacted household.

[5]No substantial time effects are evident for the variables across this period.

[6]I conducted factor analyses using LISREL VII. The fit of this three-factor structure does not differ substantially for male and female respondents (goodness of fit index = .99 for males, .98 for females).

each of these three summary indices, I present mean scores by gender, separately for black and for white respondents. I also test the significance of the interaction between race and gender in predicting these scores.

Along with these bivariate analyses of agreement, I estimate regression equations to show whether a significant gender difference is present within each racial group, net of the effects of other factors. For the work and action indices, these are ordinary least squares regression equations. For the home index, which has a more limited range (0 to 2), I estimate gender coefficients using ordered logistic regressions.[7] The controls included in all regression equations are a set of factors that one could expect to affect the development of men's and women's ideological beliefs (and some of which one could expect to be internally divisive *among* men and *among* women respectively as groups): education, age, marital status, the presence of children, class identification, employment status, and family income.[8] I also offer tests of the significance of the difference in gender coefficients across racial groups, using race/gender interaction terms from separate equations estimated for all respondents. These equations include the main effects of gender, race, and all controls along with the interactions of each of the independent variables with race.

For all of these analyses, I include only respondents identified as either black or white, a step that excludes less than 5 percent of the sample. The number of black respondents in the study is not large: approximately 140, or just over 8 percent of the sample.[9] As a result, the patterns that I document in the data should be interpreted cautiously, although they suggest clear conclusions regarding the role of race and gender in shaping gender attributes.

Results

Table 1 shows means for each of the gender-attitude summary measures by gender, within racial groups.

Table 1 documents that disagreement between men and women is greater among whites, whereas black men and women are much more likely to agree in their attitudes toward gender stratification. The magnitude of the gender differences among whites is not large, but it is clearly larger than that for black respondents. In addition, white men's and white women's means differ significantly (at $p = .01$) for all three attitude summary measures, whereas none of the difference-of-means tests is statistically significant for black respondents. Measuring agreement between the sexes with differences in means by gender presumes that standard deviations do not differ substantially by gender. Men and women could have identical means resulting from very different distributions, in which case the lack of significant mean differences would not actually indicate agreement. Table 1, however, documents that men and women have nearly identical standard deviations for all three of the summary measures; therefore differences in means by gender are a valid indicator of

[7]The ordered logistic regression model assumes that the effects of independent variables are similar across cutpoints in the distribution of dependent variables. I conducted tests of the applicability of this assumption, and found the coefficients for gender to be similar across cutpoints among both black and white respondents. The effects of some of the control variables were less consistently similar across cutpoints, but that finding does not affect the results presented here because only the gender coefficients are central to my analysis.

[8]Education is measured with five categories (less than high school, high school, some college, college degree, graduate or professional degree). Age is coded in years. Marital status, presence of children, and employment status are dummy variables; positive values respectively indicate: currently married, respondent has children living at home, and currently employed. Class identification is coded as poor, working class, or middle/upper middle class. Family income is measured in $10,000 categories (up to $120,000).

[9]This figure is somewhat lower than the percentage of blacks in the population of the United States, probably because of lower contact rates and/or lower response rates for black respondents.

TABLE 1 ■ MEANS FOR GENDER-ATTITUDE SUMMARIES, BY RACE AND GENDER

Variable	White men	White women	Black men	Black women	Gender/race interaction (p-value)
Work-related gender attitudes (Range = 0–4)					
Mean	1.95**	2.63**	2.60	2.81	.03*
(SD)	(1.34)	(1.34)	(1.35)	(1.31)	
N	689	788	62	80	
Home-related gender attitudes (Range = 0–2)					
Mean	1.13**	1.33**	1.21	1.23	.07†
(SD)	(0.75)	(0.72)	(0.73)	(0.60)	
N	689	788	62	80	
Gender-related social action (Range = 0–4)					
Mean	1.85**	2.19**	2.85	2.85	.04*
(SD)	(1.19)	(1.18)	(1.01)	(0.95)	
N	689	788	62	80	

†p < .10.
*p < .05.
**p < .01.

NOTE. Significance of difference of means by gender based on t-test (one-tailed, predicted direction: women's scores higher); significance of gender/race interaction based on regression equations including only gender, race, and their interaction as predictors (predicted direction: gender difference larger for white).

agreement. For both work-related attitudes and social-action orientations, the interaction between race and gender is statistically significant at p = .05. (For home-related attitudes, the interaction is in the expected direction but is significant only at p = .10.)

The greater agreement found between black men and women is agreement on a more critical interpretation of existing gender inequalities than that held by white men and women. As Table 1 shows, black women tend to have the highest means of any of the four groups, followed closely by black men. In contrast, for all three summary measures, white men rank as the least critical and most traditional of the four groups. Item-by-item distributions for the 10 variables that constitute the summaries document the same pattern: black women are the most critical or most egalitarian group for more than half of the items, and white men are the least critical for nine of the 10 items (data not shown).[10] The overall pattern reflects the hierarchy of privilege created by racial and gender stratification: black women (the least privileged group) offer the most critical reactions to the gendered status quo, black men and white women follow, and white men (the most privileged group) consistently offer the least critical interpretation.

The most notable departure from this pattern is found in the home-related summary

[10]In addition, black women are the most likely of any group to endorse a separate movement by women. This finding confirms the suggestion that any disinterest black women may have felt toward the mainstream women's movement was based on the white middle-class biases of that movement rather than on any resistance to the notion of women acting collectively (Dill 1983; Lewis 1980; Stone 1979).

measure, for which black women and all men express less criticism than white women. Lower means for black respondents on this measure stem from the fact that all blacks are more likely than white women to attribute women's home-making abilities to nature rather than to society (data not shown). Perhaps this is the case because black women are less likely than white women to be full-time homemakers; therefore blacks may be envisioning a more limited set of child-care and housework activities in responding to this question. This finding also may reflect a more positive and more strength-oriented image of women's role in reproduction and child rearing, like that described by Collins (1990) in her treatment of black women's domestic labor as at least partially a form of resistance to racial oppression.

The general pattern evident in Table 1—that of greater criticism and greater agreement regarding gender relations among black men and women than among white men and women—is linked closely to another pattern. For both the work and the social action measures, race is associated more substantially with men's attitudes than with women's (on the basis of difference of means tests by race, within gender groups; data not shown). Blacks are generally more critical than whites, especially on issues related to group-based social action; this finding suggests that criticism of racial inequality indeed may influence their orientation to gender inequality. In addition, that racial difference, is particularly large for men, an indication that race and gender interact in shaping gender-related attitudes. I will consider this issue more fully below, in my discussion and conclusions.

Table 2 presents estimates of the magnitude of gender differences for blacks and for whites from ordinary least squares and ordered

TABLE 2 ■ ATTITUDES TOWARD GENDER STRATIFICATION: GENDER COEFFICIENTS FROM REGRESSIONS BY RACE

Variable	Gender coefficient		Gender/race interaction
	Whites	Blacks	
Work-related gender attitudes			
Coefficient	.724**	.223	−.501*
(SE)	(.069)	(.238)	(.251)
N	1,460	135	1,595
Home-related gender attitudes			
Coefficient (OL)	.637**	.052	−.604†
(SE)	(.106)	(.397)	(.430)
N	1,460	135	1,595
Gender-related social action			
Coefficient	.326**	.015	−.311†
(SE)	(.063)	(.180)	(.255)
N	1,460	135	1,595

†$p < .10$.
*$p < .05$.
**$p < .01$.

NOTE. Findings are net of the effects of education, age, marital status, presence of children, class, employment status, and income. One-tailed tests, predicted directions positive for all gender coefficients (0 = male, 1 = female) and negative for all gender/race interactions (negative interaction coefficients indicate a smaller gender effect among black than among white respondents).
OL = ordered logistic coefficients; all others are OLS.

logistic regression equations, net of the effects of other factors.

The pattern documented in Table 2 is very similar to that noted above: after controlling for a variety of factors associated with gender-related attitudes, disagreement between men and women remains greater among white respondents for all three summary measures.[11] This difference between the gender coefficients across racial groups is statistically significant at p = .05 for one summary measure and at p = .10 for the other two measures. The latter significance level admittedly is high, but this pattern offers strong suggestive evidence that in a sample including a larger number of black respondents, significant gender/race interactions might be evident even when one uses lower probability levels.

Discussion and Conclusions

The results of these analyses suggest that race and gender intersect in shaping gender ideologies, and that disagreement between the sexes in their attitudes toward gender stratification is greater among whites than among blacks. In addition, the greater agreement evident among black respondents tends to represent a shared *critical* interpretation of gender inequality.

White men express the least critical and most traditional attitudes in these analyses. This finding is not surprising because white men, in general, are the most advantaged group in the social hierarchy created by racial and gender inequality (although this finding differs from Ransford and Miller's [1983] conclusions, which I consider below). If we view white men's responses as a baseline, it becomes clear how race and gender play a role in shaping gender ideologies. Being black is associated with greater criticism of the gendered status quo, especially among men; this attitude draws them closer to black women. Being a woman also is associated with greater criticism, especially among whites; this attitude draws white women farther from white men and leads to greater gender disagreement among whites. As a result, white men are left as the least critical group, black men and white women occupy the middle of the criticism hierarchy, and black women are generally the most critical group. Although the intersection of race and gender as social locations is considerably more complex than a simple sum of advantages and disadvantages, this hierarchy of criticism clearly mirrors the social status hierarchy created by race and gender.

Two points are especially relevant to my present inquiry: not only the ranking of these four race/gender groups but also the relative distances between them in this criticism hierarchy. These distances cause a variation in agreement between the sexes across racial groups: black men and women display similar degrees of criticism, whereas white women often are significantly more critical of gender relations than are white men. One logical hypothesis regarding race and agreement might have been that black women's relative independence and greater labor market activity would lead to especially critical attitudes among black women and therefore to greater disagreement between black men and black women. I have argued, however, that these factors also play a role in shaping black men's gender attitudes; the evidence presented here suggests that interdependence and shared resistance to racial inequality encourage black men to develop critical interpretations similar to those of black women.

Identifying the attitudinal domains for which racial (as opposed to gender) differences are particularly evident helps to explain how such shared resistance may shape agreement between black men and women in their attitudes toward gender stratification. Analyses

[11]The same pattern is documented by separate logistic regressions carried out on the component items that make up the summaries.

conducted for the entire sample (data not shown) suggest that race, more than gender, is predictive of attitudes toward social action. In contrast, race and gender are roughly equal in their associations with work-related attitudes, and gender is associated more strongly than race with the items on home-related issues. The particular importance of race for items addressing social action may reflect black Americans' attitudes toward remedies for racial inequality rather than representing a distinct interpretation of gender inequality; this point is consistent with my expectation that shared resistance to racial inequality might draw together black men and women in their reactions to gender inequality. This pattern also highlights the importance of considering a broad array of gender-related attitudes in determining how race shapes attitudes toward gender stratification. The role-related items analyzed by Ransford and Miller (1983) indeed may suggest greater traditionalism among black men than among white men, but survey questions addressing group-related social action clearly reveal black men's criticism of gender inequality. In addition, Ransford and Miller's (1983) data were collected in the 1970s, whereas mine are much more recent. Thus it is also possible that black men no longer would express more traditional role-related attitudes than white men on Ransford and Miller's items.

In interpreting black men's criticism of gender inequality, however, it is important to recall that the attitude items analyzed here refer only to gender inequality. Possibly more of a rift between black men and black women would be evident if racial and gender inequality were posed as competing priorities for social action, because gender inequality is less salient to black Americans than racial inequality (Gurin et al. 1980). In the past, some commentators stressed the destructive impact of the myth of black matriarchy, arguing that it pits black men and women against one another (see, for example, Wallace 1979). Referring to the myth, Staples (1971) asserts that it is "functional for the white ruling class . . . to create internal antagonisms in the black community between black men and women, to divide them and to ward off effective attacks on the external system of white racism" (p. 158). Similar themes of antagonism between black men and women are echoed in Collins's (1990) more recent work, but she also emphasizes that such antagonisms coexist with a deep sense of solidarity.

Although the analyses I present here do not speak to attitudes about the relative importance of racial and gender inequality, they suggest that the experience of racial oppression and discrimination increases black men's sensitivity to gender stratification. In addition, black women's greater labor force participation may increase not only their own awareness but also black men's awareness of occupational gender inequality. This conclusion is supported by the particularly strong gender/race interaction evident for work-related gender attitudes. Black women's greater economic and decision-making power in the family (relative to white women) may allow them to be critical of the gendered status quo while it also encourages black men to attend to the negative outcomes of gender inequality.

Racial differences in the level of agreement between the sexes in their attitudes toward gender stratification also offer intriguing clues for speculation about the forces shaping the degree of similarity in men's and women's gender ideologies. White men and black women occupy opposite ends of the criticism hierarchy described here. Although I believe that interdependence, along with shared resistance to racial inequality, may draw black men toward the critical end of that hierarchy occupied by black women, it is also possible that greater dependence draws white women toward the end occupied by white men. In other words, dependence may discourage white women from developing the degree of critical interpretation held by black women; such an outcome would be consistent with my contention that men's dominance and women's dependence can discourage criticism of the gendered status quo. Although white Americans show disagreement between the sexes in their attitudes toward gender stratification, these gender differences are not large. Whites also are clearly less critical than blacks. In addition, for many of the individual items that constitute the summaries analyzed here, white women's attitudes are closer to those of white men than to those of black women (data not shown).

The small number of black respondents in this study suggests the importance of exploring these issues with larger samples. Even so, the clear evidence that criticism and agreement are greater for black men and women than for white men and women, along with evidence that racial differences often are larger for men than for women, document that race and gender are intertwined in shaping gender ideologies. These patterns in the data also show that the variation in gender relations across racial subgroups translates into differential levels of agreement between the sexes. Finally, my analyses offer suggestive evidence of the role of dependence (versus interdependence) in shaping both levels of criticism and the extent of disagreement between the sexes in their attitudes toward gender stratification.

References

Abercrombie, Nicholas, Stephen Hill, and Bryan S. Turner. 1980. *The Dominant Ideology Thesis.* London: George Allen and Unwin.

Almquist, Elizabeth M. 1979. "Black Women and the Pursuit of Equality." Pp. 430–50 in *Women: A Feminist Perspective*, edited by Jo Freeman. Palo Alto. Mayfield.

Cherlin, Andrew and Pamela Barnhouse Walters. 1981. "Trends in U.S. Men's and Women's Sex-Role Attitudes: 1972–1978." *American Sociological Review* 46:453-60.

Collins, Patricia Hill. 1986. "Learning from the Outsider Within: The Sociological Significance of Black Feminist Thought." *Social Problems* 33:S14–S32.

———. 1989. "The Social Construction of Black Feminist Thought." *Signs* 14:745–73.

———. 1990. *Black Feminist Thought.* Boston: Unwin Hyman.

Davis, Angela Y. 1983. *Women, Race, and Class.* New York: Vintage.

Dill, Bonnie Thornton. 1983. "On the Hem of Life: Race, Class, and the Prospects for Sisterhood." Pp. 173–88 in *Class, Race, and Sex: The Dynamics of Control*, edited by Hanna Lessinger and Amy Smerdlow. Boston: G.K. Hall.

Dugger, Karen. 1988. "Social Location and Gender-Role Attitudes: A Comparison of Black and White Women." *Gender and Society* 2:425–48.

Farley, Reynolds and Walter Allen. 1987. *The Color Line and the Quality of American Life.* New York: Russell Sage.

Fulenwider, Claire Knoche. 1980. *Feminism in American Politics.* New York: Praeger.

Gramsci, Antonio. 1971. *Selections from the Prison Notebooks.* London: Lawrence and Wishart.

Gurin, Patricia, Arthur H. Miller, and Gerald Gurin. 1980. "Stratum Identification and Consciousness." *Social Psychology Quarterly* 43:30–47.

Gutman, Herbert G. 1976. *The Black Family in Slavery and Freedom: 1750–1925.* New York: Vintage.

Hill, Robert B. 1971. *The Strengths of Black Families.* New York: Emerson Hall.

King, Mac C. 1975. "Oppression and Power: The Unique Status of the Black Women in the American Political System." *Social Science Quarterly* 56:116–28.

Klein, Ethel. 1984. *Gender Politics.* Cambridge, MA: Harvard University Press.

Kluegel, James R. and Eliot R. Smith. 1986. *Beliefs about Inequality.* New York: Aldine de Gruyter.

Lewis, Diane K. 1980. "A Response to Inequality: Black Women, Racism, and Sexism. Pp. 532–51 in *Issues in Feminism*, edited by Sheila Ruth. Boston: Houghton-Mifflin.

Macke, Anne Statham, Paula M. Hudis, and Don Larrick. 1978. "Sex-Role Attitudes and Employment among Women." Pp. 129–54 in *Women's Changing Roles at Home and on the Job*, edited by I. Sawhill. Washington, DC: U.S. Government Printing Office.

Marcuse, Herbert. 1964. *One-Dimensional Man.* Boston: Beacon.

Martin, Patricia, Marie Osmond, Susan Hesselbart, and Meredith Wood. 1980. "The Significance of Gender as a Social and Demographic Correlate of Sex Role Attitudes." *Sociological Focus* 13:383–96.

Quarm, Daisy. 1983. "The Effect of Gender on Sex-Role Attitudes." *Sociological Focus* 16:285–303.

Ransford, H. Edward and Jon Miller. 1983. "Race, Sex and Feminist Outlooks." *American Sociological Review* 48:46–59.

Simon, Rita J. and Jean M. Landis. 1989. "Attitudes about a Woman's Place and Role." *Public Opinion Quarterly* 53:265–76.

Sorenson, Annemette and Sara McLanahan. 1987. "Married Women's Economic Dependency, 1940–1980." *American Journal of Sociology* 93:659–87.

Staples, Robert. 1971. "The Myth of the Black Matriarchy." Pp. 149–59 in *The Black Family*, edited by Robert Staples. Belmont, CA: Wadsworth.

Stone, Pauline Terrelonge. 1979. "Feminist Consciousness and Black Women." Pp. 575–88 in *Women: A Feminist Perspective,* edited by Jo Freeman. Palo Alto Mayfield.

Thornton, Arland, Duane F. Alwin, and Donald Camburn. 1983. "Causes and Consequences of Sex-Role Attitude Change." *American Sociological Review* 48:211–27.

Wallace, Michele. 1979. *Black Macho and the Myth of the Superwoman*. New York: Dial.

Appendix

Index Construction and Attitude Items

Summary Index Construction: Each of the three summary indices is constructed as a count of the number of critical or egalitarian responses (each of which is italicized in the text below) offered across items.

Work-Related Attitudes: This index combines four items.

1. *Occupational Egalitarianism:* A measure of the discrepancy between desired and perceived job opportunities, with critical values indicating the assessment that *women ought to have equal opportunities but do not*, created from the following questions: (a) In general, women in this country should be given equal job opportunities with men; and (b) In general, women in this country actually are given equal job opportunities with men.
2. *Origins, Work:* Men have more of the top jobs because they are born with more drive and ambition than women. OR *Men have more of the top jobs because our society discriminates against women.*
3. *Women's Influence:* Thinking of women as a group, would you say women have too much influence, just about the right amount of influence, or *too little influence* in society?
4. *Men's Influence:* And, thinking about men as a group, would you say men have *too much influence,* just about the right amount of influence, or too little influence in society?

Home-Related Attitudes: This index combines two items.

5. *Child-Care Discrepancy:* A measure of the discrepancy between desired and perceived division of labor, with scores indicating the assessment that *men and women ought to share but women actually take responsibility* considered "critical," created from the following questions: (a) If a man and a woman have children, do you think that taking care of the children should be mainly a woman's responsibility or that it should be a man's responsibility as much as a woman's?; and (b) How do you think most men and women actually divide child care: do you think most women are actually responsible for taking care of children or do you think most men actually take equal responsibility?
6. *Origins, Home:* By nature, many women are better than men at making a home and caring for children. OR *Our society, not nature, teaches women to be better than men at homemaking and child care.*

Gender-Related Social Action: This index combines four items.

7. *2 Option Collective Action:* the best way to handle problems of discrimination is for each woman to make sure she gets the best training possible for what she wants to do. OR *Only if women organize and work together can anything really be done about discrimination.*
8. *3 Option Collective Action:* If women want to change their position in America, which of the following do you think is the best way for them to do it? (1) *women should organize as a group with men and women.* OR (2) each woman should work to get ahead on her own. OR (3) *women should organize as a group with other women.*
9. *Gov't Effort, Jobs:* Think of how much the federal government is doing to make sure women have the same job opportunities as men; would you say the federal government is doing too much, about the right amount, or *too little* about this?

10. *Gov't Effort, Day Care:* Next, think of how much the federal government is doing to provide day care centers for the children of working parents; would you say the federal government is doing too much, about the right amount, or *too little* about this?

Emily W. Kane is Assistant Professor of Sociology at the University of Wisconsin—Madison. Her current research focuses on gender ideology, particularly the factors associated with men's and women's beliefs about gender inequality in the United States and cross-nationally.

Quantitative Studies with Eight or More Locations: Separate Group Analysis

In this section I included two articles that rely on separate group analysis for eight or more social locations. Hill and Sprague in "Parenting in Black and White Families: The Interaction of Gender with Race and Class" conduct Type I analysis with the race and class of parents and the gender of their children the independent variables. They are primarily interested in how gender is constructed in black families compared with white families. Class is measured by combining the education and income of parents into a three-level variable: working class, lower middle class, and upper middle class. The dependent variables are a variety of measures of gender socialization, operationalized in multiple ways, including parents' rankings of long-term goals for their children, their rankings of immediate priorities for their children, as well as their rankings of their own parenting roles. Because this is a Type I analysis there are no other independent variables, nor are there any control variables in this study.

Tables are constructed from the intersections of race × class × gender. Because class has three categories rather than two, there are a total of 12 distinct social locations. With a sample of 202 black and 204 white parents, this distribution results in some cells as small as 12 and 19 cases. Still, using logit models Hill and Sprague do find some significant differences across social locations. The authors' conscious use of the intersectional approach is underscored by the following statement: "Multicultural feminist theory leads us to predict that gender, class, and race will all have an impact on parenting goals and strategies, in interacting ways" (p. 320). No doubt a larger sample would have yielded even more significant interactions.

The article by Alexander, Entwisle, and Bedinger, "When Expectations Work: Race and Socioeconomic Differences in School Performance," is rather complicated, but it is of interest primarily because of the authors' search for significant interactions at the intersections of race, class, and gender. As is often the case, class is represented as socioeconomic status (SES), which is only a rough measure of class but is commonly found in the sociological literature. The authors use two measures of SES, family economic level measured by those whose children receive free or reduced-price meals compared with those who do not, and parents' education level (less than high school, high school, and greater than high school). The latter, education, is the best proxy for occupation as a class measure, although the actual categories used in research often differ according to the population being studied. In this study, using a sample in which 67 percent of the children are eligible for free or subsidized lunch, the researchers create subdivisions within the working class: parents with less than a high school education and parents with a high school education. These two measures are used separately rather than combined as was done in the article by Hill and Sprague. Alexander et al. acknowledge that [t]hese subdivisions lead to relatively small sample sizes" (p. 343), a problem that prompted them to "focus more closely on trends than on specific tests of significance" (p. 343). Still they do uncover a number of significant relationships that are reported in Tables 2 and 3 (pp. 344 and 345), and they note that "[t]he expectation coefficients reported . . . differ—significantly across racial/ethnic and SES lines in seven of 16 comparisons" (p. 343). It should be noted that only two way interactions between race and gender, and between race and class are used. These are reported by subgroups in Tables 2 and 3. However, it is not clear whether these were calculated using interaction terms in multiple regression models or through subgroup analysis.

Parenting in Black and White Families
The Interaction of Gender with Race and Class

SHIRLEY A. HILL
JOEY SPRAGUE
University of Kansas

REPRINT REQUESTS: SHIRLEY A. HILL, *Department of Sociology, 716 Fraser Hall, University of Kansas, Lawrence, KS 66045-2172: e-mail: hill@falcon.cc.ukans.edu.*

It is widely believed that gendered expectations are communicated to children in the process of socialization. However, there is reason to ask whether and how gender is constructed in Black families. An early perspective that still continues to inform some contemporary research is assimilationism, which assumes that Black people embrace and pass on to their children the gender norms of the dominant white society. The Afrocentric perspective challenges this view, maintaining that the unique historical experiences of Blacks have militated against an emphasis on rigid gender distinctions, and that relative gender neutrality exists in Black families' child-rearing practices. The development of multicultural feminist theory, which argues that the impact of race on gender varies by social class, implies that both assimilationism and Afrocentrism may be overgeneralizations. Yet, little systematic research has been done on whether race makes a difference in how parents view gender. The authors use data from surveys completed by a nonrandom sample of parents in 202 African American and 204 white families in two large metropolitan school districts to examine the impact of gender, race, and class on parents' self-reports of their immediate priorities and long-term goals for their children, their view of the parenting role, and their discipline strategies. The findings are consistent with multicultural feminist theory: Race and social class interact to shape the intergenerational construction of gender in families.

AUTHORS' NOTE: *Both authors shared equally in the creation of this article. We would like to thank Margaret Green, Shirley Harkess, Joane Nagel, Beth Schneider, and anonymous reviewers for comments on an earlier draft.*

A central focus in the feminist analysis of gender has been understanding how gender is socially constructed, perpetuated, and passed on to children. Families are held to be the first agents of gender socialization; they not only pass gender norms on to children explicitly but also organize work, roles, and identities along gender lines (Chodorow 1978; Johnson 1988; Lytton and Romney 1991; Weitzman 1979). By age 4 or 5, children have learned to prefer the behaviors and activities deemed appropriate for their sex (Bem 1983). In a summary of previous studies on gender differences in socialization, Block (1983) reported that parents typically emphasize achievement, competition, independence, and education more for sons, whereas daughters are expected to be kind, loving, well-mannered, and have good marriages. So, while it is understood that the construction of gender is an active, ongoing process throughout the life course (West and Zimmerman 1987), we also know that it is important to understand the specific construction of gender in childhood.

There is reason to ask whether the idea of gender socialization might be racially specific and may not apply to African American families. For example, scholars have argued that the gender roles prescribed by the dominant white society have never been fully institutionalized among Black people because of the way race shapes social positions (Collins 1990; King 1988). Some have pointed out that a relative degree of gender neutrality exists in the socialization of Black children (Lewis 1975; Ferguson Peters 1988; Reid and Trotter 1993), especially arguing that Black girls are taught from an early age to be independent, strong, and resourceful (Collins 1990; Dill 1988; Scott 1993). Yet, the evidence with regard to these assertions is sketchy and inconsistent.

The literature on African Americans includes themes that imply conflicting claims about gender socialization in Black families. Claims of assimilation to the dominant culture suggest African Americans will communicate hegemonic gendered expectations to children. Afrocentrists, on the other hand, maintain that the African heritage and American experience have curtailed the development of patriarchy and strict gender norms among Blacks. Multicultural feminist theory may resolve the conflict. In arguing that the impact of race on gender varies by class, multicultural feminist theory implies that both assimilationism and Afrocentrism may be overgeneralizing from specific intersections of race and class.

We review what is claimed and what is known about racial diversity in gender arrangements and about gender socialization in African American families. Then, we examine one set of indicators of gender socialization in families at diverse intersections of race and class. We look at parents' reports of immediate priorities and long-term goals for children, their view of the parenting role, and their discipline strategies, and whether these vary when talking about a son or a daughter.

Race and the Construction of Gender

During the 1960s, gender was problematized in contrasting ways for white and Black families. White feminists argued that the traditional Eurocentric conceptualization of gender was harmful, particularly the marginalized, secondary roles assigned to women and the notion of women as innately domestic, dependent, and submissive (see Weitzman 1979). Black women, on the other hand, pointed out that the Eurocentric ideology of patriarchal families and separate spheres for men and women had never become a tradition in their families. They argued that the history of labor force participation of African American women militated against full-time domesticity as the norm for Black women, as did the fact that Black families were often headed by women or organized around female-centered kinship networks (Jones 1985; Stack 1974). Racial discrimination and exclusion, on the other hand, presented significant barriers to Black men in their attempt to become the sole economic provider for their families, and their inability to fulfill this role diminished their power, esteem, and participation in families (Ladner 1971; Stack 1974).

The failure of low-income Black families to conform to dominant notions of gender was seen by some as pathological, a view that was popularized in a controversial study published by Moynihan in 1965. Moynihan attributed the perpetuation of racial inequality in the United States to Blacks' confusion about gender roles, which, he said, undermined the stability of their families. In his opinion, the economic roles and authority of Black men had been usurped by Black women, who, freed from male control through work or welfare, had illegitimate children and ran families. Moynihan described Black women as matriarchs and Black men as weak and ineffective, and he suggested that Black males would benefit by enlisting in the armed forces, "a world away from women, a world run by strong men of unquestioned authority" (1965, 42).

The burgeoning Black family literature of the era challenged the Moynihan thesis by arguing that women were perfectly capable of heading families, that women's efforts inside and outside the home had been vital to the survival of Black families, and that the broader roles of women had reduced the importance of gender in the organization of family work and in child socialization strategies (Hill 1972; Lewis 1975).

The widely held view of relative gender neutrality or equality among Blacks, however, is based more on the experiential reflections of a few people than on systematic research. It rests heavily on the fact that Black women often combine economic and family roles, with less analysis of whether these behaviors express ideological convictions or are solely the result of economic necessity. What research exists tends to focus on selected groups of women, especially those who are poor and/or single mothers, revealing little about how other factors, such as social class, affect gender ideologies. Most studies continue to view Blacks as a monolithic group, despite evidence of growing social class diversity (Billingsley 1992).

One of the most glaring deficiencies in studies of gender among African Americans has been the failure to include the experiences of men. Black males have only rarely been accorded the esteem or power associated with masculinity in the broader society or patriarchal privileges that result from being the primary breadwinners for their families. Although there has been a proliferation of research on Black women, usually emphasizing traditions of strength and independence among women (Collins 1990; Dill 1988; Giddings 1984; King 1988), little can be said about the contention of gender neutrality among Blacks when men are absent from the equation. As Hunter and Davis (1992) have pointed out, it is tacitly assumed that whereas adversity and oppression led Black women to forge strong, multidimensional roles, these same factors essentially stripped Black men of the prerogatives of manhood. Carr and Mednick (1988) have suggested that although daughters may benefit from nontraditional gender roles, such roles lessen the achievement motivation of males.

Studying Gender Socialization among Blacks

Since the late 1960s, there has been a proliferation of research on gender socialization in families, although few studies have included adequate samples of African Americans. Two perspectives—assimilationism and Afrocentrism—persist in the literature with contrasting implications for gender socialization among Blacks.

The earliest research on Black families was assimilationist in focus. It argued that Black families, especially those who achieved middle-class status, had essentially the same attitudes and child-rearing values as white families (Davis and Dollard 1940; Davis and Havighurst 1946). The idea that Black parents embrace the values and priorities of the dominant white culture, even though poverty and social inequality make adherence to those ideals difficult, persists to the present (Allen 1981; Taylor et al. 1990; Thornton et al. 1990).

Studies of gender ideologies show that Blacks are more likely than whites to support the breadwinner-homemaker family (Doyle 1989), have traditional views about the male role in the family (Binion 1990), believe that married women should not be employed (Smith and Seltzer 1992), and say a woman's real fulfillment in life comes from motherhood (Lyson 1986). Empirical research also has shown that Black couples divide housework along traditional gender lines (Hossain and Roopnarine 1993; Wilson et al. 1990). These studies indicate that African Americans have accepted the gender norms of the dominant society, implying that, at least by example, they will pass these norms on to their children.

A contrasting perspective, expressed largely by ethnographic researchers and Afrocentric theorists, is that, as opposed to the Moynihanian view of culture as pathology, African and African American cultural norms have been a source of strength, resiliency, and survival for Black families (Billingsley 1992; Hill 1972; Stack 1974). In the Afrocentric framework, the historic participation of Black women in economic work, both in Africa (Burgess 1994) and in the United States (Dill 1988), produced greater gender role equality among Black males and females. Proponents argue that gender is not a crucial factor in Black child socialization and only minimally affects the behaviors children are taught and the work they are expected to perform (Nobles 1985).

In an early expression of this view, Lewis argued that "the black child, to be sure, distinguishes between males and females, but unlike the white child he [sic] is not inculcated with standards which polarize behavioral expectations according to sex" (1975, 228). According to Lewis, all Black children are taught to "mother" and are instilled with similar traits of assertiveness, willfulness, and independence. A more recent study by Scott, focusing on the difficulty of socializing girls, pointed out that African American girls "are socialized to be at once independent and assertive as well as familistic and nurturant . . . to be sexually assertive . . . to be as authoritative, individualistic and confident as African American sons are, and as economically self-sufficient and personally autonomous as sons are" (1993, 73). More recently, Peters (1988) has argued that age and competency are more likely than sex to be the basis for defining children's roles in Black families.

Some research has supported this Afrocentric view of gender equality among Blacks. A recent study by Hunter and Sellers (1998) reported significant attitudinal support among Black men and women for gender equality and feminist ideologies, and Reid and Trotter (1993) found Black children exhibited less gender stereotypical behavior than white children.

There are three major weaknesses in this literature. First, little attention is paid to the specific question of the gender socialization of children, especially by those who argue for assimilationism. Second, especially in the area of Black family scholarship, there has been an inordinate focus on the roles of Black women rather than Black men. Yet, research has shown that Black males face numerous obstacles to success (Gibbs 1988; Madhubuti 1990; Majors and Billson 1992) and find it difficult to adhere to the gender norms of white males (Blake and Darling 1994; Cazenave 1981). Third, Blacks are viewed as a monolithic group, in spite of growing class diversity.

The development of multicultural feminist theory,[1] largely by Black feminists and other feminists of color, has broadened feminist theory by showing that race and class shape how gender gets played out in peoples' lives. For example, capitalism and patriarchy exploit women in race- and class-specific ways (Aptheker 1989; Davis 1993; Dill 1979; Espiritu 1997; Glen 1992; King 1988; Mies 1986). Whereas economically privileged white women were being relegated to unpaid, devalued reproductive roles in the family, and working-class white women had some hope of seeing their daughters rise above their class position, African American women were being heavily exploited for their labor, first as slaves and later by their long-term concentration in menial, low-paying labor market jobs (Davis 1993; Glenn 1992; hooks 1984). The way gender and race interacted to constrain the economic opportunities of Black women made it impossible for them to be defined as weak and dependent. Indeed, as Collins (1990, 67) has pointed out, the dominant culture developed a race-specific set of gendered images to control Black women by distorting and demeaning their strengths.

Multicultural feminism acknowledges that both race and class inequality have shaped the gendered options of African Americans. Black women traditionally have helped provide the nurturance and material necessities for their families and, presumably, have taught their own daughters to be strong, resourceful, and self-reliant (Collins 1987; Ladner 1971). Black men, especially those who are poor, often find the route to masculinity as defined by Eurocentric gender norms to be quite narrow, since they lack the economic and social power to cash in on the "patriarchal dividend" (Connell 1995) and benefit from female subordination (Dill 1988). Even at an early age, these barriers lead many poor young Black males to express their "masculinity" by rejecting the importance of conventional norms like getting a good education (Fordham and Ogbu 1986) and focusing on sexuality (Anderson 1989) or "cool pose" (Majors and Billson 1992) as alternative sources of esteem. Male denigration then becomes common, especially in low-income Black communities, where men are often viewed as irresponsible and unreliable (Connor 1988; Ladner 1971; Stack 1974; Wilson 1996). This view of Black manhood may shape the expectations parents have for their children along gender lines. Indeed, studies have shown that low-income Black parents often have higher expectations for their daughters than for their sons (Blau 1981; Hill and Zimmerman 1995; Staples and Boulin Johnson 1993). Thus, race and social class are clearly central factors in the social construction of gender opportunities and ideology. Yet, we know little about how they affect gender socialization processes in families.

Multicultural feminist theory provides a framework that resolves the competing themes of assimilationism and Afrocentrism. The questions of whether Black families teach their children gendered expectations similar to those prevalent among whites becomes transformed. We are directed to ask how the sex of a child influences parents' values and parenting strategies in different intersections of race and class.

Data

The data used in this analysis are from surveys completed by a nonrandom sample of parents of elementary school students during the 1993–94 school year. Seven schools in two large, urban, predominantly Black school districts participated in the study.[2] Students[3] in these schools carried letters to their parents explaining the study and asking them to complete and return the survey. The survey return rate ranged from 10 to 40 percent.[4] In all cases, parents were asked to focus on *one child* in completing the survey—the child who brought the survey home.[5] Parents provided some demographic data on that child and responded to a broad array of questions on their goals and strategies in rearing that child.

We excluded three surveys that did not indicate the sex of the child and analyzed the remaining 406 surveys: 202 Black parents and 204 white parents.[6] Demographic details about these families are reported in the appendix. Respondents range from 22 to 67 years old and are overwhelmingly women and mothers. Although grandparents and others are also among our respondents, we will call them parents, assuming that the person who completed a form brought home from school is intimately involved in caretaking; that is, we are using "parent" to indicate a social role, not a biological relationship.

Although nearly half (49 percent) of the Black parents are married, Blacks are more likely to be single parenting than are white respondents, 58 percent of whom are married. The average number of children per family is 2.8, but the range is wide: The largest single category for Blacks and whites is two children, with 72 percent having no more than three children. The very largest families are Black, with 8 percent having eight or more children. The white families have comparable numbers of children, the only striking difference being among the outliers. The children described in this study were fairly evenly divided between daughters (50 percent of Blacks, 46 percent of whites) and sons. The children range in age from 5 to 18, with an average age of about 10 years, and more were in the fifth grade than in any other.

Economic differences between Blacks and whites in this sample are less a reflection of population characteristics than an expression of the way race and class interact in residential patterns, on which school districts are organized. More Black parents than white parents are employed, and Black parents overall have a slightly higher education than do white parents. Although Black and white parents are equally likely to have completed high school, Blacks are slightly more likely to have attended or graduated from college. Family incomes for this sample are roughly comparable across race. Most families have less than $30,000 a year, and more than one-third are in the lowest income bracket, earning less than $15,000 per year. Whites are somewhat more likely than Blacks to earn more than $30,000 a year.

The current research compares the responses of parents who indicated they were reporting about their rearing of sons to those who indicated their target child was a daughter. Of course, what people say is not necessarily what they do in particular situations. We are assuming that these parents are making a good faith effort to report the principles that they try to follow—no doubt imperfectly—as they go about parenting on a daily basis. Our confidence in the strength of the connection between these self-reports and daily practices is increased because our questions are posed in fairly concrete terms and use categories and language drawn from the way parents have actually discussed these matters in qualitative interviews. Still, as we shall see, we have reason to suspect that at least in some cases, parents are attempting to give a socially desirable response.

Measures of socialization practices

The survey administered to these parents includes several questions that can be used as indicators of their approach to parenting. The survey questions, constructed specifically for this study, draw their general structure and content from the classic child-rearing studies of Kohn (1963). They also incorporate some of the issues raised in Black family studies and in-depth interviews with Black parents (Hill 1999). In this article, we report an analysis of responses to four items that have parallel structures. In each case, a child-rearing issue is posed and the parent is asked to rank the relative importance to him or her of three positions on that issue. Although most parents did rank order three options from 1 (their top priority) to 3 (their lowest priority), a few parents gave a rank of 1 to more than one option in a question and a few others ranked only one or two options.[7] For this analysis, we converted each response option to a dichotomous variable with a value of 1 if the respondent indicated it as a top priority and 0 in all other cases.

Two of the questions address parents' reported goals for their children. To tap long-term parenting goals or future hopes parents have for their children, we asked parents to rank the following outcomes in terms of importance: (1) getting a good education and a good job (EDJOB), (2) having a strong, loving family (FAMILY), and (3) having a kind and compassionate personality (KIND). To get a sense of current priorities, parents were asked to rank three values in terms of how important they are for the child who brought the survey home: (1) being happy and feeling good about himself or herself (HAPPY), (2) being obedient and respectful (OBEY), and (3) doing well in school (SCHOOL). The other two questions deal with approaches to parenting. To identify respondents' understanding of their own role, they were asked to rank three parental roles in terms of their importance: (1) being a teacher and guide (TEACH), (2) being a disciplinarian (DISCIPLINE), or (3) being a provider (PROVIDE). Finally, we examine discipline strategies used by asking parents to rank three discipline strategies in terms of which they relied on the most: (1) the loss of privileges (PRIVIL), (2) spankings (SPANK), or (3) the use of reason or logic (REASON).

Measures of independent variables

We are using the gender of the child as an indicator of gender as a causal force. To the extent that gender is being constructed through parenting practices in these families, the responses given by parents of sons will differ from those given by parents of daughters. If parents are responding more generally and not thinking of a specific child, then we should find no relationship between the gender of the child and the responses of the parent.

However, we believe it is unlikely that the gender of the child interacts significantly with any reporting discrepancies. Although parents did indicate the sex of the child they were thinking of, it was in the context of a series of demographic questions about children and their parents. The parenting questions themselves do not suggest that gender comparisons are being made. Thus, although these data, and survey data in general, cannot accurately reflect actual parenting practices, any systematic differences between parents of sons and parents of daughters can reasonably be attributed to gendered belief systems that support gendered practices.

Race is measured by self-identification in a question that offered five response alternatives (Black, white, Hispanic, Asian, and other). Sex of child (SEX) is also coded by the respondent (son, daughter). Cases with missing values on RACE and/or SEX ($n = 3$) were excluded from the analysis.

Our data include two indicators of parents' class, respondent's education, and total family income, which are strongly related, $X^2(9) = 117.6$, $p = .00$, $\gamma = 0.55$. We combined information on income and education to create a three-level measure of class.[8] The modal family in the lowest class level, which we are calling "working class," includes a high school graduate and has a household income less than \$15,000. The modal "lower-middle-class" family includes a parent with some college education and has an annual income of \$15,000 to \$30,000. The modal "upper-middle-class" family includes a college graduate and has an income of \$30,000 to \$50,000. There is no relationship between race and class in this residence-based sample, $X^2(2) = 0.52, p = .77$.

Analysis

Multicultural feminist theory leads us to predict that gender, class, and race will all have an impact on parenting goals and strategies, in interacting ways. To examine this prediction, we need to look at parents' responses by gender, class, and race. The cross tabulation of the proportion of parents placing a top priority on a particular response option by our measures of these independent variables generates a complex ($2 \times 2 \times 3 \times 2$) frequency table for each of the three choices offered in each question. The predicted interactions between race, gender, and class generate still more complexity in the data.

To get a clearer picture of the effects of each independent variable, we used log linear analysis, specifying a series of logit models using direct and interaction effects of class, race, and gender (sex of child) to predict each dichotomously coded response (see Norušis 1985; Tabachnick and Fidell 1989).[9] We then looked for the model that seemed to have the best fit across the three choices for each question. We will first report the findings by question. Then, we will look at the pattern of causal relationships that seems to emerge across questions.

Results

Table 1 reports the rankings of all parents within each of the four child-rearing issue categories—long-term goals, current priorities, parental roles, and disciplinary strategies—both overall and by sex of child. Looking at long-term goals, most parents gave top priority to their child's getting a good education and a good job. The second most commonly cited long-term goal was having a strong and loving family. The least often cited priority, having a child grow to be a kind and compassionate person, was the first choice of only 1 in 5 parents. The sex of the child has no effect on parents' ranking of these goals. In evaluating more immediate priorities, the top choice for most parents is that their children be happy and feel good about themselves. Having their child be obedient and respectful was the second most important current priority for parents, with parents of boys more likely those of girls to emphasize this priority. Doing well in school was ranked as less important than obedience and respect.

The majority of parents see their primary role as that of a teacher. Only 30 percent see themselves primarily as providers, and very few see themselves as primarily disciplinarians. The most popular disciplinary strategy among these parents is the use of reason and logic. However, withdrawing privileges is favored by a substantial minority of parents. Primary reliance on spanking as a disciplinary strategy is a rare event, although social desirability biases are probably depressing this figure. Only 22 parents ranked spanking as their sole primary approach to discipline.

To the extent that a global form of gender socialization is occurring, parents' responses to these measures should be significantly associated with the sex of the child. However, there are only two places where gender makes a significant difference, even allowing for a generous margin of error ($\alpha = .10$). Those who place their top current priority on the child's being

TABLE I ■ Measures of Dependent Variables, Labels, and Proportion of Parents Indicating Each as a Top Priority, Overall and by Sex of Child

Question	Label	All	Girls	Boys
Long-term goal for child				
Getting a good education and a good job	EDJOB	.53	.51	.54
Having a strong, loving family	FAMILY	.32	.34	.30
Having a kind and compassionate personality	KIND	.23	.21	.25
Current priority				
Being happy and feeling good about himself or herself	HAPPY	.58	.61	.55
Being obedient and respectful	OBEY	.29	.25	.33*
Doing well in school	SCHOOL	.23	.21	.25
Role as parent				
Being a teacher and guide	TEACH	.68	.65	.72
Being a disciplinarian	DISCIPLINE	.09	.10	.07
Being a provider	PROVIDE	.30	.30	.29
Discipline strategy				
The loss of privileges	PRIVILEGE	.43	.39	.47*
Spankings	SPANK	.05	.07	.04
The use of reason or logic	REASON	.53	.54	.52

*$p < .10$.

obedient and respectful and those who rely on the loss of privileges as a disciplinary strategy are more likely to be parents of boys. Of course, if the form of gender socialization varies by race and/or class, as multicultural feminists contend, those differences could be canceling one another out in global comparisons. Thus, we must examine the gender dynamics of these four measures in a race and class sensitive context.

Long-term goals

The distribution of parents' long-term goals for their children across race, class, and gender appears in Table 2. The logit analysis revealed that gender does not predict parents' long-term priorities and that class and race do in interaction.

The top panel of Table 2 shows that education and a job are more of a priority for Black than for white parents overall, and the next three panels show that among both Blacks and whites, this emphasis decreases as class increases. Lower-middle-class Blacks are more likely to place a top priority on family than their white class peers. The strongest race contrasts are among the upper-middle-class parents, where family is the top priority for white parents and education and jobs are the top long-term goals for Black parents. Whereas class does not have much impact on whether Blacks place importance on their children growing up to be kind persons, the likelihood of making this a priority increases with class among whites.

TABLE 2 ■ PARENTS' RANKINGS OF LONG-TERM GOALS FOR THEIR CHILDREN: PERCENTAGES BY RACE OF PARENT AND SEX OF CHILD, OVERALL AND WITHIN CLASS LEVELS

	Parents are		Black parents		White parents	
	Black	White	Girls	Boys	Girls	Boys
Overall						
Long-term goal						
EDJOB	58	49*	56	58	47	51
FAMILY	34	31	35	33	34	27
KIND	25	22	23	27	20	24
Within class levels						
Working class	$n = 56$	$n = 62$	$n = 33$	$n = 22$	$n = 31$	$n = 29$
Long-term goal						
EDJOB	82	71	79	86	65	79
FAMILY	20	18	18	18	19	14
KIND	21	13	15	27	13	14
Lower middle class	$n = 110$	$n = 104$	$n = 55$	$n = 54$	$n = 59$	$n = 45$
Long-term goal						
EDJOB	48	48	45	50	47	49
FAMILY	43	32*	45	41	34	29
KIND	27	22	27	28	22	22
Upper middle class	$n = 36$	$n = 38$	$n = 12$	$n = 22$	$n = 19$	$n = 19$
Long-term goal						
EDJOB	50	13***	42	50	16	11
FAMILY	28	50**	33	27	58	42
KIND	22	34	25	23	26	42

NOTE. Class and race have independent effects.

*$p < .10$. **$p < .05$. ***$p < .01$.

Although class has some systematic effects—working-class parents are more likely to emphasize education and jobs—once parents get into easier economic situations, racial differences become more striking. Black parents maintain the same ordering of priorities across class, whereas the priorities among whites in the upper middle class are quite different from other whites. This interaction effect could be expressing a more narrow, class-specific cultural difference than alleged by the Afrocentrists' perspective: Differences based on culture emerge among the relatively privileged economically.

Gender has no statistically significant effect on long-term goals for either racial group, however, even when looking within levels of class. Although there are too few parents in this category to draw any conclusions, it is interesting to note that the biggest gender differences appear among upper-middle-class whites. Here, a clear majority of parents of daughters emphasize the goal of a strong family, whereas parents of sons are evenly split between having a good family and being a kind person.

Current priorities

The distribution of parents' current priorities for their children across race, class, and gender appears in Table 3. This measure had detected one global gender difference: Parents of sons are more likely to emphasize obedience and respect. The logit analysis suggests that gender does

TABLE 3 ■ PARENTS' RANKINGS OF IMMEDIATE PRIORITIES FOR THEIR CHILDREN: PERCENTAGES BY RACE OF PARENT AND SEX OF CHILD, OVERALL AND WITHIN CLASS LEVELS

	Parents are		Black parents		White parents	
	Black	White	Girls	Boys	Girls	Boys
Overall						
Current priority						
HAPPY	52	63**	53	53	69	57*
OBEY	37	21***	35	38	16	28**
SCHOOL	30	17***	26	33	17	16
Within class levels						
Working class	$n = 56$	$n = 62$	$n = 33$	$n = 22$	$n = 31$	$n = 29$
Current priority						
HAPPY	46	48	42	50	52	48
OBEY	36	29	33	36	19	41*
SCHOOL	41	23**	33	50	26	14
Lower middle class	$n = 110$	$n = 104$	$n = 55$	$n = 54$	$n = 59$	$n = 45$
Current priority						
HAPPY	56	65	60	54	75	53**
OBEY	39	18***	36	43	15	22
SCHOOL	28	18*	24	31	14	24
Upper middle class	$n = 36$	$n = 38$	$n = 12$	$n = 22$	$n = 19$	$n = 19$
Current priority						
HAPPY	50	79***	50	55	79	79
OBEY	33	16*	33	27	11	21
SCHOOL	17	5	17	18	11	

NOTE. Class, race, and gender have independent effects.

*$p < .10$. **$p < .05$. ***$p < .01$.

enter into parents' current priorities and that race and class also have independent impacts.

Even though the best model to describe the structure of responses specifies direct effects of gender, gender differences on specific priorities reach statistical significance only among whites. In general, whites are more likely to emphasize happiness for daughters and obedience for sons. A look at the impact of class reveals that this gender difference in current priorities among whites exists among working-class whites, who emphasize obedience/respect for boys, and lower-middle-class whites, who emphasize happiness and self-esteem for daughters. Blacks seem to make fewer gender distinctions overall. This global pattern of nongendering among Blacks may be masking race- and class-specific gendering. Among the poorest Black families, more parents of sons report top priorities on both being happy and doing well in school. Their white class peers are placing a greater emphasis on school for girls and obedience for boys. Then, in the lower middle class, where the largest gender distinctions exist among whites, the same pattern seems to occur in a more muted way among the Black parents. Both Black and white parents in the upper middle class seem to be making the fewest gender distinctions.

Overall, white parents are more likely than Blacks to emphasize the child's happiness and self-esteem, whereas Blacks outnumber whites among those placing top priorities on obedience or school performance. There are significant race differences at each class level. As class status increases, whites' emphasis on happiness increases while the importance of school performance decreases. On the other hand, the proportion of Black parents putting top priority on happiness and obedience is relatively stable across class. The importance of school performance to Black parents does decline as class increases, although it is always more important to Blacks than to whites.

Several have argued that European American culture is more individualistic and focused on self-esteem, whereas African American culture is more group oriented and places a higher value on education (Collins 1990; hooks 1994). White priorities on happiness and self-esteem and Black priorities on obedience, respect, and doing well in school are consistent with that cultural contrast. However, class also makes a systematic difference here. Parents at higher class levels do not have to worry as much about whether their children will be able to get a good education and job; poorer parents seem to rely more on the potential for education to help their children move into higher class levels.

Parental role

Parents' rankings of their own roles by race and class of parent and sex of child are reported in Table 4. Parents who identify first as disciplinarians are rare, constituting only 36 of the 406 parents. Because there are so few in this category, logit modeling is statistically inadvisable. However, the models that best predict the observed pattern of parents putting a top priority on being a teacher or a provider indicate that gender interacts with race and class in shaping parents' role conceptions.

There are strong gender differences among working-class whites: Parents of sons are very likely to see themselves as teachers, whereas all the disciplinarians are parents of daughters. On the other hand, white parents in the other two classes do not seem to be making gender distinctions in their roles. In fact, the role priorities of upper-middle-class white parents of daughters and sons are identically distributed.

Although there are no statistically significant gender differences among Black parents, there are some indications of gendering in both the lower middle class and upper middle class. In both cases, the nature of the disparity parallels that among whites—more emphasis on teaching boys and providing for girls. Although there are too few in this category to draw any conclusions, it is intriguing that the distribution of role preferences among upper-middle-class Black parents of sons is very similar to that of

TABLE 4 ■ Parents' Rankings of Their Own Roles: Percentages by Race of Parent and Sex of Child, Overall and within Class Levels

	Parents are		Black parents		White parents	
	Black	White	Girls	Boys	Girls	Boys
Overall						
Role as parent						
TEACH	64	72*	61	68	69	75
DISCIPLINE	14	3***	14	13	6	1*
PROVIDE	35	25**	34	35	27	23
Within class levels						
Working class	$n = 56$	$n = 62$	$n = 33$	$n = 22$	$n = 31$	$n = 29$
Role as parent						
TEACH	52	60	45	59	42	76***
DISCIPLINE	16	8	12	18	16	**
PROVIDE	48	31**	39	59	42	21
Lower middle class	$n = 110$	$n = 104$	$n = 55$	$n = 54$	$n = 59$	$n = 45$
Role as parent						
TEACH	68	73	69	67	76	69
DISCIPLINE	15	***	18	13		
PROVIDE	33	28	31	35	25	31
Upper middle class	$n = 36$	$n = 38$	$n = 12$	$n = 22$	$n = 19$	$n = 19$
Role as parent						
TEACH	72	89*	67	82	89	89
DISCIPLINE	8	5		9	5	5
PROVIDE	19	5*	33	9	5	5

NOTE. Gender interacts with race and class as causes.

*$p < .10$. **$p < .05$. ***$p < .01$.

whites in the same class. On the other hand, Black upper-middle-class parents of daughters are more like Black parents in other class levels.

There are global race differences in parents' role priorities. White parents are even more likely to see themselves as teachers, whereas more Black than white parents see their primary role as providing for their children. Most of the parents who identify primarily as disciplinarians are Black: 14 percent of Blacks compared with 3 percent of whites list as a top priority their role as disciplinarian.

Class also has a systematic impact on these choices. As class status increases among both Black and white parents, there is increasing emphasis on the teacher role; as class status decreases, there is a greater tendency to emphasize the provider role. That is, the more a parent's ability to provide is threatened by his or her economic situation, the more likely to prioritize this role.

In general, then, parents' determination of their roles is shaped in complex ways by their race and class, as well as their notions about gender. Gendering takes the form of emphasizing teaching boys and providing for—and sometimes disciplining—girls. It is most salient among lower-middle-class whites, but there are signs it may be happening among working-class and upper-middle-class Blacks.

Whether through constraints, opportunities, or culture, class also shapes what parents understand they can and must do for their children. Race has an impact as well. We see signs of cultural differences in the importance of discipline. We also see that simply being in a more comfortable class location does not keep Blacks from worrying about providing for their children. This may be because they have access to African American cultural discourses that help them understand that racism makes their class position insecure, and because they live in a social structure that has failed historically and is failing to meet the needs of Black children.

Disciplinary strategies

The disciplinary strategies that parents rely on, by race and class of parents and sex of child, are reported in Table 5. This is the other measure on which we observed a global gender difference: Parents of sons were more likely to rely on the withdrawal of privileges. Here, again, one of the options, spanking, was rarely selected as a top priority, so we cannot reliably fit a logit model to predict that choice. In the case of the other two choices, the model that best predicts the pattern of choices on each specifies that they are shaped by class in interaction with race and with gender.

In the case of disciplinary strategies, the only significant gender differences are among Black parents. Overall, Blacks are more likely to withdraw privileges from sons than from daughters, even though their use of reason and spanking is almost the same regardless of the

TABLE 5 ■ PARENTS' RANKINGS OF DISCIPLINARY STRATEGIES: PERCENTAGES BY RACE OF PARENT AND SEX OF CHILD, OVERALL AND WITHIN CLASS LEVELS

	Parents are		Black parents		White parents	
	Black	White	Girls	Boys	Girls	Boys
Overall						
Discipline strategy						
PRIVILEGE	42	44	34	49**	43	45
SPANK	8	3*	9	7	5	1
REASON	51	54	53	54	54	54
Within class levels						
Working class	$n = 56$	$n = 62$	$n = 33$	$n = 22$	$n = 31$	$n = 29$
Discipline strategy						
PRIVILEGE	32	45	24	41	45	48
SPANK	9	3	9	9	6	
REASON	61	50	55	68	48	52
Lower middle class	$n = 110$	$n = 104$	$n = 55$	$n = 54$	$n = 59$	$n = 45$
Discipline strategy						
PRIVILEGE	45	48	38	50	47	49
SPANK	6	4	4	9	5	2
REASON	51	50	58	44	51	49
Upper middle class	$n = 36$	$n = 38$	$n = 12$	$n = 22$	$n = 19$	$n = 19$
Discipline strategy						
PRIVILEGE	50	29*	42	55	26	32
SPANK	11	**	33	**		
REASON	39	71***	25	45	74	68

NOTE. Class interacts with race and gender as causal effects.

*$p < .10$. **$p < .05$. ***$p < .01$.

sex of the child. This tendency for Black parents to withdraw privileges more from sons than daughters is relatively consistent across class. The most marked differences are among upper-middle-class Black parents, where the differential use of spanking on daughters is striking. White parents are not using gender to determine disciplinary strategies. The proportions of parents of sons and daughters relying on each strategy are nearly identical overall and within each class.

The only global race difference in disciplinary strategies is that Blacks predominate among the very few parents who report relying on spanking. The largest race differences emerge within the upper middle class, where the vast majority of whites rely on the use of reason, whereas more Blacks use the withdrawal of privileges. The only upper-middle-class parents who rely on spanking to discipline are Black parents of girls.

Class also seems to shape disciplinary strategies among these parents, but in different ways for Blacks and whites. As class status increases, Black parents decrease their reliance on reasoning with their children and increase their use of the withdrawal of privileges. Whites in the working class and lower middle class are roughly evenly balanced between using reason and withdrawing privileges. In the upper middle class, however, the vast majority of white parents rely on the use of reason. These findings tend to contradict claims that gendering is minimized among Blacks, at least in the way that parents respond to problematic behavior in children. It could be that this differential withdrawal of privileges is a kind of ceiling effect of another cultural difference. If Blacks accord fewer privileges to girls than boys, they have less to withdraw for disciplinary purposes.

Discussion and Conclusions

Do the self-reports of parents in this study reveal that parents' priorities, future hopes, views of the parenting role, and discipline strategies vary based on whether they are responding for a son or a daughter? What we have found is that gender does get constructed in the goals and values in Black and white families, but in race- and class-specific ways.

First, we note that the overall ranking of the three options given for each child-rearing issue—long-term goals, current priorities, parenting role, and discipline strategies—are the same for Black and white parents as a group. This is evidence of a common culture and significant overlap in values and beliefs. Still, white parents were significantly more likely than Black parents to emphasize happiness as a current value for their children and being a teacher as their most important parenting role. Black parents, on the other hand, were significantly more likely than white parents to indicate doing well in school and obedience as their most important current values, having their children get a good education and job as their most important long-term goal, and being a disciplinarian and provider as their most important parenting roles. These findings are consistent with studies showing that Black parents place a high value on the education of their children (Willie 1988) and stress the importance of discipline and obedience (McAdoo 1988; McLoyd 1990).

These global racial differences in priorities, taken together, suggest that white parents, perhaps more secure about their children's current status and future success, focus more on their children's psychological well-being and are less concerned about instilling strict conformity in their children. The child-rearing priorities of Black parents, however, might be influenced by their perception of greater challenges to success: Controlling, providing for, and educating children become more salient aspects of their parenting work.

Central to our analysis is whether the sex of the child influenced the behaviors or goals of parents. Gender had some overall effect. Compared to the parents of girls, the parents of boys emphasized obedience and respect more frequently as a current value and were more likely to use loss of privileges as a discipline strategy. These overall gender differences, however, turn out to be largely the product of strong, race-specific effects. The emphasis on obedience for sons more than for daughters occurs among white parents but not among Black parents. The tendency to discipline boys more than girls by withdrawing privileges appears among Black parents but not among white parents. That is, these data show that gender socialization is not a monolithic phenomenon.

Yet, how much, and even in some cases the way in which, Black and white parents differ on each of these issues varies quite a bit across class. When we observe differences between Blacks and whites in gendering practices, we may sometimes be seeing an artifact of the way race corresponds to class in American society.

We see several instances of significant gender differences occurring at specific intersections of class and race. Poor whites are particularly likely to emphasize obedience in their sons. This emphasis seems to be a benevolent one; poor white parents of sons overwhelmingly see their own role as primarily a teacher, and none of them see themselves as disciplinarians. Poor white parents of daughters might be a little more likely to see themselves as providers and emphasize school performance. There are no statistically significant gender effects in the practices reported by poor Black parents.

There is only one statistically significant gender effect among parents in the lower middle class: Whites are much more likely to emphasize happiness and self-esteem for their daughters than for their sons. Across the two lower classes in this sample, we see gendering more markedly among whites than among Blacks. The only exception is the overall Black use of privileges as a disciplinary strategy for sons more than daughters. Among upper-middle-class parents, on the other hand, gendering seems to occur among Blacks but not whites. If upper-middle-class Blacks admit to spanking as a form of discipline, they do it to daughters and not to sons. In contrast, the reports of white parents on all four measures of goals and strategies tend to be remarkably similar across sex of child.

Overall, gender does not seem to be a salient feature in parents' long-term goals for their children. On the other hand, gender seems quite salient in the choice of disciplinary strategies for Blacks and in current priorities for whites. Long-term goals are fairly abstract, distant from the daily experience of parents of elementary school age children, whereas current priorities and disciplinary strategies are much more concrete. So, one way of interpreting these findings is that gender may not be salient when parents think about their values, but it may be embedded in their daily practices, where it will have concrete consequences for children.

Studies of gender among African Americans often point to a tradition of gender neutrality in child socialization, but, as we have pointed out, most of these studies focus on expanded roles for women while ignoring the roles of males. Although some previous studies have suggested that Black parents may have diminished expectations for their sons, our findings do not support that contention. We found that in each social class, there was no statistically significant difference in current priorities or long-term goals between Black parents of sons and those of daughters.

There are important caveats to take into consideration about this analysis. First, these findings rely solely on the *reported* attitudes and behaviors of parents. The desire to appear in a "good light" as parents probably influenced at least some of their responses. Another consideration is the fact that respondents were overwhelmingly female. Johnson (1988) argues that it is men, not women, who impose gender socialization on children. Thus, gender socialization may be more pervasive than we see here, and what we are observing is that even among the parents who are less likely to gender their children, race and class shapes socialization priorities and practices.

These findings could be expressing a selection bias in drawing a residentially based sample when race still makes a big difference in freedom to choose a residence. It seems reasonable to ask whether upper-middle-class parents who choose to live in and/or school their children in communities that are predominantly working class and poor, especially whites, who do not have racial discrimination in housing as a barrier, may differ significantly from their class-race peers in values and practices (Massey and Denton 1993). We need to explore how parents who live in more privileged residential areas rear their children.

Finally, statistics on the fit of the logit models indicated that even when models fit very well, they do not explain much of the variation among parents on these questions. The best model, predicting EDJOB, still explains only about 14 percent of the variance using the more generous assessment. This is no doubt partially because of the errors in measurement of the variables. It also seems quite likely that there are other important independent variables we are not taking into account in these models. It may be that these unspecified variables are also artifacts of interactions between gender, race, and class.

Still, on the basis of these data, it seems reasonable to conclude that there is no simple answer to the question of how gender gets constructed in parents' child-rearing practices. Parents operate within their own specific economic and social constraints. Within these constraints, they try to develop an approach that coincides with gendered expectations—both their own and the ones they read in others—of their children. In struggling within these constraints and expectations, they draw on the values they learned from their own families and communities, which are marked by race and class. In parenting, and probably in the rest of life, race, class, and gender dynamics interact.

APPENDIX

Characteristics of Sample

	Black Families		White Families	
	n	%	n	%
Respondent				
Mother	165	82	167	82
Father	22	11	22	11
Grandmother	4	4	6	3
Other	11	3	9	4
Marital status				
Never married	58	29	29	14
Married	98	49	113	58
Divorced	36	18	39	19
Separated	6	3	15	7
Widowed	3	2	7	3
Number of children				
1	32	16	23	11
2	75	37	70	34
3	39	19	58	28
4	30	15	37	18
5	15	7	9	4
6 or more	11	6	7	3

	Black Families		White Families	
	n	%	n	%
Gender of focus child				
Female	100	50	93	46
Male	98	49	106	53
Employment status of parent				
Employed	133	66	120	59
Unemployed	47	23	68	33
Retired	3	2	2	1
Other/not specified	19	10	14	7
Education of parent				
Did not complete high school	20	10	27	12
High school graduate	70	35	72	35
Some college	70	35	68	33
College graduate	40	20	33	16
Annual family income				
< $15,000	72	36	71	35
$15,001–$30,000	67	33	56	27
$30,001–$50,000	41	20	43	21
> $50,000	17	8	28	14

NOTES

1. This body of work has also been referred to as multiracial feminist theory and intersectional theory.
2. Of the 12 schools invited to participate in the study, 5 declined: Four had other studies already under way and 1 was not interested. The 7 schools included were not randomly selected but do reflect some of the racial and class diversity in the two cities.
3. Initially, surveys were sent only with students between the ages of 10 and 12, since these are considered important developmental years. In three of the seven schools, surveys were sent home with all children.
4. The actual response rate is probably higher. Given the number of children in the families in this sample, many parents probably had more than one child at the school but were asked to completely only one survey.
5. The purpose of having a focus child was twofold: the recognition that parents of more than one child may have different strategies for different children and the necessity of identifying a specific sample of children.
6. Surveys completed by Asian Americans and Hispanics were omitted from this analysis because there were too few to analyze. We intend to analyze larger data sets in the future to allow for more complete cross-ethnic comparisons.
7. Our interpretation of these cases is that the scales' rank order requirement does not validly measure the beliefs of these parents, that they legitimately refuse to weigh one option over another. That is, these "ties" are substantive and should be retained in the analysis. Thus, the proportions reported do not always add up to 1.0.
8. To construct a measure of class, we used a cross tabulation of our measures of education and income to create a three-level variable. In the lowest level are families with an income of less than $30,000 and less than a high school diploma and families with high school graduates but an income of less than $15,000 a year. In the highest class level are those with a college degree and an income of at least $30,000 and all households with incomes over $50,000. Those cases missing on income were assigned class based on the modal income for their education level and vice versa.
9. To fit, a model had to predict cell frequencies that did not diverge too far from those observed

in the data. We judged fit in two ways: globally by the likelihood chi-square statistic (where we set an alpha level of .20) and for each cell by the size of standardized residuals, where we would tolerate no more than two cells (10 percent) with a significantly poor fit. If two nested models fit the data adequately, we chose the model with fewer causal terms unless a statistical test showed that its fit was significantly poorer. Details on the fit of various models are available upon request.

REFERENCES

Allen, W. R. 1981. Moms, dads and boys: Race and sex differences in the socialization of male children. In *Black men*, edited by L. E. Gary. Beverly Hills, CA: Sage.

Anderson, E. 1989. Sex codes and family life among poor inner city youths. *Annals of the American Academy of Political and Social Science* 501:59–78.

Aptheker, B. 1989. *Tapestries of everyday life: Women's work, women's consciousness, and the meaning of daily experience.* Amherst: University of Massachusetts Press.

Bem, S. L. 1983. Gender schema theory and its implications for child development: Raising gender-aschematic children in a gender-schematic society. *Signs: Journal of Women in Culture and Society* 8:598–616.

Billingsley, A. 1992. *Climbing Jacob's ladder: The enduring legacy of African-American families.* New York: Simon & Schuster.

Binion, V. J. 1990. Psychological androgyny: A Black female perspective. *Sex Roles* 22:487–507.

Blake, W. M., and C. A. Darling. 1994. The dilemmas of the African American male. *Journal of Black Studies* 24:402–15.

Blau, Z. S. 1981. *Black children/white children: Competence, socialization, and social structure.* New York: Free Press.

Block, J. H. 1983. Differential premises arising from differential socialization of the sexes: Some conjectures. *Child Development* 54:1334–54.

Burgess, N. 1994. Gender roles revisited: The development of the "woman's place" among African American women in the United States. *Journal of Black Studies* 24:391–401.

Carr, Peggy G., and Martha T. Mednick. 1988. Sex role socialization and the development of achievement motivation in Black preschool children. *Sex Roles* 18:169–80.

Cazenave, N. A. 1981. Black men in America: The quest for "manhood," In *Black Families,* edited by H. P. McAdoo. Beverly Hills, CA: Sage.

Chodorow, N. 1978. *The reproduction of mothering.* Berkeley: University of California Press.

Collins, P. H. 1987. The meaning of motherhood in Black culture and Black mother-daughter relationships. *Sage* 4:3–10.

———. 1990. *Black feminist thought.* Cambridge, MA: Unwin Hyman.

Connell, R. W. 1995. *Masculinities.* Berkeley: University of California Press.

Connor, M. E. 1988. Teenage fatherhood: Issues confronting young Black males. In *Young, Black, and male in America: An endangered species,* edited by J. T. Gibbs. Dover, MA: Auburn House.

Davis, Angela Y. 1993. Outcast mothers and surrogates: Racism and reproductive politics in the nineties. In *American feminist thought at century's end*, edited by Linda S. Kauffman. Cambridge, MA: Blackwell.

Davis, A., and J. Dollard. 1940. *Children in bondage: The personality development of Negro youth in the urban South.* New York: Harper & Row.

Davis, A., and R. J. Havighurst. 1946. Social class and color differences in child-rearing. *American Sociological Review* 2:698–710.

Dill, B. T. 1979. The dialectic of Black womanhood. *Signs: Journal of Women in Culture and Society* 4:545–55.

———. 1988. Our mother's grief: Racial ethnic women and the maintenance of families. *Journal of Family History* 13:415–31.

Doyle, J. A. 1989. *The male experience.* Dubuque, IA: W. C. Brown.

Espiritu, Yen Le. 1997. *Asian American women and men.* Thousand Oaks, CA: Sage.

Fordham, S., and J. Ogbu. 1986. Black students' school successes: Coping with the "burden of 'acting white.'" *Urban Review* 18:176–206.

Gibbs, J. T. 1988. Young Black males in America: Endangered, embittered, and embattled. In *Young, Black, and male in America: An endangered species,* edited by J. T. Gibbs. Dover, MA: Auburn House.

Giddings, P. 1984. *When and where I enter: The impact of Black women on race and sex in America.* New York: Bantam Books.

Glen, E. N. 1992. From servitude to service work: Historical continuities in the racial division of paid reproductive labor. *Signs: Journal of Women in Culture and Society* 18:1–43.

Hill, R. 1972. *The strengths of Black families.* New York: Emerson Hall.

Hill, S. A. 1999. *African American children: Development and socialization in families.* Thousand Oaks, CA: Sage.

Hill, S. A., and M. K. Zimmerman. 1995. Valiant girls and vulnerable boys: The impact of gender and race on mothers' caregiving for chronically ill children. *Journal of Marriage and the Family* 57:43–53.

hooks, bell. 1984. *Feminist theory: From margin to center:* Boston: South End Press.

———. 1994. *Teaching to transgress: Education as the practice of freedom.* New York: Routledge.

Hossain, Ziarat, and Jaipaul L. Roopnarine. 1993. Division of household labor and child care in dual-earner African-American families with infants. *Sex Roles* 29:571–83.

Hunter, A. G., and J. E. Davis. 1992. Constructing gender: An exploration of Afro-American men's conceptualization of manhood. *Gender & Society* 6:464–79.

Hunter, A. G., & S. L. Sellers. 1998. Feminist attitudes among African American women and men. *Gender & Society* 12 (1): 81–99.

Johnson, Miriam. 1988. *Strong mothers, weak wives: The search for gender equality.* Berkeley: University of California Press.

Jones, J. 1985. *Labor of love, labor of sorrow: Black women, work, and the family from slavery to the present.* New York: Basic Books.

King, Deborah K. 1988. Multiple jeopardy, multiple consciousness: The contest of Black feminist ideology. *Signs: Journal of Women in Culture and Society* 14:42–72.

Kohn, Melvin L. 1963. Social class and parent-child relationships. *American Journal of Sociology* 63:471–80.

Ladner, J. A. 1971. *Tomorrow's tomorrow: The Black women.* Garden City, NY: Doubleday.

Lewis, Diane K. 1975. The Black family: Socialization and sex roles. *Phylon* 36:221–38.

Lyson, Thomas A. 1986. Race and sex differences in sex role attitudes of southern college students. *Psychology of Women Quarterly* 10:421–28.

Lytton, Hugh, and D. M. Romney. 1991. Parents' differential socialization of boys and girls: A meta-analysis. *Psychological Bulletin* 109:267–96.

Madhubuti, Haki R. 1990. *Black men: Obsolete, single, dangerous? The Afrikan American family in transition.* Chicago: Third World Press.

Majors, R., and J. M. Billson. 1992. *Cool pose: The dilemmas of Black manhood in America.* New York: Lexington Books.

Massey, D., and N. A. Denton. 1993. *American apartheid: Segregation and the making of the underclass.* Cambridge, MA: Harvard University Press.

McAdoo, J. L. 1988. The roles of Black fathers in the socialization of Black children. In *Black families,* edited by H. P. McAdoo. Newbury Park, CA: Sage.

McLoyd, V. C. 1990. The impact of economic hardship on Black families and children: Psychological distress, parenting, and socioemotional development. *Child Development* 61:311–46.

Mies, Maria. 1986. *Patriarchy and accumulation on a world scale.* London: Zed Books.

Moynihan, D. P. 1965. *The Negro family: A case for national action.* Washington, DC: Department of Labor.

Nobles, Wade W. 1985. *Africanity and the Black family: The development of a theoretical model.* Oakland, CA: Institute for the Advanced Study of Black Family Life and Culture.

Norušis, M. 1985. *SPSS-X advanced statistics guide.* New York: McGraw-Hill.

Peters, Marie Ferguson. 1988. Parenting in Black families with young children: A historical perspective. In *Black families,* edited by H. P. McAdoo, Newbury Park, CA: Sage.

Reid, Pamela Trotman, and Katherine Hulse Trotter. 1993. Children's self-presentations with infants: Gender and ethnic comparisons. *Sex Roles* 29:171–81.

Scott, Joseph W. 1993. African American daughter-mother relations and teenage pregnancy: Two faces of premarital teenage pregnancy. *Western Journal of Black Studies* 17:73–81.

Smith, Robert C., and Richard Seltzer. 1992. *Race, class, and culture: A study of Afro-American mass opinion.* Albany: State University of New York Press.

Stack, C. 1974. *All our kin: Strategies for survival in a Black community.* New York: Harper & Row.

Staples, Robert, and Leanor Boulin Johnson. 1993. *Black families at the crossroads: Challenges and prospects.* San Francisco: Jossey-Bass.

Tabachnick, B. G., and L. S. Fidell. 1989. *Using multivariate statistics.* 2d ed. New York: Harper & Row.

Taylor, Robert Joseph, Linda M. Chatters, M. Belinda Tucker, and Edith Lewis. 1990. Developments in research on Black families: A decade review. *Journal of Marriage and the Family* 52:993–1014.

Thornton, Michael C., Linda M. Chatters, Robert Joseph Taylor, and Walter R. Allen. 1990. Sociodemographic and environmental correlates of racial socialization by Black parents. *Child Development* 61:401–9.

Weitzman, Lenore J. 1979. *Sex role socialization: A focus on women.* Palo Alto, CA: Mayfield.

West, C., and Don Zimmerman. 1987. Doing gender. *Gender & Society* 1:125–51.

Willie, C. 1988. *A new look at Black families.* Bayside, NY: General Hall.

Wilson, W. J. 1996. *When work disappears: The world of the new urban poor:* New York: Vintage Books.

Wilson, M. N., T.F.J. Tolson, I. D. Hinton, and M. Kiernan, 1990. Flexibility and sharing of childcare duties in Black families. *Sex Roles* 22:409–25.

Shirley A. Hill is an associate professor of sociology at the University of Kansas. She teaches classes on the family, health and medicine, and social inequality. Her research interests include family caregiving, gender and race inequality in health, and child socialization.

Joey Sprague is an associate professor of sociology at the University of Kansas. Her research and teaching focus on theories of gender, methodology, and the sociology of knowledge. She and her partner have been trying to raise children in nongendered ways for the last 20 years.

When Expectations Work:
*Race and Socioeconomic Differences in School Performance**

KARL L. ALEXANDER
DORIS R. ENTWISLE
SAMUEL D. BEDINGER
The Johns Hopkins University

Why are expectations for future performance realized more often by some people than by others, and why are such differences in the efficacy of performance expectations socially patterned? We hypothesize that differences in attentiveness to performance feedback may be relevant, reasoning that follow-through behaviors will be less well conceived when expectations are formed without regard to evaluation of previous performance. Using data from Baltimore fourth-grade students and their parents, we find that expectations anticipate marks more accurately when recall of prior marks is correct than when it is incorrect. Because errors of recall (mostly on the high side) are more common among lower-SES and minority children and their parents, their school performance is affected most strongly. Research on school attainment processes from a motivational perspective must give more attention to the additional resources that facilitate successful goal attainment, given high expectations. Our perspective focuses on resources internal to the individual, but external constraints also are important. The discussion stresses the need for further work in both areas.

*Data collection for this research was supported by W. T. Grant Foundation Grant 83079682 and by National Institute of Child Health and Development Grant 1 R01 16302. The analysis was supported by National Science Foundation Grant SES 8510535 and by National Institute of Child Health and Development Grants 1 R01 21044, 5 R01 23738, and 5 R01 23943. We thank the children, parents, teachers, principals, and other school system employees who have given us such splendid cooperation in all phases of this research.

"When Expectations Work: Race and Socioeconomic Differences in School Performance" by Karl L. Alexander, Doris R. Entwisle, and Samuel D. Bedinger *Social Psychology Quarterly* 1994, Vol. 57, No. 4, 283–299.

Ambition often begets success (e.g., Spenner and Featherman 1978), but not all goals are fulfilled. For reasons not clearly understood, minority and economically disadvantaged youths seem less successful than others at converting high goals into high attainments (e.g., Entwisle and Hayduk 1978; Kerckhoff and Campbell 1977; Kilgore 1991; Thornton 1977). Entwisle and Hayduk's (1978) research with primary-grade children offers a vivid illustration. In their data, middle-class children, African-American children, and white children from lower-SES families all held high expectations for their future marks, but expectations did not predict performance level as well for blue-collar and inner-city children as for middle-class children. Differences in regression results predicting marks from parents' and children's mark expectations showed that lower-SES youths were personally less effective in realizing their intentions and that their parents were less effective as agents of their children's academic socialization.

Why should high aspirations yield less for children from less advantaged backgrounds? One reason may be that their goals are grounded less securely in a proper understanding of the "means-ends" relationships that govern achievement striving in the school and the workplace than are the goals of their more favorably situated peers. It is well established that such understandings are not universally shared. Kerckhoff (1977, 563), for example, observes that "unrealistic ambitions appear to reflect ignorance of the association between antecedents and attainments." Hoelter (1982, 32) finds that youths attending black segregated schools often express seemingly "irrational" career aspirations because they fail to acquire key information about how the status attainment process works: "of particular importance is access to knowledge used to weigh information relevant to the planning process. . . . Thus, for example, ignoring academic performance or ability in planning for future education should be considered nonrational given that these variables have some predictive utility for future educational attainment."

In the above quote, Hoelter is concerned with college students and how they view their future prospects, but failure to heed relevant cues when constructing achievement goals has been observed much earlier in the life cycle as well. Consider again Entwisle and Hayduk's (1978) study of elementary school achievement processes. When expectations for future performance were taken as *dependent variables,* those of minority and lower-SES children and parents were less responsive to report card feedback about past performance (i.e., prior marks) than were the expectations of their more advantaged counterparts. Children's high performance expectations persisted even though their ideas were not validated by high or improving marks; the same general pattern also is seen among older youths. It is reflected in the "paradoxical" (e.g., Mickelson 1990) persistence of positive academic attitudes among African-American adolescents despite low academic achievement, and in the disjuncture among many African-American youths between expressed support for traditional academic goals and the behaviors needed to attain those goals (e.g., Ogbu 1988).

Young children often exhibit free-floating optimism in the face of failure and other setbacks (Diggory 1966; Heckhausen 1967), and this attitude can be healthy up to a point. In the early elementary years, however, children typically begin to "integrate their experiences accumulatively in forming expectancies" (Parsons and Ruble 1977, 1076); that is, they become both more self-reflective and more sensitive to feedback in their realm of experience (e.g., comparisons with others in their class, teachers' comments and body language, evaluations of past performance). Attending to such signals helps children to distinguish more effective from less effective strategies and can trigger constructive self-corrective actions that should facilitate goal attainment in the long run.

"Unrealistic" ambitions, in the sense used by Kerckhoff, and "irrational" ambitions, in the sense used by Hoelter, are descriptive characterizations—not evaluative, and certainly not pejorative. The labels apply less to the goals themselves than to the context in which they are framed. The very same expressions of intent will be more or less "realistic," more or less "rational," more or less "appropriate," depending on whether they seem sensible in light of prior experience and attainable in the face of prevailing constraints. Resignation to failure will not bring success, but neither will wishful thinking. The problem with "too great expectations," to borrow Entwisle and Hayduk's phrase, is that they lack conditionality and hence are not likely to serve as a useful guide to action.

But why should such differences in the character of goals be socially patterned? We propose that they result from, and reflect, social marginality. "The most cruel aspect of discrimination and disadvantage lies in its ability to deprive the individual of that competence which is essential to effective functioning once the formal barriers to free competition have been breached" (Inkeles 1966, 65). For many of the poor especially, the edifice of the school is intimidating. The rules and conventions that prevail in schools are foreign to them, and the aura of middle-class professionalism leaves them subordinate. Whereas middle-class parents often involve themselves in curriculum planning and in decisions about their children's educational placements (Baker and Stevenson 1986; Singer et al. 1986; Useem 1991), poor parents, who themselves often struggled in school, tend to defer to the schools, relying on the professional authority of the institution to do what needs to be done (Lareau 1987).

In these respects lower-SES and minority parents and their children are less adept in interacting with the school bureaucracy, in understanding the flow of information from school to home, and in relating that understanding to their own situations. These skills and understandings can be regarded as aspects of human and social capital (e.g., Coleman 1988); when they are relatively lacking, as is more often than not the case in lower-SES households, the supporting infrastructure is less conducive to following through on conventional success goals. In Baker and Stevenson's research, for example,

> . . . mothers with higher socioeconomic status were more likely to *have accurate knowledge about their child's schooling* and to have contact with the school. If their child was performing poorly or had a school related problem, they were more likely to know about the problem and to know the school personnel to contact. . . . Parents must do a long series of small things to assist their child toward maximum educational attainment . . . high-SES students do better in the system partly because their parents have better management skills (1986, 164–65; our emphasis).

High performance goals probably give all children an edge in school competitions, but to implement an effective plan of action requires more: among other things, a willingness to persist in the face of obstacles, a sense that success is within one's reach, familiarity with the rules of the game, and a mental roadmap of how to reach the place where one wants to be (e.g., Weiner 1984, 1986). When goals lack these supports, they often prove hollow.

In the present study we examine the efficacy of expectations for future school performance within a stratification framework. Our purpose is to learn whether attentiveness to performance feedback from home to school is socially patterned, and whether differences in the use of such feedback in framing expectations for future performance help to distinguish more predictive from less predictive (i.e., effective) expectations. Report card marks are the feedback we examine. The report card is the school's major vehicle for communicating with parents about their children's progress. It identifies areas of strength and weakness, and is intended to prompt realistic self-assessment. We expect follow-through to be more successful when parents' and children's thinking about children's future prospects takes account of how previous efforts have been received—one aspect of the "conditionality" discussed above.

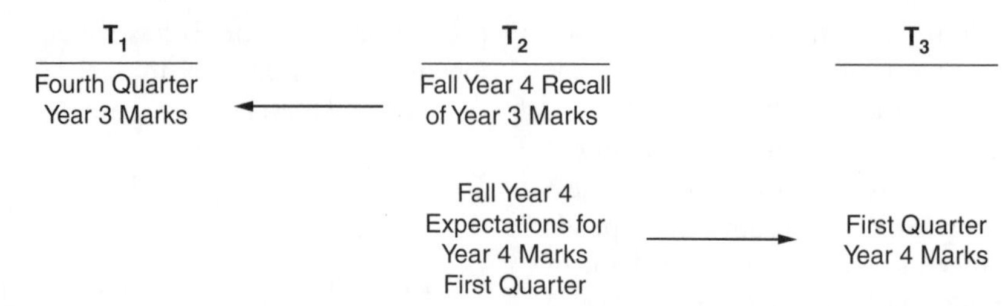

FIGURE I ■ TIME LINE FOR LINKING PAST PERFORMANCE, RECALL OF PAST PERFORMANCE, FUTURE PERFORMANCE EXPECTATIONS, AND FUTURE PERFORMANCE

These ideas are tested with data from children and their parents on expectations for fourth-grade report card marks in light of recall of third-grade marks.[1] Figure 1 maps the data sources used. Report card marks in reading and math from the end of Grade 3 anchor the comparison (T_1). Parents' and children's recall of the previous year's marks and their anticipation of upcoming fall marks appear next; these were obtained in the early fall of Grade 4 (T_2). The marks received later that fall complete the cycle (T_3).

Weaving these sources together, we can see 1) whether low-SES and minority youths and their parents are less accurate in their recall of the previous year's marks than are their more advantaged counterparts, 2) whether the mapping of expectations onto future performance is stronger when recall is accurate, and 3) whether differences in the predictive power of expectations along SES and racial lines can be attributed to differences in the accuracy of recall by SES and race. Our central hypothesis is that performance expectations and accuracy of recall interact in predicting future performance.

PROCEDURES

In the Beginning School Study (BSS), a large, diverse sample of Baltimore children is being followed prospectively from the time they started Grade 1 in fall 1982. A stratified random sample of 20 schools in the Baltimore City system yielded a sample divided about equally by race and representing all socioeconomic levels in the school system. Schools were chosen randomly from within SES and racial composition strata; children were chosen randomly within schools from kindergarten rosters for the 1981–1982 school year and from rosters of first-grade classrooms the following fall. Parents' permission was obtained for 97 percent of the children. The number of subjects so chosen was 838, but elimination of kindergarten and Grade 1 repeaters resulted in a final sample of 790–the BSS "grade cohort."

The BSS children, their parents, and their teachers have been interviewed many times over the years. This analysis uses data sources mainly from project years 3 and 4. During the first two years of the project, children were tracked only if they remained in the original 20 schools. Beginning in Year 3, children were tracked throughout the Baltimore City Public School System (BCPS); in Year 5 we began tracking children outside as well as inside the city system, thus retrieving many cases lost in the early years. During the period covered by the present analysis, most missing data reflect sample attrition due to transfer. We have compared the pattern of first-year data for children who remained in the study throughout with that of lost cases, and in general we find few

[1]For ease of expression here and throughout we refer to the various benchmarks as *grades*, but the more proper term would be *year of school*. All members of the sample were beginning Grade 1 in fall 1982, but over time many were held back. At any later date, the original cohort spans two or more grade levels.

systematic differences. We observe some social selection—whites and upper-SES families leave the BCPS often—but few other differences. Relationships among variables are practically invariant. (More highly detailed attrition analyses are reported in Alexander, Entwisle, and Dauber 1994.)

Children's expectations for their upcoming report card marks and their recall of marks from the previous spring are taken from individual interviews conducted before fall report cards were issued. Most of the parent data comes from self-administered questionnaires sent out during the summer before Year 4 and continuing into the early fall. Personal interviews—about 20 in all—were conducted when requested by parents. As with children, all fieldwork with parents was completed before report cards were issued in the fall. Information on parent's education is taken from the first year. Report card marks, California Achievement Test scores, and the family's eligibility for reduced-price meals at school are taken from school records.

Marks, mark expectations, and mark recall

Report card marks. Reading and math marks from the end of the third school year and from the first quarter of the fourth year were obtained from school records. These are E (excellent), G (good), S (satisfactory), or U (unsatisfactory), coded from 4 for excellent to 1 for unsatisfactory.

Mark expectations. Students, interviewed individually in school, were asked in two separate questions, "I'd like you to guess what marks you are going to get on your first report card this year, in November. What mark do you think you're going to get [in math?/in reading?] excellent, good, satisfactory, or unsatisfactory?" The questions for parents were identical, but were phrased in terms of their sons' or daughters' expected marks.

Mark recall. We obtained this information from parents and children using the same format as for expectations, but it was referenced to the "last report card, when school let out for summer vacation." Recall and expectation items were separated in the interview to minimize contamination from one to the other.

Background information and control variables

Race/ethnicity. African-Americans are coded 1; others, most of whom are white, 0.

Sex. Girls are coded 1; boys, 0.

Parent's educational level. Measured as the number of school years completed for the parent respondent (86% mothers or stepmothers, 9% fathers, 5% guardians), these data are taken from the first-year questionnaires.

Family economic level. Families are classified as high-income (coded 1) or low-income (coded 0) on the basis of their eligibility for reduced-price or free meals at school during the 1983–1984 school year. Meals are partially subsidized for families with incomes below 1.85 times federal poverty guidelines (based on family size and income); they are free at 1.3 times federal poverty guidelines. Sixty-seven percent of the sample received meal subsidies, 87 percent of which were free meals.[2]

California achievement test scores. Test data from the end of first grade, available through systemwide testing, are used to control for differences in verbal and quantitative competencies that predate both marks and expectations. The CAT-R is a 20-item subtest in reading comprehension; the CAT-M is a 36-item subtest in mathematics concepts and reasoning.

[2]Though a crude indicator of family economic level, the meal subsidy classification has been used, and has proved useful, in many studies (e.g., Farkas et al. 1990; Hallinan 1992).

In the analysis we first describe parents' and children's expectations and recall of marks for reading and math. Here we are interested in seeing how often expectations are "too high," and whether inaccurate forecasting and inaccurate recall are socially patterned. Then we use a simple school process model to predict marks from mark expectations. The model addresses two key hypotheses: first, that expectations will be differentially effective across racial/ethnic and SES lines; second, that the efforts of expectations will be stronger when recall of prior marks is accurate than when recall of prior marks is "too high." By making subsample comparisons, we can learn whether differences across groups in the use of performance feedback account for differences across groups in the potency of expectations as a determinant of marks.

Results

Accuracy of expectations

We begin by comparing expected marks with marks received. At this point, parents and children had been in the city school system three years; at the time of our inquiry, most of the children were a month or so into the current semester. Even so, expectations overshot marks by a wide margin.

Results for reading give a clear sense of the overall pattern because the results for math are similar to these. In a sample where reading marks center on "satisfactory" (averaging 2.1; see Table 1, upper right-hand panel), children expect marks of "good" (3.1 on average). This is a full unit too high, almost 1.3 standard deviations above the average mark received. Parents also have high expectations: their average of 2.8 is well above "satisfactory," shaded toward "good," and just below a full standard deviation above the actual average.

More detailed comparisons, not presented here because of limited space, underscore the exaggerated optimism reflected in these large mean differences. At the low end, more than one-fifth of the children receive failing marks in reading, but this is anticipated by only 3 percent of the students and by 4 percent of their parents; at the other extreme, only 5 percent receive marks of "excellent," but almost one-third of the youths and more than one-fifth of their parents anticipate such high ratings.

The subsample comparisons in Table 1 reveal both similarities and differences: all groups' expectations are higher than warranted, but some are more inaccurate than others. This is the case mainly because of differences in marking levels, because expectations are high throughout. For example, though white children's expectations are slightly above African- Americans' (3.2 versus 3.0), those of the latter are farther off target because their marks are lower (2.3 versus 1.9). African-Americans' expectations are 1.1 units above their actual mark; those of whites are .8 unit above. For African-Americans this is 1.6 standard deviations "too high," in contrast to 1.0 standard deviation for whites.

The picture is much the same when white and African-American parents are compared. White parents' average expectation (2.9) is .6 marking unit (.7 standard deviation) above the white average mark (2.3); African-American parents' average expectation (2.8) is .9 marking unit (1.3 standard deviations) above the African-American average mark (1.9). Despite moderately large differences in marking distributions by race, comparisons not displayed in the tables show that white and African-American parents actually have very similar percentages in the extreme expectation categories: 4.3 and 4.1 percent respectively for "unsatisfactory," and 24.9 and 22.5 percent respectively for "excellent." In contrast, 14.4 percent of white children fail reading as, compared with 26.5 percent of African-American children; 10.1 percent of whites receive marks of "excellent," as compared with 1.6 percent of African-Americans.

Trends are similar when the sample is divided along SES lines. Two indicators of family

TABLE I ■ Recall of Previous Reading and Math Marks, Expectations for Future Reading and Math Marks, and Actual Marks, for Parents and Students, with Subsample Comparisons

	Recall of previous year's marks			Expectation for future marks		
	Parents' recall	Actual mark	Students' recall	Parents' expectation	Actual mark	Students' expectation
Total sample						
Reading						
$\overline{X}$	2.7	2.3	2.9	2.8	2.1	3.1
N	(453)	(536)	(524)	(452)	(517)	(527)
SD	[.905]	[.861]	[.855]	[.832]	[.778]	[.794]
Math						
$\overline{X}$	2.8	2.4	3.0	2.8	2.2	3.2
N	(452)	(540)	(522)	(452)	(513)	(526)
SD	[.852]	[.833]	[.865]	[.774]	[.807]	[.723]
White						
Reading						
$\overline{X}$	2.8	2.5	3.0	2.9	2.3	3.2
N	(185)	(218)	(214)	(185)	(208)	(216)
SD	[.943]	[.927]	[.855]	[.824]	[.842]	[.745]
Math						
$\overline{X}$	2.8	2.5	3.0	2.9	2.4	3.3
N	(184)	(219)	(214)	(184)	(208)	(216)
SD	[.890]	[.915]	[.863]	[.822]	[.826]	[.717]
African-American						
Reading						
$\overline{X}$	2.7	2.2	2.8	2.8	1.9	3.0
N	(268)	(318)	(310)	(267)	(309)	(311)
SD	[.874]	[.789]	[.848]	[.835]	[.688]	[.821]
Math						
$\overline{X}$	2.7	2.3	2.9	2.8	2.0	3.2
N	(268)	(321)	(308)	(268)	(305)	(310)
SD	[.824]	[.756]	[.862]	[.739]	[.748]	[.728]
Some meal subsidy						
Reading						
$\overline{X}$	2.5	2.1	2.7	2.7	1.9	3.0
N	(295)	(360)	(351)	(294)	(347)	(354)
SD	[.872]	[.715]	[.884]	[.809]	[.637]	[.825]
Math						
$\overline{X}$	2.6	2.2	2.9	2.7	2.0	3.2
N	(295)	(362)	(351)	(294)	(343)	(353)
SD	[.807]	[.747]	[.895]	[.7674]	[.721]	[.745]
No meal subsidy						
Reading						
$\overline{X}$	3.1	2.8	3.1	3.1	2.5	3.2
N	(154)	(172)	(169)	(154)	(166)	(169)
SD	[.856]	[.901]	[.734]	[.787]	[.879]	[.711]
Math						
$\overline{X}$	3.0	2.7	3.0	3.1	2.6	3.3
N	(153)	(174)	(167)	(154)	(166)	(169)
SD	[.856]	[.901]	[.734]	[.787]	[.879]	[.711]
Parent's education < high school						
Reading						
$\overline{X}$	2.5	2.0	2.7	1.9	1.9	3.1
N	(161)	(205)	(200)	(161)	(193)	(201)
SD	[.894]	[.776]	[.930]	[.786]	[.680]	[.819]
Math						
$\overline{X}$	2.6	2.1	2.9	2.6	2.0	3.3
N	(161)	(205)	(200)	(160)	(190)	(201)
SD	[.813]	[.754]	[.928]	[.764]	[.719]	[.732]

TABLE I ■ (*CONTINUED*)

	Recall of previous year's marks			Expectation for future marks		
	Parents' recall	Actual mark	Students' recall	Parents' expectation	Actual mark	Students' expectation
Parent's education = high school						
Reading						
$\overline{X}$	2.7	2.4	2.8	2.8	2.1	3.0
N	(164)	(194)	(191)	(163)	(189)	(193)
SD	[.886]	[.738]	[.825]	[.823]	[.736]	[.797]
Math						
$\overline{X}$	2.8	2.5	2.9	2.8	2.3	3.2
N	(165)	(195)	(191)	(164)	(188)	(192)
SD	[.821]	[.789]	[.827]	[.743]	[.831]	[.785]
Parent's education > high school						
Reading						
$\overline{X}$	3.0	2.6	3.0	3.1	2.3	3.2
N	(128)	(137)	(133)	(128)	(135)	(133)
SD	[.853]	[1.005]	[.747]	[.851]	[.889]	[.747]
Math						
$\overline{X}$	3.0	2.7	3.1	3.0	2.3	331
N	(126)	(140)	(131)	(128)	(135)	(133)
SD	[.821]	[.789]	[.827]	[.743]	[.831]	[.758]

SES are used: parent's educational level and family economic level (as indicated by the family's meal subsidy status). Expectations are considerably above marks in all comparisons, but the gap is greater at lower SES levels and greater for children than for parents. Children of school dropout parents, for example, expect to receive marks of "good" (3.1), even though their actual marks fall below "satisfactory" (1.9 on average). Their expectations are 1.2 marking units too high, or almost 1.8 standard deviations. Children whose parents have some college education also expect "good" (3.2) marks, but their actual marks (at 2.3) are merely above "satisfactory." Consequently their expectations are "only" .9 unit off, or just under one full standard deviation.[3]

The reasons for such uniformly high expectations are not entirely clear. The pattern, however, is not peculiar to this study (see Entwisle and Hayduk 1978). These responses almost certainly contain an element of social desirability. Also, young children tend to be less self-reflective than older children, and to take less account of cues from teachers and of comparisons with others in weighing their competencies. Young children instead evince optimism, partly because their abilities are developing at a remarkable pace: in comparison with their capabilities a year earlier, most have made enormous strides. (Developmental changes in children's thinking and information processing are reviewed in Eccles, Midgley, and Adler 1984; Stipek 1985; Weisz and Cameron 1985.)

Immaturity does not account fully for the phenomenon of "too high expectations," however; parents' expectations show the same pattern. Performance expectations, whether high or low, do not necessarily imply a well-conceived

[3]Not only inflated expectations are socially patterned. Analyses not reported here show that expectations are accurate beyond chance expectation more often in the white and upper-SES subsamples than in the African-American and lower-SES subsamples, although none of the groups are found to be especially adept at forecasting marks beyond chance. This is indicated in kappa coefficients, calculated on the expectations-by-mark 4 × 4 cross-classifications. Because mark distributions differ across groups and expectations tend to be high throughout, failure to adjust for marginals could give an exaggerated impression of accuracy: high expectations, by chance, would correspond more closely to high marks. For the same reason, simple correlation coefficients would not give a reliable picture. Most kappas are quite small, .10 or less.

plan of action for following through, but some expectations presumably are better conceived than others; they are not merely wishful thinking, a buoyant attitude, or putting on a good face. How can we tell the difference? The left-hand side of Table 1 presents data on recall of prior marks that may help to clarify matters.

Accuracy of recall

Report cards provide feedback from school to home on children's academic progress. Attentiveness to these messages is reflected in parents' and children's recall of marks in the major academic subjects from the most recent report card. These signals are intended, among other things, to reinforce good work habits and to encourage corrective action where improvement is desired. Ideally, then, report card marks would be known by virtually everyone, but unfortunately they are not. Again, reading and math results are similar, so we focus on the former.

Although the gap between recalled marks and the marks received on the last report card is smaller than the gap between expectations and marks, the general trend is similar: recall of past performance is skewed high, and children's recall is farther off target than is parents'. Throughout the sample, the final reading mark averaged 2.3, whereas the recalled averages were 2.9 among students (a difference of .63 sd) and 2.7 among parents (a difference of .47 sd). Overall, pupils and parents report about half as many failing marks and twice as many excellent marks as were assigned.

Subsample comparisons also generally mirror the pattern for expectations, although differences between groups sometimes are small. African-American youths' recall of marks, for example, is about three-quarters of a standard deviation too high (.6 unit); the average for whites is one-half standard deviation too high (.5 unit). When findings are grouped according to parent's education, however, reports from the children of high school dropouts are much less accurate than those from children whose parents had at least some college education. Among the former, the average remembered mark of 2.7 is .7 marking unit above the actual average (or just over .9 sd); among the latter, the average recalled mark of 3.0 is .4 marking unit (.4 sd) above the actual average. In all groups the trends for the parent subsample parallel those for their children, except that parents' reports generally are more accurate.[4]

Comparisons in this and the previous section show that both performance expectations and recall often fall wide of the mark (mainly too high), and that the responses of minority and disadvantaged parents and children are most often inaccurate.[5] High expectations could

[4]As in the case of expectations, kappa coefficients show that accuracy of recall beyond chance expectation also is socially patterned. These kappas are considerably larger than those involving expectations (generally in the .2 to .5 range). In every instance the kappas for whites and upper-SES groups exceed those for African-Americans and lower-SES groups, often by a factor of 2 or more.

[5]Ceiling constraints are a concern here, however, as well as in the next section, where recall of past marks is used in an interaction analysis. In both reading and math, about 10 percent of the children received marks of "excellent." These marks *cannot* be overstated. This is an issue because prior marks are socially patterned: 18 percent of whites but only 7 percent of African-Americans had reading marks of "excellent"; for children whose parents have education beyond high school and those whose parents are high school dropouts, the percentages are 27 and 4.4 respectively. We are interested here in overreporting of prior marks as a substantive process. Children who are doing well in school (and their parents) probably also are better attuned to what is happening there, and for that reason their recall would be expected to be more accurate. Yet ceiling constraints also make it more likely that they will report past marks correctly. There is no sure way of separating "artifactual" from "real" differences across groups in reporting errors, but as a check we reran all analyses, excluding children with prior marks of "excellent." In this way everyone can overreport marks. Relationships are somewhat attenuated with this exclusion, but the trends, including significant differences, still parallel those reported. We found very few exceptions.

reflect a generally positive but realistic outlook. When this is the case, we would expect them to prove useful. High expectations, however, also could be largely fanciful, poorly informed by previous performance evaluations, and detached from appropriate follow-through behaviors; in such a case they would prove less useful. The latter pattern is consistent with the "too great expectations" assumption, but to evaluate it properly one must consider how recall, expectations, and performances are joined in individuals' thinking and experience over time. We do this in the next section.

Recall of marks and the productive role of expectations

We presume that members of advantaged groups differ from those of disadvantaged groups in possessing social skills and resources that allow them to interact more effectively with the school bureaucracy and to forge closer, more productive home-school partnerships. Such resources can be regarded as elements of human and social capital that originate in differences in class background and in attendant differences of life experience. Home-based skills and resources affect children's educational prospects in many ways. Highly educated parents are generally more sophisticated advocates of their children's interests at school and are better able to support and reinforce traditional academic goals (e.g., Hess and Holloway 1984; Slaughter and Epps 1987). Recall of marks is only one aspect of this complex issue, and a limited indicator of parents' activities. For example, parents high in social and human capital are likely also to attend to the many cues other than marks which indicate how well their child is doing, and they probably focus more closely on the academic domain than do parents outside the middle-class mainstream. Entwisle and Hayduk (1982), for example, found that middle-class parents judged their children's ability to do school-work mainly on their reading marks, whereas blue-collar and inner-city parents relied more strongly on conduct marks. This difference in emphasis between "doing well" and "being good" is consistent with the class differences in "focal values" described by Kohn (1977).

Prior marks might be reported in error for many reasons, including an unconscious desire to shore up self-regard when performance is low (see on the protective role of high self-esteem in the face of stigmatizing circumstances), deliberate falsification in order to maintain face, and lack of understanding or interest in respect to the issues. Here we are concerned mainly with information processing. Parents and children who do not use relevant feedback from school are not able to frame appropriate expectations for future performance, and inappropriate expectations can undermine prospects for successful follow-through. According to this line of reasoning, performance expectations should predict future performance more accurately among parents and children who remember past marks correctly than among those whose recall of past marks is mistaken. In addition, because the accuracy with which past marks are recalled is socially patterned, we anticipate a reduction of racial and SES differences in the strength of the relationship between expectations and marks when accuracy of recall is taken into account.

We test these ideas in the context of a simple, multivariate school process model. Our purpose is to understand more clearly the circumstances that make the very same expressions of intent productive for some youths but "too high" for others, and particularly why high performance expectations more often precede high marks in advantaged than in disadvantaged groups.

Performance expectations from early in the school year are used to predict later marks, with controls for social background (race, gender, parent's education, and family economic level)[6] and standardized test scores in the same domain (CAT level on the Verbal Comprehension subtest for reading marks; CAT level on the Math Reasoning subtest for math marks). As shown in Figure 1, the outcome measure is the first-quarter mark from Grade 4. Mark expectations were elicited early in the first quarter; timing is less critical for the other measures. The data on meal subsidy came from school records two years earlier, the parent's educational level was obtained three years earlier, and the CAT test controls dated from the spring of Grade 1.

Results are reported in Table 2 for reading and in Table 3 for math. Both metric and standardized coefficients are provided. The general framework is similar to that used in many studies that link school performance to performance expectations.

We are interested mainly in the expectation effects, but other influences warrant at least brief mention. In reading, reasonably large coefficients are obtained for all predictors except gender; in math, we find exceptions for gender and for parent's education. Youths with high test scores receive considerably higher marks than those with low scores; youths from families not on meal subsidy fare better than those receiving subsidy; African-Americans' marks, on average, fall slightly below whites'; and in reading but not in math, high parent's education is an important asset.

Mark expectations exercise a significant independent influence on performance levels, even after adjusting for these other factors. As might be anticipated, these effects are larger for parents than for children (compare metric coefficients: .259 versus .132 in reading [see Table 2]; .300 versus .175 in math [see Table 3]). As stated earlier, however, young children are not especially self-reflective, and to us it seems noteworthy that their performance expectations stand out as useful at all. In an earlier study using a roughly similar framework to predict first- and second-year marks, children's expectations were marginally significant (at the .10 level) in just one of four instances, with a standardized coefficient of .06 (Alexander and Entwisle 1988: Table A4). In this study, however, the standardized coefficients for both reading and math show that by their fourth year in school, children's expectations are about as important as other significant predictors, except for test scores.

The remaining columns of Tables 2 and 3 present results separately for the several criteria for comparison: African-American versus white, by family income level, and by parent's education. These subdivisions lead to relatively small sample sizes (see figures reported in the last row for each panel). This problem is even more severe in Table 4, where each group is subdivided further on the basis of recall accuracy. For this reason, and because of the complicated line of reasoning that directs attention to these comparisons, we focus more closely on trends than on specific tests of significance. The expectation coefficients reported in Tables 2 and 3 differ significantly across racial/ethnic and SES lines in seven of 16 comparisons. Three of these involve children and four involve parents.

The complete within-group regressions are presented in Tables 2 and 3, but we wish mainly to see how performance expectations affect marks. Generally these effects are larger in "advantaged" groups, as can be seen by

[6]We also experimented with measures of mother's occupational status and household composition, but these were not significant in any of the regression analyses. Also, the former resulted in additional sample loss (N = 610 versus 745 for mother's education and 702 versus 745 for the meal subsidy variable). The SES measures are intercorrelated substantially (e.g., in the .43 to .65 range); for this reason, no doubt, occupational status proved redundant. Correlations involving household composition (i.e., two-parent versus other arrangements) were smaller, but household composition as a predictor of schooling outcomes is often nonsignificant when SES measures are controlled as well (e.g., Entwisle and Alexander 1994).

TABLE 2 ■ Regression Results Predicting First-Quarter Reading Marks from Social Background, Test Performance, and Performance Expectations, for Parents and Students and Separately by Subgroup (Standardized Coefficients in Parentheses)

		Race		Meal subsidy		Parent's education		
	Total	White	African-American	Some	None	< High school	High school	> High school
Parents								
Race	−.366***	—	—	−.297***	−.407***	−.327**	−.272*	−.530**
	(−.23)			(−.22)	(.23)	(−.25)	(−.18)	(−.26)
Sex	.083	.033	.115	.078	.137	.100	.026	.051
	(.05)	(.02)	(.08)	(.06)	(.08)	(.07)	(.02)	(.03)
Meal subsidy	.231*	.233	.223	—	—	.300	.261	.257
	(.14)	(.14)	(.14)			(.15)	(.17)	(.14)
Parent's education	.062***	.060*	.058**	.048*	.062**	—	—	—
	(.20)	(.21)	(.19)	(.14)	(.20)			
CAT level	.003***	.004*	.003*	.003***	.002	.003*	.002	.004
	(.18)	(.20)	(.16)	(.22)	(.09)	(.20)	(.12)	(.20)
Reading expectations	.259***	.323***	.222***	.150**	.534***	.194**	.327**	.313**
	(.26)	(.30)	(.26)	(.19)	(.44)	(.22)	(.33)	(.30)
Constant	−.391	−.729	−.446	.016	−.702	1.324	.562	.061
Adj. R^2	.376***	.397	.255***	.155***	.376***	.230***	.262***	.413***
N	356	143	213	234	122	139	118	103
Students								
Race	−.279***	—	—	−.225**	−.301*	−.329**	−.094	−.436**
	(−.18)			(−.17)	(−.18)	(−.24)	(−.06)	(−.23)
Sex	.133*	.007	.208**	.125	.109	.121	.076	.125
	(.09)	(.00)	(.16)	(.10)	(.07)	(.09)	(.05)	(.07)
Meal subsidy	.287**	.286*	.288**	—	—	.248	.392**	.348*
	(.18)	(.17)	(.18)			(.12)	(.26)	(.20)
Parent's education	.051***	.051*	.046*	.026	.062**	—	—	—
	(.17)	(.18)	(.15)	(.07)	(.22)			
CAT level	.004***	.005***	.004***	.004***	.006***	.005***	.004**	.006***
	(.26)	(.28)	(.24)	(.27)	(.26)	(.29)	(.23)	(.31)
Reading expectations	.132**	.191*	.108*	.090*	.235*	.047	.213**	.151
	(.14)	(.17)	(.13)	(.11)	(.20)	(.05)	(.24)	(.13)
Constant	−.449	−.758	−.449	.088	−1.10	.264	.070	−.446
Adj. R^2	.314***	.314***	.221***	.119***	.258***	.194***	.250***	.354***
N	423	177	246	289	134	168	150	108

* ≤ .05; ** ≤ .01; *** ≤ .001.

comparing coefficients across the "Reading expectations" and "Math expectations" rows.

In reading, the expectation effects are only slightly larger for whites than for African-Americans, but in math the disparities are sizable: .310 versus .081 among children and .514 versus .149 among parents. In the SES comparisons, differences also are as expected, especially when families are distinguished by economic level. Among parents the metric coefficient for reading in the "no subsidy" group is almost four times as large as for the subsidy group; among

TABLE 3 ■ REGRESSION RESULTS PREDICTING FIRST-QUARTER MATH MARKS FROM SOCIAL BACKGROUND, TEST PERFORMANCE, AND PERFORMANCE EXPECTATIONS, FOR PARENTS AND STUDENTS AND SEPARATELY BY SUBGROUP (STANDARDIZED COEFFICIENTS IN PARENTHESES)

		Race		Meal subsidy		Parent's education		
	Total	White	African-American	Some	None	< High school	High school	> High school
Parents								
Race	−.363***	—	—	−.466***	−.131	−.369**	−.346*	−.354*
	(−.22)			(−.31)	(−.08)	(−.26)	(−.21)	(−.20)
Sex	.075	.063	.091	.058	.145	.118	−.053	.154
	(.05)	(.04)	(.06)	(.04)	(.09)	(.08)	(−.03)	(.09)
Meal subsidy	.212*	.004	.338**	—	—	.230	.240	.099
	(.13)	(.00)	(.21)			(.11)	(.14)	(.06)
Parent's education	.021	.012	.015	.043	−.008	—	—	—
	(.07)	(.04)	(.04)	(.11)	(−.03)			
CAT level	.005***	.006**	.006***	.004**	.009***	.004*	.005*	.007**
	(.23)	(.23)	(.27)	(.20)	(.320)	(.20)	(.19)	(.29)
Math expectations	.300***	.514***	.149*	.213***	.510***	.213**	.408***	.281*
	(.28)	(.50)	(.15)	(.22)	(.44)	(.22)	(.37)	(.25)
Constant	−.658	−1.208	−.678	−.121	−2.042	.035	−.384	−.700
Adj. R^2	.327***	.377***	.193***	.179***	.384***	.178***	.334***	.348***
N	360	143	217	233	127	134	128	101
Students								
Race	−.275***	—	—	−.319***	−.131	−.268*	−.228	−.313
	(−.17)			(−.21)	(−.08)	(−.19)	(−.14)	(−.19)
Sex	.064	.055	.079	.115	.008	−.200	−.040	−.049
	(.04)	(.03)	(.05)	(.08)	(.01)	(−.20)	(−.02)	(−.03)
Meal subsidy	.268**	.221	.316*	—	—	.233	.381**	.110
	(.16)	(.14)	(.17)			(.11)	(.22)	(.07)
Parent's education	.033*	.039	.023	.055*	0.0	—	—	—
	(.10)	(.14)	(.07)	(.14)	(.00)			
CAT level	.008***	.007***	.008***	.007***	.010***	.006***	.008***	.101***
	(.34)	(.32)	(.35)	(.32)	(.38)	(.29)	(.34)	(.40)
Math expectations	.175***	.310***	.081	.057	.547***	.063	.256**	.256*
	(.15)	(.26)	(9.08)	(.06)	(.41)	(.06)	(.23)	(.19)
Constant	−1.345	−1.691	−1.221	−.824	−2.694	−.195	−1.346	−1.700
Adj. R^2	.298***	.328***	.180***	.152***	.393***	.156***	.313***	.321***
N	415	178	237	281	134	169	146	102

* ≤ .05; ** ≤ .01; *** ≤ .001.

children it is more than twice as large. When groups are distinguished on the basis of parent's education, coefficients for the high school dropout sample always are the smallest of the three: in reading and in math, for parents and for children. In fact, expectation effects among the children of high school dropout parents fall short of significance in both marking areas.

As anticipated, then, high expectations consistently are least effective among the disadvantaged. No exceptions to this finding occur in Tables 2 and 3, although when college-educated

TABLE 4 ■ METRIC PERFORMANCE EXPECTATION EFFECTS ON FIRST-QUARTER MARKS, SEPARATELY FOR "ACCURATE RECALL" AND "TOO HIGH" RECALL SUBSAMPLES, STUDENTS AND PARENTS AND BY SUBGROUPS

		Race		Meal subsidy		Parent's education		
	Total	White	African-American	Some	None	< High school	High school	> High school
Parents								
Accurate recall sample								
Expectation effect	.354*	.466*	.312*	.186*	.669*	.189**	.559*	.442*
Adj. R^2	(.458)	(.486)	(.327)	(.223)	(.437)	(.309)	(385)	(.465)
N	[200]	[93]	[107]	[119]	[81]	[68]	[71]	[64]
Too high recall sample								
Expectation effect	.237*	.349*	.215*	.232*	.320**	.309*	.194	.234**
Adj. R^2	(.221)	(.238)	(.171)	(.137)	(.095)	(.224)	(.117)	(.142)
N	[156]	[50]	[106]	[115]	[41]	[71]	[47]	[39]
Diff. bet. 1 & 2	*	NS	NS	NS	*	NS	*	*
Accurate recall sample								
Students								
Accurate recall sample	.354*	.466*	.312*	.186*	.669*	.189**	.559*	.442*
Adj. R^2	(.428)	(.418)	(.337)	(.154)	(.329)	(.317)	(252)	(.462)
N	[213]	[96]	[117]	[122]	[91]	[71]	[81]	[62]
Too high recall sample								
Expectation effect	.106**	.108	.097	.102	.102	.079	.217*	−.020
Adj. R^2	(.101)	(.106)	(.067)	(.079)	(−.059)	(.096)	(127)	(.048)
N	[210]	[81]	[129]	[167]	[43]	[97]	[69]	[46]
Diff. bet. 1 & 2	*	**	**	NS	*	NS	NS	*
Math								
Accurate recall sample								
Expectation effect	.486*	.665*	.348*	.436*	.586*	.353*	.626*	.547*
Adj. R^2	(.407)	(.482)	(.244)	(.261)	(.452)	(.258)	(424)	(.407)
N	214	90	124	130	84	68	78	71
Too high recall sample								
Expectation effect	.194*	.335*	.079*	.098	.521*	.159	.288*	.115*
Adj. R^2	(.213)	(.166)	(.162)	(.127)	(.234)	(.101)	(194)	(.202)
N	146	53	93	103	43	66	50	30
Diff. bet. 1 & 2	*	*	*	*	NS	NS	*	*
Students								
Accurate recall sample								
Expectation effect	.263*	.382*	.173*	.098	.713*	.063	.354*	.488*
Adj. R^2	(.447)	(.452)	(.369)	(.308)	(.421)	(.254)	(436)	(.421)
N	193	93	100	111	82	56	82	56
Too high recall sample								
Expectation effect	.112**	.209*	.032	.048	.358*	.056	.203**	.021
Adj. R^2	(.116)	(.116)	(.020)	(.069)	(.257)	(.122)	(104)	(.029)
N	222	85	137	170	52	113	64	46
Diff. bet. 1 & 2	*	*	**	NS	*	NS	**	*

* ≤ .05; ** ≤ .10, one-tailed test.

parents and their children are compared with high school graduates, the differences either are quite small or favor the latter. Hence the trend by educational level is not linear. Rather, the high school dropout parents, and especially their children, stand out from the others. Why is this so? Do differences in the accuracy of mark recall matter?

We explored this possibility in Table 4, where parents and children with correct recall of prior marks are separated from those with mistaken recall. The model described above is used again, although in this case we report only the coefficients for performance expectations—our central concern. Parents' results are displayed in the upper panel; children's results, in the lower panel.

If inaccurate recall is the factor undermining the usefulness of high goals for minority and low-SES parents and their children, then differences in the size of expectation effects by race and SES levels should be smaller within accuracy-of-recall categories than in Tables 2 and 3, where accuracy of recall was not controlled. Also, when recall is correct, expectations should be more effective than when recall is wrong. Many of the trends in Table 4 accord with these hypotheses, but we find exceptions as well.

In the total sample, effects of parents' and children's expectations are larger when recall of marks is accurate than when it is inaccurate. All four of the interaction terms are significant at the .05 level,[7] though the differences are smaller in reading (.354 versus .237 for parents; .191 versus .106 for children) than in math (.486 versus .194 for parents; .263 versus .112 for children). Overall, then, expectations appear to be more efficacious for both parents and children when both groups understand correctly how past performance was received.

This general pattern is reflected in most subgroup comparisons as well. Among parents, expectation effects are larger when recall is accurate for both African-Americans and whites in predicting math marks, for higher-income parents in predicting reading marks, and for more highly educated parents (with at least a high school education) in predicting both reading and math marks. All these differences are significant at the .05 level. The exceptions occur mainly at the lower SES levels, where most expectation coefficients are small regardless of recall accuracy.[8]

The results for children mirror those of their parents in most respects. As with parents, larger coefficients usually obtain for the subsamples with correct recall of prior marks, but because expectation effects and sample sizes are small, fewer of the differences by recall status are significant. All four within-race interactions reach significance at the .10 level. So do five of 10 comparisons within SES group that involve distinctions at the upper SES levels: children of parents with some postsecondary education and children from nonsubsidy households who correctly report their previous report card marks derive more advantage from their high expectations than do their counterparts from similar SES levels whose recall of prior marks is mistaken. Among lower-SES youths, on the other hand, expectation coefficients are small throughout, most are nonsignificant, and recall status seems largely irrelevant.

Insofar as the potency of performance expectations differs as a function of recall accuracy,

---

[7]We determined significance of the expectation-recall interaction in regression analyses using the full sample. We added a product term to the main effects equations; this included, in addition to the predictors used throughout (race, gender, parent's education, family economic level, and CAT score in the outcome domain), a dichotomy distinguishing accurate from inaccurate recall. A one-tailed test is used in determining the significance level for the interaction term.

[8]An exception is the significant difference in math among low-income parents, where the accurate recall coefficient is four times the "too high" recall coefficient (.436 versus .098).

these results are consistent with our hypotheses. We also anticipated, however, that controlling for accuracy of recall would attenuate differences between advantaged and disadvantaged groups in the size of expectation effects. The differences diminish when recall of past marks is mistaken because the expectation coefficients are small throughout (e.g., children's results in reading). More striking, however, are the increases in coefficients when social advantage is *combined with* correct recall. These large effects occur for whites, for parents (and their children) who are at least high school graduates, and for higher-income families. Among these groups, and almost exclusively among them, it matters a great deal whether one expects to do well or poorly. In these instances all but one of the expectation effects are above .3; among parents, most effects are in the .5 to .7 range.

Where social standing is low or where recall is mistaken, the coefficients generally are small. Only a handful are above .3; just one reaches .4 (the math effect for parents with accurate recall who receive meal subsidies). Low-SES youths appear especially ineffective in capitalizing on their performance expectations: only one of eight expectation effects is significant for these children regardless of recall status, and the exception (the .118 coefficient in math for accurate-recall low-income children) is quite small. By way of comparison, all four effects for low-SES parents are significant for reading, and two of four (those for the accurate-recall subsamples) are significant for math.

Despite low income and little formal schooling, parents still can make a difference as agents of positive academic socialization (see Seginer 1983). In the present results their attitudes matter, especially when they are attuned to the flow of relevant feedback from school to home (e.g., effects in math). Lower-SES youths, on the other hand, do not realize their high expectations, whether or not they are grounded in reality. The rational model of goal-directed behavior implicit in the actor-oriented status attainment framework (e.g., Horan 1978) thus appears not to fit disadvantaged youths especially well. The children studied here are on average about age 10: they could change (e.g., Parsons and Ruble 1977), but by that age the more advantaged among them already appear to be engaging in effective self-regulation of their academic behavior. One cannot determine from these data alone whether disadvantaged children's personal development in this respect is merely delayed or actually divergent.[9] For children reared in low-SES households, however, performance expectations bear little resemblance to outcomes; this could be an especially pernicious consequence of growing up in disadvantaged circumstances.

Discussion

The present results replicate Entwisle and Hayduk's (1978, 1982) description of children's and parents' performance expectations in Grades 1 and 2 in several key respects: early performance expectations tend to be high overall, these expectations are socially patterned, and lower-SES and minority parents and their children take less account of prior performance evaluations in forming expectations than do upper-SES and white parents and children. Schools and students were selected randomly into the Beginning School Study from throughout the Baltimore City Public Schools, whereas the earlier project, though also based in Baltimore, was conducted at only three sites. Therefore this replication is important. It suggests that Entwisle and Hayduk's characterization of "too great expectations" in the early grade levels has considerable generalizability. (For a more general

[9] Stronger evidence on this point will be available when we are able to evaluate similar models at different benchmark ages. The BSS cohort now is in high school and is still being tracked.

comparison of early achievement processes in the two data sets, see Entwisle et al. 1986).

Also important are the ways in which the present project extends Entwisle and Hayduk's earlier work. The main purpose of their analysis was to explore how expectations take form: initially amorphous, over time they become increasingly responsive to situational feedback, at least among middle-class whites. In their data, children's expectations had no impact on later performance, so their being "too high" incurred no particular cost at that point in the children's schooling. (The same, however, was not true of parents' expectations, which were influential from the beginning.) This pattern also is replicated in the BSS in Grades 1 and 2 (e.g., Alexander and Entwisle 1988). The present analysis evaluates achievement patterns later in the primary grades; by Grade 4 we obtain significant effects of children's expectations on marks, both overall and in most subsamples. This is an important developmental milestone because it signals children's maturation as effective "producers of their own development" (e.g., Lerner and Busch-Rossnagel 1981). Apparently, however, not all children mature on the same schedule or in the same way: we did not obtain significant expectancy effects in all subsample comparisons.

In their earlier work, Entwisle and Hayduk intimated the possibility of differences in the way performance feedback is taken into account, but they did not test this possibility directly. They merely observed weaker ties between prior marks and future expectations among disadvantaged (i.e., minority and lower-SES) parents and children than among their more advantaged counterparts. This finding suggested to them a cycle which, over time, could undercut the development of an effective "internal control function": "Children with unrealistically high expectations apparently insulated themselves from mark feedback, and marks, in turn, displayed insulation by not responding to excessively high expectations. . . . Too big a gap between low marks and high expectations is a situation with a bad prognosis" (Entwisle and Hayduk 1978, 175–76). Why was the prognosis so poor? Because, when they ignore how previous efforts were evaluated, children and their parents miss signals that might guide corrective actions.

In the present analysis we saw *direct evidence* of differential attentiveness to prior feedback through marks (i.e., accurate versus inaccurate recall) along racial/ethnic and SES lines. We received some indication that this difference contributed to the differential effectiveness of forward-looking expectations as resources for future marks. Our analysis considered only one relevant signal on only one occasion; even so, differences in the recall of past marks seemed to alter the link between expectation and performance, to the detriment of those whose recall was mistaken.

In most research, the only link is that between expectations or aspirations and outcomes, much like the regression results reported in Tables 2 and 3. When these effects are large, as they often are, it is easy to simply conclude that high goals facilitate their realization. But when the yield from high goals or expectations is far greater for some youths than for others, we must consider more generally what else is required to make expectations "work."

Our interpretation directs attention to the broader motivation-goal-behavior nexus that frames effective goal-directed behaviors. Expectations can help to bring about the desired outcomes only by setting into motion actions that are reasonably appropriate to the task at hand. This "mental roadmap" usually is left implicit in research on achievement processes, but the supporting infrastructure may not always be present.

The "value expectancy" framework on motivation and striving for achievement is the conceptual backdrop to most achievement models. According to this approach, the drive toward a goal or object is a joint function of the value placed on that outcome and the perceived probability of success (e.g., Atkinson and Feather 1966; Atkinson and Raynor 1974; Feather 1986). In the typical survey study, the object or goal is identified through expressed expectations or aspirations (e.g., going to college, earning a mark of "excellent" on the upcoming report card). The motivational dynamic, however (assessed prospect and value), is simply inferred. In fact, goal, expectancy, and value are separate (and separable) considerations: goals deemed unattainable regardless of one's best efforts ("the deck is stacked against me, so why bother?") or relatively low in one's preference hierarchy (e.g., star athlete versus star student) may command little effort.

According to Werner (1984 27), "[E]xpectancy of success . . . influences a variety of motivational indexes such as the direction of goal-related activity, or the intensity, quality and persistence of behavior." His perspective (also see Weiner 1986) emphasizes the role of causal attributions ("Is the outcome under my control? Is it governed more by ability or by effort?") and affective responses (e.g., guilt, anger, pride), which combine in complex ways to determine when and how vigorously goals are pursued. In the case of minority and economically disadvantaged groups, discriminatory barriers, and other obstacles (Ogbu 1988), fatalistic attitudes (e.g., Coleman et al. 1966) and related feelings of low personal efficacy in academic competitions (Hughes and Demo 1989) would be expected to undermine *the pursuit* of academic goals (e.g., Bandura 1986; Schunk 1984; Weiner 1986), even when they are held sincerely. This is one reason why the connection between expectation and attainment of aspirations might be attenuated.

Another consideration is whether the *plan of action* adopted is well suited to the goal at hand. Even with identical goals and comparable commitment to their pursuit, different groups would not be expected to achieve at similar levels because the strategic resources they can bring to bear on the competition will differ. The social and personal resources that empower parents and their children in the academic realm involve many understandings and skills—about how schools work and what criteria determine success, about getting along in a complex bureaucracy, about relating present actions to future interests, and so on. These skills are socially patterned.

When high expectations are detached from such resources, they prove less useful. It is dubious, for example, whether parents who give unconditional encouragement will be as effective as those who selectively reinforce the behaviors, attitudes, and values that produce results. When parents themselves have been successful in school (e.g., highly educated) and in the workplace (e.g., higher income and high job status), high expectations are more likely to be coupled with appropriate activities at home and with the tangible resources needed to realize those expectations.[10] Indeed, the purpose of parent involvement programs and home-school partnerships is to help parents acquire precisely these kinds of "skills and understandings" so that they might support their children's schooling more effectively. The problem is not that parents' goals are too low; typically they are high, but the wherewithal for effective follow-through is often lacking. It is encouraging that some of the programs designed to help parents acquire these resources have succeeded in moderating the characteristic strong positive relationship between family SES level and school performance (for an overview, see Epstein 1991, 1992). We would guess that participation in high-quality home-school partnership programs also would strengthen relationships between expectations and performance.

[10]We believe that this is indicated in the exceptionally large expectation effects seen in Table 4, when accurate recall combines with high family SES level.

A clearer sense of the motivational character of expectations may permit a fuller accounting of the role of expectations in achievement processes. Yet even the best-conceived plan of action or the most supportive family environment will not guarantee success. Obstacles outside the motivational framework—for example, lack of ability, hostile teachers, inadequate opportunities to learn rooted in school practices—also limit prospects for success. These, too, may be socially patterned. The motivational framework does not provide all the answers, but it is possible to improve the way the motivational model is applied to problems within its purview.

We conclude that holding "too high expectations" does not serve the interests of minority and lower-SES parents and their children especially well. Does it follow that they should lower their sights? Because high expectations are associated with better performance for everyone except lower-SES children, this probably is not advisable. For ethical and other reasons one would be reluctant to undermine young children's optimistic outlook unless it is highly probable that doing so would serve a useful purpose. Some minority and low-SES children do succeed, after all, and high expectations, even if unreasonably high, may help children maintain a positive level of self-esteem. In the extreme case, it makes little sense to inflict on young children the sense that they are failures. This would not be healthy at any time; certainly it should be avoided in the early primary grades, when ideas about self and school are beginning to take form.

A more effective approach might be to shift the feedback upward. Perhaps marks in the early primary grades could emphasize effort or progress over mastery, at least initially; absolute standards of evaluation could be phased in gradually. This arrangement would allow more children to come close to fulfilling their high expectations and would encourage in their parents the attitude that success indeed is within their children's reach. More positive reinforcing feedback in the first few years of school would be expected to engage parents' and children's energies, and over time might help children to develop a more effective internal control function. As their efforts meet with reasonable success, they learn what is required to continue succeeding and are encouraged in their desire to do so; these are key considerations within the value-expectancy framework. Teachers would have to be careful, however, not to move children along without sufficient preparation for the work ahead. Because children are sharply attuned to feedback, challenges that proved too challenging could easily undermine their confidence.

Some downward adjustment of overhigh expectations also might be beneficial. At issue is the "net yield" from expectations, which is determined not only by their level (high versus low, where high generally is better) but also by their efficiency in producing results (as gauged by slope estimates, which are larger when expectations are "reasonably realistic"). The solution, however, is not simply to deflate inflated goals or to coach minority and lower-SES parents and their children on how to read report cards. These are merely surface considerations.

Parents and children who hold to inflated goals and fail to take account of pertinent feedback are not closely attuned to the way the system works; thus they find it harder to achieve success within the system through self-regulating behavior. Expectations do not "work" under such circumstances because, to paraphrase Baker and Stevenson (1986), whom we quoted earlier, they are detached from the "long series of other small things" that help make them work. Within the scope of the motivation framework, we need to understand more clearly the relevant contexts surrounding expectations and how these either impede or facilitate successful follow-through. That "contexts" is plural is the key consideration: certainly processes internal to the individual and constraints external to the individual both play a role.

REFERENCES

Alexander, Karl L. and Doris R. Entwisle. 1988. "Achievement in the First Two Years of School: Patterns and Processes." *Monographs of the Society for Research in Child Development* 53(2).

Alexander, Karl L., Doris R. Entwisle, and Susan Dauber. 1994. *On the Success of Failure: A Reassessment of the Effects of Retention in the Primary Grades.* Cambridge, MA: Cambridge University Press.

Atkinson, John W. and Norman Feather, eds. 1966. *A Theory of Achievement Motivation.* New York: Krieger.

Atkinson, John and Joel O. Raynor. 1974. *Motivation and Achievement.* New York: Wiley.

Baker, David P. and Dario L. Stevenson. 1986. "Mothers' Strategies for Children's School Achievement: Managing the Transition to High School." *Sociology of Education* 59:156–66.

Bandura, Albert. 1986. "The Explanatory Power and Predictive Scope of Self-Efficacy Theory." *Journal of Social and Clinical Psychology* 4:359–73.

Coleman, James S. 1988. "Social Capital in the Creation of Human Capital." *American Journal of Sociology* 94:S95–S120.

Coleman, James S., Ernest Q. Campbell, Carol J. Hobson, James McPartland, Alexander Mood, Frederic D. Weinfeld, and Robert L. York. 1966. *Equality of Educational Opportunity.* Washington, DC: U.S. Government Printing Office.

Crocker, Jennifer and Brenda Major. 1989. "Social Stigma and Self-Esteem: The Self-Protective Properties of Stigma." *Psychological Review* 96:608–30.

Diggory, J. 1966. Self-Evaluations: *Concepts and Studies.* New York: Wiley.

Eccles, Jacquelynne S., Carol Midgley, and Terry Adler. 1984. "Grade-Related Changes in the School Environment: Effects on Achievement Motivation." Pp. 283–331 in *The Development of Achievement Motivation,* edited by John G. Nicholls. Greenwich, CT: JAI.

Entwisle, Doris R. and Karl L. Alexander. 1994. "A Parent's Economic Shadow: Poverty and Family Structure Influences on Early School Achievement." Unpublished manuscript.

Entwisle, Doris R., Karl L. Alexander, Doris Cadigan, and Aaron M. Pallas. 1986. "The Schooling Process in First Grade: Two Samples a Decade Apart." *American Educational Research Journal* 23:587–613.

Entwisle, Doris R. and Leslie A. Hayduk. 1978. *Too Great Expectations: The Academic Outlook of Young Children.* Baltimore: Johns Hopkins University Press.

———. 1982. *Early Schooling: Cognitive and Affective Outcomes.* Baltimore: Johns Hopkins University Press.

Epstein, Joyce L. 1991. "Effects on Student Achievement of Teachers' Practices of Parent Involvement." Pp. 261–76 in *Literacy through Family, Community, and School Interaction,* Vol. 6, edited by Steven Silvern Greenwich, CT: JAI.

———. 1992. "School and Family Partnerships." Pp. 1139–51 in *Encyclopedia of Educational Research,* 6th ed., edited by Marvin Alkin. New York: Macmillan.

Farkas, George, Robert P. Grobe, Daniel Sheehan, and Yuan Shuan. 1990. "Cultural Resources and School Success: Gender, Ethnicity, and Poverty Groups within an Urban School District." *American Sociological Review* 55:127–42.

Feather, Norman T. 1986. "Bridging the Gap between Values and Actions: Recent Applications of the Expectancy-value Model." Pp. 151–92 in *Handbook of Motivation and Cognition: Foundations of Social Behavior,* Vol. 2, edited by E. Tory Higgins and Richard M. Sorrentino. New York: Guilford Press.

Hallinan, Maureen T. 1992. "The Organization of Students for Instruction in the Middle School." *Sociology of Education* 65:114–27.

Heckhausen, Heinz. 1967. *The Anatomy of Achievement Motivation.* New York: Academic Press.

Hess, Robert D. and Susan D. Holloway. 1984. "Family and School as Educational Institutions." Pp. 179–222 in *Review of Child Development Research,* Vol. 7: *The Family,* edited by Ross D. Parke. Chicago: University of Chicago Press.

Hoelter, John W. 1982. "Segregation and Rationality of the Black Status Aspiration Process." *Sociology of Education* 55:31–39.

Horan, Patrick M. 1978. "Is Status Attainment Research Atheoretical?" *American Sociological Review* 43:534–41.

Hughes, Michael and David H. Demo. 1989. "Self-Perceptions of Black Americans: Self-Esteem and Personal Efficacy." *American Journal of Sociology* 95:132–59.

Inkeles, Alex. 1966. "Social Structure and the Socialization of Competence." *Harvard Educational Review* 56:50–68.

Kerckhoff, Alan C. 1977. "The Realism of Educational Ambitions in England and the United States." *American Sociological Review* 42:563–71.

Kerckhoff, Alan C. and Richard T. Campbell. 1977. "Black-White Differences in the Educational - Attainment Process." *Sociology of Education* 50:15–27.

Kilgore, Sally B. 1991. "The Organizational Context of Tracking in Schools." *American Sociological Review* 56:189–203.

Kohn, Melvin L. 1977. *Class and Conformity.* Chicago: University of Chicago Press.

Lareau, Annette. 1987. "Social Class Differences in Family-School Relationships: The Importance of Cultural Capital." *Sociology of Education* 60:73–85.

Lerner, Richard M. and Nancy A. Busch-Rossnagel, eds. 1981. *Individuals as Producers of Their Development: A Life-Span Perspective.* New York: Academic Press.

Mickelson, Roslyn A. 1990. "The Attitude-Achievement Paradox among Black Adolescents." *Sociology of Education* 63:44–61.

Ogbu, John U. 1988. "Class Stratification, Racial Stratification, and Schooling." Pp. 163–82 in *Class, Race, and Gender in American Education,* edited by Louis Weis. Albany: SUNY.

Parsons, Jacquelynne E. and Diane N. Ruble. 1977. "The Development of Achievement-Related Expectancies." *Child Development* 48:1075–79.

Schunk, Dale H. 1984. "Self-Efficacy Perspective on Achievement Behavior." *The Educational Psychologist* 19:48–58.

Seginer, Rachel. 1983. "Parents' Expectations and Children's Academic Achievements: A Literature Review." *Merrill-Palmer Quarterly* 29:1–23.

Singer, Judith D., Judith S. Palfrey, John A. Butler, and Deborah K. Walker. 1986. "Variation in Special Education Classification across School Districts: How Does Where You Live Affect What You Are Labeled?" *American Educational Research Journal* 26:261–81.

Slaughter, Diane T. and Edgar G. Epps. 1987. "The Home Environment and Academic Achievement of Black American Children: An Overview." *Journal of Negro Education* 56:3–20.

Spenner, Kenneth and David L. Featherman. 1978. "Achievement Ambitions." Pp. 373–420 in *Annual Review of Sociology,* edited by Ralph H. Turner, James S. Coleman, and Reneé Fox. Palo Alto: Annual Reviews, Inc.

Stipek, Deborah J. 1985. "The Development of Achievement Motivation." Pp. 145–74 in *Research on Motivation in Education,* Vol. 1: *Student Motivation,* edited by Richard Ames and Carole Ames. Orlando: Academic Press.

Thornton, C. Larence. 1977. "The Educational Attainment Process: Some Interactional Effects." *The Black Sociologist* 6:40–57.

Useem, Elizabeth L. 1991. "Student Selection into Course Sequences in Mathematics: The Impact of Parental Involvement and School Policies." *Journal of Research on Adolescence* 1:231–50.

Weiner, Bernard. 1984. "Principles for a Theory of Student Motivation and Their Application within an Attributional Framework." Pp. 15–38 in *Research on Motivation in Education,* Vol. 1: *Student Motivation,* edited by Richard Ames and Carol E. Ames. Orlando: Academic Press.

———. 1986. *An Attributional Theory of Motivation and Emotion.* New York: Springer-Verlag.

Weisz, John R. and Anne M. Cameron. 1985. "Individual Differences in the Student's Sense of Control." Pp. 93–139 in *Research on Motivation in Education,* Vol. 2: *The Classroom Milieu,* edited by Richard Ames and Carole Ames. Orlando: Academic Press.

Karl L. Alexander is Professor of Sociology at the Johns Hopkins University, where he served as Chair from 1985 to 1993. Using data from the BSS, he and Doris Entwisle presently are working on an analysis of the long-term process of school disengagement and dropout. The BSS now is in its thirtieth year.

Doris R. Entwisle is Professor of Sociology at The Johns Hopkins University. Her major research interest is in how social structure affects children's cognitive development and well-being.

Samuel D. Bedinger is a doctoral candidate at the John Hopkins University. His recent research interests include educational disadvantage and attainment, and education policy.

Quantitative Studies with Six or More Locations: Interaction Analysis

In the introduction to their article, Kohr et al. refer to reviews of educational research that argue for employing an intersectional approach:

> Reyes and Stanic . . . pointed out that when race-related differences are investigated without taking SES into consideration there is a likelihood that race and SES are confounded. This is reflected by a disproportionate number of minority group members who are low in SES and, similarly, a disproportionate number of majority group members who are high SES. The end result of ignoring SES when comparing the behavior of whites and blacks can be the unintentional comparison of economically advantaged white students with economically disadvantaged black students. The conclusions drawn in such a study can certainly lead to misconceptions about racial differences. (p. 356)

With this thought in mind, the authors set out to examine the effects of race, gender, and class (SES) on mathematics achievement. The results are reported in their article, "The Relationship of Race, Class, and Gender With Mathematics Achievement for Fifth-, Eighth-, and Eleventh-Gade Students in Pennsylvania Schools." SES was trichotomized into low, middle, and high, yielding a 3 × 2 × 2 intersectional pattern of 12 different social locations similar to those in the article by Hill and Sprague in the previous section. To estimate the effects of race, gender, and class Kohr et al. employed a three-factor ANOVA model (Table 2), and run four such models for each of the three grade levels. (Analysis of variance is a technique that facilitates the search for significant interaction effects across a large number of social locations.) In Table 2 (p. 363) they report a number of significant two-way and one three-way interactions but in general find relatively few significant ones. Most significant interactions are found at the intersection of class and race, with one significant class by gender and one significant race by gender interaction.

Although most studies struggle with the problem of small sample sizes that result in insufficient numbers of minorities in some social locations, this study faced the opposite problem: very large samples that sometimes produced substantively trivial significant coefficients. The number of students in each SES grade level ranges from 22,094 to 30,703. These are certainly large numbers, but it is not clear how they are distributed across the 16 social locations: consequently, it is difficult to know how serious a problem it is with interactions involving race. Nevertheless, the analysis confirms the need to analyze race, gender, and class simultaneously in studies of this type.

The final article in this section, "Women's STD Prevention and Detection Practices: The Specificity of Social Location," by Erika Laine Austin, is a Type I analysis of the variation in sexual health practices among women at the intersections of race and class. Because the focus is on women's sexual health practices, gender does not appear in any of the interaction terms; however, Austin's analysis includes three racial groups: Hispanic,[11] African American, and white women. Together with a dichotomous class variable of middle and working class, these interactions yield a 3 × 2 model with six social locations. Race and class are the principal independent variables, and there are a number of control variables. Using logistic regression with interaction terms, Austin tests three models for each of four dependent variables of sexual health practices (Tables 4, 5, 6 and 7; pp. 380–87).

Employing interaction terms proves a bit more complicated than separate group analysis. Austin calculates a total of six separate equations, one for each social location, isolating the effects of race and class by setting the values of all control variables at their means. This approach uncovers a number of differences in sexual health practices across social locations. Austin remarks, for instance, "that middle class African-American women are actually more likely that middle class European-American women to have undergone a Pap test in the previous year" (p. 381). Practices of working-class Hispanic women also differ significantly from that of women in other social locations. While some of Austin's findings parallel those of earlier research, a number of new findings emerge from the use of intersectional analysis.

The Relationship of Race, Class, and Gender with Mathematics Achievement for Fifth-, Eighth-, and Eleventh-Grade Students in Pennsylvania Schools

RICHARD L. KOHR
JAMES R. MASTERS
J. ROBERT COLDIRON
ROSS S. BLUST
EUGENE W. SKIFFINGTON

All authors were, at the time this article was written, staff members in the Division of Educational Testing and Evaluation, the Pennsylvania Department of Education, Harrisburg, PA.

Abstract

This integrative study of student socioeconomic status (SES), race, and gender focused on mathematics achievement derived from the Pennsylvania Educational Quality Assessment Program for the years 1981 through 1984. Analyses were conducted at the 5th, 8th, and 11th grade levels. Replicable achievement differences in mathematics were observed across grade levels for student SES and race, but not for gender. White students were found to score higher than black students and achievement varied directly with student SES level. The only replicable interaction to emerge was a relatively

---

The authors gratefully acknowledge the invaluable assistance provided by Dr. Paul Games of The Pennsylvania State University who reviewed the statistical methodology and offered many helpful suggestions regarding general approach measurement issues, and statistical treatment.

[11]Whether Hispanics should be classified as a race or ethnic group is a matter of debate. Foner and Fredrickson (2004) note that the initial census classification of Mexicans in 1930 as a "race" was later changed to "white" after protest from the Mexican government, and the new category "Hispanics" was introduced. However, African Americans, Asians, and Hispanics are all considered "minority groups" today. Because "race" is no longer accepted as a "scientific" term, it would probably be more accurate to use ethnicity rather than race for all these groups.

Richard L. Kohr et al. "The relationship of race, class, and gender with mathematics achievement for fifth, eighth and eleventh grade students in Pennsylvania schools" *Peabody Journal of Education* 66(2):147–171. Reprinted by permission of Lawrence Eribaum Associates.

weak but persistent SES by race effect that occurred for all analyses involving students attending low SES schools. This was a function of the fact that, although achievement increased across student SES level for both white and black students the increment tended to be slightly larger for white students. Supplementary analyses of mathematics achievement incorporating school SES, student SES, and race were also performed. In addition to significant results for each main effect, several interactions were found, the most prominent being a race by school SES effect, which occurred at each grade level. This was due to the fact that the difference between white and black student achievement was greater in low SES schools than in high SES schools, possibly indicating that black students were hurt more than white students by the environment of a low SES school. Overall, the significant effects of the study did not account for large amounts of variance in student achievement. At each of the three grade levels, only about 10% of the variance in mathematics achievement was found to be related to student SES, race, or gender.

Introduction

Grant and Sleeter (1986) presented a review of research literature which focused upon investigations involving the variables of race, class, and gender in educational research. They summarized the results of studies in the *American Educational Research Journal, Harvard Educational Review,* the *Review of Educational Research* and the *Teachers College Record* for the years 1973 through 1983. Grant and Sleeter concluded from their review of the 71 studies that few investigators had integrated the three factors in their designs and analyses. Rather, the great majority had attended to only one or at most two of the three factors. They argued that this lack of integration of race, gender, and SES oversimplifies the analysis of student behavior in school. It provides a narrow focus, treating individuals as if they are members of just one group and ignoring the joint contribution of each of the factors.

Reyes and Stanic (1985) presented similar arguments. They pointed out that when race-related differences are investigated without taking SES into consideration, there is a likelihood that race and SES are confounded. This is reflected by a disproportionate number of minority group members who are low in SES and, similarly, a disproportionate number of majority group members who are high in SES. The end result of ignoring SES when comparing the behavior of whites and blacks can be the unintentional comparison of economically advantaged white students with economically disadvantaged black students. The conclusions drawn in such a study can certainly lead to misconceptions about racial differences.

Articles such as those just discussed provided the motivation for this article. It was recognized that the conclusions drawn by Grant and Sleeter and by Reyes and Stanic were in agreement with the findings of Pennsylvania's statewide student testing program. It was also recognized that the extremely large data base available at the state level in Pennsylvania and the routine collection of SES, gender, and racial information on all tested students, provided a readily available situation for carrying out a study in which all three factors could be statistically controlled, thereby eliminating the confounding which has plagued past research. The study to be described was performed at grades 5, 8, and 11 using student mathematics achievement results. In addition, since it is well known that the type of school a student attends is a contributing factor to his or her achievement, analyses were performed for two separate samples of students, those attending low SES schools and those attending high SES schools.

Review of Related Research

Mathematics achievement studies focusing upon race and SES

Throughout this article, the term "black" will be used rather than "African American" because this is how students identified themselves on the answer document for the Pennsylvania statewide testing program.

For a number of years, the National Assessment of Educational Progress (NAEP) has served as a major vehicle for studying differences in achievement of specific groups. NAEP reports have indicated that, over the years, black students and students from economically depressed homes have made a great deal of progress. For example, NAEP (1979) reported that in the first assessment, which took place in 1973, black 9-year-olds scored, on the average, 15% points below the national average in mathematics. In the 1978 testing this difference had decreased to 10% points. Similarly, black 13-year-olds had decreased the degree to which they scored below the national average from 21% points in 1973 to 18% points in 1978. After examining NAEP results from these years, Burton and Jones concluded that there was a "rather steady decline in the average white-black achievement difference with advancing year of birth, regardless of learning area or age of assessment" (1982, 12).

As reported by NAEP (1979), low SES students were found to have gained in a similar manner to blacks from 1973 to 1978. The gain for 9-year-olds was from 13% points below the national average in 1973 to 9 below in 1978; for 13-year-olds the gain was from 18 to 14.

In the third NAEP testing of mathematics in 1982, black students again progressed. Jones (1984) reported that in this testing blacks scored well below the national average, but that the difference between whites and blacks had decreased even more from 1978 to 1982 than it had from 1973 to 1978. This difference was interpreted as primarily the result of increases in test scores for black students rather than declines for white students. The increase in mathematics achievement for black students was larger in schools composed of at least 40% minority students than in schools composed of less than 40% minority students. Jones indicated that a portion of the difference remaining between black and white student mathematics achievement could be due to differences between them in the degree to which they enrolled in mathematics courses in high school, such as algebra and geometry courses, since at age 17 the best predictor of mathematics achievement for both boys and girls was the number of mathematics courses completed. On the average, students who took 2 years of algebra and 1 year of geometry answered 82% of the items correctly; whereas, students who did not take these courses answered 47% of the items correctly. Jones also described the finding that SES variables such as parents' occupational status and the amount of reading material in the home did relate to student performance.

In the 1986 NAEP testing of mathematics, Dossey, Mullis, Lindquist, and Chambers (1988) and Johnson (1989) reported similar trends to those of past testings. Black students continued to narrow the performance gap between their achievement and that of white students. As was the case in the past, this was primarily due to improved performance on the part of black students and relatively constant performance by white students. Analysis of the results by levels of proficiency indicated that most of the increases for black students occurred in the lower proficiency levels—those which reflect the most basic content areas. In addition, as was described for the 1982 assessment, SES variables such as parent's educational level and the amount of reading material in the home were found to relate positively to student performance.

White (1982) discussed a meta-analysis investigation in which SES and achievement were related in 101 studies. The average correlation for all studies was .25, but there were major differences between the results of individual student correlations and correlations involving aggregated units of analysis. In studies in which the student was treated as the unit of analysis, correlations between achievement and SES averaged .22. These correlations decreased as students became older. White found, however, that when the school or community served as the unit of analysis, the correlations were much higher, averaging .73. He concluded that, contrary to the beliefs of many that SES is strongly related to measures of academic achievement, the relationship is actually a weak one for individuals. Results from Pennsylvania Department of Education studies have supported this conclusion. As one example, Kohr (1986) reported individual student correlations between parental education and a composite index of student achievement of .25 at the grade 5 level, .29 at grade 8, and .30 at grade 11. When school building means for these two variables were used, these correlations increased to .52, .48, and .51 at grades 5, 8, and 11, respectively. In summarizing such results, Reyes and Stanic (1985) stated: "Thus, SES appears to account for less than 10% of the variance in mathematics achievement when the student is the unit of analysis and considerably more when the school or community is the unit of analysis" (p. 5). Their overall conclusion was that no definitive study had yet been conducted with respect to the contribution of SES to mathematics achievement.

Results such as those just cited raise questions about the degree to which the specific characteristics of students are important determiners of their achievement and the degree to which the type of school and student population are important. The widely known Equality of Educational Opportunity Survey (EEOS), also referred to as the Coleman report (Coleman et al. 1966), examined such questions. It has been the subject of debate for a number of years and such debate has resulted in a variety of reanalyses of the data. Bradley and Bradley (1977) described the major finding of this study as the conclusion that ". . . black students in desegregated schools may acquire the achievement-related values of white students and thereby increase their own achievement levels" (p. 401). Cohen, Pettigrew, and Riley (1972) questioned the degree to which the results found were a consequence of racial differentials in level of social class rather than solely a function of racial composition. Their analyses revealed that school social class and racial composition shared much of the same variance and this confounding was an important factor in attempting to interpret the results.

The EEOS study made it very clear that the variables being studied were complex and highly correlated. A general conclusion of the original study was that the "schools bring little to bear on a child's achievement that is independent of his background and social context" (Coleman et al. 1966, 325). This conclusion was questioned by the Mayeske, Okada, and Beaton (1973) reanalysis, which concluded that the percentage of achievement which could be associated statistically with family background was only 48 and the percentage associated with type of school was 10. The remaining 42% was found to be common to both sets of factors. More recently, Morgan and McPartland (1981) raised the issue of whether the grouping factor of interest should really be the classroom rather than the school. They found that tracking or ability grouping tended to reduce the opportunities for cross-racial contact in classrooms of integrated schools.

The same types of concerns as those described above led to the conclusions of recent writers who were examining the research on the relationships between student achievement and both race and SES. Fleming and Malone (1983), in reviewing science achievement research, pointed out that in the studies they reviewed, race and SES were likely to be confounded, since the authors did not tend to report subjects' SES. Scott-Jones and Clark (1986) stated that investigators should describe their subjects in terms of race, gender, and SES in future studies of achievement. They warned that researchers must seek to avoid confounding the variables of race and socioeconomic status.

Mathematics achievement studies focusing upon gender

Studies of gender differences in mathematics achievement have not faced as many difficulties as those involving race and SES. This is true because few differential results have been found which would lead to conclusions that gender differences could be a function of some other major organismic variable. As an example of this type of result, the findings from a special 1975–1976 NAEP mathematics study can be described. In this investigation, a subset of mathematics exercises were adapted from the 1973 assessment to measure mastery of basic mathematical concepts in a variety of areas. At each of ages 13 and 17, approximately 85 mathematics exercises were administered, half to one national sample of 5,000 students and half to another. As summarized by Jones (1984), 13-year-old black females and males did not differ in their mathematics achievement, and this same result was found for white males and females. By age 17, however, significant gender differences favoring males occurred for both blacks and whites. But the difference between the two racial groups was five times as large as the gender differences within racial groups.

Meyer (1989) summarized gender differences on the regular NAEP testings of the past decade. At age 9, no differences were found in 1986 although females had scored somewhat higher than males in both 1978 and 1982. At age 13, males scored slightly higher than females in both 1982 and 1986. Females had scored slightly higher in 1978. And, at age 17, males scored significantly higher than females in 1978, 1982, and 1986. At this level both females and males made significant gains from 1982 to 1986. In the age 17 testing similar percentages of males and females attained the lower proficiency levels, but significantly larger percentages of males than females achieved the higher levels of 250, 300, and 350 on the NAEP scale. Meyer (1989) stated that this finding suggested that "the gender differences in mathematics achievement result from the best males performing at higher levels than the best females" (p. 152). Analyses of the results of content subscales revealed differences at all three grade levels. Females achieved a consistent advantage on the knowledge and skills subscale of numbers and operations. This subscale measures performance of straightforward, routine manipulations. On the higher-level applications subscale, however, males outscored females. This subscale measures the ability to solve a problem through completing an appropriate strategy. Males also outperformed females at all three grade levels on the measurement subscale and at grade 11 on the geometry subscale. Meyer (1989) concluded: "Equity for males and females in mathematics has not been realized, and efforts to achieve this goal should not be relaxed until all differences in outcomes have disappeared" (p. 159).

Reviews of other research on gender have tended to find some differences between males and females in mathematics achievement, but not generally until above the elementary school level. Fleming and Malone (1983) described cognitive achievement differences attributable to race as three times as great as those attributable to gender. Fox (1977), after reviewing the research literature, concluded that gender differences on tests of mathematics achievement were repeatedly found in adolescent and adult populations. Fennema (1977) reviewed the mathematics research literature in 1976 and concluded that: (a) regardless of cognitive level no gender-related differences were evident in elementary school years; (b) after elementary school years, differences did not always occur; (c) differences sometimes begin to appear at about the seventh grade, typically favoring males, particularly on tasks involving higher level cognitive skills; (d) gender-related differences in mathematics achievement in high school may not be as large in 1976 as they were in previous years; and (e) conclusions regarding male superiority tended to be reached in older studies or from investigations not controlling for the number of mathematics courses taken. Her latter conclusion is especially important since males having 2–4 years of high school mathematics were being compared to females with 1–3 years of mathematics coursework.

More recently Hyde, Fennema, and Lamon (1990) conducted a meta-analysis involving 100 studies in which they conclude that general statements about gender differences are not warranted since important complexities become obscured. They found that the gender difference was small and that since 1974, the magnitude of the difference had declined. Furthermore, no differences were noted on mathematics concepts regardless of age level while female superiority in computation declined to zero by high school. Differences favoring males began to emerge on problem solving items at the high school level. In another meta-analysis of gender differences, Friedman (1989) also found the overall effect size to be close to zero along with a steady decline in the magnitude of differences, even in high school and college samples where rather substantial differences occurred in previous years.

The SAT quantitative test, or SAT-M, has served as a major instrument for examining gender differences in mathematics achievement. The national publications produced by the College Entrance Examination Board (CEEB) over the past 15 years (1972–1986a) have shown rather major male-female differences on the SAT-M. These differences have been of the order of 40 to 50 points, with the largest difference, 52, occurring in 1977 and the smallest difference, 42, occurring in both 1973 and 1974. A similar pattern of difference took place in Pennsylvania over this time period. However, as reported in the CEEB publications for the state of Pennsylvania (1972–1986b) the male-female differences in Pennsylvania have not been quite as large as those found nationally. These have not exceeded 46 points and, from 1972 through 1975, were less than 35. The greatest magnitude of difference, 46, took place in both 1982 and 1983. In the years 1985 and 1986, differences of 42 and 43 occurred. However, Linn and Hyde (1989) point out that the SAT-M scale contains idiosyncratic gender differences that can be attributed to differential patterns of high school mathematics course selection and an overabundance of items having a context more familiar to males. They also cite evidence that females may have a greater tendency to use strategies on word problems that interfere with reaching solutions quickly, a process that is necessary in earning high scores. The authors caution against making generalizations about differential quantitative abilities from the SAT-M, and emphasize the need for studies that would clarify the processes leading to high performance.

Method

Pennsylvania's Educational Quality Assessment (EQA) program has provided a school building assessment since 1970. The present study focused on mathematics assessment results from the years 1981 through 1984, a time period during which all school districts in the state participated at least once. During these years students at grades 5, 8, and 11 were tested in 14 areas, half of which were cognitive and half noncognitive. Data were also collected on a series of student background variables such as parental education and occupation, amount of reading material in the home, race, gender, and so on. Every building in participating school districts housing a 5th, 8th, or 11th grade underwent assessment during the first 2 weeks of March involving all students at those grade levels. Multiple matrix sampling was utilized to reduce testing time for individual students.

Data from 4 years, 1981 through 1984, were selected for inclusion in the analysis. Since school district participation was voluntary, strong efforts were made to insure geographic balance and representativeness in terms of district size and wealth. The number of districts involved in assessment was 228 in 1981, 216 in 1982, 239 in 1983 and 186 in 1984. Since the Commonwealth has a total of 500 school districts the percentage of districts involved in any given year ranged from 37% to 48%. The number of students tested at a given grade level ranged from about 35,000 to 50,000 per year.

Student outcome measure of mathematics

At each grade level a 60-item multiple choice mathematics test was used to measure achievement. Three cognitive levels were tested: conceptual, computational, and problem solving. The items were from the content areas of number systems, numeration, notation, geometry, measurement, number patterns, relationships, and other topics. An extensive description of these instruments and the rest of the test package along with technical properties is given in the test interpretation manuals *Getting Inside the EQA Inventory* (Kohr, Hertzog, & Seiverling, 1984) and *EQA Manual for Interpreting School Reports* (Hertzog & Seiverling, 1984a, 1984b, 1984c). Previous research found that the EQA mathematics test correlated between .76 and .89 with similar measures in six major commercial standardized test packages when school mean data from spring testing were analyzed (Blust & Kohr, 1981). Student outcome scores were converted into standard scores with a mean of zero and standard deviation of one in order to control for slight differences that occur depending on which form a student received. The matrix sampling technique employed by EQA involved three forms at grade 5 and four forms at grades 8 and 11. During test administration, booklets were distributed in such a way that an essentially random third (or fourth) of the students within each testing room received a given form. All students responded to an equal number of items on each of the areas assessed. For instance, there were 60 items in mathematics in the overall school assessment, with each form consisting of a different set of 20 (or 15) items. Thus, a 5th grade student would have responded to 20 items and an 8th or 11th grade student, 15 items. The original allocation of items to forms was done in such a way as to minimize form to form differences in difficulty.

Student background variables

An index of student socioeconomic status was developed by combining data collected from the EQA student questionnaire on parental education, parental occupation, and amount of reading material in the home. Parental education was measured on a scale ranging from zero (some grade school) to nine (Ph.D. or professional degree). Occupational level was a weighted score ranging from 1 to 99 which reflected socioeconomic level. Amount of reading material in the home was a weighted score based on student responses to five items. For this study, student scores on the three socioeconomic measures were converted into standard scores (z-scores) and summed. The distributions of summed or combined z-scores were then partitioned into low, middle, and high student socioeconomic subgroups defined as the lowest 30%, middle 40%, and highest 30%. In the article this index is referred to as student SES. The final two student characteristics involved in the study were gender and race. Only two racial groups were studied, black and white.

School socioeconomic status

Another variable incorporated in the study was school SES defined in terms of the percentage of low income families in the area served by the school. In contrast to student SES, which is represented by a score unique to the individual student, school SES is a constant value for all students within a particular school. For grades 5 and 8, a low SES school was defined as having 30% or more of its students classified as from low income families. At grade 11, 20% was the cutoff used. If a school had 10% or less of its students classified as from low income families, it was defined as a high SES school. Students attending schools falling between the Low-High cutoff points were excluded from the analysis.

Data analysis

To examine the effect of student SES, race, and gender a three factor analysis of variance (ANOVA) model was selected. A $3 \times 2 \times 2$ design was employed since student SES was partitioned into three levels and the factors of race and gender consisted of two groups each. A regression approach to ANOVA was taken in order to appropriately control for the correlation between student SES and race. The general linear model has been advocated and described in a number of sources such as Games (1975) and Cohen and Cohen (1975). In this approach, the descriptive means are inappropriate for examining an effect and must be replaced with the least squares estimates of the effect means. It should be borne in mind that when examining tables with estimated z-score means, they will not "balance out" to zero. A regression approach to ANOVA has the convenient by-product of yielding the percentage of explained variance for each main and interaction effect. This helps in estimating the magnitude of an outcome and to evaluate its "practical significance." School SES was treated separately rather than as an additional factor in ANOVA because of the added complexity of having to interpret potential three and four way interactions.

Considering that 18 ANOVAs were conducted, each with seven main or interaction effects, a grand total of 126 significance tests were performed. With alpha set at .01, it could be anticipated that one or two significant results could occur by chance. Furthermore, there is an even larger number of follow-up tests for simple effects subsequent to a significant main or interaction effect. In this study approximately 250 follow-up tests were conducted. Two or three of these tests may have reached significance by chance.

Characteristics of the sample

When the data were initially examined it was noted that, despite the large number of students in each year's assessment, certain cells contained relatively few cases. For instance, in high SES schools the number of male and female black students classified as having a high SES family background (student SES) was rather small, ranging between 70 and 100 for a particular gender grouping. To bolster the stability of results for the smaller cells, all analyses were conducted on combined data from two consecutive years. Thus, the analysis samples were for 1981 and 1982 combined and for 1983 and 1984 combined. Table 1 presents a breakdown of

TABLE I ■ COMPOSITION OF ANALYSIS SAMPLE IN TERMS OF STUDENT SES, RACE, AND GENDER FOR EACH YEAR AND SCHOOL SES

		Percentage of the analysis sample in each category						
School	N of	Student SES level			Race		Gender	
year/SES	students	Low	Middle	High	White	Black	Male	Female
Grade 5								
81/82 Low	22,094	37.2%	51.0%	11.7%	83.9%	16.1%	50.6%	49.4%
83/84 Low	24,414	36.9	50.5	12.6	77.1	22.9	50.4	49.6
81/82 High	27,012	11.0	48.6	40.3	97.0	3.0	51.2	48.8
83/84 High	23,226	11.1	47.9	41.0	96.1	3.9	50.9	49.1
Grade 8								
81/82 Low	23,713	33.9%	51.7%	14.4%	83.6%	16.4%	50.4%	49.6%
83/84 Low	30,703	32.1	52.1	15.8	76.7	23.3	50.4	49.6
81/82 High	25,294	14.8	47.3	37.9	96.3	3.7	51.0	49.0
83/84 High	25,751	13.6	46.0	40.4	96.0	4.0	50.9	49.1
Grade 11								
81/82 Low	23,682	33.1%	52.9%	14.0%	88.5%	11.5%	49.4%	50.6%
83/84 Low	22,502	31.8	53.4	14.8	82.8	17.2	49.7	50.3
81/82 High	28,548	15.7	49.0	35.3	96.8	3.2	50.0	50.0
83/84 High	22,343	15.9	48.0	36.1	95.9	4.1	50.3	49.7

each analysis sample, giving the number of cases and the percentage of students in each student SES, race, and gender category.

RESULTS

Summarized in Table 2 are the F-ratios derived from ANOVA for each main and interaction effect. Results are presented for the four ANOVAs conducted at each of the three grade levels. Most striking was the high consistency of results across grade levels, particularly the statistically significant main effects for student SES and race observed in all 12 analyses. Gender was significant only twice and at different grade levels. Most of the interaction effects were weakly and sporatically significant with one important exception. Very consistent was the statistically significant result for the student SES by race interaction which occurred for students attending low SES school at each grade level.

Presented in Table 3 are the least squares estimates of mean scores for the statistically significant student SES and race main effects. Displayed in Table 4 are the least squares estimates of mean scores for the significant student SES by race interaction observed at all three grade levels for students attending low SES schools.

TABLE 2 ■ F-RATIOS FOR STUDENT SES, RACE, GENDER, AND THEIR INTERACTIONS FOR MATHEMATICS GRADE 5, 8, AND 11 STUDENTS FROM LOW SES SCHOOLS AND HIGH SES SCHOOLS

	Student SES	Race	Gender	Student SES × Race	Student SES × Gender	Race × Gender	Student SES × Race × Gender
Grade 5							
Low SES schools							
1981/1982	130.38*	570.44*	9.92*	8.88*	0.59	4.50	0.50
1983/1984	178.59*	909.17*	4.74	11.21*	0.20	12.06*	0.58
High SES schools							
1981/1982	61.40*	98.14*	0.00	0.40	0.77	0.42	1.19
1983/1984	57.31*	113.74*	1.88	1.20	4.90*	0.23	6.53*
Grade 8							
Low SES schools							
1981/1982	226.75*	1449.42*	0.03	34.51*	1.81	0.09	0.37
1983/1984	323.68*	2915.99*	10.26*	95.24*	1.10	2.72	0.79
High SES schools							
1981/1982	177.85*	116.41*	0.04	0.39	0.44	0.01	2.44
1983/1984	184.16*	132.45*	1.01	0.21	0.57	0.06	1.00
Grade 11							
Low SES schools							
1981/1982	134.57*	961.44*	5.77	12.86*	1.46	0.92	0.14
1983/1984	137.87*	1403.90*	2.92	32.04*	1.24	1.33	0.14
High SES schools							
1981/1982	186.54*	133.77*	0.77	5.21*	1.65	0.02	2.45
1983/1984	129.78*	171.19*	0.11	1.07	2.61	0.57	1.81

*$p < .01$

TABLE 3 ▪ LEAST SQUARES ESTIMATES OF MATHEMATICS MEAN SCORES FOR SIGNIFICANT MAIN EFFECTS

	Low SES schools		High SES schools	
Main effect	1981/1982	1983/1984	1981/1982	1983/1984
Grade 5				
Student SES/Low	−0.377	−0.372	−0.062	0.014
Student SES/Middle	−0.125	−0.173	0.162	0.188
Student SES/High	0.047	0.078	0.465	0.471
Race/White	−0.097	−0.084	0.271	0.300
Race/Black	−0.733	−0.657	−0.108	−0.089
Grade 8				
Student SES/Low	−0.391	−0.428	−0.225	−0.207
Student SES/Middle	−0.159	−0.218	0.129	0.181
Student SES/High	0.130	0.040	0.596	0.606
Race/White	−0.074	−0.071	0.266	0.315
Race/Black	−0.787	−0.817	−0.096	−0.066
Grade 11				
Student SES/Low	−0.303	−0.335	−0.328	−0.209
Student SES/Middle	−0.119	−0.155	0.063	0.094
Student SES/High	0.190	0.096	0.561	0.521
Race/White	−0.057	−0.049	0.190	0.219
Race/Black	−0.751	−0.780	−0.210	−0.236

To interpret the results it is important to recognize that with extremely large samples the degrees of freedom are likewise very large, which often leads to small, relatively trivial differences reaching statistical significance. The regression approach to ANOVA has the added benefit of yielding estimates of test score variance accounted for by the model. The full rank regression analyses were quite consistent in revealing a slightly larger percentage of variance accounted for within the samples of students attending low SES schools. Averaging the results for the 81/82 and 83/84 analysis samples for low SES schools, we find that the model accounts for 9, 13, and 10% of the test score variance for grades 5, 8, and 11 respectively. Parallel percentages of variance for students attending high SES schools were 4, 9, and 9 respectively for grades 5, 8, and 11.

The reduced rank regression model testing the significant student SES by race interaction effect averaged just one percent of test score variance at grades 5 and 11 and 4% at grade 8. By contrast, reduced rank models testing the main effects consistently found student SES to account for approximately 1.1 to 1.7% of the variance in low SES schools and from 0.4 to 1.3% in high SES schools. The race main effect was slightly stronger than the student SES main effect in low SES schools as the percentage of explained variance averaged 2.8% at grade 5, 6.7% at grade 8, and 4.6% at grade 11. For students attending high SES schools the race main effect was very stable at approximately 0.4 to 0.5% across grade levels.

For all three grade levels, contrasts between the low-middle and the middle-high student SES groups were statistically significant. Obviously, the low-high contrasts were significant as well. For students attending low SES schools the magnitude of the differences between SES groups

TABLE 4 ■ LEAST SQUARES ESTIMATES OF MATHEMATICS MEANS FOR THE SIGNIFICANT SES BY RACE INTERACTION EFFECT FOUND IN LOW SES SCHOOLS

	Low SES schools			
	1981/1982		1983/1984	
	White	Black	White	Black
Grade 5				
Student SES/Low	−0.330	−0.845	−0.286	−0.778
Student SES/Middle	−0.016	−0.655	−0.014	−0.651
Student SES/High	0.213	−0.541	0.214	−0.378
Grade 8				
Student SES/Low	−0.359	−0.876	−0.361	−0.870
Student SES/Middle	−0.038	−0.733	−0.055	−0.757
Student SES/High	0.366	−0.560	0.366	−0.661
Grade 11				
Student SES/Low	−0.287	−0.838	−0.302	−0.833
Student SES/Middle	−0.028	−0.727	−0.019	−0.755
Student SES/High	0.347	−0.486	0.327	−0.599

*$p < .01$

was very similar for the 81/82 and 83/84 analysis samples. While the size of the differences was slightly larger, a similar pattern occurred for the two analysis samples within the high SES schools. White students outscored black students by a rather large amount which was nearly identical on the two analysis samples. Although smaller in magnitude, similar differences were observed for students attending high SES schools.

The relative weakness of the SES by race interaction suggests that the most interpretable result is to be found in the main effects. That this is the case may be seen from an examination of the estimated means presented in Table 4. Increases in mathematics achievement scores across student SES levels occurred for both black and white groups, although the magnitude of increase was generally slightly less for black students. Overwhelmingly the greatest difference in estimated mean scores occurred for the groups based on race and student SES.

Summary of mathematics results

The analytic strategy employed in this study utilized two analysis samples as a way of strengthing generalizability. Findings were reported and discussed whenever both analysis samples revealed the same results. A number of consistent findings were observed for mathematics achievement across grade levels. Significant student SES and race main effects occurred for all analyses. Not surprisingly, these results conformed to well-established evidence from previous studies of SES and race. Specifically, mathematics achievement increased as student SES increased and white students scored at a higher level than black students. Gender differences only occurred in 2 of the 12 analyses, neither of which was a replicable finding. The only replicable interaction to emerge was a relatively weak but persistent effect that occurred for all analyses dealing with students attending low SES schools. Although achievement increased across student SES level for both white and black students, the increment tended to be slightly larger for white students. Stated another way, the differences between white and black mathematics scores showed a small but progressive increase across student SES levels. Typically, the difference between white and black z-scores was approximately .50 for the low student SES level, about .70 at the middle student SES level, and about .90 for the high student SES level. This effect did not occur for analyses dealing with students attending high high SES schools.

Analyses incorporating school SES

A separate analysis was conducted which incorporated school SES along with student SES and race. It should be emphasized that the context of this analysis was *not* that of estimating the magnitude of variance accounted for by school SES. This would obviously be underestimated due to the fact for this study the variable had been reduced to a dichotomy of high/low and much of its relationship with student achievement attenuated. The analysis was performed primarily to permit a comparison of black-white performance for each level of student SES within the two types of schools (high and low SES). Since gender was found to be a nonsignificant effect generally, it was dropped and replaced by school SES. Once again a regression approach to a three-factor ANOVA was performed with SES, race, and school SES serving as factors. Student SES is obviously correlated with school SES and since the former is an organismic variable of imperfect reliability, regression effects must be considered when interpreting the interaction means, especially in cells combining low student SES and high school SES or vice versa. Table 5 contains the ANOVA results for each grade level and Table 6 summarizes the least squares estimates of the means for significant main and interaction effects.

Replicable results included significant main effects for student SES, race, and school SES at all grade levels. The full rank regression model accounted for approximately 12% of the test score variance at grade 5, 16.5% at grade 8, and 11.5% at grade 11. The reduced rank model

TABLE 5 ■ F-RATIOS FOR STUDENT SES, RACE, SCHOOL SES, AND INTERACTION TERMS FOR MATHEMATICS

	Student SES	Race	School SES	Student SES × Race	Student SES × School SES	Race × School SES	Student SES × Race × School SES
Grade 5							
1981/1982	110.22*	477.72*	240.20*	2.64	3.29	29.05*	1.35
1983/1984	139.85*	532.88*	272.80*	3.82	0.30	19.29*	0.17
Grade 8							
1981/1982	351.27*	831.02*	357.74*	7.87*	16.15*	79.72*	8.89*
1983/1984	395.74*	1061.00*	544.93*	19.91*	30.09*	107.71*	16.24*
Grade 11							
1981/1982	328.71*	749.13*	162.53*	0.06	26.64*	51.43*	13.36*
1983/1984	259.34*	932.65*	208.89*	10.37	18.27*	51.07*	4.17*

*p < .01

TABLE 6 ■ LEAST SQUARES ESTIMATES OF MATHEMATICS MEANS FOR SIGNIFICANT MAIN AND INTERACTION EFFECTS

	Grade 5		Grade 8		Grade 11	
Main Effects	81/82	83/84	81/82	83/84	81/82	83/84
Student SES/Low	−0.199	−0.183	−0.286	−0.319	−0.292	−0.267
Student SES/Middle	0.043	0.004	0.008	−0.018	0.002	−0.015
Student SES/High	0.280	0.269	0.379	0.322	0.397	0.326
Race/Black	−0.412	−0.387	−0.454	−0.482	−0.476	−0.520
Race/White	0.098	0.094	0.090	0.085	0.073	0.075
School SES/Low	−0.146	−0.139	−0.148	−0.183	−0.105	−0.129
School SES/High	0.215	0.205	0.209	0.223	0.150	0.152
Interaction Effects						
Student SES × Race						
Low student SES/Black			−0.729	−0.748		−0.740
Low student SES/White			−0.286	−0.297		−0.271
Mid student SES/Black			−0.485	−0.487		−0.558
Mid student SES/White			0.059	0.044		0.050
Hi student SES/Black			−0.164	−0.240		−0.265
Hi student SES/White			0.479	0.478		0.441
Student SES × School SES						
Low stud SES/Low schl SES			−0.418	−0.432	−0.349	−0.346
Low stud SES/Hi schl SES			−0.197	−0.208	−0.296	−0.216
Mid stud SES/Low schl SES			−0.185	−0.224	−0.164	−0.163
Mid stud SES/Hi schl SES			0.159	0.187	0.108	0.104
Hi stud SES/Low schl SES			0.105	0.030	0.146	0.089
Hi stud SES/Hi schl SES			0.610	0.612	0.587	0.535
Race × School SES						
Black/Low schl SES	−0.660	−0.593	−0.709	−0.745	−0.675	−0.720
Black/High schl SES	−0.173	−0.157	−0.184	−0.159	−0.276	−0.300
White/Low schl SES	−0.025	−0.020	0.003	0.002	0.017	0.013
White/High schl SES	0.211	0.233	0.191	0.227	0.128	0.155
Student SES × Race × School SES						
Lo schl/Lo stud/Black			−0.876	−0.867	−0.838	
Lo schl/Lo stud/White			−0.359	−0.361	−0.288	
Lo schl/Md stud/Black			−0.732	−0.758	−0.728	
Lo schl/Md stud/White			−0.039	−0.055	−0.029	
Lo schl/Hi stud/Black			−0.558	−0.668	−0.481	
Lo schl/Hi stud/White			0.368	0.364	0.346	
Hi schl/Lo stud/Black			−0.582	−0.587	−0.779	
Hi schl/Lo stud/White			−0.212	−0.193	−0.241	
Hi schl/Md stud/Black			−0.238	−0.175	−0.313	
Hi schl/Md stud/White			0.156	0.185	0.102	
Hi schl/Hi stud/Black			0.230	0.228	0.243	
Hi schl/Hi stud/White			0.591	0.632	0.504	

testing each main effect found that student SES accounted for approximately 0.5% of the variance at grade 5 and about 1.1% at grades 8 and 11. Race accounted for about 1.5% at grade 5 and 1.5% at grades 8 and 11. School SES was highly consistent across grade levels, accounting for 0.4 to 0.7% of the variance. An examination of the least squares estimates of means in Table 6 revealed familiar SES and black-white patterns of mathematics achievement. Z-score differences between the lowest and highest student SES levels averaged about .46 at grade 5, and .65 at grades 8 and 11. Black-white differences averaged about .50 at grade 5, .55 at grade 8, and .57 at grade 11.

The pattern of significant interaction effects differed across grade levels and were characterized by some degree of inconsistency. Reduced model tests of the interactions revealed that the significant effects were relatively weak compared to the main effects. The only interaction to be significant in all analyses was race by school SES, which accounted for about .05% of the variance at grade 5, approximately .15% at grade 8, and .10% at grade 11. Least square estimates of means revealed that the black-white discrepancy was characteristically greater in low SES schools than in high SES schools. In low SES schools, the z-score difference averaged about .60 at grade 5, and approximately .72 at grades 8 and 11. By contrast, the differences in high SES schools ranged from about .38 at grades 5 and 8 to about .43 at grade 11.

Discussion

The mathematics achievement results of the study were very consistent across grade levels. At all three levels, whites scored significantly higher than blacks and achievement varied directly with the SES level of students. Replicable gender differences were not found at any of the three grade levels.

A strength of the present study was that race, SES, and gender were investigated within the framework of a common analysis. This analysis approach made it possible to statistically control for the confounding of race and SES which inevitably takes place because of the high degree of relationship between these variables. Thus, the observed racial differences were unconfounded by SES and the observed SES differences were unconfounded by race.

The differences in mathematics achievement related to race and SES are consistent with those reported by NAEP and by investigators who compiled analyses of the NAEP results (e.g., Burton & Jones, 1982; Dossey et al. 1988; Johnson, 1989; Jones, 1984). However, the NAEP results over time could not be compared to the results of the present study since the intent of the study was not to investigate whether differences between groups have increased or decreased. An analysis of Pennsylvania's statewide data for racial and SES trends across time would have some potential for adding to the knowledge base about the question of differential performance for these groups.

The general lack of significant interaction effects in the present analysis is consistent with the findings of Strauch (1975), who investigated Jensen's (1971) hypothesis regarding a sex by race by ability interaction in cognitive performance. To extend generalizability of results, Strauch utilized several data bases as replications. These included mathematics and verbal skills data from the Pennsylvania Educational Quality Assessment program along with the WISC-R standardization data and Project Talent data. Analyses failed to find evidence in support of any of the interaction effects; however, significant differences were found for SES and race in all instances, with the largest differences occurring for race.

The gender findings both agree and disagree with the results of past investigations. More specifically, the finding of no significant difference between the mathematics performance of male and female fifth graders agrees with the general finding of many past studies for elementary school level students (e.g., Fennema, 1977). The finding of no significant gender differences for grade 8 students agrees with those of some investigators (e.g., Jones, 1984; Pallas & Alexander, 1983) and disagrees with others (e.g., Benbow & Stanley, 1980). The 11th grade finding of no significant gender differences in mathematics achievement, however, disagrees with the findings of the majority of studies of high school age students (e.g., Benbow & Stanley, 1980; Fox, 1977; Jones, 1984; Meyer, 1989; Pallas & Alexander, 1983).

It is not clear at this point why no significant gender differences were found for high school students in this study. As described above, Pennsylvania's SAT results have shown the same type of differential between males and females as has been found nationally, so there is no reason to expect a study performed at the high school level to differ from other similar studies performed at other places in the country. The test used to measure mathematics achievement can best be described as one which assesses a variety of types of skills, including both basic calculations and higher level applications. It does not, at face value, seem to differ greatly from either the NAEP measures or commercial standardized achievement tests used in past studies of gender differences.

The statistical approach in the present investigation included the calculation of the amount of variance in mathematics achievement accounted for by the SES, race, and gender variables studied. It should be emphasized that these variance components were very small (i.e., generally less than 10%). Although significant differences were found for the race and SES variables and although the adjusted means compared in these analyses were often different by one-half standard deviation or more, the variables being compared were not of major importance in explaining student mathematics achievement. These results agree with the statements of such investigators as White (1982), Kohr (1986), and Reyes & Stanic (1985) with respect to the impact of SES upon student achievement.

Thus, the SES and race differences which were found in mathematics achievement were large enough to warrant an effort to understand them, but the variables investigated certainly do not tell the complete story. Variables more directly related to the learning of mathematics would be expected to be more highly related to the achievement of individual students. Such variables as student mathematics ability, the quality of instruction received, the amount of time engaged in mathematics instruction, and the particular curriculum studied all are important factors which would be expected to impact upon student performance.

To obtain valuable comparative information, the variables of student race, SES, and gender were studied in both low and high SES schools. The mathematics results were, in general, very similar in the high and low SES school samples. The only real exception to this was an interaction between student SES and race found in only the low SES schools. Examination of this finding revealed that in low SES schools the achievement differences favoring white students were significantly greater for high SES students than they were for low SES students. Although achievement increased across student SES level for both white and black students, the increment tended to be slightly larger for white students. Stated another way, the differences between white and black mathematics scores showed a small but progressive increase across student SES levels. Typically, the difference between white and black z-scores was approximately .50 for the low student SES level, about .70 at the middle student SES level, and about .90 for the high student SES level. This effect did not occur for analyses dealing with students attending high SES schools. These results would tend to suggest that black high SES students may be more negatively affected than white high SES students by the generally low achieving environment of a low SES school.

The original analysis plan for the study called for examining the variables of race, student SES, and gender separately for low and high SES schools. After these analyses had been completed, question still remained about the very complex relationships existent among the individual student variables and the school SES variable. Supplementary analyses were performed to address some of these questions. The most interesting finding of these analyses was a race by school SES interaction, found at all three grades and replicated for both the 1981–82 sample and the 1983–84 sample. This interaction was a function of the fact that the differences between the mathematics achievement scores of white and black students were much greater in low SES schools than in high SES schools. This finding was primarily due to black students achieving much more poorly in low SES schools than in high SES schools. White students' scores were lower in low SES schools than in high SES schools, but the magnitude of this difference was not great. These results are similar to others that have found very low achievement for black students in low SES schools. The problem remains as to how environments in these schools can be changed to produce better achievement or whether students must be moved to more promising learning environments.

Overall then, this large-scale study of student mathematics achievement tended to support past research in which it was concluded that SES differences are related to student achievement. It also provided a methodology for studying differences between racial groups which were not confounded by their SES level. The achievement of white students was found to be higher than that of black students, especially within the environment of a low SES school. Many black students attend such schools in our urban areas and, as has been documented in the past, their achievement appears to be suffering somewhat because of this attendance. What must be stated very strongly, however, is that the differences which were found in the study are not of major magnitude. It was not possible to account for a high proportion of the variability in student mathematics achievement on the basis of their gender, their race, or their SES level. The particular schools students attend, the teachers who instruct them, and the content they are taught all would be expected to better explain achievement differences than would the variables which were investigated.

It is clear, however, that students in schools with high percentages of disadvantaged students tend to have a higher likelihood of educational failure than students in other schools. The consequences of social class inequities need our continued attention, not only in monitoring achievement, but also in allocating additional resources to improve instruction. Identification of schools which exceed a certain threshhold of disadvantaged students would appear to be a way of channeling resources to the appropriate unit. In addition to the continued search for ways of improving mathematics achievement in such schools, affective factors linked to motivation are highly important (Dossey et al., 1988). For example, there needs to be an increased emphasis on portraying careers in science and technology as attractive and possible for *all* students. Thus, the concept of educational equity, as outlined by Meyer (this issue), is an essential ingredient in changing the instructional environment in ways that facilitate mathematics achievement for all students.

References

Benbow, C. P., & Stanley, J. C. (1980). Sex differences in mathematics ability: Fact or artifact. *Science, 210:* 1262–1264.

Blust, R. S., & Kohr, R. L. (1981). *An examination of the relationship between school scores derived from commercial achievement tests and those from statewide assessment.* Paper presented at meetings of the National Council on Measurement in Education, Los Angeles.

Bradley, L. A., & Bradley, G. W. (1977). The academic achievement of black students in desegregated schools: A critical review. *Review of Educational Research, 47:* 399–449.

Burton, N. W., & Jones, L. V. (1982). Recent trends in achievement levels of black and white youth. *Educational Researcher, 11:* 10–14.

Cohen, D. K., Pettigrew, T. F., & Riley, R. T. (1972). Race and the outcomes of schooling. In F.

Mosteller & D. P. Moynihan (Eds.) *On equality of educational opportunity.* New York: Random House.

Cohen, J., & Cohen, P. (1975). *Applied multiple regression/correlation analysis for the behavioral sciences.* Hillsdale, NJ: Lawrence Erlbaum.

Coleman, J. SK., Campbell, E.Q., Hobson, C. J., McPartland, J., Mood, A. M., Weinfeld, F. D., & York, R. L. (1966). *Equality of educational opportunity.* Washington, DC: U.S. Government Printing Office.

College Entrance Examination Board. (1972–1986a). *National report: College-Bound seniors.* New York: Author.

College Entrance Examination Board. (1972–1986b). *Pennsylvania report: College-Bound seniors.* New York: Author.

Dossey, J. A., Mullis, I. V. S., Lindquist, M. M., & Chambers, D. L. (1988). *The mathematics report card: Are we measuring up? Trends and achievement based on the 1986 national assessment.* Princeton, NJ: Educational Testing Service.

Fennema, E. (1977). Influences of selected cognitive, affective and educational variables on sex related differences in mathematics learning and studying. In *Women and Mathematics: Research Perspectives for Change.* NIE Papers in Education and Work: 8, 79–135.

Fleming, M. L., & Malone, M. R. (1983). The relationship of student characteristics and student performance in science as viewed by meta-analysis research. *Journal of Research in Science Teaching, 20,* 481–495.

Fox, L. H. (1977). The effects of sex role socialization on mathematics participation and achievement. In *Women and Mathematics: Research Perspectives for Change.* NIE Papers in Education and Work: 8, 79–135.

Friedman, L. (1989). Mathematics and the gender gap: A meta-analysis of recent studies on sex differences in mathematical tasks. *Review of Educational Research, 59,* 185–213.

Games, P. A. (1975). Confounding problems in multifactor AOV when using several organismic variables of limited reliability. *American Educational Research Journal,* 12, 225–232.

Grant, C. A., & Sleeter, C. E. (1986). Race, class, and gender in education research: An argument for integrative analysis. *Review of Educational Research, 56,* 195–211.

Hertzog, J. F., & Seiverling, R. (1984a). *EQA manual for interpreting elementary school reports.* Harrisburg, PA: Pennsylvania Department of Education.

Hertzog, J. F., & Seiverling, R. (1984b). *EQA manual for interpreting intermediate school reports.* Harrisburg, PA: Pennsylvania Department of Education.

Hertzog, J. F., & Seiverling, R. (1984c). *EQA manual for interpreting secondary school reports.* Harrisburg, PA: Pennsylvania Department of Education.

Hyde, J. S., Fennema, E., & Lamon, S. J. (1990). Gender differences in mathematics performance: A Meta-analysis. *Psychological Bulletin, 107,* 139–155.

Jensen, A. R. (1971). The race × sex × ability interaction. In R. Cancro (Ed.), *Intelligence: Genetic and environmental influence.* New York: Grune & Stratton.

Johnson, M. L. (1989). Minority differences in mathematics. In M. M. Lindquist (Ed.), *Results from the fourth mathematics assessment.* Reston, VA: National council of Teachers of Mathematics.

Jones, V. L. (1984). White-Black achievement differences: The narrowing gap. *American Psychologist, 39,* 1207–1213.

Kohr, R. L. (1986). *Correlates of cognitive student outcomes.* Paper presented at the annual meetings of the American Educational Research Association, San Francisco.

Kohr, R. L., Hertzog, J. F., & Seiverling, R. (1984). *Getting Inside the EQA Inventory.* Harrisburg, PA: Pennsylvania Department of Education.

Linn, M. C., & Hyde, J. S. (1989). Gender, mathematics and science. *Educational Researcher, 18,* 17–19, 22–27.

Mayeske, G. W., Okada, T., & Beaton, A. E. (1973). *A Study of the Achievement of Our Nation's Students.* Washington, DC: U.S. Government Printing Office.

Meyer, M. R. (1989). Gender differences in mathematics. In M. M. Lindquist (Ed.), *Results from the Fourth Mathematics Assessment.* Reston, VA: National Council of Teachers of Mathematics.

Morgan, P. R., & McPartland, J. M. (1981). The extent of classroom segregation within desegregated schools. Baltimore, MD: Johns Hopkins University, Center for Social Organization of Schools.

National Assessment of Educational Progress Newsletter. (1979). *Math achievement is plus and minus, 5,* 1–7. Denver, CO: Author.

Pallas, A. M., & Alexander, K. L. (1983). Sex differences in quantitative SAT performance: New evidence on the differential coursework hypothesis. *American Educational Research Journal, 20,* 165–182.

Reyes, L. H., & Stanic, G. M. A. (1985). *A review of the literature on Blacks and mathematics* (Research/Technical Rep. 143). Paper presented at the annual meeting of the American Educational Research Association, Chicago.

Scott-Jones, D., & Clark, M. L. (1986). The school experiences of Black girls: The interaction of gender, race, and socioeconomic status. *Women in Education*, 521–526.

Strauch, A. B. (1975). *An investigation into the sex × race × ability interaction.* Unpublished doctoral dissertation, The Pennsylvania State University, University Park, PA.

White, K. R. (1982). The relationship between socioeconomic status and academic achievement. *Psychological Bulletin, 91,* 461–481.

WOMEN'S STD PREVENTION AND DETECTION PRACTICES: *The Specificity of Social Location*

ERIKA LAINE AUSTIN

School of Public Policy & Social Research University of California, Los Angeles

ADDRESS: *School of Public Policy and Social Research, 3250 Public Policy Building, Box 951656, Los Angeles, CA 90095-1656. Email: elaustin@ucla.edu*

ABSTRACT

Limited research has focused on women's prevention and detection of sexually transmitted diseases (STDs), due to the emphasis on the prevention of unwanted pregnancies. Existing public health research on women's sexual health practices treats race/ethnicity and social class as separate explanatory factors, with a focus on the practices of minority and impoverished women. This work uses an intersection approach to problematize the traditional use of race/ethnicity and social class in public health research by creating multiplicative interaction terms to represent the unique social locations created by the intersection of the systems of patriarchy, racism, and capitalist exploitation. Logistic regression models reveal several significant interaction terms, suggesting that race/ethnicity and social class interact in meaningful ways to predict women's sexual health practices.

KEYWORDS

race, gender, class, intersection theory, women's health, sexually transmitted diseases

Women frequently bear serious long-term consequences as a result of infection with sexually transmitted diseases, including infertility and, in the case of HIV/AIDS, a significantly poorer prognosis compared to men (CDC, 2001b). The steady increase of sexually transmitted diseases among women, including a significant rise in the heterosexual transmission of HIV/AIDS, point to the continuing need for sexual health interventions targeted directly at the prevention

---

Erika Laine Austin is currently a postdoctoral fellow in the NIMH Training Program in HIV/AIDS at the University of California, Los Angeles. Her research focuses primarily on sexuality and health, and she is currently working on a study of adolescents' perceptions of their susceptibility to HIV/AIDS.

The author wishes to thank Robert Bozick, Jonathan Sklar, and Bart Landry for their insightful comments.

and early detection of STDs in women (CDC, 1998). Many public health efforts designed to increase awareness of STDs and provide support for testing and treatment are aimed at specific groups of women, namely racial/ethnic minorities and those in poverty. While these targeted intervention efforts are no doubt motivated by the higher rates of sexually transmitted diseases among these groups of women (CDC, 2001a), such efforts ignore the meaningful ways in which race/ethnicity, class, and gender interact to produce women's experiences with STD prevention and detection in the United States. In this article I attempt to develop a more nuanced sociological understanding of American women's sexual health practices through an examination of the unique social locations produced by the intersection of race/ethnicity and class.

RACE/ETHNICITY, CLASS, AND PUBLIC HEALTH RESEARCH

Much public health research has sought to clarify the roles of race/ethnicity and class in women's rates of sexually transmitted diseases. More precisely, research on women's sexual health has sought to identify the specific mechanisms (such as education, health behavior, and access to medical care) through which race/ethnicity and class influence women's sexual health practices (Freiman, 1998; Santelli et al., 2000b; Tanfer et al., 1995). Research has also focused on disentangling the unique effects of race/ethnicity from those of class. This effort is complicated by a number of conceptual problems characteristic of most public health research, most notably the absence of clear and consistent definitions of both race/ethnicity and social class (LaVeist, 1994; Weeramanthri, 2000; Williams et al., 1994). Though the U.S. government collects health data by racial and ethnic group, membership in these categories is often unclear and variable over time, suggesting a lack of any underlying, shared definition of race and ethnicity (LaVeist, 1994; McKenney and Bennett, 1994). Social class is similarly difficult to pin down, as no clear boundaries for inclusion in specific classes exist. Class is thus commonly measured by such variables as education, receipt of public assistance, membership in a single-parent household, mother's education, or income (Finer & Zabin, 1998; Santelli et al., 2000b; Singh et al., 2001; Sionéan et al., 2001). More problematic, health research often uses race/ethnicity as a proxy measure of socioeconomic status, which renders a comparison of the direct effects of race/ethnicity and social class impossible (LaVeist, 1994).

The examination of race/ethnicity and class effects is further complicated by the tendency of public health research to consider only the health practices of minorities (especially African-Americans and Hispanics) and those in poverty (see, for example, Soler et al.'s work on condom use among low income ethnic minority women). This limited approach to race/ethnicity and class is deterimental for a number of reasons. First, such an approach implicitly links poor health practices with minority status and poverty, implying that the "blame" for poor health lies in the hands of minorities and the impoverished as individuals (Armstrong, 1995; Zenilman, 1998). Moreover, focusing only on minority or impoverished women misses the very real sexual health risks that European-American and economically advantaged women may also face. Examining only the sexual health practices of those groups of women believed to be at risk places improper emphasis on the consequences of race/ethnicity and social class, rather than the causal mechanisms through which these factors become salient in individuals' lives.

I suggest that the question of interest is not how best to isolate the effects of race/ethnicity and class in health research; rather, I believe that crucial insight can be gained from looking directly at the intersections of race/ethnicity, class, and gender. By considering the unique social locations created by these intersections, we may move closer to the goal of creating policies and programs which meet the health needs of all women. More importantly, considering the specific social locations created by these intersections fully and unequivocally recognizes that race/ethnicity, class, and gender are wholly social in nature, rather than biological (American Academy of Pediatrics, 2000). Such understanding is essential to moving beyond the traditionally paternalistic approach to women's health issues.

Development of Intersection Analysis

The majority of research on women's sexual health derives from an epidemiological approach, the primary goal of which is the determination of prevalence rates of various conditions and the discovery of covarying characteristics of health behaviors (Wagstaff et al., 1995). Women's sexual health practices occur within the context of specific cultures and ideologies, however, and in the case of modern Western society, that context is characterized by women's permanent inequality in society (Amaro, 1995). A sociologically-informed analysis of women's sexual health thus offers a unique tool for considering the impact of sociocultural influences on women's health practices (Scambler & Higgs, 1999).

The intersection approach, characterized by the simultaneous consideration of the systems of patriarchy, racism, and capitalist exploitation, has developed in response to concerns that mainstream feminist scholarship failed to consider the experiences of women outside of the European-American middle class. The emphasis on women's shared experiences under patriarchy, articulated most clearly by radical feminists (see, for example, Shulamith Firestone's The Dialectic of Sex, 1970) suggested an essential, universal experience of gender, an experience that many women (especially minorities, the economically disadvantaged, and lesbians) did not share. As a result, many theoretical approaches arose in the late 1970s and 1980s which sought to address the multiple ideological forces that work together to shape women's lives; for example, socialist-feminists critiqued the mutually reinforcing systems of capitalism and patriarchy (Eisenstein, 1979; Hartmann, 1981), while many African-American feminists emphasized their unique oppression under white supremacy and patriarchy (Giddings, 1984; hooks, 1984).

Although attempts to consider the theoretical interaction of patriarchy with racism and capitalist exploitation helped to move feminist theorizing forward, these developments suffered from a tendency to privilege a single system of oppression over others. Socialist-feminism, for example, was harshly critiqued for allowing class analysis to subsume gender, viewing women's exploitation solely as a function of their relation to the market (Young, 1981). Critiques were also leveled against theorists who suggested that African-American women's experiences could be conceptualized as resulting from their "double jeopardy" under white supremacy and patriarchy, which implied that experiences of oppression could be added up to determine an individual's degree of subjugation (Spelman, 1988).

Intersection analysis, emerging in reaction to these critiques, starts from the perspective that no system of oppression can be considered in isolation from others; moreover, as systems of power, specific forms of oppression (e.g, sexism, racism, class exploitation) cannot be ranked as more or less destructive, though their salience may be situationally dependent (Brewer, 1993). Through interaction at the macrolevel, these systems of oppression create unique social locations which individuals experience at the microlevel (Zinn & Dill, 1996). This perspective therefore points to what has been called the "simultaneity of oppression," recognizing the theoretical impossibility of isolating the unique effects of any one form of oppression in an individuals' lived experiences. By focusing on the unique experiences of individuals at specific sites of intersection, this perspective seeks to move beyond the traditional dominant/subordinate bifurcation, allowing a more fluid, nuanced understanding of individuals' situation-specific experiences with power and powerlessness.

While the preliminary theoretical development of intersection analysis has focused on intersections of gender, race, and class, it is clear that intersectionality by definition can be expanded to include any system of oppression which proves to be salient in individuals' lives. Therefore in the case of women's sexual health practices, the interaction of sexuality as a system of oppression must also be considered. Following Patricia Hill Collins (2000 128), I conceptualize sexuality as a "site where heterosexualism, class, race, nation, and gender as systems of oppression converge." While women's experiences with sexuality (constrained by compulsory heterosexuality and the powerlessness resulting from traditional performances of femininity) have been extensively considered, the implications of the additional layers of race/ethnicity and class are yet to be investigated systematically in the context of women's sexual health practices.

Of course, women's sexuality and sexual behavior have always been viewed through the lenses of race/ethnicity and class. The United States has a long and disturbing history of seeking to control minority women's sexuality for the "good" of society; indeed, the eugenics movement of the early 20th century and the forced sterilization it engendered exemplify society's fear of minority women's uncontrolled sexuality (Roberts, 1997). This fear is often double-sided, however, as minority women's sexuality (particularly that of African and Asian women) is eroticized in Western culture (Samuels, 1995). Moreover, poor women's sexuality is frequently exploited through prostitution. European-American and middle class women's sexuality is also dramatically shaped by the social construction of race/ethnicity and class, as these women's expressions of sexuality and sexual behavior are viewed as deviant or are hidden from society (Solinger, 2000).

STDs AND WOMEN'S SEXUALITY

Relatively little research has focused on women's experiences with sexually transmitted diseases, relative to the extensive research on women's fertility and childbearing (Santelli et al., 2000b). A brief consideration of the reasons for this disparity is illustrative of the importance of considering women's sexual health from an intersection perspective. More to the point, this disparity has very real consequences for women's health.

First, it must be noted that the prevention of sexually transmitted diseases and the prevention of unwanted pregnancy are often at odds, both in practice and in health promotion. Given the aforementioned concern with controlling the fertility of minority and poor women, these groups have traditionally been pushed to use those forms of contraception that are most effective at preventing pregnancy (and which, by no small coincidence, also give women the least amount of control over their own bodies). In particular, long-acting methods such as Depo-Provera and Norplant are used more frequently among minority women, due at least in part to health providers' efforts to encourage their use in minority communities (Malat, 2000; Petchesky, 1990). These hormonal methods, designed for the prevention of pregnancy, do not prevent the spread of STDs and may even increase the potential for infection due to physiological changes in the female reproductive tract.

Normative views of women's sexuality also undermine efforts to decrease women's risks of sexually transmitted diseases. Certain sexual behaviors (such as anal intercourse or having multiple sex partners) dramatically increase women's exposure to STDs (Lindberg, 1999), but historically these behaviors have been largely ignored, perhaps in an effort to maintain the view of women as sexually pure. More fundamentally, addressing women's potential exposure to STDs implies tacit approval for sexual relations outside of marriage. While attitudes toward women's non-marital sexuality are liberalizing, there remains a normative belief that women ought only to experience sexual intercourse in the context of long-term monogamous relationships (Tanenbaum, 2000).

Data and methods

Sample and measures

This analysis uses the 1995 National Survey of Family Growth (NSFG Cycle V), a nationally-representative survey of civilian, non-institutionalized women ages 15 to 44 (Mosher, 1998). This wide-ranging survey gathers information on a variety of issues related to sexual and reproductive health, including contraceptive use, pregnancy history and family formation, sexual partner history, and use of medical services. A total of 10,847 women completed interviews between January and October of 1995 (Mosher, 1998). The complex sample design requires that post-stratification weights be employed to obtain nationally-representative results; I have conducted my analyses using Stata 8.0 to correctly estimate standard errors (Potter and Iannacchione, 1998).

In this analysis I seek to locate women's sexual health more firmly in its sociocultural context through an examination of race/ethnicity and social class differences in a variety of STD prevention and detection practices. As suggested by the intersection approach, this is best accomplished through the creation of multiplicative interaction terms which represent the unique social locations specified by race/ethnicity and social class. The NSFG includes a constructed variable which identifies respondents as Hispanic (of any race), non-Hispanic African-American, and non-Hispanic European-American. Each of these categories is transformed into dichotomous dummy variables, with European-Americans serving as the reference category.

The conceptualization of social class suffers from a considerable lack of clarity, necessitating a brief discussion of how I use the concept in this work. Following Weber's 1921 discussion in "Class, Status, Party," I take social class to be the situation in which "a number of people have in common a specific causal component of their life chances . . . represented exclusively by economic interests in the possession of goods and opportunities for income" (Gerth & Mills, 1946 181). Weber identifies occupation as the foundation on which the class system is built (Parkin, 1971), which in our modern society translates into two broad class divisions: those individuals whose work primarily involves the production and manipulation of knowledge (the middle class); and those whose work is manual (the working class). From the Weberian perspective, occupation is the most appropriate measure of social class, as it represents an individual's objective relation to the market system. The use of women's occupation as a proxy for social class status is problematic with these data, however, due to the number of women who do not participate in the formal job market.

Social class is thus operationalized in this analysis by respondent's education, which I have recoded into two categories: high school or less (12 or fewer years of education), and 13 or more years of education; these categories represent working class and middle class, respectively. The decision to use education as an indicator of social class is based on the stability and robustness of education as a predictor (Santelli et al., 2000a; Williams et al., 1994); moreover, the qualitative social differences resulting from educational attainment make it more attractive for this research than other potential indicators of social class. The use of education as a proxy for social class is consistent with Weber's conceptualization, as education is a key mechanism determining life chances by providing the credentials and skills necessary to enter the various occupations.

A number of additional demographic, behavioral, and attitudinal variables are also included in my analyses. Current labor force participation and marital status are used to clarify women's degree of financial independence, which may mitigate the effects of social class. Age at first voluntary heterosexual intercourse and the total number of male sex partners are included, as these variables are known to be inversely related with overall sexual health (Levinson et al., 1995; O'Donnell et al., 2001); overall health status is also included. A dummy variable for

Catholic affiliation is included to account for the possibility of lower contraceptive use among Catholic women.

Finally, I include two Gender Ideology Scales to capture variations in women's acceptance of the norms of patriarchal society. My decision to include these scales is motivated by the belief that although all women's lives are constrained by the structure of gender relations in society, the extent to which women support these norms and enact them in their lives is likely to vary (Amaro, 1995). The data set includes 18 attitudinal questions on issues relating to women's role in society. I used exploratory factor analysis to extract two substantively meaningful sets of variables, from which I created two separate scales. The first scale represents views on the role of women within the home (including responsibility for the care of family and children) and is thus referred to as "Women Inside the Home." The Cronbach's alpha, a measure of the internal validity, is .67 for this scale. The second scale, "Women Outside the Home," taps views on the role of women in the work place and has an alpha of .74. Both alpha coefficients are sufficiently high to suggest that each scale measures some coherent underlying belief about the role of women. For both scales, higher scores represent more conservative views toward the role of women.

Analyses

This work is an examination of four sexual health practices directly related to the prevention and early detection of sexually transmitted diseases, including having had a Pap test in the last 12 months, having had an HIV antibody test in the past 12 months, having used any form of protection at first heterosexual intercourse, and having ever used condoms. As this work is exploratory in nature, I propose few formal hypotheses; rather, I simply seek to determine whether race/ethnicity and social class interact to predict women's sexual health behaviors. To determine if differences exist, I first present bivariate results on the relationship between all social location variables and several correlates of sexual health. I then present the results of nested logistic regression models predicting the probability of undertaking each sexual health practice. The first reduced regression model includes only the social location variables, including interaction terms. Model 2 introduces the other demographic and behavioral factors, and Model 3 (the full model) adds the Gender Ideology Scales.

Finally, I have calculated the predicted probabilities of undertaking each sexual health practice based on the full logistic regression model (Model 3). As with any regression equation, logistic regression equations can be solved for particular subgroups by substituting specific values for each variable. I have isolated the effects of race/ethnicity and social class by setting the values of all other predictors at their means, solving six separate equations to represent the six unique social locations of interest. This technique allows the direct comparison of the predicted probabilities associated with specific social locations, as well as a comparison of the relative probabilities across outcome variables. It is important to note, however, that these predicted probabilities are sample-specific and cannot be used to make inferences to the general population. In each of my analyses I use middle class European-Americans as the comparison group, in order to determine the extent to which the behaviors of individuals at other social locations differ from what is commonly depicted as the "ideal."

RESULTS

Table 1 presents the demographic distribution of the 1995 National Survey of Family Growth. A total sample of 10,482 women is used in the analyses; 365 respondents are excluded due to missing or inconsistent race/ethnicity data. As the table indicates, the majority of respondents are European-American. Within race/ethnicity, a greater proportion of African-American and

TABLE 1 ■ SAMPLE DISTRIBUTION BY RACE/ETHNICITY AND SOCIAL CLASS, 1995 NATIONAL SURVEY OF FAMILY GROWTH (CYCLE V)

	Percentage	N
African-American	23.3	2446
European-American	61.9	6483
Hispanic	14.8	1553
Working-class	52.7	5522
Middle-class	47.3	4960
Working-class African-American	14.0	1468
Middle-class African-American	9.3	978
Working-class European-American	29.1	3045
Middle-class European-American	32.8	3438
Working-class Hispanic	9.6	1009
Middle-class Hispanic	5.2	544
Total Sample = 10482 (unweighted cases)		

Hispanic respondents fall into the working class (defined as 12 or fewer years of education), while slightly more of the European-American respondents are categorized as middle class.

To begin the investigation of within group differences (by race/ethnicity and social class), I conducted difference of means tests (for continuous variables) or Chi-square tests (for categorical variables) on each of the independent variables. Only two variables are found *not* to differ significantly within groups. For European-Americans, there is no class difference in the percentage of women who have ever been married. Additionally, there is no class difference in the average number of male sex partners for African- and European-American women. Hispanic women, however, differ by social class on all variables.

An examination of within group differences on selected sexual health practices suggests further differences based on social class. The percentage of respondents having received a Pap test, using contraceptives at first intercourse, and ever having used condoms all differ by class within racial/ethnic categories. Again Hispanic women's health practices stand out as being especially different by class: 21.8 percent more middle class Hispanic women report ever having used condoms compared with working class Hispanics; the difference by class is a mere 6.2 percent for European-Americans and only 8.0 percent for African-Americans. The results from Tables 2 and 3 suggest the importance of considering social class and race/ethnicity simultaneously when examining women's sexual health practices, and the logistic regression models in the next section will examine the statistical significance of these interactions in predicting the probability of various sexual health practices.

Pap test in previous year

The first analysis reports the results of a nested logistic regression model predicting women's probability of having undergone a Pap test in the 12 months preceding the interview (Table 4). The Pap test (a screening procedure routinely performed during gynecological exams) is a highly effective method for identifying numerous sexually transmitted diseases including HPV, the primary cause of cervical cancer (Couto & Dailard, 1999). The Pap test therefore serves as a primary means of diagnosing sexually transmitted diseases in women, who often do not present external symptoms of infection.

TABLE 2 ■ MEAN SCORES AND STANDARD ERRORS OR PERCENTAGE DISTRIBUTIONS ON SELECTED VARIABLES OF WOMEN AGES 15–44, BY RACE/ETHNICITY AND SOCIAL CLASS

	African-American		European-American		Hispanic	
	Working	Middle	Working	Middle	Working	Middle
Catholic	5.7	8.5 *	25.2	30.1 *	71.1	65.8 *
Ever Married	41.3	55.0 *	67.7	69.6	65.0	66.9 *
Currently Employed	51.0	77.7 *	63.8	79.3 *	43.9	73.7 *
Overall Good Health	83.3	92.6 *	92.1	96.8 *	86.2	93.2 *
Age (at interview)	29.5 (.22)	31.8 (.23) *	29.7 (.17)	32.1 (.13) *	29.1 (.27)	30.7 (.30) *
Age at First Heterosexual Intercourse	16.1 (.07)	17.5 (.27) *	16.8 (.05)	18.3 (.05) *	17.8 (.11)	18.9 (.16) *
Total Number of Male Sex Partners	9.9 (.95)	9.2 (.87)	7.6 (.52)	7.7 (.39)	4.0 (.34)	5.8 (.61) *
Views on Women's Role Outside the Home	9.7 (.06)	8.6 (.08) *	9.6 (.05)	8.5 (.04) *	10.4 (.08)	9.1 (.11) *
Views on Women's Role Inside the Home	10.5 (.06)	9.3 (.08) *	10.8 (.05)	9.7 (.04) *	10.1 (.03)	10.3 (.03) *

*Within-group differences statistically significant at $p < .05$

TABLE 3 ■ PERCENTAGE DISTRIBUTION OF WOMEN'S STD PREVENTION AND DETECTION PRACTICES, BY RACE/ETHNICITY AND SOCIAL CLASS

	African-American		European-American		Hispanic	
	Working	Middle	Working	Middle	Working	Middle
% Received Pap test in last 12 months	66.4	77.4*	55.5	71.1*	48.3	64.6*
% Received HIV antibody test in last 12 months	31.4	27.8	14.2	14.7	22.2	22.3
% Used any protection at first intercourse	42.4	55.7*	56.3	68.5*	29.2	51.7*
% Ever used condoms	77.7	85.7*	81.5	87.7*	59.9	81.7*

*Within-group differences statistically significant at $p < .05$

TABLE 4 ■ LOGISTIC REGRESSION COEFFICIENTS AND STANDARD ERRORS SHOWING THE LIKELIHOOD OF HAVING RECEIVED A PAP TEST IN THE LAST 12 MONTHS

	Model 1 coefficients (standard errors)			Model 2 coefficients (standard errors)			Model 3 coefficients (standard errors)		
African-American	.136	(.090)		.216	(.098)	*	.214	(.098)	*
Hispanic	−.191	(.129)		−.254	(.129)	*	−.227	(.130)	#
Working-class	−.502	(.059)	***	−.524	(.062)	***	−.479	(.064)	***
Working-class African-American	.186	(.143)		.259	(.149)	#	.259	(.149)	#
Working-class Hispanic	−.241	(.168)		−.201	(.169)		−.200	(.171)	
Age				−.029	(.004)	***	−.028	(.004)	***
Catholic				.158	(.063)	**	.154	(.063)	**
Ever married				.386	(.068)	***	.407	(.069)	***
Currently employed				.285	(.056)	***	.255	(.056)	***
Reporting overall good health				−.054	(.095)		−.071	(.096)	
Age at first heterosexual intercourse				−.007	(.009)		−.005	(.001)	
Total number of male sex partners				.004	(.002)	*	.003	(.002)	*
Views on women's role outside the home							−.023	(.012)	*
Views on women's role inside the home							−.019	(.011)	#
Constant	1.021			1.575			1.933		
Log likelihood	−6703.78			−5842.37			−5539.38		
Model Chi-square	0.001			0.001			0.001		
Pseudo R-square	0.024			0.025			0.027		
N = 9099									

#$p < .10$ *$p < .05$ **$p < .01$ ***$p < .001$

In Model 1 (the intersection model), none of the interaction terms appear to be significant predictors of having a Pap test. The class variable, a main effect, is relatively large and significant, suggesting that working class women are less likely to have had a Pap test in the past year than their middle class counterparts. The effect of class holds regardless of race/ethnicity, suggesting that race/ethnicity and social class do not interact to create unique social locations in this case. In Models 2 and 3, the independent effect of class status remains significant, and race/ethnicity also gains significance once the other control variables are added to the model. African American women are more likely to have had a Pap test compared to European American women, while Hispanic women are significantly less likely. Interestingly, the interaction effect representing working class African-American women edges toward significance in the full model, suggesting that social location may work in a limited way to predict having a Pap test once other sociodemographic and attitudinal variables are taken into account.

In addition to the persistent effect of social class, Catholic affiliation, ever having been married, and being employed all significantly increase the probability of having had a Pap test in the previous year. Older women are slightly less likely to have had the test, while having more male sex partners increases the probability; the magnitude of both effects is minimal however. Both of the Gender Ideology Scales are marginally significant in Model 3, indicating that women with more liberal gender attitudes are more likely to have had a Pap Test.

An examination of the predicted probabilities of having a Pap test (based on the full model) provides the first challenge to the traditional view that minority status is associated with poor health practices. In Table 4a we see that middle class African-American women are actually more likely than middle class European-American women to have undergone a Pap test in the previous year. Additionally, working class African-Americans and middle class Hispanics are more likely to have had a Pap test compared with working class European-Americans.

TABLE 4a ■ PREDICTED PROBABILITY OF HAVING RECEIVED A PAP TEST IN THE LAST 12 MONTHS

Middle-class African-Americans	.770
Middle-class European-Americans	.729
Working-class African-Americans	.727
Middle-class Hispanics	.681
Working-class European-Americans	.624
Working-class Hispanics	.520

HIV antibody test in previous year

From the outset of the AIDS epidemic, HIV antibody testing has been a primary means of preventing the spread of infection. This is especially true among heterosexually-active women, as sex with infected men accounts for approximately 40 percent of all new cases among women (CDC, 1998). Evidence also suggests that HIV testing and the associated counseling often result in safer sexual practices in the future (Exner et al., 2002). As new cohorts of women become heterosexually active, early detection of HIV infection will remain a crucial means of controlling the spread of the disease, particularly among vulnerable populations.

In the case of HIV antibody testing, there is no evidence of differences based on the unique social locations created by the interaction of race/ethnicity and social class; none of the interaction terms is significant. The results in Table 5 clearly challenge the notion that minority status consistently results in poor health practices, however, African-American women and Hispanic women are significantly more likely than European-Americans to have had an HIV antibody test in the previous year; these findings persist in Models 2 and 3. Social class gains significance in the full model, suggesting that working class women have a lower probability of being tested relative to middle class women, once attitudinal and behavioral measures are

TABLE 5 ■ LOGISTIC REGRESSION COEFFICIENTS AND STANDARD ERRORS SHOWING THE LIKELIHOOD OF HAVING RECEIVED AN HIV ANTIBODY TEST IN THE LAST 12 MONTHS

	Model 1 coefficients (standard errors)			Model 2 coefficients (standard errors)			Model 3 coefficients (standard errors)		
African-American	.736	(.089)	***	.635	(.096)	***	.635	(.097)	***
Hispanic	.422	(.134)	***	.452	(.128)	***	.446	(.128)	***
Working-class	−.001	(.078)		−.161	(.082)	*	−.170	(.082)	*
Working-class African-American	.188	(.131)		.168	(.134)		.168	(.137)	
Working-class Hispanic	.162	(.160)		.209	(.168)		.207	(.166)	
Age				−.044	(.004)	***	−.045	(.004)	***
Catholic				−.154	(.074)	*	−.154	(.077)	*
Ever married				.018	(.074)		.015	(.078)	
Currently employed				−.125	(.065)	*	−.121	(.065)	#
Reporting overall good health				−.140	(.103)		−.137	(.101)	
Age at first heterosexual intercourse				−.043	(.013)	***	−.044	(.013)	***
Total number of Male Sex Partners				.008	(.002)	***	.008	(.002)	***
Views on women's role outside the home							.011	(.015)	
Views on women's role inside the home							−.002	(.013)	
Constant	−1.647			0.749			0.678		
Log likelihood	−4977.76			−4583.38			−4394.97		
Model Chi-square	0.001			0.001			0.001		
Pseudo R-square	0.027			0.056			0.057		
N = 9068									

#$p < .10$ *$p < .05$ **$p < .01$ ***$p < .001$

TABLE 5a PREDICTED PROBABILITY OF HAVING RECEIVED AN HIV ANTIBODY TEST IN THE LAST 12 MONTHS

Working-class African-Americans	.272
Middle-class African-Americans	.272
Working-class Hispanics	.244
Middle-class Hispanics	.237
Middle-class European-Americans	**.165**
Working-class European-Americans	.143

taken into account. As might be expected, older women are less likely to have been tested, as are women who identify as Catholic and women who are currently employed. Women who experience sexual debut at later ages are less likely to have been tested, and though the total number of male sex partners is significant the magnitude of the effect is minimal.

A comparison of the predicted probabilities for HIV antibody testing reported in Table 5a reveals the most striking results of this study. African-American and Hispanic women are much more likely to have been tested in the past twelve months compared with European-American women. Interestingly, working class individuals, regardless of race/ethnicity, are more likely than their middle class counterparts to have been tested. These unusual results call into question whether the decision to be tested for HIV infection is truly an individual-level health decision. It may be that minority and impoverished women are encouraged to undergo testing by their health care providers, regardless of whether or not they actively request such screening.

Use of protection at first heterosexual intercourse

A primary goal of comprehensive sexuality education has been to encourage the use of protection during first heterosexual intercourse, with the aim of developing a pattern of consistent use. Indeed, use of protection at first intercourse is a strong predictor of future sexual health behavior (Kirby, 1992). The results in Table 6 are therefore among the most interesting in this study. Here we see an extraordinarily strong and persistent negative effect for Hispanic women, who are much less likely than European-Americans to have used protection at first intercourse. Moreover, working class Hispanic women are even less likely to have used protection relative to middle class Hispanic women; this interaction effect holds in the full model. It is possible that the significance of this social location (working class Hispanic) is a result of differential acculturation into American society (Newcomb et al., 1998). Though not empirically testable in this study, it may be that middle class Hispanics are more integrated into American society, sharing the sexual behaviors and health practices of their similarly situated European-American counterparts. The possibility of an acculturation effect is supported by the fact that the interaction term for working-class African-Americans is not a significant predictor of use of protection at first heterosexual intercourse.

A number of other factors are also significant predictors of having used protection at first heterosexual intercourse. Women who consider their overall health status to be good are more likely to have used protection. Women whose sexual debut occurred at later ages are more likely to report protected first intercourse, a result which lends support to educational and policy efforts aimed at delaying the age at sexual debut. While a greater number of sexual partners reduces the probability of having used protection at first intercourse, the effect is so small as to be meaningless. The Gender Ideology Scales are both significant predictors in Model 3; women with more liberal attitudes are slightly more likely to have used protection at first sexual intercourse, compared with their more conservative peers.

The predicted probabilities in Table 6a present a clear pattern, with middle class women within each racial/ethnic group more likely to have used protection than their working class

TABLE 6 ■ LOGISTIC REGRESSION COEFFICIENTS AND STANDARD ERRORS SHOWING THE LIKELIHOOD OF HAVING USED PROTECTION DURING FIRST HETEROSEXUAL INTERCOURSE

	Model 1 coefficients (standard errors)			Model 2 coefficients (standard errors)			Model 3 coefficients (standard errors)		
African-American	−.556	(.094)	***	−.553	(.096)	***	−.559	(.102)	***
Hispanic	−.810	(.105)	***	−1.003	(.110)	***	−.971	(.117)	***
Working-class	−.519	(.057)	***	−.408	(.059)	***	−.356	(.061)	***
Working-class African-American	.056	(.116)		−.003	(.120)		−.006	(.127)	
Working-class Hispanic	−.319	(.138)	**	−.352	(.136)	**	−.355	(.147)	**
Age				.061	(.003)	***	−.061	(.003)	***
Catholic				−.001	(.055)		−.020	(.054)	
Ever married				−.125	(.069)		−.087	(.070)	
Currently employed				.165	(.054)	***	.129	(.057)	*
Reporting overall good health				.215	(.089)	**	.190	(.090)	*
Age at first heterosexual intercourse				.101	(.009)	***	.111	(.010)	***
Total number of male sex partners				−.004	(.001)	**	−.005	(.002)	*
Views on women's role outside the home							−.023	(.010)	*
Views on women's role inside the home							−.026	(.011)	*
Constant	0.818			0.662			1.085		
Log likelihood	−6144.45			−5849.71			−5551.87		
Model Chi-square	0.001			0.001			0.001		
Pseudo R-square	0.043			0.085			0.091		
N = 8883									

#$p < .10$ *$p < .05$ **$p < .01$ ***$p < .001$

TABLE 6a Predicted Probability of Having Used Protection During First Heterosexual Intercourse

Middle-class European-Americans	.681
Working-class European-Americans	.599
Middle-class African-Americans	.550
Working-class African-Americans	.459
Middle-class Hispanics	.447
Working-class Hispanics	.284

peers. European-Americans are most likely to have used protection, followed by African-Americans and middle class Hispanics. The predicted probability for working class Hispanics is dramatically lower than at any other social location, further highlighting the distinguishing role of social class among Hispanic women.

Use of condoms

Aside from complete sexual abstinence, condoms are recognized as the most effective means of preventing the transmission of STDs. The continued high rate of sexually transmitted diseases suggest, however, that the use of condoms remains below what is needed to effectively control the spread of STDs (Bankole et al., 1999). Women often must negotiate the use of condoms, and their ability to do so is dependent both on their power within the relationship and their own cultural and ideological views on the use of condoms (Worth, 1989). Previously, minority women were believed to be less likely to demand condoms, but empirical research suggests that the condom usage rates of minority women now parallel that of European-American women (Soler et al., 2000).

Of the four health practices examined in this study, my model works best to explain the probability of ever having used condoms based on pseudo-R^2 values; this may be a result of the increasing public awareness of HIV/AIDS among heterosexual women (Table 7) (Finer & Zabin, 1998). My results show a significant interaction between race/ethnicity and social class, as the coefficient for working class Hispanic women is large and significant. Hispanic women across the board exhibit low rates of condom use, and working class Hispanic women are notably less likely to have ever used condoms compared to African- and European-American women. Indeed, the coefficient for working class Hispanic women is nearly twice as large as that for working class African-American women and three times as large as that for European-American women of working class status. Interestingly, this social location effect does not disappear when Catholic identification is included in the full model, challenging the popular notion that Hispanic women's rejection of condoms is religiously based.

These race/ethnicity and social class effects remain strong in the full model, and many additional control variables also attain significance. Being employed increases the probability of having used condoms, as does overall good health. Women who were older at sexual debut are less likely to ever have used condoms, possibly because they have better access to those forms of contraception available through health care providers (Finer & Zabin, 1998). A greater number of male sex partners significantly increases the probability of using condoms, a heartening result given that more partners results in more potential exposure to sexually transmitted diseases (Levinson et al., 1995). As my gender hypotheses predict, women with conservative views on women's role *within* the home are significantly less likely to report ever having used condoms (Mane & Aggleton, 2001; Worth, 1989). It is interesting to note that views on women's role outside the home do not predict condom use.

The predicted probabilities in Table 7a suggest that the use of condoms is closely associated with social class, as middle class respondents regardless of race/ethnicity have higher condom use than working class respondents. The predicted probabilities for ever having used condoms do not vary as dramatically as for the use of protection

TABLE 7 ■ LOGISTIC REGRESSION COEFFICIENTS AND STANDARD ERRORS SHOWING THE LIKELIHOOD OF EVER HAVING USED CONDOMS

	Model 1 coefficients (standard errors)		Model 2 coefficients (standard errors)		Model 3 coefficients (standard errors)	
African-American	−.145	(.120)	−.309	(.131) **	−.332	(.133) **
Hispanic	−.542	(.155) ***	−.549	(.169) ***	−.497	(.162) ***
Working-class	−.495	(.082) ***	−.563	(.086) ***	−.487	(.090) ***
Working-class African-American	−.077	(.156)	−.128	(.164)	−.125	(.166)
Working-class Hispanic	−.569	(.188) **	−.548	(.189) **	−.531	(.186) **
Age			−.062	(.005) ***	−.069	(.005) ***
Catholic			−.060	(.090)	−.069	(.089)
Ever married			−.254	(.090) **	−.214	(.093) *
Currently employed			.221	(.067) **	.150	(.070) *
Reporting overall good health			.249	(.092) **	.227	(.092) **
Age at first heterosexual intercourse			−.048	(.013) ***	−.044	(.013) ***
Total number of male sex partners			.035	(.007) ***	.032	(.007) ***
Views on women's role outside the home					−.006	(.013)
Views on women's role inside the home					−.069	(.014) ***
Constant	2.023		4.596		5.277	
Log likelihood	−4421.87		−4130.08		−3889.41	
Model Chi-square	0.001		0.001		0.001	
Pseudo R-square	0.037		0.097		0.100	
N = 9099						

#$p < .10$ *$p < .05$ **$p < .01$ ***$p < .001$

TABLE 7a ■ PREDICTED PROBABILITY OF EVER HAVING USED CONDOMS

Middle-class European-Americans	.901
Middle-class African-Americans	.867
Middle-class Hispanics	.849
Working-class European-Americans	.847
Working-class African-Americans	.779
Working-class Hispanics	.666

at first intercourse, though in both cases the probabilities of middle class European-American women are higher than the probabilities at all other social locations and working class Hispanic women the lowest.

DISCUSSION

This article presents the results of logistic regression models predicting the probability of undertaking four STD prevention and detection practices, with particular attention to the role of race/ethnicity, social class, and their intersections in predicting sexual health practices. A number of patterns emerge, and while many are predicted by previous empirical findings, several unanticipated relationships bear further discussion.

Many of my results point to race/ethnicity or class as predictors of health practices. As expected, middle class status is associated with greater use of condoms, a higher probability of having used protection at first intercourse, and a greater probability of having had a Pap test in the previous year. Hispanic and African-American women were found to be less likely to have had protected first intercourse and to have ever used condoms compared to European-American women, though this effect may be due to the use of long-acting methods (such as Norplant) among minority women (Malat, 2000). These findings concur with traditional public health research, which commonly associates minority and poverty status with poor health practices.

Several results stand in contrast to this view, however, suggesting that the typical treatment of minority and poverty status as health risk factors may miss the true significance of social location. Most notable is the finding that minority women actually appear *more* likely than European-American women to report HIV antibody testing; minority women are almost twice as likely as European-Americans to have been tested. African-American women are also more likely to have had a Pap test in the previous year compared to European-Americans, though both groups report higher rates than Hispanic women.

Social class also works to mitigate the effect of race/ethnicity in many cases. Middle class Hispanic women, for example, are notably different from their working class counterparts, with a much greater probability of using condoms; this social location is also associated with greater use of protection at first heterosexual intercourse. These results point clearly to the fact that the *specificity of social location matters*. It is not enough simply to say that minority and poverty status directly predict poor sexual health practices; my results point to cases where this is simply not true.

In sum, it appears that women's sexual health practices are influenced by the individual social locations created by the intersecting systems of patriarchy, racism, and capitalist exploitation. Intersection analysis derives from a discussion about the fluidity of power, however; rather than simply classifying individuals as privileged or oppressed, intersection analysis pushes us to consider the relative power or powerlessness engendered by specific social locations. My results clearly illustrate that interaction terms can capture the unique effects of social location on women's sexual health practices, in the statistical sense at least. A more complicated task is determining what these social location indicators suggest theoretically and how this impacts women's lives. I speculate that social location may enter into women's sexual health practices in at least two distinct ways: through the negotiation of power within interpersonal relationships, and in relation to women's ability to advocate for their own health.

The use of condoms is, by virtue of their design, entirely dependent on men's cooperation (Amaro, 1995). Of course, women exercise some degree of control over whether they engage in sexual relations in the absence of condoms. This control is a function of women's power, however, which is often dependent on the social locations created by the intersecting systems of race/ethnicity, class, and gender. Women of all social classes have historically relied on men for economic security, as the patriarchal-capitalist market consistently rewards men with greater opportunities and higher wages. While previous empirical work finds that women who exchange sex for money or drugs are less able to require the use of condoms with male partners (Mane & Aggleton, 2001), little attention has been paid to the economic dependency of middle and upper class women and the resulting negotiation of condom use. Future research into the role of economic dependency in women's negotiation of condom use is necessary to clarify the ways that patriarchy and capitalism interact to shape this sexual health practice.

Women's sexual health practices may be influenced by social location in more subtle ways as well. Women who must struggle daily for survival often exhibit a present-time orientation, making concerns regarding the future consequences of STDs meaningless in comparison (Worth, 1989). In addition, the sense of powerlessness and despair many women experience as a result of racism and poverty may also reduce their regard for their own well-being, making them less able to "advocate for self" by demanding consistent condom use and testing for STDs. Peggy Matteson (1995) points out, however, that the ability to demand recognition of health concerns may be limited for women in general, given the historical tendency of health care providers to construe women's health concerns as hysterical and hypochondriacal.

While women as a group experience systematic inequality in society, it is important to recall that women do not share a single, consistent experience of womanhood. Though society has constructed rigid ideological boundaries for the appropriate performance of feminity, women's adherence to these standards is by no means total. My inclusion of the two Gender Ideology Scales in the logistic regression analysis is designed to capture this variability and consider its meaning for women's sexual health practices. Though the scales are not significant predictors of health practices in every case, the use of condoms is associated with views on the role of women. Those women whose attitudes are more ideologically conservative are less likely to require that their male partners use condoms, perhaps because making such demands could be seen as unfeminine (Holland et al., 1996).

Conclusions and Future Directions

In this article I have attempted to demonstrate the sociological insight provided by an intersection analysis of women's sexual health practices. As in any study, there are a number of data limitations which must be addressed in future research. The use of only three racial/ethnic categories is less than ideal, as significant differences may have been missed in my analysis. This is particularly true in the case of Hispanics, as empirical evidence suggests that the health behaviors of various Latin American groups differ dramatically. It would also be useful to capture the degree of acculturation of individual Hispanics, as this may also influence sexual health practices.

If the specificity of social location matters, as my results indicate it does, the question becomes where to go with these findings. First, it is clear that the traditional use of race/ethnicity and social class as predictors in health research must continue to be challenged. Race/ethnicity and social class are not the all-encompassing, monolithic determinants they are often depicted to be. Moreover, race/ethnicity and social class must not be construed to have social meaning only in the lives of minorities and the poor. In the case of sexual health practices, there is ample theoretical and empirical evidence to suggest that the experiences of European-American and/or middle class women are constrained by the ideology of sexuality, though potentially in ways which differ from their minority and impoverished counterparts.

This research also has clear implications for public health interventions designed to decrease the incidence of STDs among women. Much public health literature calls for "culturally sensitive" interventions, but little guidance is offered as to what this means in practice. This intersection analysis of women's sexual health practices is a first step toward identifying distinct cultural practices associated with unique social locations, potentially offering a starting point for the development of interventions that acknowledge the ways that race/ethnicity and social class interact—rather than operate separately or monolithically—in women's lives.

Bibliography

Amaro, H. (1995). Love, sex, and power: Considering women's realities in HIV prevention. *American Psychologist,* 50(6):437–447.

American Academy of Pediatrics. (2000). Race/ethnicity, gender, socioeconomic status—Research exploring their effects on child health: A subject review. *Pediatrics,* 105(6):1349–1351.

Armstrong, K. (1995). The problems of using race to understand sexual behaviors. *SIECUS Report,* 23(3):8–10.

Bankole, A., Darroch, J. & Singh, S. (1999). Determinants of trends in condom use in the United States, 1988–1995. *Family Planning Perspectives,* 31(6):264–271.

Brewer, R.M. (1993). Theorizing race, class, and gender: The new scholarship of Black feminist intellectuals and Black women's labor. In J. Stalie & A. Busia (eds.), *Theorizing Black feminism: The visionary pragmatism of Black women,* pp. 13–30 Routledge.

CDC. (1998). HIV/AIDS surveillance report. Centers for Disease Control and Prevention.

______. (2001a). Special focus profiles: STDs in racial and ethnic minorities. Centers for Disease Control and Prevention.

______. (2001b). Special focus profiles: STDs in women and infants. Centers for Disease Control and Prevention.

Collins, P.H. (2000). *Black feminist thought: Knowledge, consciousness and the politics of empowerment.* Routledge.

Couto, I. & Dailard, C. (1999). Wanted: A balanced policy and program response to HPV and cervical cancer. *The Guttmacher Report on Public Policy,* 2(6).

Eisenstein, Z. (1979). Developing a theory of capitalist patriarchy and socialist feminism. In Z. Eisenstein (ed.), *Capitalist Patriarchy and the Case for Socialist Feminism,* pp. 5–40. Monthly Review Press.

Exner, T., Hoffman, S., Parikh, K., Leu, C.S., & Ehrhardt, A. (2002). HIV counseling and testing: Women's experiences and the perceived role of testing as a prevention strategy. *Perspectives on Sexual and Reproductive Health,* 34(2):76–83.

Finer, L. & Zabin, L.S. (1998). Does the timing of the first family planning visit still matter? *Family Planning Perspectives,* 30(1):30–33, 42.

Firestone, S. (1970). *The dialectic of sex: The case for feminist revolution.* Bantam.

Freiman, M. (1998). The demand for healthcare among racial/ethnic subpopulations. *Health Services Research,* 33(4):867–890.

Giddings, P. (1984). *When and where I enter. The impact of Black women on race and sex in America.* William Morrow.

Hartmann, H. (1981). The unhappy marriage of Marxism and feminism: Towards a more progressive union. In L. Sargent (ed.), *Women and revolution: A discussion of the unhappy marriage of feminism and Marxism,* pp. 1–41. South End Press.

Holland, J., Ramazanoglu, C., Sharpe, S., & Thomson, R. (1996). Reputations: journeying into gendered power relations. In J. Weeks & J. Holland, (eds.), *Sexual cultures: Communities, values, and intimacy,* Macmillan Press.

hooks, b. (1984). *Feminist theory: From margin to center.* Boston:South End Press.

Kirby, D. (1992). Sexuality education: It can reduce unprotected intercourse. *SIECUS Report,* 21(2): 19–25.

LaVeist, T. (1994). Beyond dummy variables and sample selection: What health services researchers ought to know about race as a variable. *Health Services Research,* 29:1–17.

Levinson, R.A., Jaccard, J., & Beamer, L. (1995). Older adolescents' engagement in casual sex: Impact of risk perception and psychosocial motivations. *Journal of Youth and Adolescence,* 24:349–365.

Lindberg, C. (1999). Sexual behavior and condom use among urban women attending a family planning clinic in the United States. *Health Care for Women International,* 20:303–314.

Malat, J. (2000). Racial differences in Norplant use in the United States. *Social Science and Medicine,* 50:1297–1308.

Mane, P. & Aggleton, P. (2001). Gender and HIV/AIDS: What do men have to do with it? *Current Sociology,* 49:23–37.

Matteson, P. (1995). *Advocating for self: Women's decisions concerning contraception.* New York: Haworth Press.

McKenney, N., & Bennett, C. (1994). Issues regarding data on race and ethnicity: The Census Bureau experience. *Public Health Reports,* 109:16–25.

Mosher, W.D. (1998). Technical note: Design and operation of the 1995 National Survey of Family Growth." *Family Planning Perspectives,* 30:43–46.

Newcomb, M., Wyatt, G., Romero, G., Tucker, B., Wayment, H. Vargas, J., et al. (1998) Acculturation, sexual risk taking, and HIV health promotion among Latinas. *Journal of Counseling Psychology,* 45:456–467.

O'Donnell, L., O'Donnell, C. & Stueve, A. (2001). Early sexual initiation and subsequent sex-related risks among urban minority youth: The Reach for Health Study. *Perspectives on Sexual and Reproductive Health,* 33:268–275.

Parkin, F. (1971). The Dimensions of class inequality. *In Class inequality and political order: Social stratification in capitalist and communist societies,* pp. 13–47. London: MacGibbon & Kee Ltd.

Petchesky, R.P. (1990). *Abortion and woman's choice: The state, sexuality, and reproductive freedom* (Rev. ed.). Boston: Northeastern University Press.

Potter, F., & Iannacchione, V. (1998). Sample design, sampling weights, imputation, and variance estimation in the 1995 National Survey of Family Growth. *Vital Health Statistics,* 2(124).

Roberts, D. (1997). *Killing the Black body: Race, reproduction, and the meaning of liberty.* New York. Pantheon.

Samuels, H. (1995). Sexology, sexosophy, and African-American sexuality: Implications for sex therapy and sexuality education. *SIECUS Report,* 23(3):3–5.

Santelli, J., Duberstein Lindberg, L., Abma, J., Sucoff McNeely, C., & Resnick, M. (2000). Adolescent sexual behavior: Estimates and trends from four nationally representative surveys. *Family Planning Perspectives,* 32:156–165, 194.

Santelli, J., Lowry, R., Brener, N., & Robin, L. (2000). The association of sexual behaviors with socioeconomic status, family structure, and race/ethnicity among U.S. adolescents. *American Journal of Public Health,* 90:1582–1588.

Scambler, G. & Higgs, P. (1999). Stratification, class and health: Class relations and health inequalities in high modernity. *Sociology,* 33:275–287.

Singh, S., Darroch, J., & Frost, J. (2001). Socioeconomic disadvantage and adolescent women's sexual and reproductive behavior: The case of five developed countries. *Family Planning Perspectives,* 33:251–258, 289.

Sionéan, C., DiClemente, R., Wingood, G., Crosby, R., Cobb, B., et al. (2001). Socioeconomic status and self-reported gonorrhea among African-American female adolescents. *Sexually Transmitted Diseases,* 28:236–239.

Soler, H., Quadagno, D., Sly, D., Riehman, K., Eberstein, L. & Harrison, D. (2000). Relationship dynamics, ethnicity and condom use among low-income women. *Family Planning Perspectives,* 32:82–88, 101.

Solinger, R. (2000). *Wake up little susie.* New York: Routledge.

Spelman, E.V. (1988). *Inessential woman: Problems of exclusion in feminist thought.* Boston:Beacon.

Tanenbaum, L. (2000). *Slut! Growing up female with a bad reputation.* New York: Harper Collins.

Tanfer, K., Cubbins, L., & Billy, J.O.G. (1995). Gender, race, class, and self-reported sexually-transmitted disease incidence. *Family Planning Perspectives,* 27:196–202.

Wagstaff, D., Kelly, J., Perry, M., Sikkema, K., Solomon, L., Heckman, T., et al. (1995). Multiple partners, risky partners, and HIV risk among low-income urban women. *Family Planning Perspectives,* 27:241–245.

Weber, M. (1946). Class, status, party. In H.H. Gerth & C.W. Mills (eds.), *From Max Weber: Essays in sociology,* pp. 180–195. New York: Oxford University Press.

Weeramanthri, T. (2000). Ethnicity not race: A public health perspective. *Australian Journal of Social Issues,* 35:1–13.

Williams, D., Lavizzo-Mourey, R., & Warren, R. (1994). The concept of race and health status in America. *Public Health Reports,* 109:26–41.

Worth, D. (1989). Sexual decision-making and AIDS: Why condom promotion among vulnerable women is likely to fail. *Studies in Family Planning* 20:297–307.

Young, I. (1981). Beyond the unhappy marriage: A critique of the dual systems theory. In L. Sargent (ed.), *Women and revolution: A discussion of the unhappy marriage of Marxism and feminism*, pp. 43–69. Boston: South End Press.

Zenilman, J. (1998). Ethnicity and sexually transmitted infections. *Current Opinion in Infectious Diseases*, 11:47–52.

Zinn, M.B., & Dill, B.T. (1996). Theorizing difference from multiracial feminism. *Feminist Studies*, 22:321–331.

Quantitative Studies Using Separate Group Analysis with *t*-Tests

In this section I include three articles that use separate group analysis with *t*-tests. As I argued previously, separate group analysis with *t*-testing of coefficients across social locations offers the best alternative to interaction terms. This is especially true when the study includes more than four social locations. Four social locations may be easily incorporated into a statistical model with one first-order interaction term: race × gender, race × class, or gender × class. The inclusion of race, gender, and class requires a third-order interaction term, race × gender × class, which is very difficult to interpret but may be facilitated by using one interaction term with four groups. In a Type II analysis, one can employ one interaction term that includes an independent variable other than race, gender or class (e.g, gender × education) with four separate groups (pp. 222).[12] However, the use of separate group analysis with *t*-tests is also useful with fewer than eight social locations, as some of the following articles will demonstrate.

The first article, by Kei M. Nomaguchi, "Are There Race and Gender Differences in the Effect of Marital Dissolution on Depression?" is a Type II analysis of the relationship between marital dissolution and depression. Race and gender are the principal control variables, but there are a number of other control variables as well. Although scholars have conducted research on, this subject, they have primarily focused on gender differences. As Nomaguchi notes, "little research has explicitly examined whether there are race *and* gender differences in the effect of marital dissolution on mental health" (p. 396). It is the search for significant differences in the relationship of marital dissolution and depression across the intersections of race and gender that makes this intersectional analysis.

Nomaguchi approaches the analysis in three ways. She first tests for significant differences of means at the bivarate level among all variables in the model (Table 1) across the four social locations: black men, black women, white men, and white women. She then estimates a

[12]A third-order interaction requires the inclusion of all second-order interactions in the model, greatly increasing the risk of multicollinearity.

number of OLS regression models with three second-order and one third-order interaction term (Table 2). Only the marital dissolution by race interaction term is significant. It should be pointed out that marital dissolution is a dischotomous variable, coded 1 for those who were separated or divorced, and 0 for those who remained married. As in many previous articles, the number of black males and females in the sample is far smaller than the number of whites, especially in the separated/divorced category: 42 black males and 34 black females. With such a small number of black males and females in this category it would be difficult for the third-order interaction term, marital dissolution × gender × race, to rise to significance even if it were so.

In Table 3 we find the results of the OLS regression estimates for each of the four social locations. This table also contains the results of *t*-tests of significant coefficients: comparisons with black men, black women, white men and white women. Two of these *t*-test comparisons are significant at the $p \leq .05$ level: black men compared with white women, and white men compared with white women. Two *t*-tests are significant at the $p \leq .10$ level: black men compared with black women, and black women compared with white men. Nomaguchi concludes:

> [U]sing interaction terms on the full sample, I found that there were gender differences in psychological responses to marital dissolution, but there were no race differences in the effect of marital dissolution on depression. Using separate subgroup regressions and *t*-tests of differences in the effects of marital dissolution on depression, I found that white women were more vulnerable to marital dissolution than black men and white men, but there was no difference between white women and black women, and no difference between white men and black men. (pp. 405–407)

It would appear that separate group analysis with *t*-tests detected one race difference in the effect of marital dissolution on depression (black men and white women) that had not been detected using OLS regressions with interaction terms. In addition to greater ease of interpretation, separate group analysis appears to detect interaction with fewer cases than in models using interaction terms.

"Generalized Expectancies for Control among High-School Students at the Intersection of Race, Class, and Gender," by Brett A. Magill, is a Type I analysis of the effects of race, class, and gender on high school students' perceptions of locus of control. Age is the only control variable. Magill estimates OLS regression models with one class × gender interaction term for separate gender subgroups (Table 4).

Both models were statistically significant as measured by *F*-tests. As noted by Magill, there were significant main effects of class and gender on perceptions of locus of control, with class being more influential than gender or race. Although in the regression models the effects of class and gender appear to differ by race, *t*-tests for differences in coefficients across race were not significant, leaving one to conclude that there was no interaction between class and race or gender and race. Since the interaction term for class × gender was also nonsignificant, there was no third-order interaction. This article underscores the need to calculate *t*-tests for the significance of differences in coefficients across social locations. Without the *t*-tests one would have been tempted to conclude that there was at least a race difference in the effect of gender, and perhaps also in the effect of class; *t*-tests demonstrate otherwise. These results of *t*-tests are likely robust, given that the smallest social location, black working-class males, has a frequency of 285 (Table 5).[13]

[13]There is nevertheless one reason to be cautious in this interpretation. The coefficient for gender in the black subgroup (−.32) is actually larger than for the white subgroup (−.24). However, the standard error for the black subgroup is more than half the size of the coefficient, whereas in the white subgroup it is only .09. This is somewhat surprising given the size of all black social locations (Table 5).

The last article in this section, "Race, Gender, and Class Variation in the Effect of Neighborhood Violence on Adolescent Use of Violence," by Castro and Landry, is a Type II analysis. The authors explore the relationship of experiencing neighborhood violence on adolescents' own use of violence. Having witnessed violence and having been personally victimized are the principal independent variables, with use of violence as the dependent variable. Gender, race, and class are the intersectional control variables. There are also a number of other controls. Because parental occupation was not available in the data set, parental education was used as a proxy. Those with some college or more were coded as middle class, and all others were coded as working class.

The principal analysis is found in Table 4, with two interaction terms (gender × witnessed violence and gender × violent victimization) and four subgroups: white middle class, black middle class, white working class, and black working class. The only significant interaction terms are the two for the white middle class at $p \leq .001$ and a far weaker one ($p \leq .05$) for the white working class. In the former, the two significant interaction terms indicate that among adolescents in this social location, white middle-class males are more like to use violence than white middle-class females. The same is true for white working-class adolescents, among whom males exposed to violent victimization are more likely than females to use violence themselves.

To test the significance of differences found between subgroups, the authors compared the interaction coefficients for neighborhood violence within the white middle class with the coefficients from each of the other subgroups. Because the most significant interactions were found within the white middle class making comparisons with this group seemed to be a reasonable option. Results indicate that the only significant difference was between white and black middle-class adolescents. Overall there were findings of gender, race, and class differences. Although main effects indicate that all adolescents exposed to violence either as witness or victims are *more likely* to themselves use violence than those not so exposed, there are differences in the strength of this likelihood by race, gender, and class. Of those adolescents exposed to violence within their neighborhoods, white middle-class *males* (R,Cl,G) were found to be more likely to use violence than white middle-class *females*. In only one other social location was this gender difference found, among white working-class youth; but this relationship was not significantly different from that found within the white middle class. This is interesting, since the coefficient for white working-class adolescents (.093) is much smaller than that for white middle-class adolescents (.194). This may simply be the effect of subsample size, as the number of white middle-class adolescents is almost twice as large as the number of white working-class youth. Finally, among black adolescents exposed to neighborhood violence, no *gender* or *class* differences were found in propensity to use violence. Although these findings for black adolescents are substantively counterintuitive and therefore difficult to explain, it is only through the use of intersectional analysis that they were possible.[14]

[14]From everything that is known about greater male aggression, one would certainly have expected a gender difference among blacks similar to the one found among whites. Given the large error terms for all the black interaction coefficients (and the white-working class coefficients), however, one would have to conclude that this finding needs testing with much larger subsamples.

Are There Race and Gender Differences in the Effect of Marital Dissolution on Depression?

KEI M. NOMAGUCHI
Sociology
Northen Illinois University

ADDRESS: *Department of Sociology, Northern Illinois University, DeKalb, IL 60115. Email: knomaguchi@niu.edu*

Abstract

In this article, I examine whether there are race and gender differences in the effect of marital dissolution on depression, using panel data of a nationally representative sample of black and white Americans. To examine group differences, two procedures are used, including (1) OLS regression models with interaction terms on the full sample, and (2) t-tests of differences in coefficients for the effect of marital dissolution on depression from separate subgroup regression models. Results suggest that regardless of race, women are more likely than men to increase depression upon becoming separated/divorced, and there are no significant race differences within each gender, and there is no interaction between gender and race. Although black-white differences in gender relations in marriage led to speculations that blacks may differ from whites in gender difference in psychological responses to marital dissolution, results suggest that regardless of race, women are more vulnerable than men to marital dissolution.

Keywords

depression, gender, interactions, marital dissolution, race, gender, class, RGC perspective

In this paper, I examine whether the effect of marital dissolution on depression varies by race and gender. Many studies have suggested that women's psychological well-being is more vulnerable than men's to marital dissolution (Aeltine & Kessler, 1993; Horwitz, White, & Howell-White, 1996; Marks & Lambert, 1998; Simon & Marcussen, 1999), although some studies have found no gender differences (Booth & Amoto, 1991; Menaghan & Lieberman, 1986). The women's greater psychological vulnerability to martial dissolution is explained in part by gender differences in various aspects of marriage, such as the division of labor in the household, social support, and emotional life (Aseltine & Kessler, 1993, Simon & Marcussen, 1999). For example, women tend to be more economically dependent on their spouse than men. Women invest more time and energy on the marital relationship and family work than men. Because of the greater economic dependency on their spouse and the greater commitment to the marital relationship, when marriage ends, women are more likely than men to find themselves economically less self-sufficient and feel a greater sense of loss in their important adult roles.

It is not clear, however, whether such gender differences in psychological vulnerability to marital dissolution are robust regardless of race

---

Kei M Nomaguchi is an Assistant Professor in the Department of Sociology at Northern Illinois University. Her research interests include work and family, family transitions, and parenthood, with special emphasis on variations by gender, culture, and socioeconomic statuses.

I wish to thank Bart Landry and an anonymous reviewer for helpful comments on earlier drafts of this article.

and ethnicity. To date, the effect of separation/divorce on mental health has been studied by using white samples (Aseltine & Kessler, 1993; Booth & Amato, 1991; Doherty, Su, & Needle, 1989) or, by comparing whites to nonwhites altogether (Menaghan & Lieberman, 1986; Simon & Marcusen, 1999). Although some researchers suggest that the greater emotional vulnerability of women than men to marital dissolution does not vary by race (e.g., Williams, Takeuchi, & Adair, 1992), few studies have *explicitly* examined whether black women differ from black men in their responses to marital dissolution.

The race, gender, and class "intersection" perspective, or the RGC perspective, has emphasized that researchers should be mindful about the possibility of variations by race, gender, class, and culture in individuals' daily experiences, life events, and their influence on well-being (Brewer, 1993; Collins, 1998; Zinn & Dill, 1996). The basic idea of the RGC perspective was derived from black feminists' criticism of the "false universalization" of gender and family issues by middle-class, white scholars (Dugger, 1996). The RGC scholars suggest that historically black and other minorities in the United States have experienced different patterns of gender in families; and thus studying variations by race-gender groups should have a lot to offer in analysis and theorizing gender and families in American society (Dugger, 1996; Zinn, 1990)

Research on black families has suggested that black couples' experiences in economic, social, and psychological aspects of marriage often differ from whites couples (for a review, see Taylor, Chatters, Tucker, & Lewis, 1990). For example, the division of labor in black families is more egalitarian than in white families (Collins, 1991; John, Shelton, & Luschen, 1995). Black wives tend to have strong connections with their extended families and communities, and hence they are more independent from their spouse than white wives (Collins, 1991; Landry, 2000). In short, black wives are less dependent on their marriage than white wives, both economically and emotionally.

Given such black women's lower dependency on marriage than white women, it is possible that black women may not be as emotionally vulnerable as white women when their marriage ended in separation or divorce. If we compare the four race-gender groups of blacks and whites, white women may be the most disadvantaged in psychological reactions to marital dissolution, because they seem to be most dependent on marriage in terms of economic, social, and psychological aspects of adult lives among the four groups.

In this article, using a nationally representative sample of black and white Americans, I examine whether there are differences in the effect of marital dissolution on depression among the four race-gender groups—black women, black men, white women, and white men. It has been challenging for researchers to empirically assess the RGC perspective with a national sample. One issue is that in a nationally representative sample, sample size for minority groups tends to be very small. When subgroups are broken down in multivariate analysis, sample size typically becomes too small to conduct meaningful analysis. Recently, however, more surveys have been collected with oversampling of minorities. Data for this paper are drawn from the two waves of the National Survey of Families and Households (NSFH) in which blacks (and other ethnic minorities) are oversampled.

Another challenge is how to assess group differences in regression models. RGC researchers have overwhelmingly used regression models with interaction terms, such as race × gender, race × class, and race × gender × class. However, the use of interaction terms can provide several issues, including the possibility of multi-collinearity and the difficulty in interpreting results. In this paper, I use two procedures to examine group differences in OLS regression models. First, as often used in RGC research, I use interaction terms with the full sample. Second, following Hardy's (1993) suggestion, I conduct separate subgroup regression models and assess whether subgroup differences in coefficients of the effect of marital dissolution on depression are significant.

Gender, Race, and the Effect of Marital Dissolution on Mental Health

Many agree that separation/divorce is one of the most stressful, undesirable events in adult lives. Research has suggested that marital dissolution has a great negative influence on mental health (e.g., Menaghan & Lieberman, 1986; Simon & Marcussen, 1999). The extent to which marital dissolution affects individuals' psychological well-being varies by social locations, however. Gender has been one of the major social factors researchers have focused on, with many suggesting that women are more vulnerable than men to marital dissolution (Aseltine & Kessler, 1993; Horwitz, White, & Howell-White, 1996; Simon & Marcussen, 1999).

Relatively little is known, however, whether there are variations by race/ethnic groups in the gender gap in psychological vulnerability to marital dissolution. Some scholars have found that gender difference in emotional vulnerability to marital dissolution is universal and cross-racial, and crosses socioeconomic status (Simon & Marsussen, 1999; Williams, Takeuchi, & Adair, 1992). However, little research has explicitly examined whether there are race *and* gender differences in the effect of marital dissolution on mental health. Furthermore, with few exceptions, the exploration of racial differences in the effect of marital dissolution on mental health, has been neglected. For example, Menaghan and Lieberman (1986) found that whites are more likely to suffer from separation/divorce than other races in terms of depression; yet race difference was not the focus of their study and thus little discussion was devoted to it.

Explanations about gender differences in responses to marital dissolution are twofold. The first explanation assumes that the influence of stressful life events on people's mental health is event-specific. In the case of marital dissolution, its effect on men's and women's mental health may be different because marriage provides different costs and benefits, experiences, and meanings for men's and women's lives (Simon 1995; for a similar argument, see Umberson, Wortman, & Kessler, 1992). The second explanation assumes that gender differences in responses to stressful life events are *not* event-specific. Rather, it emphasizes that men and women are different in their styles of expressing distress: men tend to show behavioral disorders, such as alcohol and drug use, as responses to undesirable events, whereas women tend to show internal disorders such as depression (Robbins & Martin, 1993).

Empirical studies have provided more support for the former explanation (e.g., Mirowsky & Ross, 1995). Examining two indicators of psychological well-being, Horwitz and his colleagues (1996) found that, upon becoming divorced, women tended to increase depression, but they did not find gender differences in changes in alcohol use. When the effects of various types of stressful life events on depression are examined, researchers tend to find different patterns of gender differences. For example, contrary to the case of separation/divorce, women are *less* likely than men to increase depression in widowhood (Umberson, Wortman, & Kessler, 1992). Women are also less likely than men to increase depression when they lost their job (Wheaton, 1990). These findings suggest that gender differences in emotional responses to stressful events may not be simply due to general differences in styles of expression of distress, but due to differences in experiences of particular life events between men and women.

Hence, in this article, I focus on gender differences in various aspects of marriage as the major causes of gender differences in the effect of marital dissolution on depression. In the following, I discuss several aspects of marriage that may lead women to be more disadvantaged than men when their marriage ends, including economic activities, social relationships, and psychological involvement. For each aspect of marriage, I then discuss that such gender differences in marriage may not be as common in black families as in white families.

Instrumental aspects of marriage

Financial strain is one of the major stressors that many people experience upon becoming separated/divorced. Research has suggested that people who have their own sources of income or potential resources to earn money suffer less from divorce emotionally than those who do not have such economic resources (Booth & Amato, 1991). When people perceive a greater deterioration in standards of living after divorce, they tend to be more depressed than those who perceive fewer changes in their economic standings (Menaghan & Lieberman, 1986).

After divorce, the economic well-being of women tends to become much worse than men's (Bianchi, Subiya, & Kahn, 1999). As neoclassical household economic theory suggests (e.g., Becker, 1981), marriage is an economic function where a husband and wife specializes in the division of labor—the man works for money, while the woman stays at home to take care of her family—based on their rational choice to maximize the economic well-being of the household. In the 1990s, such specialization is no longer common among U.S. married couples. In 1997, 64 percent of married women in the United States were employed (Casper & Bianchi, 2002: Figure 10.3), compared with only 30 percent in 1970. Yet, marriage still tends to lead women to be economically dependent on their spouses. Married women are much more likely than married men to drop out of the labor force or reduce work hours in order to take care of the home and children, especially when they have young children (Casper & Bianchi, 2002). Even among professional couples, it is more often wives than husbands who slow down their career achievements when childrearing is intensive (Becker & Moen, 1999). Married women spend much more time than married men on housework (Shelton, 2000) and childcare (Bianchi, 2000), which curtail time for work and occupations. Although couples in which wives earn more than husbands are slowly increasing, on average, wives often suffer from a "wage penalty of motherhood" (Budig & England, 2001; Waldfogel, 1997) and they earn less than their spouse (Waite & Gallagher, 2000). Thus, when marriage ends, women tend to face not only a loss of their main source of income, but also find themselves disadvantaged in the job market due to their disrupted work history. On the contrary, upon becoming separated/divorced, men generally face much fewer changes in their economic and career standings than women in part because far fewer men quit their jobs or reduce their work hours while married. Marriage and fatherhood tend to encourage men to work more and earn more as a major way through which men express their love to their children and wife (Townsend, 2002), although the causal direction between marriage and earnings is not clear, i.e., men with a greater earning potential are more likely than those with a less earning potential to get married (Oppenheimer, 2000).

The division of labor in the household among black couples is generally more egalitarian than among white couples. Historically the gender gap in the labor force participation rates has been much smaller among blacks than whites partly because of black men's higher unemployment rates (Spain & Bianchi, 1996). Because black men tend to have lower-paying jobs compared with white men, the male-female gap in earnings has also been much smaller among blacks than whites (Spain & Bianchi, 1996). Although economic necessity may be the driving force of black wives' high rate of labor force participation, cultural factors also play a role: Self-reliance and economic autonomy has been traditionally emphasized as the virtue of womanhood among black women (Collins, 1991; Landry, 2000). Collins (1991) suggests that U.S. black women's attachment to paid work is derived from the West African tradition which emphasizes that not only caring for their children but also providing for their children is essential part of motherhood. The egalitarian relationship in marriage among blacks does not stop at economic roles. At home, more black husbands than white husbands share housework with their wives (John, Shelton, & Luschen, 1995; Ross 1987; Landry, 2000). Thus, the economic life of black wives is not as dependent on their spouse as that of white wives.

Interpersonal and psychological aspects of marriage

A loss of the marital relationship is another major aspect of strain for individuals who became separated or divorced. Because of the gendered cultural expectations which emphasize that it is central for adult women to take care of their husband and raise their children, women tend to invest more time and energy than men on organizing their families' daily life and maintaining the marital relationship. Even when couples believe that they share housework and childcare equally, in reality, wives often "run" domestic work and decide what their husbands should do and when it should be done in family work (Hochschild, 1989). Indeed, women do an enormous amount of "hidden" psychological work to manage their families' lives, such as planning dinner each day, making appointments for doctor check-ups for each family member, arranging time and date for home repairs, arranging childcare, organizing family gatherings, and monitoring the health and well-being of family members (Devault, 1991; Mederer, 1993; Stolzenberg, 2001). Women tend to provide more social support to their spouses than men (Kessler, McLeod, & Wethington, 1985; Waite, 1995).

How such daily "psychological demands" of marriage affect women's well-being has been debated. Stress research has suggested that married women are more depressed and less happy than married men (e.g., Cleary & Mechanic, 1983). Because of the greater responsibility for caring for other family members, family issues matter more for women's mental health than men's (Williams, 1988). Hence, as research has suggested in the case of widowhood, when marriage ends, it may "release" women from the emotional burdens of daily life (Umberson, Wortman, & Kessler, 1992). Women's work for their families has complex meanings for women, however. Although it may be repetitive, tiresome, and less enjoyable, it is "embedded" in family relations and closely linked with women's love and care towards their family members (Thompson & Walker, 1989). Because women invest so much more time and energy than men on enhancing the well-being of their marriage and family life, they may experience a greater sense of loss than men when their marriage ends by divorce. Simon (1992, 1997) suggests that the extent to which individuals suffer from undesirable events in a certain role domain depends on individuals' commitment to the role. Women may suffer from a loss of the marital relationship more than men because women tend to be more committed to the marital relationship than men.

If women have alternative role domains in which they are emotionally involved, they may suffer less from a loss of their marital relationship. Because of black men's lower status position than white men, black women get smaller returns than white women by investing to their marriage (Waite, 1995). Instead, black wives may rely on other places for social relationships where they exchange material and non-material supports with other women, including workplace, extended families, and communities. Social relationship at paid work seems to matter more greatly for black wives than white wives. For example, Waldron and Jacobs (1989) found that employment is not beneficial for white married women's mental health, but it is for black married women's mental health, and noted that this is perhaps because social support at the workplace is essential for black wives who may not get as much support from their marriage as white wives. Research on black people's extended family and their informal social supports among kin networks and close friends has suggested that blacks have stronger social supports from outside of the marital relationship than whites (Benin & Keith, 1995; Hogan, Hao, & Parrish, 1990; Taylor, Chatters, Tucker, & Lewis, 1990). The alternative sources of social and emotional support may help black women cope with a loss of their marital relationship. Indeed, there is some evidence that people who have someone, other than their spouse, whom they can count on for understanding and advice are more likely to be emotionally damaged by divorce than those who have no close supportive relationship (Menaghan & Lieberman, 1986).

It has been also suggested that black women are less likely than white women to have "traditional" gender role attitudes (Beckett & Smith, 1981; Dugger, 1996; Malson, 1983). The meaning of motherhood and the ideal womanhood in black families differ from those in white, middle-class families. Black women's identity and their ideal womanhood lie not only in being a good wife and a good mother, but also in being a good worker and a good "mother" in the community (Collins, 1991; Landry, 2000). The "threefold commitment"—to family, to career, and to community/social activities—has been the virtue of womanhood in the black community (Landry, 2000). Thus, because of the multiple sources of identities in black women's lives, a loss of marital role may not be as detrimental for black women as for white women.

In sum, researchers have suggested that women are more psychologically vulnerable than men to marital dissolution, because marriage leads men and women to specialization in the division of economic and caring roles, which leads women to be more dependent on their spouse than men. However, such specialization may be less common among black couples than white couples. Black wives are more self-sufficient and have more alternative sources of social support and identity than white wives. Given such independence of black wives from the spouse, it is possible that marital dissolution may not lead black women to as many disadvantages as those experienced by white women, and thus black women may not be as distressed as white women upon becoming separated/divorced.

Research questions

In this article, I empirically examine the following question: Are there differences by race and gender groups in adults' psychological responses to marital dissolution? More precisely, after controlling for demographic and socioeconomic characteristics, are white women more emotionally vulnerable to marital dissolution compared with black women, black men, and white men, because of their greater dependency on marriage than these three other groups? In doing so, I pay special attention to a methodological issue: How can we compare group differences in regression models? Many RGC researchers have used interaction terms with regression models on a full sample. An interaction term indicates that the relationship is not additive but multiplicative (Blalock, 1979), and thus this may be an appropriate way to test the RGC perspective's primary argument. Previous studies have suggested that this procedure is not always useful because of several issues, however. For example, interaction terms are sometimes difficult to interpret. Adding several interaction terms in one regression model may increase the possibility of multi-collinearity problems. Furthermore, small sample size for a minority group often leads to limited statistical power to examine the effects of interaction terms. I thus use another equivalent procedure to assess subgroup differences in the effect of marital dissolution on depression that I will discuss in the method section.

METHODS

Data and sample

Data for this study are drawn from two waves of the National Survey of Families and Households (NSFH) (Sweet & Bumpass, 1996). The first interview was conducted in 1987–88 with a national probability sample of 13,017 respondents, including over samples of Blacks, Puerto Rican, Mexican-American, and single parent families, step-families, cohabiting couples, and persons who were recently married. Questions were asked either in face-to-face interviews or by a respondent's self-administered questionnaire. The second interview was conducted in 1993–1994, and 10,005 respondents were re-interviewed.

From the 10,005 respondents, I selected black and white respondents who were married in the first interview (n = 5,069). I excluded the 28 respondents who did not have information about changes in marital status between the two interviews. I also excluded 211 respondents who became widowed and 139 respondents who divorced but remarried by the second interview (n = 4,691). Excluding those who have missing values in variables used in regression analysis, my sample consists of 4,232 respondents including 232 black men, 221 black women, 1,686 white men, and 2,093 white women.

MEASURES

Dependent variable

The dependent variable is a depression scale measured in the second interview (Time 2). The NSFH includes the 12 items from the Center for Epidemiological Studies Depression Scale (CED-D) which is a commonly used measure of psychological well-being (Radloff, 1977). Respondents were asked how many days during the past week they had experienced such things that they: (a) "felt bothered by things that usually do not bother them"; (b) "did not feel like eating"; (c) "felt that they could not shake of the blues even with help from their family or friends"; (d) "had trouble keeping their mind on what they were doing"; (e) "felt depressed"; (f) "felt that everything they did was an effort"; (g) "felt fearful"; (h) "slept restlessly"; (i) "talked less than usual"; (j) "felt lonely"; (k) "felt sad"; and (1) "felt they could not get going." The response for each item ranges from 0 to 7 days. A scale is created by averaging the sum of scores in the 12 items. The Cronbach's alpha for this depression scale is $\alpha = .93$.

Independent variables

The primary independent variables include: *marital dissolution* between Time 1 and Time 2 where respondents whose marriage ended in divorce or separation by Time 2 are assigned 1 and others are assigned 0. *Gender* is a dichotomous variable where women are coded as 1. *Race* is a dichotomous variable where blacks are coded as 1 and whites are coded as 0.

Control variables

I use the following demographic and socioeconomic characteristics as controls, based on their associations with depression that previous studies have suggested. Two demographic variables are included. Studies have found that aging has enhancing effects on psychological well-being (Glass & Fujimoto, 1994; Lennon, 1987; Ross, Mirowsky, & Huber, 1983). *Age at Time 2* is measured in years. Parenthood is related to adult mental health, although empirical findings are inconsistent (see the review in Nomaguchi & Milkie, 2003). *Parental status at Time 2* is a dichotomous variable where those who live with at least one child aged 18 or younger are coded as 1.

Socioeconomic status is greatly related to psychological well-being. Research has suggested that higher education, being employed, and higher income are related to lower depression (Yu & Williams, 1999). *College education* is a dichotomous variable where those who have some college education or more are coded as 1 and others are coded as 0. *Employment status at Time* 2 is a dichotomous variable where those who are employed at Time 2 are coded as 1. *Annual household income at Time 2* is a continuous variable measured as the log of household income to avoid distortion caused by extreme outliers. Before the transformation, cases with less than $100 household income were recorded as $100, and a dummy variable indicating whether income data were imputed was included in the model. Those with missing data were assigned the median household income by gender and race subgroup, and another dummy variable indicating whether income data were imputed was also included in the model. *Household income at Time 2 relative to household income at Time 1* is a continuous variable in which the log of household income at Time 2 was divided by the log of household income at Time 1.

Finally, to eliminate selection effects (i.e., people who are more depressed may be more likely to divorce than those who are less depressed), *depression at Time 1* is included in the models as a control.

Analytical plan

I use OLS regression models to examine race and gender differences in the effect of marital dissolution on depression, controlling for other demographic and socioeconomic characteristics discussed above. As mentioned above, two different procedures are used. The first one is conventional: I examine the race and gender effect using two-way and three-way interaction terms (race × martial dissolution, gender × martial dissolution, and race × gender × martial dissolution) on the full sample. The second one is relatively less common in RGC research. I conduct the same regression models for the four subgroups (i.e., black men, black women, white men, and white women) separately. Then, following Hardy's (1993) suggestion, I examine whether differences in the coefficients for the effects of marital dissolution on depression in subgroup samples are statistically significant. This involves two steps. The first step is to test homogeneity of variance between two subsamples in order to examine whether the OLS assumptions are met (Hardy, 1993 53–56). The equation for the *F*-test of homogeneity of variance can be written as:

$$F_{a,b} = \frac{RSS_1/n_1 - k_1 - 1}{RSS_2/n_2 - k_2 - 1} \tag{1}$$

where RSS stands for residual sum of squares, $a = n_1 - k_1 - 1$ and $b = n_2 - k_2 - 1$, n_1 and n_2 are the number of cases, and k_1 and k_2 are the number of variables in the subgroups. The numerator is the larger value, whereas the denominator is the smaller value. The second step is to test whether the difference in the coefficient for martial dissolution between given two subgroups are statistically significant (Hardy, 1993 48 – 53). The equation for the *t*-test can be written as follows:

$$t = \frac{B_1 - B_2}{S_{pooled}\left[\frac{S^2 B_1}{S^2_1} + \frac{S^2 B_2}{S^2_1}\right]^{1/2}} \tag{2}$$

where B_1 and B_2 are coefficients for marital dissolution, s^2_{B1} and s^2_{B2} are the variances of B_1 and B_2, and s^2_1 and s^2_2 are the mean residual sums of squares from the subgroup regressions, i.e., $RSS/n - k - 1$ in Equation (1). Assuming that variances are equal between two subgroups, s^2_{pooled} is estimated as the variance for the pooled sample which is written as:

$$s^2_{pooled} = \frac{(n_1 - k_1 - 1)s^2_1 + (n_2 - k_2 - 1)s^2_2}{N - (k_1 + k_2 + 2)} \tag{3}$$

This *t*-test allows us to examine whether differences in coefficients for marital dissolution between the two subgroups (i.e., $B_1 - B_2$) are statistically significant.

Results

Bivariate results

Table 1 presents weighted means for variables for black and white Americans who were married at the first interview, by race, gender, and whether

TABLE 1 ■ WEIGHT MEANS (STANDARD DEVIATIONS) FOR VARIABLES BY RACE, GENDER, AND MARITAL DISSOLUTION BETWEEN TIME 1 AND TIME 2 FOR BLACK AND WHITE AMERICANS WHO WERE MARRIED AT TIME 1 ($n = 4,232$)

	Black men		Black women		White men		White women	
	Remain married	Marital loss	Remain married	Marital loss	Remain married	Marital loss	Remain married	Marital loss
Depression at Time 2	1.15	1.53	1.29	2.21 ***	0.73	1.27 ***	1.04	1.88 ***
	(1.11)	(1.31)	(1.04)	(1.31)	(1.02)	(1.28)	(1.15)	(1.49)
Depression at Time 1	1.07	1.68 *	1.11	1.42	0.76	1.18 ***	1.05	1.46 ***
	(1.17)	(1.55)	(0.97)	(0.89)	(1.17)	(1.19)	(1.17)	(1.21)
Differences in depression (Time 2 − Time 1)	0.09	−0.15	0.17	0.79 *	−0.03	0.09	−0.01	0.43 ***
	(1.20)	(1.54)	(1.12)	(1.28)	(1.26)	(1.47)	(1.28)	(1.70)
Age at Time 2	49.60	43.59 **	47.37	37.18 ***	51.84	42.75 ***	48.46	38.35 ***
	(11.17)	(9.49)	(9.39)	(6.92)	(15.83)	(9.88)	(13.08)	(8.34)
Have children < 18 at Time 2	0.56	0.27 ***	0.57	0.73 +	0.45	0.19 ***	0.48	0.55 +
	(0.42)	(0.37)	(0.37)	(0.36)	(0.55)	(0.38)	(0.48)	(0.44)
College education at Time 2	0.37	0.47	0.40	0.34	0.55	0.49	0.43	0.43
	(0.41)	(0.42)	(0.37)	(0.38)	(0.55)	(0.48)	(0.48)	(0.44)
Employed in Time 2	0.69	0.70	0.65	0.73	0.72	0.74	0.55	0.72 ***
	(0.39)	(0.38)	(0.36)	(0.36)	(0.50)	(0.42)	(0.48)	(0.40)
Household income in Time 2 (logged)	10.11	10.26	10.26	9.81 +	10.67	10.26 ***	10.49	9.99 ***
	(1.24)	(0.49)	(1.04)	(0.75)	(1.15)	(1.37)	(1.27)	(0.95)
Missing data in income at Time 2	0.02	0.24 ***	0.02	0.14	0.003	0.10 ***	0.01	0.12 ***
	(0.12)	(0.36)	(0.10)	(0.28)	(0.06)	(0.29)	(0.08)	(0.29)
Household income at Time 2 relative to Household income at Time 1 (logged)	1.01	1.01	0.99	0.98	1.02	1.00 +	1.00	0.97 *
	(0.16)	(0.07)	(0.13)	(0.08)	(0.16)	(0.16)	(0.13)	(0.12)
Number of cases	190	42	187	34	1,526	160	1,898	195
% marital dissolution		18.1		15.4		9.5		9.3

NOTE: Differences by marital status at Time 2 are significant at $+p < .10$; $*p < .05$; $**p < .01$; $***p < .001$.

they experienced marital dissolution between the first and second interviews. Of those who were married in the first interview (Time 1), 9.3 percent of white women became separated/divorced by the second interview (Time 2), compared with 9.5 percent of white men, 15.4 percent of black women, and 18.1 percent of black men.

Those who were separated/divorced at Time 2 report significantly higher levels of depression than those who remain married, except for black men. It is noteworthy that those who became separated/divorced had already been more depressed than their counterparts who remained married at Time 1, that is, before their marriage ended, although the differences are not statistically significant for black women. When changes in depression between the two interviews are compared, we find that women who experienced marital dissolution show a significant increase in depression compared to those who remained married, regardless of race. However, men who were divorced at Time 2 do not differ from those who remained married in changes in depression between the two interviews, regardless of race.

Those who became separated/divorced differ from their counterparts who remain married in several demographic and socioeconomic characteristics. Regardless of race, those who experienced marital dissolution are younger than their counterparts who remained married, probably because, as suggested in previous studies, marital dissolution tends to occur among those who married at younger ages and/or at relatively early stage of marriage (Morgan & Rindfuss, 1985). Not surprisingly, regardless of race, men who are separated or divorced are less likely than those who remain married to live with children: Whereas 56 percent of black men and 45 percent of white men who remain married live with at least one child in the second interview, only 27 percent of black men and 19 percent of white men who experienced marital dissolution live with at least one child in the second interview. There are no significant differences in the level of education when it was measured by whether respondents have some college education. Only among white women, there are differences in the labor force participation rate between those who remain married and those who became separated/divorced: Only 55 percent of those who remain married are employed at Time 2, whereas 72 percent of those who became separated/divorced are employed at Time 2. Those who became separated/divorced averaged a lower level of income than those who remain married at Time 2, except for black men. Explanations for the lower level of household income among those who are separated/divorced than among those who remain married can be twofold: first, those with a lower level of household income are more likely to experience marital dissolution than those with a higher level of household income perhaps because of stresses and martial conflict caused by economic strain (Hoffman & Duncan, 1995); and second, those who got separated/divorced tend to lose a large source of income, especially women (Bianchi, Subiya, & Kohn, 1999). In this sample, only white women show that those who became separated/divorced experienced a significant decline in household income between the two interviews compared with their counterparts who remain married.

Multivariate results

Table 2 presents OLS regression results predicting depression at Time 2 using the full sample. I examined three models. Model 1 includes main effects of marital dissolution, gender, and race, controlling for demographic and socioeconomic variables, such as age, parental status, education, employment status, household income, and changes in household income between Time 1 and Time 2, and depression at Time 1. Model 2 adds three two-way interaction terms, including marital dissolution × gender, marital dissolution × race, and gender × race. Model 3 adds a three-way interaction term among marital dissolution, gender, and race.

Model 1 suggests that even after controlling for demographic and socioeconomic

TABLE 2 ■ OLS Regression Coefficients and Standard Errors for Depression at Time 2 Regressed on Marital dissolution, Gender, Race, Interactions, and Other Variables for Black and White Americans Who Were Married at Time 1 (n = 4,232)

	Model 1				Model 2				Model 3			
	b	*SE*	β		*b*	*SE*	β		*b*	*SE*	β	
Marital dissolution (1 = separated/divorced)	0.46	0.06	0.11	***	0.28	0.09	0.07	**	0.29	0.09	0.07	**
Gender (1 = women)	0.18	0.03	0.08	***	0.15	0.04	0.06	***	0.15	0.04	0.06	***
Race (1 = black)	0.22	0.06	0.05	***	0.23	0.09	0.05	**	0.25	0.09	0.05	**
Gender × race					0.01	0.13	0.002		−0.03	0.14	−0.004	
Marital dissolution × gender					0.38	0.12	0.06	**	0.34	0.13	0.06	**
Marital dissolution × race					−0.06	0.17	−0.01		−0.18	0.23	−0.02	
Marital dissolution × gender × race									0.27	0.35	0.02	
Age	−0.005	0.002	−0.06	**	−0.005	0.002	−0.06	**	−0.005	0.002	−0.06	**
Have children < 18 at Time 2	−0.03	0.04	−0.01		−0.04	0.05	−0.02		−0.04	0.05	−0.02	
College education	−0.14	0.03	−0.06	***	−0.14	0.03	−0.06	***	−0.14	0.03	−0.06	***
Employed in Time 2	−0.16	0.04	−0.06	***	−0.16	0.04	−0.07	***	−0.16	0.04	−0.07	***
Household income in Time 2 (logged)	−0.07	0.02	−0.07	***	0.07	0.02	−0.07	***	−0.07	0.02	−0.07	***
Missing data in income at Time 2	0.20	0.14	0.02		0.20	0.14	0.02		0.21	0.14	0.02	
Household income at Time 2 relative to household Income at Time 1 (logged)	0.22	0.15	0.03		0.21	0.15	0.03		0.21	0.15	0.03	
Depression at Time 1	0.33	0.01	0.34	***	0.33	0.01	0.34	***	0.33	0.01	0.34	***
Constant	1.42	0.19	0	***	1.46	0.19	0	***	1.45	0.19	0	***
Adjusted R-square		0.189 ***				0.190 ***				0.190 ***		

+p < .10; *p < .05; **p < .01; ***p < .001.

NOTE: Regressions are weighted.

characteristics, and level of depression at Time 1, adults who experienced marital dissolution were more likely than adults who remain married to report higher levels of depression at Time 2. As suggested in previous studies, women are more likely than men to have higher levels of depression (e.g., Mirowsky & Ross, 1995). Black are more likely than whites to have higher levels of depression. Black-white differences in depression have been debated (e.g., George & Lynch, 2003), and the discussion is beyond this article. Model 2 shows that there is a significant interaction effect between gender and marital dissolution. The positive sign of the coefficient for the interaction term of marital dissolution × gender suggests that women are more likely than men to be vulnerable to the effect of marital dissolution on depression. This result is consistent with several previous studies such as Horswitz et al. (1996) and Simon and Marcussen (1999). In contrast, there is no significant interaction effect between race and marital dissolution. Finally, Model 3 shows that there is no significant three-way interaction effect among gender, race, and marital dissolution, suggesting that gender and race do not interact in the effect of martial dissolution on depression. I examined the degree of multicollinearity, using the variance inflation factor (VIF), a common way to detect multi-collinearity (Belsley, Kuh, & Welsch, 1980).

The VIF are 2.45 both for the interaction term of marital dissolution × gender and for the interaction term of marital dissolution × race, and 2.39 for the three-way interaction term of marital dissolution × gender × race (data not shown). This suggests that I can be relaxed about multi-collinearity problems in this model.

Table 3 presents OLS regression results for depression at Time 2 using the same variables in Table 2 (except for gender and race) for subgroups separately. The coefficients for marital dissolution are 0.11 (not significant) for black men, 0.67 ($p < 0.05$) for black women, 0.30 ($p < 0.01$) for white men, and 0.61 ($p < 0.001$) for white women, suggesting that those who experienced martial dissolution reported a significantly higher level of depression than those who remained married, except for black men. To examine whether these sub-group differences in the coefficients for marital dissolution are significant, I examined t-tests of differences in the coefficients, as discussed earlier. The results are shown in the bottom half of Table 3. I examined whether black men, black women, and white men differ from white women in their psychological responses to marital dissolution. The test of homogeneity of variance, using Equation (1), suggests that the null hypothesis of equality in variance between each combination of two samples failed to be rejected ($F = 1.12$ for black men and white women samples, $F = 1.19$ for black women and white women samples, and $F = 1.25$ for white men and white women samples). The t-values for group differences, using Equations (2) and (3), suggest that differences in the coefficients for marital dissolution on depression are significant between black men and white women ($t = -1.73$, $p < 0.05$), and between white men and white women ($t = -2.22$, $p < 0.05$), but not significant between black women and white women ($t = 0.21$). I also examined whether black men differ from white men in their psychological responses to marital dissolution. The test of homogeneity suggests that the null hypothesis of equality in variance failed to be rejected between black men and white men samples ($F = 1.12$). The t-value is -0.73, suggesting that there are no significant differences between black men and white men in the effect of marital dissolution on depression.

In sum, using interaction terms on the full sample, I found that there were gender differences, but none race differences, in psychological responses to marital dissolution, but there were no race differences in the effect of marital dissolution on depression, and race and gender did not interact in the effect of marital dissolution on depression. Using separate subgroup regressions and t-tests of differences in the effects of marital dissolution on depression, I found that white women were more vulnerable to marital dissolution than black men and

TABLE 3 ■ OLS REGRESSION COEFFICIENTS AND STANDARD ERRORS FOR DEPRESSION AT TIME 2 FOR RACE-GENDER SUBGROUPS

	Black men			Black women			White men			White women		
	b	*SE*	β	b	*SE*	β	b	*SE*	β	b	*SE*	β
Marital dissolution (1 = separated/divorced)	0.11	0.25	0.03	0.67	0.27	0.17*	0.30	0.09	0.08**	0.61	0.10	0.13***
Age at Time 2	−0.01	0.01	−0.12	−0.01	0.01	−0.05	−0.01	0.002	−0.15***	−0.002	0.003	−0.02
Have children < 18 at Time 2	0.01	0.23	0.003	0.37	0.25	0.12	−0.03	0.06	−0.02	−0.07	0.07	−0.03
College education at Time 2	−0.15	0.17	−0.05	−0.17	0.20	−0.06	−0.12	0.05	−0.06*	−0.17	0.05	−0.07**
Employed at Time 2	−0.38	0.22	−0.13 +	−0.53	0.23	−0.17*	−0.36	0.06	−0.17***	−0.03	0.06	−0.01
Income in Time 2 (logged)	−0.06	0.08	−0.06	−0.05	0.10	−0.05	−0.02	0.03	−0.02	−0.12	0.03	−0.12***
Missing data in income at Time 2	−0.08	0.37	−0.01	0.24	0.54	0.03	0.11	0.22	0.01	0.33	0.21	0.03
Household income at Time 2 relative to Household income at Time 1 (logged)	−0.56	0.63	−0.07	0.68	0.83	0.07	0.08	0.18	0.01	0.55	0.29	0.06+
Depression at Time 1	0.39	0.06	0.43***	0.39	0.07	0.34***	0.28	0.02	0.31***	0.35	0.02	0.35***
Constant	2.80	0.90	0***	1.18	1.00	0	1.48	0.28	0***	1.57	0.28	0***
Adjusted R-square		0.208***			0.194***			0.153***			0.177***	
Residual sum of squares (RSS)		234.31			210.89			1,593.08			2,475.17	
Mean residual sum of squares		1.06			1.00			0.95			1.18	
Number of cases		232			221			1,686			2,093	
Subgroup differences in the effect of marital dissolution on depression:												
Difference in *b* s (compared with white women)		−0.50			0.06			−0.31			—	
t-value of difference		−1.73*			0.21			−2.22*			—	
Difference in *b* s (compared with black women)		−0.56			—			−0.37			−0.06	
t-value of difference		−1.52 +			—			−1.34 +			−0.21	
Difference in *b* s (compared with white men)		−0.19			0.37			—			0.31	
t-value of difference		−0.73			1.34 +			—			2.22*	

$+p < .10$; $^{*}p < .05$; $^{**}p < .01$; $^{***}p < .001$.

NOTE: Regressions are weighted.

white men, but there was no difference between white women and black women, and no difference between white men and black men. Thus, I would conclude that in contrast to my expectations, black women are as distressed as white women upon becoming separated/divorced, and it appears that women are more psychologically vulnerable to marital dissolution than men regardless of race.

Discussion

The goal of this study was to assess whether there are race and gender differences in the effect of marital dissolution on depression, using a national sample of black and white Americans. Many scholars have suggested that women are more vulnerable than men to marital dissolution, because separation/divorce is different events for women and men due to gender differences in material, psychological, and interpersonal aspects of marriage. Because of the gendered division of labor and the gendered cultural expectations regarding marital roles, women tend to be more dependent than men on the marital relationship as a source of economic resources, social support, and the meaning of life. The RGC perspective suggests, however, that researchers should be mindful that marriage, families, and cultural expectations towards women's roles are different between blacks and whites (Collins, 1991; Zinn, 1996). The black-white differences in economic, social, and psychological aspects of marriage led to speculation that blacks might differ from whites in gender differences in psychological responses to marital dissolution. I expected that women's greater vulnerability to marital dissolution relative to men's would be more pronounced among whites than among black; and thus white women would be particularly vulnerable to marital dissolution among the four groups by race and gender.

My findings suggest that contrary to expectations, black women were as vulnerable to marital dissolution as white women, whereas both black men and white men were less vulnerable than white women, and there was no race difference in the effect of marital dissolution on depression among men. Black couples seem to be less "gendered" in their marital relationship; yet, when it ends, the "gender pattern" in psychological responses is found for both blacks and whites. One possibility is that although I assumed that the extent to which individuals would *lose* the benefits of marriage after divorce is the major cause of the variations in the effect of marital dissolution, what individuals can do in the coping process may better inform us about variations in the impact of marital dissolution on mental health. For example, Gerstel (1988) suggests that divorce leads men more than women to greater opportunities to create new social networks in informal settings, such as in bars and restaurants, or in organized social settings such as sports clubs or church activities. In contrast, women tend to have greater ties in social networks with old friends and relatives. Newly expanded social contacts, which presumably give adults opportunities to have new relationships and new experiences, may help divorced people cope with the stressful event and changes. Another possibility is that, as Gilligan (1982) suggests, women are more relationship-oriented than men in U.S. culture; and this may be true for both blacks and whites. Because of the greater emotional involvement in relationships with others, especially with their spouse, women may be more affected by undesirable events in close relationships than men (Kessler & McLeod, 1984), which certainly include their marriage.

This article also aimed at demonstrating an alternative method to examine group differences in regression models that may be useful for RGC researchers. In the past decades, RGC research has developed its theoretical work and qualitative studies. Relatively fewer efforts have been made in quantitative studies with a national sample, however. Researchers have often used interaction terms on the full sample in regression models to assess group differences, but it has not always been successful because of several issues, I discussed earlier. In this article, in addition to the "conventional" method, I demonstrated an alternative way to examine group differences, which examines differences in coefficients in the effect of marital dissolution on depression from separate subgroup regression models, using Hardy's (1993) suggestion. Whereas the two procedures produce equivalent results, the separate regression models allow researchers to compare the four groups by race and gender and interpret the results more simply than the full sample models with interaction terms.

This study has the same limitation as RGC research tends to have. I was unable to explore possible mediators of the link between marital dissolution on depression that stress process models suggest, such as perceived strains, social support, and psychological resources (Pearlin, Lieberman, Menaghan, & Mullan, 1981), largely because of data limitations: Adding an additional variable into regression models would have reduced the number of cases because of missing cases. Nevertheless, further efforts to empirically assess the RGC perspective are warranted, as one of the key future directions in RGC research.

Bibliography

Aseltine, R. H. & Kessler, R. C. (1993). Marital disruption and depression in a community sample. *Journal of Health and Social Behavior,* 34:237–251.

Becker, G.S. (1981). *A treatise on the family.* Cambridge, MA: Harvard University Press.

Becker, P.E. & Moen, P. (1999). Scaling back: Dual-earner couples' work-family strategies. *Journal of Marriage and Family,* 61:995–1007.

Beckett, J.O., & Smith, A.D. (1981). Work and family roles: Egalitarian marriage in black and white families. *Social Service Review,* 55: 314–326.

Belsley, D.A., Kuh, E., & Welsch, R.E. (1980). *Regression diagnostics: Identifying influential data and sources of collinearity.* New York: John Wiley & Sons.

Benin, M., & Keith, W. M. (1995). The social support of employed African American and Anglo mothers. *Journal of Family Issues,* 16:275–297.

Bianchi, S.M. (2000). Maternal employment and time with children: Dramatic change or surprising continuity? *Demography,* 37:401–414.

Bianchi, S.M., Subiya, L., & Kahn. J.R. (1999). The gender gap in the economic well-being of nonresident fathers and custodial mothers. *Demography,* 36:195–203.

Blalock, H.M, Jr. (1979). *Social statistics.* Revised second edition. New York: McGraw-Hill, Inc.

Booth, A., & Amato, P. (1991). Divorce and psychological stress. *Journal of Health and Social Behavior,* 32:396–407.

Brewer, R.M. (1993). Theorizing race, class and gender: The new scholarship of black feminist intellectuals and black women's labor. In S.M., James & A.P.A. Busia (eds.), *Theorizing black feminisms: The visionary pragmatism of black women,* pp. 3–30. London: Routledge.

Budig, M.J., & England, P. (2001). The wage penalty for motherhood. *American Sociological Review,* 66:204–225.

Casper, L.M., & Bianchi, S.M. (2002). *Continuity and changes in the American family.* Thousand Oaks, CA: Sage Publications.

Cleary, P.D., & Mechanic, D. (1983). Sex differences in psychological distress among married people. *Journal of Health and Social Behavior,* 24:111–121.

Collins, P.H. (1991). The meaning of motherhood in black culture and black mother-daughter relationships. In P. Bell-Scott (ed.), *Double Stitch,* pp. 42–60. Boston: Beacon Press.

Collins, P.H. (1998). Some group matters: Intersectionality, situated standpoints, and black feminist thought, In P.H. Collins, *Fighting word: Black women and the search for justice,* pp. 201–228. University of Minnesota Press.

Devault, M.L. (1991). *Feeding the family: The social organization of caring as gendered work.* Chicago: University of Chicago Press.

Doherty, W.J., Su, S., & Needle, R. (1989). Marital disruption and psychological well-being. *Journal of Family Issue,* 10:72–85.

Dugger, K. (1996). Social location and gender-role attitudes: A comparison of black and white women. In E. N. Chow, D. Wilkinson, & M. Baca Zinn (eds.), *Race, class & gender: Common bonds, different voices,* pp. 32–51. Thousand Oaks: Sage.

Gerstel, N. (1988). Divorce, gender, and social integration. *Gender & Society,* 2:343–367.

Gilligan, C. (1982). *In a different voice.* Cambridge, MA: Harvard University Press.

Glass, J., & Fujimoto, T. (1994). Housework, paid work, and depression among husbands and wives. *Journal of Health and Social Behavior,* 35:179–191.

George, L. K., & Lynch, S. M. (2003). Race Differences in depressive symptoms: A dynamic perspective on stress exposure and vulnerability. *Journal of Health and Social Behavior,* 44:353–369.

Hardy, M.A. (1993). *Regression with dummy variables.* A Sage University Paper, 07–093. Newbury Park, CA: Sage Publication.

Hochschild, A.R. (1989/1997). *The second shift.* New York: HarperCollins.

Hoffman, S.D., & Duncan, G.J. (1995). The effect of income, wages, and AFDC benefits on marital dissolution. *Journal of Human Resources,* 30:19–41.

Hogan, D.P., Hao, L., & Parrish, W.L. (1990). Race, kin networks, and assistance to mother-headed families. *Social Forces,* 68:797–812.

Horwitz, A.V., White, H.R., & Howell-White, S. (1996). The use of multiple outcomes in stress research: A case study of gender differences in responses to marital dissolution. *Journal of Health and Social Behavior,* 37:278–191.

Kessler, R., & McLeod, J. (1984). Sex differences in vulnerability to undesirable life events. *American Sociological Review,* 49:620–631.

John, D., Shelton, B.A. & Luschen, K. (1995). Race, ethnicity, gender, and perceptions of fairness. *Journal of Family Issues,* 16:357–379.

Kessler, R.C., Jane D. McLeod, J.D., & Wethington, E. (1985). The costs of caring: A perspective on the relationship between sex psychological distress. In I.G. Sarason & B.R. Sarason (eds.), *Social support: Theory, research, and applications.* Dordrecht: Martinus Nijhoff.

Landry, B. (2000). *Black working wives.* Berkeley: University of California Press.

Lennon, M.C. (1987). Sex differences in distress: The impact of gender and work roles. *Journal of Health and Social Behavior,* 28:290–305.

Malson, M.R. (1983). Black women's sex roles: The social context for a new ideology. *Journal of Social Issues,* 39:101–113.

Marks, N.F., & Lambert, J.D. (1998). Marital status continuity and change among young and midlife adults. *Journal of Family Issues,* 19:652–686.

Mederer, H.J. (1993). Division of labor in two-earner homes: Task accomplishment versus household management as critical variables in perceptions about family work. *Journal of Marriage and the Family,* 55:133–145.

Menaghan, E.G., & Lieberman, M.A. (1986). Changes in depression following divorce: A panel study. *Journal of Marriage and Family,* 48:319–328.

Mirowsky, J. & Ross, C.E. (1995). Sex differences in distress: Real or artifact? *American Sociological Review,* 60:449–468.

Morgan, S.P., & Rindfuss, R.R. (1985). Marital dissolution: Structural and temporal dimensions. *American Journal of Sociology;* 90:1055–1077.

Nomaguchi, K.M., & Milkie, M.A. (2003). Costs and rewards of children: The effects of becoming a parent on adults' lives. *Journal of Marriage and Family,* 65, 356–374.

Oppeinheimer, V.K. (2000). The continuing importance of men's economic position in marriage formation. In L.J. Waite (ed.), *The ties that bind: Perspectives on marriage and cohabitation,* pp. 283–301. New York: Aldine de Gruyter.

Pearlin, L.I. (1989). The sociological study of stress. *Journal of Health and Social Behavior* 30:241– 256.

Pearlin, L.I., Lieberman, M.A., Menaghan, E.G., & Mullan, J.T. (1981). The stress process. *Journal of Health and Social Behavior,* 22:337–356.

Radloff, L.S. (1977). The CES-D scale: A self-report depression scale for research in the general population. *Applied Psychological Measurement,* 1:385–401.

Robbins, C.A. & Martin, S.S. (1993). Gender, styles of deviance, and drinking problems. *Journal of Health and Social Behavior,* 34:302–321.

Ross, C.E. (1987). The division of labor at home. *Social Forces,* 65, 816–833.

Ross, C.E., Mirowsky, J., & Huber, J. (1983). Dividing work, sharing work, and in-between: Marriage patterns and depression. *American Sociological Review,* 48:809–823.

Shelton, B. A. (2000). Understanding the distribution of housework between husbands and wives. In L.J. Waite (ed.), *The ties that bind: perspectives on marriage and cohabitation,* pp. 343–355. New York: Aldine de Gruyter.

Simon, R.W. (1992). Parental role strains, salience of parental identity and gender differences in psychological distress. *Journal of Health and Social Behavior,* 33:25–35.

______. (1995). Gender, multiple roles, role meaning, and mental health. *Journal of Health and Social Behavior,* 36:182–194.

______. (1997). The meanings individuals attach to role identities and their implications for mental health. *Journal of Health and Social Behavior,* 38:256–274.

Simon, R.W., & Marcusen, K. (1999). Marital transitions, marital beliefs, and mental health. *Journal of Health and Social Behavior,* 40:111–125.

Spain, D. & Bianchi, S.M. (1996). *Balancing act: Motherhood, marriage and employment among American women.* New York: Russel Sage Foundation

Stolzenberg, R.M. (2001). It's about time and gender: Spousal employment and health. *American Journal of Sociology,* 107:61–100.

Sweet, J.A., & Bumpass, L.A. (1996). *The national survey of families and households—waves 1 and 2: Data description and documentation.* Center for Demography and Ecology, University of Wisconsin-Madison. Retrieved March 27, 2005, from http://www.ssc.wisc.edu/nsfh/home.htm.

Taylor, R.J., Chatters, L.M., Tucker, M.B., & Lewis, E. (1990). Development in research on black families: A decade review. *Journal of Marriage and Family,* 52:993–1014.

Thompson, L., & Walker, A. J. (1989). Gender in families: Women and men in marriage, work, and parenthood. *Journal of Marriage and Family,* 51:845–871.

Townsend, N.W. (2002). *The package deal: Marriage, work and fatherhood in men's lives.* Philadelphia: Temple University Press.

Umberson, D., Wortman, C.B., & Kessler, R.C. (1992). Widowhood and depression: Explaining long-term gender differences in vulnerability. *Journal of Health and Social Behavior,* 33:10–24.

Waite, L.J. (1995). Does marriage matter? *Demography,* 32:483–507.

Waite, L.J., & Gallagher, M. (2000). *The case for marriage.* New York; Broadway Books.

Waldfogel, J. (1997). The effect of children on women's wages. *American Sociological Review* 62:209–217.

Waldron, I., & Jacobs, J. A. (1989). Effects of multiple roles on women's health: Evidence from longitudinal study. *Women & Health* 15:3–19.

Wheaton, B. (1990). Life transitions, role histories, and mental health. *American Sociological Review,* 55:209–223.

Williams, D.G. (1988). Gender, marriage, and psychological well-being. *Journal of Family Issues,* 9:452–468.

Williams, D.R., Takeuchi, D.T., & Adair, R.K. (1992). Marital status and psychological disorders among blacks and whites. *Journal of Health and Social Behavior,* 33:140–157.

Yu, Y, & Williams, D.R. (1999). Socioeconomic status and mental health. In C.S. Aneshensel and J.C. Phelan (eds.), *Handbook of the Sociology of Mental Health.* New York: Kluwer Academic/Plenum Publishers, pp. 151–166.

Zinn, M. (1990). Family, feminism, and race in America. *Gender & Society,* 4:68–82.

Zinn, M.B., & Dill, B.T. (1996). Theorizing difference from multiracial feminism. *Feminist Studies,* 22:321–331.

Generalized Expectancies for Control among High-School Students at the Intersection of Race, Class, and Gender

BRETT A. MAGILL

Department of Public Policy
Saint Louis University

ADDRESS: *Office of Planning and Decision Resources, Saint Louis University, DuBourg Hall, Room 351, 221 N. Grand Blvd, Saint Louis, Missouri 63103. Email: magillb@sbcglobal.net*

Brett A. Magill is a Ph.D. student in the Department of Public Policy Studies at Saint Louis University where he also conducts institutional research as part of the Office of Planning and Decision Resources. Brett's interests include race, housing segregation, urban poverty, mental health policy, and program evaluation.

I am grateful to Bart Landry for his support and encouragement—both while at Maryland and after. In addition, I would like to thank the anonymous reviewer whose comments helped improve this article.

"Generalized Expectancies for Control Among High-School Students at the Intersection of Race, Class and Gender" by Brett A. Magill is reprinted by permission of the author.

Abstract

The present study examines the effects of race, class, and gender on perceptions of control among high-school students from the perspective of intersection theory. Using a subset of data from the 1979 cohort of the National Longitudinal Study of Youth (N = 4818) and a four-item measure of internality-externality, attributions of control were examined as they vary by race, class, and gender. Interaction effects were also examined and age was used as a control. Statistically significant but small main effects were found for race, class, and gender with blacks, working-class individuals, and women demonstrating greater externality than whites, individuals of higher class situation, and men. Statistically significant age effects were also noted while no interaction effects were found. It is concluded that racism, patriarchy, and capitalism as systems of power create inequalities in the lives of individuals that diminish the degree to which individuals see themselves in control of their experiences.

Keywords

locus of control, internality, externality, race, gender, class, intersection theory

The notions of "Internal" and "External" control have enjoyed a significant amount of attention in the psychological literature and have been associated with many different individual outcomes. This construct was initially described by Rotter (1966) who, drawing on his social learning theory, described what he called internal and external expectancies for control of reinforcement, more commonly called locus of control. Locus of control refers to the degree to which an individual perceives behavioral reinforcements as determined by their own actions or contingent upon forces that are outside of their control. These perceptions are based on patterns of reinforcement that form an expectancy, a belief that a given behavior will produce (or fail to produce) rewards in the future (p. 1). Individuals will differ in the degree to which they attribute rewards to their own actions based on a personal historical pattern of reinforcement (p. 2). When an individual believes that a reinforcement is not the direct result of their behavior, it is typically attributed to luck, chance, fate, or the influence of powerful others—this reinforcement is said to have an external locus of control. Likewise, a reinforcement that is attributed to one's own actions is said to be internally controlled (p. 1). This is well stated by Lefcourt (1966, 207):

> As a general principle, internal control refers to the perception of positive and/or negative events as being a consequence of one's own actions and thereby under personal control; external control refers to the perception of positive and/or negative events as being unrelated to one's own behaviors in certain situations and thereby beyond personal control.

A wide body of literature has examined both the effects of, and the influences on, locus of control, with a distinct emphasis on the former. Studies that do examine the antecedents of internal and external control expectancies include a number of investigations of the impact of race, class, and gender. However, few studies have examined the simultaneous influences of these social locations on perceptions of control. Those studies that have undertaken such an effort have been inadequate. Further, there is a great deal of disparity, both in results and in the instruments used to measure perceived control, in the existing literature. The present study is an attempt to extend the literature on race, class, and gender effects on locus of control from the perspective of intersection theory, an emerging paradigm in the study of inequality, using data from a nationally representative sample of high—school youth.

Race, class, gender and locus of control

Several studies have taken as their focus the independent effects of race or gender alone, among varied populations and using different instruments to measure locus of control. None of the research reviewed examined class differences independent of race or gender. Early in the literature, one of the construct's greatest proponents, Herbert Lefcourt, along with Gordon Ladwig examined the effects of race on locus of control among 120 inmates in two correctional facilities (Lefcourt & Ladwig, 1965). This study used multiple measures of control including Rotter's (1966) scale. Finding that on all measures, blacks were more externally oriented than whites, they suggest that segregation and discrimination facilitate the development of external attributions of control. Gender has also been examined independently of race and class, however the results are far from conclusive. Wehmeyer (1993) used the adult Nowicki-Strickland Internality-Externality scale to examine gender effects among 104 students with learning disabilities, finding females more externally oriented than males. Wood, Hillman, and Sawilowski (1996) used the same scale with contradictory results. Among 117 African-American students who were at risk for dropping out of high-school and enrolled in a program to develop academic and job skills, their data suggests that males demonstrate greater externality than females. Finally, this time using the Nowicki- Strickland scale for children, Chubb, Fertman, and Russ (1997) undertook a longitudinal study of gender and locus of control. Following a group of 174 ninth-grade students over a period of four years, these authors found no significant gender effects; however, the pattern of means that they present shows that females were more likely to make external attributions of control across each of the four years of the study, leading one to question the statistical power in the research design.

Other research has examined two of the social locations of race, class, and gender simultaneously in different combinations, with some addressing their interactions. Along with Esther Battle, Julian Rotter examined the effects of race and class among 80 sixth and eighth grade children using a projective measure of locus of control (Battle & Rotter, 1963). Their data suggested significant class effects along with a significant interaction among race and class. Overall, children from the working class demonstrated more externality than children in the middle class. Although no race main effects were found, they did find that black working-class children were more likely to make external attributions of control than were whites of the same class. Although not tested, this suggests an interaction between race and class, with class a stronger predictor of locus of control among blacks than whites. These authors concluded that race and class, as markers of access to the material rewards offered in a culture are important as antecedents of control attributions. Louden (1978) and Wenzel (1993), among different populations and with different measures, examined race and gender effects with similar results. The first of these two studies used Levenson's Internal–Powerful Others–Chance scale which produces three separate scores for each respondent, while the latter used the Norwicki-Strickland Internality-Externality scale. Both studies found significant main effects for race, with no significant main effects for gender. Louden's (1978) study was conducted in Britain with a sample of 375 adolescents, finding that minority students were more externally oriented than English students. Likewise, Wenzel (1993) found that blacks were more externally oriented than whites with higher scores on both the Chance and Powerful Others scales, however they found no differences for Hispanics in this sample of 70 adults in employment training. Neither of these studies examined the interaction of race and gender.

Of those studies reviewed, only one examined the simultaneous effects of race, class, and gender on locus of control. Guagano, Acredolo, and Hawkes (1986) used Levenson's three dimensional Internal–Powerful Other-Chance scale mentioned previously with a representative sample of 652 California residents age twenty-one or older. Although they found statistically significant main effects for race, class, and gender, they concluded that only class was strongly related to locus of control. Specifically, they found that as income increased, internal attributions of control increased while Chance and Powerful Others scores decreased. Put another way, individuals of lower social class demonstrate greater externality than those in the middle and upper-classes. Interactions were also found between education, income, and race as well as between gender, income, and race. In any case, Guagano, Acredolo, and Hawkes (1986) suggested that with the exception of class, the effects were small. Although these authors defend their results with a power analysis showing that better than 80% of the time, for most analyses, their results would detect differences as small as 3%, their class sizes present a problem for this study nonetheless. The total number of respondents in the minority groups surveyed ranged from a maximum of fifty-two (Hispanics) to a minimum of twenty (Native Americans). In all, only 136 of the 652 participants were minority group members. Even if large enough to detect main effects, subdividing these groups further to examine interactions is questionable. The cell sizes reported in their results to demonstrate the interaction of race, class, and gender range from a low of four respondents to a maximum of fifteen, not nearly enough to suggest an accurate group average locus of control score.

As we have seen, the literature on race, class, and gender effects on locus of control provides no clear consensus. Nonetheless there is some support for significant main effects and significant interaction effects for race, class, and gender. The nature of these effects is not uncontested; however, most of the previous research supports the position of the present study—that blacks, individuals of the working class, and women are more externally oriented than middle-class white males. All but one of the studies reviewed fell short of examining these locations simultaneously. Most used small samples and only one was nationally representative. The present research is an attempt to overcome some of the shortcomings of previous research with regard to sample size and representativeness in undertaking an examination of the simultaneous impact of race, class, and gender on locus of control. Furthermore, it employs a unique perspective for understanding these effects.

THEORETICAL BACKGROUND

Under a variety of names, black feminist theorists have called attention to the simultaneous impact of race, class, and gender on the lives of working-class minority women. Whether we label this position "Multicultural Feminism" (Zinn & Dill, 1996) or "Standpoint Theory" (Hill-Collins, 1990) or simply refer to such things as "Interconnectedness", "Intersectionality" (Amott & Matthae, 1991), or "Simultaneity" (Brewer, 1993), what these perspectives have in common is an emphasis on the impact of racism, capitalism, and patriarchy as interlocking systems of power that create the life conditions of individuals. Brewer (1993:13) states:

> What is most important conceptually and analytically in this work is the articulation of multiple oppressions. This proclivity of multiple social locations is historically missing from analyses of oppression and exploitation in traditional feminism, Black studies and mainstream academic disciplines.

For the moment, we will depart from what will be called "Intersection Theory" to situate race, class, and gender as systems of power. We will then return to "Intersection Theory" to examine how these systems of power interconnect to affect the life chances of individuals, and from this perspective formulate a set of hypotheses about the effects of these multiple oppressions on locus of control that will inform the present study.

Race

"... [R]ace is a concept which signifies and symbolizes social conflicts and interests by referring to different types of human bodies" (Omi & Winant, 1994:55). Racial categories are organized through the process of "racial formation", a "sociohistorical process" through which these categories are created and destroyed via the interaction of macro and micro cultural and structural processes (p. 55–56). Contemporary race relations in the United States from this perspective developed out of a complex history of colonization, exploitation, and "racial politics" embodied in the "racial state" composed of institutions and policies-either implicitly or explicitly racial-that serve to support and justify the micro processes within which the state operates. Within its specific sociohistorical situation, "[t]he broad sweep of US history is characterized not by racial democracy, but by racial despotism, not by trajectories of reform, but by implacable denial of political rights, dehumanization, extreme exploitation, and policies of minority extirpation" (p. 79). Thus, in the case of the US, race is a socially and historically constructed system of categorizations embodied in the state and its polices which oppress minorities, either implicitly or explicitly, and shapes the conditions of their lives.

Class

According to Max Weber (Gerth & Mills, 1946:181), class or "class situation" has three defining elements. The first of these is a common causal component of the life chances of individuals. Second, this causal component is defined by economic interests and more specifically by the possession of goods and opportunities to generate income. Finally, these economic interests that determine life chances are situated within the commodity or labor markets. "'Property' and 'lack of property' are therefore the basic categories of all class situations" (Weber in Gerth & Mills, 1946:182). Thus, class situations according to Weber, express " . . . the typical chance for a supply of goods, external living conditions, and personal life experiences, in so far as this chance is determined by the amount and kind of power, or lack of such, to dispose of goods or skills for the sake of income in a given economic order" (p. 181). Within a competitive market system, non-owners are excluded from competition for valued goods as they come into competition with those who have resources (upper class) to secure such goods, creating the life chances of individuals (p. 181). As such, capitalism is viewed as a system of power and oppression in which individuals occupy varying class situations. Among those without property, valued skills provide greater access to opportunities (middle-class occupations) for income; while those with relatively fewer skills have relatively less access (working-class jobs) to economic rewards.

Gender

"We are born female and male, biological sexes, but we are created woman and man, socially recognized genders" (Hartmann, 1981 17). Gender relations are organized in a hierarchical fashion based on historical patterns of exclusion and oppression, a hierarchy through which men dominate women. The material base of patriarchy is men's control of women's labor power, placing men in a higher position in the hierarchy. Control is maintained by excluding women from access to material resources and by restricting women's sexuality. Hartmann (1981) continues to suggest that patriarchal relations, although not reducible to economic forces, must be understood within the system of capitalism as it currently exists. While these perspectives provide clues to the effects of the systems and statuses of race, class, and gender on the lives of individuals, in isolation, each provides only a partial understanding. Herein lies the power of intersection theory, whose explanatory strength lies with the analysis of multiple intersecting systems and the multiplicity of unique locations created from them. This leads us to a further examination of intersection theory proper.

Intersection theory

Intersection Theory suggests that, in isolation, any one of the above perspectives is inadequate to explain the life chances of individuals, calling for an examination of the simultaneous effects of racism, capitalism, and patriarchy. Chow (1996: xxi) has summarized this position well proposing a number of emergent themes, of which we will examine those that are most relevant to the current study. The first of these is that race, class, and gender are interlocking or intersecting categories that embody multiple systems of domination and oppression which shape the life experiences of individuals. These systems of oppression are interactive, reciprocal, and cumulative. Moreover, intersection theorists eschew simple additive models and along with them terms such as "double" and "triple jeopardy" suggesting that such perspectives are missing essential structural connections and countering that instead, the interconnections are multiplicative or geometric in their effects. Another theme to emerge from this body of work, Chow (1996:xxii) suggests, is that race, class, and gender are equally important "in describing and interpreting the intricacies of social structure and self" (p.xxii). This is not to suggest that race, class, and gender affect individuals to the same degree, but rather that, as analytical perspectives, they are all equally important in understanding the link between systems of oppression and the lived experiences of individuals. Their interconnections produce unique social locations based on an individual's position within these larger social systems.

From this perspective we can formulate a number of hypotheses about the specific effects that race, class, gender, and the systems of power that are embodied in these statuses, have on an individual's perceptions of personal control. First, racism, capitalism, and patriarchy as systems of power limit the options of individuals. This suggests that minority group members, individuals of lower class situation, and women will be more likely to make external attributions of control than will majority group members, individual of higher class situation, and men. Second, these systems of power intersect to produce unique social locations based on an individual's position within all three of these systems of power. Thus, we can expect to find that locus of control varies by race, class, and gender simultaneously in such a way that individuals who experience inequality along multiple dimensions demonstrate greater externality than those who are in positions of relative advantage. This should be true for all combinations of race, class, and gender categories with majority group males of higher class situation demonstrating the least externality and minority group females of lower class situation demonstrating the largest degree of externality. Finally, the effects of capitalism, patriarchy, and racism reach beyond simple additive models and are instead multiplicative in nature. As such, the effects of race, class, and gender cannot be explained simply by the combination of the singular inequalities of race, class, and gender locations. Instead, it is suggested that these locations, in combination, will produce effects on locus of control that are greater than the sum of the parts; in other words, race, class, and gender will interact.

DATA AND METHODS

Data for this study were drawn from the 1979 cohort of the National Longitudinal Study of Youth (NLSY) data set collected by the Center for Human Resources Research at the Ohio State University. The NLSY is a probability sample of 12,686 males and females born between 1957 and 1964 and who were between the ages of fourteen and twenty-two years old; blacks, Hispanics, and economically disadvantaged whites were over sampled. Youth in this sample were interviewed annually from 1979 to 1986, however items related to locus of control were asked only in the 1979 interviews. Data for the present study were limited to black and white

TABLE I ■ FOUR SELECTED ITEMS FROM ROTTER INTERNALITY-EXTERNALITY SCALE USED IN NATIONAL LONGITUDINAL SURVEY OF YOUTH INTERVIEWS

Pair 1:	• What happens to me is my own doing; or • Sometimes I feel that I don't have enough control over the direction my life is taking.
Pair 2:	• When I make plans, I am almost certain that I can make them work; or • It is not always wise to plan too far ahead, because many things turn out to be a matter of good or bad fortune anyhow.
Pair 3:	• In my case, getting what I want has little or nothing to do with luck; or • Many times we might as well decide what to do by flipping a coin.
Pair 4:	• It is impossible for me to believe that chance or luck plays an important role in my life; or • Many times I feel like I have little influence over the things that happen to me.

students who were enrolled in grades nine through twelve in 1979. The resulting sample consisted of 4952 high-school youth; eliminating all cases with missing data further reduced the working sample size to 4818.

Measuring locus of control

Rotter (1966) proposed a set of twenty-nine items to capture the degree of internal versus external locus of control. Of these, four items which were the most powerful empirical indicators of internality-externality were selected by NLSY researchers to be included in the 1979 interview. Each item consists of a set of two statements which are presented in Table 1, below. For each set of two statements, students were asked to select the one which was closest to their own opinion and then to indicate whether the statement selected was slightly closer to their opinion or much closer. Responses to each pair of statements were combined to form a four-point scale for each of the four sets of two statements. The result was summed across all four pairs to produce a scale score with a potential range of four to sixteen with higher scores reflecting greater internality and lower scores reflecting a greater degree of externality. The scale score, hereafter referred to as the Rotter Score, was used as the dependent variable in the analyses.

Although internal consistency reliability for these four items is low, with Cronbach's alpha = .30, it is consistent with the expected internal consistency reliability based on the Spearman-Brown prediction formula (Rosenthal & Rosnow. 1991):

$$R = (nr)/(1 + (n - 1)r)$$

Where R is the expected reliability coefficient, n is the factor by which the test is lengthened or shortened, and r is the average inter-item correlation (Alpha reliability) for the original set of items. The reported internal-consistency reliability for a combined group of high-school males and females for the original set of twenty-nine items was .69 (Rotter, 1966). Applying the formula above, we find that the expected internal-consistency reliability for the abbreviated Rotter used in this study is approximately .24. In other words, this set of four items actually performs better than would be expected based on the original inter-item correlations, reflecting the fact that they were selected empirically as the best measures of the construct by NLSY staff. Furthermore, principal components factor analysis suggests that these four items do load on a single factor and are, in fact, measuring a single construct. We can conclude from this that these four items are tapping the larger construct, Locus of Control, as proposed by Rotter; however, they are not doing it as well as the larger battery of items, i.e., there is more measurement error. As a result, the estimated effects will be "attenuated," making it more difficult to reject the null hypothesis of no difference (Osborne, 2003). Naturally, the degree of attenuation is an inverse function of the reliability of the measurement. Attenuation of effects is a particular problem in the case of interaction terms where unreliability is compounded. While corrections for attenuation, or methods for "disattenuation," exist (see Osborne, 2003, for a review), when reliability is very low we run the risk of over-correction. Therefore, no correction was applied in this study. Given the very low reliability, this measure can be viewed as a conservative measure of Locus of Control suggesting that any effects found in the present study would be more prominent using a more reliable measure.

Independent and control variables

The Independent and control variables, their coding schemes, and their sources are presented in Table 2. The respondent's race was coded by the interviewer as either black, white, or other; respondents coded as "other" were not used in the analyses. The student's class position was based on the educational attainment of their parents as reported by the student. Students who had at least one parent who completed high-school were considered "middle class". If both parents completed fewer than twelve years of education or if the student only reported the educational level of one parent who had completed less than high school they were considered "working class." The last independent variable is gender which was coded by the interviewer as either male or female. The literature also suggests consistent and substantial age effects (for example, Chubb, Fertman, & Ross, 1997), so this variable was included in the models as a control. The student's age at the time of the interview was constructed by NLYS staff based on the student's self-reported date of birth.

Descriptive statistics were calculated for all of the variables in the analysis. Ordinary Least Squares (OLS) regression was used to model the effects of race, class, and gender along with their interactions on the Rotter Score while controlling for the effects of age. Age was centered by subtracting the overall mean from each individual's age such that the centered mean for age is equal to zero and each individual's age is expressed as a number of years above or below the mean. Because regression coefficients represent the estimate while holding other terms in the model constant at zero, this allows the other estimates to be interpreted as the value of the Rotter score at the mean age while preserving the original scale for age. Following the regression analysis, a table of age adjusted means by race, class, and gender was produced using the estimated regression model.

It would seem natural to include a three-way interaction term to model the interaction

TABLE 2 ■ Independent and Control Variables Used in the Analyses and their Coding Schemes

Independent Variables	Race	Interviewer Coded: Student's Race: White=0 Black=1
	Class	Student Report of Parent Education: Completed High-school=0 Did not complete high-school=1
	Gender	Interview Coded: Student's Gender: Male=0 Female=1
Control Variable	Age	Student Self Report: Student's Age: Years

of race, class, and gender on the Rotter score. However, because an interaction term—the product of two or more original variables—is a nonlinear function of the original variables, it is frequently the case that there is a strong correlation among the terms. This could result in a high degree of collinearity and affect the quality of the parameter estimates in the model (Friedrich, 1982). Though this is only a problem in the most extreme cases, the problem is compounded with a three-way interaction which includes not only the three-way term but two lower-order interaction terms as well, all of which are related to the original variables. In addition, interpretation of such a three-way interaction can be difficult.

For these reasons, rather than a single regression model with multiple interaction terms, two separate regression models were produced, one for each racial group—black and white. A single "class by gender" interaction term was used in each model. The result is the equivalent of a three-way interaction among the terms in the model. To test for significance of the interactions across racial groups, the regression coefficients were tested for equality across models using the procedure advocated by Paternoster et al. (1998). After reviewing a number of alternative tests for equality of regression coefficients, these authors suggest that the test that utilizes the correct, unbiased estimate of the standard error is as follows:

$$Z = (b_1 - b_2)/(SEb_1^2 + SEb_2^2)^{1/2}$$

Where b_1 and b_2 are the regression coefficients and SEb_1 and SEb_2 are their respective standard errors. The resulting Z is referred to a normal distribution to produce a probability value p.

An Alpha level of $p = .05$, two-tailed, was used to assess statistical significance for all of the analyses conducted. Although a one-tailed test is justified given the directional hypotheses stated, a two-tailed test is viewed as more conservative and is thus favored. All analyses were conducted using R, an open-source dialect of the S language for data analysis and graphics (Ihaka and Gentleman, 1996).

RESULTS

Descriptive statistics for the independent and control variables used in the analyses are presented in Table 3. Twenty-nine percent of the students in the sample were black and 31 percent were of working-class, meaning that their parents attained less than twelve years of education. There were slightly fewer females in the

TABLE 3 ■ DESCRIPTIVE STATISTICS FOR ALL VARIABLES USED IN THE ANALYSES ($N = 4818$)

	Means*	Standard Deviation	Minimum	Maximum
Race Black = 1	0.29	—	—	—
Class Less than High-school = 1	0.31	—	—	—
Gender Female = 1	0.49	—	—	—
Age	16.0	1.3	14	21
Rotter Score	11.1	2.4	4	16

*The mean for race, class, and gender—dichotomous variables coded either 0 or 1—represents the proportion of the respondents in the category coded 1.

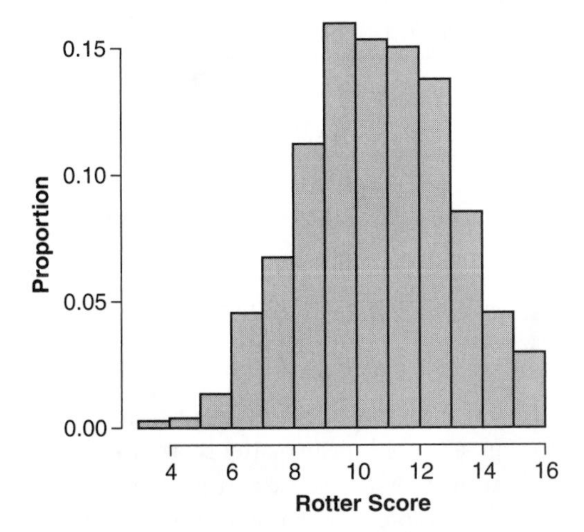

FIGURE 1 ■ HISTOGRAM OF ROTTER SCALE SCORE

sample (49%) than males (51%). The students' ages ranged from 14 to 21 with a mean age of 16.0 years old. A frequency histogram for the Rotter score is presented in Figure 1. The distribution of scores is approximately normal with a slight negative skew. Responses ranged from 4 to 16 with a mean of 11.1 and a standard deviation of 2.4.

The OLS regression models are presented in Table 4. Separate models were run for each racial group. For both models, the overall *F* test was statistically significant with an achieved R^2 of 2% in Model 1 (white) and 3% in Model 2 (black). Due to the coding of the variables and the centering of age about its mean, the intercept can be interpreted as the mean Rotter score for a middle-class male of average age. For whites, $b0_{white} = 11.46$ and for blacks $b0_{black} = 11.20$. Testing for equality of the intercepts using the method suggested in Paternoster et al. (1998) represents the test for the main effect of race, which results in $z = 1.94$, $p = 0.0526$. The effect of class was statistically significant across both models, as was the covariate for age. The effect for gender was only significant in Model 1 (white). While the absolute magnitude of the coefficient for gender was greater for black students (Model 2), the test was not significant, a result of the combination of smaller group size and larger standard error. Of the three main effects—race,

TABLE 4 ■ OLS REGRESSION MODELS BY RACE: ROTTER SCORE ON CLASS, GENDER, AND THEIR INTERACTION CONTROLLING FOR AGE EFFECTS

	Model 1: *b*	White[1] *t*	Model 2: *b*	Black *t*	Test for Equality[2] *z*
(Intercept)	11.46	178.5***	11.20	95.3***	1.94*
	(.06)		(0.12)		
Class	−0.65	−5.1***	−0.46	−2.5**	−0.83NS
	(.13)		(0.19)		
Gender	−0.24	−2.6**	−0.32	−1.9NS	0.42NS
	(.09)		(0.17)		
Age (Centered)	0.16	5.0***	0.23	4.7***	−0.37NS
	(.18)		(0.05)		
Class* Gender	0.19	1.1NS	−0.03	−0.1NS	0.68NS
	(.18)		(0.27)		
R^2	0.02		0.03		

NS $p \leq .05$ * $p \leq .05$ ** $p \leq .01$ *** $p \leq .001$

[1]Numbers in parentheses are the standard errors for the parameter estimate.

[2]Based on Paternoster et al 1998

TABLE 5 ■ AGE ADJUSTED MEAN ROTTER SCORES BY RACE, CLASS, AND GENDER

	Working Class		Middle Class	
	Female	Male	Female	Male
Black	10.39	10.74	10.88	11.20
	(306)	(285)	(382)	(439)
White	10.76	10.81	11.22	11.46
	(469)	(433)	(1203)	(1301)

class, and gender—class shows the largest effect with a coefficient of $bclass_{white} = -0.65$ and $bclass_{black} = -0.46$. The class by gender interaction was not significant in either of the race-specific models. Further, none of the tests for equality of the regression coefficients across models à la Paternoster et al. (1998) were statistically significant, implying no higher-order interactions. In summary, there were statistically significant differences in the degree of externality expressed by race and class. Gender differences in externality were also present and in the predicted direction; while there was no meaningful difference in the size of the effects, gender differences in externality were significant for whites, but not for blacks. Age was associated with externality in both models. No statistically significant interactions were observed.

The statistically significant main effect for race suggests that, on average, white students demonstrated greater internality than black students. Black students are more likely than whites to attribute control of occurrences in their lives to forces external to themselves. Of the independent variables, class showed the largest effect on Rotter scores, with students whose parents were of a higher class situation being more likely to attribute control to internal forces, while those with parents of a lower class situation demonstrated greater externality. Finally, male students were more likely to make internal attributions than females who expressed a greater degree of externality.

Based on the estimated regression models, the age-adjusted mean Rotter scores for the intersection of race, class, and gender are presented in Table 5. Examination of the means shows a distinct pattern in the Rotter score as it varies by race, class, and gender simultaneously. One can trace the pattern of means in the table from white males whose parents completed high-school or better with an age-adjusted mean Rotter score of 11.5 to black females whose parents did not complete twelve years of education with an age-adjusted mean of 10.4—a difference of a full point on the Rotter score. Without exception, for each layer of inequality added, there is a drop in the Rotter score.

A note on effect size

Although no formal tests of effect size were conducted, it is clear from the presentation of means in Table 5 that the effects of race, class, and gender are small. In the most extreme case, the difference is approximately one point between black females whose parents did not complete high school and white males whose parents did complete at least twelve years of education. In contrast, the range of scores on the Rotter scale was 4 to 16 with $s.d. = 2.3$. Thus, while statistically significant, the practical significance of such an effect is left to question. Nonetheless, these results are congruent with previous research which has repeatedly found small and mostly consistent effects with respect to race, class, and gender on locus of control.

CONCLUSIONS

Race, class, and gender differences exist in individual perceptions of the degree of control they have over their life experiences. Specifically blacks, individuals of lower class situation, and women are more likely than whites, individuals of relatively higher class situation, and men to attribute control to forces that are external to themselves. These differences are the result of inequality that is experienced by individuals based on their location within the larger systems of racism, patriarchy, and capitalism as they exist in the United States. These systems of inequality limit the life chances of individuals, affecting the degree to which they see themselves in control of their experiences.

Furthermore, we see that the intersecting nature of these systems of oppression creates unique social locations based on an individual's position within them. As each layer of experienced inequality is added, marked by the individual's race, class, and gender internal attributions of control are diminished. This suggests that failing to examine the intersecting nature of these systems and statuses provides an incomplete picture of the life experiences of individuals. All of the statuses, embedded in systems of power, affect the degree to which high-school students feel that they are in control of the things that happen to them and produce unique experiences for each combination of race, class, and gender.

Consistent with previous research, and in opposition to what was proposed in the present study, no interaction effects were found for race, class, and gender or any two-way combination of these categories. Thus, these data do not support the assertion that the simultaneous experience of inequality embodied in race, class, and gender locations produces effects on attributions of control beyond the additive effects of the observed race, class, and gender differences in locus of control scores. It is possible that a more sensitive measure with greater internal consistency, and thus less measurement error, would detect any such effects if they do in fact exist.

Race, class, and gender differences in locus of control are not an inconsequential matter. As Ellen Skinner (1996, 549) notes in a review of constructs of control:

> Both experimental and correlational studies have shown that across the life span, from earliest infancy to oldest age, individual differences in perceived control are related to a variety of positive outcomes, including health, achievement, optimism, persistence, motivation, coping, self-esteem, personal adjustment, and success and failure in a variety of life domains.

Thus, to the degree that minorities, women, and individuals of lower class situation experience a diminished sense of personal control as the result of the inequalities experienced in their relation to racism, patriarchy, and capitalism as system of power, their access to such positive outcomes is diminished as well.

Certainly intersection theory has proved valuable in understanding the effects of racism, capitalism, and patriarchy on individual's perceptions of control. It is clear that examining one or even two of these systems as they are articulated through race, class, and gender is inadequate as we attempt to understand the life experiences of individuals. As we have seen, these systems of power overlap to produce unique social locations based on an individual's position within these systems. However, the suggestion that these systems of power produce effects that are not merely additive but rather that are multiplicative in nature was not supported. Further research is needed to better evaluate this assertion and assess its utility as this perspective continues to emerge.

Bibliography

Amott, T. & Matthae, J. (1991). Race, class, gender, and women's works: A conceptual framework. In *Race, Gender and Work: A multicultural economic history of women in the United States.* Boston: South End Press.

Battle, E.S. & Rotter, J.B. (1963). Children's feelings of personal control as related to social class and ethnic group. *Journal of Personality,* 31:482–490.

Brewer, R.M. (1993). Theorizing race, class, and gender: The new scholarship of black feminist intellectuals and black women's labor. In S.M. James & A.P. Busia (eds.), *Theorizing Black feminisms: The Visionary Pragmatism of Black Women.* London: Routledge.

Chow, E.N. (1996). Introduction: Transforming knowledgement: Race, class, and gender. In E.N. Chow, D. Wilkinson, & M. Baca Zinn (eds.), *Race, class, and gender: Common bonds, different voices.* Thousand Oaks: Sage.

Chubb, N.H., Fertman, C.I., & Ross, J.L. (1997). Adolescent self-esteem and locus of control: A longitudinal study of gender and age differences. *Adolescence,* 32:113–129.

Collins, P.H. (1990). *Black feminist thought: Knowledge, consciousness, and the politics of empowerment.* New York: Rutledge.

Friedrich, R.J. (1982). In defense of multiplicative terms in multiple regression equations. *American Journal of Political Science,* 26:797–833.

Gerth, H.H. & Mills, C.W. (1946). *From Max Weber: Essays in sociology.* New York: Oxford University Press.

Guagnano, G. Acredolo, C., Hawkes, G.R., Ellyson, S., & White, N. (1986). Locus of control: Demographic factors and their interactions. *Journal of Social Behavior and Personality,* 1:365–380.

Hartman, H. (1981). The unhappy marriage of Marxism and feminism: Towards a more progressive union. In L. Sargent (ed.); *Women and revolution: A discussion of the unhappy marriage of Marxism and feminism.* Boston: South End Press.

Ihaka, R. & Gentleman, R. (1996). R: A language for data analysis and graphics. *Journal of Graphical and Computational Statistics,* 5:299–314.

Lefcourt, H.M. (1965). The American Negro: A problem in expectancies. *Journal of Personality and Social Psychology,* 1:377–380.

———. (1966). Internal versus external control of reinforcement: A review. Psychological Bulletin, 65:206–220.

Louden, D. (1978). Self-esteem and locus of control in minority group adolescents. *Ethnic and Racial Studies,* 1:196–217.

Omi, M. and Winant, H. (1994). *Racial formation in the United States: From the 1960s to the 1990s.* New York: Routledge.

Osborne, J. W. (2003). Effect sizes and the disattenuation of correlation and regression coefficients: lessons from educational psychology. *Practical Assessment, Research, and Evaluation, 8* (11). Retrieved July 14, 2003 from http://edresearch.org/pare/getvn.asp?v=8&n=11.

Paternoster, R., Brame, R. Mazerolle, P., & Piquero, A. (1998). Using the correct statistical test for the equality of regression coefficients. *Criminology,* 36:859–66.

Rosenthal, R. & Rosnow, R.L. (1991). Standards of reliability and validity. In *Essentials of Behavioral research: Methods and data analysis.* (Second Edition). Boston: McGraw-Hill.

Rotter, J.B. (1966). Generalized expectancies for internal versus external control of reinforcement, *Psychological Monographs: General and Applied,* 80:1–28.

Skinner, E.A. (1996). A guide to constructs of control. *Journal of Personality and Social Psychology,* 71:549–570.

Wenzel, S.L. (1993). Gender, ethnic group, and homelessness as predictors of locus of control among job training participants. *Journal of Social Psychology,* 133:495–505.

Wehmeyer, M.L. (1993). Gender differences in locus of control scores for students with learning disabilities. *Perceptual and Motor Skills,* 77:359–366.

Wood, P.C., Hillman, S.B., & Sawilowsky, S.S. (1996). Locus of control, self-concept, and self-esteem among at-risk African-American adolescents. *Adolescence,* 31:597–604.

Zinn, M.B. & Dill, B.T. (1996). Theorizing difference from multicultural feminism. *Feminist Studies,* 22:321–331.

Race, Gender, and Class Variation in the Effect of Neighborhood Violence on Adolescent Use of Violence

JENNIFER CASTRO
Criminology and Criminal Justice

BART LANDRY
Sociology
University of Maryland at College Park

Please address correspondence to Jennifer Castro, Urban Institute, 2100 M Street NW, Washington, DC 20037.
E-mail: jcastro@ui.urban.org

Abstract

Over the past few decades, countless youth have been exposed to chronic neighborhood violence, yet few studies have examined the effect of this exposure on adolescents' own assaultive behavior. Whether and how exposure to neighborhood violence increases the likelihood of adolescent violence has importance to criminological theory and policy. Furthermore, there is reason to believe that the strength of this effect may vary by the race, gender, and class of the adolescent. To date, no known quantitative analyses have examined the effect of neighborhood violence on adolescent use of violence across intersections of race, gender, and class. By conceptualizing neighborhood violence as a source of negative and noxious strain, the present study integrates elements of general strain theory with an intersectionality approach. Using multivariate regressions, we analyze the effect of neighborhood violence on adolescent use of violence across intersections of race, gender, and class—while controlling for other predictors of adolescent violence. We conduct our study using self-report data from 3,214 juveniles interviewed as part of the 1995 National Survey of Adolescents (Kilpatrick & Saunders, 1995). Results provide support for intersectional variation in the effects of experiencing and witnessing neighborhood violence on adolescent use of violence.

Keywords

race, gender, class, intersectionality, neighborhood violence, general strain theory

Over the past few decades, countless inner-city neighborhoods have been ravaged by violence—including drive-by shootings, violent street fighting, drug-related robberies, and so forth—leaving many neighborhood youth exposed to chronic community violence. Yet to date, few quantitative studies have examined the effect of neighborhood violence on the adolescent and

---

Jennifer Castro is a Research Associate in the Justice Policy Center at the Urban Institute in Washington, D.C. She is pursuing a doctoral degree in the Department of Criminology and Criminal Justice at the University of Maryland. Her research interests include the study of neighborhood and individual violence, as well as crime prevention and program evaluation.

Bart Landry is Professor of Sociology at the University of Maryland, College Park. His research interests include stratification, family, race, gender and class, and technology and society. Currently his research focuses on the New Economy, especially software startups in the United States and Brasil.

most focus only on the emotional damage that can result from exposure to violence, such as posttraumatic stress and fear. Relatively few studies have looked at how community-level violence might increase adolescents' own assaultive behavior, and no previous *quantitative* analyses have examined the possibility of variation in this effect across intersections of race, gender, and class.

By conceptualizing neighborhood violence as a source of negative and noxious strain, the present study integrates elements of general strain theory (GST) with an intersectionality approach. GST postulates that anger generated by strain must be internalized or externalized, and previous research suggests gender and race differences in the likelihood that anger will be externalized in illegitimate, even violent ways. Lacking a measure of anger in the present study, we instead look for a direct link between exposure to neighborhood violence (strain) and adolescent use of violence (externalized illegitimate coping). Using multivariate regressions, we analyze the effect of neighborhood violence on adolescent use of violence across intersections of race, gender, and class while controlling for other predictors of adolescent violence. The main question addressed is whether adolescents from violent neighborhoods exhibit more violence than adolescents from nonviolent neighborhoods when other individual-level predictors are controlled. Supplemental to this question is an examination of how the criminogenic effects of living in a violent neighborhood vary by intersections of race, gender, and class.

The organization of this paper is as follows. The first section articulates the theoretical framework for the present analysis and postulates the two hypotheses tested in the present study. Then, previous research on the effect of neighborhood violence on individual violence is reviewed with a specific focus on findings of race, gender, or class variation in this effect. Third, the research design for the present study is discussed, and analytical results for each intersectional group are presented. Finally, the study's major findings are interpreted in light of the theoretical predictions and an agenda for future research is proffered.

Theoretical Framework

This section lays out the theoretical framework for the present study by incorporating the ideas of intersectionality with the principle tenets of general strain theory and by describing how this integrated approach can be applied to the study of neighborhood and individual violence. This section also identifies the main hypotheses tested by the present study.

Intersectionality

In the past two decades, a new theoretical and methodological approach to the study of human behavior has emerged, one that focuses on the intersections of race, gender, and class. Although this approach has been referenced by many different names, the most popular term and the one employed in this paper is *intersectionality* (Crenshaw, 1993).

The ideas of intersectionality evolved from the writings of African-American feminist scholars who argued that the unique experiences of economically disadvantaged black women were being ignored in academia. Scholars argued that poor black women suffer simultaneous oppressions of race, gender, and class— suffering that is not captured by looking only at sexism, racism, or classism (Collins, 1993; King, 1988; Brewer, 1993). To examine sexism, racism, or classism in isolation and to make analogies among and between them is to assume a commonality in the discriminations felt by each subordinate group, when in fact there are substantive differences in individuals' experiences with oppression even when they share common gender, race, or class categorizations. For example, black women have experienced sexism and advocated feminism in ways and for reasons that are very different from those of white women (King, 1988).

Intersectionalists argue that race, gender, and class must be conceptualized as three socially constructed, interlocking systems of oppression that mutually support and define elements of one another (Collins, 1998, 209; Zinn, and Dill, 1996, 326). Racism, patriarchy, and capitalism simultaneously exemplify and perpetuate existing, unjust power relations and are therefore relevant to every analysis of human behavior, although the relative significance of each will depend on the "social historical context and the social phenomenon under consideration" (King, 1988). This interdependence and simultaneous existence creates unique, social experiences for each intersectional group that must be examined individually through interactive (multiplicative) analyses (Collins, 1993; King, 1988; Brewer, 1993). Statistically speaking, the authors argue for interactive (multiplicative) analyses that focus on race, gender, and class variations in the effects of independent variables (e.g., neighborhood violence) on dependent variables (e.g., individual violence).

Although intersectionality research originated with a focus on the experiences of poor black women, the idea of conducting interactional race, gender, and class research is relevant for all individuals. Because sexism, racism, or classism simultaneously affect how all individuals are treated, it is imperative to examine the experiences of all groups in order to understand how race, gender, and class structure social experiences (Collins, 1993). According to Collins, every individual both suffers from and perpetuates varying amounts of oppression, and "each of us carries around the cumulative effect of our lives within multiple structures of oppression" and privilege (Collins, 1993, 564; Zinn & Dill, 1996, 327). Therefore, all possible intersections warrant theoretical and empirical attention, and each group has its own distinctive sociohistorical context for understanding and experiencing life events, situations, and social movements (King, 1988). Social or historical context may cause individuals to be affected by one type of oppression more than another, but all three should be assumed present and relevant to every social situation (Collins, 1993). Race, gender, and class thus have the power to influence and structure all social relations.

General strain theory

The present study attempts to integrate the ideas of intersectionality with Robert Agnew's general strain theory by conceptualizing race, gender, and class variation in the effect of neighborhood violence on individual violence. Robert Agnew's general strain theory (GST) provides an understanding of why neighborhood and individual violence might be linked and how this general pattern could vary by intersections of race, gender, and class (Agnew, 1992, 1999). The main tenet of GST is that strain, in the form of failure to achieve positive goals, removal of positive stimuli, and/or presentation of negative or noxious stimuli, generates negative affect within individuals, pressuring them to cope through either legitimate or illegitimate means (Agnew, 1992:59–60). The negative affect generated by strain may be either inner-directed (taking the form of depression, disappointment, and guilt) or outer-directed (taking the form of anger and frustration), depending on whether an individual blames herself or blames others for the infliction of strain. From a criminological standpoint, outer-directed anger is the most important type of negative affect, because it is most likely to lead to illegitimate behavioral coping, such as violent delinquency. This is because anger "increases the individual's level of felt injury, creates a desire for retaliation/revenge, energizes the individual for action, and lowers inhibitions" (Agnew, 1992:59–60).

The coping strategies adopted by individuals may be cognitive, behavioral, or emotional in type and are constrained by a number of social and psychological factors (Agnew, 1992: 66–73). Cognitive strategies involve conscious reinterpretations of strainful events so as to minimize their offensiveness (Agnew, 1992:66).

Members of violent neighborhoods may cognitively justify acts of violence as victim-deserved or victim-precipitated to make themselves feel better about their own chances of violent victimization, or they may mentally reduce the severity of the violence to make the act more acceptable (Anderson, 1999:125-126). Emotional coping strategies focus on ways of coping with the emotional damage inflicted by strainful events (Agnew, 1992:69–70). Positive forms of emotional coping include physical exercise and meditation, while negative forms include use of illicit drugs to achieve temporary, narcotic escapes from painful feelings. Behavioral coping strategies "seek to minimize or eliminate the source of strain [or] satisfy the need for revenge" (Agnew, 1992:69). Clearly, behavioral responses to neighborhood violence, especially vengeful behavior, may be delinquent in nature (e.g., shootings, street fights, gang retaliations). Strain-generated anger (and frustration) is the negative affect most likely to lead to illegitimate, behavioral coping strategies, such as violent delinquency.

Neighborhood violence can be conceptualized as a source of strain and is best categorized as noxious stimuli. Individuals who reside in violent neighborhoods are at an increased likelihood of forming relationships with people who present noxious or negative stimuli (in the form of violence). This negative stimuli includes acts of aggression aimed directly at neighborhood members (through personal violent victimizations) and acts of aggression presented indirectly to them (through witnessing others' violent victimizations and assaultive behaviors). Furthermore, neighborhood violence seems the type of strain that is highly likely to generate feelings of anger in the individuals it affects (Jenkins & Bell, 1997; Osofsky 1997). Acts of violence that are experienced or witnessed by neighborhood members will likely generate feelings of anger and a desire to "attack or escape from the source of adversity" (Agnew, 1992:49). Such noxious stimuli can lead to the use of violence when individuals try to "terminate or alleviate the negative stimuli [or] seek revenge against the source of the negative stimuli or related targets" (Agnew, 1992:58; Jenkins & Bell, 1997). Therefore, it seems theoretically plausible from a GST point of view that neighborhood violence could increase adolescents' own violent behavior, and this effect would be mediated by feelings of anger and frustration. This conclusion leads to our first hypothesis stated below:

Hypothesis (1): Experiencing and witnessing neighborhood violence will have a positive effect on the likelihood of physical violence by all adolescents, regardless of gender, race, or class.

Intersectionality and general strain theory

The ideas of intersectionality and general strain theory can be integrated through an explanation of intersectional (gender, race, and class) differences in anger, attributions of blame, and choice of coping strategies. In this way, general strain theory offers a promising explanation for intersectional variation in violent delinquency resulting from exposure to neighborhood violence.

Gender differences in strain Of the three classification systems, gender has occupied the most attention in psychological stress research. A number of studies have shown that although males and females are equally likely to react to strain with anger, the nature of this anger and strategies for coping with it can vary dramatically (Broidy & Agnew, 1997; Campbell, 1993; Mirowsky & Ross, 1995). Males are more likely to blame others for adversity and to externalize feelings of anger, while females (especially white females) are more likely to internalize anger and blame themselves (Broidy & Agnew, 1997; Campbell, 1993; Ogle et al., 1995). Female anger is typically accompanied by feelings of guilt, anxiety, fear, and depression. Girls/women often view anger as an indication that they have lost control, or they "worry that their anger might lead them to harm others and jeopardize valued relationships" (Campbell, 1993; Broidy and Agnew 1997; Eagly and Steffen 1986; Ogle et al., 1995; Agnew & Brezina, 1997). Boys/men, on the other hand, are "less concerned about hurting others or disrupting relationships, and they often view anger as an affirmation of their masculinity" or as a means of gaining control over the precipitating situation or individual (Broidy & Agnew, 1997; Messerschmidt, 1993; Campbell, 1993). Male anger is typically experienced as moral outrage and contempt (Broidy & Agnew, 1997). Under the principles of general strain theory, boys would be more likely to engage in aggressive behavior directed toward others (e.g., violent delinquency) as a result of their externalized anger, while girls would be more likely to direct their negative affect inward to alleviate internalized feelings of guilt, shame, and anxiety (e.g., through drug use or suicide).

Differences in male/female social support networks also contribute to gender differences in the use of violence as a response to strain. Female support networks typically emphasize rules, morals, and compassion, and discourage violent responses to disputes or confrontation (Broidy & Agnew, 1997). Male support systems, on the other hand, are frequently characterized by competitive and physical interaction and strong approval for rule-breaking (Thorne & Luria 1986; Broidy & Agnew, 1997). Male peer networks, particularly those in economically disadvantaged inner-city communities, often encourage aggressive responses to confrontation as a way of affirming masculinity and achieving status and respect (Anderson, 1999; Bennett & Fraser 2000; Messerschmidt, 1993). Male peers can, therefore, both model and encourage violent behavior, especially on the street. Furthermore, recent evidence suggests that inner-city African-American females are increasingly being drawn into the street code of using violence to maintain respect (Baskin & Sommers, 1998; Anderson, 1999). Therefore, although gender differences in social support systems contribute to the likelihood that males (and not females) will respond to strain with violence, the difference appears to be increasingly less pronounced among disadvantaged, inner-city and disproportionately black populations.

Race Differences in Strain Empirical research on race differences in reaction to strain is far less established than research on gender variation. Racial differences in reaction to strain might stem from any number of economic and/or cultural sources: (1) African-Americans may disproportionately occupy neighborhoods that are characterized by higher levels of strain than whites; (2) blacks may be more likely than whites to aggressively cope with strain because of differences in neighborhood social support for violence; or (3) blacks may be more likely to externalize blame for neighborhood disadvantage/strain if they see it as a long-term consequence of racism and slavery in the United States. Racial discrepancies in the amount of violence committed by blacks and whites (with blacks engaging in greater amounts of violence) suggest that blacks may be more exposed to certain stressors than whites. Alternatively, when exposed to strain, African-Americans and whites may react with similar levels of anger, but blacks may be more likely to externalize this anger as violence.

Ethnographic research in inner-city African-American communities has shown that aggressive responses to verbal and physical confrontation can be encouraged and even viewed as a way of achieving status and respect in the neighborhood (Anderson, 1999; Baskin & Sommers, 1998; Bennett & Fraser, 2000; Messerschmidt, 1993). For many inner-city youth, there may be "role models" of violent behavior living in the neighborhood, and use of violence may have become a socially acceptable coping strategy for dealing with various sources of strain.

Class Differences in Strain From a theoretical viewpoint, any existence of class differences in reaction to strain would likely stem from differential access to legitimate coping resources. Poor and working-class residents may be financially unable to move out of violent neighborhoods and escape legally from neighborhood adversity (Wilson, 1987). Middle-class residents, on the other hand, are less financially restricted and may have greater access to coping services such as counseling or physical recreation. Working-class individuals exposed to neighborhood violence may therefore be at an increased likelihood of reacting with illegitimate coping strategies (e.g., engagement in violent delinquency), simply because they have no better legitimate alternatives (Agnew, 1992; Agnew & White, 1992).

Intersectional Differences in Strain From the research discussed above, there are fairly strong reasons to expect intersectional differences in reaction to neighborhood violence. Clearly, most previous research has focused on gender differences and would predict that adolescent males should be more apt to react to neighborhood violence by engaging in violent delinquency than adolescent females. This prediction leads us to our second hypothesis stated below:

Hypothesis (2): Experiencing and witnessing neighborhood violence will have a stronger positive effect on the likelihood of physical violence by adolescent males than by adolescent females.

Although we expect males to be more likely to externalize anger they experience as a result of neighborhood violence and females to be more likely to internalize anger, much of the research upon which this second hypothesis is based was conducted on predominantly white populations (Broidy & Agnew, 1997; Eagly & Steffen, 1986). We do, however, have some reason to expect greater similarity than difference in strain's effect on the assaultive behavior of working-class white males and working-class black females. A number of criminological studies have found similar patterns and rates of violent behavior between white males and black females (Simpson, 1991; Chilton & Datesman, 1987; Hill & Crawford, 1990; Kruttschnitt, 1994; Hindelang et al., 1981; Sampson & Lauritsen, 1994; Cernkovich & Giordano, 1979). However, the exact way in which these findings affect gender differences in reaction to neighborhood strain across intersections of race and class remains an issue to be empirically explored. Toward this end, we state our third and final hypothesis in exploratory rather than predictive form:

Hypothesis (3): Gender differences in the effect of experiencing and witnessing neighborhood violence on the likelihood of adolescent physical violence will vary by intersections of race and class.

To test this third hypothesis in our analyses, we explore whether significant gender differences exist across four subgroups of youth—white middle-class, black middle-class, white working-class, and black working-class. In this way, our research constitutes the first known quantitative analysis of intersectional differences in the effect of neighborhood violence on individual violence.

Studies of negative and noxious stimuli

Relatively few studies have examined the effect of neighborhood-level variables on individual-level outcomes, and even fewer have examined the effect of neighborhood violence on individual violence or how race, gender, and class interact with this effect (Elliott & Wilson, 1996; Miller et al., 1999:3; Mazza & Overstreet, 2000:91). The most relevant previous research includes at least four criminological studies of negative and noxious stimuli and several psychological studies on the exposure to community violence and aggression. Within this first category, empirical studies that provide some support for a positive effect of neighborhood violence on individual violence; however, no study has examined race, gender, and class variation in this main effect.

Agnew and White (1992) found that a measure of negative life events, which included experiences of personal violent victimization, had a significantly positive effect on concurrent violent delinquency among 1,380 male and female adolescents. However, another measure of neighborhood problems, which tapped into adolescents' feelings of safety in their neighborhood, failed to significantly predict concurrent violent delinquency. Although Agnew and White controlled for gender and socioeconomic status (using parental education and income) in their analyses, they failed to examine intersectional variation in the effect of neighborhood violence on delinquency. Nor did they did control for or examine variation by race since their sample was predominantly (90%) white (1992:485 n.4). They did, however, suggest that "future studies should . . . determine if there are age, sex, class, race, and other subgroup differences in the impact of strain" on violent delinquency (1992:494).

A second study by Paternoster and Mazerolle (1994) replicated the study by Agnew and White (1992) and found that a measure of neighborhood problems, which included assaults and muggings in the neighborhood, had a significantly positive effect on concurrent and subsequent (one year later) general delinquency among 1,525 male and female adolescents interviewed in the first and second waves of the National Youth Survey. Their measure of delinquency included both violent and nonviolent offenses. Although they included gender as a control variable in their analyses, they failed to examine gender variation in the effect of neighborhood violence on delinquency. They also omitted any discussion of race or class.

A third study by Mazerolle (1998) explicitly examined gender variation in the effect of strain on violent delinquency using some of the same data analyzed by Paternoster and Mazerolle (1994). Mazerolle (1998) found that neighborhood problems positively predicted concurrent general delinquency among males, but not among females in a sample of 1,498 adolescents (National Youth Survey, 1976–1977). The difference between the two coefficients was not significant. In his longitudinal analyses, however, Mazerolle (1998) found that neighborhood problems failed to predict subsequent (one year later) violent delinquency among either males or females, and there was again no significant difference between the two effects (Mazerolle, 1998:83). Similar to Paternoster and Mazerolle (1994), Mazerolle (1998) failed to control for or examine variation by race or class in the effect of neighborhood problems on delinquency.

Finally, a fourth study by Broidy (2001) examined gender variation in the effect of individual-level noxious stimuli on anger and other negative emotions, as well as in the effect of negative affect on both legitimate coping and on delinquency in a sample of 896 male and female undergraduate students. Broidy found that a measure of stressful life events, which included criminal victimization and physical or sexual abuse, positively predicted subsequent levels of strain-induced anger, which in turn positively predicted concurrent general delinquency. Furthermore, she found that males and females were equally likely to react to strain with anger, but that females were more likely to experience other negative emotions as well (2001:22–23). Broidy also found that males were more likely to engage in general delinquency and females were more likely to seek legitimate coping strategies, even after differences in strain-induced anger and other negative emotions and race were controlled (2001:24–27). Broidy failed to test for race, class, or intersectional variation in the effect of noxious stimuli on anger and subsequently on delinquency (although she did include race and class as control variables).

Studies of community violence and aggression

Within the second category, several psychological studies have linked exposure to community violence and experiences of violent victimization with concurrent and subsequent aggression and antisocial behavior, especially among adolescent males (Jenkins & Bell, 1997; Scarpa, 2001; Miller et al., 1999; Morrison, 2000; Hawkins et al., 2000). Schwab-Stone et al. (1995) examined the effects of exposure to violence (yearlong frequency of witnessing somebody get shot or stabbed) and feeling unsafe around the home, school, or neighborhood on adolescents' willingness to use physical aggression and aggressive and antisocial behavior (measured by items such as fighting, arrest, vandalism, theft, and carrying a gun) in a sample of 2,248 adolescents in urban public schools. A majority (61%) of the sample was African-American, only 16% was Caucasian, and the remaining 22% was Latino. Schwab-Stone et al. (1995) found that students who reported having committed violence (i.e., "hurt someone seriously enough to warrant attention by a doctor or nurse") also reported significantly greater exposure to violence in the community. They also found that exposure to violence and, to a lesser extent, feeling unsafe positively predicted adolescents' willingness to use physical aggression and concurrent engagement in aggressive and antisocial behavior. Although Schwab-Stone et al. (1995) controlled for gender, race, and economic disadvantage (measured as receipt of free school lunches), they failed to examine intersectional variation in the effect of exposure to violence on aggression and antisocial behavior.

Notably, Schwab-Stone et al. (1999) presented results from a 2-year follow-up of a subset of the sample analyzed in Schwab-Stone et al. (1995). In the sample of 1,093 male and female adolescents surveyed in both 1994 and 1996, Schwab-Stone et al. (1999) found that self-reported exposure to violence at Time 1 was positively correlated with self-reported externalizing problem behavior at Time 2 (two years later). Schwab-Stone et al. (1999) also reported results for the cross-sectional tests of association between exposure to community violence and externalizing problem behavior for the full sample of adolescents interviewed in 1994 (N=2,748) as well as the full sample interviewed in 1996 (N=2,600).[1] In their cross-sectional analyses, Schwab-Stone et al. (1999) tested for the moderating effects of gender and race separately. They found that exposure to community violence significantly and positively predicted concurrent externalizing problem behavior for the full sample as well as for each gender and race subgroup, with no significant between group differences. Thus, the effect of community violence on concurrent aggression and antisocial behavior was similar for males and females and for blacks and whites. However, Schwab-Stone et al. (1999) failed to examine variation by *intersections* of gender and race. Also, although Schwab-Stone et al. (1999) measured parental education (a frequently used proxy for class), they failed to control for this variable in any analyses or to examine class variation in the effect of community violence on externalizing problem behavior.

Duckworth et al. (2000) examined the effects of two different aspects of neighborhood violence—direct victimization and witnessing violence using self-report data from 181 African-American male and female adolescents in low-income urban communities with moderate to high levels of crime. They found that direct victimization positively predicted general behavior problems (which included items of aggression and delinquency) (Duckworth et al., 2000:815–819). They also found that witnessing violence positively predicted behavior problems, but this effect was mediated by a measure of community chaos (overall neighborhood criminality and disorganization). Duckworth et al. (2000) failed to control for gender or class or to examine such variation in the effects of violence exposure on behavior problems, and they could not examine race variation because the sample was entirely African-American.

DuRant et al. (1994) found that exposure to community violence was the strongest predictor of adolescent use of violence in a sample of 225 African-American male and female adolescents living in or around urban public housing projects (1994:615–616). DuRant et al. (1994). also conducted interaction analyses to test whether the effect of community violence on use of violence varied significantly by gender, and they found no significant difference between the effect for black males and the effect for black females (1994, 615). Notably, their measure of community violence also included drug selling, burglary, and weapon carrying (as well as actual physical violence) in the neighborhood. DuRant et al. (1994) could not examine race or class variation because the sample was entirely African-American and poor or working-class.

In another cross-sectional study, Scarpa (2001) examined the effects of witnessing and of being victimized by community violence on concurrent physical aggression for a sample of 54 male and female college students. Her sample was 64% female, 66% white, and only 8% black (Scarpa, 2001:39). Scarpa (2001) found that students in the "high-victim" group and students in the "high-witness" group reported significantly greater levels of physical aggression, meaning that both witnessing and being victimized by neighborhood violence were significantly related to reports of physical aggression.

In a longitudinal study, Miller et al. (1999: 7–8) found that witnessing community violence was positively related to concurrent antisocial behavior and positively predicted subsequent changes in antisocial behavior in a sample of 97 young urban boys with delinquent siblings. Virtually the entire sample was comprised of ethnic minorities (51% African-American and 45% Hispanic). Although Miller et al. (1999) measured parental education, they failed to control for this variable in any analyses or to examine class variation in the effect of witnessing violence on antisocial behavior. Because of the lack of variation in gender and race, Miller et al. could not examine variation by gender or race.

A second longitudinal study by Farrell and Bruce (1997) examined the effect of exposure to community violence on the frequency of violent behavior in a sample of 436 African-American, male and female adolescents in an urban school. They found a positive relationship between exposure to community violence and concurrent violent behavior among both males and females. In their longitudinal results, however, Farrell and Bruce found a significant gender interaction with this main effect. Exposure to community violence positively predicted subsequent changes in violent behavior for African-American girls, but not for boys. Farrell and Bruce (1997) failed to examine class variation and could not examine race variation in this effect.

Finally, a third longitudinal study by Gorman-Smith and Tolan (1998) examined the effect of exposure to community violence on aggression in a sample of 245 African-American and Latino adolescent boys (ages 11 to 15) from economically disadvantaged inner-city neighborhoods in Chicago. Gorman-Smith and Tolan (1998) found that exposure to violence positively predicted subsequent aggressive behavior one year later, even after controlling for early aggressive behavior. Because of the lack of variation in race, gender, and class, Gorman-Smith and Tolan (1998) could not examine intersectional variation in this effect.

Summary of previous literature

Collectively, previous studies of noxious stimuli, community violence, and aggression provide some support for the hypothesis that exposure to neighborhood violence will positively predict adolescent engagement in individual violence. These research findings can be summarized into four broad categories. The first category includes studies that have focused on the effect of general neighborhood violence—both victimization and witnessing violence—on individual violence. Studies within this category have found that neighborhood violence has a significant and positive effect on *concurrent* individual violence and that there is some support for gender variation (Paternoster & Mazerolle, 1994; Attar et al., 1994; Farrell & Bruce, 1997; Mazerolle, 1998 (effect is significant for males, but not for females); DuRant et al., 1994 (effect is significant for black males and black females, with no significant gender difference in size of the effect); Bell & Jenkins, 1993 (effect is significant for boys, but not for girls); Schwab-Stone et al., 1999 (effect is significant for blacks and whites and males and females with no significant differences in effect size). Some studies within this category have also found that neighborhood violence has a significant and positive effect on *subsequent* changes in individual violence (Paternoster & Mazerolle, 1994; Gorman-Smith & Tolan, 1998; Farrell & Bruce, 1997 (effect is significant for girls, but not for boys)). Only one study found no significant longitudinal effect for either males or females (Mazerolle, 1998).

The second category includes studies that have focused on the effect of violent victimization on individual violence. Studies within this category have found that violent victimization has a significant and positive effect on concurrent individual violence (Agnew & White, 1992; Duckworth et al., 2000; Scarpa 2001; Broidy, 2001 (effect is significantly stronger for males than for females)). Only one study found that violent victimization predicted internalizing behavior problems, but not externalizing behavior problems (such as individual violence) (Shahinfar et al., 2000). The third category includes studies that have focused on the effect of witnessing violence on individual violence. Studies within this category have generally found that witnessing violence has a significant and positive effect on concurrent individual violence (Schwab-Stone et al., 1995; Duckworth et al., 2000; Scarpa, 2001; Shahinfar et al., 2000; Miller et al., 1999). One study found that witnessing violence also has a significant and positive effect on subsequent changes in individual violence (Miller et al., 1999). Finally, the fourth category includes studies that have focused on the effect of feeling unsafe in the neighborhood on individual violence. One study found that feeling unsafe had a significant and positive effect on concurrent individual violence (Schwab-Stone et al., 1995), while another study found no significant effect (Agnew & White, 1992).

On the whole, previous studies have largely ignored gender, race, and class variation in the effect of neighborhood violence on individual violence; and no known quantitative analyses have examined the possibility of intersectional variation in this effect. The present study attempts to fill this gap by conducting an exploratory quantitative analysis of intersectional variation among a sample of adolescents.

Research design

Our research involves a quantitative analysis of the effect of neighborhood violence on individual violence with explicit examination of intersectional variation by gender, race, and class.

Sample

Data for the present study came from the National Survey of Adolescents conducted in 1995 by Kilpatrick and Saunders (1995) and was downloaded directly from the Inter-University Consortium for Political and Social Research (ICPSR) website. This self-report data was collected via telephone interviews with a representative sample of adolescents age 12 to 17 years living in United States households and residing with a parent or guardian. Among other things, the adolescents were asked about their lifetime experiences with being victimized by or witnessing violence in their neighborhood, as well as their own use of physical violence. After variables relevant to the present study were selected, respondents with missing values on any variable were removed. Additionally, because race variation was restricted to a comparison of non-Hispanic whites and blacks, adolescents of other races were removed. The final sample consisted of 3,088 individuals (out of an original 4,023). Table 1 presents a demographic breakdown of the intersectional social locations analyzed in the present study.

TABLE 1 ■ SAMPLE DISTRIBUTION OF EIGHT SOCIAL LOCATIONS CREATED BY INTERSECTIONS OF RACE, GENDER, AND CLASS, 1995 NATIONAL SURVEY OF ADOLESCENTS

	Males		Females		
	Working class	Middle class	Working class	Middle class	Total
Black/African-American	4.4% n = 135	4.3% n =133	4.5% n = 140	4.6% n = 141	18% n = 549
White/Caucasian	15.5% n = 478	26.2% n = 808	15.7% n = 485	24.9% n = 768	82% n = 2539
Total	50.3% n = 1554		49.7% n = 1534		100% N = 3088

Variables

Twenty-five variables were selected for analysis in the present cross-sectional study, eighteen of which were subsequently reduced to four summated factor scales, resulting in a final total of eleven variables. Each of these eleven variables is described in detail below and descriptive statistics for all variables are presented in Table 2.

The dependent variable of interest, *Individual Violence,* consists of a 3-item scale measuring adolescent lifetime participation in gang fights, robberies, or assaults with intent to maim or kill. The two independent variables of interest measure aspects of neighborhood violence. The first independent variable, *Witnessed Violence,* consists of a 7-item scale measuring incidents in which adolescents witnessed somebody being shot, stabbed, sexually assaulted, robbed, beaten up, or threatened with a gun/knife. This scale also includes an item measuring whether adolescents believe violence is a problem in their neighborhood or not. Cronbach's alpha for the *Witnessed Violence* scale was .609. The second independent variable, *Violent Victimization,* consists of a 6-item scale measuring adolescent experiences of violent victimization (incidents of being attacked with or without a weapon, being beaten up with an object or with fists, being assaulted in one's neighborhood, or being threatened with a gun/knife). Cronbach's alpha for the *Violent Victimization* scale was .685.

Three dichotomous variables are used to measure the intersectional constructs of gender, race, and class. *Gender* is coded as 1 for males and 0 for females. *Race* is coded as 1 for blacks and 0 for whites. *Class* is coded as 1 for working class and 0 for middle class; however, it is important to understand exactly how class is measured in the present study. From a Weberian perspective, an individual's class is determined by position in the commodity (wealth) or labor (occupations) market. Therefore among the propertyless the best indicator of an individual's class position is his or her occupation. In the case of adolescents, the highest occupation held by the adolescent's parents is an appropriate indicator of the adolescent's class. In the present data set, no such measure of parental occupation was available; therefore, parental educational attainment (which is highly correlated with occupation) was used as the best available proxy for class. If the parent that was present at the time of the interview had attended at least some college, the adolescent was coded as middle class. If the present parent had not attended any college, then the adolescent was coded as working class.

Finally, five other predictors of individual violence were employed as control variables in the present study. *Age* represents the age of the adolescent and ranges from 12 to 17. *Single-Parent Household* is a variable coded 1 if the adolescent

TABLE 2 ■ MEAN SCORES AND DESCRIPTIONS OF SELECTED VARIABLES OF ADOLESCENTS AGED 12–17

Variable	Possible Values	Description	Mean
Individual violence	0 thru 1	Respondent use of violence scale (e.g., gang fights, robberies, and assaults with intent to mail/kill) (alpha = .504)	.04
Witnessed violence	0 thru 1	Respondent witnessed violence scale (e.g., seeing someone cut/stabbed, sexually assaulted/raped, mugged/robbed, threatened with gun/knife, beaten up/hit/punched) and whether respondent believes violence is a problem in their neighborhood (alpha = .609)	.24
Violent victimization	0 thru 1	Respondent victimization by violence scale (e.g., attacked with or without a weapon, threatened with gun/knife, beaten up with object or fists and hurt badly, assaulted in neighborhood) (alpha = .685)	.06
Gender	0,1	Gender of respondent (1 = male, 0 = female)	.50
Race	0,1	Race of respondent (1 = black, 0 = white)	.18
Class	0,1	Class of respondent (1 = working, 0 = middle)	.40
Age	12 thru 17	Age of respondent	14.6
Single-parent	0,1	Respondent lived in single-parent household	.65
Urban	0,1	Respondent lived in urban neighborhood	.39
Violent friends	0,1	Respondent had violent friends (i.e., friends who hit or threatened to hit someone)	.20
Other strain	0 thru 1	Respondent experienced other strain scale (e.g., problems with family or friends, health, or work)	.05

has *not* always lived with both biological parents, and 0 if the adolescent has. *Urban Neighborhood* is coded as 1 if the adolescent lives in an urban neighborhood (city or large town) and 0 if the adolescent does not. *Violent Friends* is coded as 1 if the adolescent had friends who hit or threatened to hit someone. *Other Strain* is a 3-item scale measuring adolescent problems with family or friends, health, or work. All five control variables are expected to have a significantly positive effect on individual violence.

Methodology

Ordinary least squares (OLS) regression analyses were used to measure the effect of neighborhood violence on individual violence for the full sample and for each intersectional analysis. Tests of gender variation in the main effect of neighborhood violence on individual violence were conducted through inclusion of a gender interaction term in the regression equations. The two independent variables of interest—*Witnessed Violence* and *Violent Victimization*—were centered (recomputed as deviations from the mean) to reduce problems of multicollinearity.[2]

The analytical strategy adopted in the present study involved three main steps. The first step (Model A) was to run a regression of *Individual Violence* on all ten independent variables with no interaction terms included. The

TABLE 3 OLS STANDARDIZED REGRESSION COEFFICIENTS PREDICTING INDIVIDUAL VIOLENCE IN THE FULL SAMPLE (N = 3,088)

	Standardized beta coefficients[1]	
Variable	**Model A**	**Model B**
Witnessed violence	.192***	.144***
Violent victimization	.263***	.169***
Gender (1 = male)	.069***	.071***
Race (1 = black)	.025	.025
Class (1 = working)	.032*	.033
Age	.043**	.044**
Single-parent	−.044**	−.045**
Urban	.007	.009
Violent friends	.112***	.113***
Other strain	.125***	.129***
Gender × witnessed violence		.069**
Gender × violent victimization		.111***
R-Square	.271	.280

* = $p \leq 0.05$, ** = $p \leq 0.01$, *** = $p \leq 0.001$, all tests one-tailed.

second step (Model B) was to run a regression of *Individual Violence* with two interaction terms measuring gender variation in the effects of *Witnessed Violence* and *Violent Victimization.* The third and final step (Models C through F) was to run separate regressions of *Individual Violence* with gender interaction terms on the four race and class subgroups of youth—white middle class, black middle class, white working class, and black working class.

FINDINGS

Table 3 presents the standardized beta coefficients and R-squared values obtained from the first two regression analyses conducted on the full sample of adolescents (Models A and B).

Model A represents a regression of *Individual Violence* on all ten independent variables with no interaction terms included. Looking at the results, both measures of neighborhood violence had significant and positive effects on concurrent *Individual Violence* regardless of gender, race, or class (which were included as control variables). This finding is in accordance with Hypothesis (1). Being victimized by violence had the strongest association with using violence (standardized bet = .263***), and witnessing violence had the second strongest association (standardized bet = .192***). Other results from Model A reveal that gender and class (but not race) continued to have significant associations with *Individual Violence* even after exposure to neighborhood violence and other variables were controlled. Witnessing and experiencing neighborhood violence failed to fully explain the greater tendency of working-class and male adolescents to engage in violent behavior.

Model B represents a regression of *Individual Violence* on the same predictor variables as Model A except that two gender interaction terms are now included. Looking at the results for Model B presented in Table 3, *Violent Victimization* and *Witnessed Violence* continue to exhibit the strongest associations with adolescent use of violence. Most notable, however, both gender interaction terms are significant and positive—indicating that the effect of witnessing and/or being victimized by violence is stronger for males than for females. This finding

TABLE 4 ■ OLS UNSTANDARDIZED REGRESSION COEFFICIENTS AND STANDARD ERRORS PREDICTING INDIVIDUAL VIOLENCE BY INTERSECTIONAL SUBGROUPS

	Unstandardized Beta Coefficients[2]			
Variable	Model C	Model D	Model E	Model F
Subgroup	White middle-class (n = 1,576)	Black middle-class (n = 274)	White working-class (n = 963)	Black working-class (n = 275)
Witnessed violence	.067***	.240***	.088**	.125*
	(.022)	(.060)	(.033)	(.068)
Violent victimization	.074*	.252**	.178***	.216*
	(.035)	(.085)	(.044)	(.116)
Gender (1 = male)	.018***	.025	.023**	.034
	(.005)	(.018)	(.008)	(.022)
Age	.001	.000	.005*	.014**
	(.001)	(.005)	(.003)	(.006)
Single-parent	−.006	−.056***	−.012	−.008
	(.006)	(.017)	(.009)	(.020)
Urban	.001	−.022	.005	.032
	(.005)	(.017)	(.009)	(.019)
Violent friends	.026***	.029	.055***	.051**
	(.007)	(.019)	(.011)	(.021)
Other strain	.087***	.031	.123***	.199***
	(.016)	(.049)	(.022)	(.061)
Gender × witnessed violence	.082**	−.109	.043	.136
	(.029)	(.079)	(.047)	(.092)
Gender × violent victimization	.194***	.086	.093*	.126
	(.042)	(.115)	(.056)	(.146)
R-square	.236	.333	.289	.359

* = $p \leq 0.05$, ** = $p \leq 0.01$, *** = $p \leq 0.001$, all tests one-tailed.

provides support for Hypothesis (2). There is as yet no way to ascertain whether gender variation in reaction to strain holds true for blacks as well as for whites, or for working-class as well as for middle-class adolescents. For this reason, we next conduct regressions on social locations defined by race and class to examine intersectional variation in the effect of neighborhood violence on individual violence.

Table 4 presents the unstandardized beta coefficients and R-squared values obtained from regression analyses conducted on each race and class subgroup of adolescents (Models C through F). Looking at the results from these four regressions, both witnessing violence and being victimized by violence have significant and positive associations with adolescent use of violence within each intersectional group. The strength and significance of other variables' associations vary by subgroup and sample size. Of primary interest to the final hypothesis, however, are the interaction terms representing gender variation in the effect of neighborhood violence on individual violence. These interaction terms are significant within the subgroup of white middle-class adolescents, and one interaction is significant among white working-class adolescents, but none are significant among black middle- or working-class adolescents. In all models, the interactions are in the expected positive direction, with one exception: the gender interaction with witnessing violence among black middle-class adolescents. The negative coefficient indicates that black middle-class females who witness violence in their neighborhood are more likely to use violence than males; however, because this coefficient does not achieve statistical significance, we ultimately find no gender difference in the likelihood that black males and females will react to neighborhood violence by engaging in violence themselves.

To further explore intersectional variation in reaction to neighborhood violence, we followed the procedure spelled out in Paternoster et al. (1998) to test for differences in the magnitude of the gender interaction coefficients.[3] We compared the interaction coefficients for neighborhood violence within the white middle-class group with the coefficients from each of the other subgroup regressions. Our comparisons yielded only one statistically significant difference: the gender interaction coefficient for witnessing violence was significantly larger in the white middle-class subgroup than it was in the black middle-class subgroup ($t = 2.28$, $p < .05$, two-tailed). Simply put, white middle-class males who witnessed neighborhood violence were more likely to use violence than white middle-class females; whereas a significantly smaller (and statistically nonexistent) gender effect was found among black middle-class adolescents. It is also noteworthy that the gender effect among black middle-class adolescents was significantly smaller than that among black working-class adolescents ($p < .05$), but was not significantly different from that among white working-class adolescents. These findings provide support for our exploratory Hypothesis (3).

Collectively, our regression findings support all three of our hypothesized predictions and provide fairly strong evidence of intersectional variation in the effect of neighborhood violence on adolescent use of violence. Experiencing and witnessing neighborhood violence had a positive effect on the likelihood of physical violence by all adolescents, regardless of gender, race, or class. These effects were statistically stronger for males than females in the white middle-class subgroup; and this gender variation was significantly different among white middle-class adolescents than it was among black middle-class adolescents (at least with regard to witnessing violence in one's neighborhood).

Conclusion

The present study examined the effect of living in a violent neighborhood on individual violence across intersections of gender, race, and class. Results confirmed the hypothesized general strain theoretical prediction that witnessing and experiencing neighborhood violence would have a significantly positive effect on concurrent engagement in violent delinquency. Adolescent reports of having witnessed or having been victimized by violence were significantly related to adolescent reports of having used physical violence, and this finding was true for all intersections of race, gender, and class.

The intersectional analyses performed in the present study also provide support for the fundamental proposition of intersectional theorists—namely, that the effects of certain factors on social behavior may vary by intersections of gender, race, and class. White middle-class males who witnessed or experienced neighborhood violence were significantly more likely to engage in violent behavior than white middle-class females. Alternatively, no such significant difference was observed among black middle-class or black working-class males or females. Furthermore, the non-significant gender difference among black middle-class adolescents was significantly smaller than the positive gender difference found among white middle-class adolescents.

These findings appear to support the existence of race differences in the process of gender socialization, at least among middle-class adolescent youth. White middle-class females may be more likely than black middle-class females to internalize strain-generated anger, or the environments in which they are reared may be less supportive of female aggression. Alternatively, black middle-class adolescents may be reared in environments characterized by stronger (or more equal) social support for aggressive conflict-resolution, regardless of the adolescent's gender. Unfortunately, we lack sufficient information in the present cross-sectional data to explore the way in which these mechanisms play out. Future studies should attempt to conduct intersectional analyses using a prospective longitudinal study of neighborhood violence and individual violence so that proper temporal ordering can be established, and studies should include measures of the mediating mechanisms of negative affect generated by strain and other types of coping strategies employed by adolescents.

Our findings do definitively illustrate the importance of conducting intersectional analyses in all areas of social science research. If our analyses of gender variation in the present study had been conducted only on the full sample of adolescents, we would have missed the fact that neighborhood violence appears to affect black males and black females more similarly than it does white males and white females. If the analyses had been confined solely to variation by race, we would have missed the fact that neighborhood violence sometimes affects males more (or less) strongly than females. Future research in this area should attempt to expand the categories of intersectionality to include other races and should incorporate a more reliable measure of class (e.g., parental occupation).

Notes

1. Although never explicitly stated, presumably results for 2,248 adolescents in the 1994 sample were also reported in Schwab-Stone et al. (1995).
2. Once centered, each variable included in the regressions had a variance inflation factor (VIF) of less than four and most were less than two, indicating that multicollinearity was not a significant problem.
3. This formula—$(B1 - B2) / SQRT(SE_{B1}^2 + SE_{B2}^2)$ — yields results comparable to those produced using more complicated procedures outlined in Hardy (1993).
4. Standardized coefficients allow within-model comparisons of the relative strength of each predictive effect.
5. Unstandardized coefficients allow between-model comparisons of the relative strength of each predictive effect.

Bibliography

Agnew, R. (1992). Foundation for a general strain theory of crime and delinquency. *Criminology,* 30(1):47–87.

———. (1999). A general strain theory of community differences in crime rates. *Journal of Research in Crime and Delinquency,* 36(2):123–155.

Agnew, R. & Brezina, T. (1997). Relational problems with peers, gender, and delinquency. *Youth and Society,* 29(1):84–101.

Agnew, R. & Raskin White H. (1992). An empirical test of general strain theory. *Criminology,* 30(4):475–499.

Anderson, E. (1999). *The code of the street: Decency, violence, and the moral life of the inner city.* New York, NY; W.W. Norton.

The authors wish to thank an anonymous reviewer for helpful comments on an earlier draft of this paper. An even earlier draft was presented at the American Society of Criminology conference in Chicago, Illinois. November 16, 2002.

Attar, B. K., Guerra, N.G., & Tolan, P.T. (1994). Neighborhood disadvantage, stressful life events, and adjustment in urban elementary-school children. *Journal of Clinical Child Psychology,* 23:391–400.

Baskin, D.R. & Sommers, I.B. (1998). *Casualties of community disorder: Women's careers in violent crime.* Boulder, CO: Westview Press.

Bell, C.C. and Jenkins E.J. (1993). Community violence and children on Chicago's southside. *Psychiatry,* 56:46–54.

Bennett, M.D., Jr. & Fraser, M.W. (2000). Urban violence among African American males: Integrating family, neighborhood, and peer perspectives. *Journal of Sociology and Social Welfare,* 27(3):93–117.

Brewer, R.M. (1993). Theorizing race, class and gender: The new scholarship of black feminist intellectuals and black women's labor. In S.M. James & A.P.A. Busia (eds.), *Theorizing Black feminisms: The visionary pragmatism of Black women.* London: Routledge.

Broidy, L.M. (2001). A test of general strain theory. *Criminology,* 39(1):9–35.

Broidy, L. & Agnew, R. (1997). Gender and crime: A general strain theory perspective. *Journal of Research in Crime and Delinquency,* 34(3):275–306.

Campbell, A. (1993). *Men, women, and aggression.* New York, NY: BasicBooks.

Cernkovich, S.A. & Giordano, C. (1979). A comparative analysis of male and female delinquency. *Sociological Quarterly,* 20:131–145.

Chilton, R. & Datesman, S.K. (1987). Gender, race, and crime. *Gender and Society,* 1:152–171.

Collins, P.H. (1993). Toward a new vision: Race, class and gender as categories of analysis and connection. *Race, Sex, and Class,* 1(1).

Crenshaw, K. (1993). Beyond racism and misogyny: Black feminism and 2 Live Crew. In M. Matsueda, C. Lawrence III, R. Delgado, & K. Crenshaw (eds.), *Words that wound.* San Francisco, CA: Westview Press.

Duckworth, M.P., Hale, D.D., Clair, S.D., & Adams, H.E. (2000). Influence of interpersonal violence and community chaos on stress reactions in children. *Journal of Interpersonal Violence,* 15(8):806–826.

DuRant, R.H., Cadenhead, C., Pendergrast, R.A., Slavens, G., & Linder, C.W. (1994). Factors associated with the use of violence among urban Black adolescents. *American Journal of Public Health,* 84:612–617.

Eagly, A.H. & Steffen V.J. (1986). Gender and aggressive behavior: A meta-analytic review of the social psychological literature. *Psychological Bulletin,* 100(3):309–330.

Elliott, D.S. & Wilson, W.J. (1996). The effects of neighborhood disadvantage on adolescent development. *Journal of Research in Crime and Delinquency,* 33(4):389–426.

Farrell, A.D. & Bruce, S.E. (1997). Impact of exposure to community violence on violent behavior and emotional distress among urban adolescents. *Journal of Clinical Child Psychology,* 26:2–14.

Gorman-Smith, D. & Tolan, T. (1998). The role of exposure to community violence and developmental problems among inner-city youth. *Development and Psychopathology,* 10:101–116.

Hardy, M.A. (1993). *Regression with dummy variables.* Newbury Park, CA: Sage, pp. 48–53.

Hawkins, J.D., Herrenkohl, T.I., Farrington, D.P., Brewer, D., Catalano, R.F., Harachi, T.W., & Cothem, L. (2000). Predictors of youth violence. *Juvenile Justice Bulletin.* Washington, DC: U.S. Department of Justice, Office of Juvenile Justice and Delinquency Prevention.

Hill, G. & Crawford, E. (1990). Women, race, and crime. *Criminology,* 28:601–623.

Hindelang, M.J., Hirschi, T., & Weis, J.G. (1981). *Measuring delinquency.* Beverly Hills, CA: Sage Publications.

Jenkins, E.J. & Bell, C.C. (1997). Exposure and response to community violence among children and adolescents. In J.D. Osofsky, (ed.), *Children in a Violent Society.* New York, NY: The Guilford Press.

Kilpatrick, D.G. & Saunders, B.E. (1995). National survey of adolescents in the United States. Washington, DC: National Institute of Justice.

King, D.K. (1988). Multiple jeopardy, multiple consciousness: The context of a black feminist ideology. *Signs,* 14(1).

Kruttschnitt, C. (1994). Gender and interpersonal violence. In A.J. Reiss, Jr. & J.A. Roth (eds.), *Understanding and preventing violence,* Volume 3. Washington, DC: National Academy Press.

Mazza, J.J. & Overstreet, S. (2000). Children and adolescents exposed to community violence: A

mental health perspective for school psychologists. *School Psychology Review*, 29(1):86–101.
Mazerolle, Paul (1998). Gender, general strain, and delinquency: An empirical examination. *Justice Quarterly*, 15(1):65–91.
Messerschmidt, James W. (1993). *Masculinities and crime: Critique and reconceptualization of theory.* Lanham, MD: Rowan and Littlefield.
Miller, Eleanor M. (1986). *Street Women.* Philadelphia, PA: Temple University Press.
Miller, Laurie S., Wasserman, Gail A., Neugebauer, Richard, Gorman-Smith, Deborah, and Dimitra Kamboukos (1999). Witnessed community violence and antisocial behavior in high-risk, urban boys. *Journal of Clinical Child Psychology*, 28(1):2–11.
Mirowsky, John and Catherine E. Ross (1995). Sex differences in distress: Real or artifact? *American Sociological Review*, 60:449–468.
Morrison, J.A. (2000). Protective factors associated with children's emotional response to chronic community violence exposure. *Trauma Violence, and Abuse: A Review Journal,* 1(4):299–320.
Ogle, Robbin S., Maier, Daniel Katkin, and Thomas J. Bernard (1995). A theory of homicidal behavior among women. *Criminology*, 33(2):173–193.
Osofsky, J.D. (1997). *Children in a Violent Society.* New York, NY: The Guilford Press.
Paternoster, R., Brame, B., Mazerolle, P., & Piquero, A. (1998). Using the correct statistical test for the equality of regression coefficients. *Criminology,* 36(4):859–866.
Paternoster, R. & Mazerolle, P. (1994). General strain theory and delinquency: A replication and extension. *Journal of Research in Crime and Delinquency,* 31 (3):235–263.
Sampson, R.J. & Lauritsen, J.L. (1994). Violent victimization and offending: Individual-, situational-, and community-level risk factors. In A.J. Reiss, Jr. & Roth, J.A. (eds.), *Understanding and preventing violence,* Vol. 3. Washington, DC: National Academy Press.
Scarpa, A. (2001). Community violence exposure in a young adult sample: Lifetime prevalence and socioemotional effects. *Journal of Interpersonal Violence,* 16(1):36–53.
Schwab-Stone, M.E., Ayers, T.S., Kasprow, W., Voyce, C., Barone, C., Shriver, T., and Weissberg, R.P. (1995). No safe haven: A study of violence exposure in an urban community. *Journal of the American Academy of Child and Adolescent Psychiatry,* 34(10):1343–1352.
Schwab-Stone, M., Chen, C., Greenberger, E., Silver, D., Lichtman, J., & Voyce, C. (1999). No safe haven II: The effects of violence exposure on urban youth. *Journal of the American Academy of Child and Adolescent Psychiatry,* 38(4):359–367.
Shahinfar, A., Fox, N.A., & Leavitt, L.A. (2000). Preschool children's exposure to violence: Relation of behavior problems to parent and child reports. *American Journal of Orthopsychiatry,* 70(1):115–125.
Simpson, S.S. (1991). Caste, class, and violent crime: Explaining difference in female offending. *Criminology,* 29(1):115–135.
Thorne, B. & Luria, Z. (1986). Sexuality and gender in children's daily worlds. *Social Problems,* 33:176–190.
Wilson, W.J. (1987). *The truly disadvantaged: The inner-city, the underclass and public policy*. Chicago, IL: University of Chicago Press.
Zinn, M.B. & Dill, B.T. (1996). Theorizing difference from multiracial feminism. *Feminist Studies,* 22(2):321–331.

Summary

If the intersectional approach is to achieve its goal of promoting the simultaneous analysis of race, gender, and class, it is important to understand its application in quantitative studies. The multiplicative assumption is of special importance here. I have argued that statistically the multiplicative notion is *statistical interaction* and that the idea of multiplicative rather than additive relationships is an assumption that must be tested. Testing for statistical interactions, however, is challenging because of problems of multicollinearity and of interpretation in the case of higher-order interaction terms. Subgroup analysis using *t*-tests of interaction coefficients across groups together with one or more interaction terms offers a viable alternative to the sole use of interaction terms. A number of *t*-tests are readily available, particularly the ones by Hardy (1993) and Paternoster et al. (1998). I have tried to explain the basics of such an approach, as well as provided examples of this approach, in a number of the articles included in this text.

ENDNOTES

i $Y = b_0 + b_1R + b_2G + b_3Cl$ [3.1]

where Y = income; G represents gender, coded 0 for females and 1 for males; R stands for race, coded 0 for blacks and 1 for whites; and Cl represents class, coded 0 for working class and 1 for middle class.

ii $Y = b_0 + b_1G$ [3.2]

iii $Y = b_o + b_1Ed + b_2G$ [3.3]

iv $Y = b_0 + b_1Ed + b_2G + b_3EdG$ [3.4]

v To accomplish this statistically, we calculate two equations, one when the value of G equals 0 (females), the other when G equals 1 (males). We then test whether each equation is significantly different from zero and whether the two equations are significantly different from each other. *The first test will indicate whether education is related to income attainment for males and for females,* the latter test will reveal whether the effect of education on income varies across the simple locations of male and female. If the two equations differ significantly from zero and from each other, we can be confident that females and males receive different income returns for the same education. If the two equations are not significantly different from each other, we will have to conclude that the effect of education on income is the same for females and males. Statistically, the slope of the regression of income on education depends on the particular value of G at which the slope is considered. Since G is a dichotomous variable, we need to solve two equations, one for the slope of income on education when G is female, the other for the slope of income on education when G is male.

vi $Y = b_0 + b_1Ed + b_2G + b_3R$ [3.5]

vii $Y = b_0 + b_1Ed + b_2G + b_3R + b_4EdG + b_5EdR$ [3.6]

viii $Y = b_0 + b_1Ed + b_2G + b_3R + b_4Cl + b_5EdG + b_6EdR + b_7EdCl$ [3.7]

ix $Y = b_0 + b_1R + b_2G + b_3Ed + b_4RG$ [3.8]

x This requires calculating coefficients for each of the four social locations, testing the significance of each, and calculating *t*-test of the difference between each group.

xi $Y = b_0 + b_1Ed + b_2R + b_3G + b_4EdR + b_5EdG + b_6RG + b_7EdRG$ [3.9]

xii $Y = b_0 + b_1Ed + b_2R + b_3G + b_4EdG$ [3.10]

xiii $Y = b_o + b_1Ed + b_2R + + b_3G + b_4Cl + b_5EdR + b_6EdG + b_7EdCl + b_8RG + b_9RCl + b_{10}GCl + b_{11}EdRG + b_{12}EdRCl + b_{13}EdGCl + b_{14}EdRGCl$ [3.11]

xiv $Y = b_0 + b_1Ed + b_2R + b_3G + b_4EdG$ [3.12]

REFERENCES

Agresti, Alan, and Barbara Finlay. 1997. *Statistical methods for the social sciences.* Upper Saddle River, NJ: Prentice Hall.

Aiken, Leona S., and Stephen G. West. 1991. *Multiple regression: Testing and interpreting interactions.* Newbury Park, CA: Sage.

Brod, Rodney L. 1999. Logistic regression modeling of race, gender and class: Illustrated by gender bias in wages." In *ASA Resource Materials for Teaching,* 81–93. Washington, DC.

Foner, Nancy, and Geroge M. Fredrickson, eds. 2004. *Not just black and white: Historical and contemporary perspectives on immigration, race, and ethnicity in the United States.* New York: Russell Sage Foundation.

Hardy, Melissa A. 1993. *Regression with dummy variables.* Newbury Park, CA: Sage.

Paternoster, Raymond, Bobby Brame, Paul Mazerolle, and Alex Piquero. 1998. Using the correct statistical test for the equality of regression coefficients. *Criminology* 36 (4): 859–66.

Notes on Teaching RGC Methodology to Undergraduates

Today a large number of instructors are introducing intersectional theory to undergraduates. These classes often exist alongside courses on race and ethnicity and courses on gender. Given the number of texts on gender and on race/ethnicity that continue to be published, it is clear that these courses will endure. The task of RGC instructors, therefore, is not to eliminate gender or race/ethnic courses, but to demonstrate the advantages of combining race, gender, and class within the same course and to introduce the methods of RGC research. Because many instructors of upper-division courses require students to engage in some research, it should not be too great a leap to introduce RGC methods.

"Doing" RGC Research

It goes without saying that any attempt to teach RGC methodology should be preceded and/or accompanied by instructions on the theory. A stand-alone methodology would make little sense without some understanding of the basic simultaneity and multiplicative assumptions of RGC theory; however, these concepts will be better understood when illustrated with appropriate empirical examples.

The research process can be divided into three stages: design/planning, data collection, and analysis. In discussing each of these three stages, I shall focus on the issues that I believe are most relevant for intersectional research. The methodological practices basic to any qualitative or quantitative project are easily accessible in the many undergraduate texts on the market and will not be covered here.

Study Design and Simultaneity: Perhaps the most basic step in teaching RGC methodology to undergraduates is to stress that intersectional research requires the inclusion of race, gender, and class in the study design. This is the principle of simultaneity, one of the cornerstone concepts of the RGC approach. What does this mean in practice to the researcher? Fundamentally this means that the researcher should include all relevant individuals in the data being collected, or—in the case of secondary analysis[1]—they should represented in the data being used. But since intersectional analysis focuses on the *groups* (social locations) that are formed at the *intersections* of race, gender, and class, it is first necessary to identify the relevant groups. This is the uniqueness of the intersectional approach in contrast to the traditional focus on race, or gender, or class.

To simplify the discussion, we first consider a study design with only two of the three identities, race and gender.[2] We identify the groups that must be included in our sample by mapping out the intersections involved, as illustrated in Table 1. This example

TABLE I

	RACE	
GENDER	Latino	White
Males	LM	WM
Females	LF	WF

[1]*Secondary analysis* refers to the use of existing data that were collected by someone else.

[2]Although it is true that all three should be included whenever possible, in reality the nature of the specific research may exclude one of the three identities. For instance, if the goal is to research pregnancy, only females are of concern. A study of masculine identity would naturally omit women.

reproduce the one in the Introduction, with the substitution of Latino for black.

The intersections of race and gender are identified by creating a cross tabulation of race by gender. The table reveals the existence of four distinct groups or social locations: Latino males, white males, Latino females, and white females. It is from these complex social locations that persons observe the world, interact with other individuals, and are perceived by others.

Including all three identities and also dichotomizing class into middle and working class results in the social locations shown in Table 2.

TABLE 2

	CLASS			
	Middle		Working	
GENDER	RACE		RACE	
	Latino	White	Latino	White
Males	McLM	McWM	WcLM	WcWM
Females	McLF	McWF	WcLF	WcWF

Thus adding middle class and working class to each of the previous four social locations gives middle-class Latino males, middle-class white males, middle-class Latino females, middle-class white females, working-class Latino males, working-class white males, working-class Latino females, and working-class white females.

Data Collection: The most important consideration in research design is careful planning to collect data on a sufficient number of individuals from each of the social locations, whether interest is in four or eight social locations. In a qualitative study, the researcher should interview individuals in each of the social locations involved. A researcher using secondary data should take care to identify a data set containing sufficient cases in each social location. If either class or race/ethnicity[3] includes more than two categories, the number of social locations is increased. For instance, three categories of race (black, Latino, and white) and two categories each for gender and class would yield 12 social locations (3 × 2 × 2). As noted in my analysis of articles in this text, RGC analysis often appears to be an afterthought, a decision taken after the data have already been collected. The result can be insufficient cases for analysis in one or more social locations.

In practice, identifying and including individuals in each social location can be very challenging. Although gender and race are relatively easy to identify (ethnicity is more difficult), recognizing an individual's class position is not straightforward. I usually follow the Weberian tradition in micro analysis, using occupation as the indicator of class. From this perspective, individuals with white-collar occupations are members of the middle class, and those in blue-collar or unskilled service jobs fall into the working class. Ideally, then, the student researcher must solicit occupational information from interviewees. If respondents are themselves students, it is their parents' class position that identifies their own. In the absence of occupational data or when it is too difficult or impossible to obtain, education is the best proxy. Parents with at least some college can be identified as middle class, with all others falling into the working class.[4]

Alternatively, we may assign college graduates to the upper middle class, those with some college or technical training beyond high school to the lower middle class, and those with a high school degree or less to the working class.

Analysis Analytic strategies depend on whether the research is qualitative or quantitative; quantitative research can be descriptive or inferential. Qualitative research has the advantage of providing considerable depth. In interviews the researcher can ask a number

[3]There is some confusion over the terms *race* and *ethnicity.* Although it is widely accepted in social science that race is an inappropriate concept, since there are no pure races, the term has become such an important part of our lexicon that it continues to be used. Ethnicity is a broader concept that refers to cultural, linguistic, and national differences. In practice, Latinos (or Hispanics) are sometimes thought of as a race, sometimes as an ethnic group.

[4]Sometimes a researcher may wish to identify those in the upper middle class. These are individuals in professional or managerial/executive occupations, whereas lower-middle-class individuals occupy clerical, sales, or technical positions.

of probing questions to elucidate the response to a question rather than having to guess at the meaning of a significant correlation, as often occurs in quantitative analysis. On the negative side, qualitative research typically involves small, nonrepresentative samples and therefore yields nongeneralizable findings.

In reporting results the RGC qualitative researcher should report not only the sample size but also the number of cases in *each* social location. Without this information the reader cannot evaluate the strength of the findings. In quantitative analysis, it is customary to require a minimum of 20 cases in each cell (i.e., in this case, social location), owing to the demands of the statistical tools used in the analysis. Because qualitative data are not subjected to tests of significance, such a criterion would be inappropriate. I would suggest, however, that the number of cases in each cell (social location) be balanced, that is, equal or nearly equal. The size of the entire sample—and of the individual cells—should be guided by the objective of the researcher. All things being equal, the larger the sample—and the frequencies in the individual social locations—the better. However, given the labor-intensive nature of qualitative research, sample size is usually a compromise between time and resources. For a student project using four social locations, 5 to 10 individuals in each social location (a total of 20–40 cases) might suffice. Sample sizes can be increased as time and resources allow.

Analysis of the data gained from interviews should focus on making comparisons among the various social locations. In reviewing a large number of published qualitative RGC articles I have been struck by the degree to which this is not done. Rather, there is a tendency for authors to compare across simple social locations: race or gender or class; that is, comparisons are made between males and females, blacks and whites, or middle-class and working-class respondents. This is not RGC analysis. RGC research is concerned with variation across complex social locations such as. Asian males, white males, Asian working-class males, black middle-class females, or Latino middle-class females. How is such analysis accomplished?

In qualitative research, data exist in the form of quotes from respondents. These quotes are to qualitative analysis as frequency counts are to quantitative analysis. The researcher therefore seeks to identify quotes that are answers to or comments on a particular question asked and to compare these answers and comments across social locations. "Do you believe that outsourcing is harmful to American workers?" "Do you think the death penalty should be abolished?" "Do you feel that you were well prepared for college by your high school?" Whatever the question, the goal of the RGC researcher is to be able to make statements like the following. "It was found that Latino working-class males felt less prepared for college than Latino middle-class males" or "Working-class black males and females were found to be more opposed to the death penalty than working-class white males and females." Of course, it is possible—and even advisable—to aggregate these responses and report percentage differences on to use language such as "a few," "most," or "all."

Strategies: Upper-class undergraduates usually have not had sufficient quantitative training for the more complex multivariate RGC research presented in this text. However, they can use less complex quantitative techniques that are usually taught in undergraduate statistics courses. I illustrate one possible approach, ANOVA (analysis of variance), next.

ANOVA is ideally suited to RGC analysis, since it allows the comparison of multiple groups rather than just two, as is the case with *t*-tests of two group means. Although it is possible to calculate repeated *t*-tests of pairs, doing so greatly expands the amount of work and increases the risk of a Type I error (rejecting the null hypothesis of no difference when it is true). In contrast, ANOVA decreases the amount of work and reduces the possibility of a Type I error. However, ANOVA is appropriate only when the dependent variable is interval level. This level of measurement is often encountered in sociological, educational, and psychological research. In the latter case (as in some sociological studies) an attitude may be measured on an interval scale and groups compared on their agreement with or support for a specific position (attitude). In measures of educational achievement a variable such as grade point average might be used. Although ANOVA cannot be used in all situations it is appropriate for any number of research questions in which the dependent variable can be reduced to means.

In these cases the social locations created at the intersections of race, gender, and class are the independent variables, and the researcher wishes to explore the relationship between social locations and some dependent variable. More specifically, he/she wants to test the null hypothesis that the groups (social locations) are equal on the characteristic, attitude, or achievement of interest.

In my own teaching my objective is to give students a feel for RGC research compared with the more

TABLE 3 ■ MEAN EDUCATIONAL ATTAINMENT BY SEX AND RACE IN 2000

Groups	All ages	25–35 yrs
Males	10.64	12.85
Females	10.79	13.11
Asians	11.62	14.53
Blacks	9.83	12.71
Latinos	8.20	10.44
Whites	11.24	13.44
Middle class	13.84	14.10
Working class	11.54	11.74

traditional approaches they may have used or encountered in their readings. To illustrate the methodology, I use data from the IPUMS[5] 2000 *small* sample. IPUMS offers the option of downloading samples of different sizes to meet the researcher's unique needs. Given the number of subgroups used in intersectional analysis, the *tiny* sample of about 5000 adults is usually too small. The 1% and 5% samples contain millions of cases and are usually not needed.[6] For many purposes the *small* sample of approximately 50,000 cases is just about right.

In the following example I use mean educational attainment as the dependent variable and explore the extent to which educational attainment varies across specific social locations (RGC groups). Education has been recoded to allow a more intuitive interpretation, so that 12 equals high school, and 16 equals a BA/BS degree. To illustrate the difference between the RGC and the traditional approach, I first present the mean educational attainment for the simple social locations of sex, race, and class for individuals of all ages and for those 25 to 35 years old in 2000 (see Table 3).

What do we learn from these statistics? There is only a slight difference in educational attainment between males and females, whether one considers all ages together or the more restricted group of 25- to 35-year-olds. The higher educational attainment of the younger cohort reflects increasing educational opportunity over time in the United States. The 25- to 35-year-olds have two to three years more education on average than individuals of all ages combined. Although this is informative, we do not know if these sex differences in educational attainment exist within the individual racial groups. For instance, is the gender gap between Asian males and females the same as, larger than, or smaller than the gender gap between *all* males and females combined? Similarly, what about class differences within race? Are they similar to the class differences of all individuals combined, or are class differences larger or smaller among whites than among Asians, African Americans, or Latinos?

Table 3 also reveals some striking differences in the educational levels of racial groups; however, we cannot tell whether these racial differences exist across gender or class. For instance, among those 25 to 35 years old, Latinos have an average of four years less education than Asians (4.09). Is this gap the same between *male* Asians and Latinos or between *female* Asians and Latinos? To answer these questions we must focus on the intersections of race and gender.

I now turn to an example using ANOVA to illustrate how it can be used to answer such questions in a very direct and parsimonious manner. For this example I first examine educational attainment for the eight groups at the intersections of race, gender, and class (Table 4).[7]

One of the most striking aspects of Table 4 is the difference in some of the means compared with those in Table 3. Part of the answer to this seeming anomaly is the "content" of these categories. Males and females include individuals of all races of the respective genders. Each racial group in Table 3 includes both males and females of that group, and middle class and working class both encompass males and females of all racial groups combined. It would require a great deal of laborious calculations to untangle all of this. ANOVA simplifies the task.

The ideal strategy for untangling these interactions begins with tests of the significance of the entire model, the three main effects (race, gender, and class), the three two-way interactions, and the one three-way

[5]IPUMS (Integrated Public Use Microdata Series) is an online compilation of census data from 1850 to 2004 developed at the University of Minnesota. It is a user-friendly database that can be accessed online at www@IPUMS.org.

[6]Although there is no inherent problem with using the 1% and 5% samples, their sheer size makes computing an unnecessarily slow process. Such large samples also are more likely to yield significant results.

[7]All tables were created using SPSS-PC. Version 12 allows one to click on a table and copy and paste into a Microsoft Word document. Of course, SAS can also be used for these calculations.

TABLE 4 ■ MEAN EDUCATIONAL ATTAINMENT BY COMPLEX SOCIAL LOCATIONS FOR ALL AGES IN 2000

R × C × G	Mean	N	Std. deviation
WMcM	14.3168	7676	2.43857
WMcF	13.7572	10388	2.15574
BMcM	13.5292	633	2.24831
BMcF	13.2763	1331	2.18489
WWcM	12.0273	7311	2.00220
WWcF	11.9631	3534	2.11382
BWcM	11.6010	1186	2.23975
BWcF	11.6749	858	2.17019
Total	13.1551	32917	2.41405

interaction. The null hypotheses are tested using a statistic called the *F ratio.* If significant, the overall *F* statistic is an indication that at least one of the population means is significantly different from the others. In Table 5 the *F* ratio for the overall model (Corrected model) is significant ($p < .001$), signaling that it is appropriate to continue the analysis. (Had the *F* ratio lacked significance—signaling the absence of group differences—we would then stop and report nothing else.) Likewise, the *F* ratios for the three main effects—race (W), gender, and class—are also significant, indicating that each is related to the dependent variable, education; that is, blacks and whites have significantly different mean education, as is likewise the case between males and females, and middle- and working-class groups. Because two-way interaction terms represent *four* groups, formed at the intersection (as seen in Table 1) of two variables (e.g., race × gender.), a significant *F* ratio indicates that at least one of the four group means is significantly different from the other three. This logic can be extended to the three-way interaction of race × gender × class, except in this case we have eight different groups, as seen in Table 2. It should be noted that the *F* statistic for the three-way interaction is not significant (.277), probably owing to discrepancy in the size of some of the groups as well as multicollinearity. For example, there are more than 16 times as many white middle-class females (10,388) as black middle-class males (633). One of the limitations of the *F* ratio is its sensitivity to inequality in group size; however, it is clear that there is a great deal of significant variation in educational attainment among groups.

In the case of RGC analysis the foregoing tests are simply a "warm-up" for the more important task of comparing educational means among groups. To accomplish this we turn to the ANOVA analysis in Table 6, which is an output of the Tukey statistic. Given the large sample size, I used the most conserva-

TABLE 5 ■ TWO WAY ANALYSIS OF VARIANCE OF DIFFERENCES IN EDUCATIONAL ATTAINMENT AMONG RACE, GENDER, AND CLASS SOCIAL LOCATIONS IN 2000

Source	Type III sum of squares	df	Mean square	F	Sig.	Noncent parameter	Observed power[a]
Corrected model	33296.981[b]	7	4756.712	987.463	.000	6912.243	1.000
Intercept	2092595.983	1	2092595.983	434409.694	.000	434409.694	1.000
BW	788.586	1	788.586	163.705	.000	163.705	1.000
Gender	129.227	1	129.227	26.827	.000	26.827	.999
Class	11624.495	1	11624.495	2413.172	.000	2413.172	1.000
BW X gender	39.676	1	39.676	8.237	.004	8.237	.819
BW X class	61.545	1	61.545	12.776	.000	12.776	.947
Gender X class	135.551	1	135.551	28.140	.000	28.140	1.000
BW X gender X class	5.692	1	5.692	1.182	.277	1.182	.192
Error	158526.023	32909	4.817				
Total	5888309.830	32917					
Corrected total	191823.004	32916					

[a]Computed using alpha = .05

[b]R squared = .174 (adjusted R squared = .173)

TABLE 6 ■ COMPARISON OF MEAN EDUCATIONAL ATTAINMENT AMONG SOCIAL LOCATIONS IN 2000, WITH ALL AGES INCLUDED (TUKEY HSD)

R × C × G (I)	R × C × G (J)	Mean difference (I−J)	Std. error	Sig.	99.9% confidence interval	
					Lower bound	Upper bound
WMcM	WMcF	.5595*	.03303	.000	.4235	.6955
	BMcM	.7875*	0.09076	.000	.4138	1.1613
	BMcF	1.0404*	.06517	.000	.7721	1.3088
	WWcM	2.2894*	.03587	.000	2.1417	2.4371
	WWcF	2.3537*	.04462	.000	2.1699	2.5374
	BWcM	2.7157*	.06848	.000	2.4338	2.9974
	BWcF	2.6418*	.07901	.000	2.3165	2.9671
WMcF	WMcM	−.5595*	.03303	.000	−.6955	−.4235
	BMcM	.2280	.08985	.180	−.1420	.5980
	BMcF	.4809*	.06390	.000	.2178	.7440
	WWcM	1.7299*	.03351	.000	1.5919	1.8679
	WWcF	1.7941*	.04274	.000	1.6181	1.9701
	BWcM	2.1562*	.06727	.000	1.8792	2.4332
	BWcF	2.0823*	.07796	.000	1.7613	2.4033
BMcM	WMcM	−.7875*	.09076	.000	−1.1613	−.4138
	WMcF	−.2280	.08985	.180	−.5980	.1420
	BMcF	.2529	.10597	.248	−.1835	.6892
	WWcM	1.5019*	.09093	.000	1.1274	1.8763
	WWcF	1.5661*	.09473	.000	1.1761	1.9562
	BWcM	1.9282*	.10804	.000	1.4833	2.3731
	BWcF	1.8543*	.11500	.000	1.3807	2.3278
BMcF	WMcM	−1.0404*	.06517	.000	−1.3088	−.7721
	WMcF	−.4809*	.06390	.000	−.7440	−.2178
	BMcM	−.2529	.10597	.248	−.6892	.1835
	WWcM	1.2490*	.06541	.000	.9797	1.5183
	WWcF	1.3132*	.07058	.000	1.0226	1.6039
	BWcM	1.6753*	.08764	.000	1.3144	2.0362
	BWcF	1.6014*	.09609	.000	1.2057	1.9971
WWcM	WMcM	−2.2894*	.03587	.000	−2.4371	−2.1417
	WMcF	−1.7299*	.03351	.000	−1.8679	−1.5919
	BMcM	−1.5019*	.09093	.000	−1.8763	−1.1274
	BMcF	−1.2490*	.06541	.000	−1.5183	−.9797
	WWcF	.0642	.04497	.844	−.1209	.2494
	BWcM	.4263*	.06871	.000	.1434	.7092
	BWcF	.3524*	.07920	.000	.0262	.6785
WWcF	WMcM	−2.3537*	.04462	.000	−2.5374	−2.1699
	WMcF	−1.7941*	.04274	.000	−1.9701	−1.6181
	BMcM	−1.5661*	.09473	.000	−1.9562	−1.1761
	BMcF	−1.3132*	.07058	.000	−1.6039	−1.0226
	WWcM	−.0642	.04497	.844	−.2494	.1209
	BWcM	.3621*	.07365	.000	.0588	.6654
	BWcF	.2882	.08353	.013	−.0558	.6321

TABLE 6 ■ (*CONTINUED*)

R × C × G (I)	R × C × G (J)	Mean difference (I−J)	Std. error	Sig.	99.9% confidence interval Lower bound	Upper bound
BWcM	WMcM	−2.7157*	.06848	.000	−2.9977	−2.4338
	WMcF	−2.1562*	.06727	.000	−2.4332	−1.8792
	BMcM	−1.9282*	.10804	.000	−2.3731	−1.4833
	BMcF	−1.6753*	.08764	.000	−2.0362	−1.3144
	WWcM	−.4263*	.06871	.000	−.7092	−.1434
	WWcF	−.3621*	.07365	.000	−.6654	−.0588
	BWcF	−.0739	.09837	.995	−.4790	.3311
BWcF	WMcM	−2.6418*	.07901	.000	−2.6971	−2.3165
	WMcF	−2.0823*	.07796	.000	−2.4033	−1.7613
	BMcM	−1.8543*	.11500	.000	−2.3278	−1.3807
	BMcF	−1.6014*	.09609	.000	−1.9971	−1.2057
	WWcM	−.3524*	.07920	.000	−.6785	−.0262
	WWcF	−.2882	.08353	.013	−.6321	.0558
	BWcM	.0739	.09837	.995	−.3311	.4790

Based on observed means

*The mean difference is significant at the .001 level.

tive test of significance at 99.9% ($p < .001$). ANOVA is an excellent tool for this type of RGC analysis, since it allows comparisons of each group (social location) with every other social location. The output in Table 6 from SPSS-PC analysis automatically provides all comparisons. Although this comparison is certainly convenient, I have argued elsewhere in this text that comparing each group with all others is not necessarily the best approach. It is best to be guided either by theory or by one's objective in the study. For instance, comparing Latina females with females of other races is probably more enlightening than comparing Latina females with Asian or African American males.

Although any number of different comparative approaches can be taken, I shall suggest several possible ones that answer some of the questions raised earlier. Because white males are often used as the norm in comparisons such as in the case of income attainment, I start with this approach. Examining the statistics in Table 6 we find that the mean educational attainment of white males is significantly different—and higher—than that of all other groups, including white females. This appears to be the case from an examination of the means in Table 4, where we find that the mean for the white middle-class males is 14.32, with the next highest being that of white middle-class females, 13.76. But without testing the null hypothesis of no differences between these two means, we cannot be sure. In the case of white *working-class* males, however, we find that their mean education is significantly different from that of all other groups except white working-class females.

Other interesting comparisons can be made *within* race, gender, or class, for instance, within the middle or the working class. Because most comparisons reveal significant differences between group means, we can focus on those cases that are not significantly different. Within the middle class these cases are between white middle-class females and black middle-class males, and between black middle-class males and black middle-class females. In both cases the null hypothesis must be rejected, indicating that black middle-class males (13.53) and white middle-class females (13.76) have the same educational achievement on average. An identical conclusion can be made for black middle-class males (13.53) and black middle-class females (13.28). The latter finding is perhaps contrary to the general impression that black males lag black females, an impression that arises because, historically, a higher proportion of black females than males attend college. This finding suggests that at least among *middle-class* blacks there is educational parity between males and females and that black middle-class males are likewise on a par with white middle-class females.

Similarly, comparisons can be made across working-class groups and between gender groups. In the latter case, for instance, it can be noted that among females, white (11.96) and black (11.67) working-class females have approximately the same level of education, whereas the mean education of white middle-class females (13.76), statistically, is significantly higher (although not by much) than the educational attainment of black middle-class females (13.28).

These comparisons should be sufficient to illustrate how ANOVA can be used for RGC analysis. Instructors can guide students in assignments of this type using the same or other dependent variables and show them how to consider carefully which comparisons are relevant to the particular objective of their study.

Homogeneous Subsets Another useful output of the Tukey HSD statistic is the homogeneous subsets (Table 7). These subsets are groupings of social locations that are most alike on the dependent variable, in this case their mean educational attainment. The six groupings found in Table 7 provide a convenient summary of some of our earlier observations. Each of the first five groups is a pair of social locations whose mean education are most alike. White middle-class males are in a "group" all by themselves, since their mean education is significantly different from that of all other groups. Although these pairs are "statistically" significant groupings, they may or may not be substantively meaningful. Certainly, the observation of the educational equality of black working-class males and females (subset 1) and of black middle-class males and females (subset 4) is informative, as is that of white and black working-class females (subset 2). Subset 5, consisting of black middle-class males and white middle-class females, is perhaps less interesting. Thus, although these homogeneous subsets are useful, the researcher should still be guided by theory and research interests rather than the statistical groupings alone.

One additional example illustrates intersections of race and gender that includes multiple racial/ethnic groups: Asians, African Americans, Latinos, and whites. In this case I use only those in the 25 to 35 age cohort and show only the group means and the results of the Tukey HSD post hoc test (Tables 8 and 9); and rather than education, I use wage and salary income as the dependent variable. The null hypothesis is that all eight groups have the same mean income. Although we know from previous research that this cannot be

TABLE 7 ■ HOMOGENEOUS SUBSETS OF SOCIAL LOCATIONS BASED ON MEAN EDUCATIONAL ATTAINMENT IN 2000 (TUKEY HSD)

		Subset					
R × C × G	N	1	2	3	4	5	6
BWcM	1186	11.6010					
BWcF	858	11.6749	11.6749				
WWcF	3534		11.9631	11.9631			
WWcM	7311			12.0273			
BMcF	1331				13.2763		
BMcM	633				13.5292	13.5292	
WMcF	10388					13.7572	
WMcM	7676						14.3168
Sig.		.981	.005	.992	.024	.064	1.000

Means for groups in homogeneous subsets are displayed. The error term is mean square (error) = 4.817.

[a]Uses harmonic mean sample size = 1604.476.

[b]The group sizes are unequal. The harmonic mean of the group sizes is used. Type I error levels are not guaranteed.

[c]Alpha = .001.

TABLE 8 ■ MEAN INCOME BY COMPLEX SOCIAL LOCATIONS FOR INDIVIDUALS AGED 25–35 IN 2000

Social location	Mean	N	Std. deviation
White males	36490.7319	3047	30084.76985
White females	23744.9704	2706	21547.74704
Black males	26491.5049	412	21528.51520
Black females	22368.0619	485	13378.69711
Asian males	39812.7778	198	36182.17910
Asian females	26093.6842	171	20357.88264
Latino males	23075.3591	543	20271.40419
Latina females	18093.7017	362	13578.64102
Total	28852.7196	7924	25775.33272

TABLE 9 ■ COMPARISON OF MEAN INCOME AMONG SOCIAL LOCATIONS IN 2000, FOR INDIVIDUALS AGED 25 TO 35 (TUKEY HSD)

(I) Social location	(J) Social location	Mean difference (I-J)	Std. error	Sig.	99.9% confidence interval	
					Lower bound	Upper bound
White males	White females	12745.7614*	657.70294	.000	10036.3229	15455.2000
	Black males	9999.2270*	1306.99272	.000	4615.0084	15383.4457
	Black females	14122.6700*	1217.26735	.000	9108.0793	19137.2607
	Asian males	−3322.0459	1826.08610	.607	−10844.6944	4200.6026
	Asian females	10397.0477*	1956.77756	.000	2336.0094	18458.0859
	Latino males	13415.3728*	1159.82858	.000	8637.4038	18193.3417
	Latina females	18397.0302*	1384.22188	.000	12694.6623	24099.3981
White females	White males	−12745.7614*	657.70294	.000	−15455.2000	−10036.3229
	Black males	−2746.5344	1316.76500	.424	−8171.0104	2677.9416
	Black females	1376.9086	1227.75400	.952	−3680.8824	6434.6996
	Asian males	−16067.8073*	1833.09316	.000	−23619.3218	−8516.2929
	Asian females	−2348.7138	1963.31824	.933	−10436.6966	5739.2691
	Latino males	669.6113	1170.82980	.999	−4153.6777	5492.9003
	Latina females	5651.2688	1393.45266	.001	−89.1257	11391.6633
Black males	White males	−9999.2270*	1306.99272	.000	−15383.4457	−4615.0084
	White females	2746.5344	1316.76500	.424	−2677.9416	8171.0104
	Black females	4123.4430	1668.24360	.208	−2748.9658	10995.8518
	Asian males	−13321.2729*	2153.11108	.000	−22191.1164	−4451.4294
	Asian females	397.8206	2265.01111	1.000	−8933.0003	9728.6416
	Latino males	3416.1457	1626.80645	.415	−3285.5608	10117.8523
	Latina females	8397.8032*	1793.70207	.000	1008.5622	15787.0442
Black females	White males	−14122.6700*	1217.26735	.000	−19137.2607	−9108.0793
	White females	−1376.9086	1227.75400	.952	−6434.6996	3680.8824
	Black males	−4123.4430	1668.24360	.208	−10995.8518	2748.9658
	Asian males	−17444.7159*	2099.85646	.000	−26095.1745	−8794.2574
	Asian females	−3725.6224	2214.44918	.699	−12848.1510	5396.9063

TABLE 9 (CONTINUED)

(I) Social location	(J) Social location	Mean difference (I-J)	Std. error	Sig.	99.9% confidence interval Lower bound	Upper bound
	Latino males	−707.2973	1555.63783	1.000	−7115.8213	5701.2267
	Latina females	4274.3602	1729.41520	.208	−2850.0480	11398.7684
Asian males	White males	3322.0459	1826.08610	.607	−4200.6026	10844.6944
	White females	16067.8073*	1833.09316	.000	8516.2929	23619.3218
	Black males	13321.2729*	2153.11108	.000	4451.4294	22191.1164
	Black females	17444.7159*	2099.85646	.000	8794.2574	26095.1745
	Asian females	13719.0936*	2599.35296	.000	3010.9355	24427.2517
	Latino males	16737.4187*	2067.08967	.000	8221.9445	25252.8928
	Latina females	21719.0761*	2200.84702	.000	12652.5822	30785.5701
Asian females	White males	−10397.0477*	1956.77756	.000	−18458.0859	−2336.0094
	White females	2348.7138	1963.31824	.933	−5739.2691	10436.6966
	Black males	−397.8206	2265.01111	1.000	−9728.6416	8933.0003
	Black females	3725.6224	2214.44918	.699	−5396.9063	12848.1510
	Asian males	−13719.0936*	2599.35296	.000	−24427.2517	−3010.9355
	Latino males	3018.3251	2183.40278	.866	−5976.3065	12012.9567
	Latina females	7999.9826	2310.43623	.013	−1517.9694	17517.9345
Latino males	White males	−13415.3728*	1159.82858	.000	−18193.3417	−8637.4038
	White females	−669.6113	1170.82980	.999	−5492.9003	4153.6777
	Black males	−3416.1457	1626.80645	.415	−10117.8523	3285.5608
	Black females	707.2973	1555.63783	1.000	−5701.2267	7115.8213
	Asian males	−16737.4187*	2067.08967	.000	−25252.8928	−8221.9445
	Asian females	−3018.3251	2183.40278	.866	−12012.9567	5976.3065
	Latina females	4981.6575	1689.47905	.063	−1978.2318	11941.5468
Latina females	White males	−18397.0302*	1384.22188	.000	−24099.3981	−12694.6623
	White females	−5651.2688*	1393.45266	.001	−11391.6633	89.1257
	Black males	−8397.8032*	1793.70207	.000	−15787.0442	−1008.5622
	Black females	−4274.3602	1729.41520	.208	−11398.7684	2850.0480
	Asian males	−21719.0761*	2200.84702	.000	−30785.5701	−12652.5822
	Asian females	−7999.9826	2310.43623	.013	−17517.9345	1517.9694
	Latino males	−4981.6575	1689.47905	.063	−11941.5468	1978.2318

Based on observed means

*The mean difference is significant at the .001 level.

true, we do not know the exact means of these groups in 2000, nor do we know the positions of these groups relative to one another. Normally, the median rather than the mean is used for income, because the mean is sensitive to extreme outliers in the distribution; however, in some cases this feature of means may actually be desirable. In the present example the likelihood that white individuals rather than those of other races possess the higher incomes is part of the reality of income inequality. In the IPUMS 2000 sample being used, 0.8 percent of all individuals (excluding those with 0 incomes, who include many housewives and children) had wage and salary incomes greater than $300,000. Among the 23 individuals 25 to 35 years old in this subsample, with incomes over $300,000, there were 16 white males, 5 white females, and one each among

Asian and Latino males.[8] This does not mean that there are no black males or females with incomes over $300,000 in this subsample, but it is likely that they are older than 35. Indeed, analysis of the entire IPUMS *small* sample for 2000 yields the following frequencies for those groups with individuals having incomes of $300,000 or higher: 221 white males, 37 white females, 9 black males, 5 black females, 8 Asian males, 4 Asian females, 4 Latino males, and 1 Latina female. Although each group has one or more individuals earning $300,000 or above, 76% of the 289 individuals with this income are white males. Among those individuals 25 to 35 years old, 68% of the $300,000 + income holders are white males.

Turning now to the mean distribution in Table 8, we note that the groups with the highest mean income are Asian and white males, black males, and Asian females. Without further analysis we do not know whether all these individuals are salaried or are entrepreneurs reporting salaries from their own business. Black males have a higher mean income than black females, again calling into question the myth that black females fare better in the market because they fulfill two affirmative action goals for race and sex.

Turning to Table 9 we find the Tukey statistic comparisons of all groups. I include the statistics for homogeneous subsets, although in this case they do not work as well because of extreme inequality in group size. It is clear, however, from both Tables 9 and 10 that white males differ significantly from all other groups except Asian males. White females have a significantly different mean only from those of white males, Asian males, and Latina females. Latina females have the lowest mean income of all groups, reflecting their high concentration in the unskilled service sector. These are some of the highlights that can be observed from the comparisons in Table 9. Further analysis is possible, of course, but will not be pursued here. In Tables 11 and 12, I provide—without comment—the income means and Tukey comparisons for the eight groups formed at the intersections of race, gender, and class. Analysis of these tables can be used as student assignments.

Conclusion

I have attempted to provide some assistance to instructors who teach or may wish to teach upper-

TABLE 10 ■ HOMOGENEOUS SUBSETS OF SOCIAL LOCATIONS BASED ON GROUP MEAN INCOMES IN 2000 FOR INDIVIDUALS AGED 25 TO 35 (TUKEY HSD)

		Subset		
R×G	N	1	2	3
Latino females	362	18093.7017		
Black females	485	22368.0619	22368.0619	
Latino males	543	23075.3591	23075.3591	
White females	2706	23744.9704	23744.9704	
Asian females	171		26093.6842	
Black males	412		26491.5049	
White males	3047			36490.7319
Asian males	198			39812.7778
Significance		.034	.292	.582

Means for groups in homogeneous subsets are displayed. The error term is mean square (error) = 619962533.282.
[a]Uses harmonic mean sample size = 386.673.
[b]The group sizes are unequal. The harmonic mean of the group sizes is used. Type I error levels are not guaranteed.
[c]Alpha = .001.

[8]Removal of those individuals earning $300,000 or more reduced the white male mean by $1541, the white female mean by $551, the Asian male mean by $1371, and the Latino male mean by $548. The sharp reduction of the Asian male mean is a result of the small number in that age group, 198 compared with 3047 white males.

TABLE 11 ■ MEAN INCOME BY COMPLEX SOCIAL LOCATIONS FOR INDIVIDUALS AGED 25–35 IN 2000

R × C × G	Mean	N	Std. deviation
WMcM	43737.3670	1485	36455.14744
WMcF	26076.6414	2111	22899.19475
BMcM	31857.5887	141	30853.83410
BMcF	24706.9508	305	13107.73454
WWcM	29565.7306	1492	20451.96648
WWcF	15339.8291	585	12846.48961
BWcM	23325.4183	251	13836.99422
BWcF	17950.8092	173	12734.81875
Total	29660.9140	6543	26352.90173

TABLE 12 ■ COMPARISON OF MEAN INCOME AMONG SOCIAL LOCATIONS IN 2000, FOR INDIVIDUALS AGED 25 TO 35 (TUKEY HSD)

					99.9% confidence interval	
(I) R × C × G	(J) R × C × G	Mean difference (I−J)	Std. error	Sig.	Lower bound	Upper bound
WMcM	WMcF	17660.7256*	844.18804	.000	14182.6500	21138.8012
	BMcM	11879.7784*	2196.46449	.000	2830.2903	20929.2664
	BMcF	19030.4162*	1566.93171	.000	12574.6188	25486.2136
	WWcM	14171.6364*	913.64710	.000	10407.3878	17935.8851
	WWcF	28397.5379*	1216.69217	.000	23384.7361	33410.3398
	BWcM	20411.9487*	1701.02804	.000	13403.6711	27420.2263
	BWcF	25786.5578*	2002.36241	.000	17536.7751	34036.3404
WMcF	WMcM	−17660.7256*	844.18804	.000	−21138.8012	−14182.6500
	BMcM	−5780.9473	2168.03964	.133	−14713.3242	3151.4297
	BMcF	1369.6906	1526.83156	.986	−4920.8932	7660.2744
	WWcM	−3489.0892*	843.02471	.001	−6962.3718	−15.8065
	WWcF	10736.8123*	1164.59412	.000	5938.6558	15534.9689
	BWcM	2751.2231	1664.16226	.718	−4105.1666	9607.6127
	BWcF	8125.8322*	1971.14050	.001	4.6845	16246.9798
BMcM	WMcM	−11879.7784*	2196.46449	.000	−20929.2664	−2830.2903
	WMcF	5780.9473	2168.03964	.133	−3151.4297	14713.3242
	BMcF	7150.6378	2538.30995	.091	−3307.2620	17608.5376
	WWcM	2291.8581	2196.01764	.968	−6755.7889	11339.5051
	WWcF	16517.7596*	2338.39310	.000	6883.5222	26151.9970
	BWcM	8532.1703	2623.21155	.025	−2275.5261	19339.8668
	BWcF	13906.7794*	2827.93169	.000	2255.6309	25557.9279
BMcF	WMcM	−19030.4162*	1566.93171	.000	−25486.2136	−12574.6188
	WMcF	−1369.6906	1526.83156	.986	−7660.2744	4920.8932
	BMcM	−7150.6378	2538.30995	.091	−17608.5376	3307.2620
	WWcM	−4858.7797	1566.30526	.041	−11311.9962	1594.4367
	WWcF	9367.1218*	1760.36956	.000	2114.3556	16619.8879
	BWcM	1381.5325	2124.16043	.998	−7370.0610	10133.1260
	BWcF	6756.1416	2372.34407	.084	−3017.9747	16530.2578

TABLE 12 ■ (*CONTINUED*)

(I)R×C×G	(J)R×C×G	Mean difference (I−J)	Std. error	Sig.	99.9% confidence interval	
					Lower bound	Upper bound
WWcM	WMcM	−14171.6364*	913.64710	.000	−17935.8851	−10407.3878
	WMcF	3489.0892*	843.02471	.001	15.8065	6962.3718
	BMcM	−2291.8581	2196.01764	.968	−11339.5051	6755.7889
	BMcF	4858.7797	1566.30526	.041	−1594.4367	11311.9962
	WWcF	14225.9015*	1215.88529	.000	9216.4240	19235.3790
	BWcM	6240.3122	1700.45099	.006	−765.5879	13246.2124
	BWcF	11614.9213*	2001.87223	.000	3367.1582	19862.6844
WWcF	WMcM	−28397.5379*	1216.69217	.000	−33410.3398	−23384.7361
	WMcF	−10736.8123*	1164.59412	.000	−15534.9689	−5938.6558
	BMcM	−16517.7596*	2338.39310	.000	−26151.9970	−6883.5222
	BMcF	−9367.1218*	1760.36956	.000	−16619.8879	−2114.3556
	WWcM	−14225.9015*	1215.88529	.000	−19235.3790	−9216.4240
	BWcM	−7985.5893*	1880.72390	.001	−15734.2183	−236.9603
	BWcF	−2610.9802	2157.10019	.929	−11498.2863	6276.3260
BWcM	WMcM	−20411.9487*	1701.02804	.000	−27420.2263	−13403.6711
	WMcF	−2751.2231	1664.16226	.718	−9607.6127	4105.1666
	BMcM	−8532.1703	2623.21155	.025	−19339.8668	2275.5261
	BMcF	−1381.5325	2124.16043	.998	−10133.1260	7370.0610
	WWcM	−6240.3122	1700.45099	.006	−13246.2124	765.5879
	WWcF	7985.5893*	1880.72390	.001	236.9603	15734.2183
	BWcF	5374.6091	2462.97336	.363	−4772.9021	15522.1203
BWcF	WMcM	−25786.5578*	2002.36241	.000	−34036.3404	−17536.7751
	WMcF	−8125.8322*	1971.14050	.001	−16246.9798	−4.6845
	BMcM	−13906.7794*	2827.93169	.000	−25557.9279	−2255.6309
	BMcF	−6756.1416	2372.34407	.084	−16530.2578	3017.9747
	WWcM	−11614.9213*	2001.87223	.000	−19862.6844	−3367.1582
	WWcF	2610.9802	2157.10019	.929	−6276.3260	11498.2863
	BWcM	−5374.6091	2462.97336	.363	−15522.1203	4772.9021

Based on observed means

*The mean difference is significant at the .001 level.

division undergraduate courses in RGC analysis. The underlying premise of this appendix is that we must move beyond discussions of the theory to its application in qualitative and quantitative research. I have highlighted some of the principal issues that are relevant to RGC research at each stage of the process: design, data collection, and analysis. For the latter I have provided examples of quantitative data analysis that should be accessible to students who have or are taking a standard statistics course for the social sciences. These texts are likely to include analysis of variance; if they do not, it should not be too great a stretch to teach the fundamentals of this technique in a statistics course. It is hoped that having students conduct empirical research from the RGC perspective, however limited, will further their understanding of this approach. Of course, the ANOVA examples presented are useful for graduate students as well. Finally, for those students without statistical training, it is hoped that my comments on design, data collection, and analysis will assist them in conducting qualitative research projects.